FAITH AND FEAR

AMERICA'S RELATIONSHIP
WITH WAR SINCE 1945

GREGORY A. DADDIS

OXFORD
UNIVERSITY PRESS

Oxford University Press is a department of the University of Oxford.
It furthers the University's objective of excellence in research, scholarship,
and education by publishing worldwide. Oxford is a registered trade mark of
Oxford University Press in the UK and in certain other countries.

Published in the United States of America by Oxford University Press
198 Madison Avenue, New York, NY 10016, United States of America.

© Oxford University Press 2025

All rights reserved. No part of this publication may be reproduced, stored in a retrieval system, transmitted, used for text and data mining, or used for training artificial intelligence, in any form or by any means, without the prior permission in writing of Oxford University Press, or as expressly permitted by law, by license or under terms agreed with the appropriate reprographics rights organization. Inquiries concerning reproduction outside the scope of the above should be sent to the Rights Department, Oxford University Press, at the address above.

You must not circulate this work in any other form
and you must impose this same condition on any acquirer.

Library of Congress Cataloging-in-Publication Data
Names: Daddis, Gregory A., 1967– author
Title: Faith and fear: America's relationship with war since 1945 / Gregory A. Daddis.
Other titles: America's relationship with war since 1945
Description: New York, NY : Oxford University Press, [2025] |
Includes bibliographical references and index.
Identifiers: LCCN 2024055405 (print) | LCCN 2024055406 (ebook) |
ISBN 9780197804223 hardback | ISBN 9780197804230 epub | ISBN 9780197804254
Subjects: LCSH: United States—History, Military—20th century | War and society—United States |
War—Psychological aspects | United States–Military policy | Militarism—United States |
National security—United States
Classification: LCC E181 .D225 2025 (print) | LCC E181 (ebook) |
DDC 355.00973/0904—dc23/eng/20250401
LC record available at https://lccn.loc.gov/2024055405
LC ebook record available at https://lccn.loc.gov/2024055406

DOI: 10.1093/oso/9780197804223.001.0001

Printed by Marquis Book Printing, Canada

For Cameron

Contents

Preface and Acknowledgments   ix

Introduction   1

I. WAR TO DEFEAT EVIL

1. Freedom from Fear?   21
2. The Cold War Comes   30
3. Militarizing the Cold War   49
4. The Cold War Comes Home   62

II. WAR TO DETER WAR

5. Winning Here or Losing Everywhere   73
6. A Brave (and Frightful) New World   87
7. Below the Nuclear Threshold   107

III. WAR TO BUILD NATIONS

8. Undertaking a Hemispheric Crusade   123
9. War (and Fear) along the New Frontier   132
10. War as a Transformative Power   147
11. Faith and Fear on the Road to Vietnam   158

IV. WAR TO PRODUCE PEACE

12.	War and the "Peace You Desire"	175
13.	Managing Détente	185
14.	War for Peace?	199
15.	The Limits of Peace	212

V. WAR TO RESTORE HONOR

16.	Fear of War, Fear of Weakness	225
17.	Rebuilding (and Re-Militarizing) America	232
18.	Renewing Faith in "Low-Intensity" War	240
19.	Contemplating the "End"	255

VI. WAR TO CREATE ORDER

20.	Desperately Seeking Stability	277
21.	War in an Era of Triumphant Liberalism	285
22.	War in a Globalized World	300
23.	War on the Cheap?	317
	Conclusion	327

Notes	345
Index	462

Preface and Acknowledgments

I've been thinking about America's relationship with war for most of my adult life. I served in the US Army for more than twenty-five years and have taught military history in academic institutions for over two decades now. I became engrossed with the implications of America's failed war in Vietnam during my studies at the University of North Carolina. And I've been immensely fortunate to work alongside intellectually gifted veterans, scholars, and students. In many ways, war has become an integral part of my professional identity.

And yet, all this time, a long-ago conversation with my wonderful PhD advisor Richard H. Kohn lingered in the back of my mind. As I neared my departure from Chapel Hill, Dick posed what seemed like a challenge, even if he never would engage in such provocation. If you're going to stay in academia long enough, he offered, you should aspire to write a "big idea" book at least once in your career. Well, this is my response to one of the best academic mentors in the field, my "big idea," if you will.

For the longer I became immersed in war, whether in overseas deployments or in the pages of scholarly books and veterans' memoirs, the more I came to see a fundamental binary in my nation's increasingly dysfunctional relationship with war. To me, Americans' martial bonds have been informed by deep-seated frictions between faith in and fear of war and its consequences. This "big idea" is more than simply recasting Thucydides' time-honored argument of fear, honor, and interest driving state policy. In the years and then decades following the Second World War, Americans formed a special—and deeply flawed—relationship with war that rested on inherent tensions between faith and fear.

What follows is a culmination of two careers merging together to form a rumination on war and America. Both my experiences in uniform and my time in academia have highlighted a recurring pattern, a dialectic, so to speak. Americans are exhilarated by war's potential to make them safe while transforming the world, yet are fearful, acutely so, of what war might unleash upon them. For me, this pattern led me to ask a central, "big" question: what drove Americans' relationship with war in the latter half of the twentieth century?

In many ways, the duality between faith and fear crept into policy debates and public conversations—and remained constant—because focusing on war often was the easiest, most compelling argument to make. For civilian policymakers and senior military officers alike, it proved far simpler to focus on preparing for war than on sustaining nonmilitary programs and policies that didn't demonstrate progress against an evil enemy supposedly intent on global domination. Americans thus ushered military force to center stage of US grand strategy and foreign policy. But, as I found, there was much more to the story.

Faith and Fear, then, is an exploration of sorts. I wanted to survey the political and cultural tendencies of how Americans conceived of war, how they valued and placed their faith in it, and how they feared it and what it might leave behind. And I wanted to assess how these tendencies evolved over time, even as Americans' core assumptions about war remained firm. Essentially, *Faith and Fear* offers a new interpretation of America's long Cold War, one that dwells less on systems and ideologies and more on human actors' fraught emotional relationship with war.

Given this largely is a work of thematic synthesis, I have relied on the work and generosity of so many others, both within and outside of academia. First and foremost, my immense gratitude to Dick Kohn, who remains the very embodiment of professional scholar and mentor. There are days I'm still in disbelief that I had the chance to work with Dick. And so too with Paul Miles, a champion and counselor bar none. Our weekly conversations have become indispensable as we cover everything from Vietnam history to contemporary events. I treasure our friendship.

PREFACE AND ACKNOWLEDGMENTS

After serving more than a quarter century in uniform, two other fellow veterans have remained, like Paul, lasting friends. Rob Young, my brother and favorite Jersey "tuff guy," and Cotton Puryear taught me a simple lesson long ago: to be a good leader, be a good person. They are the best of both.

In Southern California, my heartfelt thanks to the USS Midway Foundation, whose leadership generously endowed a chair in military history at San Diego State University that has allowed me—and my students—to explore the past in ways relevant to the present. I also am indebted to those colleagues at SDSU who value sanity in the madcap world of academia, foremost among them Pierre Asselin, who has taught me far more than just Canadian cusswords. I don't know anyone more passionate about history or committed to doing right by our students than "P." And, thankfully, the indomitable David Cline proved a true and loyal friend when needed most. These two have been my rocks in San Diego. My sincerest thanks also go to Melissa Bacci, Keely Bamberg, Grace Cheng, Beth Pollard, Adriana Putko, Latha Varadarajan, Andy Wiese, and, at UCSD, Danny Widener.

There also are a host of scholars for whom my admiration knows few bounds. On the wars in Vietnam, I have learned so much from Pierre, Bill Allison, Amber Batura, Larry Berman, John Burns, Martin Clemis, Fred Logevall, Ron Milam, Kathryn Statler, Jim "You Weren't There Man" Willbanks, and the late George Herring and Marilyn Young. I've also been fortunate to build relationships with Andrew Bacevich, Gian Gentile, Richard Immerman, Lloyd Gardner, Frank Costigliola, and Mary Elizabeth Waters that have helped me better understand the ups and downs of US foreign policy and, importantly, the limits of American power overseas. A special shout-out to Amy Rutenberg, Andrew Preston, Beth Bailey, and Kara Dixon Vuic for offering invaluable feedback on the manuscript's final drafts.

My sincere thanks to the Fulbright Commission. A distinguished-scholar award offered me an opportunity to spend a term at Pembroke College of Oxford University and finalize the outline of this book which, as you'll see below, became pretty important to my family. While in

England, I had the good fortune to spend quality time with Andrew Preston, Susan Carruthers, Sir Hew Strachan, Patrick Porter, Gary Gerstle, Leo McCann, and the faculty associated with Pembroke's Changing Character of War Centre. To my great fortune, Brian and Dinny Linn were in town at the same time; I couldn't have asked for better—pun intended—fellow travelers.

Thanks also to Andrew Byers who, despite being a Duke alum (Go Heels!), facilitated a Stand Together Trust Research Grant in US Grand Strategy and Foreign Policy that aided greatly in my work. Because of this grant, I was able to work with some truly amazing student research assistants at SDSU: Julien Paschal Vedrene, Jack Matura, Laura "The Book Mule" Scott, Sara Anne Guthrie, Rachel Layton, and Noah Levy. Noah offered superb feedback on the final draft and caught more than a few errors. All are talented young scholars in their own right and should offer us all hope for the future.

Being part of the Department of History at West Point set the intellectual foundation for the scholar I have become and the book that follows. It's the only place I've been where incoming faculty are taught how to teach. It remains a highlight of my army career, thanks to working with the likes of Casey Doss, Josiah Grover, my dear friend Jen Kiesling, Rory McGovern, Cliff Rogers, Chuck "Maximus" Steele, Steve Waddell, and Jackie Whitt. As does the history department at Chapman University for my academic career. Brother Alex Bay ("yeah, yeah, yeah"), Jerry Josephs, Jennifer Keene, the late (and truly great) Bob Slayton, Charissa Threat, Shira Klein, and Mateo Jarquín challenged me to expand my horizons and understand the value of recognizing the deep relationships between war and society. I always will be grateful for my time in Orange County.

I also want to thank the Society for Military History, a superb organization of terrific people with shared interests who are generous with their time and research. I had the immense good fortune to lead a Summer Seminar in Military History—dubbed "Camp Clausewitz" by participants—and spend quality time with some of the brightest young military historians in the nation. It was there that many of the ideas in this book solidified over three weeks of thought-provoking conversations.

And, of course, my sincere thanks to the stellar team at Oxford University Press. This is my fourth outing with OUP and, as before, it's been a pleasure working with the ever-professional and tremendously supportive Dave McBride. My gratitude as well to Alexcee Bechthold for her first-rate assistance.

Among all these people, to whom I owe so very much, five stand apart. When the pandemic hit full force in 2020, a group of us began texting. It became (and remains) a near-daily chat session, a ray of light as we collectively hunkered down in a dim world. At one point, my daughter, who had escaped from her tiny, shared New York City apartment to come home, rolled her eyes and said we were texting like a bunch of "high school friends." The name stuck and when we finally got together in person, the t-shirts were ready. So, to my closest colleagues and my very best high school friends—Beth Bailey, Bob Brigham, Debbie Gershenowitz, Dave Kieran, and Kara Dixon Vuic—it is nowhere near an overstatement to say I cherish you all like family.

And that says something given how fortunate I am to have the family I do. My mom continues to encourage with her strength of will and amazing good humor. As does the memory of my dad. Beyond question, my wife Susan remains my closest companion and confidante. If what follows is my "big" idea, then marrying her was the very best idea. And because she wouldn't want it any other way—"thanks, babe"—this book's "d@mn outline" is dedicated to her and her alone. Even if our constant feline companions George and Beatrice also were present from beginning to end.

Finally, there is nothing more rewarding than being a dad to a truly astonishing daughter. We all find inspiration from people in our lives and, without question, Cameron inspires her mom and me the most. She is a phenomenally talented, compassionate human being, and she makes her parents immensely proud on a daily basis. This one's for you, Cam. Pooda loves the Pada.

Introduction

War to Liberate the World

The war was over. No doubt Douglas MacArthur felt chiefly responsible for its outcome. Who else deserved the lion's share of credit for the ultimate victory he had helped achieve? In the general's telling, his World War II offensive through the Southwest Pacific proved a master class in operational military planning. To MacArthur, the island-hopping campaign melded air, naval, and ground forces to a degree unlike any other in the history of warfare. The logistical effort alone to support such an ambitious strategy was staggering. Operation Cartwheel, for instance, involved some thirteen separate actions along the coast of New Guinea and through the Solomon Islands in 1943. Never reluctant to inscribe his achievements into the annals of history, the five-star general exulted in his performance as a military virtuoso. A self-congratulatory MacArthur recalled "leaping forward" in his westward drive "from one success to another," helping the Japanese armed forces write the last chapters in their "epic story of defeat."[1]

MacArthur's flair for the dramatic didn't end with the war. As the proconsul responsible for rebuilding and reforming a defeated Japan, the general extolled his unbending faith in American power. And not just military power. Rather, MacArthur hailed the supposed transformative capacities of the United States to reconstitute a new Asia, to usher in a "revolution" that would "restore the dignity and freedom of the common man" in Japan. Nor was this just rhetorical bluster. The US military occupation force held as its central mission that Japan would "not again become a menace to the peace and security of the world" and that it would be readmitted "as a responsible and peaceful member of the family of nations."[2]

MacArthur wasn't alone in this faith. In 1947, the head of the American Civil Liberties Union, Roger N. Baldwin, effusively praised democracy's rise in post-surrender Japan. (Had not war ushered in that very democracy?) Returning from a three-month inspection trip of Asia, at MacArthur's invitation, Baldwin lauded how Japan was reacting "like a liberated country. As a result there is little danger that democracy will be overcome by a dictatorship of the Left or Right." To return the general's favor, the ACLU director spoke highly of MacArthur and of how he was "justified in his sense of accomplishment." American occupation troops apparently had changed the very thinking and cultural norms of Japanese society.[3] Democracy, it seemed, had been hand-delivered by a benevolent general and his army to a clearly grateful people.

This faith in US power, however, stood in stark contrast to many Americans' wartime fears of the Japanese. In fact, these fears had penetrated into the very fabric of domestic society, leading to the conflation of Japanese Americans with a foreign enemy. Under the auspices of the 1942 War Relocation Authority, some 122,000 Japanese Americans living on the West Coast had been forced into internment camps, incarcerated and relocated into makeshift detention centers from Arizona to Arkansas. Fears of internal subversion, based on little more than racial prejudices, ran deep. The California attorney general deemed the Japanese "an unassimilable people," while the Arkansas governor protested the resettlement of "enemies of my country in my state." When Franklin D. Roosevelt signed Executive Order 9066 less than two months after the attacks on Pearl Harbor, authorizing "every possible protection against espionage and against sabotage," there seemed little doubt about the target of his presidential decree.[4]

The mass incarceration of their own citizens suggested something rather profound about how Americans saw themselves at the midpoint of the twentieth century. Despite victory in World War II and the confidence that it inspired, fears persisted about America's place in the world. Not long after the global conflict ended, famed journalist Edward R. Murrow suspected that "seldom, if ever, has a war ended, leaving the victors with such a sense of uncertainty and fear, with such a realization that the future is obscure, and that survival is not assured." By 1957, MacArthur himself was decrying how "our government has kept us in a perpetual state of fear—kept us in a continuous stampede of patriotic fervor—with the cry of a grave national emergency." We might momentarily overlook how the general's own past warnings about the threat posed by a communist China—he deemed it a "military power hostile to the United States"—had led to an expansion of war in Korea.[5]

Still, MacArthur's rhetoric intimated two important, often overlooked, themes that have been shaping America's paradoxical relationship with armed force ever since the end of World War II: a faith in—yet fear of—war.

Standard diplomatic histories of what drove US Cold War foreign policy don't probe very deeply into America's larger relationship with war. Certainly, war is present in these narratives. Yet the rhetoric of the Cold War often serves as a substitute for looking into war itself, save for conflicts in places like Korea or Vietnam. Diplomatic surveys instead concentrate on policies aimed at spreading democratic ideals or securing resources in an ever-antagonistic world. War surely was a means to these ends—while sustaining a profound sense of American exceptionalism—but it often remains just out of view.[6]

Of course, ideals and interests matter. They have since the republic's founding. To paraphrase Thomas Jefferson, American policymakers long have wrestled with competing ideas over "theory"—the principles of liberty and democracy—and "tastes"—the hunger for commerce and open markets. Nor has this competition ever been static. Arguably, all presidents have acted to satisfy national interests, even as idealistic notions changed dramatically between, and sometimes within, their own administrations.[7]

Faith in the American experiment certainly came easy when its inheritors felt they represented the "chosen nation." Yet American-style liberalism also could be worrisomely intolerant of other political ideologies. Here were inklings of a corresponding relationship between faith and fear that would inform US policies for decades to come. Americans might have faith in their ideological exceptionalism being protected by war, yet they feared any threat, ideological or otherwise, that might undermine the United States' privileged economic and military position. Wielding or threatening the use of force thus became an integral component of how Americans related with the outside world. Fear of failure reinforced a fragile faith in what military power might achieve.[8]

As the Cold War solidified, Wilsonian internationalism appeared to some a model worthy of emulation in this new global contest for safety and security. Americans would lead under the banners of "democracy" and "self-determination," all while ensuring a global order that facilitated US access to foreign markets and raw materials. And for those who feared the coming of yet another ideological contest so soon after World War II, Wilsonian ideals seemed as relevant as ever. Indeed, high school students in the former president's home state of New Jersey argued in 1956 that the best way to defeat communism was to "help educate other nations in the best way to achieve democracy and equality." As the state's governor, Robert B. Meyner, argued at the Phillipsburg Youth Forum that winter, "Freedom for mankind would be impossible with communism in the ascendancy."[9]

And here is where war came in. Higher democratic ideals often were eclipsed by concerns over "national security"—always a relative term—that delineated Americans' place in the world. War shaped post-1945 views on both crusading idealism and hard-power realism. Many citizens saw World War II as an inflection point, a critical moment demanding a new and expansive role for the United States and its armed forces in perilous times. Cold Warriors at once could embrace a faith that "American expansion naturally improved the world," while also fearing that that world was a "dangerous place," as realists warned. Not surprisingly, policymakers from George Kennan to Lyndon Johnson, from Henry Kissinger to Madeleine Albright, would all attempt to balance idealist and realist notions as they considered war's relationship to US foreign policy.[10]

Yet surveyors of that foreign policy often have focused less on war and more on competition within a larger international system. These systemic arguments surely still carry weight.[11] On one side, they account for early Cold War realists like Hans J. Morgenthau who insisted international politics was a "struggle for power." On the other, they interrogate the United States' search for "extraregional hegemony" in a competitive world, spotlighting the aftereffects of using "raw power" to achieve global dominance and of overestimating threats to US foreign policy. Writing in the mid-1950s, for instance, historian William Appleman Williams argued, not without merit, that unless American hegemonic pursuits "were modified to deal with [their] own consequences, the policy was certain to produce foreign policy crises that would become increasingly severe."[12]

Without question, ideology, interests, and the international system all informed US foreign policy in the decades following World War II. However, if we reframe Cold War debates around more basic human motives, an oft-unspoken truth emerges.[13]

In the second half of the twentieth century, another set of tensions guided US policies abroad—and, just as often, at home—on a far more practical, far more human level. Throughout these decades, Americans' individual and collective relationship with war remained central to their very identity, and thus to how they waged the Cold War and beyond. Understanding that relationship allows us to better evaluate the Cold War as both a lived experience and a historical era.[14]

What I am arguing is that faith in and fear of war became the keystones of US grand strategy in the years after 1945, if not the main influencers shaping American foreign policy. Again, notions of ideology, national security, and open access to markets were important. But what influenced whether ideology or interests would take precedence? What propelled these topics in both public debates and private policy discussions? I contend the answer can be found in America's relationship with war, in the inherent tension between faith in war and fear of its consequences.

In a sense, I am asking what motivated state behavior and individual decision-making when it came to the Cold War competition. I suggest that for many Americans living throughout the long decades of this era, high-minded debates about liberalism or alliance structures held far less sway than what they thought about war. Their vision of, if not faith in, what was possible at the conclusion of World War II collided sharply with deep-seated, "primitive" fears over what war might bring in the atomic era.[15]

I maintain that a secular faith in war to solve US foreign-policy problems, coupled with fears of America's enemies laying waste to the nation's interests, indelibly shaped policy choices aimed at containing communism around the globe. At times, faith and fear determined the path of policy, even when ideology and interests also were at play. Americans held to their faith that war would be utilitarian, a "rational means" for attaining their desired ends. And yet, constantly present was a fear, intertwined with ideology, in perennial arguments for an ever-stronger military. As Chairman of the Joint Chiefs of Staff Omar N. Bradley testified in 1949, the United States faced an "antagonistic" ideology that was "attempting to penetrate into the very homes we cherish." As the general argued, if war was "thrust upon us," the nation had to respond "by all means at our disposal." The stakes were so high because there was "no second prize for the runner-up."[16]

In such castings, war might bring chaos or a loss of prestige, but it also lured with the promise of influence, even dominance, the chance to reshape or control whole swaths of the globe. If faith and fear helped shape foreign policy—and, as we'll see, popular culture—in the Cold War era, how were such concepts expressed in a global conflict which seemingly posed an existential threat to the nation? How did policymakers explain war's potential benefits? How did average Americans conceive of war's destructive power after witnessing the final, fiery blows of World War II?[17]

My focus on faith and fear is meant not to displace existing historical frameworks or to buck welcome trends that are globalizing Cold War history. Rather, I wish to complement these interpretations by concentrating on war's deeper relationship to American Cold War society, not just to structural interpretations of policymaking decisions. At its core,

I am arguing that faith in and fear of war defined the cognitive framing of American foreign policy and grand strategy throughout the entirety of the Cold War era, with enormous social and cultural implications that rippled across the post–World War II decades.[18]

By faith, I am not referring to religious determinants in US foreign policy. For sure, we shall encounter church leaders using their pulpits in service to both God and the anticommunist cause. And, of course, religion intersected political ideologies and nationalist ideas not just in the United States but across the globe during these years. Instead, I express faith as an anecdote to policymakers' unwavering trust and confidence in war, as a vital tool for achieving their strategic objectives, however defined. In many ways, both religious and secular faith require believing in something without evidence. Cold War Americans shared a deep faith in war while hoping it might eliminate that of which they were deeply afraid. At times, they proselytized their faith to mask fears over losing their position as the world's most powerful nation. At others, they sent soldiers out as quasi missionaries to save humanity from itself.[19]

Notably, there were some among the policymaking elite who did not blindly embrace war for its positive aspects, whose faith could be shaken by what war might unleash. Wary of their faith-based colleagues, they saw war mostly as a defensive imperative, a necessity, but a bad one nonetheless. Others, like political scientist Harold Lasswell, went further, arguing that so much power in the hands of so few could perpetuate a "caste-like garrison-police state." Yet, too often these voices were drowned out by a faith in war. The United States had to generate power, so the argument went, and then use that power to advance its political and economic aims against an unyielding enemy. In this way, strategists in and out of uniform sought to make war usable for the nation, to wield force for fulfilling their aspirations and for combating their fears.[20]

Importantly, these convictions transcended policy circles. Faith in war was not just propagated as a means toward national security ends, but, more broadly, could be crafted as a redemptive social and cultural force as well. The relationships between faith and fear worked, in large part, because of these intersections between the foreign and domestic.

Throughout the Cold War, war helped produce "cultural meaning," a way for Americans to make sense of the world around them and their place in it. Terms like "national defense" and "national security" mattered. Both politicians and their constituents grappled with their connotations, thought about their implications, and debated how their very identity as Americans was bound up in the meaning of war. Thus, we need to examine not only foreign policy and military establishments but the influence of (and war's impact on) the American public and popular culture as well.[21]

As we'll see, Americans' faith in war remained at odds with the historical record. Faith ignored the tangible limits to American power abroad. Faith discounted the reality that war rarely delivered as much as policymakers desired from it. (We might ask if anything ever does.) But faith also partnered well with politics. No politician could hope to win office by campaigning on the limits of American power when facing an evil, expansionistic communist threat. Instead, eager candidates extolled the nation's military capabilities, minimizing the costs of war while worshiping its benefits. In the process, as one critic has argued, Americans with a "power problem" consistently expressed "outsized expectations" of what military force could achieve. Seldom did they consider the possibility that military intervention might make matters worse, exacerbating problems abroad instead of solving them.[22]

Perhaps unsurprisingly, those who didn't accept this compulsory faith were branded as unpatriotic heretics. During the 1960 presidential campaign, for example, Democrats accused Republican candidate Richard Nixon of seeking to "impute disloyalty or lack of patriotism" to anyone who criticized the nation's foreign policy. John F. Kennedy combatively weighed in, condemning the Eisenhower administration for not doing *more* to support defense readiness. In such ways, faith in war, taken to its extreme, could breed hyper-patriotism, xenophobia, and militarism. Dissent could be driven to the political periphery. It seemed far easier, and far more patriotic, to embrace false promises of effortless, if not eventual, victory when the nation committed itself to war.[23]

INTRODUCTION 9

Alongside this essentialist faith in war hovered a fear that nearly all national security threats, both external and domestic, were existential ones. Cold War Americans fastened their faith in war to a kind of primal, Hobbesian fear of the unknown. They tended to agree with the English philosopher that the human "state of nature" was one of endemic "warre." Thus, only a strong, militarized state could provide the security needed to dampen their post–World War II fears while achieving their interests abroad.[24]

Those viewing the Cold War conflict through systemic or ideological lenses have recognized fear's role in shaping the trajectory of American foreign policy. Political scientist John Mearsheimer contends that fear might be seen as the "central aspect of life in the international system." In competing for influence and limited resources, great powers tend to distrust and fear one another. And, of course, fear of communist ideology surely colored Americans' views of the Soviet Union in the aftermath of World War II. Nor were these worries unique to the United States. National security fears also played an important role in Joseph Stalin and Mao Zedong's worldviews—and the eventual Sino-Soviet ideological break—as the Cold War unfolded.[25]

But what were Americans afraid of? What left them in a near-constant state of Cold War paranoia? Well, everything. They feared atomic war and "unconventional" war. They feared an anarchic international system seemingly under threat by global communist forces. They feared arms races and missile gaps, threats abroad and threats at home. They feared depressions and recessions, the future and the past. They feared Soviet spies and Cuban "revolutionaries." And, perhaps worst of all, they feared each other. Rather than adopting a "realistic, war-preventing fear," Americans displayed a "neurotic anxiety" born of perpetually exaggerated fear. If they thought about grand strategy helping answer the question "What is our power for?" then many conceivably would have answered, "To keep us safe from what we fear."[26]

Historical precedence surely carried weight. Pearl Harbor remained on Americans' minds long after their World War II victory. The surprise Japanese attack exposed a lack of preparedness that arguably set Cold

War fears indelibly in motion. Vast oceans no longer served as inviolable barriers from America's enemies. The US armed forces now would have to project power far from their shores. In many ways, "never again" became a sort of mantra of the Cold War era. On the tenth anniversary of the "day that would live in infamy," Vice President Alben W. Barkley illustratively counseled at a Honolulu memorial ceremony that Americans had to pledge "there will never be another such day in the country's history. We must be constantly prepared and ever watchful," the Kentucky native declared. The wreckage of battleships like the USS *Arizona* thus served as "a somber and terrible warning that we must never again be heedless or complacent."[27]

This chilling sense of vulnerability and the need for "absolute security" helped to redefine what war meant for Americans. In an age when World War II seemingly had fractured present from past, when the Soviets had tested their first atomic bomb (in 1949), and when communist spies were thought to be everywhere, any real or imagined era of "free security" appeared a distant pipe dream. No longer could citizen-soldiers demobilize after war, setting the foundations for a permanent security state at odds with some of the Founding Fathers' fundamental ideals.[28]

If Americans were to achieve the "total defense" of which Franklin D. Roosevelt had earlier spoken, then preparation for war would have to be continuous, an enduring activity embedded into their very way of life. Once more, apparently existential threats to their security justified their fears. Communist expansion, national and ethnic rivalries, and nuclear proliferation all purported to destabilize an international system in which national security was far from certain. Insecurity became ingrained as fears of a "future imbalance of power" rattled military and civilian alike.[29]

As the Cold War endured, shrewd politicians and opportunistic policymakers realized that fear could be useful for persuasion and propaganda. If the Soviet Union already had "declared psychological warfare against the United States," according to one information-agency official, then should not Americans respond in kind? Taken to its politicized extreme, fear could coerce a form of consensus and breed obedience.

When Senator Barry Goldwater (R-AZ) argued in 1960 that he and his fellow Americans might become "slaves" if the United States lost to the Soviet Union, he clearly was positioning himself as a stalwart defender of the nation worthy of election to the highest of offices.[30]

Raising alarm about imaginary fifth columnists also could burnish the credentials of those wishing to be seen as "tough" on communism, helping build political solidarity among their constituents. Exploiting fears in the fight against evil would propel eager politicians into the national spotlight, Senator Joseph McCarthy (R-WI) and Congressman Richard Nixon (R-CA) being two leading examples. Fellow politicians might privately revile the antics of "Tailgunner Joe," yet Republicans increasingly took McCarthy's side as more and more Americans came to support his anticommunist crusade. Serving on a Subversive Activities Control Board, as one example, could boost aspiring politicians' careers as they held public hearings to root out "Communist action" or "Communist front" groups.[31]

Big business likewise could profit from fear. Not only could companies reap financial rewards by hawking "bomb havens" that allegedly protected against the "blast, heat and radiological effects" of a nuclear attack. Just as importantly, the nation's increased military posture benefited major defense firms by awarding them contracts for vast weapons programs, and the insidious relationships between legislators and the lobbyists for these firms would become a hallmark of Cold War politics. As one journalist noted in 1960, the purposes of the military-industrial complex fit "neatly in the atmosphere of crisis, since World War II, as the United States continued to be held in the grip of wartime thinking." In successive presidential administrations, social-welfare programs would suffer because of this forced imbalance within the national budget.[32]

Consequently, it would be mistaken to argue, as esteemed historian John Lewis Gaddis does, that only communist ideology depended, "for its functioning, upon the creation of fear." The other ideology, democratic capitalism, "had no need to do so." For Gaddis, the underlying basis of the US government during the Cold War era, unlike the Soviet

Union, "would be hope, not fear." Reexamining these years through a slightly different lens reveals that the United States relied just as much on the construction and propagation of fear as did its ideological foe.[33]

Such a focus on faith and fear requires us to embrace a comprehensive approach to America's relationship with military might, one that expands beyond Clausewitzian views of war as a means to political ends. Of course, the nineteenth-century Prussian military theorist understood that human dynamics like passion, hatred, and reason were integral to war. My aim, however, is to outline war more as a social phenomenon, a "form of human interaction," as it were. Back in the early 1990s, British military historian John Keegan famously critiqued Clausewitz's thought as "incomplete," suggesting that his answer to the question "What is war?" was "defective." While I dare not tempt the Prussian gods with similar impertinence, I do believe it useful to broaden our evaluation of America's relationship with war beyond just the political realm. And we need to broaden our definition of "war" beyond just a synonym for "military force."[34]

This more comprehensive definition of war matters because, for Americans living in the post–World War II era—the "American Century," as publishing magnate Henry Luce called it in early 1941—war became part of their identity. War sustained their vision of national self as the protector of global peace. And war, along with the military force required to wage it, enabled access to foreign trade and markets. In many ways, Luce was foreshadowing immediate post–Cold War claims of the United States being the "indispensable nation" in global affairs. Neither Luce nor future Secretary of State Madeleine Albright believed America to be uniquely warlike, even if the nation-state had been born from armed conflict. Yet they likely would have agreed that war retained a special place in Americans' understanding of nationalism and patriotism as the Cold War endured.[35]

In this light, *Faith and Fear* examines war not just from those working in the Pentagon or serving in military units across the globe, however important they were during the Cold War. Rather, we will look at generals and diplomats, presidents and movie directors, and those ordinary

Americans who engaged with the sometimes vague yet always pervasive, even systemic, relationships between war and society. None of these actors was working in isolation from one another. Crucial decisions on defense and national security evolved through conversations between policymakers, in uniform and out, as well as with the general public. War cohered American society as it seeped across social, political, and economic boundaries.[36]

This holistic approach seems necessary, for war appeared an encompassing force in these decades. As George Kennan, the father of "containment," saw it in 1951, "many people in this country are coming to believe that war is not only unavoidable but imminent." (We might note that by 1950 Kennan's fears were as much about American strategic shortcomings as about Soviet perfidy.) Decades of reflection hardly had altered his views. Looking back more than thirty years later, the State Department diplomat recalled that Americans were "threatened by the outside world" that had arrived in 1950, so much so that they "seemed to be able to think of little else but this danger."[37]

All the while, these fears were complemented by a near-messianic faith in American power and innocence. Cold War security policies could be fashioned as part of a longer historical mission justifying immense defense budgets. Americans took faith that their liberal ideology, coupled with military might, offered stability, if not peace, within the international system. They assumed their nation stood apart from its imperialistic European partners, even as some critics wondered aloud if they were an "empire in denial." Perhaps unsurprisingly, "Why do *they* hate us?" would become a popular refrain, especially at the opening of the twenty-first century as America confronted a new enemy that seemed as vicious as Cold War communist hordes.[38]

These tensions between faith and fear matter because they delineated Americans' thinking about strategy in the modern era. If strategy is about choices, we must ask how much faith in and fear of war contributed to policymakers rendering decisions about the threat and use of military force. Surely, these Cold War choices involved balancing bold political aspirations with limited military or economic means. But if grand strategy is an "intellectual architecture that gives form and structure to foreign policy," as Hal Brands proposes, then it's vital to examine how ideas on war influenced these designs.[39] Any state's relative power derives from a host of resources, from economic to demographic. I submit, however, that during the Cold War, Americans more often than not defined "power" in military terms because of their faith in and fear of war.[40]

It then followed, almost logically, that US foreign policy became increasingly militarized as the global conflict endured. Faith and fear elevated war to a preeminent position among the nation's other instruments of power. In such an environment, diplomatic means easily became devalued in relation to military ones. Still, the interplay between blind faith and existential fear somehow seemed dissatisfying, even absurd to some. British historian Arthur Bryant put the matter succinctly in early 1955. "War may be necessary to save freedom," he argued. "Yet modern war is so materially destructive and so socially and spiritually disintegrating that it can destroy civilization and freedom in saving them."[41] Might war not be all that it was cracked up to be?

What follows is not a comprehensive historical overview of the Cold War, but rather a reflection on how war was conceptualized throughout the turbulent decades following World War II. What I offer is a new window into thinking about American behavior during these Cold War years. Within the national security state, war became central to basic definitions of security, foreign policy, and even national identity at a time when many Americans saw themselves participating in a global struggle against an evil, ideologically driven foe.

Further, because my main concern lies with how Americans perceived the utility and dangers of armed force during the Cold War, neither is this an all-inclusive global military history. We will examine only tangentially, for instance, the nationalist struggles and decolonization efforts in places like India, Africa, and Indonesia, three crucially important sites for how the global conflict unfolded in the twentieth century.[42]

Without question, these regions mattered. Along what many policymakers dismissively judged the "periphery"—and what some contemporary strategists called "gray areas"—the United States remained perennially engaged in destructive wars that showcased both faith and fear.[43] Two sides of the same coin were integral to America's military interventionism. Faith in war led high-minded Americans to see it as a socially transformative force capable of remaking "traditional" societies abroad. Meanwhile, fear of losing influence to communist competitors drove US armed forces and civilian officials across the Global South, where the vast majority of Cold War deaths occurred. Violence thus became a fundamental aspect of the United States' global presence, even as General Dwight D. Eisenhower warned in 1950 against "dispersing American power all over the globe."[44]

Moreover, as we shall see, American-sponsored development programs in the "Third World" went hand in hand with the application of military force. For fearful Americans, the very course of history seemed in jeopardy. What if the intended recipients of great-power benevolence chose poorly and threw in their lot with communist fraudsters? This "civilizing mission," backed by armed force, ironically denied the self-determination that US policymakers so openly pledged to support.[45] Thus, as Soviet, Chinese, and US officials all tested their own modernization experiments abroad, they contributed to and intensified the violence that became endemic to the Cold War Global South. For Americans in particular, their faith in liberal ideas and capitalist institutions sat uneasily aside fears that their ideology might not win approval of those who apparently needed democracy most. Hubris and horror, though, made for a violent world outlook. Outside the confines of Western Europe, the Cold War hardly could be called an era of "long peace."[46]

In short, we need to wrestle with the role and consequences of a militarized American state during the latter half of the twentieth century. A "cold" war did not mean the absence of violence, and far too often the United States had a heavy hand in propagating that violence across the globe.[47]

Since Americans from across the political and social spectrum—legislators, military planners, journalists, and film producers, to name but a few—largely embraced this faith and fear, it is important, then, to ask how all this happened. Without question, the general public could be manipulated into accepting a wartime mentality. Policy elite or big business adeptly promoted notions of a Cold War carrying great risks because political and financial rewards could be found within an increasingly militarized American society.

Even as some resisted this militarization, far too many bought into arguments that war at once could bring them harm yet, simultaneously, keep them safe. In 1952, Supreme Court Justice William O. Douglas warned that a "concentration on military means" was breeding "fear and insecurity." The jurist bemoaned the "military thinking" that was playing such a "dominant role in our domestic affairs." A similarly minded editorialist in the *Hartford Courant* argued that confronting the communist threat through loyalty purges, censorship, and suppression was "the very stuff of which the police state is made. If we resort to them, we will fasten upon ourselves the very chains we want to keep off." But such warnings too often fell flat. In an antagonistic Cold War culture, few citizens questioned the role that war played in their lives.[48]

Perhaps there were two reasons why this faith in war rested uneasily with a parallel fear of war: a fervid search for security after decades of depression and global conflict, and an insecurity over the United States' status after its emergence as a postwar superpower. Addressing an audience at the University of North Carolina in Chapel Hill, Senator J. William Fulbright deplored the "vast diversion of energy and resources from the creative pursuits of a civilized society to the conduct of a costly and interminable struggle for world power." (Notably, the Arkansas Democrat would become a fierce critic of US escalation in Vietnam.) William Faulkner equally lamented the "general and universal physical fear" and its consequences. "There are no longer problems of the spirit," the American writer argued. "There is only the question: When will I be blown up?"[49]

Paradoxically, the more the nation spent on defense, the more vulnerable its citizens felt. Many Cold War Americans thus feared not only war but also its consequences. What if war didn't deliver on its assurances?

Would the nation lose its influence overseas? Would national security be threatened?⁵⁰

There were, of course, dissenters. As early as 1950, the *New York Times* editorialized that, in the search for security, fear was undermining democracy itself. The challenge lay in suppressing those fears. "There is a security in the faith that does not shiver at every shadow or at the whistle of every wind."⁵¹

These critics are important for our story. They shone a reasoned light on their nation's flawed relationship with war. And their inability to resist the culture of war helps us understand why the United States maintains such an unhealthy, dysfunctional relationship with war to this day. Theologian Reinhold Niebuhr stood tall among these critics, arguing that an inability to grapple with the limits of their own power had left Americans anxious about the future. The ethicist maintained it wasn't easy "for an adolescent nation, with illusions of childlike innocence, to come to terms with the responsibilities and hazards of global politics in an atomic age." As a result, powerful nations like the United States tended to "use the weak as instruments of their purposes." What Niebuhr was suggesting in the early 1950s rings true today. Fear that the United States might not endure as a global power, coupled with a faith in military power itself, has left Americans dependent on war and all that it promises.⁵²

Faith and Fear thus situates the concept of war as central to American foreign relations during the second half of the twentieth century and to the domestic atmosphere shaping that concept. I see faith and fear as linchpins of my reconsideration since so much of Cold War policy fixated on America's confidence in and doubts about its own military power.

Alternating between diplomatic, military, and cultural history, I suggest that Americans' relationship with war since 1945 has rested on an uncritical faith in their own military strength and the supposed advantages of using it. Beside this faith sat irrational fears guiding policy elite toward war without regard to the consequences of relying so instinctively on raw military power.

Ultimately, the horrific experiences of World War II had left Americans grappling with an uncomfortable legacy. War might safeguard them against dangerous enemies—both at home and abroad—but new adversaries always seemed lurking, ready to destroy what young American GIs had fought so hard to secure in a supposedly "good war" to help liberate the world.[53]

PART I

War to Defeat Evil

CHAPTER 1

Freedom from Fear?

Veteran journalist Theodore H. White was struck by the number of stars that Sunday morning. White had traveled widely during the Second World War, serving admirably as *Time* magazine's China correspondent during the global conflict. He had seen famine and war, and in his bestselling book *Thunder Out of China* reported on the growing communist movement in Asia's largest country. Aboard the USS *Missouri* on September 2nd, 1945, however, White couldn't help but comment on the stars. The ship's veranda "bristled" with them. Douglas MacArthur wore five. Behind him were "five full four-star generals... eleven three-star generals backing up the four-stars, followed by twenty two-star generals and fifteen one-stars." Nor did these numbers include the navy admirals, marine corps generals, or cluster of allied officers aboard the *Missouri* that morning. Clearly, the Japanese surrender ceremony was a command performance not to be missed.[1]

Not surprisingly, MacArthur came prepared for his part. The "master of the Pacific," as White called him, began by proclaiming a "solemn agreement" had been made "whereby peace may be restored." MacArthur then shared his hope of a better world emerging "out of the blood and carnage of the past—a world founded upon faith and understanding." His final remarks that morning, now aimed at his fellow countrymen, warned of a new era dawning. "Even the lesson of victory," the general cautioned, "brings with it profound concern, both for our future security and the survival of civilization." With scientific discovery revising the "traditional concept of war"—atomic bombs had obliterated two Japanese cities less than one month prior—MacArthur feared that future policy failures would mean "Armageddon will be at our door." The path to peace could no longer lead through the "crucible of war."[2]

Ever the showman, MacArthur emotionally concluded that America's sons and daughters, who had served "well and faithfully," were now "homeward bound." "Take care of them," he ended. As he did, White watched as some 400 B-29 bombers and 1,500 fleet planes roared overhead. "There they were, speckling the sky in flecks of scudding gray; it was American power at its zenith."[3]

But was it? If the *Missouri* ceremony represented the height of American power, then why was an architect of the World War II victory warning that mankind's future lay at risk? What did MacArthur's warning portend for those Americans who had sacrificed so much during the war? Had evil been vanquished? Had "freedom from fear" been realized with the defeat and occupation of Germany and Japan? Perhaps the unconditional surrender of America's enemies had not established an absolute condition of peace. Perhaps what came after war only increased obligations for securing the nation, if not the world, from future threats.[4]

Here lies the paradox of victory in World War II: the United States had become a world power, but an immensely insecure one. American policymakers and citizens warily accepted that in the wake of such a destructive global conflict, only they could assume the mantle of international leadership. Europe lay in ruins, Japan prostrate, and China wracked by civil war.[5]

The war had extracted gargantuan human costs. And so, despite its concrete results, victory appeared incomplete. President Franklin D. Roosevelt had not lived to cherish the fruits of his labor, and his faith in globalizing America's liberal ideas seemed already falling short by 1945. As historian Daniel Sargent notes, what "emerged after the Second World War was not the integrated, liberal world order that American planners hoped to build, but a world divided, not only between East and West but also between north and south."[6]

Nor was it clear wartime alliances would endure after the guns fell silent. The implications of new technologies surely didn't help matters. Soviet leader Joseph Stalin feared Americans would use their atomic monopoly "to force us to accept their plans on questions affecting Europe and the world." For their part, US policymakers saw the Grand Alliance coming apart well before MacArthur spoke aboard the *Missouri*. Admiral William D. Leahy, the president's military chief of staff, had warned FDR at the February 1945 Yalta Conference of Russian ambitions in Eastern Europe. Soviet protocols on Poland, the admiral cautioned, were "elastic." Reasonably, territorial disputes might once more lead to military conflict. Thus, with World War II still raging, Americans foresaw a future far less peaceful than they had hoped.[7]

Afraid of that future, some Americans also feared the past. Relapsing into another economic depression after war's end proved most unsettling. While not as dire as in Great Britain, whose national debt had quadrupled during the war, US economists still worried about inevitable job losses as the troops came home. (Disgruntled, out-of-work veterans long had been a concern in American history.) With the US economy nearly doubling during the war and pulling the nation out of the Great Depression, what would happen when defense spending cooled? Roosevelt's successor, Harry S. Truman, hinted at these fears in his January 1946 State of the Union address. The peacetime task ahead, the president maintained, was to achieve "the full utilization and development of our physical and human resources that were demonstrated so effectively in the war." Not surprisingly, State Department officials equated "full employment and prosperity" at home with the acquisition of markets abroad.[8]

The physical devastation that war had wrought overseas, specifically in Europe, fanned these economic fears and gave them political import. Winston Churchill spoke of a European "charnel house" and how war's aftermath might turn into "a breeding ground of pestilence and hate."

The dislocation of so many people, with little immediate prospect for normalcy, portended economic instability and, worse, socialist and communist takeovers in places like France, Italy, and Greece. So too in Asia. Could not wartime ally China, engulfed in a brutal civil war, fall to the communists now that the common Japanese threat had been expelled? Everywhere, it seemed, economic privation had the potential of encouraging despondent war victims to embrace communism and once more pit the United States against oppressive, authoritarian enemies.[9]

Among these fears, however, lay a burgeoning faith in an American-dominated global economy facilitating social reform and, with it, long-term political stability preventing future wars. It was an enduring faith, from underpinning the European Recovery Program—popularly known as the Marshall Plan—to efforts at globalizing the US economy during the 1990s. Not long after his surprising 1948 reelection, Truman described poverty as "a handicap and a threat" communists would exploit if the United States remained passive. The president expressed his faith that if Americans worked alongside "peace-loving peoples" around the world, they could "help them realize their aspirations for a better life." Republican Jacob Javits agreed, but discerned a competition against sheer evil. As the New York congressman warned, those suffering in war-ravaged areas and seeking help might adopt "communist doctrine and philosophy." Americans had to "meet that challenge successfully," Javits advised, or lose out in an increasingly zero-sum game.[10]

As faith in the power of economic development preventing war gained purchase among US policy elite, some encouraged exporting New Deal policies abroad. Might FDR-era programs, they asked, remake the postwar world according to American values: free trade and open-door economic alliances, participatory democracy, and a commitment to collective security? Implicit were expectations of the United States dominating such a liberal world order. If Javits correctly inferred that the Soviets would contest US hegemony around the world, Americans evidently had few alternatives. With little questioning, then, faith in New Deal liberalism fit neatly alongside fears that Americans were entering a new global conflict against an erstwhile ally and now ideological foe.[11]

The fraying US-Soviet relationship surely alarmed American policymakers. FDR had intended to work with Stalin upon war's end, to set up a "machinery of peace," as he called it. Ideological differences, he felt, need not impede cooperation and collective security. While Roosevelt wasn't some starry-eyed idealist—he accepted his nation's limited influence over events unfolding in Eastern Europe—the president still believed democratic capitalism would appeal more than communism in the postwar world. His successor, however, took a more pessimistic view. For Truman, Russia no longer was an ally but an enemy. To budding Cold Warriors, Truman more lucidly saw the threat already confronting the United States in 1945. Admiral Leahy found the new president's views "more than pleasing," while Republican Senator Arthur H. Vandenberg trumpeted in his diary that "FDR's appeasement of Russia is over." Suspicion and anticommunism fast were becoming cornerstones of American foreign policy.[12]

Added to these burgeoning Cold War fears was an awareness, in Pearl Harbor's aftermath, that Americans no longer could assume the geographical advantages provided by two vast oceans. Security is a relative concept, but World War II appeared a breaking point in how Americans conceived of its idea and practice. The supposed "lessons" of Pearl loomed large in the late 1940s. Americans now needed a "global military presence" to derail future attacks, a worldwide structure of military bases to defend "in depth," and an intelligence machinery to avoid another "sucker punch" from treacherous enemies. In language reminiscent of the post-9/11 era, policymakers argued that anticipating threats abroad offered far more safety than reacting to them once they struck home. If there ever was an era of "free security," Pearl Harbor had disabused Americans of that illusion. After World War II, war would occupy a place in the American psyche that it never fully would relinquish.[13]

The emerging postwar era thus seemed different, even if war always had been embedded in Americans' collective psychological DNA. In many ways, America's relationship with war hadn't been as central to basic definitions of foreign policy, security, and national identity prior to the Second World War. Certainly, war had been part and parcel of US policy since the nation's founding; but after two global wars in the first half of the twentieth century, war now dominated policy elites' conceptions of what was needed for the state to prosper, and indeed even to survive.

With this developing reliance on war, policy leaders drew other "lessons" from World War II. For one, any postwar demobilization spelled doom for global peace and security. In late 1946, former Marine Corps Commandant Holland M. Smith castigated Washington policymakers for discharging men in uniform. By demobilizing America's armed forces, he argued, "one of the greatest implements for world peace disappeared." Of course, bored and disgruntled GIs overseas were clamoring that the demobilization process was taking too long. "We want to go home" slogans sat uneasily aside claims that the United States needed to be strong if it wanted to be safe. Thus, when senior military officers like Air Force General Curtis LeMay warned against dropping "our guard" after wars ended, Americans took heed.[14]

In fact, most citizens embraced a growing conviction that the United States was now, and must remain, a global military power. After World War II, they assumed their nation was a force for unqualified good. They were not alone. Washington elite coupled faith in American virtue with global leadership and the imposition of order, if not through democracy then by force. They justified this shift as necessary to ease their fears of a perilous world. In the process, American internationalism became reliant upon military supremacy. But this faith in armed force extended beyond its foreign-policy implications. Military power, in Andrew Bacevich's view, had deeper social and cultural consequences as it became "evidence of a larger American superiority." Faith in military power, as much as fear of war, was becoming linked to Americans' sense of self.[15]

Such a framing, however, required a redefinition of national defense. Military theorists would wrestle with these reinterpretations, especially as the atomic era dawned. To strategist Bernard Brodie, continuous "essential security" had to be "expansible" and move "beyond simple self-defense." If threats were ideological—and thus global—they would require a massive military infrastructure that rivaled the most expansive of empires. Indeed, World War II already had established a useful model. By war's end, the United States had built up a "global base network" of some 2,000 sites. When MacArthur offered his ceremonial remarks aboard the *Missouri*, the US Navy had constructed and occupied nearly 200 bases to support the Pacific campaign alone—thanks largely to local labor. As one study from the Joint Chiefs of Staff tersely concluded, the United States had to be "capable of applying armed force at a distance."[16]

While fear helped drive this military-imperial network, contemporary internationalists saw an "unparalleled opportunity to mold the postwar international system," especially given the "power vacuum" in places like Western Europe. Of course, economic benefits attended a permanent military presence overseas, and business leaders were quick to mention how internationalism supported open markets and alleviated fears of another depression. Moreover, at least some foreigners actively pursued a US security blanket. Reporting from Paris in early 1951, the *New York Times* bureau chief claimed that while Europeans might hold a "fear and distrust of American power," more clearheaded observers worried that Soviet "conquest" might alter the international system in Moscow's favor. Thus, America, with its "unique power," had a "responsibility toward regions whose safety has been officially defined as vital to the United States." Defining "vital" would become an enduring (and volatile) national debate.[17]

In these early postwar years, then, Americans were establishing an intellectual, if not emotional, framework for the Cold War era, one founded upon military activism. The tension between faith and fear was foundational to this structure, while also encouraging the emerging ideological competition. International-relations theorist Hans Morgenthau, seeing the Cold War as an "all-or-nothing struggle," argued that it threatened to become hot because "unresolved political issues serve as a tangible focus upon which the fears and suspicions of the cold war can concentrate, seeking release in armed conflict." Alarmingly, Morgenthau spoke in global terms, maintaining that the communist challenge and the West's response concerned "the future political and social organization of the world."[18]

This global competition of ideologies surely made sense to those who saw World War II in a similar light, as a battle between American democracy and Nazi fascism or Japanese militarism. With recent history in mind, the Cold War easily could be construed as an existential conflict between two "incompatible systems," both with "global aspirations." Not surprisingly, both sides would accuse the other of expansionistic designs and craft policies accordingly. And while many US policymakers held faith that democratic capitalism would win out in the end, even in these early Cold War years, a fear pervaded Washington leaders that capitalist institutions might not take root in barren postwar landscapes abroad.[19]

While ideology mattered—popular historian Stephen Ambrose later would claim that democracies were so superior that they even produced better soldiers—the power of free-market capitalism, bound to grand strategic objectives, equally informed notions of ultimate Cold War victory. American technical production ostensibly had saved the day in World War II, demonstrating the value of liberal capitalism in harnessing humankind's intellect, ingenuity, and spirit of volunteerism to defeat evil. In this way, Cold Warriors might cite the Second World War as a guide for securing victory in the inevitable conflict ahead. As one *Washington Post* journalist argued in early 1949, "Russian cold war tactics" had placed a "greater emphasis on the economic phases of preparedness," and the United States must reply in kind.[20]

Whether economic or ideological, tensions between faith and fear would become a hallmark of the immediate postwar years and influence how policymakers saw the coming Cold War as a fundamental struggle between good and evil. In short, national security became *the* national interest. As one historian has argued, faith in America's moral goodness became a kind of "civil religion" within the United States. And, no doubt, the myth of the "greatest generation" later would converge with Americans' faith in assuming the mantle of world leadership, of being *the* righteous protector for defeating evil wherever it seemed to lurk.[21]

This sense of moral obligation to save the postwar world from the evils of global communism would infuse itself into foreign-policy debates and later buoy social-science theories promoting American-led "modernization" programs. Indeed, war and development would become uneasy partners during the Cold War era, as Americans would fight their war against evil with far more than just military tools, even if they preferred those tools most. They also would come to find that nation building and war making often made for poor bedfellows.[22]

But most Americans didn't think all that much about the consequences of wielding their military power on a global scale. World War II–era strategists argued that "power politics" demanded a "readiness for war," and by the 1950s, few questioned this prevailing narrative. Why would they when they saw a benevolent United States bravely defending the "free world" against a new and dangerous menace? There seemed little incentive, then, for Cold War policymakers to question this faith or, for that matter, their own fears.[23]

CHAPTER 2

The Cold War Comes

When did the Cold War begin? It depends on which historian you ask. And, in truth, those who witnessed its genesis weren't so sure either. There were no sudden war-opening battles, no Pearl Harbors around which to rally the nation, no public declarations separating peace from war. To most observers, this new power struggle pitting the United States against the Soviet Union had roots preceding World War II, perhaps even the creation of the Union of Soviet Socialist Republics (USSR) itself. British writer George Orwell's first use of the term "cold war" in 1945 intimated a "new world system," but the transition from old to new remained blurry, an indistinct passage from one era to the next.[1]

Undeniably, the essence of the Cold War's ideological competition was evident well before the 1940s. With the Russian monarchy's fall during the 1917 Bolshevik Revolution, a symbolic challenge to the capitalist world order came hazily into view. Perhaps, it now seemed, the Great War might not deliver on its promise "to end all wars" after all. Woodrow Wilson, seeking to imprint his own vision on the postwar international system, saw Bolshevism as a "mistake" that "must be resisted as all mistakes are resisted." But clearly this all appeared more threat than mistake. The Bolsheviks were promoting a universalistic ideology that contrasted starkly with the Wilsonian ideals of liberal, democratic capitalism. Already, it seemed, any coming contest would be a global one.[2]

Vladimir Lenin certainly thought so. In 1919, the Russian leader exhorted his followers to "arouse the working masses to revolutionary activity" and to "translate the true Communist doctrine . . . into the language of every people." That same year the Third Communist International formed in Moscow. Dubbed Comintern, Lenin's revolutionary organization sought an end not only to class domination but to imperialism itself. Communist parties soon began emerging in Europe, and in 1921 Lenin's organization sponsored the founding of the Chinese Communist Party. Everywhere one turned, the red tentacles of communism looked to be protruding outward from Moscow.[3]

While the Bolshevik Revolution resonated abroad, adding to the trauma of World War I, it also exposed the need for greater security and intelligence networks at home. As the war came to its bloody end, Lenin reached out to "class-conscious" American workers and promoted "overthrowing the bourgeoisie," leading the US attorney general, A. Mitchell Palmer, to proclaim that "the blaze of revolution was sweeping over every American institution of law and order" like a "prairie-fire." Cold War commentators, looking back on this moment from the 1950s, beheld the launch of communism's "permanent revolution." While Leninists saw capitalism as producing imperialism and war, Americans perceived Lenin's Bolsheviks as militant insurrectionists acting as a "vanguard of world revolution."[4]

This budding ideological contest led to America's first "red scare" in the 1920s. Critics charged that the "twisted brains of Moscow" were seeking to fill workers' minds with "socialist and communist jargon." In truth, the communist party didn't appeal to many Americans after World War I. Yet in both 1920s popular culture and political discourse, radical ideologues were lurking in the background awaiting their moment to pounce. One red scare critic thought it "primarily a domestic disease" born of "overwrought emotionalism." But such fears weren't dismissed so easily. Thirty years later, when a new, more potent red scare enveloped the United States, one reviewer suggested that modern America had become a "land of stampeding neuroses," with another depicting the nation in "chronic crisis" as a "consequence of our national insecurity."[5]

Thus, much of the anticommunist culture of fear so characteristic of the 1950s had its origins well before World War II. These fears, however, seemed perpetually overstated. As one critic of the Cold War argued, the communist party in America was "ridiculously weak." Indeed, it would never attract more than one-tenth of one percent of the nation's adult population. Yet such frailty mattered little to the nation's self-sworn defenders. In 1920, future FBI director J. Edgar Hoover, then working in the Justice Department's "Radical Division," apocalyptically declared that in communism "civilization faces its most terrible menace of danger since the barbarian hordes overran West Europe and opened the Dark Ages." Forty years later, Senator Barry Goldwater would echo similar sentiments, arguing that communism had "captured, enslaved, and exploited one billion people against their will" and that it was destroying "freedom, liberty, independence, human rights and dignity wherever possible." In the Arizona Republican's eyes, these were the "clear, inescapable truths about our enemy."[6]

Historical truths, though, are rarely so straightforward. After World War II, fear of communism easily could be manipulated by comparing former allies to former enemies. Policymakers and journalists alike compared communism to Nazism, publicly asking if "the man in the Kremlin" was "just another Hitler." One editorial maintained that Soviet leader Joseph Stalin, the "most powerful dictator in modern history," had become "the symbol of a cult, fanatically worshiped by the world's Communists as a leader who can do no wrong." Such assumptions, however, misconstrued Soviet intentions. State Department diplomat George Kennan felt it mistaken to conclude that Stalin and Hitler were "animated by the same lusts for military conquest" or that "they had the same sort of timetables for external military aggression." Despotic comparisons, though, demonstrated how easily fear-mongering could replace earlier versions of the "good Russian" once the US-Soviet alliance had crumbled. Almost effortlessly, fear could be stage-managed to adapt to any situation.[7]

It would be wrong, however, to assume these fears were falsely constructed. They rested upon genuine anxieties about future wars, informed by cogent "lessons" of the past. For many Americans worried about security in the new Cold War era, the most important lesson of World War II was that any negotiation with one's enemy meant "appeasing" evil. This Munich analogy, foregrounding fears of a maniacal authoritarian bent on global domination, would become a truism among US politicians and senior military leaders alike. Never mind that British Prime Minister Neville Chamberlain's supposed failure to stand up to Hitler at Munich in 1938 was a unique moment in history, not a universal instruction guide for future policymakers. The message was clear. Complacency led to appeasement; appeasement led to disaster.[8]

The upshot? Cold War policy quickly became militarized as a precaution against imagined would-be Hitlers. To military men like Curtis LeMay, only preemption guaranteed Americans' safety. According to LeMay, the United States shouldn't merely be preparing for war; it already was at war. It made sense, then, to eliminate the threat "at its source rather than at its destination." The challenge, of course, was determining if, when, and where the United States faced an imminent attack requiring preemption. But since communists couldn't be trusted, they left no choice but to maintain a posture of strength for deterring war and preparing for its eventuality. Campaigning for president in 1952, former Supreme Allied Commander Dwight D. Eisenhower relayed a line that American politicians would mimic throughout the Cold War. "The vital lesson is this," the general declared. "To vacillate, to appease, to placate is only to invite more war—vaster war—bloodier war."[9]

In the process, politicians assumed the United States was "more threatened than threatening." One Republican senatorial candidate in 1950 railed against his political opponents for giving "aid and comfort to Moscow." What was needed was more "courage and backbone in meeting the Red menace," he argued. Three years later, Michigan Senator Homer Ferguson charged that 1952 Democratic presidential nominee Adlai E. Stevenson was advocating "appeasement" of communism simply for suggesting high-level conferences with the Soviet Union. Part of this brashness no doubt stemmed from convictions that the United States was an unmitigated force for good on the world stage. As the Cold War endured, many foreign leaders would question such assumptions. But as US politicians on both sides of the aisle would find, it was far easier, and far more advantageous, to argue that evil communists were the aggressors when seeking support for one's own agenda.[10]

Even before World War II ended, Americans were convinced of the expansionist designs of their "quasi allies." At the July 1945 Potsdam Conference, American and British leaders knew that Stalin was seeking to extend Russian influence eastward while "liberating" Nazi-occupied territory in places like Poland, Hungary, and Czechoslovakia. Postwar critics, especially Republicans, latched onto this historical moment, claiming that FDR and Truman had sacrificed democracy in Eastern Europe while granting Stalin a "sphere of influence" there. One historian writing from the vantage point of 1964 believed Americans had come to several "disquieting" conclusions not long after World War II ended: that the Soviet Union "was not a peace-loving nation," and that Soviet policies were "prompted by aggressive rather than defensive designs."[11] It would not take long for those same Americans to place their faith in war as a shield for protecting their own sense of shared innocence.

Assertions of Soviet aggressiveness weren't hard to make when coupled with claims that the United States now faced a "permanent crisis" in global affairs. When historian Arthur M. Schlesinger, Jr. published *The Vital Center* in 1949, he spoke of such a crisis, that it would "test the moral, political and very possibly the military strength of each side." This state of enduring emergency—paired with the psychological impacts of living in a modern, consumeristic society—led to a "reign of insecurity" and a "fear of isolation." Looking back fifty years on, Schlesinger remembered how "the future of democracy seemed problematic" because World War II had "shattered the international order." As the Harvard professor recalled, a "struggle for the future was inevitable."[12]

Creation of the United Nations in October 1945 hardly assuaged these fears of perpetual war. Before his death, FDR had worried that war's end would evaporate commitments to cooperation and collective security. His successors, however, saw need in building an organization that would sustain American hegemony by providing stability to the postwar international order. The United States hadn't fought a global war simply to relinquish its global dominance. No doubt Stalin felt similarly. Within the two superpower camps, then, fearful skeptics looked across the ideological divide and accused those on the other side of only paying "lip service" to international cooperation and peace.[13]

In truth, fears in Moscow mirrored those running rampant in Washington. While Americans saw the Soviets' drive for increased territorial security as proof of their globalist designs, Stalin and his successors worried about capitalist encirclement in the wake of a destructive European war. For Stalin, recent history mattered. Russia had suffered tremendous losses during the war. Throughout 1943 and 1944, Moscow leaders exasperated over their allies' delay in opening a second front, suspecting that the bloodletting on the Eastern Front was welcomed by British and American officers. The lack of trust cut both ways. Thus Stalin, the "cautious expansionist," sought to expand Russia's western borders for bolstering his own security, all while US policymakers saw these moves as validating communist plots for global domination. Such expansionism, however, did not necessarily mean the Red Army was preparing for World War III. But convincing fearful Americans otherwise never came easily during the Cold War era.[14]

Stalin's ruthlessness at home provided further evidence of what Soviet communism might bring if left uncontested. Here, ideology loomed large. Interpreting Marxist thought literally, US policymakers assumed Stalin and his followers were committed to world revolution aimed at subverting the capitalist global order. But how well could pragmatism and ideology coexist in the war's aftermath? Stalin faced a broken economy, ruined cities, and a war-weary population. Marxism might suggest that war was an "external manifestation of internal class struggle," but the Soviet Union seemed ill-positioned to lead a global revolution in the late 1940s. Washington policymakers would struggle with this fundamental question for years to come. How committed were Stalin and his successors to radical visions of Marxist revolutionary thinking? Uncertain, contemporary policy advisors simply inferred that Moscow leaders were driven principally by "suspicion, distrust, and an abiding cynicism," attitudes that conceivably could lead to war.[15]

Stalin's own fears of being encircled by western imperial powers surely were part of this deadly equation. Moscow saw Eastern Europe not just as a "war trophy" but as an essential strategic buffer zone. In many ways, faith and fear developed inside the Soviet Union just as they did within the United States. Stalin's anxieties over the potential for renewed German military aggression seemed well founded given the massive destruction of World War II. As the Soviet leader argued, Russia and its allies "must retain possession of the important strategic points in the world, so that if Germany moved a muscle she could be rapidly stopped." All the while, Stalin held faith in Soviet military power keeping newly attained European satellites in check as Russia's "social system" extended throughout its sphere of influence.[16]

Perhaps unsurprisingly, this insecurity alienated Soviet satellites and set a tense relationship between "border states" and the Moscow politburo. The threat of Russian military intervention loomed over Eastern Europe, leaving Stalin's sphere a brittle one. Americans, though, often dismissed these tensions in favor of perceiving a coordinated, aggressive, and global communist threat. They increasingly viewed the Red Army not just as a tool for repression but as a potential force for revolution in Eastern Europe and beyond. Some maintained that the Soviet Union was practicing "puppet-government imperialism" and had forcibly "liberated" places like Albania, Romania, and Poland "into subservience." Yet the Soviet bloc never became as homogenous as US policymakers feared, even if Stalin prevented these newly won territories from entering into the postwar capitalist system.[17]

The question, then, was simple. Did Stalin want war? Unsure, Americans decided it best to err on the side of caution. Stalin's own security aims—in many ways, less ideological than assumed—clearly looked expansionistic from the outside. Making matters worse, it became increasingly difficult to assess what lurked behind the "Iron Curtain." When former British Prime Minister Winston Churchill first uttered this ominous phrase during a 1946 speech in Fulton, Missouri, he claimed the Soviets desired, if not war, at least "the fruits of war in the indefinite expansion of their power and doctrines." Surely, communists wanted more than just security, no? Unable to find clear answers to apparently existential questions, there seemed little choice but to gird for another global military conflict.[18]

Given so many ambiguities, we might ask how much of American grand strategy throughout the Cold War was speculative, formulated less on dispassionate analysis and more on emotion and conjecture. Intelligence chief Richard Helms recalled that "our knowledge of what the other side was up to, their intentions, their capabilities, was nil, or next to it." One CIA report agreed, acknowledging that the agency "had few methods of collecting intelligence on the Soviet Union and felt compelled to exploit every opportunity, however slim the possibility of success or unsavory the agent." Was the Red Army merely rebuilding after World War II or actually readying for global conquest? Without clear intelligence, rational policymakers decided to assume the latter.[19]

But fear can prejudice rationality. Certainly, not all Washington analysts believed Stalin was ready or willing to launch a new war. Some were aware of the "pitiful" conditions inside Russia precluding military aggression. Yet despite countervailing evidence, fear continued to guide US policy. Many within the Washington, DC orbit understood, as one historian has conjectured, that Stalin had a "pathological predisposition to create enemies internally and externally." Policy elite tended not to question whether their fears were overwrought given most people living within the Soviet orbit—if not throughout Europe—simply wanted to lead better lives after World War II. For ordinary Russians, the global competition between socialism and capitalism often mattered less than their desires for housing, health care, and a general sense of well-being.[20]

Enter George Kennan, the State Department diplomat and Sovietologist, who arguably shaped Cold War grand strategy more than any individual. The Milwaukee native had served on the American ambassadorial staff in Moscow during the 1930s and in 1944 became the embassy's deputy chief of mission. In many ways, prior to Kennan's writings, US policy toward Moscow had been "piecemeal." Kennan, though, had found his moment. His views on the Soviet "threat"—and its proper response—arrived just in time for them to hold purchase with both policymakers and the public at large. They also would become, to his lasting frustration, misrepresented and warped by those promoting military means as the only sensible response to the global communist menace.[21]

In short, Kennan maintained that Soviet power was, by nature, expansionist yet, paradoxically, inherently weak. Written from Moscow in February 1946, his "Long Telegram" to Washington colleagues painted the Soviet regime as one "accustomed to think primarily in terms of police power." While the communist state "did not take unnecessary risks," Kennan believed it was, nonetheless, "impervious to logic of reason" and thus "highly sensitive to logic of force." In his view, the threat was far more political than military, a point quickly losing credence after the Korean War began in 1950. Communism might be a "malignant parasite," but it could be best obstructed by the "health and vigor of our own society." Kennan may have demonized the Soviet Union in his telegram, but he also called for a confident response to Moscow's own sense of insecurity that eschewed fear-based militarism.[22]

The following year, Kennan took his views public, writing "The Sources of Soviet Conduct" for *Foreign Affairs* under the pseudonym "X." Herein lay the conceptual framework for what would become the decades-long Cold War grand strategy of "containment." After offering a tutorial on ideology, Kennan asserted that Moscow's "basic antagonism" toward capitalism, while perhaps "not founded in reality," was here to stay "for the foreseeable future." "This means," he argued, "that we are going to continue for a long time to find the Russians difficult to deal with." Such antagonisms did not mean war was inevitable. Rather, the "X Article" called for a policy relying on a "long-term, patient but firm and vigilant containment of Russian expansive tendencies." Kennan believed that Russia was "by far the weaker party," and thus Americans should be confident in confronting Soviet moves with an "unalterable counter-force at every point where they show signs of encroaching upon the interests of a peaceful and stable world."[23]

Kennan made sure to highlight Moscow's security fears in his calculus. In his view, Soviet insecurity trumped communist ideology, thus requiring "steady pressure" over the long haul. Of course, as Kennan himself acknowledged at the time, distinguishing "security" from "world domination" could be tricky. Which was Stalin truly pursuing? Moreover, it seemed likely that Moscow would view "containment" as nothing but a hostile policy of "encirclement," a debate resurfacing in the 1990s as the Clinton administration encouraged NATO's expansion after the Soviet Union's collapse. At the opening of the Cold War, however, Kennan's views corroborated those seeing America's relationship with war as central to its foreign policy. Power politics predicated on military response would become an unintended consequence of Kennan's call for patient yet resilient containment.[24]

The Long Telegram and "X Article" also highlighted the State Department's crucial role during the Cold War's early years. While Department of Defense influence would skyrocket over successive presidential administrations, Kennan and his peers helped set the foundation for America's faith in and fear of war. Diplomats like Charles "Chip" Bohlen and Elbridge Durbrow, while initially seeking a more cooperative, less militaristic relationship with the Soviet Union, became prominent architects of containment policies. Even Bohlen, who sympathized with the Russian people and their culture, concluded the world had become divided into "two irreconcilably hostile camps." Such changes of heart illustrated both fear's power and its pervasiveness, elevating apprehensions beyond the routine anxieties of nervous military officers.[25]

Certainly, Truman's secretary of state, Dean Acheson, saw two hostile camps. If Kennan was the theoretical architect of containment, Acheson became one of its earliest advocates. Against the threat of communist aggression, he proclaimed his generation's responsibility to "take up again the defense of freedom against the challenge of tyranny." As Acheson saw it, containment was a logical response to the "mortal threat" of the "Soviet menace." Underlying such language rested a largely imperceptible aspect of containment. More a broad concept than a detailed grand strategy, containment had developed into a faith-based pattern of thought. Freedom-loving Americans now could depict Moscow-led communists as the new belligerents of the postwar international system.

Facing a hostile ideology seemingly bent on military conflict enabled postwar Americans to rationalize both their faith and their fears.[26]

As key players at State developed and nurtured a culture of fear, it soon meshed effortlessly with the military and cultural components of the budding Cold War. For American strategists, however, the problem was applying this containment theory on a global scale. How does one devise a grand strategy with few, if any, geographic limitations? Truman and his advisors wrestled with just such a question, even as they continued to define US interests—and the threats to them—in sweeping terms. Still, the broad brushstrokes of containment offered a path forward, a sort of "middle ground" between war and appeasement. An expansionistic Soviet Union might pose an existential threat to the United States, but few in Washington had much appetite for war with yet another totalitarian regime so soon after World War II.[27]

Kennan's views, unsurprisingly, had a counterpart among Russian diplomats. In September 1946, Nikolai Novikov, the Soviet ambassador in Washington, cabled a telegram to Moscow outlining American intentions. He argued that US foreign policy reflected "imperialistic tendencies" and contained "broad plans for expansion." Mirroring US policymakers' strident language, Novikov alleged that a "desire for world domination" characterized Truman's approach. As evidence of America's aggressive policies, the ambassador pointed to the "establishment of a system of naval and airbases stretching far beyond the boundaries of United States." From the Soviet perspective, Novikov wasn't wrong. American military bases and outposts *were* dotting the globe. Thus, when Stalin received a copy of Kennan's "X Article" the following year, the word "containment" had been translated into the Russian word for "strangulation." Fear worked both ways.[28]

The same month Novikov's telegram made its way to Moscow, presidential counsel Clark Clifford and his aide George Elsey delivered Truman a report on Soviet foreign policy. In soon-to-be standard language, Clifford and Elsey deemed peaceful coexistence between communist and capitalist nations impossible. Mimicking Novikov in reverse, the two advisors portrayed the Soviets as baldly pursuing world domination and the "ultimate destruction of capitalist states." Moreover, they claimed these "disciples of power politics" only understood the "language of military power." Distorting Soviet behavior and intentions, Clifford and Elsey implicitly placed their faith in war to deter Stalinist aggression while basing their evaluation on deep-seated fears tipping toward paranoia. And, by relying on savages-only-understand-force argumentation, the two embedded an us-versus-them mentality into Cold War foreign policy.[29]

Both the Truman Doctrine and the Marshall Plan would codify these nascent ideas of power politics based on faith and fear. When Truman asked a joint session of Congress in March 1947 to extend aid to Greece and Turkey, both supposedly threatened by communist overthrow, he called for the United States "to support free peoples who are resisting attempted subjugation by armed minorities or by outside pressures." In short, the president was responding to local threats by universalizing the American response to communist aggression. Putting containment into practice, aid to Greece and Turkey would display America's commitment to stopping Soviet expansion. The *Washington Post* editorialized that Truman's speech demonstrated how security in the modern era "must be based on global concepts." "In this atomic age," the newspaper lectured, "freedom cannot be secure in one hemisphere alone." Such language pitting "freedom" versus "totalitarianism" would be a mainstay for Cold War politicians from that point forward.[30]

Politics as they were, critics panned Truman's speech, with some judging the doctrine "not a product of any actual international 'crisis'" but rather "primarily a formula to insure Mr. Truman's reelection in 1948." From the left, former Vice President Henry Wallace accused the president of "reckless adventury" that would consign the world to "a century of fear." On the right, Ohio's Republican Senator Robert Taft faulted Truman for dividing the world into two antagonistic camps. Even Secretary of State George C. Marshall worried the president might be "overstating the case a bit," as the speech intimated an open-ended strategic commitment. But we might consider Truman's principal audience. Was he speaking to communist adversaries, worried allies, foreign leaders on the fence over which side to support, or a domestic audience increasingly fearful of its ideological foe? As the Cold War hardened, each group would require attention—and incur obligations. For Truman, the challenge was one of balancing these commitments while arguing the nation held a special responsibility to defend freedom across the globe.[31]

The president's new doctrine held immense, long-term implications that would inform nearly all of Truman's successors and, seemingly, require each of them to craft "doctrines" of their own. "Seeds of totalitarian regimes" could be found anywhere as Truman and future White House occupants, guided by fear, linked "peace of the world" to "the welfare of this nation."[32]

Meanwhile, the Marshall Plan rested on a faith that the American economy could serve as a foundation for remaking postwar Europe, if not the world. In the process, war and economic development became uneasy allies in the struggle against communism. After World War II, administration officials feared "deteriorating" European economies might collapse the global economic order. Germany's revival thus became a key target of the European Recovery Plan. Yet such aims brought their own fears. Would a recuperated Germany once more threaten European security or would it partner in containing communism? Here, Marshall agreed with Kennan. Rehabilitating Europe and other key industrial areas mattered just as much, if not more, than any military-centric grand strategy. Only an integrated economic order could resist the communist threat. Stalin, of course, saw the Marshall Plan in a far different light, a device to "destroy Soviet military and political hegemony over Eastern Europe."[33]

From Moscow, the American commitment to European recovery undeniably seemed imposing. Between 1948 and 1952, the United States obligated more than $13 billion to one of the most ambitious aid programs in history. But what was Marshall suggesting when arguing that American policy was "directed not against any country or doctrine, but against hunger, poverty, desperation, and chaos"? Was poverty just as implacable an enemy as communism? In recovery advocates' eyes, the two surely were interrelated. Fear of economic dislocation leading to labor unrest instigated larger worries about confronting communism in Western Europe. Moreover, because fueling European recovery depended on Middle East oil and raw materials from former colonies, economic instability had become a global concern. The Marshall Plan, like Truman's doctrine, fast was committing the nation to new and unaccustomed international obligations.[34]

Some politicians, like Ohioan Robert Taft, doubted whether economic aid would deter European countries from falling to communism. If the Marshall Plan led to "dissatisfaction, inflation and depression in the United States," the senator questioned, how could it offer any real assistance to Europe? Republicans like Taft also worried about the domestic costs of maintaining a permanent military footing to reinforce Marshall's plan, fearful that economic inflation might run rampant while supporting the western alliance. Other critics thought the administration was expecting too much of the recovery plan, of the hope to "produce a United States of Europe."[35]

Yet faith prevailed. Free trade, backed by a strong military, would foster global economic stability all under the benevolent supervision of wizened US policymakers. Indeed, Americans embraced their role in setting an example for the world to follow, an extraordinary responsibility bestowed upon them after World War II. Here, in a sense, was the modern incarnation of Manifest Destiny, an "ideology of expansion" for the twentieth century.[36]

If Americans were engaging in a form of expansionism while decrying communists for the same offense, they rarely acknowledged the irony. Rather, programs like Radio Free Europe and Voice of America highlighted the ideals of freedom, democracy, and "people's capitalism." While communists employed "psychological warfare," the Voice of America, supporters maintained, instead merely translated "our point of view" to embattled peoples resisting authoritarianism. There seemed little choice but to "negate the lies and distortions spread about us by the Communists." Sustaining the war for hearts and minds took on a crucial supplementary role to both economic and military initiatives.

Thus, selling the "American way of life" became an integral component of attempts to "pierce the Iron Curtain."[37]

Still, an element of fear pervaded these inspirational propaganda messages. What if, Americans asked, they could not stabilize European nations devastated by war? Might the discontented turn to communism as their savior? While the Marshall Plan extolled a faith in American economic superiority, fear that recovery programs wouldn't be enough to stanch communist expansion underlay calls for increased military preparedness. When the Korean War broke out in 1950, the Marshall Plan all but receded into political obscurity. Military defense of "critical points" now took precedence, even as policymakers worried over committing enough resources to defend them on a global scale. Economic stability mattered, for sure, but increased defense expenditures in the early 1950s suggested that military crises were becoming far more important than financial ones.[38]

The Truman administration didn't have to wait long for evidence of communist subversion in Europe. In 1948, the Italian elections loomed as a test case in which postwar economic hardships might translate into communist political power. Americans feared the worst. An armed uprising seemed plausible enough that the newly formed CIA began channeling money to pro-Western Christian Democrats. (It wouldn't be the last time the agency interfered in local elections.) And although the prospect of communists taking power in Italy may look overstated in hindsight, George Kennan himself feared that American troops might have to intervene if an Italian civil war broke out. Even after anticommunist parties scored victories that April, the *New York Times* continued to run stories declaring that the "danger of communism" was "still grave in Italy."[39]

If the Italian elections were crafted as a political contest between democracy and totalitarianism, the Pentagon saw things through a standard militaristic lens. The Joint Chiefs of Staff already had initiated a series of studies in late 1945 exploring how to wage war against the Soviet Union. Code-named Pincher, the planning "envisioned war breaking out in the eastern Mediterranean or Near East and spreading rapidly across Europe." For nervous military strategists in the Pentagon, a communist electoral victory in Italy conceivably could have sparked another global inferno. They were not alone in their fears. Some 930 miles north of Rome, the military governor of the US zone in Berlin, Lucius Clay, worried that any "indication of weakness on our part would jeopardize our position in central Europe." For senior officers like Clay, "Soviet domination" inevitably would follow any Allied withdrawal from major European cities like Berlin or Rome.[40]

Of course, from the Soviet view, US economic and military initiatives exemplified American imperialism unleashed on a global scale. The editor of the communist newspaper *Pravda* scored the "expansionistic designs" of the United States in a 1949 speech honoring Lenin, proclaiming that the Marshall Plan "brought enslavement to Western Europe." Soviet Minister of Foreign Affairs Vyacheslav Molotov likewise denounced the plan, arguing it was "nothing but a vicious American scheme for using dollars to buy its way" into European affairs. With American troops remaining in the Middle East after World War II and US naval ships keeping close watch on the Formosa Strait in the South China Sea, Moscow needed little added incentive to view itself as the defender of "people's democracies" in an "era of crushing capitalism."[41]

The birth of the international Communist Information Bureau further underscored the finger-pointing, and shared assumptions of wrongdoing, between Moscow and Washington. Two years before *Pravda*'s editor railed against US foreign policy, the Cominform sought to foster closer ties among European communist parties. Its manifesto spoke of confronting the "camp of imperialism and anti-democratic forces" and accused America's "ruling circle" of embarking upon a "crusade against Communism." Soviet leaders stressed how the United States was creating "numerous bases and vantage grounds situated at great distances from the American continent against the USSR." With US air and naval bases in Egypt, Iran, Turkey, and Greece, it wasn't hard for Stalin and his lieutenants to denounce Washington's policy of Soviet encirclement.[42]

As the Truman Doctrine had implied, though, Americans were obliged to resist the very kind of expansionism of which they were being accused. Here, morality and geography combined to incite action. Policymakers in DC imagined smaller nations in southeastern Europe and western Asia as potential victims of communist revolutionary activity; thus, they perceived a moral obligation to defend anticommunist governments, especially as former colonial powers Britain and France were receding from the global scene. Henceforth, the Middle East and Mediterranean would grow in strategic importance as US military planners viewed access to oil and trade routes crucial for fighting the Cold War. As events in Greece, Turkey, and Iran suggested, not all problems could be solved by economic or political means alone.[43]

In Greece, a civil war between communist-led guerrillas and right-wing government forces emerged as the Cold War's first engagement, inspiring Truman to pronounce his doctrine. With a cash-strapped London reducing its support in the Mediterranean, Washington, fearing a power vacuum, saw potential for regional disaster. As Secretary of State Acheson opined, "corruption of Greece would infect Iran and all to the east" if the communist threat was left uncontained. American advisors soon were aiding their first of many Cold War counterinsurgency efforts. Yet their focus on external communist aggression diminished the role that local politics played in explaining violence in the first place. Looking back, US advisors clearly overestimated Stalin's interest in aiding Greek guerrillas. But the apparent successes of the counterinsurgency effort mattered most. Never mind the Greek population was either neutral or openly opposed to a communist regime. A Cold War domino had held firm.[44]

While contemporary historians hailed their fellow Americans for "shoring up" the Greek government in this "critical hour," nearby Turkey seemed equally vulnerable to the Kremlin's grasp. In 1946, the US ambassador nervously reported on Soviet troop movements, submitting that their objective was "to break" the present government, install a friendly one, and close the "Turkish gap" in the Soviet security belt. From the Baltic to the Black Sea, the ambassador related, Moscow was endangering western influence in the region. Symbolically, Truman ordered the USS *Missouri* to the straits. More decisively, however, rumors of Soviet aggression circulated in Istanbul, leading angry nationalist demonstrations to convince Stalin the time was not yet ripe for an advance. Once more, Americans learned from a potentially explosive episode that employing or threatening military force prevented communists from obtaining "full mastery" of contested territory.[45]

Similar fears of communist expansion and faith in military power to contest it permeated US policy for the Middle East, another early Cold War flashpoint. With fossil fuels proving their strategic worth in World War II, the Iranian oil industry, still under British control, became a lucrative Cold War object of desire. Violating a 1941 treaty, Stalin had left Soviet troops in the Iranian province of Azerbaijan after war's end. Just as ominous, the local Tudeh party, with its close ties to the Soviet Union, seemingly posed a threat to Iran's political stability. Worried American planners considered the oil rich country a "testing ground" for communist influence, while one *Washington Post* columnist editorialized that what happened in Iran would "throw light on Russian ambitions" in a region of "vast strategic importance." Given the potential for direct conflict with an intervening United States, Stalin backed off. Still, the episode reinforced Americans' resolve that their newfound global interests must be protected at all costs.[46]

Finally, the creation of the Jewish state, born of war in 1948, also held long-term implications, as a regional Arab-Israeli conflict would threaten to undermine global stability for decades to come. If Truman's decision to recognize Israel made sense given Americans' historical pro-Zionist leanings, it also helped them pardon a violent settlers' war against indigenous, homeless Palestinians. This Israeli-Palestinian history surely preceded Cold War antagonisms. And, for the first few decades after Israeli statehood, the contest over Israeli settlements would remain peripheral to the larger US-Soviet competition. Yet Arabs' resentment over what they saw as western imperialism loomed constantly, stoking American fears that the Soviet Union might manipulate this bitterness and justify its own encroachments into the Middle East.[47]

In fact, even in 1948, US policy elite like former Treasury Secretary Henry Morgenthau, Jr. argued that backing Israel aided the fight against communism and facilitated a "hard core of resistance" against the Soviet courtship of local Arab allies. Here, one final theme would emerge in these early Cold War years. Washington policymakers consistently would mistake anticolonialism in the Middle East—as elsewhere around the globe—for communist affiliation. Coupled with fears of losing access to strategic oil reserves and military outposts, these officials saw few alternatives but to intervene in a region already wracked by local conflict. While they never lost their faith in bringing peace to the Middle East, US policymakers mostly viewed the region as a volatile one threatening other global priorities.[48]

The 1948 war ultimately left Israel in a perpetual state of conflict, in many ways making it a strategic liability for the United States despite leaders' hopes otherwise. The ensuing Israeli-Arab wars would further demonstrate how the superpowers' militarization of the Cold War tended to exacerbate local tensions rather than help resolve them. But whether in the Middle East or Southeast Asia or Latin America, fearful Americans convinced themselves they were up against a truly evil, truly global communist threat. The safest option, then, was to demonstrate resolve by arming themselves for what many worried was a coming global war.[49]

CHAPTER 3

Militarizing the Cold War

In a world where the prospect of war seemed an unavoidable part of American life, what did "resolve" mean against a global communist enemy? Would Americans be up to the task of long-term containment? Would the nation's credibility, its very existence, be threatened any moment Americans let their guard down? By the early 1960s, politicians like Barry Goldwater no longer believed the United States was engaged in "a cold war but a real war." To the Arizona Republican, if Americans lost this conflict—a "death struggle," he surmised—it would mean "the end of freedom as we know it."[1]

Still, at least some critics of such perceptions had emerged in the two decades prior. They denounced a militarized US foreign policy to confront an overhyped menace. Supreme Court Justice William O. Douglas, for instance, decried how "military policy has so completely absorbed our thoughts that we have mostly forgotten that our greatest strength, our enduring power is not in guns, but in ideas." To Douglas, the communist threat had been "magnified and exalted far beyond its realities." The politics of militarization, however, had a nasty habit of embracing fear even when significant security threats never existed as advertised.[2]

Influential journalist Walter Lippmann equally lamented containment's militaristic turn. He worried not only about the national security state's expansion, but of overcommitting to far-flung places around the globe. Back in late 1947, Lippmann, now a convert from his earlier pro-interventionist views, unleashed his fury against Kennan's "X Article" and US foreign policy more generally. While he conceded that Soviet power must be prevented from expanding, he nonetheless saw containment as a "fundamentally unsound" strategy. Believing it surrendered the initiative to the Russians, Lippmann argued in a series of syndicated editorials that the policy committed the nation "to an enormous effort without offering any concrete objective that can be attained." Worse, in Lippmann's eyes, American military power was "unsuited to a policy of containment which has to be enforced persistently and patiently for an indefinite period of time." In short, this "strategic monstrosity," as the journalist called it, likely would lead to geopolitical exhaustion.[3]

Lippmann wasn't a lone voice. From a practical standpoint, senior military leaders struggled to match limited resources to ever-expanding security requirements. As one Joint Chiefs of Staff study warned in the early 1950s, current resource allocations "to military purposes are generally inadequate . . . to meet the threat of Soviet military power predicted for . . . 1954–1955, which is considered to represent a very dangerous period." Here was a key challenge for any nation's grand strategy: matching limited means to attainable ends. The task proved especially daunting when fear-induced military requirements became global in scope.[4]

Yet prowar, anticommunist crusaders retained their influence in politics and popular culture. It didn't take long for a secular faith in war to be infused with strident religious undertones. Reverend Billy Graham, for instance, used his pulpit to call for the merging of Christianity and anticommunism. During one Los Angeles revival, Graham proclaimed that communism was a religion "inspired, directed and motivated by the Devil himself who has declared war against Almighty God." Episcopalian Leland Henry similarly judged the Cold War a clash between "irreconcilable theologies." War might be an evil, but communists defying God surely were worse. No wonder that Eisenhower's Presbyterian secretary of state, John Foster Dulles, would denounce communism as an "alien faith."[5]

In a just war of self-defense against a godless evil, religious groups eagerly morphed into activist political associations. In historian Michael Sherry's words, "the sword was lashed to the Bible." Clergy proclaimed the Cold War a "spiritual clash," dismissing any moral quandaries about advocating for war. But a paradox underlay their fighting faith. In an atomic era, how could war be just if it potentially led to humanity's demise? The Vatican would wrestle with such questions throughout the Cold War, often maintaining that nuclear war posed a greater threat than atheistic communism. For fearful Americans, though, pacifism held no place in an existential struggle against evil. Moreover, what better way to prepare for Armageddon than by redeeming one's soul beforehand? The politics and religion of militarization seemed ready-made for each other. In the thinking of religious leaders like Billy Graham and Francis Cardinal Spellman, loyal, patriotic Americans were loyal, patriotic Christians.[6]

If anticommunism had become a kind of "sacred focus," a shorthand for distinguishing good from evil, that focus also hinted at unspoken issues with Americans' faith in war. In short, faith in martial dominance sat beside fears that military and economic means alone might not be enough to defeat the Soviet threat. Thus, George Kennan spoke of the need for a "spiritual vitality" to support containment policies, while J. Edgar Hoover warned against materialism and antireligious sentiments. Vilifying the "Godless, Communist way of life," Hoover was following firmly in the footsteps of earlier evangelists who promoted a "muscular Christianity." Spiritual mobilization thus became a sacred adjunct to military preparedness.[7]

The National Security Act of 1947 showcased how these societal fears could inform a massive reorganization of US defense institutions. Replacing an "antiquated defense setup," the act formally established the Joint Chiefs of Staff, a National Security Council, and a Central Intelligence Agency. Not surprisingly, the CIA quickly added covert and paramilitary operations to its core intelligence-gathering mission. Only later would Senator Mike Mansfield raise concerns that the agency had become a global "Gestapo" force unchecked by legislative oversight. The bureaucratic shakeup, though, intimated how the very architecture of US security organizations might be insufficient in serving the Cold War national interest.[8]

Once accepted that "godless," savage communists only understood the threat of force, it didn't take long to craft a philosophy for this newly designed security structure. Three years after its birth, the National Security Council delivered to Truman a seventy-page document on safeguarding American security. Labeled NSC-68, the report, principally authored by Paul Nitze, painted a grim picture in which the Soviet Union, animated by a "fanatic faith," was threatening the "destruction not only of this Republic but of civilization itself." In a war pitting freedom against slavery, merely checking "the Kremlin design" wasn't adequate. Over and over, Nitze's report leaned into the phrase "world domination" when assessing Moscow's objectives. And because communists were "inescapably militant," the United States had to match the threat in kind, which, as Nitze warned the president, wasn't happening. It was clear, he argued, "that our military strength is becoming dangerously inadequate." The only way forward was "a rapid and sustained build-up of the political, economic, and military strength of the free world . . . to wrest the initiative from the Soviet Union."[9]

Exaggerating the threat, Nitze's militarism moved well beyond what the father of containment had originally advised. To Kennan, it was "not Russian military power which is threatening to us, it is Russian political power." Nitze disagreed, arguing in NSC-68 that "one of the most important ingredients of power is military strength." Indeed, "power" became central not just to Nitze's framework but to more enduring Cold War narratives, an end unto itself. The risk seemingly warranted this unprecedented search for strength. For Nitze, the Kremlin's pursuit of world domination had left Americans no choice but to arm themselves for war. Whatever the costs.[10]

In militarizing containment, NSC-68 might be seen as a microcosm of the larger, decades-long tensions between faith and fear. Arguably one of the most paranoid documents of the entire Cold War era, Nitze's report assumed the United States could fund enduring global offensives if it just had the will to do so. Previous National Security Council documents, like NSC 20/4, equally highlighted the "hostile designs of the USSR" and sought to reduce Soviet "power and influence." Yet Nitze was calling for a military-centric approach based on raw power. Kennan, for his part, railed against this "alarmist militarism" and would become a constant critic of how his ideas had been hijacked by those advocating a more militarized foreign policy. He also had less faith in globalizing US interests, knowing that, because the country's national resources were finite, its interests should be restrained. But faith in military power and fear of war prevailed over Kennan's concerns. Incidentally, Americans living outside the DC beltway continued to view themselves as traditionally anti-militaristic even while supporting these increasingly costly security policies.[11]

In the end, NSC-68 demonstrated how easily means of defense could be turned into means of aggression and power projection. When the Korean War erupted only months after the panic-laden report hit Truman's desk, Nitze seemed prophetic. (The president had initially rejected the report out of hand.) Accordingly, the defense budget quadrupled. Defensive containment no longer seemed sufficient. And, unsurprisingly, the term "national security" eclipsed that of "national defense," an indication that assuming the "strategic defensive" naively handed the initiative to evil communists. Policy hawks went one step further. Relying on a fear-based perception that "free institutions" around the world were under assault, saber-rattlers like John Foster Dulles soon began arguing that "rollback" of communism and the "liberation" of democratic-leaning peoples should replace "containment" as America's grand strategic aim. Kennan's view of patient defense was falling out of favor.[12]

In fact, those opposing offensive action easily were branded political heretics, a fraught status at a time when many believed domestic communists were lurking in every shadow. It didn't matter if threats now were defining interests. Nor did many question, as did theologian Reinhold Niebuhr, how American ambitions might be transmuting "means of defense" into "means of aggression." In Niebuhr's eyes, a "sense of superior virtue" too easily led to a "misuse of our power." While he saw the need for vigilance against the communist threat, he warned against exaggerated fears being used to support nearly any expansion of American presence abroad. In short, Niebuhr warned of a classic security dilemma. Unsure of communist intentions and fearing war, the United States was arming itself so much that it threatened the Soviets, leading them to increase their own military spending and thus creating a vicious cycle. Fear of war had the potential to breed war itself.[13]

While NSC-68 depicted a global threat, many Americans still viewed Europe as the Cold War's most dangerous continent, further validating the militaristic turn in US foreign policy. The question of what to do with Germany, in particular, worried US policymakers looking back upon two recent world wars. Even a "neutral," denazified Germany seemed perilous, either susceptible to an internal revolution, as had happened after the First World War, or likely to set an example for other "neutralist" states which then might break free from American influence. Even worse, a unified Germany might fall into the Soviet camp, leaving a key industrial and population center in communist hands. As Soviet intentions in Eastern Europe became clearer, Americans drew a hard line. There could be no unified Germany under present conditions.[14]

As these more theoretical questions simmered, a crisis in Berlin offered tangible proof, if any was needed, of Soviet aggression. In the waning days of World War II, Germany had been divided into occupation zones with Berlin, subdivided into four sectors, falling inside the Soviet domain. When the French and British-American zones unified in western Germany in late 1947 and early 1948, Stalin responded by closing communication routes into Berlin. The ensuing blockade placed Europe at the heart of Cold War competition, raising fears of what came next. Truman worried in his diary that "we are very close to war," while future West German Chancellor Willy Brandt lamented that Berliners "lived in a besieged fortress." A massive airlift followed, as allied air forces began delivering thousands of tons of supplies daily to Berlin's citizens. Still, fear gripped senior American officials. The US commander in Berlin, General Lucius Clay, believed the German city "was now drawn as tight as a steel spring," and, in March 1948, dreaded war "may come with dramatic suddenness."[15]

Yet the Berlin Airlift also illuminated a new kind of faith, that of deterring war. As the crisis escalated, the Truman administration used its nuclear monopoly to dissuade the Soviets from militarily interdicting the airlift. (It would not be the last time a US president rattled the nuclear saber.) Deterrence, however, never quite delivered what it promised. Truman saw the airlift only as an interim solution, a way to maintain options while seeking a more permanent resolution with Moscow. Others viewed the Berlin operation through a martial lens. To military commentators like Hanson W. Baldwin, the airlift strengthened the US arsenal, as a "weapon" to be wielded, opening a "new chapter in the history of air power." This friction between averting war and preparing for war would endure, especially in Europe.[16]

Even after the Kremlin lifted its blockade in May 1949, tensions surrounding Berlin would catalyze further US defense spending. Once more, fearful Americans believed they had no choice. Two competing German states demanded a US military commitment to Europe. The 1941 Atlantic Charter may have conceptualized an American-European partnership, but the Berlin crisis compelled those ideas into lasting reality. Stalin's blockade offered seemingly irrefutable proof, once and for all, that Moscow was less worried about securing borders than hell-bent on expanding communism.[17]

The creation of the North Atlantic Treaty Organization (NATO), with its focus on mutual defense and collective security—including a rearmed Germany—demonstrated that fear of a future European war outweighed any final arguments for American "isolationism." NATO codified a long-term transatlantic partnership. More importantly, the treaty's Article 5 considered an attack on one party an attack against all signatories. The United States had committed itself to European defense. If membership broke time-honored American ideas on entangling alliances, NATO demonstrated the ways in which US policymakers sought to defend the nation as far from its shores as possible. In an age of airpower and strategic missiles, "forward defense" became a national security mantra. Once more, fear and faith intermingled in US decision-making—fear of the Soviets invading Europe coupled with a burgeoning faith in collective security. Once more, Kennan acknowledged that while the Russians posed "a military danger" to Western Europe, their basic intent remained conquest by "political means."[18]

Not surprisingly, Soviet officials denounced the planned rearmament of Germany. World War II hero Marshal Georgy Zhukov saw American proposals as "fulfilling their [own] aggressive behaviors" while reviving German militarism. The Soviet ambassador in Washington, Alexander Paniushkin, viewed NATO as a treaty directed against the USSR, one "designed to frighten states which do not agree to submit to the dictates of the Anglo-American grouping of powers." When West Germany formally joined NATO in May 1955, *Pravda* declared the German state was "being turned into a bridgehead for the deployment of large aggressive forces." The World War II Grand Alliance had met its demise.[19]

Given Soviet fears of American aggressiveness, it's notable how both NATO and a divided Germany helped stimulate East-West confrontation, as did US plans for using nuclear weapons against Soviet targets in the advent of war. Fear of hostilities, both real and imagined, led to military policies raising anxieties rather than ameliorating them—the rearmament of Germany, the deployment of US strategic bombers to Europe, the creation of a military alliance directed toward Russia and her satellites. Fear, in short, was driving strategy in Western Europe.[20]

So too across the globe. Local events in Asia further raised anxieties over the United States' ability to contain its communist foes alone. The long civil war in China resumed with full fury in 1946, with Mao Zedong's communist forces making gains each successive year. When Mao proclaimed three years later that China would "lean to one side" and "ally ourselves with the Soviet Union," the possibility of a Sino-Soviet communist bloc shook excitable members of Congress and pundits in the media. The same month that Mao declared his alliance with Moscow, the World War II Flying Tigers commander, Major General Claire L. Chennault, declared that a "third and more horrible world war is inevitable if the United States permits Communism to conquer China." The remarks were telling. Not only did Chennault foresee "a billion enemies" if the nationalist government fell to its communist enemies, but he also had faith the United States could do something about it.[21]

Then the hammer fell. In December 1949, Mao declared victory in the Chinese civil war. The nationalists fled to the island of Formosa, while Americans recoiled at how quickly their former wartime ally had fallen to its communist foe. Political accusations were not long in coming. Secretary of State Dean Acheson might argue that nothing the United States "could have done within reasonable limits of its capabilities" would have changed the result, but Truman's political opponents saw an opening. Republicans railed against "stupidity at the top—treason just below." They saw links between the "giveaway" at Yalta and the "betrayal" in China. They blamed Truman for "losing" China. And, in a precursor to the domino theory, some Americans even worried that the "Red" triumph in China posed a "real danger" of communist "infiltration" into India and beyond. The potential for a Sino-Soviet alliance became a policy nightmare.[22]

The "loss" of China portended more bad dreams to come. What if other developing nations turned to Moscow and Beijing as their Cold War partners? A commitment to self-government surely informed US foreign policy after World War II, but what if budding nationalists in India or Pakistan or across the African continent freely chose the "wrong" side? With the August 1947 dissolution of British rule in India, the fear of global economic centers potentially falling under communism's spell seemed real enough. Moscow, not Washington, might end up commanding key strategic resources. Local leaders like India's Jawaharlal Nehru proposed keeping "away from the power politics" that led to past world wars, but in an increasingly zero-sum contest, such lofty proposals were difficult to carry out as Cold War tidal waves crashed above.[23]

The prospect of Indonesia, Indochina, Malaya, Burma, and neighboring countries of China falling to communism globalized American fears. The Cold War no longer was being fought over Western

Europe alone. China's "emergence as a revolutionary country" meant that peoples across Asia and the Pacific, in Kennan's words, might be "dangerously vulnerable to communist penetration." It didn't help that their "political immaturity" left them with "stubborn misconceptions" about colonialism and imperialism. Kennan hardly stood alone in such arrogant views; Americans throughout the era would look down upon the very people they were trying to draw away from the clutches of communism. In the process, militarized nation-building efforts would suffer from a sense of hubris heightened by a culturally entrenched fear of the "other."[24]

Mao's victory also raised a key question for Washington's policy elite. With an anti-American alliance ostensibly forming in the communist camp and Moscow seeking "world domination," how much of a threat did China truly pose? Some analysts doubted whether an impoverished, war-torn China could ever compete militarily with the United States. Yet the Chinese, like the Russians, were now calling for a "world revolution" and "proletarian internationalism." Moreover, as one policy paper surmised, the Chinese communists were "both adjuncts of the Kremlin and the popularly preferred leaders of the Chinese revolution." But were they pawns of Moscow or self-directed revolutionaries? Erring on the side of supposed safety, US policymakers tended toward the former view, at least early on. Such an aggressive stance, though, reinforced Mao's own fears that the United States would never accept the Guomindang's civil war defeat. Security dilemmas were becoming routine.[25]

So too were Americans' fears of the "rural peasant," who presumably played a vital role in communism's march. Exploiting local grievances on land reform, income inequality, and governmental corruption, Mao had turned poor farmers into fierce revolutionaries. Perhaps Lenin had it right that a proletarian revolution, at least a rural one, was possible. These fears would inform America's future relationship with war, with more thoughtful US officers realizing that "military force by itself will not eliminate communism." Economic and political reforms would have to be orchestrated in tandem with battlefield actions, perhaps even transcend them. As such, the lowly peasant assumed global power, with global implications. One member of Moral Re-Armament, a faith-based international network, no doubt spoke for many Americans when arguing that Asia was "the Number 1 treasure of the Communist heart.... If China goes, half the world will go."[26]

With Americans paradoxically both fearful and dismissive of politically "immature" peasants, we should note that racial attitudes also fed into fears of Chinese communism. Alarm over the "Yellow Peril" long had informed western perceptions of Asia. No doubt some Americans conflated Red fanaticism in China with Japanese banzai charges or kamikaze attacks during World War II. Recent experiences must have confirmed bigoted opinions that all Asians were "savages" who only understood the threat of force. Moreover, the coming conflict in Korea, seeing Chinese wave attacks against allied positions, would strengthen earlier evaluations from US military officers that "human life all over Asia is cheap." In dealing with irrational, primeval barbarians, only "the fear of prompt, immediate, and unfailing punishment" would hold them in check. Not surprisingly, echoes of these racialist sentiments later would be heard in the aftermath of 9/11.[27]

As in the case of Russia, fears of communist fanaticism tended to outweigh deeper analysis of the intricacies and implications of the Chinese civil war. The Soviets' successful atomic-bomb testing the same year as Mao's victory only compounded a sense of dread in the West. Fear of communism's global advance thus weighed heavily on those thinking about Cold War grand strategy. As one American general advised, a "China dominated by Chinese communists would be inimical to the interests of the United States." It would not be the last time US policymakers misread the origins of and support for Asian social revolutions.[28]

Anxious American strategists meanwhile viewed the Maoist revolutionary-warfare model as directly threatening their global policing mission. Mao had weaponized his people through "political mobilization and winning the sympathy of the masses," both "indispensable to the success of the military struggle." If his methods were to be adopted by others, US foreign-policy strategists feared, a bleak future likely lay ahead. According to one Pakistani scholar, the military potential unleashed by "a moral explosion among the disinherited, disenchanted masses in underdeveloped countries" could be "unprecedented." American officials thus interpreted any revolutionary movement through a conspiratorial lens, believing all were inspired by and controlled from Moscow. One National Security Council report even depicted Chinese communism as an "instrument for the extension of Soviet influence," one that might strengthen similar movements across the Global South.[29]

While the Chinese threat led to calls for Japanese rearmament—fear of former enemies can be fleeting if they offer the promise of newfound security—it also inspired alarm over what post–World War II decolonization efforts might foreshadow for a stable global order. Whether in Asia, Africa, or Latin America, local leaders seeking independence, or simply social and economic reform, now appeared as potential agents of chaos. Worse, their societal revolutions were exposing their peoples to communist influence. American strategists thereby assumed a confrontational approach to the Global South, comprehending local events through their own rivalry with the Soviet Union.[30]

Meanwhile, anxious Europeans fretted over their relative decline as colonial holdings slipped from their grasp in a rapidly changing, politically fragmented world. Such a world appeared incredibly violent, as revolutionaries from Mao Zedong to Ernesto "Che" Guevara deemed armed conflict essential for imperialism's elimination. Others believed violence crucial to their independence movements. National liberationists like Frantz Fanon, for instance, regarded violence as a "cleansing force" that freed the "native from his inferiority complex" and restored his "self-respect." No doubt such talk exacerbated fears among Pentagon officials already concerned about waging a global conflict with their already overstretched military resources.[31]

All the while, economic anxieties united foreign and domestic policies. Open global markets and access to resources, popular arguments went, required the overseas projection of military power. Commerce and force seemed two sides of the same coin. Writing in the late 1950s, historian William Appleman Williams unfavorably judged leaders "who began by thinking about the United States and the world in economic terms" and then came "to define the United States in military terms as an embattled outpost in a hostile world."[32]

Thus, a seemingly endless list of fears lengthened every time Americans looked abroad. Economic instability. Soviet military capabilities. Chinese-backed revolutionary movements. Communists' drive for world domination from Greece to Turkey, from Berlin to Korea. And, as if these fears weren't enough, Americans then turned inward so that fear itself took on a new, more ominous dimension.

CHAPTER 4

The Cold War Comes Home

Back at home, fear and faith mixed in volatile ways. During the late 1940s and throughout the following decade, anticommunism became a "national fetish," inducing a form of "social warfare" that turned suspicious Americans against one another. Wisconsin Senator Joseph R. McCarthy ranked first, and most infamous, of these political fearmongers demanding "loyalty" to the nation as an anticommunist litmus test. Given enemies were believed to be lurking within, loyalty and security became intertwined, with fear tying them together. Never mind how blacklists and accusations of "un-American" activities suppressed domestic dissent and inhibited cultural advancement. McCarthy's sordid methods enticed because they rested on a widely accepted faith that fighting communism offered potential benefits. In short, the "Red Scare" could be politically useful.[1]

McCarthy excelled in connecting foreign fears to domestic ones. To the Wisconsin Republican, traitors lurked in the halls of government as he accused the Truman administration of "deceit and dishonesty." Nor did Eisenhower escape the senator's wrath. In late 1954, McCarthy attacked the president, reproaching Ike for a "shrinking show of weakness" in combatting communism. Critics labeled McCarthy a "stuffed shirt" who destructively inflamed "ignorant people," but his self-styled crusade took root across the nation. In the fight against godless communism, strength sold, especially after the "loss" of China. And, as anticommunist impresario, McCarthy played to his audience. Leaning into bigoted vernacular after the Chinese civil war, the senator lambasted "egg-sucking phony liberals whose 'pitiful squealing . . . would hold sacrosanct those Communists and queers' who had sold China into 'atheistic slavery.'"[2]

McCarthy was not alone. Richard Nixon won his 1946 congressional campaign against Horace "Jerry" Voorhis by red-baiting the Democratic incumbent, and his rebuke against Truman for being soft on communism demonstrated how eager electoral candidates could profit politically from such accusations. Four years later, in his successful bid for a senate seat, Nixon impugned the loyalty of his opponent, Helen Gahagan Douglas, and charged that she was "pink right down to her underwear." No cruelty could be excessive when deployed against alleged subversives and communist fellow travelers. When voters elevated Nixon to the vice presidency in 1952, the California Republican embraced the anticommunist crusade, becoming Eisenhower's "attack dog" to shore up his boss's right flank.[3]

Privately, Nixon might have conceded he was oversimplifying international affairs, but publicly he and fellow Cold War politicians actively pursued the political rewards of supporting war over peace. In one White House strategy session, Senator Arthur H. Vandenberg (R-MI) counseled Truman that the best way to gain financial support for Greece and Turkey was to "scare the hell out of the American people." Ominously, few citizens rebuffed the idea that communists at home should be treated like war criminals, giving politicians further leeway. Some critics, like political scientist Harold Lasswell, called out officials for promulgating "war scares." But far more Americans agreed with Eisenhower when he claimed in his first inaugural address that the "forces of good and evil are massed and armed and opposed as rarely before in history."[4]

Arguing that politicians simply fabricated anticommunist anxieties, however, misleads. If McCarthyism looked like a neurosis, both its causes and its symptoms seemed real enough to many Americans. The 1954 Department of Defense "Know Your Communist Enemy" series, for instance, instructively examined the teachings, aims, and methods of international communism. Readers learned of "communist imperialism" and how the "communist bag of tricks" included "systematic espionage for the Soviet Union" and the creation of "'front' organizations with innocent-sounding names to trap the unwary." Alleged infiltration into trade unions, political societies, and civic organizations permeated political debates. In popular discourse, the United States stood as both an obstacle to and target of communist advances. As such, Americans had to steel themselves against the false promises of an evil ideology. As one pamphlet warned, communism appealed to "weaklings and maladjusted persons who want to be told what to do or to escape from personal problems."[5]

If the threat of communist infiltration might paradoxically result in a US surveillance state, larger societal fears of future war raised questions about Americans' ability to defend the nation after World War II. A faith in war building boys into "men" accompanied fears of a "feminized" postwar society unable to confront danger. Once more, potential gain tempted political candidates and officeholders alike. Republicans admonished Democrats for being "soft on communism," scoring their rivals for "moral flabbiness" and wondering aloud why their nation was "losing the victory that we have won with so much sacrifice in 1945." Appearing warlike, in George Kennan's words, was the best way for politicians to "take protective action" against charges of being "'soft on communism,' however meaningless the phrase or weak the evidence."[6]

Yet the phrase did have meaning. Fears abounded that a conformist, affluent, consumeristic society was, at its core, soft and weak. McCarthy saw the nation "in a position of impotency" thanks to his rivals' "traitorous actions." While Truman condemned McCarthyism as "the corruption of truth," at least one supporter approved of the Wisconsin senator's "raw courage" while deriding liberal "soft-brained pseudo intellectuals." As the no-doubt aspiring strategist noted, "You can't stop a barroom brawl with a law book." Nor were such views mere local editorial offshoots. In Robert A. Heinlein's award-winning 1959 sci-fi novel *Starship Troopers*, the protagonist's high-school teacher tells the graduating class that "violence, naked force, has settled more issues in history than has any other factor, and the contrary opinion is wishful thinking at its worst." Nations survived because they were strong militarily, plain and simple.[7]

With little effort, the hard–soft dichotomy tied political transgressions to sexual ones. Fears of communism's links to homosexuality made for titillating reading during the Cold War, resting on baseless assumptions that emotional instability and psychological maladjustment contributed to both "conditions." One report on American communists maintained that "sex-role confusion" often could be found among party members. Another exposé highlighted a young woman who joined the party because "the Communist doctrine of sexual equality helped her reject her femininity." As early as 1950, a senate resolution called for a full-scale investigation of "homosexuals and other moral perverts" working in federal service. Against such threats, eating away at the very foundation of American government, it seemed only strong, heterosexual men were capable of defending the nation.[8]

Even into the mid-1960s, Senator Barry Goldwater was arguing that his "faint-hearted" political opponents "offer nothing but weakness." The Arizonan frequently spoke of America's need to "achieve superiority in all of the weapons," suggesting how the nation's relationship with war crossed political, economic, and social boundaries. Passivity promised peril. Thus, Americans had to embrace a muscular, militarized approach to the existential struggle in which they found themselves after World War II. Preparing for war, it appeared, made sense for reasons of both national security and moral constancy.[9]

Not only did a gender component inform these debates, but a racial one as well. Fears of a "Red Menace" and a "Yellow Peril" worked in tandem with the imagined threat of Black violence at home. Supporters of discriminatory Jim Crow policies, for example, attacked the growing civil-rights movement by claiming it had been infiltrated by communists. Of course, such protests sought to disrupt Black activism and maintain the postwar racial status quo. As writer Ralph Ellison remarked, "any Negro demand for justice" could be viewed as "treasonable" and "any Negro act of self-defense as an assault against the state." Anticommunism thus became a convenient tool for white supremacists, with segregationists like South Carolina Governor George Bell Timmerman, Jr. arguing that enforcing "Negro voting rights" not only would "make a mockery of the Constitution" but promote the "cause of Communism" as well.[10]

It didn't take long for civil-rights organizations to self-censor, demonstrating how anticommunist crusading could delineate acceptable Cold War behavior. Against conservative backlash, African Americans sought to demonstrate their loyalties, as if service in World War II hadn't been enough. Only five years after that war's end, the National Association for the Advancement of Colored People (NAACP) adopted a resolution directing local chapters to "eradicate" any communist elements within the organization. The decree mattered little to segregationists. In 1958, the Arkansas attorney general publicly sought to "neutralize" the NAACP, in part, because it was "benefitting Communist Russia." Fears of subversion from within were fueling not just a burgeoning national security state but those individuals and offices aggressively seeking to maintain the racial status quo.[11]

In such a phobic environment, any person of color might be suspect. The 1950 Internal Security Act, for instance, included provisions for a "preventive detention program" allowing authorities to detain any person who might "probably" conspire with others to engage in acts of espionage or sabotage. Such egregious attacks on civil liberties, though, weren't enough. Two years later, the act's sponsor, Nevada Senator Patrick McCarran, backed an Immigration and Nationality Act that allowed for the "'denaturalization' of any naturalized aliens found to have been Communist sympathizers at the time of their citizenship proceedings." The National Council of Churches of Christ condemned the discriminatory act as "outmoded" and "unworthy of America," but both the House and Senate overrode Truman's veto. A sign of the times, McCarran denounced the president's stand as "one of the most un-American acts I have ever witnessed in my career."[12]

Even "peace" itself became cause for fear as the House Un-American Activities Committee (HUAC), the congressional manifestation of

Cold War anxieties, investigated the activist group Women Strike for Peace. Thenceforth, even pacificism assumed a threatening tenor. HUAC chairman Clyde Doyle asserted that it was "a basic Communist doctrine to 'fight for peace,'" leaving little room to argue against the militarization of American policies or society. Any pursuit or activity could be assessed as an "instrument of Soviet subversion." Nor did the odds favor dissenters. When the Federal Bureau of Investigation began allying with HUAC by passing confidential security reports to committee members, peace activists often had to defend themselves against wild charges of disloyalty and sedition. For fearful Americans, the cost to civil liberties seemed worth the national security benefit. Moscow's "masters of deceit" could be hiding anywhere.[13]

Political commentators of the day took critical notice of the frenzy, indicating that not all Americans found fear persuasive. Editorial cartoonist Herbert Block, a biting satirist, found the Red Scare dangerous. In one cartoon for the *Washington Post*, Block drew a gasping man, water bucket in hand and "Hysteria" penciled down his leg, feverishly climbing a ladder toward the Statue of Liberty's torch. Prominent attorney Richard Scandrett equally lamented the growing threat to civil liberties. "Even to suggest in a whisper here nowadays that every Russian is not a cannibal is to invite incarceration for subversive activities." While backers of a new senatorial Subversive Activities Control Board, created in 1951 to investigate communist infiltration into American society, consented to the persecution of their fellow citizens, clearly not all citizens bought into the witch-hunting. By the early 1960s, the hysterics being fanned by McCarthyites had entered into the academic lexicon, with historian Richard Hofstadter describing such conspiratorial thinking as the "paranoid style in American politics."[14]

Accordingly, in these early Cold War years, fear became integral to patriotism and helped shape America's larger relationship with war. Fear of the evils inherent in communism informed Americanism during this era. And the fears could multiply: fear of dictators, fear of losing power abroad, fear of nonconformity at home. The list went on and on. In the mid-1950s, the American Legion even accused the Girl Scouts of selling "one world" communist ideas to youngsters. Cultural critic

H. L. Mencken wondered if there wasn't some underhanded purpose to all this fearmongering. The whole aim of politics, he alleged in 1954, was "to keep the populace alarmed (and hence clamorous to be led to safety) by menacing it with an endless series of hobgoblins, most of them imaginary."[15]

Given the specter of these skulking monsters, patriotism became performative for fear of being branded un-American and, therefore, a communist. It wasn't enough to consent to the idea of America. Citizens had to *prove* their patriotism. Thus, because communists ostensibly were exploiting constitutional freedoms for their own devious ends, the Texas legislature made Communist Party membership a felony. Federal officials followed suit. The Communist Control Act of 1954 defined the ideology as a "clear, present and continuing danger to the security of the United States" and deprived the party of all rights and privileges. Few Americans spoke out to propose that in suppressing inherent civil liberties, the nation was quickly becoming the evil it so deplored.[16]

True, perceptive critics took notice that fear only wrought more fear. Some rang loud warning bells. Accompanying the hysteria surrounding the domestic threat, they argued that a militarized "garrison state," originally intended to defeat communism, might arise. While Harold Lasswell popularized the term back in 1941, his worry of the United States, as a "global policeman," becoming a "political police state" took on added meaning in the following decade. Fears of unchecked state power running roughshod over citizens' rights ran parallel to fears of the existential threat against which that power was being wielded.[17]

During the early Cold War, however, Lasswell's apprehensions gained little traction. In fact, his words were repurposed by those seeking security in a war of "Moscow's making." Paul G. Hoffman, in charge of directing the Marshall Plan, claimed in 1949 that if Western Europe fell into the Soviet orbit, the United States would have to go on a "war footing" and become a "garrison state." Claude Putman, president of the National Association of Manufacturers, even suggested the following year that "in times of a national emergency every citizen's life, every citizen's property and every citizen's talents must be at the instant and unquestioned disposal of his government." One wonders if the irony of such arguments resonated with those supporting the anticommunist crusade.[18]

Though Lasswell's ultimate fears of a garrison state never came to pass, acceptance of the nation's first peacetime draft, introduced in 1948, hinted that Americans were willing to relinquish some of their individual freedoms in defense of the collective. Here, though, fear had its limits. While conscription became the "new normal" for age-appropriate male citizens, historian Amy Rutenberg argues that universal military training was "a level of militarization they were unwilling to accept." Selective service was one thing; forcibly conscripting all men into the armed forces for training was quite another. While the Joint Chiefs emphasized the critical importance of having well-trained forces "quickly available," the debate temporarily opened up space for deliberating what was militarily essential in the fight against communism. Imposing fear from above occasionally had its limits.[19]

In fact, the clash over and demise of universal military training hinted at larger questions about the United States' relationship with war at the midpoint of the twentieth century. Ultimately, Americans struggled with defining this new "cold war" and, just as significantly, their role in it. How much should they sacrifice to liberate the world from evil? What was needed to defend America from the domestic communist threat? And, fundamentally, if the United States was now in a continuous state of conflict against an implacable enemy, what did this suggest about the utility of war as a political instrument?[20]

Faith and fear thus revolved around opposing poles—one global, the other domestic—and turned on questions wrapped intrinsically around how Americans understood themselves. In the aftermath of a great depression and two world wars, they yearned for security. But how to achieve security in an insecure world? How to mitigate risk and ensure control in so uncertain a global environment? When war and peace blurred together into one intangible muddle, Americans' faith in leading a liberal international order seemed undermined by intense fears of an ideologically opposed foe. In the process, the global became personal. What did it mean, for example, if not even the family household could provide security against the dual—and paradoxical—threats of international communism and postwar consumerism?[21]

Finally, when would Americans know they had "won" this kind of war? Could "evil" ever truly be defeated? While some more recent historians have argued that containment of the Soviet Union had been achieved by 1949 or 1950, it seems likely most policymakers and ordinary citizens didn't feel that way at the time. For many, their fears were real enough. If "alarmism" more than empirical evidence was driving a continuation of the Cold War, new questions arose in the 1950s that made Americans' faith in and fear of war seem all the more pressing.[22]

PART II

War to Deter War

CHAPTER 5

Winning Here or Losing Everywhere

For anxious Americans in 1950, the sudden outbreak of war in Korea came as a thunderclap. Strategic surprises on this scale tended to generate their own fears. Might the Soviets be launching World War III not in Western Europe but along the global periphery in East Asia? Could China be making a bid for military supremacy throughout the region? One concerned citizen from Falls Church, Virginia claimed that the North Korean invasion of June 1950 had "electrified the American people like Pearl Harbor." The difference, however, was that this recent aggression targeted not US territory but rather "the mind and the liberties of individuals . . . anywhere in this world." Such alarmist commentary might now seem overwrought, but it certainly was a view shared by more than a few senior military officials as North Korean infantry surged across the 38th Parallel. Among them stood Douglas MacArthur.[1]

While retaining his role as Supreme Commander for the Allied Powers in Japan, MacArthur now took on the added role of leading the United Nations Command to defend South Korea. Throughout 1950, the seventy-year-old general spoke in apocalyptic terms about the regional, if not global, threat of communism on the march, an argument that found a receptive audience especially after China joined the North Koreans at year's end. In November, MacArthur sent a blistering message to Washington claiming that any limits imposed upon his military options would lead to a "calamity of major proportions." One month later, he publicly declared that a "state of undeclared war" existed between

Chinese communists and UN forces in Korea. Military analyst Hanson Baldwin went further, speaking of the communists' "determination to make the conquest of Asia complete." Not to be outdone, MacArthur maintained in early 1951 that "if we lose the war to communism in Asia the fall of Europe is inevitable." For a Truman administration hoping to limit the scope of the Cold War's first major conflict, such language posed a clear challenge to civilian authority.[2]

MacArthur's dramatic rhetoric—"We win here or we lose everywhere"—hinted at the potential gains to be realized either from extolling faith or peddling fear when it came to war. Might not Wisconsin Senator Joseph McCarthy argue he was right all along, that the Korean conflict was part of Moscow's prearranged plan for world domination? Ironically, MacArthur would deride the press and their "insensate desire for sensationalism," all while heightening Americans' larger sense of dread. Yet he wasn't alone. Even Truman, committed to containing hostilities on the Korean peninsula, spoke in ominous terms not long after Kim Il Sung's offensive began. On 27 June, the president declared that "the attack upon Korea makes it plain beyond all doubt that Communism has passed beyond the use of subversion to conquer independent nations and will now use armed invasion and war." An early Cold War turning point, it seemed, had been reached.[3]

The middling performance of the first US units to arrive in Korea—Task Force Smith collapsed in its first meeting with North Korean forces—raised fears over whether Americans could defeat the communist threat. One former officer even argued that the "poor performance" of those initial US troops sent to Korea resulted not just from inadequate training while they were stationed in Japan" but instead was "rooted in the failure of the army . . . to prepare itself during peacetime for battle." For fearful Americans in the early 1950s, the lessons were clear: The United States had entered a period of enduring war, and national security would require constant vigilance. Thus, as historian Masuda Hajima has suggested, the "imagined" and "constructed nature" of the Cold War became "reality" in the aftermath of Korea. A localized military contest was packing a huge political wallop.[4]

In many ways, the local Korean conflict held sweeping international consequences, thanks largely to false assumptions of the invasion being planned from and directed by Moscow. In truth, Stalin only reluctantly supported Kim Il Sung and had hardly pressured China to enter the conflict. Fearful Americans, however, only saw Korea as part of a "global conspiracy."[5]

The war also substantiated developing ideas about the potential of "falling dominoes" in the face of communist aggression. Dwight D. Eisenhower, then serving as the president of Columbia University, argued that failure in Korea "would encourage the outburst of similar or worse incidents somewhere along the perimeter of the area controlled by Russia." As the retired general maintained, "Any place that there is weakness they are going to go." Some military leaders took these fears a step further, contending that the Korean invasion was a ruse and the Soviets were about to strike in Europe where the "real" war would unfold.[6]

Seen in another light, though, the North Korean invasion gave Americans, and the still fledgling United Nations, a "moral legitimacy" to use military force against this "orchestrated" communist offensive. Some policymakers even glimpsed a symbiotic Cold War relationship in the making. Writing in 1956 to Dean Acheson, Truman was to argue that "there can be no U.N. without guns and guts from us." In a contest with "no rules and no umpires," force mattered. As the former president shared, "Only the iron fist with a hundred yards saber in it will be understood by Stalin's successors." Such thinking gained purchase, especially when communist North Koreans, according to one army handbook, embraced an "Oriental disregard for human life." Only a faith in war and the application of brute force could mollify fears that Americans might not be able to keep these "savages" at bay.[7]

Perhaps most importantly, at least for US policy elite, the fighting in Korea elicited a central question for waging the Cold War. What was a "vital interest" in this new, global "war"? Only after 1950 did fearful Americans come to essentialize nearly all areas of the globe. It now seems clear the Korean peninsula didn't hold much strategic value, in itself, for either the United States or the Soviet Union. Certainly, Secretary of State

Acheson intimated as much, at least publicly, in a January 1950 speech to the National Press Club when Korea was excluded from "the essential parts of the defensive perimeter of the Pacific," locales that "must and will be held."[8]

Kim's invasion, however, shifted the calculus and indicated how strategic decision-making isn't always a rational enterprise. Fearing the outbreak of World War III—nearly two-thirds of polled Americans thought they already were engaged in another global war—Truman and senior Pentagon officials believed they had to draw the line in an otherwise strategically insignificant area. (South Koreans under attack surely would have debated such an assertion.) Thus, Chairman of the Joint Chiefs of Staff Omar Bradley contended that the decision to go to war was "in a sense . . . unavoidable and inevitable." Similar assumptions about obligatory military interventions would mark US grand strategy throughout the Cold War. In order to deter a more general, direct war with the Soviet Union in Western Europe, Americans presumably would have to wield force and engage in local, peripheral wars around the globe.[9]

Some military theorists, surveying the destruction armies and air forces had wrought in the first half of the century, worried over the fickle nature of war itself. British writer B. H. Liddell Hart, for instance, intimated that war could have its own agenda. "War might come any time—even though no government desired or designed it."[10] Such speculation left an uncomfortable proposition. War might be uncontrollable. If this local outbreak was a harbinger of World War III, as some feared, then how best to contain not just the threat of communism but war itself? Therein lay the paradox to which Eisenhower alluded. The United States needed to contest communist advances through military might, but war in an atomic era had to be kept in check lest it unleash itself from human restraints. Using local wars to deter larger ones rested on an increasingly fraught relationship between faith and fear.

The war in Korea, though, still had more to give. The Chinese intervention raised questions about the larger purpose of US grand strategy. Mao hoped to avoid an American expansion of the war that would upset his plans for liberating Taiwan, but equally saw an opportunity for China to became *the* anticolonial power in international affairs. Truman, not surprisingly, viewed China's entry differently. At a November press conference, the president spoke of an aggression that threatened "not only the whole fabric of the United Nations, but all human hopes of peace and justice." Against such a vile threat, was the larger strategic aim containment or "rollback" of communism? Or, viewed through a more racial lens, defending western civilization against "hysterical" and "fanatical" savages? Even the usually sober George Kennan recalled, in dire terms, that the United States was confronting "a great, terrible, remorseless enemy, dedicated to our undoing, and holding in his hands the wherewithal to do us immense damage, even right here at home." The definition of "containment" would evolve over time, yet faith in and fear of war remained constant in Americans' views of an increasingly dangerous world.[11]

War, moreover, seemed to be fast becoming a thorny management problem, and not just for Americans. Faith and fear guided China's leadership as well. Mao worried about an American presence on China's borders—much as Stalin had feared for Russia's physical security after World War II—yet was confident that intervention in Korea would stoke a wave of revolutionary nationalism at home while bolstering his anticolonial credentials abroad.

Back in the United States, senior leaders equally wrestled with how best to craft a response to Kim Il Sung's invasion. Hardliners advocated for crossing the 38th parallel and unifying Korea, a way to reverse "the dangerous strategic trend in the Far East," as one Defense Department report argued. Others, however, cautioned that an open military confrontation with China or the Soviet Union would undermine US policy aims. As Truman maintained, direct action against China would enmesh the United States "in a vast conflict on the continent of Asia" and thus make "our task ... immeasurably more difficult all over the world."[12]

Truman's caution elicited a harsh response from a predictable source. MacArthur, who had been threatening to expand the war into China proper—while lacking the authority to do so—now began publicly criticizing his commander-in-chief. He complained that unwarranted limits imposed upon him were an "enormous handicap, without precedent in military history." In short, MacArthur's faith in American power was conflicting head-on with Truman's fears of a broader war. The Joint Chiefs ultimately recommended the general's dismissal, which the president obliged in April 1951. The Korean conflict had exposed civil-military tensions between presidents and senior military officials that would persist throughout the Cold War.[13]

Deeper questions around war's objectives in these types of "limited" conflicts also would endure. Within these interrogations, civil-military tensions were not always so clear-cut. MacArthur's linking of "winning" in Korea—there was "no substitute for victory"—to the larger defense of Europe aligned, however loosely, with Truman's fear that inaction on the part of the United States would lead to future communist aggression. As the president remarked of the communists not long after the outbreak of hostilities, "If we are tough enough now . . . they won't take any next steps. But if we just stand by, they'll move into other parts of the world in the future." Yet the eventual inability of US forces to achieve "total victory" in Korea would invite still other fears. If the United States was unable to impose its will on Korean communists, what might happen when the nation had to battle Soviet ones on the European continent?[14]

Truman's efforts to keep the Korean War localized also called into question the very purpose of war. While the president did his utmost to keep the war limited geographically and refused to authorize the use of atomic weapons, he also purposefully highlighted, if not exaggerated, the Korean threat to rally public support for the global containment of communism. It all seemed so confusing. If Americans were facing an existential evil, and possibly World War III, why was the administration limiting the war's scope and potential impact? One analyst suggested the problem was cultural. Having historically embraced a "crusading ideology," Americans remained convinced "that hostilities cannot be brought to an end before the evil enemy system has been eradicated." But the fighting in Korea clearly wasn't going to eliminate communism. So why, then, were Americans fighting at all?[15]

Not surprisingly, "limited war" became a contested term in the atomic age. In debating war's purpose in these new conflicts, scholars like Bernard Brodie contended they were now "talking about something quite new." Limiting US action to territory south of the Yalu River, for instance, seemed inconsistent with the World War II aims of unconditional surrender. Perhaps that is why the Korean conflict was temporarily redefined as a "police action," differentiating it from "real" war. (Of course, such terms reflected their users' perspective; it's unlikely that civilians living in Seoul found the fighting there "limited.") Writing from Tokyo, war correspondent Keyes Beech reported on this dissimilarity in outlooks. "The greatest source of anger and frustration here," he shared, "is Washington's apparent refusal to recognize the Korean war as a first-class war."[16]

Beech's testimonial highlighted Americans' increasingly tense relationship with war at the midpoint of the twentieth century. If the communist threat was a "revolutionary movement with an international ideology," then how could the United States only fight "limited" wars to contain it? The 1950 film *Why Korea?*, sponsored by the Department of Defense, offered few options for civilian policymakers. As the documentary warned, "If we don't fight there, we will fight here. We have no other choice." The challenge, then, was to contest communist expansionary drives while limiting the fighting so local wars didn't escalate into general—or worse, atomic—ones. As definitions of wartime success changed, so too did Americans' faith in war.[17]

Correspondent James Reston, an incisive commentator on national security issues, offered his thoughts in the immediate aftermath of the Korean invasion. Reston saw the conflict as a "costly but useful warning." These "little wars" weren't going away anytime soon, and Americans had to realize they couldn't "count on the atomic bomb to deter the Russians from limited engagements such as the Korean War." Political scientist Robert Osgood supplemented such thinking by writing a treatise on "limited war," developing an alternative to the faith that Eisenhower's administration apparently had placed in nuclear weaponry. For Osgood, a policy of containment and a reliance on nuclear weapons ceded to communism the strategic initiative. Americans instead had to become comfortable with fighting for "well-defined objectives that do not demand the utmost military effort." War, Osgood argued, was "a matter of degree."[18]

Advocates for relying on America's atomic arsenal—soon to be dubbed "massive retaliation"—agreed with "limited war" proponents in one key area: both held to their faith that the threat of military force could modify communist behavior. Eisenhower, who succeeded Truman in January 1953, believed that his own not-so-veiled threat of employing atomic weapons had led to peace on the Korean peninsula. It turned out Ike was wrong. Little if any evidence has surfaced that the Chinese were all that impressed by Eisenhower's saber-rattling.[19]

At the time, however, a faith in force united the US national security establishment. Debate might rage over how best to deter communist aggression, through either atomic or conventional means. But most agreed that containment necessitated military strength. Even those critics like Osgood, who questioned the true worth of nuclear weapons, felt coercion could reap strategic benefits if applied correctly. In this sense, Reston proved prophetic. By the mid-1950s, many if not most policymakers agreed that nuclear armaments had become more "instruments of threat" than usable weapons of war. Of course, the threat mattered only if taken seriously.[20]

This is not to suggest that limited war escaped criticism. On the contrary, detractors asked why American boys were being asked to "die for a tie" in Korea. Theorists like Brodie believed the term connoted "a deliberate hobbling of a tremendous power," while others felt that "artificial" limitations posed "exceedingly difficult theoretical and practical problems" in determining what was "necessary and sufficient" to win a war. More recently, some historians have argued, dubiously, that the concept of limited war meant policymakers didn't value victory. In this telling, "MacArthur, for all his many faults, understood the importance of victory better than Truman." A negotiated settlement indicated weakness, not restraint.[21]

Still, a key question remained: how best to deal with a stalemated war? Was the goal of war simply to inflict maximum pain on one's enemy until some political solution could be found? General Mark Clark thought so. Taking over the United Nations Command in Korea in May 1952, Clark later recalled that, since "it was not our government's policy to seek a military decision, the next best thing was to make the stalemate more expensive for the communists than for us." Cold War policymakers would wrestle with this strategic dilemma for decades to come.[22]

Clark hinted at another critique of limited war. As military officers would argue then and later, political constraints hampered military effectiveness. Dismissing the fact that North Korea had suffered horribly during the war—Pyongyang was left in rubble—some officers claimed the Soviet Union and China would see negotiations as a "concession and concession as weakness." Yet when cities now could be destroyed with one bomb, such fears dismissed war's changing character. In 1950, Liddell Hart had argued that "total warfare" was "not compatible with the atomic age." Any victory "pursued without regard to the consequences" seemed nonsensical, if not "mutually suicidal." Even Eisenhower agreed. Speaking to a group of military officers in 1954, the president wondered aloud what a general war that destroyed Moscow, Leningrad, and other cities offered the United States. "Gain such a victory, and what do you do with it?"[23]

The former general understood that even if war's character might be changing in the atomic era, translating military effectiveness into political influence remained *the* central issue for those waging war. Here, another type of faith entered into strategic calculations as military planners peered into the future. Localized wars, they hoped, would contain communism while simultaneously preventing superpower conflict. In an atomic age, limited war advocates assumed this was how war retained its utility for policymakers, a way to demonstrate strength against a supposedly global communist threat.[24]

In short, military analysts asked, could the United States use "limited wars" to deter larger ones? Hanson Baldwin believed so. In fact, he saw no other alternative. "An unlimited atomic war, obviously cannot lead to a more stable peace," the journalist maintained, "or to anything that could be called 'victory.'" Good strategy produced stability, not chaos, and thus the best way forward relied on setting "limited objectives, utilizing limited means."[25]

Senior officers like Maxwell Taylor concurred. The future salesman of "flexible response" distrusted nuclear deterrence's untested assumptions and actively promoted strategies that prepared the US armed forces to fight limited wars. Meanwhile, theorists like Robert Osgood couched their arguments by looking toward Moscow. If the communists sought to "minimize the risk of precipitating total war," then they would rely on "limited military force as a means of attaining their ambitions." Thus, the United States must prepare for conflicts "in which discrimination in the use of weapons and selection of targets would be practicable." Only in this way, Osgood argued, could the "strategic failure" of "total war" be minimized.[26]

This growing faith in limited war had a less publicized but equally important political counterpart. Though the United States had helped liberate South Korea from Japanese rule in 1945 and funded much of its budget throughout the 1950s, it could not goad the Seoul government into initiating meaningful domestic reforms. American modernizers were confident they could build a strong democracy capable of resisting communist sway. Yet Syngman Rhee's regime proved resistant to US development agendas as it struggled to gain popular support and legitimacy among a population wracked by civil war. This misplaced faith in influencing local allies' behavior portended challenges ahead. Korea became a harbinger for the problems of wartime nation building, what one historian called "a military rehearsal for the subsequent disaster in Vietnam."[27]

At the same time, Korea demonstrated how fear could lead policymakers, and the larger public, into conflating localized conflicts with the larger Cold War competition. It would be a trend that would persist, not just in Europe—where the "cement of fear" was holding NATO together, according to the State Department—but in "peripheral" areas across the globe. As the film *Why Korea?* opined, "There are no longer any geographical boundaries.... What we are defending is not geographic borders, but a way of life." Calculating politicians took note, as fear incentivized demonstrating strength given such high stakes. Senator Millard Tydings (D-MD) illustratively claimed the United States was "in deadly peril. The question now is whether we can survive.... The war in Korea has shown us how weak we are, and how strong the enemy is."[28]

Even after Stalin's death in March 1953, with the active war in Korea drawing to a close, hawkish politicians maintained their drumbeat. While it took time for Nikita Khrushchev to consolidate his power within the Soviet politburo, Eisenhower briefly hoped for a thaw in superpower relations. He would be disappointed. Subsequent changes to Soviet foreign policy did not appreciably alter Americans' perceptions of the global communist threat. In fact, as Khrushchev pushed Soviet policy toward a more internationalist stance, the move, in itself, inspired new fears. As Secretary of State John Foster Dulles shared with the president, Moscow might be more willing to take risks as a show of strength for the new leadership.[29]

Outside the White House, similar warnings echoed across the political landscape. After Stalin's death, the chairman of the Senate Foreign Relations Committee, Alexander Wiley (R-WI), alleged that the danger of communist aggression "may be actually terribly intensified." As Wiley professed, "we have to have far more than a static defense." Foreign leaders in Bonn and London also urged their allies not to relax in the face of "increased perils." West German Chancellor Konrad Adenauer implored his countrymen not to "sit idle hypnotized by the political developments in Moscow." British Foreign Secretary Anthony Eden equally encouraged the West not to change its policy after Stalin's death. "The foundations of our policy cannot change," he declared.[30]

But Kremlin leaders were seeking a change. Even before Khrushchev had prevailed in his power struggle with Georgy Malenkov in 1955, senior politburo members were speaking of a new "peace initiative," a way to relax Cold War tensions by reopening diplomatic ties with the West. True, Khrushchev retained his own deep faith in the communist system, believing it would prevail over the Soviet Union's capitalist foes. Still, he remained hopeful that open war could be avoided. All that frightened Americans heard, however, was Khrushchev declaring to western diplomats in 1956 that "we will bury you." That the First Secretary's avowal was more about the long-term future of Marxist doctrine than actual Soviet military policy didn't matter. Such combative language only reinforced the fears of those Americans who believed the "communist conspiracy" was "indigenous" to the Russian homeland.[31]

Thus, by the early 1950s, the Cold War already was being seen as a zero-sum game; any Soviet "win" necessarily meant an American "loss." No wonder the feeling of a "lost victory" in Korea left so many Americans unsatisfied and likely contributed to the conflict becoming a "forgotten war." Concerned with maintaining a global balance of power—some instead saw it as a "balance of terror"—the two superpowers consistently overreacted when local trends didn't go their way. Dean Acheson, for example, insisted the Asian conflict was not a "Korean war on either side," but rather "the global strategy of global purpose on both sides." Often dismissed was the immense destruction suffered by local peoples because of superpower interventionism.[32]

By globalizing a local (or, at best, regional) Korean conflict, US policymakers were creating a paradox. Though they saw "proof" of global Soviet designs and Chinese collaboration, they sought to avoid any broader atomic war that might destroy the United States or undermine its overseas interests. All the while, they avoided hard truths that while the Cold War might seem bipolar in nature, the United States still remained disproportionally more powerful than the Soviet Union. It appeared far safer—and politically profitable—for policymakers to exaggerate threats and play upon citizens' fears when communist aggression seemed in motion.[33]

Relying on more limited forms of war to avoid general war, however, rested on largely untested assumptions born of fear. Pursuing one form of war in hopes of deterring a presumably deadlier form of war assumed a level of control over the chaotic environment of armed conflict.

Even in Korea, some officers were recommending the use of atomic bombs if "suitable targets could be found."[34] A limited war one day could mushroom into something entirely different the next.

Existential fears, though, sat uneasily alongside a faith that limited war could achieve larger US policy objectives. Take, for instance, the increasing militancy of John Foster Dulles. In May 1952, Dulles advocated for "A Policy of Boldness" in *Life* magazine. The soon-to-be secretary of state pulled no punches arguing that the United States confronted "its gravest peril" in Soviet communism. Current policies were "*inadequate in scope*," he emphasized and, despite the nation's vast resources, the "only commodity in which we seem deficient is faith." In contesting the "dozen people in the Kremlin . . . attempting to rule 800 million human beings," Dulles argued that "common defense" came in the form of "common punishing power." Three years later, in *Foreign Affairs*, the statesman continued his call for US military power "able to retaliate at once and effectively against any aggression." What other choice given Soviet rulers' aim to "harass the existing order and pave the way for political coups which will install Communist-controlled régimes"?[35]

An evolution from containment of communism to its "rollback" fit well within Dulles's Manichaean worldview. He held faith in war remaining limited despite ever-increasing policy objectives. Properly managed, violence and the threat of its use would signal to communist leaders the strength of American will and resolve. Such a faith also corresponded to the cultural framework of American exceptionalism. When Dulles spoke of embracing an offensive foreign policy to keep "alive the hope of liberation," his words resonated with those convinced of their nation's moral—and thus ideological—superiority.[36]

Notably, not all Americans agreed with Dulles's logic, heralding future challenges to the White House sustaining popular support for "limited wars" overseas. A late 1951 Gallup poll found 56 percent of Americans agreed that the "Korean war is an utterly 'useless war.'" Uniformed officers likewise worried about waning domestic support. General Matthew Ridgway, fearing a rapid demobilization with the Korean conflict's end, expressed concern over the media using phrases like "Let's Get the Boys Back Home" and "the War Weary Troops." What if Dulles was correct in alluding to Americans' "deficient" faith?[37]

In many ways, this increasingly public debate over foreign-policy aims in Korea centered upon the inherent tensions between faith and fear. As we've seen, MacArthur's faith in military power conflicted with Truman's fear of escalating war. The general underlined these tensions by calling for a military buildup on Formosa (Taiwan), the bombing of Manchuria, and a blockade of China. But would this display of military strength intimidate the communists or incite them to higher levels of violence? Truman feared the latter. MacArthur's relief in 1951 hardly closed the debate. If Dean Acheson was correct in arguing that the United States was "facing the Soviet Union all around the world," then complacency came with unbearable costs. Still, the general's black-and-white prescriptions appeared equally alarming. After being relieved of command, MacArthur tellingly advocated for defending "every place, and I think we have the capacity to do it. If you say we haven't, you admit defeat."[38]

If the general's views lacked nuance, a Cold War consensus was, in fact, emerging from the war in Korea. Most Americans tended to agree with MacArthur's gloomy predictions that envisioned a bleak world if economically and ideologically closed to the United States. To policymakers, economics and ideology were interconnected, even if they weren't publicly explicit about such relationships. Wars might need to be limited in their scope to deter larger ones, but that didn't mean the United States should restrain itself from acting as a global, even imperial, power. A tipping point had been passed. As veteran diplomat Charles "Chip" Bohlen maintained, "It was the Korean War and not World War II that made us a world political-military power."[39]

CHAPTER 6

A Brave (and Frightful) New World

If diplomat Chip Bohlen understood the Cold War as both a political and military contest, theologian Reinhold Niebuhr worried that "the American nation [had] become strangely enamored with military might." Writing in 1955, Niebuhr conceded that military power was necessary, "particularly in moments of crisis, when the community faces recalcitrance and anarchy at home, and dispute with another community abroad." While the ethicist thought military force pertinent to international disputes, he wondered why so few Americans realized that force had its limits. To Niebuhr, far too many of his fellow citizens felt it "possible to establish order out of chaos by the assertion of military might."[1]

The unsatisfying military experience in Korea rested uneasily with Americans' faith in the application of this military might. On another level, the war's largely conventional tenor also challenged their faith in technology to solve military problems and defray the human costs of battle. Of course, technology, in the form of airpower, did matter to South Korea's survival, especially during the conflict's early days and after China's intervention. But advanced weapons of war—strategic bombers, intercontinental missiles, and a burgeoning nuclear program—all came with high price tags. Thus, Americans' faith in technology sat worryingly alongside fears that increased defense spending might undermine the nation's economic welfare.[2]

Compared to World War II innovations, Korea saw relatively few dramatic advances in military technologies. If the war's outcome proved frustrating, so too did its conduct when wielding American power. Airpower enthusiasts complained of scarce "strategic" targets on the peninsula, while those outside Korea were deemed off-limits by supposedly meddling civilian authorities. On the ground, military leaders like James Gavin, reflecting mid-century racial attitudes, bemoaned the fact that America, "with its scientific resources and tremendous industrial capacity, had to accept combat on the terms laid down by a rather primitive Asiatic army." Korea, it seemed, provided few opportunities to exploit "the technical margin of advantage" needed to win "decisively and quickly."[3]

The questionable utility of technologically superior weapons intensified parallel fears that any new technology might soon become obsolete, leaving one vulnerable to an enemy's scientific developments. This hardly was a new problem for military commanders. World War II, however, had changed the strategic calculus. The most fearsome of wartime technological advances, employed to its illogical conclusion, spelled mankind's doom.[4]

Even before Korea, Truman had acknowledged that atomic weapons likely would play a role in an eventual war against the Soviets. But he resolved they would remain under civilian control. The president recognized it was a "terrible thing" to order the use of a weapon intended to "wipe out women and children and unarmed people." "You have got to understand," Truman implored, "this isn't a military weapon." Nor were civilians alone in wrestling with these questions. Air Force General Hoyt Vandenberg wondered what targets were acceptable for atomic weapons. "In a war with the USSR is our purpose to destroy the Russian people, industry, the Communist party, the Communist hierarchy, or a combination of these?" The Pentagon and White House would wrestle with if and how best to employ nuclear weapons for years to come.[5]

Despite Truman's admonition that the atomic bomb wasn't a "military weapon," uniformed leaders increasingly believed it fell within their purview as military strategists. Chairman of the Joint Chiefs Omar Bradley, for instance, declared the bomb held "first priority" in the defense of Europe. Lower down the hierarchy, US commanders in Germany saw atomic weapons as vital to winning a future war against the Soviets. By 1953, the US Seventh Army was conducting war games to instill "atomic mindedness" among its soldiers. Three years later, the army would be experimenting with "pentomic" divisions, highly mobile units with enough firepower to fight and win on a "tactical" atomic battlefield. Of course, to retain funding within the defense budget, army leaders had to demonstrate their usefulness in the nuclear era. National security aside, service rivalries had a tendency to invite themselves into strategic calculations.[6]

The army's foray into atomic warfare suggested deeper fears over being left behind as a nuclear arms race took hold. Relying on an atomic monopoly back in 1948, Truman's National Security Council argued that if Western Europe were to "enjoy any feeling of security," it would be "in large degree because of the atomic bomb, under American trusteeship." But that monopoly didn't last for long. Senior policy advisors therefore believed they had little choice but to place their continuing faith in atomic testing and weapons accumulation. Even the head of the US Atomic Energy Commission, Lewis Strauss, argued against any test-ban treaties. Sharing with Eisenhower in 1958, Strauss thought about communism as he did about sin—"there was no compromise with it." Thus, any arms race, nuclear included, was one between "good and evil."[7]

While Strauss might appear panic-stricken by the communist threat, the context in which he spoke matters. Less than a year earlier, on 4 October 1957, the Soviet Union had launched a man-made satellite into orbit. *Sputnik* generated its own set of fears, demonstrating to some Americans the United States' vulnerability to external attack. A media frenzy followed the realization that "backward" communists had somehow stolen a march on Americans and now were able to engage in "scare diplomacy." Scientist Edward Teller declared the nation had lost "a battle more important and greater than Pearl Harbor." Meanwhile, Senate Majority Leader Lyndon B. Johnson alleged the Soviets would soon be "dropping bombs on us from space," while *Life* magazine asked its readers, "Why Did the U.S. Lose the Race?" Across the political spectrum, the *Sputnik* crisis led to anxious finger-pointing over such a momentous setback.[8]

Eisenhower did his best to calm the nation's frayed nerves, later blaming the "post-Sputnik panic" on grandstanding politicians and greedy defense specialists eager to profit from the affair. By this point, though, Ike had settled into his role as Cold War president. He knew from intelligence reports that Soviet missiles actually presented a negligible threat to the United States. And so, while accelerating the nation's long-range rocket program and sending medium-range missiles to the United Kingdom, Italy, and Turkey to quiet the political storm, the president also explored a possible nuclear test-ban treaty with his science advisors. *Sputnik* may have encouraged a new technological arms race, but Eisenhower hoped to proceed cautiously and economically.[9]

Entering office four years before the Soviet satellite launch, Eisenhower had spoken of a world in which the "forces of good and evil are massed and armed and opposed as rarely before in history." As he made clear in his inaugural address, Ike agreed with his predecessor on the need for containing the global communist threat and, perhaps because of his senior role in World War II, never doubted that the defense of Western Europe remained vital to US national security. He departed from Truman, however, in accepting as necessary a vast military buildup to confront the Soviets. Nor did Eisenhower buy into the excesses of McCarthyism. By ignoring the Wisconsin senator, he hoped—with limited success—to curb the Red Scare's intemperance. The president thus only occasionally lashed out against the "fear, threat, hysteria, and intimidation" upon which domestic anticommunism and Red-hunting depended.[10]

By the time Ike took office in 1953, fear had permeated the political landscape. Living with "the bomb" had seeped into the American psyche, even if few citizens grasped the potential for accidents and miscalculations that might trigger nuclear war. Military theorists certainly debated the possibility of "accidental nuclear escalation," and mishaps did happen. In 1958, an air force B-47, en route to England and carrying a Mark 6 nuclear bomb, accidentally released its load over Mars Bluff, South Carolina. While the device neither detonated nor released any radioactive fallout, Hanson Baldwin reported that the incident "started a chain reaction of worry," despite government officials' claims that an accidental explosion was "so remote as to be negligible."[11]

The challenge for Eisenhower, then, was reducing defense spending while also easing fears of atomic war, intentional or inadvertent. The administration's "New Look" policy aimed to facilitate these two goals. Relying on nuclear weapons to deter Soviet aggression, Ike's grand strategy would take full advantage of the nation's "atomic capability and massive retaliatory striking power." Yet its reliance on and faith in nuclear deterrence remained in tension with the public's fears of nuclear Armageddon. Moreover, deterrence, as a "political condition," could change depending on the enemy's own calculations. What was required to deter Moscow, for example, might not be the same for dissuading Beijing from aggressive action. And as the arms race continued apace—the Soviets tested their first thermonuclear device in August 1953—deterrence became not just a quantitative problem but a qualitative one as well.[12]

While Eisenhower emphasized "financial solvency and economic soundness" to support the New Look's reliance on nuclear weapons, it would be wrong to paint his strategic approach as simply one of "massive retaliation." The president relied heavily on alliance structures, psychological-warfare operations, and covert action to enhance national security. However, it was John Foster Dulles's remarks on the "deterrent of massive retaliatory power"—a euphemism for nuclear weapons—that illuminated contemporary strategy debates. Critics, like General Matthew Ridgway, worried the New Look defense budget would "leave us with less combat effectiveness than we had when we started." Democrats equally maintained that reliance on the bomb was inadequate to prepare against a Soviet menace "in a period of total danger." Faith in conventional war, even in an atomic era, still loomed large.[13]

Eisenhower's National Security Council took all this in as it developed a workable strategy for implementing the New Look. Questions over nuclear reliance mattered, but so too did other uncertainties. How could the United States reduce Soviet power "without accepting grave risks of general war"? How best to avoid a global stalemate while attempting to "build free world strength"? Under what conditions might atomic weapons actually be employed? Could they be used at all "short of general war"? Undergirding all these competing priorities was the question of what America's nuclear arsenal really was supposed to deter. Communist subversion? Limited wars like Korea? An atomic attack from Moscow's strategic air forces? Practically speaking, Ike's team had few good answers.[14]

The problem stemmed from an inability to both define and evaluate the value of "deterrence" in the atomic age. If limited war remained necessary for preventing global communist advances, what was needed to prevent a general war that might lead to nuclear exchanges? Hanson Baldwin argued that deterrence was "the sum of all its parts" and not simply a reliance on bombs and bombers, while theorist Thomas Schelling maintained it was the "skillful *nonuse* of military forces." For his part, John Foster Dulles suggested it was the "'necessary art' of risking war to keep peace." All these characterizations implied that deterrence meant persuading, even threatening, one's opponent to act—or not act—in a certain way. Fear of a general atomic war thus induced a faith in deterrence to prevent what Eisenhower deemed "the unthinkable."[15]

Once more, inconsistencies arose in how US policymakers thought about war's utility. What did deterrence suggest about Americans' overarching faith in war? If such a strategy was intended to discourage or prevent war, was this an admission that faith in war itself was misplaced? And, if deterrence failed, might not the political ends of containment become irrelevant in a nuclear war? Military historian Russell F. Weigley once called deterrence "a thoroughly negative kind of strategy." But in arming itself to the teeth, the United States positively risked inspiring fear in its enemies and provoking them into preemptive action.[16]

As military commanders and civilian policymakers wrestled with these questions, political scientists and international-relations "experts" weighed in. Harvard professor Henry Kissinger argued that in the atomic age, limited war had become "essentially a political act" because it had no "'purely' military solution." The problem, Kissinger surmised, was that no one questioned how deterrence "was to be achieved by strategic striking power" or how "victory depended on inflicting maximum destruction on the aggressor." Limited war, then, became a faith-based form of deterrence, "the only means for preventing the Soviet bloc, at an acceptable cost, from overrunning the peripheral areas of Eurasia."[17]

This relationship between deterrence and limited war mattered because it emboldened a faith that the combination would prevent the catastrophe of general nuclear conflict. As General James Gavin argued in late 1958, "by failing to provide for limited wars we invite general wars, and such a war is one that no one will win." Gavin's conception of "winning" captivated military theorists and raised yet another set of uncomfortable questions. Was a stalemate in a limited war like Korea preferable to a "victory" in a general war? Did a stalemate in one arena relegate the entire Cold War competition to an impasse? Moreover, what did "victory" even mean? Theorist Bernard Brodie believed that even the victor in an atomic war would "suffer a degree of physical destruction incomparably greater than that suffered by any defeated nation of history." "Under those circumstances," he argued, no victory "would be worth the price."[18]

But what if one's enemy deemed the risk of war worth the price? The central issue of deterrence thus became one of influencing perceptions. US policymakers had to convince their communist foes that certain limited military advances might trigger a larger war. Brodie noted the value of "deliberate restraint" in fighting limited wars, but Washington elite found utility in threatening unilateral escalation. The challenge was presenting a credible threat. Brodie concluded that war's political objectives could not be "consonant with national suicide," but deterrence theories rested on risking just that. War was fast becoming an exercise in managing the probability of expected future punishment. Would Khrushchev, as an example, find Eisenhower's faith in "massive retaliation" credible if it meant trading American cities for Soviet ones?[19]

In the larger context of the Cold War, it's worth considering whether deterrence had become *the* critical component in defining war itself. Bernard Brodie famously argued that in the atomic age, the military establishment's chief purpose was no longer to win wars but "to avert them." Yet the theorist also advised taking measures to protect the nation from the "possibility of retaliation in kind," suggesting that deterrence offered no guarantees. No wonder theoretical discussions of "brinksmanship"—what Thomas Schelling described as deliberately creating "a recognizable risk of war, a risk that one does not completely control"—seemed so frightening. If deterrence was becoming a "rigidified response" to any perceived communist encroachment, then the risk of general war actually might grow, potentially invalidating the whole point of the exercise.[20]

The increasingly undefinable nature of war confounded at least a few policymakers. Commenting on the dangers of brinkmanship and miscalculation, future Secretary of State Dean Rusk lamented that there was "no certainty in this god damn poker game." Additionally, American presidents throughout the era worried that their actions—or failures to act—might damage the nation's global standing, thus undermining the reliability of deterrence-based threats. In the process, overblown fears of losing "credibility" reinforced the United States' reliance on military might. If deterrence failed, so arguments went, then only war could save the nation. Not surprisingly, as historian John Dower has argued, "brute force" became, and remained, "the ultimate measure of credibility" for far too many Americans.[21]

Venomous debates within the military bureaucracy did not help matters. When the Department of Defense cut the budget for ships to buy more bombers, the admirals revolted, resulting in what Secretary Louis Johnson deemed a "grave danger to our national security." One rear admiral publicly condemned the air force's approach to atomic bombing as "ruthless and barbaric," an endorsement of "random mass slaughter." The critique was disingenuous. In truth, few military men had debated the liabilities of civilian bombing during or after World War II. The indiscriminate slaughter of Japanese or German civilians seems to have mattered little as long as it was helping win the war. Nor did these same military men question whether the Soviet threat truly justified an immense defense budget. Of greater significance, it seemed, was how much of the New Look budget naval leaders might lose to their air force brethren.[22]

Indeed, nowhere else did the theoretical debates on deterrence take a more corporeal form than inside the US Air Force. Faith in and fear of airpower became a central component of how the United States thought about war in the second half of the twentieth century, even if Korea had demonstrated the limits of that power. Ever since the First World War, airpower advocates had imagined planes bypassing ground resistance and attacking an enemy's "vital centers." The next global war seemingly validated such lofty assumptions, even if evidence afterward proved far less certain. (MacArthur acknowledged that perhaps "too much was expected from the air" in Korea.) As one 1947 Air Staff report hypothesized, "the long-range bomber will permit the delivery of devastating blows to the heart of the enemy without the necessity for the conquest of intermediate bases." When atomic bombs were added to the payload, aerial Cold Warriors could not help but thump their chests and declare themselves the premier guardians of national security.[23]

Not only would they deter communist aggression, airpower advocates maintained they also could coerce the enemy into surrendering if war erupted. In making armies and navies obsolete, air forces now could shorten wars, if not win them, all on their own by directly undermining the enemy's political will and destroying its "vital industrial and population centers." As the chiefs of the Strategic Air Command confidently reported in 1958, SAC could "destroy the Soviet Union and China several times over in the event of war." It all seemed so alluring, so cost-effective, and, most importantly, so empowering. War, however, has an irritating tendency to defy shortcuts. Air activists would spend the Cold War's remaining years managing the disparity between their inflated expectations and the reality of armed combat.[24]

As airpower enthusiasts championed bombs and bombers, the rise of the US Air Force's Strategic Air Command effectively blurred the lines between offensive striking power and national defense. Led by the outspoken General Curtis LeMay, SAC achieved near cult status within the armed forces and the command's mission rested on a simple prescription. "If you are strong then you maintain peace," one senior officer declared. "If you are weak, you get run over." In briefings, LeMay was clear in his purpose: "to conduct the strategic air offensive utilizing atomic weapons." He and his command would annihilate Soviet forces, prevent them from launching their own bombs or missiles, and destroy the communists' "war-sustaining resources." Any cuts to his portion of the defense budget, he argued, undermined US national security. Along the way, LeMay helped expand America's global footprint as SAC required overseas military bases to operate effectively twenty-four hours a day.[25]

LeMay's faith in airpower hid an underlying fear. He believed in the prospect, even likelihood, of nuclear war. The best way to manage that fear, then, was to instill it in his enemies. LeMay may have deemed the air force the nation's "primary deterrent," but he also declared war was about one thing—"you've got to kill people, and when you've killed enough they stop fighting." Here, the influence of extirpative war in Japan shone brightly. LeMay and his peers purposefully were blurring the lines between battlefields and home fronts, just as they had done in World War II. Cities, and the civilians living in them, became "legitimate targets for mass destruction." The envisioned level of devastation reached the absurd, putting into question the value of war. One strategic plan, for example, called for firing 1,459 nuclear weapons, which would kill an estimated 275 million people. One wonders what policy objective could have been served by so many deaths.[26]

Contemporary theorists shared LeMay's faith, even if they sought different targets for America's nuclear arsenal. Some espoused a "counterforce" strategy aimed at Soviet military forces, with Daniel Ellsberg, for one, believing it a more humane approach. Others, like future Secretary of Defense Robert S. McNamara, submitted in the early 1960s that a "no cities" strategy might incentivize Moscow to "refrain from striking our own cities." (His critics thought laughable the assumption that godless communists would limit their own nuclear attacks.) Undergirding these debates were intense disputes about the United States' capacity to absorb an enemy's preemptive first strike. If "strategic coercion" failed to deter, if threats didn't intimidate, then what might follow clearly frightened civilian theorists and military leaders alike.[27]

The fears didn't end there. Faith in deterrence theories remained in tension with deep anxieties over massive retaliation and what later would become known as "mutually assured destruction," or MAD. Ever since the Soviets first successfully tested an atomic bomb back in 1949, Cold War commentators had worried about the United States' ability to establish a "monopoly of armed strength," as one Rand analyst commented. Decisive victory in war seemed ever more elusive as Moscow filled the atomic gap. Worse, Soviet retaliation to an American attack might be just as bad as a surprise "bolt-from-the-blue" strike. No longer did strategic discussions center on limiting damage, but rather on survival itself. As a theory, MAD appeared inconsistent with winning a war, especially if a losing enemy committed themselves to unleashing a "last orgy of destruction."[28]

With Pearl Harbor memories still fresh in their minds, Americans saw themselves apart from their Soviet competitors, not only, in historian Paul Boyer's words, as a "potential threat to other peoples, but as potential victims." This sense of victimhood became more acute after theorists like Bernard Brodie came to view cities as the most valuable targets for atomic weapons. American citizens, in all likelihood, would be on the front lines of a future nuclear war. Some believed they already were, given popular stories of Soviet espionage at home. The House Committee on Un-American Activities held hearings on supposedly "shocking" security lapses in which "Soviet agents in a completely professional spy ring" had taken advantage of "misguided scientists" to steal America's "atomic secrets." Accusations that "hundreds of subversive aliens" were entering the country only further heightened existing fears at home.[29]

Given the horrors of atomic warfare and the threat of atomic spies, was war becoming too complex, too dangerous to leave to the generals? The rise of civilian "strategy intellectuals" like Brodie, Kissinger, and Herman

Kahn insinuated as much. From think tanks like the Rand Corporation, a cadre of theorists and scholars weighed into strategic debates, arguing that technological changes incumbent in nuclear war demanded a more scientific approach to its study. In the process, technical specialists steeped in "systems analysis" methods increasingly questioned the expertise of professional military officers.

The reactions were predictable. One senior officer seethed at "the pipe-smoking, tree-full-of-owls type of so-called professional 'defense intellectuals'" entering high-level strategy discussions. To military men with combat experience in World War II and Korea, it rankled that academics were approaching war as if it "could be settled on a chessboard in an ivory-covered Great Hall."[30]

But these intellectuals had a point. If professional officers were supposed to "manage violence" on behalf of the state, what happened when nuclear weapons entered this civil-military equation? Truman already had made it clear that the president made nuclear decisions. Moreover, civilians understood the implications of nuclear war just as well as their military counterparts. Bernard Brodie feared that "truly cosmic forces" had been "harnessed to the machines of war" and that an all-out war spelled the possible destruction of "the national community." Henry Kissinger equally worried that "a more flexible application of our power" might have been inhibited by the technological arms race. Scientist Edward Teller, for his part, acknowledged that the "interplay of nuclear threat and diplomacy" was "frightening" and "very complex." Surely, these civilian intellectuals realized that the nuclear arms race was altering the United States' relationship with war and potentially limiting the political payoffs that came from it.[31]

Among the more unconventional of these theorists, Herman Kahn leaned into the absurdity of it all. Directing the Hudson Institute think tank in New York, Kahn argued that Americans were "guilty of the worst kind of wishful thinking" when it came to nuclear war. He sought to shock them into confronting its likely realities, delivering public lectures with briefing charts captioned "Will the Survivors Envy the

Dead?" He employed ominous phrases like "megadeath" and "doomsday machines." He created an "escalation ladder" that included the steps "Inadvertent War" and "Catalytic War." And in 1960 he published *On Thermonuclear War*, a book one reviewer called a "moral tract on mass murder." Kahn wanted his readers to think about "the unthinkable," to confront the possibility that state leaders might not be rational actors when considering the nuclear option.[32]

In short, Kahn challenged Americans' faith in deterrence. War might be "unthinkable," but it also was statistically probable. While theorists like Brodie suggested nuclear weapons might serve as a "stabilizing force" if great powers could rely on "retaliation in kind" as a form of deterrence, Kahn had his doubts. He wasn't alone. With scholars like Kissinger writing about the potential value of "limited nuclear war," how, critics wondered, could policymakers be certain the limits they imposed would stick? Or that a "limited" war would be enough to deter an adversary from taking additional steps up Kahn's escalation ladder?[33]

While academic theorists and military officers debated nuclear war's utility, the Eisenhower administration retained its faith in the nation's atomic arsenal. Both Ike and Dulles continued to believe that nuclear weapons could help solve political problems abroad, either by reassuring their allies or demonstrating resolve to their enemies. Had not atomic bombs, they mused, efficiently if destructively ended the Second World War, while also sending a signal to the United States' erstwhile Soviet allies? And yet over all these debates hung a fundamental question when it came to nuclear weapons: how much was enough?[34]

Policymakers may have exuded confidence from their possession of nuclear weapons, yet their eagerness to pursue hydrogen bombs and a triad of delivery systems—intercontinental bombers, ballistic missiles, and submarines—intimated deeper fears about what the future might hold. If, one Texas senator maintained, the United States did not pursue a hydrogen "super-bomb," it would be "an act of delayed surrender." (The H-bomb was first detonated in November 1952 at Eniwetok Atoll in the Marshall Islands.) Given such arguments, would it ever be possible to exit from the budding arms race once it had begun? Critics might disparage the H-bomb as a "weapon of genocide," but Eisenhower and Dulles clearly thought it essential to their strategy of containment.[35]

Additionally, by Ike's second term, the administration was spending more time considering how to adjust modern weaponry to the purposes of limited war. Nuclear weapons had acquired an important strategic role, so popular theories went, but they might now solve tactical problems as well. Ike appeared willing to consider their use for ending hostilities in Korea. And with the French colonial enterprise in Indochina unraveling in 1954, Pentagon officials floated the idea of dropping "tactical A-bombs" to save the French garrison at Dien Bien Phu. While Ike retreated from such a far-reaching step, the idea seemingly held merit. Three years later, political scientist Robert Osgood would argue that there were "no rational grounds for regarding low-yield atomic battlefield warheads as any more horrible and inhumane than napalm or, for that matter, TNT." Lost in such considerations was the fact that America's nuclear arsenal had failed as an instrument of strategic deterrence or as a tool for maintaining its allies' colonial holdings.[36]

Osgood's calculations weren't mere academic musings. The Pentagon *was* planning to engage in "broken-back warfare," fighting that would continue after a nuclear exchange concluded. Army leaders even decided to arm American GIs in Europe and South Korea with low-yield atomic recoilless rifles. Weighing about fifty pounds, the "Davy Crockett" had a yield of roughly ten to twenty tons of TNT. The weapon also had an undesirable design feature: its blast radius exceeded its delivery range, meaning soldiers firing it almost immediately were exposed to radioactive fallout upon detonation. How could senior civilian policymakers control and limit nuclear war when enlisted soldiers were roaming the battlefield with mini-atomic warheads?[37]

The Davy Crockett's dubious technical merits intimated deeper issues with leaders' faith in nuclear weapons. Whether in Moscow or Beijing, Paris or Washington, policy elite interrogated the political advantages to be gained from their possession. If using atomic bombs placed mankind on the path toward Armageddon, then how valuable were they? Was any of this thinking "rational" from a policy perspective? While Stalin had scoffed at the coercive nature of atomic bombs—they were "meant to frighten those with weak nerves," he mused—they nonetheless remained appealing. Mao, for instance, may have mocked the American atomic bomb as a "paper tiger," yet he still hoped that China's own bomb, first detonated in October 1964, would win him greater international influence. The bomb might be considered an "unusable weapon" by some, but it obviously still retained substantial symbolic power.[38]

And, for Eisenhower at least, the threat of using nuclear weapons fortified a faith in coercive diplomacy and brinkmanship. This faith was put to the test in the Taiwan Strait when Chinese artillery forces shelled the Quemoy and Matsu Islands. While doubtful that Ike believed US national security truly at risk if Taiwan's offshore islands fell, he did fear a hit to US credibility if the communist assault went unchecked. Clearly, there were political benefits to be reaped at home for supporting Chiang Kai-shek's Chinese Nationalist government on Formosa. Over the course of late 1954 and early 1955, the administration publicly invoked nuclear weapons while signing a mutual defense pact with Chiang Kai-shek, engaging in weapons tests, and deploying naval carriers to the region. Then, in March, Eisenhower suggested that nuclear weapons might be employed "as you would use a bullet or anything else."[39]

While the Joint Chiefs of Staff split on whether atomic weapons should be used to defend the islands, they agreed on affording no "sanctuary" to the Reds if Formosa came under attack. Here, faith assumed laughable notions. Air force and navy pilots claimed tactical atomic weapons were more "humane" than ordinary bombing, given they could offer a "rapier-like" thrust against the enemy. This "limited retaliation" to communist aggression apparently would serve as "portent and warning" to China without the risk of a wider war. Deterrence and retaliation were becoming linked in the minds of some military leaders.[40]

Few of these officers, however, asked "For what purpose?" Why risk general war for what critics dubbed "the Staten Island of Communist China"? When Mao initiated another crisis in 1958—the first one had de-escalated after ambassadorial-level talks in 1955—the Joint Chiefs once more considered nuclear weapons for defending Taiwan. They were the "only way we can stop the Communists," one senior officer reported. Yet the Second Taiwan Crisis suggested that there were limits to America's coercive power. Mao may once more have de-escalated, yet it remains unclear whether US nuclear threats alone forced his hand. Military leaders, not surprisingly, took from the episode self-affirming lessons. General Laurence S. Kuter, commanding the US Pacific Air Forces, congratulated his service for successfully backing up "indigenous military forces," while another officer alleged that "the nuclear firepower of the force deployed to the Far East in the Quemoy emergency amounted to tremendous strength."[41]

In the end, a blind faith in atomic weaponry arose because far too few Americans, even those in uniform, had yet to confront the real destruction unleashed on Hiroshima and Nagasaki. Without doubt, the misery of living in a post-apocalyptic world elicited speculation and commentary, Herman Kahn being a prime example. But any grappling with larger policy implications seemed incomplete at best. Americans had to imagine what nuclear war would look like, all while hoping the bomb would enable them to avoid a general war with their communist foes. As journalist Walter Lippmann opined, atomic weapons became the "perfect fulfillment of all wishful thinking on military matters."[42]

Moral ambiguities also hung over debates on atomic weapons' political, social, and environmental implications. On the day the bomb first was tested, Truman had surmised that machines were "ahead of morals by some centuries." Yet the president also would inflate the number of American lives potentially saved when later justifying the weapons' use on two Japanese cities. It didn't help matters that most US citizens held little sympathy for Asian dead. The bombs had saved *Americans*, so why engage in any further moral inquiries? Thus, much of the nuclear debate required an imagining what *might* happen, a vision of "collective death" that was hard to fathom. And even with the Cold War raging, at least some Americans thought they should not have to choose between being either "red" or "dead."[43]

With moral questions set aside, popular imaginings of what the atomic world might bring led fearful Americans to question how long this "balance of terror" truly could last. In October 1951, *Collier's* ran an entire issue on "The War We Do Not Want." The editors shared their belief that war need not be inevitable, yet conceded that so long as communist "aggression persists, the threat of a needless, unwanted, suicidal war will remain." A year earlier, peace advocates abroad had spoken in similar terms. The Stockholm Appeal at the 1950 World Peace Council meeting called for outlawing atomic weapons because they were instruments of "mass murder." Eisenhower sympathized with these views, yet struggled with the competing tensions between the ideals of disarmament and the need to maintain a position of strength against the Soviet Union.[44]

It was the latent instability of this "balance" that frightened critics. The Castle Bravo atomic test in March 1954 conveyed an inability to even calculate the awesome, and fearful, power of thermonuclear weapons. The device, dubbed "Shrimp," yielded a blast equivalent to fifteen megatons of TNT, three times more than expected. The detonation left a crater 250 feet deep and more than a mile across. Some eighty miles away, a Japanese crew aboard the *Lucky Dragon* fishing trawler became exposed to massive radioactive fallout, one of them subsequently dying. A week later, Walter Lippmann felt the "whole world" had been frightened by the affair, but not simply because of "the intrinsic horror of the hydrogen bomb. The critical element of the fear, and the most dangerous to our position and influence, was the apprehension that the bombs were 'out of control.'" Speculators wondered what might happen if a similar bomb detonated inside a major US city instead of the faraway Marshall Islands.[45]

That critics cared more for American lives than for those of Pacific Islanders also signals how US exceptionalism was driving atomic debates. Policymakers concentrated far more on measuring tonnage and the psychological impact of these "terror weapons" than on the ecological or health implications of atomic testing.[46] Four years after the Bravo test, Rand analyst Albert Wohlstetter spoke of a "delicate balance of terror" and argued that deterrence was "not automatic." That same year, sociologist C. Wright Mills, in his popular work *The Causes of World War Three*, argued that in becoming "total," war had "become absurd." Much later, Daniel Ellsberg would offer frightening insights in *The Doomsday Machine*, where, according to some Pentagon plans, hundreds of millions of civilians would perish in a nuclear exchange between the United States and Soviet Union. While death might be universal, the American ones clearly mattered most to Washington elite.[47]

Outside policy circles, popular critiques did little to assuage fears of what science had wrought. Early on, John Hersey's *Hiroshima* (1946) had illuminated the aftereffects of atomic weaponry for a popular audience, highlighting the "circle of misery" that the Japanese city had become. So too a late 1945 issue of *Life*, which included an exposé on "The 36-Hour War" accompanied by a graphic illustration of GIs testing for radioactivity in a shattered American city. When the *Bulletin of American Scientists* began representing a "Doomsday Clock" on its covers two years later, the dangers of living in a nuclear age became national conversation. Fears of science gone awry blended with philosophical musings of humankind's very existence. In 1955, physicist Albert Einstein and philosopher Bertrand Russell published a manifesto on the "tragic situation which confronts humanity." Because nuclear weapons invited the "risk of universal death," they urged governments and citizens alike to acknowledge "that their purposes cannot be furthered by a world war."[48]

The idea of science unleashing unfathomable terror also could be found in science-fiction films. In movies like *World Without End*, *Attack of the 50-Foot Woman*, and *Them!*, radioactive fallout leaves behind a wake of destruction. One critic of the 1954 Japanese film *Godzilla* surely missed the movie's warnings about atomic war. This was not, he argued, a "symbol of Japanese hate for the destruction . . . descended upon Hiroshima one pleasant August morn." Rather, "Godzilla was simply meant to scare people." More serious movies, in fact, did just that. Works like *On the Beach* and *Fail-Safe* offered incisive critiques of nuclear brinksmanship, while *Dr. Strangelove* highlighted the absurdities of a technical system based on threat and fear. Each, in their own way, starkly depicted the risks and consequences of living on the edge of nuclear war.[49]

Even children confronted the horrors of atomic war in shorts like *Duck and Cover*. In the comic book version of the civil defense film, young readers were warned that "the bomb might explode and the bright flash come... without any warning." Thus, the need to "*duck* to avoid the things flying through the air... and *cover* to keep from getting cut or even badly burned." In *Atomic War!* comics fans watched as guileless Soviets, promising peace, unleashed a surprise nuclear attack on the United States, leaving New York City a "raging inferno" and Detroit a "shambles of twisted steel and blasted factories." In other comics, radioactivity might turn a young Peter Parker into the amazing Spider-Man, but if atomic war left Manhattan a "heap of twisted, broken rubble," there seemed little point in the friendly neighborhood hero spinning his web.[50]

These fears expressed across popular culture contributed to deep anxieties that not just cities, but private homes, had become "de facto military targets." Civil defense officers urged families to consider building bomb shelters—the "nation that wins the next war will be the one best prepared to withstand the effects of a nuclear attack," one New York official argued. And living in the Great Plains next to some 1,000 Minutemen missile silos brought the Cold War almost literally to some rural Americans' doorsteps. When the Kennedy administration published the pamphlet "Fallout Protection: What to Know and Do About Nuclear Attack," the message was clear. Effective civil defense required "the participation of every citizen." Mothers and children were now responsible for preparing their homes for war. To pacifist Albert Bigelow, such talk seemed ludicrous. How was it that little children had become "front line troops" in the advent of a nuclear war?[51]

Of course, civil-defense officials had to balance larger public fears of nuclear war with plausible reassurances that families could survive if properly organized. Yet doubts persisted. Could self-protection guarantee survival, or were civil-defense programs simply part of a larger "futile illusion" of families enduring a nuclear attack? Herman Kahn had no doubts on the subject, judging civil defense "the cruelest deception ever played on any people." Indeed, Eisenhower administration officials worried that "mass panic" might be even more destructive than the bomb itself. The television series *The Twilight Zone* highlighted how terror-prone suburban citizens could turn on one another in the event of a nuclear attack. In "The Shelter," an episode from 1961, a doctor's home is the only one equipped with a bomb shelter. When the false alarm of a Russian attack creates panic, neighbors turn on the doctor, demanding entry and threatening violence. While the episode also offered a not-so-subtle commentary on immigration and fear of outsiders, the show highlighted the inconsistencies in America's larger civil-defense plans.[52]

Seven years before "The Shelter" aired, Maryland Civil Defense officials had published "The H-Bomb and You." In the comic-book-styled pamphlet, a grade-school teacher leads her class in a discussion on atomic preparedness, showing a film that ends with a mushroom cloud over a destroyed city. She then invites a local civil-defense officer to speak. He offers assurances that the students and their families can survive the "H-bomb's blast, heat, radiation, and radioactive fallout" if they follow his instructions. This matters, he emphasizes, because "any spot in the United States might quickly become a battleground when war strikes." A blind faith in surviving nuclear war seemed the best, perhaps only, way for dealing with the fears of such war.[53]

CHAPTER 7

Below the Nuclear Threshold

While Americans shuddered at the "the ultra-modern horror" of mutually assured destruction, it would be wrong to suggest that the Eisenhower administration cared only about nuclear war. In fact, far below the nuclear threshold, policymakers exhibited a deep faith that war still could be useful for them, albeit in different forms. Covert actions by the CIA, as one example, became a favored paramilitary tool for rooting out and exterminating "procommunists," "fellow travelers," and "radical leftists" who were infecting local regimes in places as far afield as Guatemala and Iran. Even when the agency's record proved middling at best, Ike retained his faith in the CIA. Coups and psychological-intimidation operations offered promise as martial alternatives to both conventional war and nuclear madness.[1]

In many ways, because of Eisenhower's preference for cost-saving measures, covert operations became, according to one anthropologist, a "favored imperial tool." The president himself judged the CIA a "silver bullet in the arsenal of democracy," highlighting how faith could shape not only policy rhetoric but decision-making as well. Thus, despite subsequent depictions—as in the 1960 presidential campaign, when JFK claimed that Ike simply was "swapping threats and insults with the Russians"—the former general did not rely solely on nuclear extortion for national security. In reality, the Massachusetts senator and the Kansas general weren't far apart in their thinking about containment. When Kennedy argued in 1961 that the nation's defense "must be designed to reduce the danger of irrational and unpremeditated general war," Eisenhower likely would have nodded his head in agreement.[2]

Operating below the nuclear threshold, however, stipulated that military officials set aside moral concerns. Successful interventionism could not be obstructed by ethical misgivings. When James H. Doolittle submitted a 1954 report on CIA covert activities at the president's request, the retired Army Air Corps general advocated for security policies "more ruthless than that employed by the enemy." Because the United States was facing an "implacable" foe committed to "world domination by whatever means and at whatever cost," there could be "no rules in such a game." As Doolittle maintained, "Hitherto acceptable norms of human conduct do not apply." Such contemptuous attitudes set a dangerous precedent. American policymakers hence would declare their moral superiority while fighting communism—or "terrorism" in the following century—yet engage in the same evils against which they supposedly guarded.[3]

If moral concerns weren't an issue, business ones certainly were. Eisenhower's administration had few qualms about either allying with authoritarian regimes or undermining democratically elected governments if free enterprise could be linked to the anticommunist cause. Never mind that such an approach cultivated revolutionary violence that alarmed fearful Americans in the first place. War could be profitable for the right kind of investors. Linking Doolittle's military advice to corporate business interests, Eisenhower authorized more than 150 major covert operations in nearly fifty nations during his time in office. Throughout the Global South, national security and capitalist development would become two sides of the same containment coin for the remainder of the Cold War.[4]

Despite Ike's later forebodings of the military-industrial complex, faith underwrote notions of covert operations being discriminating tools for rooting out communist infestations abroad. Eisenhower, for one, saw the "free world" as facing multiple threats, not least of which was the "infection" of communism. Projecting the nation's anxieties ever outward, Ike and Dulles embraced the CIA's increasing preference for paramilitary action. No wonder one observer called the era a "Pax Americana enforced by terror." Clandestine operations became "worldwide in scope," fears subsidizing a growing faith that CIA programs aimed at "regime change" would further US interests abroad. Nor were these worries limited to current or potential enemies. At least some Washington insiders worried that France might accept some form of rapprochement with Moscow and undercut the allied effort at containment.[5]

Closer to home, Eisenhower worried that Latin American instability might present the Soviets a Western Hemispheric opening. In the mid-1940s, Guatemalan revolutionaries had overthrown a corrupt oligarchy, leading to claims of communist infiltration from the American multinational United Fruit Company. The 1951 election of reform-minded Jacobo Arbenz only heightened fears of Soviet collaboration. US policymakers quickly mistook any type of social justice or progressive agenda—whether improving labor codes or agrarian land reform—as a step toward communism. Ike warned of a possible communist "outpost on this continent," while other Republicans claimed that the Reds had "established a strong beachhead in Guatemala." Such threatening rhetoric was embraced, if not propagated, by the United Fruit Company, which saw reform as a danger to its profit margins. When Arbenz seemed to be leaning toward Moscow for support of his reform agenda, State Department officials bellowed that Guatemalan political institutions were "dominated and controlled by the international Communist organization."[6]

Contending with unrest at home and wary of the Americans to his north, Arbenz imprudently worked a deal to obtain Czechoslovakian arms for shoring up his government. When news broke that Guatemala was receiving Soviet-bloc weapons, anxious US policymakers envisioned the entire hemisphere turning red. One congressman equated the arms shipment to "an atom bomb planted in the rear of our backyard." Eisenhower, believing US credibility and national security to be threatened, unleashed the CIA and set in motion an American-sponsored coup whose consequences would reverberate throughout Latin America for decades to come.[7]

The operation, dubbed PBSuccess, left a checkered legacy. In the moment, Secretary of State Dulles hailed the overthrow as a "'new and glorious' victory over Red encroachments," even as he warned that communism remained a "menace everywhere." But Arbenz's downfall left the Guatemalan state in shambles, consigning the country to devastating and lasting economic hardships and a spiraling level of internecine violence. Americans' anxious search for national security and economic gain, linked to an innate sense of hubris, became a deadly combination for Guatemalan citizens supposedly on the front lines of the anticommunist effort.[8]

The administration's faith in covert action, however, soared in the coup's aftermath. In the Middle East, US policy elite saw other reform-minded leaders as opening the door to communist encroachment. When Prime Minister Mohammad Mosaddegh took steps to nationalize Iranian oil from the British-owned Anglo-Persian Oil Company, Americans immediately saw their regional position jeopardized. The Eisenhower administration once more blamed communist influence, though Mosaddegh hardly fit that role. The Iranian advocated economic independence from western influence far more than any communist political line. Not surprisingly, the British in Iran played to American fears, claiming that "the only thing to stop Persia [from] falling into communist hands is a coup d'état." With the recent Guatemalan success still fresh, it didn't take long for the CIA to jump on board.[9]

Mosaddegh's opposition to foreign intervention exposed how easy it was for fearful Americans to conflate nationalism and anti-imperialism with communism. CIA Director Allen Dulles, for instance, warned Eisenhower that if Iran "succumbed to the Communists," the results would be catastrophic, as "some 60% of the world's oil reserves would fall into Communist control." Moreover, fears of a power vacuum in the Middle East—a "military void" as Hanson Baldwin called it—filled by the local communist Tudeh party also encouraged American interventionism. The *Los Angeles Times* even ran a sensational account, the "Soviet Plot to Steal Iran," that read more like a pulp-magazine story than journalistic reporting.[10]

There seemed little reason then to doubt the justification behind or likely success of a plot to overthrow Mosaddegh. Realizing the Tudeh political threat was minimal, the CIA nonetheless allied with

British counterparts, spending money to influence Iranian newspapers and hiring local agents to break up communist rallies. In August 1953, Mosaddegh, whom Americans judged as "childlike," "moody," and "faint-prone," was removed from power and the autocratic (and anticommunist) Shah returned to his throne after being forced into a brief exile. Another presumably successful regime change solidified the CIA as a principal weapon within Eisenhower's New Look arsenal. As in Guatemala, however, the consequences of the American-supported coup would linger, reaping unwelcome rewards in the late 1970s as a new theocratic regime would unseat the royal dictatorship and open an entirely new phase of the late Cold War era.[11]

The enduring consequences of these two coups alluded to deeper issues with Americans' faith in war. Whether in Asia, Latin America, or the Middle East, military power proved frustratingly ineffective when taking a longer strategic view. Interventionism often obliged the United States to costly military occupations that further engendered ill will from local populations. Nor did a preponderance of American power deter Moscow from creating the Warsaw Treaty Organization less than two years after Mosaddegh's ousting. Just one month prior, in April 1955, General Matthew Ridgway warned Congress that the Soviet Union's army was "'equipped and disposed' to go to war on short notice." Might a faith in covert operations deterring communist aggression abroad be unjustified?[12]

Of course, the United States was not alone in using violence to serve its political aims. When Hungary's Imre Nagy denounced the Warsaw Pact and demanded neutrality from the Cold War competition following anti-Soviet demonstrations, Khrushchev responded with a brutal military crackdown. Roughly 2,500 Hungarians were killed and thousands more wounded and incarcerated. Journalist Walter Lippmann, so often a Cold War critic, shared his "bitter sorrow to see so brave a people crushed." As in Washington, Moscow's leaders equally dealt with interventionism's unintended consequences. A nonaligned India cooled toward the Soviet Union, while Khrushchev nervously worried about the true extent of his power over the Kremlin's eastern satellites.

Moreover, in the uprising's aftermath, he feared western imperialists would view any Moscow withdrawal as "weakness and go on the offensive."[13]

Khrushchev's personal fears aside, the United States vacillated in its response. Would a US military response instigate the general war Eisenhower hoped to avoid? The president condemned Russia's use of force, just as organizations like Radio Free Europe broadcast American support for those "captive nations" behind the Iron Curtain. But the administration was willing to go only so far when it came to liberating satellite states from Moscow's domination. Three years earlier, the United States had done little to support the 1953 uprisings in Czechoslovakia and East Germany, unwilling to risk a confrontation with the Soviet Union so soon after Stalin's death. The Red Army's intervention in Hungary might have been seen as a "diabolical onslaught," but fears of escalating toward nuclear war continued to cast a long shadow.[14]

The effects of the Hungarian revolution rippled far outside of Europe. In the Middle East, a new crisis emerged in Egypt as Gamal Abdel Nasser declared his intentions to nationalize the Suez Canal. The Egyptian already had roiled the United States by proclaiming neutrality in the Cold War and signing a $200 million arms deal with Czechoslovakia. Eisenhower retaliated by vetoing World Bank funds to finance the Aswan High Dam, leading Nasser to nationalize the canal in July 1956 and finance the dam project himself. Such an act of defiance—Dulles referred to Nasser as a "tin-horn Hitler"—ultimately led to a joint invasion of Egypt that October by the combined forces of Britain, France, and Israel. Eisenhower, though, fumed at the escalation, fearing war there would take the world's eyes off Hungary and incite Arab hostilities elsewhere in the Middle East. In a rare moment of Cold War unity, both Washington and Moscow condemned the attack as Ike actively pursued a ceasefire. Nasser's reputation throughout the region soared.[15]

Far from deterring Eisenhower, the Suez Crisis helped motivate a greater US presence in the Middle East. With the region holding more than half of the world's known oil reserves and the British clearly losing grip of its empire, the administration may have been frustrated with its allies but could not risk losing valuable strategic assets to the communist orbit. As Secretary of the Treasury Robert Anderson argued, "Middle East oil was as essential to mutual security as atomic warheads." Combined with Arab nationalism, the region's oil reserves mattered to Cold War calculations as much as they did to American energy needs. Further spurring US involvement, Ike's frustration with his allies generated fears that Washington had "lost Cairo to Moscow." Such worries led to increased cooperation with Arab monarchies, which put into question America's commitment to democracy as a pillar of US foreign policy.[16]

Ideology, however, could still sanction policy. In early 1957, the president decreed that he would commit the United States to resisting any communist aggression in the Middle East. This new Eisenhower Doctrine authorized assistance to and cooperation with regional actors to "secure and protect" their "territorial integrity and political independence . . . against overt armed aggression from any nation controlled by International Communism." The president hoped such a commitment would sway Arab public opinion away from Moscow while confronting Nasserism and "Arab radicalism." The doctrine would come up short on both accounts.[17]

Arab states proved frustratingly resistant to Cold War divisions and US policymakers shied away from asking whether the pursuit of Arab unity truly was "radical." Nor did they consider if Marxist-Leninist ideology made sense for the Arab states. In many ways, the Eisenhower Doctrine rested on an untested faith that the United States could secure Arab political allegiance by transcending local rivalries, especially with Israel, and diverse cultural histories. Fears of Soviet encroachment further bolstered Eisenhower's desire for guaranteed access to oil and military bases in the region. Moderating Arab behavior, however, was easier said than done.[18]

When civil war broke out in Lebanon in 1958, President Camille Chamoun, a Christian, invoked Eisenhower's new doctrine and requested American assistance to defend against Muslim "radicals." A marine contingent landed in July, staying until October after the political situation stabilized. The military foray, though, led Arab leaders across the region to question the United States' commitment to self-determination. Ike himself already was realizing the bind in which his doctrine had placed him. As he shared with his staff before the marines landed, they "would be intervening to save a nation; and yet the nation is the people, and the people don't want our intervention." He would not be the last US president to reflect this way. Nationalism proceeded fitfully throughout the Middle East, often at odds with American policies. To a frustrated John Foster Dulles, Arab nationalism was "like an overflowing stream." The best one could do was "try to keep it in bounds."[19]

Racial stereotyping, never far below the surface, didn't help matters. The impulse to remake the Arab world informed US foreign policy without much concern for the people who actually lived there. Ike groused that Arab nationalists like Nasser "simply cannot understand our ideas of freedom and human dignity." He was not alone in his disdain. George Kennan shared in his diary that if "left to their own devices," Middle Easterners either would "continue to stew in their own tantrums and furies" or "yield in one degree or another to Soviet influence." Not surprisingly, locals took a different view, quickly coming to see the United States as a vulgar, interventionist force with little regard for Arab concepts of nationalism and independence.[20]

Fearing that instability might lead to war and loss of access to the oil-rich region, Eisenhower pressed on with his interventionist doctrine. While concerned that US aid was perpetuating the "ruling class," Ike nevertheless funneled dollars into the Middle East. In the process, the administration, like so many of its successors, would back authoritarian, conservative Arab regimes because of its faith that regional stability equated to access of strategically vital oil. Whether in Iran or Saudi Arabia, Ike pursued a policy of "regime reinforcement." Between 1953 and 1960, Iran alone received over $1 billion in US economic and military aid. Similar policies would unfold in Latin America as well, especially in the oil-rich country of Venezuela. Meanwhile, critics scored the Eisenhower doctrine as "calculated to plunge the world into the nightmare of final war."[21]

As with the domestic Red Scare, foreign policy fears bled into those at home. Administration officials worried that southern segregationist policies were undercutting appeal to "third world" leaders. Without question, communist propagandists targeted US race relations and linked domestic segregation to colonialism abroad. American embassy workers in Ceylon, for example, fretted over local columnists who wrote, with some merit, that "the colour bar is the greatest propaganda gift any country could give the Kremlin in its persistent bid for the affections of the coloured races of the world." After Eisenhower sent federal troops to Arkansas in 1957 to enforce the antisegregation *Brown v. Board of Education* decision, the US ambassador to the United Nations, Henry Cabot Lodge, saw "the harm that the riots in Little Rock are doing to our foreign relations." Translating military clout into political appeal was posing immense problems for an administration attempting to define containment in global terms.[22]

These domestic fears also intensified misgivings that wielding violence abroad was militarizing American society at home. Critics warned that imbalances within the national budget could not sustain such huge military expenditures, even as the New Look sought to cut costs. (Of course, fear could rationalize nearly any cost if placed within the context of "national security.") But with McCarthyism still afflicting political discourse, such criticisms too often remained muted. Few policymakers questioned, as did Senator J. William Fulbright (D-AR) in 1958, the nation's "readiness to use the specter of Soviet Communism as a cloak for the failure of our own leadership." With US marines still in Lebanon, the Senate Foreign Relations Committee member stood firm, deriding the administration for continuing to "put one foot over the brink" while not considering that any "shooting war" might be "irrelevant" to Cold War politics.[23]

Fulbright was right. War had not served to deter war. Violence along the "global periphery" raged with few limits; indeed, it was exacerbated by the US-Soviet competition. For Koreans or Vietnamese, along with millions of others outside Western Europe, war hardly was "limited." In many cases, these local conflicts had little to do with Cold

War superpower interests. The president apparently knew as much. As Eisenhower shared with Khrushchev at a 1955 summit dinner in Geneva, "War has failed. The only way to save the world is through diplomacy." Yet Cold War fears prevailed against such rational sentiments. When Ike floated an "Open Skies" proposal that July, wherein the major powers would share information on their military installations and authorize aerial inspections, the pitch fell flat. Giving "Russians the right to inspect American bases" garnered few supporters in the age of McCarthy.[24]

Nor did Khrushchev's call for "peaceful coexistence" win many converts, either in the United States or in China. Pursuing his de-Stalinization agenda while courting Third World allies, the new Soviet premier's nod to the "forces of peace" left critics suspect of his intentions. Surely, the Kremlin hadn't abandoned its struggle between socialism and capitalism? In fact, Khrushchev had not. Rather, peaceful coexistence might be seen as a tool for drawing newly formed nations into the Soviet orbit. Skeptical Americans, of course, doubted Khrushchev's claim that when Soviets like him spoke of the "victory of Communism," they did not mean they would "wage war against any country in order to establish the regime we want by force." Nor did local leaders in decolonizing states give up on war, believing armed violence still offered them the best chance at achieving true independence.[25]

Within China, for example, the Great Leap Forward brought death and destruction on a massive scale, all in the name of modernity. While Mao's radical socioeconomic plans were intended to industrialize China and make it more competitive on the international stage, the Great Leap also helped militarize Chinese foreign policy in ways that fueled violence both at home and abroad. Mao's agenda also contributed to a growing Sino-Soviet split, as the chairman saw Moscow's rapprochement with the capitalist West as a sellout. To Mao, the Great Leap would allow China to challenge the USSR, to be seen as the "center of world revolution," and to actively promote Afro-Asian unity. Despite the program's immense failure, Americans still fretted over Mao's muscle flexing. If Third World leaders followed Beijing instead of Moscow, the end result remained the same—losing the Global South to the communist sphere.[26]

Moreover, China's fears of encirclement further fueled competition and conflict. When the United States took the lead in creating the South East Asia Treaty Organization (SEATO), seeking a regional equivalent to NATO, Mao unsurprisingly felt threatened. India's Jawaharlal Nehru called the organization, which included Pakistan, an "angry reaction" to the recent 1954 Geneva Accords on Indochina. Prince Sihanouk of Cambodia decided not to join, calling SEATO an "aggressive military alliance directed against neighbors whose ideology I did not share but with whom Cambodia had no quarrel." In fact, only two of SEATO's eight members, the Philippines and Thailand, were Southeast Asian nations, putting into question John Foster Dulles's portrayal of a "collective security arrangement."[27]

With a healthy dose of irony, critics maintained that when leaders like Nehru questioned NATO or SEATO, they had let their "emotions get the better of [their] reasoned judgment." And yet, Nehru was not alone. Senator Barry Goldwater derided collective alliances because they envisioned an "exclusively defensive strategy," like the "boxer who refuses to throw a punch." But non-Americans saw something else. Indonesia's Sukarno believed Americans were "too full of fear," to the point where even body odor and bad breath scared them. Russian Foreign Affairs Minister Vyacheslav Molotov agreed with such sentiments, complaining that US policy toward China was "dominated by emotion." If Americans hoped that alliance networks would display strength and unity in far-flung regions of the world, fears inspired by the global decolonization process were challenging their aspirations.[28]

Viewed from Washington, both decolonization and Third World nationalism were threatening violence all along the Cold War "periphery." And, in truth, many anticolonial elites maintained their own faith in war's utility to create new social and political orders. After World War II, they increasingly believed that the violence of the capitalist, colonial system had begotten and thus justified the violence of national liberation movements. If the wartime victors wouldn't deliver on their Atlantic Charter promises of restoring self-governance, then new national leaders would seize it for themselves. Political philosopher Frantz Fanon famously argued in *The Wretched of the Earth* (1961) that the "violence of the colonial regime and the counterviolence of the colonized balance each other and respond to each other in an extraordinary reciprocal homogeneity." From this perspective, the prospects for global stability looked grim indeed.[29]

This apparent instability below the nuclear threshold not only inspired fear, but, as we've seen, encouraged US policymakers to readily accept relationships with autocratic regimes and their armed forces. National liberation movements, even if popular and democratic in nature, were far too messy to support with the Cold War raging. Dictatorships, in turn, became acceptable partners so long as they were anticommunist. Thus, with Washington elite often equating "anticolonial" or "leftist" with "communist," right-leaning political leaders and military forces became the preferred recipients of US aid and assistance.[30]

Throughout the 1950s and 1960s, then, successive administrations failed to answer a key question about the developing world. Were those new states gaining independence in places like Africa a threat or an opportunity? Eisenhower favored leaving the continent, and its problems, to the Europeans. But fears of Africa being exploited by encroaching Soviets kept pulling the Americans back in. As one Pan-Africanist supporter lamented, westerners had a nasty habit of ascribing "every manifestation of political awakening in Africa to Communist inspiration." Never mind that most local leaders saw colonialism and not communism as the chief impediment to their political and economic progress. When Cuba's Fidel Castro sent support to revolutionary forces in the Congo—one of seventeen African states declaring independence in 1960 alone—there seemed little choice but to intervene. By decade's end, some thirty coups had fractured Africa's political landscape, further sowing doubt about the continent maturing into a bulwark against communist infiltration. Clearly, threats were outnumbering opportunities.[31]

If war was proving an inadequate tool for deterring war, then perhaps Americans should place their faith in developmental programs, employing social and economic uplift for fighting the Cold War on a nonmilitary plane. Fatefully, this reliance on "modernization" efforts only further militarized societies and their foreign policies, nowhere better seen than in the United States itself, where preserving the military-industrial establishment "became a kind of national addiction." As the 1950s came to a close, Americans were left in a bind. Neither atomic bombs nor covert operations had slain their "ominous existential enemies." The Cold War endured, consigning the nation to its increasingly dysfunctional relationship with war. Even the world's "free peoples" took notice, worrying that America's own emphasis on military preparedness "may lead to war" as its own policies masked "an urge to expand."[32]

Ultimately, the warnings of Eisenhower's January 1961 farewell address would go unheeded. The president's comments would popularize the phrase "military-industrial complex," as Ike warned against its "unwarranted influence" and the potential for the "disastrous rise of misplaced power." Privately, Eisenhower included Congress in this "delta of power," but shied away from any public accusations. Yet in those same remarks, Ike also maintained that a "vital element in keeping the peace is our military establishment." "Our arms must be mighty, ready for instant action," he argued, "so that no potential aggressor may be tempted to risk his own destruction." Deterrence, nuclear or otherwise, still required a faith in war.[33]

Fear, though, was never far behind. In a lesser-known address given to the American Legion Convention in 1952, then–presidential candidate Eisenhower had offered cautionary words to an adoring crowd of veterans. In New York City that August, Ike warned how fear "induced by peril is a climate that fosters militarism." Not only did the former general warn of the potential bankruptcy in "dollars and morals alike." He also offered a far grimmer prognosis for America's future. "In an era of chronic fear can be heard the death rattle of a nation."[34]

PART III

War to Build Nations

CHAPTER 8

Undertaking a Hemispheric Crusade

Looking back, it's rather astounding that a small island nation of just over seven million people in 1960 inspired so much fear within the United States. New York City alone had more residents living across its five boroughs that year. Yet Cuba aroused more revolutionary nightmares among sleeping Washington policymakers than any other small nation of the entire Cold War era. Even before World War II, Latin American intellectuals had turned to Marxist-Leninist thought as a way to make sense of US regional hegemony, of the capitalist exploitation that subjugated their economies and peoples. In the aftermath of that global war, however, it was Cuba that metamorphosed into America's southern bogeyman.[1]

When thirty-year-old Fidel Castro led a band of young revolutionaries in a guerrilla campaign against Fulgencio Batista's repressive dictatorship in 1956, the entire Western Hemisphere seemed ripe for upheaval. Had not the United States intervened in Guatemala only two years earlier to prevent it from becoming a communist "beachhead"? What if Castro served as an example to other Latin American revolutionaries? Such questions turned into real fears with Batista's ouster in January 1959. Worse, Castro immediately embarked on a thorough reform of Cuba's social, political, and economic systems. To wary US policymakers, the new leader in Havana seemed more than just a vessel for Soviet communism. Castro threatened the American-led structure throughout the entire Western Hemisphere.[2]

Yet the Cuban revolutionary moment portended something far more frightening than simply challenging American hemispheric leadership. Castro held his own faith that revolutionary war would not just propel Cuba into becoming a regional leader, but also serve as a revolutionary model for militant leftists around the globe. Meanwhile, American economic interests seemed at risk, made visible with the signing of a major commercial agreement between Cuba and the Soviet Union in early 1960. If anti-imperialism and armed revolt merged into a Cold War paradigm for the Third World, Washington elite feared, both US national security and economic viability would be in jeopardy.[3]

Castro's rise also fanned US policymakers' fears of falling Latin dominoes, of the Western Hemisphere becoming a radicalized new front in the war to contain global communism. Castro spoke publicly of creating jobs, ending social injustices, and building schools. "Our revolution is humanist," he argued, "and not Communist." Worried observers, however, believed Castro, "on direct orders from the Kremlin," was "stepping up the export of Cuba's Communist revolution to other Latin American countries." The US embassy in Havana even reported that Castro's regime should be regarded as "an extension in the Western Hemisphere of the Sino-Soviet bloc." Three years after Batista's ouster, one editorialist likened Cuba to a "Soviet fortress" just off America's shores and a "cancer throughout the hemisphere." A new and frightening Cold War theater seemed to be opening.[4]

While some journalists saw Castro as "dangerous" and "infectious," Senator J. William Fulbright (D-AR) judged the new communist regime a "thorn in the flesh; but it is not a dagger in the heart." Cuba may have become a Soviet "base for agitation," yet that hardly demanded a far-reaching interventionist response. Other introspective policymakers also questioned Moscow's military commitment to the Western Hemisphere. In reality, Khrushchev wanted to avoid war there, especially if instigated by Cuban overreach. Nor did Castro see himself as a Soviet puppet, instead aspiring to be a "third camp"—alongside Moscow and Beijing—of international communism. As in so many regions, though, local matters in Latin America became inescapably tied to global Cold War calculations.[5]

These fears of hemispheric foreign interventionism had deep roots, dating back to the Federalist era. Alexander Hamilton had spoken of the need to protect American commerce from "wanton intermeddlings" of warlike nations. The 1823 Monroe Doctrine followed suit, defining the Western Hemisphere as the United States' privileged domain and any foreign incursions as "dangerous to our peace and safety." In the early 1900s, President Teddy Roosevelt added a corollary asserting the right to exercise "international police power" in the region. Moreover, the 1901 Platt Amendment gave Washington the right to oversee Cuban finances and intervene with military force if necessary. As Governor General Leonard Wood, occupying the island in the Spanish-American War's aftermath, conceded, there was "little or no independence left Cuba under the Platt Amendment." Conceptions of security trumped those of sovereignty as Americans increasingly looked outward.[6]

If Cubans like Castro resented this baldly imperialist behavior, fearful Cold War Americans believed they had no choice but to stay the course. FDR's "Good Neighbor Policy" pledge of nonintervention may have made sense in the 1930s, but twenty years later appeared naive in the face of communist expansionism. How could Cuba be considered a good neighbor when it was radicalizing young men and women and then launching these "missiles . . . in human form" against the United States? Senator Barry Goldwater explicitly made the case for reviving the spirit of the Monroe Doctrine to keep at bay the "greatest of threats to all of Latin America from a relentless international communism." To buttress his warning, the Arizona Republican resuscitated not only Monroe but Munich. It would be "appeasement," he insisted, if the United States whittled down "its traditional legal rights to protect the persons and properties of its citizens in Latin America."[7]

At the time, fears of Latin America turning red were more than just political grandstanding. They were palpable. Revolutionary activity spread throughout the hemisphere. Reform and social justice were on the lips of many intellectuals. Freedom from US economic control became a rallying cry on the Latin American left. Once in power, Castro offered training on guerrilla warfare and political indoctrination. Thus, even if Soviet influence was negligible during the 1950s and 1960s—and it was—the hemisphere looked like a powder keg waiting to ignite. When senior US officials, like JFK's secretary of state, Dean Rusk, worried that Cuba might become a "Sino-Soviet missile base" if left unchecked, it was no wonder that plans to unseat Castro and bring the island back under American influence were set in motion.[8]

Regime change could come in many forms. The CIA toyed with taking "gangster action" against Castro or poisoning him with help from the Mafia. In the meantime, Eisenhower, now late in his presidency, broke off diplomatic relations with Cuba before bequeathing his successor a CIA plot to train Cuban exiles in Guatemala and then launch an invasion at the island's Bay of Pigs. With Castro ousted, a provisional government would be established, with US recognition and support forthcoming. Kennedy acquiesced, and in April 1961 the "makeshift armada" went forward. It failed spectacularly. As one scholar noted, "Almost no part of the plan worked in practice." No regime overthrown, no popular uprising against Castro, and no quarter given to the captured invaders. The *Washington Post* called the "Cuban fiasco" a story of "fumbling and bumbling by the Central Intelligence Agency."[9]

Kennedy's first foray wielding American military power had ended in disaster. And with Eisenhower distancing himself from the role he had played, the new president took the political aftershocks on the chin. There were, however, lessons to be learned. Fear could breed mistaken policy assumptions. Regime-change wars were not so easily pulled off. Military interventions came with unanticipated political costs. The Bay of Pigs misadventure certainly inspired JFK to question the utility of armed force in the modern era—as had his own experiences in World War II—and perhaps left the president in a strengthened position to deal with his own military advisors during the subsequent Cuban Missile Crisis.[10]

The calamity also demonstrated, yet again, Americans' unquestioning faith in their military power, diminishing the influence of these potential lessons. CIA and military planners alike convinced themselves of Castro's shaky domestic support, that a popular rebellion would emerge as soon as exiled leaders came ashore as part of the invasion force. Furthermore, they tended to focus on the cheerier lessons from past covert operations like Guatemala, rather than examine their failures in Cuba. (In doing so, they discounted the repression, economic downturn, and death squads that followed Jacobo Arbenz's overthrow.) Perhaps unsurprisingly, Castro's status skyrocketed after the Bay of Pigs, with Latin Americans hailing him as a leader who stood up to the United States and gave the imperial giant to the north a black eye.[11]

Nor would the botched operation challenge policymakers' fundamental faith in military force undermining Castro personally or, more broadly, contesting communist expansion throughout the hemisphere. The president quickly reembraced Cold War notions and, along with his brother, resumed a "virtual vendetta" against the Cuban leader. With the Bay of Pigs dust still unsettled, the administration began planning yet another operation to oust Castro, according to one CIA station chief, "whether by palace revolt, military coup, popular uprising, or assassination." Dubbed Mongoose, the scheme abruptly halted with the discovery of Soviet missiles on the small Caribbean island in October 1962.[12]

Notably, the Kennedys were not alone in their unbroken faith when it came to war. In the Bay of Pigs aftermath, the editor of the *Los Angeles Times*, Nick B. Williams, called for military action "to rid the Western Hemisphere of the cancer of communism, for the moment localized in Cuba." Williams argued that the only way to drive communism out of Cuba was to "do it ourselves," even if it required action beyond "legalistic methods." No wonder that Castro—and, to a lesser extent, Khrushchev—was convinced Kennedy would launch a second attack on Cuba. Such thinking about war's potential would ripple far beyond Latin America and long into the future. Ultimately, the Bay of Pigs fiasco would presage post-9/11 theories on preemptive wars that rested on a blind faith of threats being defeated before they actually emerged.[13]

The combative US relationship with Cuba also highlighted how fears of looking weak could propel American presidents to act in overly aggressive ways. Only six weeks after the Bay of Pigs fiasco, Kennedy flew to Vienna for his first and only summit with Khrushchev. With failure in Cuba, an unsettled conflict raging in Laos, and hostilities mounting over Berlin, now was not the time to appear vulnerable. Yet by most accounts, the Soviet premier got the better of the young president. JFK described the meetings as "somber," while Khrushchev found his American counterpart "very inexperienced, even immature." Kennedy even acknowledged in private that the Soviet leader "just beat the hell out of me." In many ways, the 1961 Vienna Summit reinforced already prevailing fears of failure. Moreover, the administration assumed that humiliation in Cuba had inspired Soviet bellicosity over Berlin.[14]

The failure to oust Castro no doubt punctured Americans' sense of invulnerability. As the imagined relationship between Cuba and Berlin suggested, fears had a tendency to reinforce one another and the expanding American Cold War empire seemed only to make matters worse. As US global responsibilities grew, so too did potential vulnerabilities. Resources might be drained. Political support might waiver. Military stalemates might endure. What is telling, however, is that such trepidations never seemed to last. Faith in American military power might be dented in places like Korea or Cuba, but never enough to completely dissuade future presidents or senior uniformed leaders from their fast-held convictions in war's capacity to deliver.[15]

Just as importantly, Americans' reactions to the Cuban revolution underscored how Cold War policymakers were seeking to contain communism by melding military power with social, political, and economic-development programs. Indeed, Eisenhower spoke in military terms when proclaiming a "hemispheric crusade for economic development" while visiting Brazil in early 1960. Discerning historians certainly took notice that the general's 1948 World War II memoir was titled *Crusade in Europe*. Ike's newest "crusade," though, intimated how war might aid in building strong nations, fortified by "the belief in democracy, freedom and self-determination of peoples." When the president spoke of "coordinated action" capable of "combating underdevelopment," he also implied combating communism.[16]

Eisenhower wasn't alone. Senator Mike Mansfield (D-MT), a former professor who had taught Latin American history, believed the powerful attraction of Castroism and communism resulted from Latin American nations' inability "to meet the needs of their people." It would become a common refrain of modernization theorists throughout this period. Economic power would be grafted onto military power as the United States guided more "traditional" societies along the path toward modernity and, ideally, anticommunism. Once more, faith and fear combined inside policy circles in harmful ways. A fear of Moscow projecting global military power and political influence led US policymakers and academics alike to seek ways in which military forces could build liberal states strong enough to withstand the supposed communist onslaught.[17]

Several problems, however, characterized this approach to nation building overseas. First, as Ambassador Chester Bowles maintained, economic aid and military assistance "rarely belonged together." Moreover, Bowles was concerned by the "narrow military perspective that even some of our ablest military leaders brought to bear on what were primarily political questions." Nor was this simply a trait among uniformed officers. The long-time ambassador to India worried about presidents' tendency to "reach for military answers to political problems," to demonstrate "they were, in fact, tough characters."[18]

Next, American policymakers' conflation of nationalist social reforms with communism drove how many of them conceived the "Third World." Senator Barry Goldwater, for instance, saw Cuba as an intolerable "bastion of communism ninety miles from our shores and in close proximity to our Latin American friends." To not act was to "accept Russian claims of invincibility." Mistaking anti-imperialism for Soviet-inspired communism thus tended to imprint a military face on modernization efforts. Contemporary historians might have argued that the "stereotype of Soviet influence or control was grossly at odds with the facts." But it seemed far more prudent, and safer, to listen to the military Joint Chiefs of Staff who forecast "disastrous consequences to the security of the Western Hemisphere" if Soviet efforts went unchecked.[19]

The Joint Chiefs might be excused for their overly cautious stance given what they saw emerging from Latin America in the 1950s and early

1960s. No doubt they cringed when young radicals like Che Guevara encouraged "armed struggle" as essential for revolutionary activity and the only way to contest US imperialism. Che felt that he had devised an insurrectionary model that could be replicated across Latin America and then exported globally. Successful revolutionary strategies would inspire guerrilla groups and the local peasantry to "merge into one single mass" for overthrowing dictatorships and imperialists alike. Here, Che believed, was a way to liberate the still-colonized world. His pronouncements, however, only heightened pressures on US policymakers, already misconstruing local dynamics in Latin American countries, to intervene militarily lest weak states inexorably fall to communist rule.[20]

Finally, these fears of communist "political penetration and internal subversion," as Goldwater warned, led to militarized policies when Americans did intervene. When social and economic programs seemed to falter, US policymakers quickly emphasized "collective security" to ensure political stability within the hemisphere. In such an environment, "neutrality" once more became suspect. In June 1961, Defense Secretary Robert S. McNamara and Chairman of the Joint Chiefs General Lyman L. Lemnitzer appealed to Congress for greater "authority to send military equipment to neutral countries to combat increased Communist infiltration." Strong economies mattered. But, as Lemnitzer argued, "you have to have the internal security forces necessary to prevent subversion and overthrow of governments." If modernization ideas rested on economic-aid programs, they also depended upon sheer military force.[21]

Internal instability thus became a pretext for US military interventionism. In the process, economic development went hand-in-hand with imperial violence. As we'll see, US counterinsurgency doctrine may have trumpeted social, economic, and political reforms, but when push came to shove, it was the military instrument that mattered most. The irony was that promoting democracy abroad, in historian Greg Grandin's words, tended to "inspire fear more than virtue." In Latin America, imperial modernization projects ended up inciting antirevolutionary security forces who equally found violence a practical tool for achieving political dominance. Not surprisingly, leftist radicals saw no other option but to reply in kind, forcing local politics into a spiraling escalation of brutality. As American nation-builders soon would find, destruction was far easier to accomplish than construction.[22]

With Americans becoming more comfortable in their imperial ways as the Cold War wore on, they relied increasingly on military might to solve their political problems. When anticipated end-states in nation building never materialized, their faith in armed force led them to amplify their martial efforts. The ever-present fear of spreading communism left few alternatives. So too an uncertain future. When John F. Kennedy accepted his party's nomination for the 1960 presidential election, he spoke of Americans facing a "New Frontier." Beyond, the Massachusetts senator cautioned, were "uncharted areas of science and space, unsolved problems of peace and war, unconquered pockets of ignorance and prejudice, unanswered questions of poverty and surplus." Now was not the time to shrink from that frontier.[23]

CHAPTER 9

War (and Fear) along the New Frontier

When Eisenhower delivered his farewell address in mid-January 1961, he hinted at the larger, potential problems of defining American power through a military lens, even while warning of future crises. The outgoing president affirmed that the nation faced a "hostile ideology—global in scope, atheistic in character, ruthless in purpose and insidious in method." For democracy to survive, though, he counseled that Americans "must avoid becoming a community of dreadful fear and hate, and be, instead, a proud confederation of mutual trust and respect." But despite Ike's calls for "peace with justice," such advice likely rang hollow for those citizens being fed a steady diet of anticommunist indoctrination.[1]

Moreover, Ike's fears of profligate war spending undermining the very foundations of American democracy were turned against him during the 1960 presidential campaign. On the trail, Kennedy lambasted the administration's New Look policy for its cost-cutting measures, arguing how national security suffered as a result. Despite the contrasts he highlighted that summer and fall, Kennedy nonetheless agreed the threat was real, leading him to advocate for a more "flexible response" to communist aggression. As with Eisenhower, JFK held faith in the White House calibrating levels of force to deter Soviet adventurism. Rather than settling for a defensive strategy, Kennedy would regain the initiative through a more flexible application of America's military arsenal.[2]

Regardless of the Kennedy-Nixon electoral outcome, which was razor close, faith in war would endure. As the Democratic candidate argued just before election day, communist doctrine regarded "military force, and the threat of force, as an integral component of the pursuit of expanded political power." Senior advisors like Ambassador Bowles might caution that the word "power" was "bandied around" Washington without a clear consensus on what it meant. But to Kennedy, the Soviets only respected strength given their "commitment to the notion of Communist world domination."[3]

Thus, the new president's offensive-minded refashioning of containment demonstrated a continuing faith in American military power overseas. This despite JFK's clear-headed view that any war came with devastating costs. To one intimate friend, Kennedy thought stupid the "romanticist point of view of war." Even in his inaugural address, he lauded the United Nations as "our last best hope in an age where the instruments of war have far outpaced the instruments of peace." And yet in that same oration, speaking of the "dark powers of destruction," Kennedy warned his fellow Americans to "dare not tempt them with weakness. For only when our arms are sufficient beyond doubt can we be certain beyond doubt that they will never be employed." Relying on war to deter war would persist as Americans embarked upon a new frontier.[4]

Of note, Kennedy also ran against Vice President Richard Nixon by claiming a nonexistent "missile gap" between the United States and the USSR. Generating fear still could reap huge political rewards. The senator claimed that Ike's "budget-firsters" had allowed Moscow to steal a march on the United States and gain an advantage in nuclear weapons. In a similar vein, JFK's colleague Stuart Symington, a Democratic senator from Missouri, asked why the Eisenhower administration had decided that "money is more important than security." In truth, a missile gap did exist—in America's favor. Not wanting to out his intelligence sources, Ike kept mum and Kennedy narrowly slid by his opponent. Less than three weeks after the inauguration, studies from the new administration "tentatively" confirmed that no gap, in fact, existed, despite Khrushchev claiming he could make missiles "like sausages." The Kennedy team, not surprisingly, quickly denied the "leaked" report.[5]

Any potential political rewards to be gained by touting nuclear superiority, however, seemed distant once the administration found itself embroiled in the Cuban Missile Crisis less than two years later. The Bay of Pigs operation may have been a political debacle. This new emergency threatened to become an existential catastrophe. And while the White House never quite gave up on deterrence, Kennedy's faith in the concept clearly weakened in October 1962. Peeking into the apocalyptic abyss tended to elevate fear over faith during the Cold War era.[6]

When Khrushchev fatefully decided to position nuclear-capable missiles in Cuba, the calculus of deterrence shifted. Soviet hopes of establishing a presence in the Western Hemisphere to deter US aggression, alongside Castro's desire to confront the United States, put into question the value of nuclear posturing, at least for the Americans. To Khrushchev, who did not want "to unleash a war," the missile deployment might serve "to intimidate, to contain the U.S. with regard to Cuba." It also could redress the missile-gap problem, while allowing Moscow to reassert itself against China as the communist camp's true global leader. However, as the Soviet premier soon would discover, Castro was willing to risk far more than Moscow deemed reasonable.[7]

In the summer of 1962, however, Khrushchev saw the missile deployment as a strategic stroke of genius, a way to keep the Americans off-balance while he settled issues in Berlin and even Southeast Asia. Yet when a U-2 overflight discovered construction sites for Soviet installations, the premier's plans quickly began to unravel. Fearful Washington, DC pundits unsurprisingly saw the missiles as offensive weapons, while the *Washington Post* declared in September that the "planting of Soviet power in Cuba" was "creating a depth of uneasiness and anxiety among the American people which can hardly be overstated." If this was a form of "red brinksmanship," the president would have to tread carefully, balancing Soviet intentions with domestic public opinion.[8]

By mid-October, the missile crisis had come to a head, and Kennedy formed an executive committee (ExComm) in hopes of developing a feasible, safe, and politically acceptable offramp. (In fact, the initial consensus was to resort to some form of military intervention ranging from massive bombing to a full-scale invasion.) Throughout nearly two weeks of tense moves, the White House wrestled with fundamental questions about war and its relationship to US foreign policy. Were the Soviet missiles more a military threat or a political one? Were "surgical" strikes advocated by the Joint Chiefs possible? Was a "no cities" doctrine still relevant with Soviet nuclear weapons so close to America's shores? As these questions were being debated in Washington, across the Atlantic British newspapers doubted the United States' "moral right" to "endanger world peace for the sake of a few real or imaginary missiles in Cuba."[9]

British editorialists might have taken a bit of comfort in knowing that Kennedy was asking similar questions about the morality of nuclear brinkmanship. The president feared his top generals weren't fully grasping the implications of nuclear conflict, given the chiefs' unanimous recommendation to launch air strikes on Cuba. To JFK, a nuclear war equated to "final failure." And, thanks in part to the Bay of Pigs fiasco, Kennedy was now willing to stand up to the military brass. His trepidations ultimately led the president to accept a quarantine solution—Curtis LeMay deemed it "appeasement"—and an undisclosed withdrawal of US missiles in Turkey in exchange for a Soviet departure from Cuba. By month's end, Kennedy and Khrushchev had decided it best to step back from the nuclear precipice and negotiate an end to the crisis.[10]

Bolstering internal White House fears of miscalculation were those of losing credibility, perhaps, cynics might argue, fears important as losing lives in a nuclear exchange. JFK's ExComm debated how to balance the twin messages of restraint and resolve. How could the threat of war be used to send a prudent political message? Secretary of Defense McNamara warned of "pushing Khrushchev to extremes," of not goading the Soviets into retaliation. Yet such counsel sat in tension with concerns over looking weak in the face of clear Soviet aggression. Speaking on behalf of the Joint Chiefs, Maxwell Taylor shared with the president on 19 October that if the United States did not "respond here in Cuba, we think the credibility of our response in Berlin is endangered." Credibility was at stake as much as American lives. It would be no coincidence that the next president would exhibit similar fears of being humiliated as he decided to intervene into a Vietnamese civil war less than three years later.[11]

Weighing its options in the debate over war's utility this close to the nuclear cliff, the administration also had to guard against claims that Soviet missile bases were an attempt to "neutralize" America's "superior power" in the Western Hemisphere. Journalist Hanson Baldwin felt that Kennedy "seemed to be risking war to prevent war." The challenge, though, came in finding a way to "back down without defeat." Such concerns mattered when the map accompanying Baldwin's essay—ominously titled "Will There Be War?"—highlighted "ten points in which the Soviet is threatening the U.S. position in the Cold War." These hotspots included not only the threat of a nuclear bridgehead in Cuba, but the threat to allied occupation in West Berlin, the threat of guerrilla war in South Vietnam, and (curiously) the threat of a UN "peace" offensive.[12]

The missile crisis went far in marring America's relationship with war. The nation's leaders seemed close to losing control of war, at least temporarily. What political objectives could they possibly have secured by launching nuclear missiles? In the aftermath, McNamara worried there was "no longer any such thing as strategy, only crisis management." Contemplating how close the world had come to the brink of nuclear conflict, major newspapers encouraged a reassessment. In arguing for increased diplomacy, the *New York Times* quipped that "thermonuclear war" was a "mere euphemism for thermonuclear annihilation," thus putting into question the very utility of war. Yet diplomacy faced its own obstacles, and not just in Washington. Beijing, for instance, blasted the Soviet leadership for "vacillation" and daring "not to win a victory that can be won."[13]

Without question, the crisis had an impact on Kennedy. The following year, while delivering a commencement address at American University, the president spoke of "world peace" because of the "new face of war." In words that might have been uttered by his predecessor, Kennedy argued that "total war" no longer made sense in an age when nuclear confrontation spelled out a "collective death-wish for the world." Peace, JFK shared, "need not be impracticable, and war need not be inevitable."[14]

In this context, it is unsurprising that Kennedy engaged with the Soviets on a Limited Test Ban Treaty. The agreement—signed by British, Soviet, and US representatives in August 1963, not long after JFK's American University speech—prohibited nuclear-weapons testing in the atmosphere, under water, and in outer space. (Underground tests remained permissible.) Equally unsurprising, critics lambasted the administration for its naïveté. Barry Goldwater, who already had warned against any "policy that may reduce our relative military strength," saw talk of limitations or disarmament as examples of the Russians "baiting a trap" rather than furthering peace. His Republican colleague from Illinois, Senator Everett Dirksen, agreed, condemning talks over nuclear testing as "an exercise not in negotiation ... but in give-away." Senior military leaders similarly feared that the Soviets would "cheat" and "attempt clandestine testing of some sort."[15]

Kennedy, however, persevered, in part because of growing consensus that "nuclear superiority" had become a pipe dream. Looking toward the 1964 election, the president no doubt felt he had the political backing to shield him from his Republican rivals' accusations of being "weak." And while Kennedy never it made it to the election, his successor would follow suit by signing the 1968 Nuclear Non-Proliferation Treaty. Johnson surely agreed with theorists like Herman Kahn who believed that the probabilities of disaster increased as more states entered the nuclear club. In urging Senate ratification, LBJ warned against the weapons' further spread, the consequences of which would lead to "nuclear anarchy" and plunge the world "into darkness." States like India, locked out of the nuclear circle, thus decided that their own path to status and security lay in mastering the atom.[16]

Yet despite his seeming loss of faith in war, Kennedy continued to see the New Frontier as a dangerous place. Incredulously, after coming so close to war over Cuba, the president authorized a CIA-run sabotage campaign against Castro that included attacks on an electric power plant and an oil refinery. Congress, in the meantime, authorized a 1963 defense budget that amounted to nearly nine percent of the nation's gross domestic product, while the Soviet leadership, stung by what they saw as a humiliating retreat from Cuba, engaged in their own new round of weapons procurement. Kennedy might publicly challenge those who saw war as inevitable, but it certainly appeared that the two superpowers had not fully lost their faith in it.[17]

Perhaps, then, tackling global threats along the New Frontier might best be served by nonmilitary efforts focused on social and economic reform to uplift "traditional" societies and tie them to the US orbit. This trust in "reformist intervention" would temporarily supplant and then reinforce Americans' faith in war. Proponents of what would become known as "modernization theory" argued that the Cold War was not just a contest between ideological systems, but economic ones as well. Thus, new "weapons"—"aid and trade"—could be brought to bear against the Soviets while vying for control in the decolonizing Global South. What is more, modernization programs could be promoted as a new "civilizing mission" whereby the United States ushered inexperienced nations into the global community.[18]

Like his predecessor, Kennedy sought ways to compete with the Soviets below the nuclear threshold, only now using war to help build nations. Both the Alliance for Progress and Peace Corps initiatives were built upon a faith in military power and, paternalistically, in setting an American example abroad as well. In supporting Latin American development, Kennedy hoped to counter communists who were seeking to "exploit discontent and misery." Promoting reform and American values would win over Cold War recruits in the Western Hemisphere. In the process, political transformations, based on American models, would guard against Castro-inspired radicalism that allegedly threatened US regional hegemony. To JFK, programs like the Alliance for Progress could "awaken the American revolution" throughout the hemisphere.[19]

The Peace Corps rested on a similar faith in the state, one in which "community development" would revitalize Latin America, all while providing life lessons for young Americans traveling abroad. Yet these two programs proved far more destructive than intended and, in many instances, helped entrench military autocracies. They rested on an underlying racism in which American volunteers could remedy local "deficiencies" simply by their presence and hard work. One US official even argued that Guatemalans, in failing to make needed reforms, had "a concept of mankind opposed to that of Western civilization." Americans might be afraid of radical nationalism across their southern border, but they equally held faith that their values were universalistic, appealing to anyone who simply had the chance to see them in person.[20]

This faith in democratic-capitalist principles, though, was combined with a fear of losing access to resources and raw materials so necessary for fighting a global war against communism. Democracies, popular thinking went, naturally would be open to American markets. Thus the notion of aid being a Cold War weapon. And the stakes could not be higher. If the Alliance for Progress failed, one journalist warned, it would bring on a "wave of military dictatorships ... itself the seedbed for communism." Predictably, when these political and economic reform efforts faltered, US policymakers embraced military assistance and security programs to shore up American presence overseas. As a result, in the words of one CIA analyst, the Alliance for Progress amounted to little more than a "broad counterinsurgency program." As with the Marshall Plan, war once again was becoming intertwined with development.[21]

The tension between faith and fear played out in now-familiar ways. JFK and modernization theorists believed they could remake entire societies in relatively short order. If they put Latin American countries on the fast track to equality and economic development, their populations would be less susceptible to the siren song coming from Cuba and the Soviet Union. Here was a policy, as one Kennedy advisor claimed, of "enlightened anti-communism." If the United States failed to act in this competition between development models, officials feared, an "economic gap" rather than a missile one would develop, and US credibility in Americans' "own backyard" would suffer. As Kennedy shared with an aide, "the whole place could blow up on us."[22]

Drawing from atomic-era lexicon, officials spoke in apocalyptic terms when discussing the stakes of modernization efforts. Walt Rostow, author of the influential *The Stages of Economic Growth* and Kennedy's national security advisor, defined communism as a "kind of disease which can befall a transitional society." Rostow conceded that such a threat had to be met "primarily by maintaining or increasing U.S. military strength," suggesting that military power remained vital for underwriting modernization efforts. Still, only through promoting the "evolution" of societies could these threats be diminished. And for some Americans, these threats were existential. According to Senator John G. Tower (R-TX), if the United States did not "win" the Cold War, the nation would not survive. "It's that simple," Tower declared.[23]

Ironically, modernization advocates ended up promoting radical social reforms of the type that had triggered "red" alarm bells in the first place. (Jacobo Arbenz called for similar initiatives in Guatemala only a decade earlier.) Apparently, land reform and social revolution were acceptable only if they proceeded under American tutelage. Otherwise, they were a reckless "threat to freedom"—and to the profits of US corporations like the United Fruit Company. Left unstated by modernization theorists was the questionable value of programs like the Alliance for Progress in Latin America. "In the first eight years of the Alliance," historian Michael E. Latham explains, "the region experienced sixteen military coups, destroying hopes for progressive middle-class revolution."[24]

American-sponsored nonmilitary programs thus ended up amplifying Latin American internal-security apparatuses, furthering the Cold War's militarization. In Guatemala, political elite used military power to suppress political dissent, despite the US focus on community-development programs. In El Salvador, $63 million of US aid between 1962 and 1965 could not prevent the National Guard and National Police from routinely violating human rights. Modernization theorists might view Latin America as a "political, social, and economic laboratory," but military regimes saw US-backed reform as destabilizing and thereby resorted to state terror for crushing local rebellions. As the "decade of development" wore on, American officials were hard-pressed to determine which was worse: terrorism against the state or by the state.[25]

In practice, promotion of democratic capitalism proved far less convincing than the threat or use of armed force. Controlling societies became more important than modernizing them. As a result, development plans turned into "political tools for control and coercion," easy to adopt (and justify) when competing against communist models. Modernization theory, in short, helped militarize US foreign policy. To some pundits, nation building abroad rested far more on imposing force than on winning "hearts and minds." According to one authority writing for *Foreign Affairs* in 1962, communists were going "far beyond political indoctrination" to "obtain effective control" of the population. As such, "the side which uses violent reprisals most aggressively will dominate most of the people, even though their sympathies may lie in the other direction." War was becoming indispensable for building nations.[26]

Alongside the Alliance for Progress and the Peace Corps, it was the military component of the New Frontier, the Green Berets, that caught the nation's attention. The US Army's Special Forces were not just anti guerrilla warriors but "armed social workers" as well, purposefully melding armed force and development. As one journalist described the "tough and versatile" men who wore the green beret, they had the "combined abilities of a paratrooper, frogman, infantryman and diplomat." Yet few Americans appreciated the civic-minded component of their mission. Rather, popular culture depicted Special Forces as super-soldiers, ultimate commandoes who had the guts and know-how to teach ravaged foreign peoples to defend against and defeat the communist threat.[27]

Of course, not only Americans found alluring the clarion call of potential military glory. Che Guevara crafted his revolutionary theory of combatting western influence through armed insurrection. By relying on a small nucleus (*foco*) of armed revolutionaries, Latin Americans could reclaim their independence against colonial exploitation. In fact, Che believed the *foco* might create conditions for revolution, independent of local land-tillers' commitment to the cause. But the Argentinian's faith in military force and his reverence for the Cuban revolution were misplaced. Both would be put to the test, and fail miserably, in Bolivia, leading to Che's capture and execution by government forces in 1967. Romantic notions of war, whether they be American or Cuban, were evaporating in the tumultuous decade of the 1960s.[28]

While JFK looked to bolster America's image across the Western Hemisphere, European problems continued to attract global attention. The Berlin Wall crisis, a year before the Cuban missile one, raised anew fears of nuclear war befalling the continent. Back in 1958, Khrushchev had issued an ultimatum that western powers withdraw from Berlin. While his deadline passed without action, tensions remained high throughout Eisenhower's presidency. The impasse, however, would not—in Moscow's eyes, *could* not—last forever. By 1961, East Germans were fleeing in droves across porous borders into West Berlin, draining vital manpower and threatening East Germany's very existence. Walter Ulbricht, head of the German Democratic Republic, implored Khrushchev to step in or face uprisings jeopardizing the USSR itself. There seemed little choice then but to close the "uncontrolled border between the socialist and capitalist worlds."[29]

With Kennedy's poor showings in the Bay of Pigs fiasco and at the recent Vienna Summit, Khrushchev decided the time was ripe for taking action. Under mounting pressure from Ulbricht, the Soviet premier authorized the building of a barrier around West Berlin, first a barbed-wire fence and then in the form of a wall. Protests erupted throughout the city, but fears of escalation kept the matter from boiling over, even after a direct showdown between US and Soviet tanks at Checkpoint Charlie along the newly erected barricade. Inside the White House, presidential advisors deemed the wall "illegal, immoral and inhumane, but not a cause for war." West German Chancellor Konrad Adenauer decided to maintain trade ties with the east, while Khrushchev, relieved the United States had not responded more forcefully, confessed that "war might have broken out."[30]

Indeed, it might have. Moscow's gamble that Kennedy wouldn't risk nuclear war over Berlin assumed a rational president weighing his options. But emotions ran high in Washington that summer. Former Secretary of State Dean Acheson, advising JFK, argued that the Berlin crisis would "go far to determine the confidence of Europe—indeed of the world—in the United States." Acheson thus recommended a general alert of the Strategic Air Command and troop movements in Europe. Henry Kissinger, then teaching at Harvard and advising the National Security Council, spoke in equally alarming terms. Though Kissinger later would argue the crisis was little more than a "demonstration of latent Soviet weakness," at the time he judged Berlin's fate as "the touchstone for the future of the North Atlantic Community." Failure in Germany, he warned, would demonstrate globally the "irresistible nature of the Communist movement." It would not be the last time Kissinger misremembered the past.[31]

Kennedy, however, decided not to overreact. Despite the hardliners clamoring for a more forceful response to what they viewed as a clear attack on US credibility, the president moved cautiously. He saw the Berlin affair as emanating from Khrushchev's own fears of East Germany "slipping away." Besides, he shared with his advisors, a wall was "no very pleasant solution," but it was "damned better than a war." To a televised audience in late July before the crisis hit its crescendo, Kennedy warned Americans not to be impatient, for "any misjudgment on either side about the intentions of the other could rain more devastation in several hours than has been wrought in all the wars of human history." Meanwhile, behind closed doors, Pentagon officials explored plans for a "limited first strike" against the Soviet Union if war broke out over Berlin.[32]

For some Europeans, like West Berlin Mayor Willy Brandt, the episode raised serious questions over whether the US nuclear umbrella provided the safety it promised. West Germans had rallied during the late 1950s in support of the "Fight Against Atomic Death" campaign. The potential of NATO dragging West Berliners into a nuclear conflict without their assent sparked new waves of protest. Such dissent, though, generated its own source of worry inside Washington. NATO strength depended on allied solidarity, and any defections threatened to undermine the alliance's defensive posture. In language that would be echoed by the first Trump administration more than five decades later, US military leaders, according to the *Washington Post*, hoped the Berlin danger would "arouse Western Europe to the need to contribute greater effort to a NATO buildup."[33]

While tensions simmered in Europe, the New Frontier continued to beckon. In August 1960, a coup in Laos threatened to destabilize Southeast Asia—already shaky given South Vietnam's ongoing political travails—and open the region to communist penetration. Nominally "neutral" since the 1954 Geneva Accords, Laos had wrestled with both an internal civil war and external infiltration of North Vietnamese troops using the country as a passageway into South Vietnam. By March 1961, Kennedy deemed the war-ravaged nation a Southeast Asian "testing ground" of global import. In a nationally televised address that month, the president warned that "no one should doubt our resolution" in keeping an independent Laos from becoming a "cold war pawn." Ambassador Chester Bowles shared Kennedy's fears, suggesting to the Joint Chiefs that Laotian instability invited the "possibility of a massive Chinese advance into Southeast Asia."[34]

The anxiety Washington elite felt over new states leaning toward communism exposed an unspoken paradox. Obviously, they feared communist enslavement of the decolonizing world. But if Americans held faith in the inherent advantages of democratic capitalism, why were they so afraid that "Third World" peoples would freely choose a communist form of government? Either way, a sense of alarm drove US policy in the Global South. When Eisenhower earlier had expounded upon the "incalculable" consequences of "falling dominoes," he revealed a deep-seated concern that global citizens might not aspire to American values. Here, in a rare moment, Henry Kissinger moved closer to the truth in describing the "mistaken belief that any country anywhere if given the opportunity would choose to be more like America."[35]

With American hubris tied to fear, local actors paid the price, as in the case of South Asia where the American alliance with Pakistan created not stability, but a heightened military threat to India. Nehru assailed those who criticized his avoidance of military alliances with foreign powers, seeking a path independent of Cold War rivalries. Washington elite, though, saw danger in such neutralist sentiments. Moreover, they worried about access to Middle Eastern oil and growing Soviet and Chinese influence in South Asia, thus necessitating Pakistan's inclusion in SEATO. Not surprisingly, the Indian prime minister viewed his Muslim neighbors' drift into the American orbit, and the military support it invited, as hostile. Nehru fumed to the UN Secretary General that giving "military aid to one party to a conflict" was "obviously a breach of neutrality." American interventionism born of Cold War fears ended up elevating already tense relations between the two most important states in South Asia.[36]

It would not be the last time American meddling exacerbated local hostilities or highlighted the disconnect between worldviews. Nehru saw lingering colonialism, not communism, as the greatest threat to world peace. American policymakers judged the Indian naive and incapable of governing. Viewed from Washington, however, regional politics mattered only insofar as they helped form a buttress to communist aggression in South Asia. Thus, both India and Pakistan's "flirtation with China" seemed precarious. Preparing for war appeared the lone remedy. As Eisenhower's secretary of defense, Thomas S. Gates, Jr., offered in May 1960, he and the Joint Chiefs were "convinced of the indispensability of military assistance as an integral part not only of our own defenses but of those of the free world." If Great Power competition expanded into South Asia, only armed force would deter further aggression, no matter the price.[37]

In the end, few US policymakers surveying the New Frontier grasped the destructive effects of their faith in military power to transform other societies, to build nations capable of resisting communist influence. Academic theories promising to "modernize" the Global South proved not nearly as practical as their originators had hoped. But faith-makers have a habit of dispensing with facts. To their minds, violence might disrupt and destroy, but it also could also reshape institutions in a positive way if channeled properly. There was more to be done. And modernization theorists weren't quite ready to suppress their appetites for winning the global Cold War.[38]

CHAPTER 10

War as a Transformative Power

By the late 1950s and early 1960s, American social scientists believed they had developed a blueprint for a rapidly changing postwar global society. Such optimistic designs mattered as Americans were "groping for some blend of force and politics to pacify" local revolutionary movements. It was more than just revolution at play, however. Modernization theorists offered what seemed a surefire way to build political institutions abroad, a means to navigate the difficult transition from colonial client state to independent nation. Infusions of US economic and military aid, properly administered, would act as stabilizers, strengthening local governments and ultimately tying them to an American-led liberal world order.[1]

Linking development to security made sense with the communist threat painted in militaristic hues. Yet modernization theory rested on assumptions bordering on ultimatums. Infused within was a faith, if not insistence, that other people copy American institutions and values to survive the Cold War. Such theories, while influential, did not go unquestioned. Writing in 1959, historian William Appleman Williams doubted the long-term value of initiating "drastic, fundamental changes" in other societies' internal affairs. Not surprisingly, Williams argued, "host" nations seemed relegated to an inferior position vis-à-vis the United States. Surely resentment would follow. As the Wisconsin professor imparted, "America's integrated reformist and economic expansion provoked trouble. And the reaction to the trouble ultimately took the form of terror."[2]

Insofar as communism was an ideology of development, scholarly views on the potential of American modernization programs were embraced outside of academia as well. The assumptions rhymed, even if the details differed. In places like Afghanistan, the *New York Times* reported, the United States and Russia were in "direct competition" over a "stagnated" population "not ideologically committed to any social or political systems." Mao's Great Leap Forward and Cultural Revolution both intended, with equally disastrous results, for China to compete internationally by relying on a noncapitalist model of internal development. A ruinous adulteration of modernizing impulses equally contributed to one of the worst genocides of the post–World War II era inside Cambodia. Modernization theorists might view development as a weapon, but it clearly was an unwieldy one at best.[3]

Notions of modernity also were embraced by Third World leaders seeking economic aid across the Cold War political spectrum. Wary of foreign strings attached to that aid, they cast a wide net in courting potential investors. Rather than welcome such competition, nervous American policymakers fretted that the communist camp would gain at the United States' expense. When Indonesian leaders, for instance, considered China as "an alternative modernity," Washington elite bristled.[4]

By the time Kennedy took office, debates over aid had become commonplace inside US foreign-policy circles. Back in 1955, the Bandung Conference had brought to Indonesia numerous newly independent Third World leaders aiming to fashion a response to western "control," whether economic, intellectual, or physical. They aspired to develop common strategies for empowerment free of and independent from superpower manipulation. As attendee Mohammed Ali of Pakistan argued, the people of Asia and Africa had to ensure those "still groaning under the heel of foreign domination [were] allowed to enjoy in full measure the fruits of freedom."[5]

The conference participants set their sights high, tackling the interrelated issues of neutralism, nationalism, and anticolonialism. In African American novelist Richard Wright's words, Bandung was meant to answer the weighty question of "how shall the human race be organized?" Predictably, Eisenhower officials were alarmed by attendees speaking of global disarmament and potential economic development ties with China. (Of note, Bandung occurred not long after the first Taiwan Strait Crisis.) The administration might take a public stance of "benevolent indifference," as one congressman shared, but the foreign-policy concerns were real. Even with the relatively quick collapse of the cooperative "Bandung Spirit," Washington kept a wary eye on participants as they mapped out new relationships with the Cold War superpowers.[6]

Coupled with Bandung, the rise of a Third World Non-Aligned Movement animated intense fears among US policymakers. In a world underwritten by fear, even neutrality was suspect. Nehru, for instance, genuinely approached both sides of the Cold War contest for economic and political inspiration, but Americans found any glance toward Moscow duplicitous. Proving one's anticommunist credentials had to be absolute and everlasting. Chester Bowles, the US ambassador to India, might see the South Asian giant as a "testing ground for democratic government in a period of rapidly receding colonial dominance," but Washington elite worried what would happen if India failed that test.[7]

While Nehru flirted with the Soviet Union as a potential model for economic planning, Yugoslavia's Tito defiantly set out on his own path of neutrality. India held certain advantages, being outside of Eastern Europe, farther away from the wrath of leaders like Stalin, who had expelled Yugoslavia from Cominform back in 1948. Both Moscow and Washington, it appeared, deemed neutrality dangerous. Setting aside Belgrade's insolent impartiality, the head of the US united labor movement argued in 1955 that Nehru and Tito were "not neutral" but "aides and allies of communism in fact and in effect, if not diplomatic verbiage." Meanwhile, policy leaders did their best to make traveling the middle road unnavigable. In language that would be repurposed by George W. Bush for another global war the following century, Truman declared as early as 1947 that "nearly every nation must choose between alternative ways of life."[8]

What if "neutralization" in countries like India, Laos, or Brazil was not enough to satisfy American policymakers' unease over communism's global march? Under Truman, the State Department had warned that the "decline and weakness" of both France and Great Britain had left a "growing vacuum" in Asia that needed to be "filled, as far as possible, by elements friendly rather than hostile to the free world." Such views would change little during the next two administrations. Both Eisenhower and Kennedy subscribed to a 1951 National Security Council assessment that the "loss of India to the Communist orbit would mean that for all practical purposes all of Asia will have been lost."[9]

Because modernization theory united military and economic efforts, it should not surprise that fears of an Indian economic collapse destabilizing the global world order informed how many US policymakers viewed South Asia. Poverty led to radicalism, theories went, which then opened the door for Soviet and Chinese incursions. Given an Indian population of more than 445 million in 1960, the entire regional balance might tip away from the United States. Observers feared that the "most ground down" people on earth could turn away from democratic practices, toward communism, and an "aping of it" that would lead to "more votes for the Communist party of India." A "Soviet economic offensive" might be just as dangerous as a military one.[10]

Underlying these fears was a misguided belief that nations resisting American ideals—and US policies of "defensive expansion"—were hostile and therefore responsible for any ensuing violence. Dissenting voices countered that US policy toward "uncommitted nations" should be dedicated to defending individual freedoms, not corporate profits. Yet for anxious Americans looking at such problems from either a military or an economic standpoint, there seemed few alternatives to attacking communist intentions in the Global South head-on. Thus, we see not just a fear of war but a contributing fear of losing influence over or access to overseas markets, all the while sitting alongside a faith in war to address these fears.[11]

Lacking detailed knowledge of local politics and histories did not help matters. How could US policymakers know if leaders like Tito, Nehru, Sukarno, or Nasser were to be trusted? Were they principally guided by a desire for economic improvement or by nationalist, anticolonial sentiment? Were their calls for global disarmament an opportunity or a threat? Too often, Americans erred on the side of excessive, seemingly desperate, caution. Journalist Drew Pearson, for example, wondered aloud if Gamal Abdel Nasser, a vocal advocate of nonalignment, was "acting Hitlerish," while largely dismissing the fact that the Egyptian leader saw western imperialism, not communist subversion, as the central threat to his nation's independence. In the process, modernization theories took on a coercive, even repressive vibe given US policymakers' fears of "communist engulfment."[12]

As modernization theorists looked to the developing Third World as a laboratory for testing their allegedly transformative ideas, few of them considered the inherent deficiencies of imprinting a universalistic theory onto any and all nations. Rarely did they take note, for instance, of India's struggle simply to define itself in a postcolonial world. The 1947 partition of the subcontinent into two separate nation-states, India and Pakistan, was a traumatic event in itself, having little to do with simmering Cold War tensions. Additionally, the lack of homogeneous communities in both states complicated fundamental questions about nationality, sovereignty, and the rights of citizens. Modernization was playing out far differently than American theorists had expected.[13]

Fear tended to guide these same theorists. Like many Americans, modernization advocates worried about the subcontinent's volatility after partition, seeing India, in particular, as a target of communist China and a potential source of global instability. According to the *New York Times*, by 1955 the communists had "made India the target of their most intensive and integrated propaganda campaign in this part of the world." A new Cold War military front threatened to open if the United States wasn't careful. Unavoidably, militarized conceptions of South Asia were reflected back, as Indian groups came to see Americans as "warmongers and backers of colonialism." When locals described Moscow as supporting "the freedom struggles of the colonized peoples" and fighting for peace, US policymakers shivered at the prospect of losing a key ally in the region.[14]

Nor could the Chinese separate the Cold War from the India-Pakistan conflict, further nurturing Americans' fears. China had clashed with

India over their border ever since its 1950 invasion of Tibet. In late 1962, after years of skirmishing along India's northeastern frontier, the territorial dispute ignited into a full-blown, albeit brief, military conflict. One month after the war began, a triumphant China declared a unilateral ceasefire, having deflated its neighbor's "arrogance" and "illusions of grandeur." While Beijing placed the border war within the context of American imperialism and military support to South Asia, the White House saw only a newly hot theater of the Cold War threatening to destabilize the international system. If India were to request additional military support to resist future Chinese incursions, however, perhaps the United States could strengthen ties with New Delhi. As one Kennedy advisor calculated, "we may have a golden opportunity for a major gain in our relations with India."[15]

Such potential gains mattered given Khrushchev's 1961 speech declaring support for the "national-liberation movement." That January, the Soviet premier publicly threw his weight behind the "active struggle against U.S. imperialism." The response from Washington was predictable. Dismissing the possibility that Khrushchev's strategy might overextend already limited Soviet resources, the White House feared the decolonizing world might turn away from the West. Self-determination no longer was a Wilsonian abstraction, but a potentially dangerous Cold War reality. Wedded to Soviet designs, anticolonial nationalism could be turned against the United States. No wonder Kennedy, only one year later, signed a national security memorandum recognizing "subversive insurgency ('wars of liberation') [as] a major form of politico-military conflict equal in importance to conventional warfare."[16]

Around the globe, however, American views held different meaning. One British correspondent reporting from Indonesia shared that "people here think 'anti-imperialist' rather than 'anti-communist.'" Indeed, Khrushchev hoped to profit off such sentiments, arguing in early 1961 that while communists were the "most determined opponents of world wars," imperialists needed them "to seize the territories of others, and to enslave and plunder other peoples." What if such a message resonated throughout the Global South? Hardliners like Barry Goldwater shot back, speaking of the global contest as a choice between "freedom or slavery." The senator lashed out against those "who cherish the false notion that by accommodating the totalitarian doctrine of communism we can continue the uneasy peace maintained since the end of World War II."[17]

Given such disparate views over the decolonizing world, might there be limits to "peaceful coexistence"? Years earlier, in 1953, the *New York Times* had editorialized that the Soviet Union had "always shouted 'peace, peace,' even when it was engaged in the most open aggression." Seemingly little had changed in the ensuing decade. Americans saw Khrushchev's support of national-liberation movements as an underhanded promotion of communist subversive activities across Asia and Africa. Meanwhile, Soviet leaders held similar fears that the recently organized Non-Aligned Movement was a US tool for capitalist expansion. Alongside these fears, both camps shared a faith that their development models, backed by military might, would transform the Global South and tilt the Cold War in their favor.[18]

At the same time, American presidents, and more than a few liberal interventionists, embraced another foreign-policy tactic in places like Latin America and the Middle East: allying with brutal anticommunist dictators who used military force to eradicate any whiff of leftism. If development policies weren't enough to tip the balance in the United States' favor, then armed force under the guise of "liberal peace-building" could be brought to bear. When "Castroite" communists threatened to seize and overthrow the Dominican Republic in 1965, President Johnson dispatched US marines and soldiers from the army's 82nd Airborne Division to the island, ostensibly to evacuate American citizens. The truth, however, had far more to do with US fears of preventing "another Cuba" and losing regional credibility as American troops sat on the cusp of deploying to South Vietnam.[19]

The Dominican Republic already had suffered through a military coup in 1963 that deposed the democratically elected and reform-minded president Juan Bosch. When, two years later, an alliance of farmers, laborers, and progressives—known as the "Constitutionalists"—called for Bosch's return, the island seemed ripe for a leftist insurrection. In ordering the troop deployment, Johnson argued he would "not permit the establishment of another Communist government in the Western Hemisphere." Yet both the president and the CIA had exaggerated the threat, to a considerable extent. In the end, the United States backed the conservative government while the CIA likely engaged in vote rigging the following year, preferencing the island's stability over its democracy. The invasion also threw into question the purpose behind deploying US troops abroad. Were they part of "peacekeeping" or "stability operations," two prevalent missions in the 1990s, or simply an instrument of "armed diplomacy"?[20]

Critics of Johnson's Caribbean foray, like Idaho Senator Frank Church, recognized "the folly of trying to impose an American solution upon every insurgency abroad." A foreign policy based solely on military might, Church felt, was a "form of self-delusion." Was the Idaho Democrat suggesting that faith in war wasn't enough for winning the Cold War? It seemed that way. Yet Kennedy- and Johnson-era policies toward the Global South also intimated that faith in war, at least partially, emanated from deep-seated insecurities over foreign elections, where local populations might voluntarily, if not misguidedly, choose communist over American-sponsored candidates. In due course, definitions of democracy became corrupted. If only noncommunist politicians were worthy of support, how committed was the United States to true electoral freedoms?[21]

Perhaps, then, the best way to combat these self-doubts was to combine war and development; theoretically the two could be mutually reinforcing. During the Korean War, the Far East Command noted how intense fighting had caused massive "socioeconomic dislocation," a central foundation of counterinsurgency theories applied later in Vietnam. Accordingly, President Johnson promised Dominicans "massive economic aid" as "an incentive to warring factions to settle their violent dispute." Economic development. Political reform. Military training and assistance. All these mutually supporting programs would fall under the larger rubric of US grand strategy and, by the early 1960s, turn the United States into *the* armed branch of global capitalism.[22]

Gnawing fears of war-induced poverty inspiring social unrest thus led to interventionist policies, taking civilian reformers and military advisors to places as far afield as Latin America and Southeast Asia. Ideology, reform, and war all became embedded into Americans' faith in their transformative powers. In nearly every theoretical model, unstable states became "fertile" breeding grounds for communism. Internal reforms required a secure environment in which to take root, yet another counterinsurgency hypothesis soon to be tested in Vietnam. Some senior policymakers, like Senator Goldwater, disagreed with the "false notion" that communism was "spawned by poverty, disease, and other similar social and economic conditions." To the Arizonan, communism was "spawned by Communists, and Communists alone." By the early 1960s, however, Goldwater, while not alone in his critique, found himself in the minority. Reformist interventionism would underwrite Americans' faith in war, with deadly consequences on the near horizon.[23]

There was a problem, though, with this faith. The same malleable peasants who ostensibly wanted to be just like Americans also were potential receptacles for communist influence. Neither modernization theorists nor grand strategists were quite certain their putative allies were up to the task of implementing their intended reforms. George Kennan, for instance, doubted whether Latin Americans had the "societal resolve" to resist communism, concluding that "harsh governmental measures of repression may be the only answer." Truman's secretary of state, Dean Acheson, had felt similarly, describing the region as a dreadful combination of "an explosive population, stagnant economy, archaic society, primitive politics, massive ignorance, illiteracy, and poverty." One might question how reform was supposed to flourish in a region that policy elite found so utterly contemptible.[24]

Faith in the power of militarized modernization thus sat in tension with fear of its recipients. Unable to decipher whether "peasants" were victims of communism or potential revolutionaries, American reformers nonetheless plowed ahead. Some three years before US combat troops began arriving in South Vietnam, journalists were reporting that the "peasant's support" would be the "deciding factor in this struggle."

In 1961, Ted Kennedy (D-MA) similarly argued that "as the peasants go . . . so Latin America will go." Still, questions remained. If military forces became engaged in fighting among the population, were they at war *for* the peasant or at war *against* the peasant? High casualty rates among noncombatants would become a destructive consequence of these uncertainties, as Americans came to view local villages as dens of anarchy and insecurity.[25]

As a consequence, landless farmers paid a high price for being the supposed targets of American developmental aid. It should have come as no surprise that land reform, when viewed as a "weapon," would become inherently destructive. Its inclusion as an element of counterinsurgency—what Robert Kennedy superficially described as "social reform under pressure"—only worsened the plight of hard-pressed locals. Modernization became an immensely violent process. Future National Security Advisor Walt Rostow might speak of "immunizing" Third World countries against the "disease" of communism, but the cure often proved worse than the original symptom. When paired with local policies of, if not exploitation by, authoritarian governments, security needs often trumped reform programs, further militarizing American interventionism.[26]

The paradoxes unfolded in rapid fashion. The United States would support social or economic reform in countries vulnerable to communist influence, but those same countries bred ideological infection that threatened US security. Hunger and poverty were opportunities to demonstrate American largesse, yet dangers to global stability. Local farmers were isolated in rural villages, yet potential collaborators with international communism. Development initiatives could uplift the people, yet security programs could destroy their social fabrics. Undergirding all these paradoxes, even after the political demise of Joseph McCarthy, was a continuing "violent anticommunism" that kept armed force central to America's global presence.[27]

In the end, modernization theory never lived up to its promises. The faith of its progenitors in the power of American aid to influence others had faltered. Local leaders often saw modernizing efforts as simply a repackaged form of imperialism. And when tied to an increasingly enticing faith in counterinsurgency, those efforts became far more destructive than many theorists had dreamed possible. The American war in Vietnam soon would demonstrate that the two ideas of development and security were hardly reinforcing and, in fact, dangerously counterproductive. War along the New Frontier was about to take a deadly turn in the already contentious region of Southeast Asia.[28]

CHAPTER 11

Faith and Fear on the Road to Vietnam

"We felt beset and at risk. This fear underlay our involvement in Vietnam." So recalled former Secretary of Defense Robert S. McNamara, who served both the Kennedy and Johnson administrations as the United States embarked upon its misguided crusade in Southeast Asia. McNamara offered a laundry list of fear-inducing events that spurred US policymakers like himself to see communism "as monolithic." Mao's victory in the Chinese civil war. The bloody conflict in Korea. The launching of *Sputnik*. Khrushchev's support for wars of national liberation. The crises in West Berlin and Cuba. McNamara surely fudged the truth in claiming he didn't see the communist danger as "overwhelming," but many of his contemporaries surely did. The borderlands along the New Frontier were frightful, dangerous places to tread.[1]

This fear of global communism long had clouded a deeper understanding of the Vietnamese anticolonial and nationalist movements unfolding in the aftermath of World War II. Washington elite worried about a decline in US credibility if a regional ally collapsed. Others, like US ambassador to South Vietnam Frederick Nolting, warned two years before ground combat troops arrived in the country that the Chinese would profit most from an American withdrawal in Southeast Asia. At the time, McNamara invoked the "domino theory" and cautioned that if the United States decided to "back down" in Vietnam, it would "encourage the regional and global spread of Communism."[2]

Such fear-based prophecies rested on the wrongheaded belief that the Vietnamese conflict, much like the Korean War, was simply an invasion of the democratic South by the communist North. US Army officers tended to portray the North Vietnamese as launching a "strategic offensive to conquer South Vietnam." This was not an internal civil war, they argued, but an external incursion. Americans equally assumed that any invasion plans were masterminded by Moscow, Beijing, or, worse, both. In reality, nationalist revolutionary leaders like Ho Chi Minh maintained their own priorities, ones that never accorded neatly with Cold War paradigms. Ho might welcome superpower sponsorship and, ultimately, commit his nation to socialist reform, but he hardly submitted to becoming a pawn of either China or the Soviet Union.[3]

Universalizing fears ultimately became a *casus belli* in Vietnam. Obsessed with losing credibility in the larger Cold War contest, Washington's policy elite spoke in ominous tones as the United States inched closer to full-scale war in Southeast Asia. Terms like "image," "honor," and "prestige" became watchwords for Cold Warriors intent on keeping America strong in the face of aggression. Lyndon Johnson, who assumed the presidency after Kennedy's assassination in November 1963, cautioned that "surrender anywhere threatens defeat everywhere." Across the political aisle, Senator Goldwater spoke comparably, arguing that if communism triumphed it was because "the American people chose to surrender." Fear fostered political consensus.[4]

The domino theory thus could be applied anywhere without an understanding of local histories or politics. When the Malayan Communist Party initiated an insurgent campaign to oust British occupiers in the late 1940s, the "emergency" drew the attention of American strategists already nervous about communism's spread. Indeed, British commanders argued they were facing a "theatre-wide" communist aggression. Over the next decade, British and Commonwealth forces fought a protracted counterinsurgency campaign, experimenting with a host of military and socioeconomic programs to root out insurgents and their supporters. Destruction became endemic to both sides' strategies. While the communists engaged in terror killings and sabotage, the British resorted to forced population resettlement—"regroupment"—in hopes of separating guerrilla fighters from their support networks. As one observer noted, the counterinsurgency effort became built around a "system of population control and area dominance." American strategists saw potential in reproducing British tactics if they too faced a future insurgency.[5]

Yet in dismissing local conditions, those same Americans tended to take the wrong lessons from Malaya. The Malayan Communist Party, populated mostly by ethnic Chinese, never succeeded in recruiting Malay and Indian supporters, making it far easier for the British to incorporate a racial plank into their counterinsurgency campaign plans. The MCP leader, Chin Peng, also launched an open armed struggle well before his forces were ready. Moreover, geography mattered. The narrow Malay Peninsula prevented communist forces from retreating into cross-border sanctuaries, while also posing difficulties for superpower benefactors wishing to provide external support. Finally, the duration of the British effort, with over a decade of military campaigning, might have exposed to Americans the challenges of fighting a protracted war far from home. Few of these details mattered, though, to those who only saw communists deriving "moral support from Red China" and drawing to "the jungle to plot seizure of power."[6]

If the British successfully had contained communism in Malaya, could not the United States, with far greater resources, do the same in Vietnam? Once more, faith in and fear of war met with predictable results. Back in 1954, with the climactic battle of Dien Bien Phu still raging, then-Senator Kennedy argued that to "pour money, materiel, and men into the jungles of Indochina without at least a remote prospect of victory would be dangerously futile and self-destructive." But ten years' worth of Cold War fears had made an impact on JFK. Speaking on the conflict in Vietnam shortly before his death, Kennedy insisted that "for us to withdraw . . . would mean a collapse not only of South Vietnam but Southeast Asia." Extolling a faith in American power, at least publicly, Kennedy in fact had expanded US military and economic assistance programs in Vietnam over the course of his presidency, all while hoping to avoid a wider war.[7]

The aftermath of JFK's death left Americans with one of the most enduring "what-ifs" of Cold War history. Had Kennedy lived and been elected to a second term, would he have committed the United States to a full-blown war in Vietnam? Counterfactuals, of course, take us only so far. Without evidence, one can only speculate, and historians often make for bad futurists. What matters here is that the advice Kennedy received illustrated the deepening relationships between faith and fear. Aides warned of "excessive fears" and of acting "indecisively," of how the "bright promise" of the New Frontier might be "sunk under the rice fields" of Vietnam. Others suggested that a withdrawal plan might be feasible "if progress in the counterinsurgency campaign warrant[ed] such action." Still others, pointing to recent British experiences, noted how Malaya demonstrated that force could be applied successfully to contain communism in Southeast Asia. The slain president bequeathed these deliberations to his successor, and for the next two years LBJ agitated over them before finally committing the nation to war.[8]

Yet these discussions remained, almost exclusively, Americentric. At worst, they were disdainful of local visions for the future. Columnist Walter Lippmann hinted at this derision, suggesting the "domino theory" was working—but in reverse. The more military power the United States applied in places like Vietnam, Lippmann argued, the more isolated it was becoming throughout Asia. Yet, for Americans fashioning the Indochinese struggle as one of "liberty against despotism," local opposition to US policies was dismissed as postcolonial naivety. Even advice from the French often went unheeded, with President Charles de Gaulle scoffing that Vietnam was a "rotten country" and that it was useless for Americans to fight there. But Asian dominoes had to hold. Freedom had to be preserved. American prestige maintained. Within such mindsets, it became easy, as one contemporary historian contended, for Americans to engage in a kind of "self-hypnosis," convincing themselves that they alone could defend Indochina against communist control.[9]

Two central problems resided within these assumptions about falling Asian dominoes. First, claims that defeat in Indochina might trigger a "chain reaction throughout the Far East and Southeast Asia" dismissed local populations' relationship with communism. Local customs and histories did not necessarily coincide with Leninist-Marxist ideals, and for many smaller nations, China posed a threat as large as the United States. Sovereignty mattered. The second issue corresponded more directly to Vietnam. The French-Indochinese war may have linked to larger Cold War currents, but the US-Sino-Soviet rivalry was not at the heart of what was, at its core, a local affair. Americans mostly viewed Vietnam as a crucial Cold War battlefield. In reality, they were intervening into a local civil war. External actors most certainly played a role in this civil conflict, but only the Vietnamese could determine its final outcome.[10]

Similar trends unfolded in North Africa, where the war for Algerian independence highlighted yet again the limits of Cold War influence. As the French departed Indochina in 1954, they immediately found themselves embroiled in another anticolonial struggle that threatened the very fabric of French nationhood. (Most French considered Algeria part of France proper rather than a colonial possession.) For the next six years, a brutal war ravaged the countryside, with both the Front de libération nationale and French forces inflicting extreme violence upon the population. True, fears of expanding international communism played out in this war, especially of pan-Arabism being tied to communism and offering a model for Middle Eastern revolutionaries to follow. However, in a struggle conceived primarily as anticolonial, participants' rationale for fighting often sat far afield from Cold War ideologies.[11]

For those Vietnamese living through their own French war, colonialism, class-oriented economic issues, and a history of resisting foreign invaders loomed far larger than the superpower Cold War competition. Children recalled their parents feeling "dirty" for having to live under French colonial rule, that the experience had somehow "reduced" them. Meanwhile, villagers saw the local insurgency as "the only political group that really loved the people." Might it be that communism had a more compelling message than colonialism? Americans, looking in from the outside, missed many of these signs. Indeed, English writer Graham Greene's 1955 novel *The Quiet American* showcased the suffering caused by superpower interventionism that escaped the grasp of idealistic yet close-minded US agents working in Vietnam.[12]

Americans like Alden Pyle, the protagonist in Greene's novel, held faith that they could succeed where the French had failed. Reality, it turned out, matched fiction. Over the next decade, US armed forces repurposed French experiences in Indochina and Algeria, mining them for examples of how—and how not—to fight counterinsurgency warfare. Military leaders and doctrine writers examined French works that laid down "basic principles" for defeating insurgencies. They assessed the relationships between the French mission and the Vietnamese people. They asked whether political instability inside France or Vietnam had caused a lack of coherent strategy. And, throughout, they assumed that the United States, eschewing colonial designs, would be welcomed as liberator, not occupier.[13]

Thus, the French defeat, if properly handled, presented an opportunity. For some advisors in the Kennedy White House, South Vietnam offered a "counterinsurgency laboratory" for testing new ideas on modernization, on development, and on military tactics. The problem should have been evident. Local Vietnamese civilians and officials weren't crude lab animals on which to test new political medicines. Ngo Dinh Diem, South Vietnam's taciturn and virulently anticommunist president, refused to be manipulated by Washington. Modernization advocate Wesley Fishel had visited Saigon back in 1954, arguing the Saigon regime was "shaky as all hell" and advocating for "administrative, economic, and social reforms." Yet Diem was no puppet. He held his own ideas about building state infrastructures to create an independent South Vietnam, frustrating US advisors in the process. In fact, Pentagon analysts later would blame the United States' "inability to exert leverage" over Saigon leaders as a principal failure of the burgeoning war effort.[14]

Had they been more perceptive in studying their predecessors' experiences, Americans might have glimpsed similarities as they waded deeper into Vietnam. The French "civilizing mission" had generated resentment among both rural farmers and urban intellectuals, and French military forces struggled to gain "control" of contested areas, especially in the countryside. In a pluralistic society like southern Vietnam, unifying ideas like "nationalism" still were being contested in the aftermath of World War II. Local leaders became adept at manipulating external aid, all while distancing themselves from their foreign benefactors. Western development theories weren't validated, but discredited. If Vietnam was to be a "test case" for American ideas, the coming report cards would disappoint.[15]

Perhaps *the* fundamental problem stemmed from Americans misjudging the internal contest over nationalism and identity within Vietnam's borders. True, communist leaders in Hanoi argued that Diem's regime was a "puppet" client state of the United States even as they sought international support from the socialist camp. But at its core, the struggle within Vietnam centered upon competing interpretations of what it meant to be Vietnamese in the postcolonial era. It seemed unlikely that any foreign force could weigh in on those questions. Nor did Diem improve matters by enacting policies far more authoritarian than democratic. Masses of rural farmers saw the regime as corrupt, especially when wealthy landlords reclaimed their properties as part of "land reform." All the while, nervous Americans worried Diem's policies were pushing southern Vietnamese into the communist camp.[16]

With the Saigon regime exacerbating local grievances rather than attending to them, the insurgency's ranks swelled. Similar infighting had occurred in the Philippines, where a Hukbalahap communist rebellion threatened the US-sponsored government in World War II's immediate aftermath. Huk insurgents, many of whom had resisted Japanese occupation, espoused a class-based anticolonial message that resonated with the rural population. Not surprisingly, Americans viewed the threat to their former Pacific holdings through an anticommunist lens. Counterinsurgency advocates dashed to the islands, armed with modernization theories born of American hubris. By the mid-1950s, the Huk threat had diminished, though far more from local leadership than US power. Of course, faith-based Americans took far different lessons from the affair. As Edward Lansdale, an air force officer working with the CIA, paternalistically concluded, foreign assistance programs could work as long as Americans were providing the proper direction to local leaders.[17]

These false assumptions from counterinsurgency advocates came home to roost in Vietnam with disastrous results. Fawning admirers of Lansdale might argue that the Huk experience illustrated how "a foreign power could stimulate improvement of an ally's counterinsurgency capabilities without adverse repercussions," but Vietnam proved otherwise. More accurate were assessments that US intervention in the Philippines only influenced "on the margins." The Huks failed more because of internal contradictions within their movement than any American supervision of Manila leaders. And while those leaders, like Ramon Magsaysay, instituted electoral reforms and civil improvements, US officers reviewing the conflict tended to focus on security-centric programs, even as they noted the importance of civic action and economic development.[18]

Interventionism therefore adopted coercive, even violent measures. Americans in Vietnam long had presumed that victory against the communist insurgency relied on more than just military force. But US modernizing programs presumed that force necessary. As McNamara put it succinctly, "Security is development." No wonder that when Diem embarked upon his own population resettlement agenda, known as the strategic hamlet program, Americans were enthusiastic that the fortified villages might limit insurgents' freedom of movement. General Paul D. Harkins, head of the US military command in Vietnam, lauded the program's expansion and its potential to "isolate guerrillas from the Vietnamese rural population." But Americans' faith was misplaced. More critical observers wondered if the communists, not the Saigon regime, were the ones benefiting from the people's forced resettlement. Nor could anyone be sure of how peasants were responding to the battle "for men's minds."[19]

With the growing US advisory effort in South Vietnam came an untested assumption that accumulation and manipulation of local cultural knowledge might answer these vital questions. Might cultural literacy lead to "control" of what many Americans saw as a "vulnerable" and "underdeveloped" Asian population? Even as senior officers debated whether the most dangerous threat to South Vietnam was internal or external, they concluded that only by controlling the population could the insurgent movement be defeated. Only through the people, military strategists assumed, could control over the enemy be achieved. But what kind of "control" was desired? Under what circumstances would "destruction or the threat of destruction bring about the desired measure of control?" Counterinsurgency theorists believed the answers could be found by appreciating the cultural landscape. Military forces could achieve control over the people, and thus power over the enemy, by understanding their culture.[20]

But there was a "legibility" issue here in translating local socio-political knowledge for use by American military forces. How were US soldiers supposed to interpret what they were seeing? Few American advisors deploying to Southeast Asia had much familiarity with Vietnam. They struggled to build working relationships with their Vietnamese counterparts. The "human terrain," as the US military would come to call it, could be as impenetrable as a triple-canopied jungle. And yet Americans continued to assume an adequate level of understanding about a society far different from their own. Contemporary critics blasted those supporting a war in which "the unknowable can be stated with certainty." But as the conflict dragged on, misplaced cultural assumptions endured. As Pulitzer Prize–winning author Thomas Powers observed, "The war refused to be won, or lost, or understood."[21]

This inability to navigate Vietnam's human terrain could be explained, in part, by Americans' enduring faith in their values' universal suitability. As just one example, LBJ held to his faith that he could somehow balance a war in Vietnam with the Great Society at home, all while exporting modernization programs and democratic ideals to a war-torn Southeast Asian nation. Looking back, the irony is palpable. American values were at once "exceptional *and* universal." Entire social structures could be refashioned on an ideal American model, helping defeat communism abroad and strengthen society at home. Faith transformed easily into delusion. With the war in Vietnam still raging, Ambassador Bowles took notice, asking a central question often discounted at the time: "why did presumably able, thoughtful American officials allow themselves to become committed to such unrealistic goals with so little understanding of the forces with which they would be called upon to contend?" Their faith in the transformative nature of American military power was partly to answer.[22]

Such faith, however, persisted alongside real fears that, without US action, South Vietnam would fall to the communist onslaught. Johnson remained adamant throughout 1964 that he wouldn't send "American boys" to fight an Asian war. But as reports emanated from Saigon the following year that the regime was tottering and would collapse without US military support, the president could not face the frightening prospect of losing Vietnam as Truman had "lost" China. To the president, deploying American troops (and values) became the inescapable choice to keep the principle of self-determination alive in South Vietnam. Nearly four decades later, George W. Bush similarly would hope to export democracy to the Muslim world after 9/11 as a way to protect American security interests and provide an "antidote" to global terrorism. Framing war as a contest over values clearly prevailed both during and after the Cold War.[23]

But not without condemnation. Reverend Martin Luther King, Jr. doubted Johnson's faith in war, assailing the administration for making the conflict in Vietnam a "'national obsession' while reducing the war on poverty to a 'skirmish.'" To King, the disproportionate investments simply didn't add up. "The security we profess to seek in foreign adventures," he argued, "we will lose in our decaying cities." And, in an example of politics making for strange bedfellows, some army officers agreed. One US Army colonel writing a searing postmortem on the war railed against the "American arrogance" embedded in the attempts to internationalize the Great Society. In the mind of Harry S. Summers, Jr., it was presumptuous "to force the world into the American mold—to act not so much the World's Policeman as the World's Nanny."[24]

If Johnson saw himself as caregiver-in-chief, such an outlook paled in comparison to personal fears of appearing weak in the face of communist aggression. Over and over, LBJ warned of not surrendering in Vietnam, of not running from the communist threat. The American people, he insisted, would "forgive you for anything except being weak." Administration officials chimed in, expressing similar fears that defeat in Vietnam would diminish US credibility, regionally and globally. As Secretary of State Dean Rusk maintained, "If the communist world found out that the United States would not pursue its commitment to the end, there was no telling where they would stop their expansionism." Coupled with these worries was a faith that if the United States could just "press on," things would work out. Of course, once American GIs started dying in Vietnam, it became even more difficult to back away from a seemingly vital commitment. Sunk-cost fallacies rested firmly upon wartime interplays between faith and fear.[25]

Debates over commitment and credibility continued after Johnson authorized a bombing campaign over North Vietnam, Operation Rolling Thunder, in early 1965, followed soon after by deployment of US ground combat troops to South Vietnam. America once more was engaged in a full-scale war. Defense Secretary McNamara confessed later that the administration chose war "because of our increasing fear—and hindsight makes it clear it was an exaggerated fear—of what would happen if we did not." The White House worried about the potential consequences if Americans signaled not strength, but a lack of resolve. If they "cut losses," in Vice President Hubert Humphrey's words. If they weren't a credible ally or a credible enemy. In the process, local allies could take advantage of their superpower sponsors' fears by indicating they might falter without more aid or support. Fear had become a ready weapon to be wielded in nearly any policy discussion or decision.[26]

Worse was to come on the ground in South Vietnam. Frustrated American GIs often faced an elusive enemy who submerged into the hamlets and jungles like a submarine at sea. They soon came to fear communist insurgents as much as the Vietnamese population they purportedly were there to protect. Army Lieutenant James R. McDonough recalled feeling "extremely vulnerable" by "exposing ourselves" in a way that demoralized his platoon. Military theorists reflected this dread, arguing that the counterinsurgent was "enveloped in an impenetrable fog" and, thus, "every person without exception, must be considered an agent." Not surprisingly, scared soldiers and marines lashed out against the people, leading to civilian atrocities and undercutting the local population's faith in American power. Meanwhile, Saigon's own policies became an outgrowth of US fears, with South Vietnamese military trials sentencing dissidents to hard labor for "having weakened the country's anticommunist spirit."[27]

By 1967, if not before, Vietnam had become a jet engine sucking everything into its maw. George McGovern assailed US policy that spring during a heated exchange on the senate floor. The South Dakotan Democrat argued that the United States was "unwittingly advancing the cause of Communism while seeking to contain it." The impacts, McGovern claimed, could be felt at home. "We are wasting human and material resources needed for the revitalization of our society." Senator Russell Long (D-LA) shot back that his colleague was developing "an argument to a point of ridiculousness." McGovern, though, had a point. As the military deadlock in Vietnam wore on, year after bloody year, with no real end in sight, an increasing number of Washington elite worried that the impasse might be demonstrating to allies and enemies alike the limits of American military power overseas.[28]

The costly stalemate left behind little but a devastated countryside. Pacification efforts intended to link the rural population to the Saigon government disappointed. Training programs to build a capable national army showed inconsistent progress. Combat operations to keep enemy main force units away from population centers ravaged the landscape. Perennial hopes that rising levels of violence would intimidate Hanoi proved illusory. All the while, the communists succeeded in effectively diversifying their resistance to US intervention. By contrast, the Americans had succeeded only in exposing their inability to undermine the will of Hanoi leaders who had, in essence, turned the Democratic Republic of Vietnam into a war state.[29]

If war is about control, then the 1968 Tet offensive exposed Americans' lack of it. In late January and early February, the communists launched a coordinated attack across the breadth of South Vietnam. White House claims of progress the previous year now appeared deceitful. The war effort seemingly had veered off the tracks. *Washington Post* correspondent Lee Lescaze argued that all "the indices of progress" had been "swept away" and that all "the old arguments and cliches have died." Inside Washington, policy leaders began questioning the return on their investment. President Johnson disapproved a troop increase requested by the US command in Saigon. Meanwhile, the enemy offensive lit a spark in the antiwar movement which already had lost faith in the capacity of the United States to act in a morally responsible manner.[30]

Faith, however, dies hard. Less than six months after the Tet offensive began, Warner Brothers released John Wayne's militaristic fantasy film *The Green Berets*, a bald attempt to shore up domestic resolve by pitting courageous Special Forces teams against sadistic Vietcong. In the actor's own words, he wanted to showcase "the mettle of the American fighting men." Wayne, however, failed in his mission. Miserably. One film critic deemed the movie "vile and insane . . . so full of its own caricature of patriotism that it cannot even find the right things to falsify." Another called it a "dismayingly clumsy patriotic gesture." "If only," critic Kevin Thomas argued, "the war in Vietnam were as simple as Wayne presents it here." Americans' faith in military heroes had been dented by their experience in Vietnam.[31]

Of course, the antiwar movement also proceeded from a place of faith, anticipating that their dissent would undermine the state's tolerance for a losing war's mounting costs. Conviction laced with hallucinogenic drugs even led some activists at a huge demonstration in Washington, DC to believe they could levitate the Pentagon and "demystify" the military's authority. Not surprisingly, FBI director J. Edgar Hoover linked this antiwar dissent—and, perniciously, civil-rights advocacy—to the communist cause. (Government officials long had labeled antiwar sentiment as apostasy, judging it blasphemous to speak out against war.) The party wanted nothing more, Hoover declared, "than to witness a continuation of widespread opposition, especially non-Communist opposition, to the Government's policy in Vietnam." At the White House, Johnson similarly tried to connect antiwar activism to international communism, with little success. In Tet's aftermath, the Cold War consensus was crumbling. Faith in war and fear of communism were losing their argumentative weight.[32]

As the implications of the Tet offensive came into sharper focus, critics wondered if the communist peril in Vietnam truly posed a mortal threat to the United States. Might America's fears have been exaggerated all along? McNamara's successor Clark Clifford believed so. Taking over the Defense Department in February 1968, the longtime Washington insider convened a study group to evaluate the war and its impact on US foreign policy. The findings dismayed. As Clifford recalled, "I couldn't get hold of a plan to end the war, there was no plan for winning the war. It was like quicksilver to me." Worse, the new defense secretary worried that the price being paid in Vietnam was undermining other foreign-policy objectives around the globe. With the United States trapped in a Southeast Asian quagmire, the Soviets might reassert themselves and challenge American influence and access throughout the Global South.[33]

Of course, as we now know, few dominoes fell in the aftermath of America's failed Vietnam adventure. It seems doubtful they would have, regardless of US intervention. Even with its focus on South Vietnam, Washington cultivated ties with other Southeast Asian nations to keep the communists at bay. More importantly, a late 1965 coup in Indonesia led to left-leaning and anticolonial Sukarno's ouster. The installment of a vicious anticommunist regime led by his successor Suharto essentially took Indonesia off the global chessboard. Over the next six months, the Indonesian Communist Party, the PKI, met its grisly demise. "Anti-PKI" massacres took on purge-like dimensions rivaling the worst of Stalin's excesses in the 1930s. The new military regime arrested, interrogated, and executed any "perpetrators" with a hint of communist affiliation. Estimates of the dead ranged from 500,000 to 1.2 million people.[34]

Few tears were shed in Washington. The destruction of the largest communist party outside of Russia and China ensured the Southeast Asian dominoes would remain upright. McNamara figured the fall of the PKI "greatly reduced America's stakes in Vietnam," throwing into question why so many had to die there for a containment strategy that no longer had any purpose. Unfortunately, there was meager incentive to probe such queries over grand strategy. The White House viewed the rapid transferal of Indonesia into the American camp as a positive realignment in the global balance of forces. Little else mattered. Few, if any, American officials expressed remorse over the PKI's slaughter. Nor did they divulge how the CIA had handed over "kill lists" to Suharto's armed forces. The United States had scored a major Cold War victory without much effort on its part.[35]

But this supposed "victory" challenged the presumption that war helped build nations. Instead of fostering new, freer political communities, the United States was participating in military campaigns that only led to their destruction. Senior policymakers and uniformed officers had committed themselves to conflicts that, far from furthering US national security interests, only brought death and misery to Indonesians, Vietnamese, Cambodians, and Laotians. They feared the potentially toxic mixture of self-determination and communism as emerging nations grappled with new identities in the postcolonial era. And they held faith, even in the face of contrary evidence, that war created a safer global environment in its destructive aftermath.[36]

PART IV

War to Produce Peace

CHAPTER 12

War and the "Peace You Desire"

They came to their altar with a faith unburdened by doubt. They accepted as true their theories and their doctrines and most of all their weapons. The airpower acolytes of the early 1960s were convinced they could win the war in Vietnam and deliver "peace." Once they forced those annoying civilian interlopers aside, they would unleash their planes against a small communist nation, break its leaders' will to endure, and deliver victory to a grateful America. It all seemed so enticing, so comparatively easier than a slogging ground war.

They knew the results would take time. Admiral U. S. G. Sharp, head of Pacific Command, acknowledged that bombing North Vietnam was a "campaign of pressure. Immediate and spectacular effects were not intended." Pilots would have to contend with harsh weather and, perhaps worse, civilian policymakers' restrictions on target selections. But Sharp and other airpower advocates also believed they had a war-winning weapon at their disposal. They could cut rail lines and destroy supply caches. They could interdict enemy forces infiltrating into South Vietnam. They could bomb fuel-storage sites and truck convoys and weaken the enemy's economy. Most importantly, they could demonstrate to the world that the United States would not tolerate communist aggression.[1]

With such an awesome display of strength, the disciples of airpower also would convince the Hanoi politburo that it could not win a war against a nation as powerful as the United States. They would deliver on the political goals of destroying North Vietnamese "will and capabilities." But muddled were those objectives on what airpower truly was supposed to achieve. To destroy the enemy's war-making capacity? To undermine northern morale? To stop infiltration along the Ho Chi Minh Trail? To prop up the Saigon regime? When Operation Rolling Thunder, the bombing campaign against North Vietnam, commenced in March 1965, neither the White House nor the Pentagon had reached any consensus. The airpower debate would continue for the remainder of America's war in Vietnam.[2]

While Rolling Thunder marked a clear escalation in Southeast Asia's Cold War, it also shone a harsh light on Americans' long-standing faith in airpower. Ever since World War II, air force leaders had sought to prove strategic bombing's war-winning merits, how they not only could deter America's enemies but coerce them into accepting defeat. Their long-standing faith that ground combat might not be necessary harkened back to the very first airpower theorists. To early military thinkers like Italian Giulio Douhet, writing in the immediate aftermath of World War I, the airplane afforded a warring nation "complete freedom of action and direction" and the ability to erase any and all distinctions between soldier and civilian. To Douhet, armed flight had triggered an "upheaval in the character of war."[3]

This was the faith that airpower enthusiasts took with them as they plunged into Vietnam. It didn't take long, however, for their assumptions to be found wanting. Only three weeks after Rolling Thunder began, White House advisors noted the situation in Vietnam was "bad and deteriorating." By April, the CIA reported that air strikes actually were hardening the enemy's attitude. One year later, Admiral Sharp admitted that the bombing campaign "did not apply adequate and steady pressure against the enemy." The enemy's "recuperative capability" had been "remarkable." Air Force General Curtis LeMay might have threatened that the United States would bomb North Vietnam "back into the Stone Age," but the results proved far less assuring. This despite some 643,000 tons of bombs dropped during Rolling Thunder alone, more than six times the amount dropped in the Pacific theater during all of World War II.[4]

What's more, faith in bombing's ability to end the war in Vietnam endured even when evidence revealed it was misplaced. President Johnson pushed back against this faith, bemoaning that his military commanders only knew how to "bomb, bomb, bomb." Indeed, his spring 1965 decision to send American ground combat troops into Vietnam hinted that the air campaign had failed. Even the combination of ground and air assets could not hide the fact that faith in airpower had been mislaid. Two years after US soldiers and marines landed in Vietnam, the Washington-based Institute of Defense Analysis found the bombing campaign against Hanoi had "not discernibly weakened the determination of the North Vietnamese leaders to continue to direct and support the insurgency in the South." As one air force command historian succinctly put it, the "American bombing of North Vietnam did not work."[5]

If some insiders questioned the efficacy of airpower theory in Vietnam, so too did those reporting on the war. *New York Times* correspondent Harrison Salisbury visited Hanoi in late 1966 and penned a series of widely read articles. Already a Pulitzer Prize–winning international reporter, Salisbury wrote from a position of authority, at least outside of Pentagon circles. What he found startled American readers. The bombing of North Vietnam had inflicted massive destruction upon Hanoi's residents, but that devastation had not translated into political progress. Nor had it dented the "fierce independence" of the North Vietnamese, who, as the journalist observed, had a "fighting tradition ... of struggle against long odds." Salisbury clearly sympathized with Hanoi inhabitants' plight, showcasing poor hotel waitresses forced to take up arms against attacking US aircraft. White House officials, meanwhile, were "furious" at the correspondent for circulating casualty statistics.[6]

Salisbury's reporting suggested how the psychological impacts of the US bombing campaign veered widely from theoretical assumptions. Worse, the international community increasingly condemned the United States for inflicting untold damage on a small Southeast Asian country, with some critics equating the air campaign to the atomic bombings of Hiroshima and Nagasaki. Even senior air force officers conceded the Hanoi politburo successfully was portraying the North "as a set-upon David fighting a bullyboy Goliath." When President Johnson declared a bombing halt in October 1968 in hopes of precipitating peace negotiations before the November election, he implied that airpower advocates' faith had been misplaced all along. Perhaps war wasn't the best tool to produce peace.[7]

On the campaign trail that fall, presidential candidate Richard M. Nixon hinted at his own secret plan to end the war, only sharing publicly that he didn't believe in a "purely military solution" in Vietnam. (McNamara had used those precise words back in 1964.) Privately, the California Republican held deep-seated fears that, if elected, Vietnam would keep him from refashioning the United States' larger Cold War relationships with the Soviet Union, and, perhaps most importantly, the People's Republic of China. In supporting Hanoi, the Soviets were encouraging "violent disorder rather than peaceful stability." Meanwhile, Beijing was attempting to shape the Vietnamese conflict's outcome for its own political advantages. Nixon might not believe a military victory possible in Vietnam, but he held faith in his ability to win the peace over his communist adversaries. He would exploit war to coerce or cajole the other side into accepting a settlement that served US interests.[8]

Nixon's stance toward Moscow and Beijing may have seemed ironic given his resumé as a political hardliner. He long had used fear as a weapon to demonstrate his Cold War credentials. Yet, in Nixon's view, only a true Cold Warrior could attempt his scheme for a historic undertaking with the communist bloc. Writing in *Foreign Affairs* in late 1967, the former vice president argued that Vietnam had "imposed severe strains on the United States, not only militarily and economically but socially and politically as well." The war there had become a millstone, keeping presidents from thinking more broadly. China could be dealt with better by bringing it "into the world community." Military power alone would not achieve this goal. Rather, the United States needed a "positive policy of pressure and persuading, of dynamic detoxification . . . to keep the peace and to help draw off the poison from the Thoughts of Mao." As the election neared, Nixon spoke increasingly of negotiating with the Soviets and of conversing with the Chinese. As James Reston reported that September, the candidate was even questioning "the advisability of future unilateral military intervention, even in the Western Hemisphere."[9]

Once in office, however, Nixon exposed his reliance on and faith in military power to extricate the United States from Vietnam with "honor." While "peace with honor" became a convenient political catchphrase for the Nixon White House, the term concealed the new president's dependence upon military might. Senior advisors may have abandoned the notion of war building a stable, independent South Vietnam, but they continued to view military force as a tool for achieving other policy objectives. Any precipitate withdrawal from Southeast Asia might call into question America's credibility on the world stage. In fact, "projecting resolve" seemed (always) far more important than securing Vietnamese independence. Only through war or the threat of war, Nixon surmised, could the United States achieve an honorable peace in Vietnam. Apparently, the president differed from the seventeenth-century French political writer Émeric Crucé, who had exclaimed, "What a miserable thing honor is if it has to be bought with bloodshed!"[10]

Perhaps brinkmanship and honor were not mutually reinforcing. Still, Nixon found utility in "excessive force" to get what he wanted. While some historians overplay the "madman theory"—the idea of persuading foreign leaders that Nixon was irrational and unpredictable and thus must not be needlessly provoked—the president maintained his faith in threatening the use of military force, including nuclear weapons. Hadn't Eisenhower ended the war in Korea, Nixon believed, thanks to nuclear saber-rattling? If Hanoi thought he "might do *anything* to stop the war," if they believed advisors couldn't "restrain him when he's angry," might they then sue for peace? After all, he did have "his hand on the nuclear button," didn't he? The challenge Nixon faced was making such madman threats credible. It seemed far-fetched that a US president would risk general nuclear war over a regional conflict in Southeast Asia. But that didn't stop Nixon or his national security advisor, Henry Kissinger, from threatening the Soviets with "dramatic" action if they continued supporting Hanoi.[11]

If Kissinger saw deterrence as a "psychological" problem, gambling on "irresponsibility" while engaging in "threats and counter-threats," Nixon found merit in direct coercive escalation. With little thought to long-term consequences, the administration authorized the "secret" bombing of Cambodia in March 1969, a sovereign and nominally neutral state, expanding a war it was trying to end. In relying on his air forces, Nixon, like Johnson before him, wanted to signal he would "go to almost any length to end the war quickly." The president even toyed with the idea of using nuclear weapons and in October placed the Strategic Air Command on a global nuclear alert. According to White House Chief of Staff H. R. Haldeman, Kissinger felt the nuclear-readiness test would serve as a "signal-type activity" to "jar the Soviets" and North Vietnam into negotiations. Apparently, the national security advisor thought there was a "good chance" of this "being the big break."[12]

While diplomatic breaks would not emerge for another three years, Nixon retained his faith in airpower, even as he lashed out against the US Air Force for not delivering the decisive blows he so desired. None of these early dalliances was a constructive use of military power. Yet Nixon returned to the same well again and again. Even long after the bulk of US combat troops had withdrawn from South Vietnam, the president would unleash his fury at the northern communists for their intransigence. In two air campaigns, Operations Linebacker I and II, Nixon affirmed that he had the power to destroy Hanoi's "war making capacity." Yet as US forces conducted at least 200 strikes a day against North Vietnam during these bombing campaigns, critics questioned their proportionality. A group of over forty religious leaders beseeched Nixon to immediately end the bombing. "Promised a generation of peace," they argued, "we have experienced not even one day of peace." Correspondent James Reston, one of the war's more insightful journalists, similarly derided the president for exercising "power without pity."[13]

Nixon's faith in military power, though, could not resolve fundamental political problems besetting the Saigon regime. Surely senior advisors overstated their case, as did one Johnson official, in arguing that South Vietnam was "a country with an army and no government." The South Vietnamese *were* engaged in deeper questions over national and political identities. They debated intensely over how much democracy or anticommunism should contribute to their political culture. Yet fundamental issues over the relationship between people and government remained unresolved. Nor did the massive display of American power convince the majority of southern Vietnamese to voluntarily throw their support behind the Nguyen Van Thieu regime. Rather, reporters blamed the unending political instability in Saigon for inhibiting military performance. Few considered how the long war may have bled southerners' popular will to resist Hanoi's bid for reunification.[14]

If military force failed to inspire political loyalties inside South Vietnam, Nixon found the same held true within the United States. Back home, the president's faith in military power to produce peace in Vietnam sat uneasily alongside personal fears that the antiwar movement was undercutting his larger aim of redefining Cold War superpower relations. Nixon might dismiss "campus radicals" and protesters as "bums"—compared to American soldiers who were "the greatest"—but the dissenters clearly weighed on the president and his inner circle. If the antiwar movement determined the endgame in Vietnam, the repercussions would be catastrophic. "If we yield," Kissinger exclaimed, "we're just inviting the Soviets into a confrontation." No wonder Nixon labeled student protesters, journalists, and other "liberals" as just a bunch of "bastards."[15]

The White House condemnation of the antiwar movement stemmed from long-held assumptions about power and credibility in the international arena. To Nixon's national security advisor—"a fundamentalist on America's duty to resist Communism in the world"—pulling the plug on South Vietnam would have dire consequences for US prestige around the world. Back in 1966, Kissinger had sung a similar tune, arguing how an "American withdrawal under conditions that could plausibly be represented as a Communist victory would be disastrous." Three years later, though, critics were growing weary of words like "honorable settlement" and "credibility." As the antiwar movement blossomed in the aftermath of the 1968 Tet offensive, many Americans became increasingly unclear what "victory" in Vietnam truly meant. Not Henry Kissinger, however. A year after Nixon took office, the former Harvard professor insisted the administration stay the course. "A nation needs many qualities," he argued, "but it needs faith and confidence above all."[16]

But confidence in combative Cold War policies was waning. And not just in America. As the 1960s limped to a close, long-standing tensions between faith and fear were being felt across the globe, amplifying the distrust young people held in their governments' moral authority. More and more social movements withheld their consent over destructive foreign policies. More and more willingly challenged a militaristic international order. National leaders, fearful of losing their grip on power amid growing unrest, tried to stabilize the situation and increasingly sought diplomatic compromise over military intimidation. The Cold War paradigm once more was shifting as new ideas of "détente" gained purchase from Washington to Moscow.[17]

What did the 1968 Prague Spring, for example, suggest for stability of the Cold War order? And not just for Soviet politburo members, but for other world leaders as well? When Alexander Dubček, the Czechoslovakian Communist Party's First Secretary, began repealing repressive measures to foster political reform, he set off a wave of nationalist and anticommunist fervor. Self-government seemed within reach. Not surprisingly, Polish and East German leaders worried about a "counter-revolution" igniting along their borders. The Moscow politburo equally feared an unraveling of its entire satellite system. Leonid Brezhnev, who had replaced Khrushchev in 1964, condemned Dubček for purveying "anti-Sovietism and anti-socialist ideas." But reformers, many taking to the streets, saw their duty as defending national sovereignty, not socialism. Soviet field armies prepared for cross-border operations. Europe once more seemed on the verge of war.[18]

In late August, a reluctant Brezhnev could countenance the challenge to Soviet leadership no longer. Unsure of NATO's reaction, he placed his missile forces on alert. Under directions from Moscow, the Warsaw Pact then invaded Czechoslovakia, one of its own members. Dubček decided not to challenge the invasion force, hoping to avoid the bloodshed Hungary had suffered back in 1956. The "rebellion" was short-lived, but the strategic implications reverberated. With Czech youth defiantly screaming at Soviet tanks in Prague streets, critics wondered if the threat of force seemed less compelling than it once did. From Beijing, Mao roasted the Soviets for acting like an imperial power. Albania withdrew from the Warsaw Pact a month later. In Washington, with a national election looming, policy specialists and military officers alike kept a wary eye on Europe, hoping the invasion would not spiral beyond Czech borders.[19]

Mimicking US presidents, Brezhnev decided to outline his own "doctrine" in hopes of avoiding future unrest along Russia's borders. In the Prague Spring's aftermath, he declared that socialist states within the Soviet orbit had only "limited sovereignty" and that Moscow retained the right of intervention to dismantle emerging threats. Yet Brezhnev wasn't just mirroring Americans' penchant for named doctrines. Like his US contemporaries, he too worried about "falling dominoes," though in Central Europe, not Southeast Asia. American critics might see the doctrine as proof of "Stalinism ascendent in Moscow" and fretted over where the new policy might lead Soviets forces to "hit next." But Brezhnev's reliance on the threat and use of force, seen differently, indicated that fear continued to drive superpower foreign policies.[20]

Such fears, however, worked to reduce tensions as much as they exacerbated them. By the late 1960s, Brezhnev knew perennially high military expenditures were taking their toll on the Russian economy. Perhaps the Cold War contest was not advancing the aims of Lenin and Marx. Perhaps reaching out to the West would offer more political and economic advantages than constant conflict. Nixon, too, felt these tensions as North Vietnamese leaders in Hanoi stubbornly resisted diplomatic overtures. These pressures, both domestic and global, thus informed how Washington and Moscow reconsidered the ways in which war correlated to a stable state of peace. Whether regionally, from Southeast Asia to Central Europe, or with regard to nuclear weapons, perhaps the Cold War competition needed a political, if not philosophical, transformation.[21]

Such aspirations were hardly new. Back in the mid-1950s, British military theorist Basil Liddell Hart defined strategy as a sort of dialectic between war and peace. Speaking on national policy objectives and military aims, he maintained that the "object in war" should be a "better state of peace." This was particularly important for grand strategists. As Liddell Hart argued, it was "essential to conduct war with constant regard to the peace you desire." George Kennan agreed. Writing in the Cold War's final decade, the senior US diplomat noted that war should be more than just a "matter of destruction, brutalization, and sacrifice." Senior policymakers and uniformed officers must ensure that any "military victory" was but a "prerequisite for some further and more positive achievement." War, in short, should lead to peace, not more war.[22]

As we'll see, though, détente never had a fighting chance. Any faith in war's capacity for producing peaceful relations between superpowers foundered as both sides feared the other might be taking advantage of thawing international relations. Ideology remained wedded to geopolitical outlooks. Military competition endured in the Third World. So too did the nuclear arms race, despite genuine attempts at imposing limitations. All the while, hawkish critics in Moscow and Washington leveled charges of appeasement against their leaders. Peace might be enticing, but fear ultimately proved central to détente's untenable position.[23]

CHAPTER 13

Managing Détente

Richard Nixon entered office with a conviction that the People's Republic of China, given its size and regional influence, must actively participate in the global community. True, there were deep ideological differences between the two nations. But as one administration official remarked, US foreign policy should be aimed at bringing "China out of its angry, alienated shell." Less true were attendant arguments that the United States wasn't seeking "to exploit for our own advantage the hostility between the Soviet Union and Communist China." Behind closed doors, that's exactly what Nixon and Kissinger were pursuing. Thus, a relaxing of Sino-American tensions offered a unique opportunity. If the president could help integrate China into the "world community" without seeming to abandon Taiwan, he might further drive a wedge between Moscow and Beijing, all to the advantage of the United States.[1]

A Sino-Soviet split long had been brewing, its origins dating back to the late 1950s. Even if the relationship between the two powers remained an "enigma" to western analysts, there were hints of discord in the communist camp throughout the following decade. Mao had publicly lashed out against Khrushchev for his lack of leadership in the Third World, for his mishandling of the Berlin Crisis, and for his broken pledge to support Castro's Cuba. By Nixon's inauguration, it was clear Moscow and Beijing were at loggerheads over nearly every aspect of their foreign policies—from competing revolutionary models for the Global South to negotiations over nuclear-weapons limitations. Whether the

Americans could take advantage of this friction remained to be seen, but the prospects enticed Nixon nonetheless.[2]

The new president sensed that Washington's policy elite had been slow to appreciate the potential implications of this split, in part because fear had encouraged them to visualize the communist threat as a monolithic one. Clearly, that wasn't the case, as Mao increasingly aired in public his grievances against Moscow. The Soviets, Beijing leveled, had been guilty of "great-power chauvinism." Not surprisingly, China's leadership deemed Maoist policies the archetype of communism that others should follow. All the while, insecurities abounded over an unfavorable international system brought about by Moscow's arrogant misapplication of traditional Marxist-Leninist thought.[3]

By the late 1960s, the Sino-Soviet split no longer could remain hidden. American newspapers, with a bit of dramatic flair, began speaking of the two communist powers divided by "an unbridgeable, indissoluble hatred" that had reached a "pitch of intensity surpassing anything ever experienced between Russia and the West." The split, American readers learned, resulted from a "compound of ideology, nationalism, fear, racial hatred, contempt, folk memory, [and] historical grievances." Here, then, were the "makings of a classical balance of power situation." If the United States reached an understanding with China, it might gain an advantage over its chief rival, the Soviet Union. Given such a cataclysmic fracturing within the communist camp, no wonder Nixon and Kissinger believed they had a chance at altering the dynamics of the Cold War international system.[4]

Just as enticing, the White House might be able to use the Sino-Soviet split as a leverage point for exerting pressure on Hanoi and ending the stalemated Vietnamese war. If editorials were true, even in the slightest, that Kremlin leaders were considering a "preventive war against China," then might not it be possible to exploit these ruptures to safely withdraw American troops from Southeast Asia? Might the United States benefit from the chaos if it played ball with China? Such a reconsideration of US policy—not just for Vietnam but for the entire Cold War—intimated that ideology, which itself had inspired so much fear throughout the years, might not be as important to international relations as previously considered. Fighting an "abstract crusade" against communism, as Nixon called it, no longer made sense.[5]

The president's surprising lack of ideological rigidity meant, to some, that a foreign policy based on "realism" had returned to White House thinking. Under Nixon, the United States would act to serve national interests, not to embark upon ideological crusades. Yet even as critics questioned the price to be paid for better relations with Beijing and Moscow, we should ask if the emerging ideas of détente differed all that much from past policies. Were Nixon and Kissinger any more "realist" than their predecessors? All previous Cold War presidents had reacted to communist threats with a fluctuating mix of conciliation and coercion. All had struggled with distinguishing vital interests from peripheral ones, with balancing realism and anticommunism inside a larger containment framework. And, notably, the Nixon White House retained a penchant for "artificially" inflating the stakes while still viewing the Cold War conflict as a zero-sum game. Détente may have departed from past tactics, but the long-standing pillars of US grand strategy remained secure.[6]

Of course, defining détente was no easy task. Nixon hoped to answer a basic yet far-reaching question: with the United States no longer shackled to a questionable client state in Southeast Asia, what were its grand strategic aims? Perhaps entering into an "era of negotiation," as the president called it, might provide some answers. Yet the strategic course alteration entailed multiple undertakings—withdrawing responsibly from Vietnam, limiting the arms race, inducing the communist powers to act with more restraint, maintaining US economic access across the globe, and restoring domestic faith in the government's national security agenda. All the while, the nation had to safeguard its predominant military might lest potential enemies assume the United States had lost its war-fighting edge.[7]

Détente, however, also could be seen as a reaction to fears of America losing its place within a changing international system. The Soviet Union had embarked upon a massive nuclear-arms buildup after the

Cuban Missile Crisis. China appeared intent on becoming more than just a regional actor. Nixon worried about the United States becoming a "second-rate power" thanks to its decline from World War II pre-eminence. Of course, the enduring stalemate in Vietnam didn't help matters, as the White House fretted daily about the nation's eroding credibility on the world stage. Détente, then, might help maintain the status quo, a conservative grand strategy sustaining a world order in which the United States preserved its power and influence.[8]

Fear, of course, worked both ways. Conservatives in Nixon's own party, driven by personal and political anxieties, accused the president of giving away the store, of not preparing for the next global war. Democrats like Washington Senator Henry "Scoop" Jackson equally slammed Nixon, styling US-Soviet détente as a "formula between governments for capitulation on the issue of human rights." Conservative reactions to Nixon's larger policies, though, hit closer to home as they once more echoed cries of appeasement. In 1971, conservative political commentator William F. Buckley, Jr. wondered aloud of President Nixon, "Is he one of us?" No doubt an intrinsically suspicious Nixon felt betrayed by such insinuations. Yet Republicans would return to a similar refrain in the 1980s as Reagan began negotiations with Gorbachev over reducing nuclear weapons. Peace, it seemed, could be as frightening as war.[9]

With tensions still simmering in Eastern Europe after the Prague Spring and the war in Southeast Asia enduring with no end in sight, perhaps it wasn't surprising that contemporaries pondered what "détente" really meant. After decades of fearmongering himself, no wonder Nixon found it difficult to convince Americans that negotiating with evil communists was in the United States' best interest. Why were Americans even talking about détente, Senator Barry Goldwater asked, when the chance of World War III was becoming "more probable by the month" thanks to the "Soviet Union's determined drive to become more powerful in all areas of military endeavor"?[10]

The Arizona senator's displeasure revealed fundamental anxieties about the nation's relationship with war and peace. Had America's faith in war been misplaced all along if the president was seeking to normalize relations with the communist camp? If Kissinger still believed the Soviets were "brutal bastards," then why was the White House entertaining discussions with them over nuclear-arms limitations? To critics like Goldwater, détente endangered a Cold War security structure founded upon confrontation between two opposing ideologies. Expansionist communism supposedly drove global conflict, the dark heart of an existential battle between good and evil. If Nixon no longer believed that, then the fundamental rationale for fighting in places like Vietnam collapsed in on itself.[11]

Détente, of course, did not mean peace or even an end to armed conflict. The policy inspired no profound departure from long-held assumptions about the meaning or goals of communism. Instead, Nixon and Kissinger wished to relax and manage international tensions even as antagonisms between the United States and the communist camp endured. The challenge facing policymakers, then, was defining the meaning of security in this potentially new era of cooperative competition. Left unstated in nearly all these conversations was an uncomfortable proposition: détente meant there might be limits to American military power overseas.[12]

Not that Nixon didn't try to wield that power. In 1970, he authorized a military "incursion" into Cambodia, ostensibly to protect the gradual withdrawal of US troops from Vietnam that had begun the year prior. In 1971, he returned to his military handbook with a similar operation into Laos. Both offensives showcased how Nixon continued to believe in war's utility, even if "military victory alone" could not solve America's problems in Vietnam. As in the past, however, faith and fear intertwined. Nixon assumed an expansion of the war would shorten it, yet also worried about the consequences of inaction. As he explained his Cambodia decision to the American people, "If we fail to meet this challenge, all other nations will be on notice that despite its overwhelming power the United States, when a real crisis comes, will be found wanting." The president conveniently remained silent on the misery these new wars were inflicting upon the peoples of Cambodia and Laos.[13]

If Nixon believed these forays outside of South Vietnam's borders would hasten the war's end, he had company. During the long conflict and after, military activists imagined that both ground and air offensives, like the 1972 Christmas bombing of North Vietnam, had helped deliver the Paris Peace Accords. Few considered that the Hanoi politburo, under Le Duan's firm control, feared Soviet and Chinese diplomatic isolation more than American bombs. Despite the middling performance of US air forces in Vietnam, the 1973 peace process only reinforced airpower champions' faith that an earlier victory was possible if only they had been unleashed. As Admiral U. S. Grant Sharp seethed in his postwar memoirs, civilian policymakers had made decisions out of "flagrant arrogance" while committing the United States to a "restrained approach of gradualism." War produced peace, Sharp argued, only when professional managers of violence were allowed to do their jobs.[14]

Yet Nixon's bid at "opening" China—the president called it "containment without isolation"—connoted that there might be limits to what military men like Sharp could achieve on the global stage. Rather, the United States must tolerate what Nixon and Kissinger deemed were "profound ideological differences" while finding a balance between cooperation and conflict. Of course, US policymakers retained their long-held fears when it came to China's potential, both military and economic, dating back to at least the Korean War. But fear also inspired Beijing to rethink its relationship with the West. China's security situation had diminished in recent years, thanks to border clashes with India in 1962 and, more foreboding, with the Soviet Union in 1969. The latter incident involved a bloody conflict between garrison forces on Zhenbao Island and even elicited fears of a nuclear exchange between the two communist giants.[15]

When Nixon famously visited China in February 1972, détente seemingly had realized the president's long-term goals of reshaping the Cold War international system. In one sense, the president's aim of driving a wedge between the two communist powers worked. Real were Soviet fears of Sino-American diplomatic relations, of Moscow once more being encircled by hostile forces. Brezhnev agonized that Washington would use China as an "anti-Soviet blade." Yet the Kremlin also was seeking a relaxation of tensions, eyeing a strained economy barely capable of sustaining exorbitant defense expenditures while simultaneously addressing domestic social priorities. If Nixon envisioned détente as preserving the status quo, so too Brezhnev, who saw emerging global threats as challenging Soviet authority. Fear was leading both Washington and Moscow toward a more cooperative relationship.[16]

Ignoring accusations that he was "yielding" to the communist camp, Nixon followed his China visit with a dramatic summit meeting in Moscow. At the first night's banquet, the Soviet leadership spoke of a "radical turn toward relaxation," while the president declared his hopes of making "peaceful cooperation a reality." From the *Washington Post*, Murrey Marder spied a "new, fluid pattern of world relations now in play among the United States, China and the Soviet Union." A chance for peace appeared enticingly within reach. And yet more sober assessments warned Americans to manage their expectations. Walter Laqueur of the Center for Strategic and International Studies, a Washington-based think tank, noted how Nixon and Brezhnev had committed themselves to avoiding collisions between the two superpowers. "But," he warned, "they have been unable to reach agreement on almost any other topic of basic importance."[17]

True, the summit failed to end the ongoing conflict in Vietnam. Nor would it prevent a new war in the Middle East the following year. Laqueur equally doubted that progress would come from a historic proposal to limit nuclear arms. At the Moscow Summit, both sides signed an interim agreement coming out of these Strategic Arms Limitation Talks (SALT). The arrangement set limits on the deployment of intercontinental and submarine-launched ballistic-missile systems, though it imposed no constraints on strategic bombers or cruise missiles. SALT also limited the number of sites protected by antiballistic missiles, though debate continued over how best to manage multiple-warhead weapons systems. The nuclear arms race had generated a dense lexicon all its own, making high-level discussions a technical matter as much as a strategic one.[18]

The negotiations leading to SALT highlighted how assumptions about, if not faith in, nuclear deterrence theories held firm after more than a quarter of a century. Hoping to keep pace with evolving technologies, specialists in Moscow and Washington aimed for stability within the nuclear arms race to avoid general war. Both sides sought "parity" for fear that any real or perceived disadvantage might provoke the other to consider a first strike. Both sides looked to define strategic "sufficiency" within their nuclear arsenals. And both sides distrusted the other to meet their treaty obligations. If arms control claimed to be a centerpiece of détente, doubts and fears over accurately evaluating enemy strength punctured Nixon's hopes of reshaping the Cold War paradigm.[19]

These fears emanated from home as much as from abroad. Once more, conservative critics unleashed their fury on the administration. William Buckley fumed at the president for "sitting in the White House while the Soviet Union is accumulating a first strike capability." Resurrecting earlier Cold War rhetoric, the *Firing Line* host accused Nixon of taking a "soft line" against Moscow. (Buckley equally judged the China opening a "staggering capitulation.") The criticism would outlast Nixon's tenure in the White House, with one virulently anticommunist interest group, the Committee on the Present Danger, claiming in 1977 that Washington had agreed to "unequal compromises unfavorable to the United States." Of course, neither side had committed to any agreement undermining their ability to conduct nuclear strikes, meaning that faith in and fear of nuclear weapons still held sway among superpower leaders.[20]

Critics like Buckley might have been on firmer ground if they had interrogated what Nixon truly meant by "détente." Washington and Moscow clearly disagreed on its meaning, portending problems for sustaining Nixon's efforts. The White House hoped to maintain the international status quo as the war in Vietnam cut into US credibility and prestige. In the Kremlin, however, Soviet leaders saw détente as a means to contain, if not control, competition with the United States, especially in the arena of nuclear weapons. Both capitals may have viewed the policy as a tool for thawing Cold War relations, but neither saw détente as an alternative to preparing for war against the other.[21]

Nor, as we have seen, was the domestic reaction to détente any less contested. The breaking of the Watergate office wiretapping story in late 1972 would muddy the foreign-policy waters and, according to the president's devotees, undermine the full realization of Nixon's visionary policy initiatives. Kissinger, for one, lamented how the White House's "political and moral authority" had been undermined by the sordid affair. Congressional critics, emboldened by a weakened executive branch, amplified their cries against an "immoral" and "inhumane" policy. Yet blaming Watergate for détente's demise overstates. Domestic attacks may have hurt Nixon's credibility as political opponents sensed blood in the water, but any policy resting on cooperation with evil communists likely had a limited American shelf life as soon as it was pronounced.[22]

While domestic politics helped weaken détente, so too did world events. Thawing superpower relations took place at a time of increasing violence in the Global South, validating claims that preparing for war still mattered in a dangerous world. As just one example, a crisis in South Asia showcased for many fearful Americans the limits of rapprochement with China. Back in March 1971, Pakistan's Yahya Khan had brutally suppressed a separatist movement in the largely Bengali region of East Pakistan. The US consul general in Dacca, Archer Blood, reported back on the atrocities while American officials recalled bodies being stacked in public spaces. In August, Senator Edward M. Kennedy (D-MA) visited refugee camps along the Indian border and denounced Pakistan's military action as "an outrage to every concept of international law." Nixon and Kissinger, however, resisted calls for US intervention into what they deemed a civil war, regardless of the bloodshed. But when Indian troops began massing along the East Pakistan border, fears abounded of an escalating war that might draw the United States into yet another regional conflict. Any pacific ideas underlying détente seemed frightfully wanting.[23]

Moreover, the Cold War's grip remained firm. Nixon hesitated to criticize Pakistan, a SEATO member, as Yahya had helped open secret negotiations with China. Now was not the time to risk jeopardizing an improving relationship with Beijing. (Kissinger saw the conflict as a "Soviet-Indian power play to humiliate the Chinese and also somewhat us.") India felt otherwise. Fearing a Sino-American-Pakistani "encirclement," New Delhi leaned toward Moscow, signing a friendship treaty in September. If détente led to this kind of chaos, perhaps a continuing faith in war was justified. With death tolls mounting until the signing of a July 1972 treaty, Kissinger fretted over a "complete collapse of the world's psychological balance of power." It would not be the last time that the United States placed geopolitical interests above humanitarian ones.[24]

Even Jimmy Carter, who entered the White House in early 1977, would struggle to reprioritize American interests outside the Cold War paradigm. Despite détente's breakdown, Carter hoped to emphasize human rights over war as a centerpiece of US foreign policy. Four years later he would leave Washington disappointed, with an increasing defense budget and an international environment as dangerous as any time during the Cold War. And, like Nixon, he too had turned away from intervening in a genocide, this one in Cambodia, where the Khmer Rouge ravaged the countryside and murdered some 1.7 million of its own people out of a population of seven million. As would be the case throughout much of the Cold War, Washington elite struggled with the tensions between human rights as an aspirational principle and an endorsed policy because intervention usually meant war.[25]

Yet White House officials feared more than just genocidal acts as détente came under fire in the early 1970s. Broadly, senior policymakers worried that continuing, even escalating, violence in South and Southeast Asia exposed the limits of imposing US will on local actors. Not even the UN could "make nations behave," according to one editorialist, thus leaving the United States to deal with "miniwars and maximurders" across Africa and Asia. Nor had Washington elite fully grasped the implications of what the wars in Vietnam, Cambodia, and Laos had wrought. Would the credibility of the United States be irretrievably damaged? Were the US armed forces capable of deterring future communist aggression given their mixed performance in Vietnam? Such questions resonated as civil wars engulfed Ethiopia, Angola, and parts of Central America.²⁶

Indeed, détente coincided with episodes of intense violence across the globe, most notably in Latin America. If Nixon aspired to ease tensions with Moscow and Beijing, he had no such intentions for Havana or Santiago. When the reformist Salvador Allende won an electoral victory in Chile in 1970, the White House fearfully equated the voting results to Castro's Cuban revolution. Once more, the hemisphere seemed under communist assault, forcing the United States, in the mind of one senior US official, into "a mortal struggle to determine the shape of the future of the world." Yet as in Guatemala two decades earlier, reality proved far more intricate. Allende sought to nationalize the Chilean copper industry, to restructure the state economy, and to reduce the US dominance over Chile's internal affairs. Castro might crow how the election demonstrated the power of Cuban influence, but Allende was far from a red-dyed, international communist. Not surprisingly, the White House saw the voting differently, with Nixon ordering the CIA to devise a plan to "save Chile."²⁷

Thus, while promoting détente with China and the Soviet Union, Nixon returned to traditional Cold War methods in Latin America. Almost inexorably, deliberations began about a possible US-supported coup against the Allende government. The White House would not stand idly by while a Marxist government came to power, even via free elections, in its own backyard. As in years past, senior policymakers viewed communism as an infective contaminant. American military dollars accordingly streamed into Chile, and an American credit blockade aimed to destabilize the Chilean economy. CIA operatives increased their disinformation campaign and began planning for a military coup. Nixon wanted "no stone unturned" to depose Allende.²⁸

The Chilean president, however, was no Soviet or Cuban puppet, and Moscow had few designs on the Western Hemisphere at this time. While Nixon, who tended to hold Latin Americans in contempt, instructed the CIA to make the "economy scream," such intentions rested on little more than old-fashioned fears of global communism. Kissinger threw in a dash of hubris, just for good measure. The national security advisor thought the United States should not have to "stand by and watch a country go Communist due to the irresponsibility of its own people." Under such external pressure and facing political and economic challenges at home—many of them US-inspired—Allende could last only so long. On 11 September 1973, a military coup under Augusto Pinochet seized power in Santiago. Allende lay dead by his own hand rather than submit to the general. For the next seventeen years, Chile would suffer under a brutal and bloody dictatorship.[29]

This US interventionism in Latin America intimated that détente, as a theory, had its limits. Thawing relations with the communist camp extended only so far. Otherwise, the United States, in Kissinger's words, might risk "appearing indifferent or impotent" if containment appeared to be wavering. The Chilean coup also highlighted Washington's penchant for mendaciousness. Publicly, CIA director William W. Colby denied the agency's direct role, only allowing that the United States had looked "forward to a change in government, but through Democratic elections by political forces." In private, the national security advisor proved more forthcoming, sharing with Nixon that it was an "absurd situation where we have to apologize for the overthrow of ... a government hostile to us." If the United States had to destabilize another country to appear strong, then so be it.[30]

A mixture of faith and fear underlay both the public lies and the private candor. At his political core, Nixon fretted that America might be squandering its greatness and thus stomached dictators like Pinochet to sustain US influence abroad. Like so many of his predecessors, he feared the "poison" of communism that was crippling the Western Hemisphere, if left untreated, might "infect" the United States. He wasn't alone. Observers worried the United States was "losing" Latin America, that radicals and revolutionaries were seeking a "breakaway" from the US sphere of influence. Thus, the enduring faith in armed might and covert activity, as both Nixon and Kissinger surmised that communists solely respected "power and strength." Only through war and the threat of war could the White House successfully manage détente.[31]

The lagging US economy of the early 1970s, however, cast doubt upon America's capacity to wield raw power on a global scale. The Nixon Doctrine, if not détente as a whole, therefore might be seen as an attempt not only to "de-ideologize" the Cold War, but also to hide the limits of American military power abroad while maintaining the international status quo. Nixon aimed to be subtle. At a July 1969 press conference on Guam, the president outlined plans to offload Asian defense responsibilities onto regional allies. Nixon stressed "self-reliance" while emphasizing that the United States would stand by its treaty commitments. The president would extend economic support to allies, but American combat troops now were off the table. Burden sharing and cost-saving measures clearly motivated the president's new doctrine. Yet so too did the goal of "avoiding future Vietnams."[32]

Faith in regional policemen became an important corollary of the Nixon Doctrine. In the Middle East, for instance, the president strengthened relations with Mohammad Reza Pahlavi, the Shah of Iran, selling him US weapons, advanced fighter aircraft, and helicopters, all for the professed goal of containing Soviet advances. Saudi Arabia equally boosted its defense spending. The American arms industry reveled in the earnings bonanza. Whether such an influx of military hardware into an already volatile region provided stability seems doubtful. Local matters, like the persistent Arab-Israeli conflict, usually eclipsed America's Cold War priorities, while leaders like Pahlavi exploited the Nixon Doctrine to lobby for more and more weapons. All along, Nixon's new foreign-policy statement masked Washington's fears that US military forces were not large enough for the nation's "global defense responsibilities."[33]

If Nixon and Kissinger retained their faith in American military power even as they engaged in burden sharing with regional allies, the stability they sought eluded them. The reasons were not hard to find. Regional actors, from southern Africa to Latin America, continued to trust in war to deliver on their political promises. Under the threat of direct superpower intervention, local leaders saw military might as vital to retaining their influence and achieving independence in the postcolonial world. During the Angolan civil war of the mid-1970s, for example, rival nationalist groups competed for political dominance over each other and against external intrusion from the Soviet Union, the United States, and even Cuba. Hardly surprising, Americans fretted over communist intervention in Angola, sparking anxieties of yet another continent being dominated by leftist forces. No wonder political columnist William Safire argued at the end of 1975 that détente was "dead" and the "Second Cold War" was under way.[34]

Had the détente experiment altered America's relationship with war? Perhaps, but arguably only at the margins and only temporarily. Nixon's approach might best be viewed as an evolution of containment doctrine, a slight drawing back from the reflexive anticommunism that had guided his predecessors. But the president and his national security advisor never lost their faith in war, even as the failure in Vietnam became clear. Both Nixon and Kissinger continued to view the world as a dangerous place in which only a strong America could survive. Détente might soften tensions with the communist camp, but the policy never could eradicate Moscow and Beijing's designs for global domination. If Nixon truly believed "the greatest honor history can bestow is the title of peacemaker," he also held a deep faith in war's role for achieving peace.[35]

CHAPTER 14

War for Peace?

"Lasting peace." "Peace with honor." "Peace at any price." As the American war in Vietnam limped to its unsatisfying conclusion, Americans spoke of peace almost as much as war. They hoped the Paris Peace Accords of 1973 finally might close a dark chapter in their nation's military history. They anticipated a new era in which the scars of a bloody foreign war might heal. A time when the United States might repair its self-image and regain its sense of purpose and global influence. A time to recommit to the nation's prosperity at home rather than military promises abroad. And yet, with the ink still damp on the Paris peace documents, the US president already was speaking publicly of the need to remain "strong militarily." Only strength, Nixon argued, would inspire "the trust of our allies and the respect of our potential adversaries in the world."[1]

There was a problem, however, with the president's calculations. In Vietnam's wake, the entire military-industrial complex had come under fire, with some critics alleging corporate profits had trumped drafted soldiers' lives in an immoral overseas war. Nixon, ever the politician, moved to check his opposition and initiated a policy ending military conscription and introducing an all-volunteer force in July 1973. His hopes of relying on a "strong" military, though, ostensibly were dashed as the army failed to meet its recruitment goals that first summer. By most accounts, the war in Vietnam had damaged Americans' faith in war, if not fatally, at least momentarily.[2]

A shaky faith in war did not mean that Americans were reflecting all that deeply upon their disappointing crusade in Southeast Asia. It was far easier to cast blame elsewhere than to examine one's own shortcomings. One popular refrain, for instance, charged that America's putative "allies" had been unreliable in the global fight against communism, that South Vietnam's government and armed forces were to blame for US failures. Scapegoating became a national pastime. Even before the fall of Saigon in April 1975, senior US military officers were claiming they could have achieved victory had it not been for a host of incompetent, if not malicious, actors: unpatriotic antiwar activists, weak-kneed US civilian policymakers, corrupt Saigon officials, or an uncommitted South Vietnamese population. If war didn't produce, it wasn't the fault of the US armed forces.[3]

Of course, such parochial arguments worked both ways. To at least some South Vietnamese, the US withdrawal from Vietnam suggested that it was the Americans who were unreliable allies, that placing faith in them had been fraught with risk because the Americans would desert erstwhile friends as soon as the relationship no longer suited the great benefactor. As one Vietnamese-born American observed, "Sixteen years of fighting had reduced the war to a troublesome liability." Senior policymakers like Nixon might appeal to honor and pride and loyalty when articulating US commitments abroad, but those words tended to ring hollow as American troops returned home with little to show for their sacrifices.[4]

Ten months after the signing of the Paris Peace Accords, war returned with a vengeance, this time in the Middle East. We must digress briefly, however, and retrace our steps back to 1967. That year the superpowers were drawn into the region by a war that hardened the lines between Israel and its Arab neighbors. While Israeli generals pressed for an expansion of their borders for security purposes, an increasingly radical Syria called for the "liquidation" of the Jewish state. As an Arab alliance took shape, Washington fell back on traditional Cold War fears. National Security Advisor Walt Rostow, for example, worried that "radical states and their Soviet backers" were going to "dominate" the Middle East if left unchecked. For both Arabs and Israelis, though, land seemed more important than peace. When Egypt's Nasser announced a blockade of Israeli shipping through the Straits of Tiran, all while trumpeting Arab solidarity, the region lurched toward full-scale war.[5]

In early June 1967, Israel decided it no longer could await an Arab blow and launched its air forces against Egyptian bases, destroying most of Nasser's fighter jets while still grounded. Syria and Jordan also joined the fray, only to have their air arms thrashed as well. From the White House, President Johnson opposed these preemptive strikes but stood by his ally as Israeli tanks and mechanized units rumbled into the Sinai and Gaza. Within six days, the war was over, with Israel having defeated three regional adversaries in quick fashion. Nasser's vision of Pan-Arabism lay in ruins. Beijing once more spit venom at Moscow for allowing the defeat of Arab allies by imperialist forces. A relieved Johnson welcomed the ceasefire, thankful the United States did not need to tackle another conflict with the war in Vietnam still boiling. Any hopes of a lasting reconciliation between Israel and its neighbors, though, were dashed as the Six-Day War ended.[6]

What followed the 1967 conflict hardly encouraged peace advocates. Israeli Prime Minster Levi Eshkol claimed that his country wanted "nothing but to live peacefully in our territory," but his conflation of civilian refugees with enemy "infiltrators" belied such pacific statements. Nasser committed himself to regaining Egypt's lost territory and prepared his citizens for another round of fighting. "That which was taken by force," he declared, "will be returned by force." Under pressure from China and Arab client states alike, the Soviet Union increased its military aid, prompting the United States to respond in kind. Perhaps worst of all, Israel leaned into its role as an occupying power, imposing harsh policies on Palestinian residents, forcing many into exile and an embrace of guerrilla tactics to fight back against their expulsion from the West Bank and Gaza Strip. War clearly was not inspiring a better state of peace that Liddell Hart had envisioned.[7]

The Palestinians' armed resistance corresponded with a rising sense of national consciousness, nourishing the roots of future conflict.

Diplomacy seemed increasingly ineffective. For every Palestinian home it bulldozed or family it exiled, Israel appeared more and more a "settler-colonial project" than an example of democracy in the Middle East. Nervous US policymakers worried that their regional ally might become a strategic liability rather than asset as the Soviets increasingly backed their Arab partners. Of course, an insatiable appetite for Middle East oil factored into Americans' thinking, even if they shrouded their lubricated desires under the category of "geostrategic concerns."[8]

Ultimately, these regional pressures would lead to another conflict in 1973, just as Nixon was hoping to put the war in Vietnam behind him. Once more, deterrence revealed its limits. Once more, fears of an escalating war drawing in the superpowers gripped the American home front. Once more, Soviet leaders seemed bent on a policy of "expansionist détente" that minimized those seeking a Cold War thaw. And once more, statesmen—this time Nasser, who hoped a new round of fighting might inspire the superpowers to initiate peace talks and force Israel to return occupied portions of the Sinai Peninsula and reopen the Suez Canal—placed their faith in war.[9]

The resulting October 1973 Yom Kippur War made plain combat's fickle nature. War rarely is a precise tool for achieving such exacting policy objectives as Nasser and his successor, Anwar Sadat, intended. When Egyptian and Syrian forces surged across the Suez Canal and into the Golan Heights, the Israelis bent under the pressure but did not break. The fighting soon devolved into a slugfest, as both the United States and Soviet Union rushed military reinforcements into the war-torn region. Israeli officers recalled facing a "forest of missiles" and participating in "simply bloody fighting." American officials admitted the war was taking a "heavy toll" on their allies, the combat so violent that it inspired the US Army to reform its doctrine and equipment for fear of not being able to compete on a modern, conventional battlefield.[10]

More frightening than the tactical bloodbath was fear of the war "getting out of hand," as Kissinger, now secretary of state, put it. Pentagon officials worried Israel might resort to nuclear weapons rather than accept defeat by the Arab coalition. Others in Washington realized the difficulties of restraining independent-minded local allies, with Israel stonewalling talks over a negotiated settlement until battlefield fortunes returned. Kissinger, meanwhile, hoped to end the fighting in a way that offered few, if any, political advantages to the Soviet Union. Apparently, as in Latin America, détente did not extend to the Middle East. Nor was Kissinger all that concerned with the fate of displaced Palestinians, leaving a major political issue unresolved and ripe for war's return.[11]

If the settlement ending the October War intimated that détente had passed a key test thanks to US-Soviet mediation, Americans at home hardly reaped the rewards. During the conflict, the Organization of the Petroleum Exporting Countries (OPEC) punished the United States for its support of Israel by embargoing oil shipments to the West. Worldwide prices per barrel skyrocketed. Critics slammed the Arab states for using oil as a "weapon," setting the stage for an elevated, and then perpetual, American presence in the Middle East. Not surprisingly, Arab public opinion soured on the United States, whose vast military expenditures had kept Israel in the fight. The rising anti-American sentiment would hit a crescendo in Iran by decade's end, but for now a more immediate fear gripped policymakers back in Washington. Both the Arab-Israeli conflict and the ensuing oil crisis stoked widespread anxieties that America's military power was proving incapable of delivering the global influence and national prosperity that Nixon so desired.[12]

While the Americans suffered through an oil embargo and an energy crisis, Siberian crude helped the Soviet Union cushion the oil shock's effects and underwrite plans for an ongoing military buildup. A few voices within the State Department raised concern over the United States' growing dependence on the Middle East, yet they were drowned out as Americans lashed out against what they saw as Arab perfidy. As in the cases of Iran and Guatemala in the 1950s, whenever local leaders nationalized their own natural resources, Americans cried foul and envisioned a global communist plot to seal off vital markets from US access.[13]

In the end, fears of growing Soviet influence in the Middle East—and across the globe—disincentivized Americans from tackling the root causes of conflict that may have led to peace. Their regional allies didn't help matters. As historian Jonathan House rightly argues, the Israelis "continued to seek military solutions to what was fundamentally a political question—the future of the Palestinians." Occupation of land became far more important to the Israelis than seeking peace. What followed, perhaps inescapably, was a superpower arms race that only further militarized an already unstable region of the globe.[14]

With the oil shock still reverberating, the final collapse of Saigon in April 1975 landed another blow upon frustrated Americans still seeking some reckoning from their failed Southeast Asian war. Mostly, they turned inward, viewing the sordid affair as an "*American* tragedy" rather than a Vietnamese one. For just a moment, armed conflict lost its luster in the jungles and rice paddies of South Vietnam. And yet hints of an enduring faith in war weren't hard to find. Predictably, Secretary of Defense James R. Schlesinger stressed that his fellow citizens must decide, "even with our disappointments of the Vietnam war," whether "we are going to maintain our position in the world and provide the necessary strengths for a worldwide military equilibrium." Any dreams of quitting the habit of war evidently remained overly optimistic.[15]

So how were Americans grappling with their first "lost" war? Not well. Public trust in government waned, especially after the Watergate scandal forced Nixon to resign from office in August 1974. Popular culture depicted returning Vietnam veterans as dangerous malcontents, psychologically damaged from their combat experiences. Washington elite fretted over the seemingly irreparable damage done to US interests throughout Asia. Military officers wondered why their supposed tactical victories had not led to strategic success. If hard fighting did not produce victory, then what was the point of war? Similar questions would loom large in the aftermath of America's future wars in Iraq and Afghanistan.[16]

Still coming to grips with Saigon's fall, the White House, now occupied by Gerald R. Ford, suffered another indignation when Khmer Rouge naval units seized the US cargo ship *Mayaguez* off the coast of Cambodia. Could it be that the United States really was a "paper tiger," as Mao had scoffed so long ago? The new president decided to act rather than suffer recriminations of weakness. Deploying a marine reaction force on a daring rescue mission, Ford assured the nation that it still had the "power and will" to protect its regional interests. Before the marines arrived, however, the Cambodian government released the *Mayaguez* crew. Worse, the subsequent raid on Cambodian territory needlessly cost 41 American lives. *Time* magazine commended the president's "resolve," but other observers proved more critical. Journalist Rod MacLeish, for example, wondered aloud if the operation resulted from "the desire of the administration which doubts its own global credibility in the tawdry aftermath of Vietnam to prove that there is still sting in the American tail."[17]

Glory and credibility depend, of course, on constructive storytelling. Thus, Ford highlighted his "decisive action" to "reassure our allies and bluntly warn our adversaries that the US was not a helpless giant." Much of the country took up the refrain, not just about the *Mayaguez* affair but about the entire experience in Southeast Asia. Rather than focusing on whether military action could have achieved its stated political goal in Vietnam, Americans refashioned the postwar narrative by highlighting how they had demonstrated the ultimate benevolence of US power by offering a new home for Vietnamese refugees. In doing so, the United States proved itself capable of fulfilling a "profound moral obligation." Not only had Americans voluntarily defended South Vietnamese from the evils of communism, but they also had rescued them from a defeated land after Saigon's fall.[18]

The scars of Vietnam, however, ran deep. So too, in the aftermath of Watergate, did Americans' distrust of the executive branch. Before Nixon left office, Congress passed the 1973 War Powers Act, which authorized legislative review over any presidential decision to send US troops into harm's way. Ford would later excoriate the act as "gutless" and a "serious mistake that will come back to haunt us." Yet the resolution suggested something deeper about elected officials' faith in the president's authority to wage war. Might Americans be wary of their own leaders when it came to making decisions about when and how to go to war? Clearly, many had lost confidence in how the commander-in-chief wielded the nation's vast power during Vietnam. How long this antimilitarist sentiment would last remained to be seen as the national security state endeavored to reinvigorate itself in the mid-1970s.[19]

It was in this global and domestic context that at least some Washington policymakers came to more fully embrace a novel proposition: that the superpower competition not only had its limits but was counterproductive to basic human rights. To be sure, traditional security and economic interests prevailed throughout the decade. But when the Helsinki Consultations began in 1972, negotiations centered on elevating human rights on a global scale. For the next three years, diplomats and advocates labored over the inherent tensions between national security, domestic politics, and international cooperation. Their efforts bore fruit. In August 1975, thirty-five nations signed the Helsinki Final Act, dubbed the "high point of détente." While critics objected to the formalization of territorial borders—particularly the West's acceptance of Russia's satellite system in Eastern Europe—supporters hailed the act's declaration to "respect human rights and fundamental freedoms."[20]

Arguably, the Helsinki Act was an "ersatz peace treaty," as one contemporary critic claimed, revealing how fears of internationalism coincided with fears of war. Leaders in both Moscow and Washington worried about foreign interference into their own domestic affairs. From their viewpoint, human rights advocates harbored the potentially dangerous idea that state sovereignty was not absolute. How could security be guaranteed, policymakers asked, if an external power could intervene in a country on grounds that the human rights of its citizens were not being respected? No matter that Americans had been doing just that since the end of World War II under the banner of anticommunism. What counted to critics was that Ford seemed intent on appeasing the communists. The Soviets, they charged, were giving lip service to "détente" while continuing their military buildup. Diplomat George Ball skewered the administration for its "capitulation" at Helsinki, arguing that détente had "become more an obsession than a policy."[21]

Genuine were these fears of Ford conceding too much at Helsinki. Inside the Kremlin, politburo members felt similarly. The focus on human rights troubled Soviet leaders anxious over losing legitimacy on the international stage. Worse, satellite states might discard their faith in the communist system writ large. Of course, recognition, even from the West, long had been a goal of Moscow, and the Helsinki Act seemingly offered as much. Yet the focus on humanitarianism led to cries that Americans were intruding on internal Soviet affairs. When Senator Henry M. Jackson (D-WA) and Congressman Charles A. Vanik (D-OH) cosponsored a bill limiting trade with countries that restricted Jewish emigration, furious Soviet leaders cried foul. So too did administration officials at home, who blamed Congress for the "large-scale breakdown of détente."[22]

In fact, despite Helsinki's cooperative pledges, détente was hobbling toward its demise. Ford no longer would speak the word, instead preferring to characterize his foreign-policy goal as "peace through strength." On the campaign trail in 1976, the president vowed to keep the US armed forces strong—"not strong for the sake of war, but strong for the sake of peace." Meanwhile, in Congress an increasingly vocal "anti-détente coalition" spoke out against Soviet mistreatment of its Jewish population. As if on cue, the self-styled realist Henry Kissinger mocked those State Department officials promoting human rights over economic and military might. It would not be the last time, in Kissinger's words, that Cold War administrations tried to find the "precise balance between the moral and the strategic elements of American foreign policy."[23]

If Kissinger tended to favor the strategic over the moral, European policymakers were working through their own Cold War calculations on the relationships between war and peace. This too raised fears in Washington. In the late 1960s, West German Chancellor Willy Brandt began exploring a rapprochement with the Soviet bloc. As his *Ostpolitik* gained steam, Brandt signed treaties with Moscow and Warsaw and took steps to increase trade with East Germany. Kissinger reeled at the implications this "new eastern policy" potentially held for containment in the heart of Europe. An independent West Germany normalizing relations with its communist neighbors might lead to "dangerous concessions" with the Soviet Union. Moreover, recognition of the German Democratic Republic, Kissinger feared, could "boost its status and strengthen the Communist regime." Once more, peace inspired as much fear as war.[24]

We might pause momentarily to note how the fear-faith binary transformed during the early 1970s. There seemed to be few fears of conventional war expanding beyond Southeast Asia. Nor did many consider the threat of nuclear escalation there all that plausible. Rather, fears of the falling Vietnamese domino intermeshed with larger fears of a failed war's consequences. A loss of international prestige arguably frightened more than war itself. And in the aftermath of Saigon's fall, while faith in war waned briefly, Americans soon would embrace it once more as the solution to that which they feared. Even a new president untarnished by Watergate-era politics and foreign-policy setbacks could not kick the nation's martial addiction.

With détente outliving its usefulness, Jimmy Carter's 1976 presidential campaign offered an alternative to the traditional Cold War competition. Georgia's governor deplored the "inordinate fear of communism," while promising a return of values and moral principles to US foreign policy. He wanted the democratic system to be "worthy of emulation," and he believed that multilateralism and trade could replace containment as "the foundation of global security." Debating Ford that October, Carter lamented how "we've lost in our foreign policy the character of the American people." He conceded the need for a strong defense—"a defense capability second to none"—but he also criticized the nation for becoming "the arms merchant of the whole world." Carter might have caught more heat for this take but, in an unforced error, Ford stole the harsh spotlight by mistakenly claiming there was "no Soviet domination of Eastern Europe."[25]

Still, Carter's idealistic humanitarian focus sat uneasily alongside America's faith in war. Despite the discouraging outcome in Vietnam, the new president confronted sharp resistance in seeking to deemphasize the militarization of American foreign policy. As Bill Clinton would find nearly two decades later, it was difficult to sell war's purpose as "humanitarian." Questions abounded. What was war's place if promoting human rights became *the* central theme of US foreign policy? Was "soft power" truly more effective than deploying military force when facing a dangerous world? Carter struggled to answer, hoping to advance arms control with the USSR while simultaneously critiquing Moscow's tainted record on human rights. Hardly surprising, leaders like Brezhnev lashed out against "interference in the internal affairs of the Soviet Union." The president faced a difficult road ahead.[26]

Carter, however, wasn't shy in accepting the challenge. In late May 1977, at a Notre Dame commencement address, the president outlined a vision for rearticulating America's purpose in the world. Americans should have faith and confidence in their "essential character as a nation," he offered. Though Vietnam had "produced a moral crisis, sapping worldwide faith in our policy," the United States could look to a future "free of that inordinate fear of Communism which once led us to embrace any dictator who joined us in our fear." The way forward, Carter maintained, was to find "our way back to our own principles and values." A commitment to human rights would reaffirm America's leadership position while restoring confidence in the democratic system. It was a bold articulation of where Carter wanted to steer the nation.[27]

Yet the Notre Dame speech also overreached by defying the nation's larger relationship with war. In describing a new world—one that "America should not fear"—Carter dismissed the real anxieties Americans felt about their place in it. True, they were "fatigued by the Vietnam War," as National Security Advisor Zbigniew Brzezinski acknowledged. And, yes, a focus on human rights might help wash away the moral stain of an ugly Southeast Asian conflict. But the allure of war remained too strong, even for Carter. While coping with a sagging economy at home, Americans looked outward and saw a dangerous planet. Abusive regimes in Asia and Africa. Political and military turmoil in Latin America. A never-ending nuclear arms race with the Soviet Union. Carter's advisors might envision links between social development, human rights, and national security, but as détente became a historical footnote, fearful Americans increasingly came to see military power as their best insurance.[28]

Some policy critics were elated to see détente go and pounced on Carter's naive faith in human rights. The neoconservative Committee of Santa Fe painted the president's foreign policy as a "sincere but desperate meandering through the woods of the world." Given the West was facing the "third phase of World War III," with "America everywhere in retreat," Carter seemed out of his league. The harshest broadside came in 1979 from Georgetown professor Jeane Kirkpatrick. In her searing essay "Dictatorship and Double Standards," Kirkpatrick turned Carter's arguments on their head, claiming that right-wing dictatorships could be moved gradually in democratic directions if the United States didn't actively meddle in their internal affairs. Under Carter, she growled, America had dangerously embraced "a posture of continuous self-abasement and apology." The critique caught the eye of a future Republican presidential nominee and landed Kirkpatrick the US ambassadorship to the United Nations under Ronald Reagan.[29]

If Carter faced national security dissidents from without, so too from within. Inside the White House, tensions between faith and fear flared among his foreign-policy team. Brzezinski saw the Soviets as opportunistically "assertive" and consistently argued to Carter that "power had to come first." Secretary of State Cyrus Vance proved more sympathetic to the president's focus on human rights and held faith that cooperation on arms control could moderate tensions with the Soviet Union. In short, an internal debate swirled around the merits of military power versus quiet diplomacy. The Brzezinski-Vance quarrel, and their competing interpretations of US foreign policy, might be viewed as a microcosm of the tensions between faith in and fear of war in the wake of American disappointments in Vietnam.[30]

Carter seemed, at least in public, to be straddling the line between his two advisors, and indeed he was. At Notre Dame, the president had spoken of his goal to "produce reciprocal stability, parity and security." One year later, speaking at Wake Forest University, he assumed a far more strident tone. Carter called out Moscow's "ominous inclination" to use its power for intervening in local conflicts. The human-rights advocate now was speaking of employing "quickly deployable" air and sea forces, of contesting the Soviet Union's military buildup, and of meeting threats to our "vital interests." While he seemed torn between seeking cooperation and threatening retaliation, he asserted that "even as we search for agreement on arms control, we will modernize our strategic systems and revitalize our conventional forces."[31]

Despite its internal squabbling, the Carter administration held to its faith that American power—not just military power—might help solve lingering problems throughout the Global South and particularly in the Middle East. According to Brzezinski, these problems were alarming. In December 1978, the national security advisor warned Carter of an "arc of crisis" extending from Iran and Pakistan to India and Bangladesh. The following May, Brzezinski argued in public that countries along this arc were struggling with "internal difficulties" that made them "vulnerable to external exploitation." Cold War rhetoric continued to rhyme across the decades. Enduring fears of global chaos and the faith in American military strength to quell it reinforced US tendencies to oversimplify regional problems by continually subsuming local issues within a superpower framework.[32]

With fearful critics seeing a crisis around nearly every corner, Carter found his humanitarian position becoming untenable. The growing, and global, antinuclear movement might equally seek to challenge America's faith in war, but the president was finding few other allies for his cause. The contradictions no doubt flummoxed Carter. He questioned whether a reliance on war would lead to lasting peace, whether war could deliver social justice or economic stability. And yet advocating human rights exposed him to claims of gullibility and weakness, hardly a winning ticket for reelection. Moreover, the president soon would find the international arena an unforgiving showground. Crisis was coming to Washington whether Carter liked it or not.[33]

CHAPTER 15

The Limits of Peace

The Carter administration's final two years left little doubt about war's place in international affairs. These were trying times for a president so genuinely committed to a more peaceful world. Looking back, it's hard not to feel that Carter had been dealt a bad hand. He successfully pursued better relations with China, arms limitations with the Soviets, and peace between Israel and the Arab states. He believed in the power of democratic principles and in the universal connections and aspirations of people across the globe. He had faith that his country could serve as a model for others if only it lived up to its founding principles. And yet as his only term in office neared an end, Carter begrudgingly had to accept the limits of peace in America's relationship with war.

The Naval Academy graduate did his best to foster cooperative relationships with the communist bloc. While exasperating the Kremlin with his insistence on improving human rights, Carter still actively sought a revised nuclear-arms agreement with the Soviet Union. As with his two predecessors, Strategic Arms Limitation Talks under Carter highlighted the limits of pushing back against the country's faith in nuclear deterrence. CIA officials and high-ranking retired naval officers warned against their government's inability to verify Soviet compliance. Conservative commentator William Buckley, Jr. once more entered the political fray, denouncing "men in America who would trust the Russians." Even the Pentagon warned of a "net loss" during SALT II negotiations. The Joint Chiefs of Staff ultimately endorsed a new strategic arms treaty, yet simultaneously advocated for greater spending to modernize the nation's nuclear arsenal.[1]

That Carter had to accept "an arms buildup in exchange for an arms treaty" illustrated how fears of nuclear war had endured since the Cuban missile affair. True, a sense of crisis had diminished. But when Carter and Brezhnev signed the SALT II treaty in June 1979, a fearful US Senate refused to ratify any document imposing limits on America's nuclear arsenal. Neoconservative critics returned to familiar Cold War talking points to warn of Carter's perfidy. Senator Henry Jackson denounced the treaty as "appeasement in its purest form," while Paul Nitze, the architect of NSC-68, called it a "bad bargain." While Nitze claimed to favor some form of stabilizing agreement with Moscow, he cautioned against paying too high a price. "To favor the institution of marriage," he argued, "is not to wish to be married to the Wicked Witch of the West."[2]

In an ironic twist, the framework of SALT II remained in place despite hardliner backlash. From the political sidelines, Ronald Reagan warned against any negotiation "clearly not in the national interest." Deterrence required not only a sense of strategic balance but a process verifying compliance of international agreements. If the United States agreed to an arms treaty that the Soviets secretly violated, stability would be jeopardized. Strategic theorists thus continued to rest their faith on sustaining military parity. The doctrine of mutually assured destruction continued to ripple across the 1970s. And yet despite condemnations of Carter undercutting US national security through "unilateral disarmament," his successor (and Moscow) would abide by the SALT II restrictions. Perceptive onlookers may have pondered whether Reagan's discreet support of the treaty hinted that his own faith in the nuclear arms race might, in fact, be wavering.[3]

Nor did Reagan differ as much as expected from his predecessor when it came to defense spending. Without question, the former California governor poured money into the armed forces once he entered the White House. But despite any visions of peace, defense budgets did not suffer all that much under Carter. In fact, spending on the armed forces increased every year of Carter's administration. Part of this surely was domestic politics, as the Democratic president found it necessary to reinforce himself against conservative attacks that he was being "soft" on national security. When, for instance, Carter negotiated a treaty in late 1977 to return control of the Panama Canal to the Panamanian government, the denunciations were fast in coming. Senator Orrin Hatch (R-UT) assailed the agreement, claiming it reflected a "pattern of surrender and appeasement that has cost us so much all over the world." Reagan, raising money for the Republican National Committee, maintained that his political rivals "time and time again" were supporting "actions that weaken our national security."[4]

The political hits kept coming. When Carter intimated that he would pursue full diplomatic relations with Beijing, furthering steps taken by Nixon, policy dissenters once more cried foul. Critics cared little that China's main focus in the post-Mao era concentrated far more on economic development and trade relations than on military competition. Nor did they share Brzezinski's optimism that closer ties with Mao's successor, Deng Xiaoping, offered leverage over Moscow and might force the Kremlin into greater concessions during the strategic arms talks. Rather, critics returned to well-rehearsed scripts. Senator Barry Goldwater slammed the decision to recognize mainland China as "one of the most cowardly acts ever performed by a president of the United States" and "a stab in the back" to Taiwan. Conservative commentator George Will piled on, calling Carter's plan a "cold-blooded act" against Taiwan, arguing there was "no need for the United States to appease China." Predictably, similar cries of "outright appeasement" would be thrown at Clinton when he deemed China a "strategic partner" in the late 1990s.[5]

And despite the realities of increasing defense budgets under Carter, critics continued to rely on fabricated fears to attack the president. Perhaps the best example was the neoconservative Committee on the Present Danger. Reincarnated from a similar Cold War policy forum in the 1950s, the CPD sought to revitalize the military principles of containment. Indeed, the committee sang in tunes that Joseph McCarthy would have found appealing. A founding document from 1976 illustratively argued that the "principal threat to our nation, to world peace, and to the cause of human freedom is the Soviet drive for dominance based upon an unparalleled military buildup." Meanwhile, members like former Under Secretary of State Eugene V. Rostow claimed that the "true moral of Vietnam" was the "failure to press for military victory." Put simply, talk of peace was as dangerous as it was naive.[6]

In many ways, the Committee on the Present Danger exemplified the relationship between faith and fear. Its members were convinced that military might, more than any other instrument of power, guaranteed the "nation's future well being." Carter, however, was squandering that power. With Moscow engaging in a military buildup that was shifting the US-Soviet balance in its favor, any attempts at "accommodation" were near-suicidal. Unless the White House took "decisive steps" to redress this imbalance, the nation's economic and military capacity would "become inadequate to assure peace with security." Carter might dismiss Nitze and his ilk as taking a "doomsday approach" to international relations, but the Committee's views gained ground in Republican circles as American confidence and credibility appeared to be ebbing.[7]

Not surprisingly, the Committee placed the Strategic Arms Limitation Talks squarely in its crosshairs. To neoconservatives, the SALT process had done nothing to restrain either the Soviet Union's "policy of imperial expansion all over the world" or its "drive for military superiority." In a clear act of fearmongering, the committee published a comprehensive report in 1978 asking, "Is America Becoming Number Two?" The assessment racked up a laundry list of concerns: the decline of US bomber superiority, the asymmetry in antiballistic missile defenses and air defense systems, the imbalance of "general purpose" forces, and so on. A policy neophyte might think the United States had no army or navy at all. In such an environment, there was little chance of reining in defense spending. As James Reston reported, "anybody who suggests a Pentagon budget cut is asked whether he wants to hand over military superiority and the balance of power in the world to the Soviet Union." As Reston quipped, this "tends to end all debate."[8]

Contemporary events seemed to validate neoconservative doomsaying and, ultimately, would contribute to Carter's political demise. The teetering regime of Mohammad Reza Pahlavi in Iran and the lingering effects of the 1973 October War eroded the potential for regional stability in the Middle East. Vietnam's invasion of Cambodia in 1978 and a Sino-Vietnamese war the following year indicated that Southeast Asia lingered as a global hotspot. The enduring energy crunch and lagging American economy instigated a crisis of capitalism at home. When the Soviet Union invaded Afghanistan in December 1979, Carter's domestic and national security policies appeared indefensible. And still, despite mounting evidence of the limits of American power, the president retained a glimmer of faith that it could be employed for virtuous aims.[9]

The Middle East, in particular, showcased the limits of both cooperating with and attempting to coerce local allies. Cold War presidents consistently had feared the potential of the Arab-Israeli conflict disrupting the international system and, vitally, US access to oil. Yet Carter hoped he could inspire Israel and its neighbors to turn a corner in their long-standing feud. As the president would find, however, the regional dispute proved especially well-suited for exposing the limits of peace. As one US advisor remarked, agreeing on any peace settlement was complicated because both Arabs and Israelis depicted their struggle as an "existential crisis."[10]

Still, Carter persisted. Hoping to keep some element of détente alive, he petitioned Moscow to serve as a co-mediator between Middle East client states. Of course, neither side in the Arab-Israeli conflict viewed itself as a superpower pawn. As had always been the case, the Cold War paradigm applied only so far here. It was Egypt's president Anwar Sadat who took the first step. In a surprise move, he approached Jerusalem in late 1977 and expressed a willingness to negotiate with Israel. An elated Carter called the decision "unprecedented" and "very courageous." Yet deep questions remained, not least of which was Israel's stance toward the Palestinians and their fate in the occupied West Bank. When bilateral talks failed to deliver results, Carter invited Sadat and Israeli Prime Minister Menachem Begin to Camp David in the fall of 1978. Perhaps, the American president dreamed, real peace was within reach.[11]

The ensuing Camp David Accords sermonized in promising language. The framework noted how security was "enhanced by a relationship of peace and by cooperation between nations which enjoy normal relations." Yet ultimately Camp David, a major accomplishment at the time, revealed the limits of peace. True, the two primary Middle East antagonists, Israel and Egypt, had signed a historic deal. But Israeli political priorities came at the cost of Palestinian freedoms and a guaranteed homeland. Moreover, while Carter lauded Sadat for his courage, Arab states chafed at the Egyptian speaking on their behalf. The Palestine Liberation Organization (PLO) equally protested Sadat's handling of issues ranging from the return of refugees to compensation for lost properties. Even Carter worried that Israel cared far more about securing a separate peace with Egypt than finding compromise with the Palestinians. It didn't help matters that Begin declared that "Palestinian" was merely another word for "terrorist."[12]

As the dust settled after Camp David, Begin confirmed Carter's worst fears by proclaiming that Israel's West Bank and Gaza settlements were permanent. If promoting self-determination had been a US foreign-policy pillar for most of the twentieth century, Israel disclosed that such ideals did not extend to Palestinians. Observers worried that the "brilliance" of the Camp David "moment was darkened almost at once by the angry reaction of most of the Arab world." Such fears were well founded. The PLO Charter from 1968 already had committed the organization to "armed struggle" as "the only way to liberate Palestine." The accords seemed only to justify such a stance as the PLO declared it would continue its "armed resistance inside the occupied territories." As had been the case in South Vietnam after the Paris peace accords, the Sadat-Begin agreement ultimately solved few of the conflict's underlying issues.[13]

If Camp David raised hopes, at least in the White House, for stability in the Middle East and surrounding regions, they soon disintegrated with the Soviet invasion of Afghanistan. Americans watched in alarm as Moscow deployed Russian troops outside of Warsaw Pact countries for the first time since World War II. Back in April 1978, a military coup had overthrown Mohammed Daoud's nationalist Afghan regime. Given that insurrectionary officers sympathized with the local communist party, it didn't take long for Americans to paint the hostile takeover in Cold War hues. Moscow, however, also viewed the coup's aftermath with unease as a rebellion soon broke out across Afghanistan. By the spring of 1979, the entire country seemed headed for open revolt. With a neighboring communist ally now at risk of collapse, the Kremlin tentatively decided at year's end upon military intervention.[14]

Carter the humanitarian bellowed in threatening disapproval. Addressing the nation in early January 1980, he deemed the invasion an "extremely serious threat to peace" and a "callous violation of international law." It seems doubtful many Americans could find the Central Asian country on a map as the president spoke. Now, however, Carter argued that his fellow citizens "must recognize the strategic importance of Afghanistan to stability and peace." Not only were the Soviets threatening Iran and Pakistan, but their invasion looked like a "steppingstone to possible control over much of the world's oil supplies." Having devoted his presidency to seeking peace, Carter would spend the final months of his administration deterring aggression.[15]

The White House response indicated that détente lay on its deathbed. As the *New York Times* reported only days after Carter's speech, "a decade of fitful East-West relaxation ... appeared headed for suspension, if not collapse." The president withdrew the SALT II treaty from the Senate's ratification process, imposed a grain embargo on the Soviet Union, and barred US athletes from participating in the upcoming Moscow Olympics. Carter also pledged a defense-budget increase and quietly approved sending covert military aid to Afghanistan and Pakistan. As détente churned in its death spiral, military "experts" even called for the United States to "revive and develop its ability to wage chemical warfare." And, as if on cue, the Committee on the Present Danger stepped in to blame the president for helping create this "world crisis" and the "relentless slide to anarchy."[16]

With little political maneuver room, Carter embraced a tougher stance to sidestep charges of "weakness." In late July 1980, he signed Presidential Directive 59, the administration's "Nuclear Weapons Employment Policy." Intended to give the president more "flexibility" during a nuclear war, the leaked document only heightened fears that the Soviet offensive in Afghanistan might trigger a catastrophic global conflict. Some Americans worried that nuclear war was "becoming more thinkable" and, fearing deaths in the hundreds of millions, asked "How can we reasonably or morally justify such a slaughter?" The apparent shift in US nuclear strategy equally alarmed Moscow, with *Pravda* reporting that a "flare-up of war psychosis in Washington" could "only be explained by a loss of common sense" and "a weakening of the sense of reality." Once more, defense analysts pondered their faith in tactical nuclear weapons and weighed the continuing tensions between deterrence, "military superiority," and the geostrategic balance of power.[17]

All the while, anxious policymakers sought comfort in preparations for war. Carter's national security advisor believed the United States was "now facing a *regional crisis*" given turmoil in both Iran and Afghanistan. As his predecessors had done during similar episodes of crisis, Brzezinski exaggerated the Soviet invasion as a test of the president's—if not the nation's—credibility and urged allies to "tangible action" against Moscow. Little did he consider that persistent Cold War fears might be driving the Kremlin's actions as well. As the situation in Afghanistan deteriorated, Soviet leaders worried that if they failed to act in dramatic fashion, they would lose ground in Central Asia and, potentially, across the Middle East. Worse, Islamic revolutionary fervor, if left unchecked, might bleed into Soviet satellites and undermine the appeal of communism throughout the region. As foreign minister Andrei Gromyko bluntly warned, "under no circumstances may we lose Afghanistan."[18]

Brzezinski and his like neglected to consider these fears. It seemingly never occurred to jittery American policymakers that Kremlin leaders might regard the invasion of Afghanistan as defensive in nature. That they too might be making decisions based on alarming visions of the future. This flawed assessment of Soviet motivations informed the American response, with the national security advisor alleging that there was broad support to "condemn the Soviets." Meanwhile, the president publicly warned Moscow to withdraw its forces from Afghanistan or face "serious consequences." According to political commentator William Safire, the president finally saw the "true Soviet colors." In Safire's estimation, the "false premise" of Carter's foreign policy, a gullible "vision of a peaceful world," had been shattered by Russian military aggression."[19]

While Nixon's former speechwriter may have overstated his case in arguing that Carter, "mistaken about Soviet intentions throughout his Presidency," now was turning to the "hawks for quick fixes," Safire hit closer to home on the White House's newfound faith in war. Carter might not be able to use war to produce peace, but he certainly could wield it to punish the Russians. Here, Moscow and Washington shared a long-held faith in military might. Both entered into Afghanistan lured by a conviction that armed force would deliver regional political objectives in a relatively efficient manner. And, in what would become a paradox of the late Cold War era, Carter would lay the groundwork for Americans exploiting Islamic fighters to defeat the Soviet threat. Nor was this a new phenomenon. As one Middle East expert maintained not long after Russian forces departed Afghanistan, the West had "became more and more convinced that Islam was the weapon to fight communism" and secure Cold War policy goals.[20]

In a sense, Carter was turning about, replacing a lost confidence in the purpose of war with a renewed faith in it. Far from his campaign trail rhetoric on advancing humanitarianism, he now called the Soviet invasion "the most serious threat to world peace since the Second World War." Perhaps the transformation was unavoidable. The totality of foreign-policy blows in 1979—the Soviet invasion of Afghanistan, the taking of American hostages in Iran, the ongoing, bloody revolution in Nicaragua—all led Carter back to a militarized conception of containment and set the stage for Reagan's early 1980s muscle-flexing. Under Carter, it seemed, American power had suffered a sharp decline since the glory days of World War II. Peace had proven its limits.[21]

We might, then, think of Carter as a reluctant belligerent. With his political life hanging in the balance, he resorted to ever more confrontational language. During his January 1980 State of the Union address, the president returned to a militarized version of deterrence for fostering stability in a chaotic world. In what would become known as the Carter Doctrine, he declared that attempts "by any outside force to gain control of the Persian Gulf region will be regarded as an assault on the vital interests of the United States of America." The president didn't mince words. He argued, with not a little exaggeration, that the Soviet Union was "attempting to consolidate a strategic position . . . that poses a grave threat to the free movement of Middle East oil." Such threats would be "repelled by any means necessary, including military force."[22]

Critics like defense analyst Leslie Gelb doubted whether the United States had the "military capability to back up our threats in the Persian Gulf area." Given continuing economic woes at home, it also seemed unlikely that Congress would approve military operations directed against the Soviet Union. Carter, however, calculated that tough talk would deter Moscow from further destabilizing the greater Middle East. It had the opposite effect. The Carter Doctrine committed the United States to a warlike posture in sharp contrast to the president's earlier commitment to human rights. Much worse, it laid the foundation for an enduring military presence in the region that arguably has done far more to damage US national security than enhanced it.[23]

Carter likely wasn't thinking about the long-term consequences of a militarized American presence in the Middle East. He had his hands full with tectonic-shifting events already engulfing the region. If Carter felt his critics' sting over the Soviet invasion of Afghanistan, then the Iranian Revolution terminally poisoned his political future. The commander-in-chief's powerlessness to force the return of fifty-two American hostages held in Tehran exhibited a "vulnerability and seeming impotence" that would cost him a second term. But far more importantly, the crisis in Iran would lay bare Carter's seemingly misplaced commitment to "peace for peace's sake." His political rivals drew in, ready to pounce. To them, the unfolding events in Iran and Afghanistan offered a rare opportunity to rekindle their own faith in war and restore it to its proper place in America's strategic arsenal.[24]

PART V

War to Restore Honor

CHAPTER 16

Fear of War, Fear of Weakness

They chanted "Death to America" in frenzied unison. They stormed the American embassy gates and brandished weapons and burned US flags. They displayed posters depicting a corpselike United States as the "Great Satan." Among the crowds, clerical groups—dubbed "the turbans" by American correspondents—fanned resentment against western culture and interference in the greater Middle East. Their religious leader appeared both mystical and maniacal. His followers "seemed possessed by madness." So engrossing had the foreign-policy humiliation become that ABC News began airing a nightly report, "America Held Hostage."[1]

The 1979 Iranian Revolution and the hostage crisis that followed shook both the Middle East and the United States. In Iran, the overthrow of the Shah and the rise of Ayatollah Ruhollah Khomeini sparked a new, potentially threatening version of political Islam. At home, the hostage crisis, perhaps more than even the collapse of Saigon, heightened fears that America had become a waning power, a paper tiger. And, despite long-standing frictions with Iran, US policymakers feared the loss of a crucial regional ally. They also worried, as always, about losing access to the Middle East's key export. As an ABC News journalist reported in November, "Despite the embassy takeover, Iran's oil pipelines to the U.S. are still open. How long that will last is up to the Ayatollah." The forfeit of control was palpable.[2]

So too the rising voices of anti-Americanism. A militant Islamic Republic was bad enough. One pledging to eliminate western presence from the Middle East, backed by Iran's military arsenal, threatened the very foundations of US economic and national security. Jimmy Carter's first news conference in the revolution's aftermath highlighted the already escalating fears. One reporter, quoting Khomeini, asked pointedly if the American president didn't "have the guts to use military force." Was the Ayatollah justified in saying that he placed no "credibility in our military deterrence"? Another correspondent asked about the possibility of "drifting into a cold war with the Islamic countries," while yet another asked if the recent series of events in Iran proved that America's power was "declining." Carter did his best to parry, arguing that the US military still was the "strongest on earth." But questions—and fears—remained.[3]

One year later, little had changed. While some spoke admiringly of US restraint as the hostage crisis wore on with no resolution, others doubted "the reliability of the United States as the guardian of world peace." Of course, volatile regional politics had generated fears before. The US complicity in Mohammad Mosaddegh's 1953 overthrow and the special American relationship with the Shah highlighted a long and sordid involvement in Iranian affairs. Throughout much of the 1950s and 1960s, an unsteady Iran had elicited concerns over possible communist infiltration there. And, of course, the nationalization of the Iranian oil industry had prompted additional worries about loss of access to a vital strategic resource. During all this time, the unwavering US support of the Shah, while promising regional access, provoked rising anti-American sentiment. Still, his overthrow in 1979 generated a sense of crisis in Washington because, in Carter's thinking, Iran had been "an island of stability in one of the more troubled areas of the world."[4]

That stability mattered to the United States' geostrategic aim of containing global communism. As National Security Advisor Zbigniew Brzezinski cautioned, the "disintegration of Iran would be the most massive American defeat since the beginning of the Cold War." Yet the revolutionary fervor in Iran centered far more on local dynamics outside the construct of the larger Cold War contest. Carter argued as much in making a comparison to Vietnam, warning against becoming "unnecessarily involved in the internal affairs of another country when our own security is not directly threatened." Such thinking was a "serious mistake," the president advised. Yet Carter's arguments, however sensible, held little sway when American civilians were being held captive in Tehran.[5]

Though Khomeini called upon all Muslims to confront the West, such rhetoric did not mean he was pro-communist. Without question, the corrupting influence of a materialistic western culture on Islamic tenets formed a central pillar of his political philosophy. But he most certainly was not "drifting into the Soviet orbit," as some Americans worried. Rather, the Ayatollah—who had been exiled by the Shah for fourteen years—focused his opening efforts against a despotic Iranian government, even as he spoke of exporting the "Islamic revolution" abroad. State socioeconomic reform mattered much more to him than delving into Cold War politics. And while Moscow initially welcomed the Shah's overthrow, its leaders quickly became disappointed in Tehran's "anti-Sovietism." The new Islamic Republic opposed superpower domination, regardless of its source. As one student activist put it, "Imperialism exploits us and dominates the whole world."[6]

While critics would blame Carter for the "disastrous American foreign policy loss in Iran," such weak analogies to Truman's "loss" of China three decades earlier mistook the underlying causes behind the Islamization of Iranian society. Nor did they account for the true limits of American power in influencing local political affairs. There seemed little chance that the United States could reverse the revolution unfolding in Tehran. Carter, for his part, was unwilling to either envision or authorize a full-scale military response, even against those he deemed "fanatics" and "terrorists." As one Middle East specialist presciently warned, "Obviously for white soldiers to go after Moslems and people of the Third World is a very severe complication. It pulls all that part of the world together."[7]

Carter's visible impotence to resolve what quickly was becoming a foreign-policy (and economic) disaster turned into a millstone as he campaigned for a second term. Politically, he wasn't on ground stable enough to sustain the added weight. When news broke back in April that the president had to fend off a "killer rabbit" while on a fishing trip in Georgia, Carter appeared a laughingstock, even to some within his inner circle. The political hits seemed relentless. Critics blasted the president for high inflation, for rising unemployment numbers and energy costs, and for his "passive" stance against communist expansionism. His inability to secure the hostages' release in Iran only added to an aura of weakness. As Carter set off on the campaign trail in 1980, it appeared as if Iranian revolutionaries had added yet another hostage to their quarry.[8]

Worse, a botched attempt to rescue the hostages seemingly offered proof that the American armed forces had atrophied in Vietnam's aftermath, that the nation was incapable of defeating aggression overseas. Carter had signed off on the risky "humanitarian mission," Operation Eagle Claw, to save the hostages in April. Evoking memories of the Bay of Pigs fiasco, nearly everything went wrong. Two of the rescue helicopters experienced mechanical failures en route to the mission staging area and had to abort, while a massive dust storm and further difficulties grounded another. With the operation abandoned, a fourth helicopter then collided with a C-130 transport plane, killing eight Americans. As the president relayed the tragic tale in a televised address, America's faith in war seemed wildly misplaced. "There was no fighting. There was no combat." And yet eight soldiers were dead and fifty-three hostages remained captive in Tehran.[9]

The aftershocks soon hit. Critics unsurprisingly questioned the US military's readiness to fight a major war. Some observers felt the "ruined aircraft and charred bodies" were "sad symbols of a new American humiliation in Iran." Still others returned to familiar gendered language, writing postmortems under titles like "America the Gulliver Mired in Impotence Again." Even the Chairman of the Joint Chiefs, General Edward C. Meyer, spoke of a "hollow army" in the ensuing months, while an official report leaked that six of the army's ten combat divisions were rated as "not combat-ready." And, predictably, the president's political opponents laid blame at Carter's feet, as did conservative columnist George Will, who charged that the military had been "ill-served by the President and his appointees."[10]

Eagle Claw, with its "major errors," inspired changes to military training, especially within the Special Forces community. Reinvigorating America's relationship with war, the public failure also provided a sense of urgency for reform, facilitating the militarization of US foreign policy during the Reagan years and beyond. Carter would reap none of these apparent rewards. His secretary of state, Cyrus Vance, resigned in protest, claiming that US interests throughout the region "could be severely damaged" by a military operation and that the "Islamic world would be outraged, causing a larger Western-Islamic conflict." Indeed, the president's political future appeared in doubt. As one senior aide remarked after hearing of the failed rescue attempt, "We just lost the election."[11]

Ronald Reagan sensed that the eight dead American soldiers could still be of service, if not to the nation then to his political campaign. Both their deaths and the hostage crisis were indicative of "a symptom of a larger crisis we face," he argued while campaigning a week after the abortive mission. "America's credibility, leadership and strengths are not only being questioned by our friends," Reagan maintained, "but increasingly are being tested by our adversaries." In other venues on the trail, he asserted that the United States had become "weak and fearful," and that Carter had made a "shambles" of the US defense posture. Relying on well-honed acting skills, Reagan profited from a self-fashioned gladiatorial image, a candidate who would be a "tough" commander-in-chief willing to use military power to redeem the nation's honor.[12]

The former California governor already had rehearsed his lines during a failed bid to be the Republican candidate four years earlier. His 1976 campaign against Gerald Ford had resurrected early 1950s alarmism with allegations that the nation was "in danger," growing "greater with each passing day." Reagan hammered the president for speaking so much of peace. "But peace does not come from weakness or from retreat," he declared. "It comes from the restoration of American military superiority." A fierce anticommunism was returning to American politics, and with it a faith in military preparedness to recuperate losses suffered under previous weak administrations. Thus, Reagan would profit politically not only from the hostage crisis but from their timely release on the day of his inauguration. The lesson seemed clear. Enemies of the United States had heard Reagan's martial message and, fearing the worst, had yielded to the new, tough-talking president.[13]

Such assumptions, of course, weren't unique to Reagan's successful White House bid. Across the political landscape, détente's dissenters grew increasingly restless and vocal, arguing that the Soviets had taken advantage of the Cold War respite to steal a march on the American defense industry. In fact, the supposed loss of US military supremacy became the raison d'être of the rising neoconservative movement. No wonder that fear became a central pillar in accusations that détente was undermining national security. The new president embraced the cataclysmal rhetoric, early on warning of Russia's goal being "world revolution and a one-world Communist state." As he did on the campaign trail before winning the 1980 election, Reagan committed himself to offering the nation a stark policy binary between an arms race against the Soviet Union and the "unacceptable choice" between surrender and defeat.[14]

For policy hawks, the choice was clear just by looking at the volatile global map. The Iranian revolution. The Soviet invasion into Afghanistan. The continuing unrest in Latin America. All this disorder confirmed that détente had been treacherously oversold. True, there were dissenters who believed that flawed strategic thinking was perpetuating a system continually pitting the superpowers against each other and legitimizing theories of mutually assured destruction. But in the Reagan administration's eyes, Carter and his predecessors had overvalued diplomacy, development, and "soft power." While on the campaign trail, Reagan called détente an "illusion" and maintained his conviction that grand strategy should rest upon three principles: a faith in the "rightness of America's cause;" a "strong economy based on a free market;" and "America's 'unquestioned capability' to keep the peace through superior weaponry." An anomaly in modern politics, Reagan stuck to his word.[15]

Thus, in an era when Americans were experiencing a "crisis of confidence" and worrying they had been weakened on the world stage, war might serve as a redeeming elixir, a way to restore the nation's honor, especially after the debacle in Southeast Asia. Indeed, Vietnam would remain a useful historical comparative for years to come, a lesson plan for students seeking tutorials on what not to do in war. Some critics would label the war there as "aggressive" or "imperialist," while others regarded the American enterprise as the "logical extension of a 'national security' policy of permanent war on a global scale." Reagan, however, was intent on flipping the script. War need not be solely destructive. It also could be redemptive.[16]

Employing his accomplished rhetorical skills, the new president made his case for leading the nation out of the 1970s' darkness. A strong military would play a vital role, and popular culture would aid his efforts in restoring, if not "re-masculinizing," post-Vietnam America. But it was on the political front where Reagan sought to make his immediate mark. During a presidential debate with Carter just before the 1980 election, the first set of questions focused on the use of military power. Reagan capitalized on the moment, arguing that America had "never gotten in a war because we were too strong." He criticized Carter for "responding late to aggressive Soviet impulses," a weak president who had little to offer beyond his own "methodical" commitment to defense. Military strength thus would become integral to Reagan's plan of ushering in an "era of national renewal."[17]

Yet a central question remained, especially when, over time, Reagan's actions did not quite match his combative rhetoric. Could military power really make Americans feel better about themselves after a decade of their confidence being shaken to the core? Certainly, some observers doubted the equation. They worried this new leader in the White House might be a "warmonger, bomb-thrower and recklessly belligerent." But others embraced a different kind of fear, a fear that under Carter the United States had become a "bumbling, stumbling giant." Might then Reagan's faith in military power help renew the American dream? Might war restore a sense of honor? Such were the two main themes confronting an anxious nation as a new administration ushered in the Cold War's final phase. As one journalist put it succinctly, "fear of war, fear of weakness."[18]

CHAPTER 17

Rebuilding (and Re-Militarizing) America

Though often derided in conservative circles for being an indecisive pacifist and naive supporter of human rights, Jimmy Carter actually increased defense spending by more than five percent during his last year in office. Americans eager to regain their lost confidence seemed content to allow Reagan and Secretary of Defense Caspar W. Weinberger to spend even more. Nor did the new White House occupant radically alter Carter's emphasis on human rights. Though Alexander Haig, Reagan's truculent secretary of state, announced how international terrorism would replace human rights as a policy focus, the president found utility in using humanitarian language as an anticommunist tool, if not a weapon. To Reagan, an emphasis on "identifiable human beings" could help restore Americans' faith in their nation's foreign policy.[1]

This repaired faith mattered because, Reagan charged, under Carter's watch the Soviet Union had been engaging in "the greatest military buildup in the history of man," one clearly "offensive in nature." In short, the president radiated a conviction that military power could rebuild America, despite the failure of its armed forces in Vietnam. Reagan said as much when calling the war in Vietnam a "noble cause," arguing that under Carter national defense had deteriorated into "shambles" and that "deserving veterans" were the main reason for a huge jump in military spending. It would become a trend for years to come. Rather than inspire deep critical thinking or reflection on the limits of

US power abroad, failed military incursions would stimulate renewed faith in the capacity of increased defense budgets solving domestic and foreign problems alike.[2]

Such convictions existed in tandem with persistent Cold War fears that a threat anywhere in the world, however small, required some form of American response. Reagan's early "Strategic Guidance" argued that "no area of the world is beyond the scope of American interest." No wonder the new administration eagerly was seeking and supporting anticommunist insurgencies from Latin America to the Middle East. Any proxy would do if it meant delegitimizing the Soviet Union. Chary observers worried that, in the new president, the "Reagan of confrontation" was pitted against Reagan "the pragmatic practitioner of power."[3]

If the president sounded like a "warmonger" to some, Caspar Weinberger's plan to "regain atomic superiority" put others on edge. The defense secretary spoke of expanding the nation's "strategic nuclear deterrent forces" by increasing the numbers of intercontinental ballistic missiles, long-range bombers, and nuclear-capable Trident submarines. When Reagan asserted in October 1981 that he could envision an "exchange of tactical weapons against troops in the field without it bringing either one of the major powers to pushing the button," allies were left "horrified and appalled." The president's speculation, however frightening, actually harkened back to the Eisenhower era, with officials pondering how nuclear threats might help underwrite a global US presence while ensuring that presence would be respected—or at least feared.[4]

For Reagan, respect mattered. It was central to his approach toward the Cold War competition. At least in his first term, the president embraced an unquestioning faith that massive military spending not only would make Americans more secure but would enhance the nation's prestige and credibility. (Brezhnev thought similarly about the Soviet Union.) Without question, hawks like Weinberger influenced the president's early thinking. So distressed was the defense secretary over the state of the US arsenal that he proposed a six-month moratorium on negotiating with the communists until America's strength had been rebuilt. Chairman of the Joint Chiefs of Staff John Vessey apparently agreed, arguing that US strategy was "one of preventing war by making it self-evident to our enemies that they are going to get their clocks cleaned if they start one."[5]

But the administration also was relying on historical precedent for its military buildup. At the opening of the twentieth century, Admiral Alfred Thayer Mahan, for instance, had maintained that sea power could "enhance national prestige, raise public confidence and morale, and promote security and prosperity." As the Cold War opened, Hans Morgenthau spoke in similar terms, reasoning that a "policy of prestige uses military demonstrations as means to achieve its purpose." Though not an advocate of using armed force, the influential political scientist still felt that since "military strength is the obvious measure of a nation's power, its demonstration serves to impress the others with that nation's power." It all seemed so easy, so formulaic. By renewing the country's commitment to and faith in military power, Reagan and his team could ensure US safety through respectability. Similar dubious reasoning would guide another American president as he embarked upon a global war against terrorism in the aftermath of 9/11.[6]

Weinberger's philosophy on the relationship between "across-the-board increases" in military spending and American global power presumed a lack of readiness among the US armed forces. The failed Eagle Claw operation offered proof of such assumptions. With détente now obsolete, defense specialists like Albert Wohlstetter warned of a growing Soviet power that might exploit "international lines of communication" and "threaten military action at various points vital to the West near its periphery." Alarmist pronouncements like these aided Weinberger in selling his massive budget on Capitol Hill. The support mattered, as critics worried about "horrendous deficits" even as the administration was substantially cutting non-defense spending.[7]

Hawks like Weinberger and Haig certainly played up the speculative association between power and respect. Militarization relies on a faith that armed might engenders deference and a sense of awe among lesser states. But the two secretaries also hedged their bets by selectively ignoring intelligence assessments of the communist threat. Both tended to dismiss CIA reports suggesting that the Soviet economy, plagued by structural problems, actually was deteriorating and that its arms buildup had been overstated. Haig was disposed to disparaging such evaluations as evidence of communist duplicity. (And, of course, the CIA never truly could be certain of Moscow's intentions.) Weinberger, meanwhile, worried that Democrats might use any declining sense of threat as an excuse to vote down vital defense spending packages.[8]

The defense secretary's uneasiness signified the crucial role of the domestic economy in Reagan's foreign policy. The links here between war and society were strong. The administration adopted a faith, akin to that of economist Milton Friedman, that tax cuts and supply-side economics not only would support the massive outlay in defense spending but would benefit all Americans as wealth trickled down to the most needy. Other economic pundits weren't so sure. Researchers warned that Reagan's fiscal program was "fatally flawed because his passion for military strength directly conflicts with his goal of economic recovery." Other analysts counseled Americans to hang onto their wallets as policymakers started "talking about future deficits and military spending." Union leader Lane Kirkland fiercely attacked "Reaganomics" by claiming that the working class was shouldering the military buildup costs while social programs fell by the wayside.[9]

Such criticisms made small impact as key neoconservative voices, from both military and economic camps, found a welcoming home inside the Reagan White House. They reignited the Cold War competition and heightened tensions with the Soviet Union, intentionally so. Brezhnev, not surprisingly, replied in kind, declaring that "peace with the imperialists is not for the asking." But with Reagan revitalizing the US defense establishment, the Soviet leader entreated the president to "see what is going on through our eyes." Brezhnev enumerated the disturbing American initiatives: a rejuvenation of US-made military alliances, the construction of new bases far from the United States' shores, an expanding American military presence abroad, and large areas of the world "being declared spheres of 'vital interest' to the U.S.A."[10]

In many ways, this renewed faith in war had the opposite of its intended effect. Instead of making Americans feel more secure and safe, the administration's bellicose rhetoric and profuse defense spending elevated hostilities and, during Reagan's first term, left the Soviet Union more convinced than ever that the United States was preparing for war.

Much of the neoconservatives' language derived from a long tradition of fear-based conjecturing, including the belief that savage communists respected "only strength." The Committee of Santa Fe offered a stark example of such thinking. In "A New Inter-American Policy for the Eighties," the right-wing group argued that war, not peace, was "the norm in international relations." Entering into "the third phase of World War III," the group insisted that Americans had to wake up to this "metaphysical" crisis. Its policy memorandum spanned the globe, identifying threats from southern Africa to the Indian Ocean, bemoaning how the United States was "everywhere in retreat" and "under attack." Worse, the Santa Fe group protested, the damage had been self-inflicted by gullible policy elite who didn't resist "the Communist commitment to utilize every available means to overthrow the capitalist order and to transform the world." Washington had to accept that the United States was at war.[11]

In the aftermath of Saigon's fall, these persuasive militaristic views gained purchase, especially after a decade in which Americans' confidence had been shaken by Vietnam, Watergate, and the oil crisis. Outside the national security establishment, citizens gradually began lashing a renewed faith in war to a basic faith in themselves. By the 1980s, with the sting of Vietnam slowly fading, military culture once more informed American identity. Reagan willingly facilitated the trend. A restored sense of American exceptionalism would again rest upon military might. As in the aftermath of World War II, martial prominence would become the "ultimate proof of American greatness."

The logic, though, seemed tainted. Was military power truly indicative of national worth? Did a nation's values stem from its arsenals? Critics were dubious. As the late historian Marilyn Young argued, the United States was "not exceptional, only exceptionally powerful."[12]

But power was popular once more. And Hollywood took notice. A new wave of blockbuster films placed heroic warriors center stage during the 1980s, rekindling a faith in war within popular culture. Sylvester Stallone and Chuck Norris returned to an imagined Vietnam in which former soldiers engaged in revenge fantasies that washed away the stains of a lost war. Arnold Schwarzenegger and Mel Gibson acquired on-screen special-forces resumés, as would Steven Segal in the following decade. *Top Gun* ruled the domestic box office in 1986, a victory for the "military-entertainment complex" as the US Navy made available two aircraft carriers for filming. Hasbro even resurrected its G.I. Joe toy line to ensure it profited from the military mania. Cultural critics fretted that "the fantasy of brute masculine force [had] grown out of all proportion to human dimension," but such worries gained few adherents in the age of Reagan.[13]

The 1980s conceptualization of militarized masculinity illustrated how faith in martial power remained a gendered concept in American popular culture. Even cultural critics of the day admitted that the "masculine principle is at heart a warrior's principle." (Sigourney Weaver's Ripley character in *Alien* might have disagreed.) Reagan embraced these views as they spread across the popular and political landscape. Yet little was new here. Within policymaking circles, Washington elite long had equated tough-minded masculinity with ability to serve the national interest and successfully pass "tests of resolve." After the 1957 *Sputnik* orbit, for instance, columnist Joseph Alsop took Eisenhower, a former general, to task for his "flaccid" leadership. Weakness was both unmasculine and, in the Cold War context, potentially dangerous.[14]

Reagan needed little convincing that military power and American honor were intrinsically tied. This, after all, was how he justified his massive re-militarization program. As historian John Lewis Gaddis argues, the president "came to this position through faith, fear, and self-confidence"—a faith in democracy and capitalism joined with a fear of nuclear war. "Peace through strength" became a popular catchphrase in conservative circles, even as critics argued that Reagan's martial policies lacked "diplomatic follow-through." Like his political beau ideal Teddy

Roosevelt, Reagan made explicit the connections between manhood, war-making capacities, and national power. The message resonated with Americans who had been primed to feel good about themselves. Yet, as in Roosevelt's day, the focus on raw power concealed an underlying fear that a weak nation might not survive in an industrialized, competitive world.[15]

One had only to gaze upon the Middle East to see the importance of regaining national honor via military hardware. The hostage release in Tehran had done little to diminish fears of Iranian revolutionary influence spreading throughout the region. Defense analysts worried that "Khomeini and his fundamentalist zealots" were intent on dominating the Middle East, upsetting the tenuous balance within the Persian Gulf region and crimping the flow of oil to the world market. Thus, when Iran and Iraq went to war in 1980, the Reagan administration held its nose to ignore the brutality of the secularist Saddam Hussein and began supplying military weapons to Baghdad in hopes of preventing the spread of Islamic radicalism. That Iraq might be weaned from its dependence on Soviet aid in the process appeared only an added benefit to Reagan officials.[16]

Meanwhile, in Moscow, similar fears of declining national strength pervaded the aging Soviet politburo. Between November 1982 and March 1985, three general secretaries—Leonid Brezhnev, Yuri Andropov, and Konstantin Chernenko—died in rapid succession. These hoary leaders had been informed by impulses similar to Reagan's as they nervously relied on military power to compensate for a sclerotic political system. Longtime Moscow correspondent Harrison Salisbury saw peril in the diminishing Soviet state. The danger to world peace, he surmised, came from the Kremlin's "reaction to failures and frustrations that stem from incurable flaws within its own creaky system." Salisbury feared that Soviet policy would seek "escape from the morass in which it is mired" through a "military-technological revolution." In such a fraught climate, the politburo's "chauvinistic military tendency" seemed certain to grow. No doubt hawks like Weinberger and Haig agreed.[17]

In an odd parallel, both Reagan and his Soviet adversaries held their faith that preparedness for war would compensate for domestic social ills and help rebuild a diminished nation for the Cold War's final round. This formulation of war as remedy would highlight a dependence that would turn into an addiction in the coming decades. War once more was becoming fashionable.[18]

CHAPTER 18

Renewing Faith in "Low-Intensity" War

Reagan's dependency on war rested on his inherent faith in its utility. Reflecting Eisenhower's thinking from the 1950s, the president reasoned that war still could be functional below the threshold of US strategic bombers and ICBMs, even as he continued seeking to enhance US nuclear forces. Under the new guise of "low-intensity conflict," the armed forces once more would engage in a broad swath of military operations, from peacekeeping to counterterrorism, all while avoiding unwelcome legislative interference. As one policy memo asserted, the United States could "apply measured force" for protecting its interests. This did "not mean 'war' in the traditional sense; rather, it is the use of military power to complement diplomacy."[1]

The post-Vietnam-era armed forces, however, were planning for war. Turning a page on their failed Southeast Asian endeavor, senior military leaders returned their focus to Western Europe and hypothetical Soviet invasion plans. With counterinsurgency out of favor, the preferred threat magically became the most dangerous threat. A new doctrine, with the name AirLand Battle, sought to restore an "offensive focus" to the armed forces by stressing "rapid, violent operations." A return to conventional warfighting, with messy and inconclusive irregular warfare happily abandoned, would salvage the nation's martial reputation. The military-industrial complex swooned as doctrine writers incorporated new attack helicopters, rocket systems, tanks, and close air support fighters into their "deep battle" plans. With AirLand Battle, the thinking went, war once more would become decisive.[2]

Hardliners argued the Soviet threat warranted a strong response and an offensive doctrine to match. As did the administration's first National Security Strategy Directive, NSDD-32. In its authors' view, the United States now was facing its "greatest danger" since World War II. Containment no longer sufficed as a grand strategic objective. Instead, the Reagan administration would seek help from allies across the globe "to encourage the dissolution of the Soviet Empire." While the directive spoke of emboldening "pro-reform forces inside the USSR," the possibility of negotiated solutions clearly took a back seat to the wielding of military and economic power. As the *New York Times* reported, Reagan's national security team favored "meeting Soviet attacks head-on."[3]

As in previous administrations, Reagan wrestled with projecting US power to adequately contest Soviet "expansionism," whether in Central Asia or Latin America. Perhaps that's why the president had few objections to inheriting and capitalizing upon the Carter Doctrine's commitment to the Middle East, even as he attacked his allegedly weak predecessor. Yet this inheritance fostered little introspection about how Carter had failed to advance US grand strategy by military means alone. Neoconservatives took note, and by early 1982 already were expressing "anguish" over the administration's emerging Middle East policy. As one critic maintained, the president's strategy amounted to little more than "Carterism without Carter." More strident denunciations were yet to come from Reagan's right.[4]

The Middle East offered still another test of American power overseas. Rising incidents of terrorism in the region underscored a new, increasingly effective tactic by its adherents, further escalating fear levels back home. Alexander Haig assumed Moscow was pulling the terrorists' strings, but CIA analysts uncovered no evidence. Their findings, though, inspired no self-confidence in the White House. The agency already had warned during Carter's tenure that "the development of a complex support base for transnational terrorist activity" was "the wave of the future." Thus, when the CIA established a Counterterrorism Center in 1986, it offered proof of another emerging threat well below the nuclear threshold.[5]

Once more, popular culture played its role in cultivating the relationship between war and American society. In the 1986 action thriller *The Delta Force*, for instance, Chuck Norris leads a Special Forces team in rescuing a hijacked plane from "New World Revolution" terrorists. Unlike the failed Eagle Claw operation, which Norris's character mentions as the film opens, "America's elite antiterrorist commandoes" are successful on the big screen. While the film suggested that Americans could defeat terrorism simply through their grit and spirit, it also advanced racialized linkages between "militant Islam" and radical violence as a popular narrative device. Left aside in this "wildly fanciful, chauvinistic fiction" were more serious questions about the nature of this new threat. For example, we might ask how much the defense establishment, into which Reagan was funneling so much of taxpayers' dollars, considered the political motivations behind the terrorist activity itself. Surely such questions mattered.[6]

Yet, like Eisenhower, Reagan retained his faith in "low-intensity" warfare despite the potential mismatch between emerging threats and present capabilities. While movies like *Red Dawn* (1984) suggested that "teen-age guerrilla patriots" could fight and win future unconventional conflicts, the US armed forces mostly concentrated on high-intensity, conventional warfare in Western Europe. True, there were fictionalized accounts of this latter kind of war that gained purchase in popular culture. Tom Clancy's 1986 novel *Red Storm Rising* offered a glimpse of what World War III might look like as American tank crews and air force pilots battled Warsaw Pact forces. In fact, Clancy's work caught the attention of Reagan, while the Naval War College in Rhode Island added the fictional account to its curriculum. Yet the administration seemed torn over how to advance its new security strategy. Should it focus on directly confronting the Soviet war machine in Western Europe or pursuing a more indirect approach along the traditional global periphery?[7]

The 1983 fiasco in Beirut only muddied the waters and showcased how Reagan could not simply purchase American security overseas with increased defense spending at home. Back in 1978, Israel had entered into the ongoing Lebanese civil war by launching a limited offensive against PLO forces in the country's southern region. Unsuccessful, Israeli Defense Forces opened a full-scale invasion four years later, laying siege to Beirut. Sensing an opportunity to reassert US influence in the region, Reagan deployed marines as part of a multinational peacekeeping force. How a small US military presence in Lebanon was supposed to facilitate the president's larger Middle East policy remained unstated. Officers later testified they were part of a "diplomatic mission" and a "presence mission," but more likely they were seen by many locals as interlopers. The mortar and rocket fire targeting marines suggested as much.[8]

In April 1983, a truck bombing at the US embassy compound in Beirut resulted in more than sixty deaths, including seventeen Americans. Tragedy then turned into catastrophe. On 23 October, another truck bombing tore into the US marine barracks, killing 241 Americans and 58 Frenchmen. By intervening in a local civil war to facilitate a lasting peace in the Middle East, all while blocking Soviet influence in Lebanon and beyond, Reagan had hoped to demonstrate strength. Instead, the deaths of so many Americans engaged in a "peacekeeping" mission undermined those hopes in a single day. The United States had projected its military power and been found wanting.[9]

The barracks bombing and American dead left Reagan an unwelcome choice: retaliate or withdraw. The president defiantly pronounced that he "was not going to cut and run" given the nation's "vital interests in Lebanon." But pressures mounted to remove US servicemen from harm's way when those interests didn't seem as vital to the American public as Reagan proclaimed. Debate swirled within the White House over how best to respond, with National Security Advisor Bud McFarlane fearing that any US withdrawal would embolden regional terrorist networks. But convincing skeptical Americans that the attacks necessitated a long-term regional presence proved beyond Reagan's reach, especially when bitter family members were charging that their loved ones had been left out like a "piece of cheese in a trap." In February and March, the remaining marines returned home.[10]

While Americans tried to make sense of what had happened in Lebanon, Israelis similarly found they could not so easily alter their own strategic situation by military means alone. It wasn't for lack of trying. In their efforts to destroy the PLO, which called for the "elimination of Zionism in Palestine," Israel's leaders also hoped to extinguish regional support for Palestinian nationalism. As was so often the case in the Middle East, the employment of military force only aroused further violence. By 1987, the Palestinians had launched an "intifada," an armed rebellion against Israel's continuing occupation of the West Bank and Gaza Strip. Not surprisingly, the United States reinforced Israeli policies assuming, incorrectly, that the PLO was aligned with the Soviets. As violence surged, the White House found—as had the Kremlin throughout the Cold War—how difficult it was to bolster one's allies while simultaneously restraining them. There were, in short, limits to exercising military leverage overseas.[11]

It seems of little coincidence then that the US invasion of Grenada came so closely on the heels of a humiliating setback in the Middle East. The small Caribbean island nation of just 110,000 people offered Reagan the chance for a "symbolic" military victory to overthrow a revolutionary government apparently intent on strengthening ties with Moscow and Havana. As one senior State Department official conceded to an interviewer, the Beirut affair had elevated the need "to demonstrate American resolve." With American medical students on the island ostensibly at risk, the White House authorized Operation Urgent Fury to restore order and, just as importantly, to validate American power and influence that looked so weakened by events in the Middle East. That Grenada's defense force included neither air nor naval forces—and only a 2,000-man army—certainly reduced the risk factors for sanctioning a military operation.[12]

In many ways, the fabrication of a hemispheric communist threat in Grenada rested on overblown fears dating back decades. By the early 1980s, though, such notions had lost some of their persuasive power. In the operation's aftermath, critics felt the idea of Grenada "serving as spearhead for international communism's attack upon the Americas" was "very hard to take seriously." Moreover, there were issues in delivering democracy "at gunpoint." And, of course, Soviet leaders saw the invasion as proof that US imperialism risked "unleashing a full-scale war for its venal class interests." Still, at least within military circles—if not the White House as well—such a "clear-cut victory" offered a welcome contrast to the Iran hostage fiasco and the shattered marine barracks in Beirut.[13]

Reagan lauded Urgent Fury as an achievement of his vision for rejuvenating the armed forces. Young Americans in uniform had delivered on his faith in war. Below the surface, however, the Grenada mission presaged deeper questions that would confront the Clinton administration well into the 1990s. For armies configured to fight in mass, industrial warfare, what did "peacekeeping" mean? If the US military was training according to AirLand Battle doctrine, planning for a climactic showdown with the Warsaw Pact in Western Europe yet engaging in peace support operations in the Caribbean and Middle East, then what was the primary wartime mission for which they were preparing? Besides, there were some who doubted the face-saving nature of Urgent Fury at all. Historian Marilyn Young believed operations like those in Grenada "were painted on too small a canvas to take the sting out of defeat in Vietnam."[14]

Preparing for general war while aiming to avoid it harkened back to the Eisenhower years, when the administration related military power, well below the nuclear threshold, to global peace and stability. Reagan did his best to link Soviet machinations to unrest in Lebanon and Grenada, arguing that Moscow "assisted and encouraged violence in both countries" and that it directly supported a "network of surrogates and terrorists." The far-ranging deployments of US troops in late 1983 suggested an ever-growing list of "vital interests" that must be defended. As in the past, fear and faith informed senior policymakers' decisions—fear these interests were imperiled, faith that a renewed military machine could protect them even as US forces were stretched thin by their global commitments. Under Reagan, peacekeeping (and peacemaking) only added to America's ever-growing self-defined responsibilities.[15]

While Pentagon officials prepared for these new "low-intensity" conflicts in the Middle East and Latin America, they continued, if not elevated, their proxy support for the war in Afghanistan. Arguably, Reagan had few strategic aims beyond inflicting maximum damage on Soviet forces there. In fact, within CIA headquarters a group known as the "Bleeders" sought to make the invasion as expensive as possible for Moscow even while the White House was calling for a Soviet withdrawal. Here, political fears of "another Vietnam" transformed into a faith that Americans might contribute to the Soviets being bled dry in the "quagmire" of Afghanistan. Rather than committing US troops, Reagan relied on the CIA to advise and support local mujahedeen forces who would serve as the tip of the spear in rolling back communist advances.[16]

The American backing of Islamist Afghan fighters suggested how reliance on proxies was now a crucial component of Reagan administration thinking about America's relationship with war. It also blurred the lines between good "holy warriors" and bad ones as counterterrorism rose in importance. Occasional voices warned of potential blowback, cautioning that increased US aid might "goad the Soviets into introducing more and more occupation troops into Afghanistan" or "sow the seeds of civil strife in Pakistan." In fact, just that happened. Soviet forces undertook "massive reprisals against towns and villages harboring mujahedeen." Not unlike their American counterparts, Russian leaders assumed that any local resistance would collapse when faced with overwhelming military force. But the CIA's Afghan operation, funneling some $700 million per year into the war-torn country by 1987, served to undercut that faith. The ghosts of the Nixon Doctrine had drifted from Southeast to Central Asia.[17]

Meanwhile, Soviet fears were driving their own continued presence in Afghanistan. Kremlin leaders initially had worried that a politically fractured satellite might ally with the West, leaving little choice for intervention. As the nine-year war dragged on, year after bloody year, new and more alarming fears emerged. Might a failed military venture in Central Asia undermine Soviet credibility among its communist allies? It certainly seemed so. As one Russian journalist wryly noted, with "each passing day, the war more and more resembled the sexual performance of an impotent." With the Russian economy showing signs of stress, if not buckling, maintaining credibility on the military front mattered as much to Moscow as it did to Washington. If the Soviet army let slip that it wasn't the vaunted military machine American analysts had feared, the entire Cold War defense framework might collapse.[18]

Along Afghanistan's western border, the continuing Iran-Iraq War equally indicated that superpower policy aims might not be as compelling as local ambitions. In the wake of the recent Iran hostage crisis, few American policymakers championed an Iranian victory. Indeed, both Washington and Moscow supported Saddam Hussein, who assumed the Khomeini regime would collapse after a quick military victory. As so often in the Cold War, though, the reality of combat sabotaged such notions. The state department quietly "de-designated" Iraq as a sponsor of terrorism. American arms and materials flowed into Baghdad. And yet the United States was playing a double game, secretly (and illegally) directing weapons to Iran in hopes of keeping the two regional powers at each other's throats.[19]

Simultaneously aiding two warring factions should have sowed doubt about Washington's public pronouncements for peace. The military aid, however, reflected National Security Council aims of advancing US strategic objectives in the Middle East—and little more. As one CIA analyst argued, Reagan's team had no "illusions about the extremely unpleasant nature of the Iraqi regime." Yet they also felt that "if Iran won the war, that would be the worst of everything—the Middle East as we knew it would soon be overrun by anti-Western fanatics." Hoping to deny "radical forces" and deter Soviet aggression, while also maintaining access to oil, proved a tricky balancing act. The administration never quite learned how to exploit this local conflict for its long-term benefit. In fact, it achieved just the opposite.[20]

The mishandled Iran-Iraq War, with its massive loss of life, would not be the last occasion when the White House poured weapons into the Middle East while managing fears of a regional conflict spiraling out of control. In fact, the war engendered deep fears over losing control.

With a frightening new "surge" of Islamic fundamentalism in the region, Washington elite worried they might not be able to direct the political outcomes once local militants committed to "holy war." Palestinian nationalism, for example, evolved in a manner often far outside of American influence. So too did Israeli reactions. Not surprisingly, the regional conflicts of the 1980s hardened political factions, militarized societies, and left Americans fearful that Islamic fundamentalism was a "growing force" in the Middle East.[21]

And yet, despite these fears, US officials retained their misguided faith that there were few, if any, long-term consequences for supporting religious extremists or autocratic regimes to fight global communism. In Saudi Arabia, as just one example, the United States found a willing partner in its anti-Soviet crusade, funneling advanced weaponry into the monarchy despite objections from pro-Israel lobby groups. And once more, fear entered into the equation. One Reagan administration official defended selling advanced missiles to Saudi Arabia in 1986 because "failure to support them will send the wrong signals everywhere in the world." Such arguments hardly were new.[22]

Back in the 1950s, the United States had supported Saudi Arabia because US officials saw Islam as a conservative religion ensuring regional stability and serving as a safeguard against Soviet communism. Given the post-9/11 vitriol and violence against Muslims, both at home and abroad, Cold War Americans' faith in Islam now appears tragically incongruous. Yet this weaponization of religion as an "ideological tool" suggested that Americans' faith in war was as ill-informed as their understanding of the religious landscape in the Middle East. The often opaque—and often assumed—relationships between nationalism, Islam, and violence certainly didn't help matters. As the Cold War neared its conclusion, Americans increasingly saw the Islamic religion as far more radical than conservative.[23]

Exploiting religious and martial faith in "low-intensity" conflicts, though, was intended to achieve a principal strategic goal for Reagan— not just containing communism but reversing Soviet expansionism. In January 1983, the administration published an internal national security directive, titled "US Relations with the USSR," that laid out such a goal. The policy statement took a hard line, even as it vaguely advocated negotiations to "eliminate, on the basis of strict reciprocity, outstanding disagreements." The new and level-headed secretary of state, George P. Shultz, expressed concern over NSDD-75's militaristic tone, but hardliners on the National Security Council had Reagan's ear. Luckily, Shultz remained committed to an "intensified dialogue" with Moscow. Still, NSDD-75 evinced a hawkish stance. Perhaps most indicative of Reagan's faith-based approach to foreign policy, the directive intimated that the United States could influence Soviet "internal affairs" if the president led from a position of power.[24]

Two years later, in his 1985 State of the Union Address, the president articulated his vision for a re-militarized America in which "faith and freedom" were the nation's "guiding stars." Reagan urged his fellow citizens that they could not remain "passive" with freedom "under siege." Thus, it was imperative to "help friendly governments defend themselves" and support "democratic forces" and "freedom fighters" whose struggle was "tied to our own security." Advocates believed this "Reagan Doctrine" to be a "highly cost-effective" strategy in rolling back communism, if not ultimately winning the Cold War. Not surprisingly, Soviet leaders heard a far more antagonistic, dangerous message emanating from the White House, especially given the president's earlier pronouncements that the West would "transcend communism."[25]

Reagan's support for "freedom fighters" waging wars from Afghanistan to Nicaragua advanced multiple political aims that alarmed Moscow. A successful proxy war in Central America, for instance, could fortify anticommunist efforts close to home. When Nicaraguan insurgent groups consolidated with the Sandinista National Liberation Front and overthrew the Somoza regime in 1979, Reagan only saw further proof of Carter's bungled foreign policy. But in chaos came an opportunity to flex America's new military muscles. Backing a winning counterrevolutionary effort against a Marxist-Leninist group also might exorcise the ghosts of Vietnam. Helping the "Contras" offered the additional chance to validate reworked counterinsurgency theories that had been discredited in Southeast Asia over the previous two decades. Shultz might judge Central America a messy "swamp" best avoided, but in Reagan's mind the risks were worth the rewards.[26]

While Democrats cautioned that the president's policies in Nicaragua might lead to another Vietnam-like political-military quagmire, Jeane Kirkpatrick pointed to a possibly more appropriate historical analogy: Munich. Deploying well-worn Cold War parallels, Reagan's ambassador to the United Nations railed against congressional recreants who opposed support to the Contras, arguing they were engaged in "self-defeating appeasement." Kirkpatrick, however, failed to acknowledge the atypical nature of Munich or the potential merits of patient diplomacy. Nor did the ambassadorial hawk reveal that the administration she served increasingly was dabbling in extralegal activities to combat the supposedly existential Sandinista threat.[27]

The "Weinberger Doctrine," based on a 1984 speech by the secretary of defense, certainly complicated these discussions, suggesting how Vietnam still informed Americans' thinking about war. Before the National Press Club, Weinberger laid out six principles for the use of military power in the aftermath of the Beirut barracks bombing. The United States, he argued, should not commit forces unless "vital national security interests" were involved. Committing those forces also required "defined political and military objectives," the support of the American public, and a "clear intention of winning." Clearly, the ghosts of Vietnam still lurked in the halls of power in Washington, DC.[28]

Weinberger's principles—journalist Bob Woodward called them "tests"—diverged sharply from Kirkpatrick's full-throated defense of Central American interventionism. Supporters claimed the secretary had constructed a "viable American strategy," one that accommodated the "imperatives of our superpower status to the realities of domestic politics." Yet questions remained. A decade after Saigon's fall, was Vietnam still a relevant historical case study? Which interests met the "vital" threshold to authorize military force? Would the president be able to guarantee public support once committing the nation to war? Officers like Colonel Harry Summers worried that the doctrine offered something different than intended, that "fear of escalation" had forced

Americans to act indecisively. "Our fears," he complained, "became a sort of self-imposed deterrent." Such constraints served the nation poorly with communism still on the march.²⁹

To resolve the Kirkpatrick-Weinberger dilemma required a reworking of language. War would be refashioned as a "moral struggle between good and evil" while paving over local differences within South and Central America. Reagan, believing that "under the domino theory, we're the last domino," justified involvement in places like El Salvador to help stabilize Nicaragua, if not the entire hemisphere. The president pitched US interventionism in now standard cataclysmic terms. El Salvador was "on the front line in a battle that is really aimed at the very heart of the Western Hemisphere," he argued, "and eventually at us." Never mind that noncommunists allied to leftist revolutionaries in El Salvador cared more about land reform than international politics. In Reagan's mind, American credibility was at stake. El Salvador had to be kept out of "enemy" hands.³⁰

These constructed fears rationalized an increased US military buildup across Central America. In the name of "national security," Americans would deploy men and materiel to assist those suffering under the boot of "communism." The CIA funneled massive military aid into Honduras, which had become a sanctuary for the Nicaraguan Contras and thus a new front in the war against hemispheric evil. Given the number of US military bases springing up in the encircled Central American country, administration officials joked that they had constructed the USS *Honduras*. The likelihood of Soviet-sponsored aggression in the Western Hemisphere, however, was small. With a brutal conflict in Afghanistan raging and the Russian economy teetering, the Kremlin had little incentive to sponsor new wars of national liberation so far from home. Yet fear of looking weak still prevailed in Washington. As one 1984 commission report held, "the triumph of hostile forces in what the Soviets called the 'strategic rear' of the United States would be read as a sign of U.S. impotence."³¹

These tensions between faith and fear became readily apparent in Reagan's Nicaragua policy. Support of the Contras represented a faith in the kind of counterrevolutionary forces that had marked previous

CIA activities in Iran and Guatemala during the Eisenhower administration. A similar faith in employing local forces to do America's heavy lifting overseas had informed the Nixon Doctrine. Yet long-held fears of communism spreading in Central America persisted. But so did fears of Reagan's policies undermining human rights. Congressional opponents claimed the Contras were vicious mercenaries helping an ousted Nicaraguan dictatorship slaughter its own population. Senator Frank Church (D-ID) went further, arguing that the idea of a communist threat being "everywhere has made our government its captive and its victim." To Church, the nation has "become so conservative—so fearful—that we have come to see revolution anywhere in the world as a threat to the United States. It's nonsense."[32]

The White House was not persuaded. Reagan claimed that Central America had become "the stage for a bold attempt by the Soviet Union, Cuba and Nicaragua, to install communism, by force, throughout this hemisphere." He thus pledged to "not break faith with those who are risking their lives." Following his Cold War predecessors, Reagan depicted local projects aimed at social uplift and land reform as communist-inspired. Yet contradictions in US policy endured. How could basic land-reform initiatives justify foreign military intervention? Did local civil wars sponsored by the United States and resulting in hundreds of thousands of deaths truly advance US foreign policy? Did political repression and authoritarianism? While the White House feared a loss of credibility on the world stage, Central Americans faced rising death rates, devastated economies, and escalating political instability.[33]

The notorious Iran-Contra affair might also be seen as a mixture of faith and fear with lasting political ramifications. As opposition to Reagan's Central American policies grew, Congress passed a series of laws, the Boland Amendment, which prohibited using funds to overthrow the Sandinista government. To circumvent what the administration believed to be legislative interference, Reagan's National Security Council concocted a bold, and quite illegal, plan. With the CIA's assistance, the White House would secretly sell arms to Iran, where the deadly Iran-Iraq war was still raging, and then use the unaccountable proceeds to fund the Contras. Oliver North, a marine lieutenant colonel on the NSC staff, directed the operation. As the scandal broke and condemnations poured in, Reagan played the unwitting patriarch duped by his hawkish brood. In leading his anticommunist crusade in Central America, the president apparently had adopted a faith based on sheer ignorance.[34]

While the sordid affair stained Reagan's second term, the Iran-Contra scandal also suggested something deeper about neoconservatives' faith in managing global anticommunist crusades. "Paramilitary enthusiasts" like Colonel North had little geostrategic experience. They simply accepted their innate power to harness counterrevolutionary forces abroad and direct them toward US foreign-policy goals. We might question, then, whether Reagan's team truly believed they were aiding, in the president's own words, the "moral equivalent of our Founding Fathers." It seems doubtful. Arguably, the administration only had faith in the Contras so long as it felt confident that Washington could finance and direct their operations. If right-wing rebel groups were little more than militarized extensions of the CIA, then Reagan's depiction of them as stalwart "freedom fighters" seemed suspect at best.[35]

Of course, dismissing contemporary anxieties over communism's spread, especially within the Western Hemisphere, would be an ahistorical mistake. Numerous policymakers inside the DC beltway genuinely feared the Soviet Union, with Cuba's help, might capitalize on the Nicaraguan civil war and secure that beleaguered Central American nation as a beachhead for communist expansion. (It also would be a mistake to discount the fact that those concerns typically were exaggerated, sometimes deliberately so.) To Reagan and his team, revolutionary groups like the Sandinistas posed a direct threat to American credibility. Could the United States maintain its prestige, the White House feared, if it allowed a band of ragtag guerrillas in Central America to sing songs calling the Yankee an "enemy of humanity"? Might not all of Latin America unite and form a bloc in opposition to US policies if left undeterred? The nightmare scenarios multiplied as easily as they reinforced one another.[36]

As in "limited war" theories of an earlier Cold War era, "low-intensity" conflict became a one-sided construct. Americans supported local clashes abroad, while indigenous proxies and their adversaries struggled for survival in society-engulfing wars. For fearful members of the Washington policy elite, global threats justified local sacrifices. Critics, however, weren't so easily convinced.

As Reagan began his campaign for a second term in the spring of 1984, esteemed historian Henry Steele Commager condemned US officials for their "historical ignorance." He wasn't speaking of the "great plague of amnesia" spreading within the executive branch as the White House fended off political attacks in the wake of Iran-Contra. Rather, the Amherst College professor maintained that interventions "dictated by the imperatives of self-defense" had been undermining American foreign policy since the Cold War's beginning. Commager cast doubt upon the reflexive justifications that fueled war after war. "Has Vietnam threatened us in any way," he queried, "any more than Cuba has threatened us, or than China has threatened us?" He asked the same question about El Salvador and Nicaragua, bemoaning that once again "we stand at Armageddon and we battle for the Lord. Will we never learn?" Commager knew his history, and the stinging critique fit. But Reagan, in a surprise move, was about to redirect his faith in a new direction that would challenge the professor's gloomy appraisal.[37]

CHAPTER 19

Contemplating the "End"

Rhetoric from the "Great Communicator" certainly helped his fellow citizens feel better about their place in the world. Without question, the president genuinely worried that America "had lost faith in itself." He also knew that uplifting, plain-spoken speeches pitting good against evil resonated given military setbacks in the Middle East and the humming background dread of nuclear war and global terrorism. And while some critics noted that the "premier political salesman" was having a hard time selling America "on the desirability of giving military aid to anti-government rebels in Nicaragua and more money to the Pentagon," Reagan still broadcast a tough image at home and abroad. To supporters, performance mattered as much as message.[1]

"Freedom" rested at the core of Reagan's political narrative. When, in a March 1983 speech to the National Association of Evangelicals, the president judged the Soviet Union "an evil empire," his followers identified with being on the right side of history. Religious faith comingled effortlessly with political faith. The Cold War would be won in church pews and fighter cockpits alike. Moreover, defining the global conflict in religious tones allowed Reagan to situate America on the moral high ground. A benevolent nation would spread freedom to those struggling under communism and offer them salvation from the Kremlin's wicked ways. Such a faith-based message resonated with evangelicals across the country. The president, if not his entire political party, took note.[2]

Casting Russia as the "focus of evil in the modern world" also helped Reagan make a direct correlation between military strength and political freedom. When the president visited the demilitarized zone separating North and South Korea in late 1983, he declared proudly that American troops there were "on the front lines of freedom." As he told a group of US infantry soldiers standing aside a bunker position, "There is no better proof of the relationship between strength and freedom than right here on the DMZ in Korea." Not surprisingly, such bombast played differently in the Kremlin than it did domestically. The following year, Soviet Minister of Foreign Affairs Andrei Gromyko told his assistants that "Reagan and his team have taken up as their aim to destroy the socialist camp. Fascism is on the march in America."[3]

Yet after the president's 1984 electoral trouncing of Walter Mondale, if not before, discerning observers might have noticed something incongruous in Reagan's martial chest-pounding. The evil-empire rhetoric was not necessarily being reflected in US foreign policy. Despite massive defense-budget increases, the commander-in-chief seemed indisposed to deploying conventional forces in combat. In fact, fears of escalation unintentionally leading to nuclear war haunted the president. As he campaigned for a second term, Reagan began to speak more and more of seeking peace and diplomatic solutions with the Soviets. "Living in this nuclear age," he declared in early 1984, "makes it imperative that we do talk."[4]

By the midpoint of the decade, while Chuck Norris and his Delta Force team were taking out plane-jacking terrorists onscreen, Reagan seemed increasingly earnest about the first half of the "peace through strength" maxim. The confrontational tenor diminished in his speeches. He spoke more of arms control and reductions in nuclear weapons. He speculated about the possibility of peaceful coexistence with the Soviet Union. And he elevated the role of diplomacy both in public and in private. This isn't to suggest that Reagan abruptly had lost his faith in military might. He most certainly had not. As Secretary of State George Shultz noted, the nation would still engage in a "parallel pursuit of strength and negotiation." But with the defense buildup secure, the president now believed he could negotiate from a position of power.[5]

With his second term locked in, political calculations arguably mattered less. True, the Californian long ago had invested in fearmongering to advance his political aspirations. Yet evidence suggests that, like British Prime Minister Margaret Thatcher, the ideals of individual liberty and identity were fundamental to his understanding of the Cold War contest. Such leanings did not bode well for those advocating government-sponsored social programs in the 1980s, especially in relation to defense spending. But from a more universalistic perspective, Reagan appeared to be resurrecting earlier Cold War critiques of atomic-era security policies. In short, Armageddon was not in the nation's best interest. Reagan thus began intimating that not just American lives mattered in a future nuclear exchange, but communist ones as well.[6]

Perhaps, the president conjectured, the risks of deterrence theory outweighed its benefits. Perhaps nuclear retaliation and national security were incompatible. With Shultz's help, he began asking tougher questions about old strategic assumptions. As a consequence, faith in military strength and fear of nuclear weapons became intertwined, not just in the president's commentary on national security issues but in his administration's formulation of US grand strategy as well. Already by 1983, Reagan believed relying on "the specter of retaliation, on mutual threat" to be a "sad commentary on the human condition."[7]

Yet deeper questions bubbled to the surface. Had Reagan lost his faith in war or just in nuclear deterrence? Or was the president contemplating something far more consequential—nuclear disarmament? Certainly, Reagan himself pushed for arms control efforts, beginning with the 1982 offer for Strategic Arms Reduction Talks. START, however, required Moscow to accept nearly all of the proposed armament cuts, leaving the Kremlin little choice but to rebuff Reagan's proposition. Given the severe economic problems within Russia and its satellite states, Soviet leaders surely had ample incentive to ease up in the global arms race. At this point, however, Reagan was not yet ready to think boldly about reducing the US nuclear-weapons cache.[8]

The president was ready, however, to break the nation's reliance on deterrence theory and mutually assured destruction. In 1983, Reagan unveiled his plans for a defensive shield to protect Americans from nuclear attack. Styled the Strategic Defense Initiative—mocking critics dubbed it "Star Wars"—SDI aimed, in Reagan's words, to build a "security shield that destroys weapons, not people." A faith in technology had reached its Cold War apogee. In arguing that it was far "better to save lives rather than avenge them," the president sought to transcend the uncertainty inherent in deterrence theory. In many ways, SDI became the epitome of faith and fear in the Reagan era: a faith in technological means saving lives coexisting uneasily alongside fears of a desperate Soviet Union employing nuclear weapons or of an accidental outbreak of nuclear war. In one technological fell swoop, the uncertainties of war would be washed away under the protective shield of a strategic defense system.[9]

Reagan's faith in countering the "awesome Soviet military threat" hardly enamored everyone. Surprised allies, whom the administration had not consulted prior to announcing the initiative, argued that SDI would undermine the 1972 Anti-Ballistic Missile Treaty and thus destabilize the geostrategic balance of power. Back at home, the president's claim that a strategic defense system might allow both the United States and Soviet Union to "do away with our nuclear missiles, our offensive missiles," left the security establishment aghast. White House officials quickly walked back Reagan's remarks, maintaining that he "was not seeking the elimination of all nuclear weapons" before any shield could be constructed.[10]

The secretary of defense also entered the fray by concentrating, as he had done so often in the past, on the communist threat. In defending SDI, Weinberger claimed that since the 1972 ABM treaty signing, the Soviets had "spent roughly as much on all forms of strategic defense as it [had] on its huge offensive program." The commitment to strategic defense was a "prudent hedge" against a "technological surprise." Yet concerns over feasibility undercut many of Reagan and Weinberger's claims. Famed writer Isaac Asimov judged SDI bad "Hollywood science fiction" and ridiculed the plan as "the wish-fulfillment dream of a shallow mind." Meanwhile, political cartoonists portrayed a becrowned commander-in-chief walking naked in public with imperial scepter in hand. A small boy shouts out, "The emperor has non-existent defense technology!"[11]

Here was a fundamental paradox embodied by Reagan—a man so fearful of nuclear war that he placed his faith in untested technology yet a president willing to push the limits of apocalyptic language, if not action. Allies and enemies alike were uncertain what to make of the contradiction. While friends on the European continent expressed their own fears of the alliance being in the hands of a "trigger-happy cowboy," Soviet politburo leaders were no less flummoxed. Though Reagan spoke of making cuts in nuclear arms, Gromyko believed that SDI "would be used to blackmail the USSR." Was the American president seeking to reduce Cold War tensions or to reignite the strategic arms race? Or was the Strategic Defense Initiative simply a Pentagon ploy to argue for more funds, even as the administration projected a $184-billion deficit for fiscal year 1984?[12]

It was in this ambiguous environment that a NATO military exercise intensified Soviet fears to fever pitch. In November 1983, the Western European allies conducted a major war game against simulated Warsaw Pact forces in which a conventional conflict would escalate to a nuclear one. Code-named Able Archer 83, the exercise was monitored by Soviet intelligence, as had become customary in similar war games. Yet the exercise's similarities to actual preparations for nuclear war unnerved some of the Kremlin's military and political leaders, especially when reports surfaced of NATO forces loading warheads and moving to "general alert" status. Was it possible that the West was preparing for a preemptive strike, that Able Archer was just a cover for a major launch?[13]

While historians and participants alike still debate the level of anxiety surging through the Soviet politburo as the war game unfolded, Moscow's response clearly impacted Reagan. In response to Able Archer, the Kremlin placed its strategic nuclear forces on alert, a worrying sign even without a major military exercise in motion. The potential for misperception and escalation—what Herman Kahn had warned about in the early 1960s—seemed real enough. When Reagan learned of the Soviet response in Able Archer's wake, he muttered pithily, "Really scary." In fact, the war game and what it had prompted so shocked the president that he renewed efforts to open up a dialogue with Moscow. As he recalled, "I was even more anxious to get a top Soviet leader in a room alone and try to convince him we had no designs on the Soviet Union and Russians had nothing to fear from us."[14]

While Weinberger spoke of the "moral obligation to defend" the "strongest nation in the history of the world," a new peace movement was pushing back against such combative rhetoric, especially if it risked an accidental nuclear war. By the mid-1980s, "freeze" activists were gaining traction by highlighting the destructive potential of antagonistic Cold War policies. The National Committee for a Sane Nuclear Policy (SANE), formed back in 1957, took up the mantle of the Vietnam-era antiwar movement and, aligning with the Nuclear Weapons Freeze Campaign, took their message across the nation. As one journalist noted, the nuclear disarmament and freeze movements had become a "coast-to-coast grass-roots crusade that commands comparison with the civil rights movement and the antiwar protests of the 1960s." *Time* reported how the freeze had attracted "broad-based support" from "across the socio-economic spectrum." Public-opinion surveys agreed. One 1983 Harris poll found that a staggering 87 percent of respondents concurred that the United States should negotiate "an effective nuclear arms agreement that would call for a real cut back" in US and Soviet arsenals.[15]

Environmentalist warnings only added to the potency of the nuclear-freeze movement's appeal. Scientists reported on diminishing life expectancies from "delayed fallout" and increased incidences of malignant diseases that would poison the human gene pool. Medical experts painted gruesome pictures of "lethal radiation syndromes" leading to central nervous system deaths, gastrointestinal deaths, and bone marrow deaths. Planetary scientist Carl Sagan and his colleagues warned of a "nuclear winter" in war's aftermath that would radically cool the earth and result in an uninhabitable planet. And in his widely read book *The Fate of the Earth*, journalist Jonathan Schell argued that a nuclear war would turn the United States into a "republic of insects and grass."

Schell extrapolated the "scenes of agony and death that took place at Hiroshima" and imagined a war with far more destructive weapons. Victims, he envisioned, would be "burned, battered, crushed, and irradiated in every conceivable way."[16]

The nuclear-disarmament campaign received another boost from popular culture. While Sagan and Schell examined the long-term ecological and environmental impacts of nuclear war, film director Nicholas Meyer took viewers to a small Midwestern city to observe what could happen in the immediate aftermath of nuclear war. In *The Day After* (1983), residents of Lawrence, Kansas, living next to Minuteman missile silos, suffer the horrific consequences of a nuclear exchange. Roughly 100 million Americans watched the made-for-television movie, some in sheer dread. After watching the broadcast special, one student claimed, "I think I'd rather die than survive a nuclear war." Reagan himself noted in his diary that the film left him "greatly depressed." Might the film have shaken the nation's faith in war? An early 1984 Gallup poll, taken only two months after the television special aired, indicated that forty-nine percent of Americans disapproved of Reagan's handling of foreign policy, more than ten percent higher than the number of those who approved.[17]

While an irritated president publicly panned *The Day After* as "anti-nuke propaganda," Washington elite continued to debate the merits of nuclear war. ABC News hosted a "Viewpoint" roundtable immediately following the film. Secretary of State Shultz believed the movie highlighted the "unacceptability of nuclear warfare." Carl Sagan agreed, suggesting the reality of war would be "much worse" than what the movie portrayed. Perhaps unsurprisingly, conservative critic William F. Buckley pushed back, arguing that Meyer was engaging in disinformation with harmful foreign-policy implications, an "enterprise debilitating to the United States." Former Secretary of State Henry Kissinger wondered aloud what the point was of "scaring ourselves to death" with such a "simple-minded notion" of a complicated question. Writer Elie Wiesel, a Holocaust survivor, opened his remarks with an admission. "I'm scared. I'm scared because I know what is imaginable can happen." To Wiesel, the film evoked uncomfortable memories. "I had seen it before, except once upon a time it happened to my people and now it happens to all people."[18]

That a television movie had garnered such a star-studded debate panel highlighted how *The Day After* had tapped into the zeitgeist of mid-1980s America. While Sagan and Buckley traded high-minded barbs, jazz composer Sun Ra took a different track. In "Nuclear War," the Afrofuturist dropped a rap/chant call-and-response song that spoke in far more direct terms. "If they push that button (if they push that button) / You can kiss your ass (you can kiss your ass). . . . / If they push that button (if they push that button) / It's a motherfucker (it's a motherfucker)." Pop musicians followed suit. In 1983 the German band Nena released an English version of "*99 Luftballons*," in which children's red balloons accidently spark a nuclear war. In "Russians" (1985), former Police front man Sting sang of "a growing feeling of hysteria" and hoped "the Russians love their children too." Clearly, larger public fears of nuclear war were eclipsing policymakers' faith in it.[19]

The lack of US-Soviet meetings over arms control during Reagan's first term had not helped matters, something which the president desperately hoped to rectify in his second term. The increased risk of misperceptions and miscalculations weighed on him as much as the public criticisms. Political scientist Robert Jervis, for instance, worried that "perceptual dynamics" might lead statesmen "to see policies as safe when they actually were very dangerous" or "to see war as inevitable, and therefore to see striking first, as the only way to limit destruction." National security analyst Arthur Macy Cox similarly believed that the greatest risk Americans faced was the "accidental launch of nuclear weapons." Meanwhile, former ambassador to the Soviet Union W. Averell Harriman openly rebuked the president for making America's "relationship with the Soviet Union more dangerous than at any time in the past generation."[20]

These pervasive fears of nuclear conflict ending both the Cold War and all of humanity with it ultimately pushed policymakers in Washington and Moscow toward each other. It would be a fitful promenade.

Wary politburo members continued to view SDI as a ruse, a way for US "ruling circles" to embark upon "a sudden application of a nuclear attack on the Soviet Union" while protecting the United States from retaliation. Back home, religious leaders entreated policy elite on both sides of the aisle to repudiate an "Armageddon Ideology" that inevitably would lead to nuclear war. Across the Soviet-American divide, political leaders, conditioned by decades of Cold War fearmongering, viewed with suspicion any claims that their ideological rivals were sincere in renouncing their faith in nuclear weapons.[21]

Yet behind the scenes, Reagan himself, thanks partly to George Shultz, was willing to be flexible, to "improvise," especially when he saw an opportunity to negotiate with a new Soviet premier. Even before Mikhail Gorbachev's rise to power, Reagan had been speaking in more moderate tones, calling for "constructive cooperation" in early 1984. Addressing the nation, he called for "peaceful solutions to problems through negotiations," a far cry from preparing for war against an evil empire. "In our approach to negotiations," the president maintained, "reducing the risk of war—and especially nuclear war—is priority number one." Had Reagan the hawk lost his faith in war? Did he no longer believe in war as the surest path to democracy's ultimate victory over communism? Had the nation's honor been restored to the point that it confidently could pursue peace? These were the questions confronting Americans as Reagan began his second term. And they were questions Moscow desperately was seeking to answer.[22]

Gorbachev's rise within a sclerotic Soviet state and party system offered an opportunity for Reagan. Finally, the American president had a counterpart with whom he could talk. Gorbachev was younger than his predecessors, less committed to the international class struggle, and agreed with Reagan that the nuclear arms race increasingly made little sense. In many ways, he too struggled with managing his own nation's relationship with war. Like his American counterpart, Gorbachev sought "strategic sufficiency" while reducing international tensions. The general secretary, though, had an added incentive to rein in defense spending and limit the global military competition. By 1985, the creaking Soviet economic system was showing signs of potential collapse. Gorbachev, quite simply, could not afford the Cold War.[23]

The new Soviet leader's rise came at an opportune time, when Secretary of State Shultz already had persuaded Reagan that dialogue could yield better results than threats. Trained as an economist, Shultz knew the Soviet economy had been stagnating for years and suggested in meetings with Kremlin leaders that globalization and the information revolution risked leaving the Soviet Union further behind. Integrating into the international economic system not only would benefit Russians but would lower tensions that risked sparking conflict. Based on this thinking, Shultz offered his boss a four-part framework for moving forward with Moscow: "bilateral relations, regional matters, arms control, and human rights." Diverging from administration hawks like Weinberger, the secretary of state believed that "patient dialogue" would yield far better results than threats and martial bluster.[24]

At the root of Gorbachev's problems, however, was not that he had to match Reagan's massive increases in defense spending. As Shultz correctly surmised, the Soviet economy's woes long predated Reagan. Sustaining the Warsaw Pact, for example, had taken a heavy toll, racking up Russian debt that only further aggravated a lethargic and overextended domestic economy. Rather, the Soviet Union had to rethink the entirety of its domestic and foreign policies, both of which had been shaped by the decades' long Cold War competition. Managing such a complex task of interrelated change proved immensely challenging. Gorbachev had to accept numerous political risks, both at home and abroad, from ending the war in Afghanistan to contending with increasingly vocal nationalist forces within the Soviet orbit. In some ways, Reagan was the least of his worries.[25]

Still, the apparently simultaneous evolution of Gorbachev and Reagan's dovishness both bewildered and threatened conservative hardliners. They railed against giving away too much to the Soviets and saw the new Kremlin leader as cut from the same cloth as his Cold War predecessors. "Let's have no illusions," Senator Dan Quayle (R-IN) proclaimed. "We are dealing essentially with the same Soviet Union that we have for the past seventy years." True, Gorbachev retained his commitment to a socialist system. It also became apparent that he was sincerely devoted to reform. Moreover, Reagan came to see that the Soviets actually feared the Americans. Given the combative tone of his first term, the epiphany might have come sooner. But old habits clung to the Washington establishment. Even as Gorbachev spoke of transforming Soviet foreign policy and restructuring the economy, DC elite doubted his motives. As one CIA specialist noted, Gorbachev was "simply a new and more clever and subtle proponent of Soviet global imperialism abroad and communism at home."[26]

In fact, the more Reagan reached out, the more hardliners cried foul, even within his own administration. Assistant Secretary of Defense Richard N. Perle proved among the most vocal. Perle had championed the Strategic Defense Initiative, thought arms reductions dangerous, and berated European allies as "mealy-mouthed." According to the *New York Times*, his "guiding light was mistrust." After resigning in 1987 over disagreements with Reagan's Soviet policy, the self-described neoconservative hawk argued that pursuing scientific exchanges with Russia was "like putting the K.G.B. into the Pentagon." To Perle, there was "not a shred of evidence" that Gorbachev desired "a respite from the burdens of military spending." As one biographer noted, Perle feared that a "naive public, led by naive politicians, would be deceived into believing [an arms control] treaty really reduced tensions." Perhaps not surprisingly, the hard right's "Prince of Darkness" would go on to become a key architect of the 2003 US invasion of Iraq.[27]

Reagan's vision of a future without fear of nuclear Armageddon, however, trumped these hawkish alarms. To be sure, the political fight proved to be an arduous one. While critics on the left berated the president for his martial rhetoric and his slashing of social programs, those on the right felt betrayed by their president as he spoke more and more of peace. The Soviets, they argued, had not changed their stripes. The war in Afghanistan raged on. The trampling of human rights continued. Had not Reagan himself called it a "massacre" and "an act of barbarism" when, back in September 1983, the Soviets mistakenly had shot down a Korean airliner, killing all 269 passengers and crew aboard? Hardliners were apoplectic over the president's change of course. But others saw it differently. Pulitzer Prize–winning journalist Anthony Lewis derided the "American right" for its obstructionism. "They have worked for years," Lewis maintained, "to keep Presidents from dealing with the Soviet Union, however responsibly."[28]

Similar fearmongering within the politburo confronted Gorbachev as the entire Soviet system seemed to be crumbling beneath him. Recalcitrant ministers pushed back against decentralization efforts. Party apparatchiks fumed over talk of expanding private property rights that reeked of capitalism. Senior military officials voiced alarm when their leader proposed cuts in defense spending. Indeed, it was Gorbachev, more than Reagan, who struggled to force his bureaucracy into accepting change. While some scholars paint the general secretary as a gullible reformist, one in need of patient American guidance, it seems more likely that Gorbachev clearly understood the true threats to his country's existence. It was no longer capitalist adversaries who posed the greatest threat. Rather, according to historian Melvyn Leffler, Gorbachev believed that Soviet security was "far more endangered by communist functionaries, economic managers, and demoralized workers than by any external foe."[29]

In this light, Gorbachev's rationale for withdrawing from Afghanistan becomes clear. The invasion had demonstrated the immense damages wrought from military interventionism based on fear and bad assumptions. The war had become, in one estimation, "a domestic burden and an international embarrassment for Moscow." As one of Gorbachev's closest aides shared, the politburo "could not go on paying such a heavy price in casualties, expenditure and isolation on the international scene." Thus, in February 1988, the general secretary announced that Soviet forces would complete their withdrawal over the following year. Gorbachev had lost faith not only in the Afghan government's ability to defeat the insurgency but in his own troops' capacity to build a socialist state in the war-torn country. As with the American experience in Vietnam, extracting Soviet forces became more important than defending what they would leave behind.[30]

More broadly, the long Soviet occupation of and fierce fighting in Afghanistan challenged Moscow's own faith in war. Rather than bolstering Russia's southern satellites, the conflict upset the delicate balance between tribal relationships, regional politics, and religious loyalties. Nor did military intervention warrant the Kremlin's faith in local proxies. As Americans would find in the coming decades, the Afghan government proved an unreliable ally. Moreover, the bloody civil war following the Soviet withdrawal only further demonstrated the painful aftereffects of miscalculated military alliances. As Gorbachev himself admitted, regional conflicts like Afghanistan were akin to "bleeding wounds capable of causing spots of gangrene on the body of mankind." In the end, the Soviet Union's final military struggle would highlight the problems of being dragged into war on the basis of bad assumptions and worse policy motivated by faith and fear.[31]

The same might be said for Americans who continued to support the Afghan mujahedeen without considering the potential long-term consequences of war destabilizing local societies simply to steal an advantage from the Soviets. For sure, an anticommunist Islamist movement had emerged even before the first Russian troops arrived. Yet the CIA's funneling of arms and money to the mujahedeen, even after the Soviet withdrawal, only furthered the breakdown of government services and the dissolution of civil society. Bit by bit, the ensuing Afghan civil war was becoming as violent as the communist invaders' scorched-earth tactics. Post-conflict cultural transformations seemed inevitable. As one Afghan-born scholar recalled, the younger generation knew "nothing but war, its ravages, and the power of the gun."[32]

Seeking stability in this broken society, Afghans turned to a new group promising to end the fractious infighting among local warlords. In 1994, the Taliban emerged and offered order in return for setting up a just Islamic system of government. War-weary Afghans accepted these "students of Islam" who presented themselves as religious saviors and social peacemakers. Faith born of war can take many forms. With the Soviet Union now defunct, though, most Americans cared little for a fearsome nation-building project taking Afghanistan in a new, potentially hazardous direction. If Central Asia remained pertinent, it only was so to US companies seduced by hypothetical profits spewing from Afghan oil fields. That Afghanistan might one day serve as a base for global *jihad*, or struggle, against the United States seemed inconceivable in the heady days of the Cold War's end.[33]

For Ronald Reagan, though, the Cold War had not yet ended. Back in 1987, the president, still under attack by hardliners for his conciliatory approach to Moscow, had traveled to West Berlin, giving one of the decade's most iconic speeches. In front of the Berlin Wall's Brandenburg Gate, the president implored Mr. Gorbachev to "tear down this wall" and emotionally declared there was "only one Berlin." The crowd roared in approval. Under "iron-gray skies," Reagan's oration shone as a pivotal moment. American leadership, rather than arousing fear, served to inspire citizens across the globe, to call for a reconsideration of the Cold War competition as Soviet reforms took hold. American ideals, the president claimed, mattered most. As Reagan grandly pronounced, the Berlin Wall "cannot withstand faith. It cannot withstand truth. The wall cannot withstand freedom."[34]

Yet behind the theatrics lay deeper questions. Did the Soviet Union's instability result more from internal factors—economic, political, or military shortcomings—or from the inherent superiority of the American cause? Reagan might trumpet his nation's faith in freedom, but how much did that truly factor into the current Soviet predicament? A faith in American democracy was one thing. Huge deficit spending to underwrite a grand re-militarization project was quite another. Without question, both elements served Reagan's larger anticommunist strategic goals, if not an innate desire to remake the world in an American image. But it seems worth probing if either of these considerations genuinely affected Gorbachev's thinking.[35]

In truth, domestic politics were as important to Gorbachev as they were to Reagan, or even more so. He continued to clash with military officials over defense cuts. Party conservatives complained that he wanted to "destroy" the socialist order. Most importantly, however, the general secretary faced staggering obstacles from an economic standpoint, isolated from the global system like few other nations. Aid to Third World countries and satellite nations within the Eastern bloc no longer were sources of security, but fiscal liabilities. Thus, fears of economic collapse were far more central to Gorbachev's thinking than Reagan's sermonizing at the Brandenburg Gate. In a moment of clarity, the American president hit upon his Soviet counterpart's dilemma. As he shared during one National Security Council meeting, "We *want* peace. They *need* peace."[36]

Gorbachev's faith in intentionally reconstituting the Soviet economy ultimately proved misguided. His aim of increased cooperation with the West made rational sense and preceded American initiatives. Surely, the general secretary believed, a "peace dividend" from disarmament would promote security while lowering the burden of massive defense outlays. But successfully balancing the Cold War competition with domestic reform left small margin for error. Gorbachev was unable to be so precise. His goals of economic decentralization were too ambitious given the capabilities of the state apparatus. Aggravating Gorbachev's woes, Central European allies began questioning their ideological ties to Moscow if Kremlin leaders were speaking of building some form of "socialist democracy."[37]

Tensions between Moscow and Warsaw Pact capitals had been building for some time. In 1980 and 1981, a wave of factory strikes had broken out in Warsaw that both challenged Soviet authority and rekindled earlier Cold War concerns about rebellious activity in Prague and Budapest. Eastern European leaders increasingly, yet carefully, looked to the West for economic assistance. Fears of political upheaval within the Soviet satellite states gripped Kremlin leaders. When, in 1987, Gorbachev deemed the Warsaw Pact a "strictly defensive alliance," he laid bare the changing nature of relationships among the Union of Soviet Socialist Republics as well. After decades of competition and conflict, the Cold War was entering, imperceptibly to many, its final act.[38]

Not all policy elite were ready to contemplate the Cold War's end. Surely, Reagan's trust in Gorbachev, especially in the face of hawkish critics, suggested the possibility of a changing international environment. Yet panic continued to grip communist party leaders in Moscow who felt humiliated that socialism had not lived up to its promises. Similar fears, from a slightly different perspective, arose in the American media. Journalist William Safire, for instance, argued that it was "safer to negotiate on the assumption that the Soviet Union has not given up its goal of world domination." Safire offered cynically that with "The Enemy"—he capitalized the term throughout one opinion piece for emphasis—gone, there would be no need for NATO, no help required for Afghanistan or Nicaragua, and "no need for a nuclear shield in space." Fear on both sides was extending the Cold War.[39]

Gorbachev and Reagan, however, persevered. At summit meetings in Geneva, Switzerland (1985) and Reykjavik, Iceland (1986), the two leaders spoke earnestly of nuclear arms reductions, SDI, and human rights. Reagan thought he finally had made a human connection with his Soviet counterpart. Yet both summits highlighted how long-standing fears could inhibit a willingness to engage. When the president revealed his desire of eliminating nuclear weapons, Washington policy elite let loose a flurry of condemnations. Strategic-arms "experts" decried the potential loss of the nuclear deterrent while arguing that Reagan's "enthusiasms" needed to be "curbed." Nixon and Kissinger, watching from the sidelines, argued that the proposals coming out of Reykjavik would reopen the "gap in deterrence," while future National Security Advisor Brent Scowcroft thought Reagan's plans an "absolute disaster."[40]

Once opened, the salvos continued to fire. The summits aroused neoconservatives to renew charges of "appeasement," while alleging that feckless politicians were undermining US national security. Clearly, they argued, Gorbachev had pulled the wool over Reagan's eyes. George Will grieved that "Reagan has accelerated the moral disarmament of the West by elevating wishful thinking to the status of political philosophy." Fellow columnist Charles Krauthammer scorned Reagan's policies as "ignorant and pathetic." Howard Phillips, chairman of the Conservative Caucus, went further, disparaging the president as a "very weak man with a strong wife and a strong staff" and a "useful idiot for Soviet propaganda." While Gorbachev spoke boldly of a "massive peace offensive," conservative critics, mimicking Fleet Admiral Gial Ackbar, saw only a trap.[41]

Yet both Reagan and Gorbachev shared a genuine desire to limit, perhaps even abolish, nuclear arms for fear of global devastation. For the Soviet general secretary, those fears already had been confirmed by the worst nuclear disaster since World War II. In April 1986, an accident at the Chernobyl nuclear power plant in Ukraine spread radioactive smoke throughout the local area, forcing the evacuation of thousands and poisoning scores of innocent civilians. The catastrophe, aggravated by the Kremlin's clumsy attempts to cover it up, shook politburo leaders. As Gorbachev lamented, "We felt the breath of a nuclear war." Moreover, long-held faith in a population's ability to guard against and survive a nuclear attack now appeared badly misplaced. Soviet physicist Evgeny Velikhov believed the disaster had "opened the eyes of all people that civil defense is nonsense." The accident had exposed the fiction of achieving "victory" in nuclear war. A contaminated, unlivable landscape seemed Chernobyl's only lasting legacy.[42]

One year later, in December 1987, Reagan and Gorbachev met for their third strategic summit, this time in Washington. With Chernobyl fresh in the public mind, the two leaders signed an arms-control treaty that actually eliminated an entire class of nuclear weapons. The Intermediate-Range Nuclear Forces (INF) Treaty offered a glimmer of hope that a desire for peace could overcome the fear of war. As in past summits, Gorbachev took the lead, proposing bold steps—and, in this case, shelving his objections of SDI—to envision a world without nuclear weapons. By now, however, Reagan had become a willing, even enthusiastic accomplice. Far from the "evil empire" activist of his first term, he had become convinced of the need to "offer a new hope for our children" by rendering "nuclear weapons impotent and obsolete." As one historian judged, Reagan had evolved into the "only nuclear abolitionist ever to be president of the United States."[43]

Contemporaries in his own party were not so kind. The summit and treaty had not inspired faith in a nuclear-free future, but instead fear of being deceived by the communist enemy. Former Secretary of Defense Caspar Weinberger argued that "Washington went mad" with disarmament talk, while another White House insider suggested that Gorbachev had "out-Reaganed Reagan." Columnist George Will complained that the president was "drunk on détente." How could he not see that Stalin, Khrushchev, and Brezhnev all had espoused similar forms of "peaceful coexistence" while engaging in the "East-West competition"? On a more practical level, worries abounded that the INF treaty might lead to a "re-nuclearization" of Europe as nations depended more and more on short-range, "tactical" nuclear weapons for their defense. Henry Kissinger, never shy about offering an opinion on US national security, feared the treaty might reduce the nation's retaliatory capabilities in a nuclear war. Age-old anxieties would obviously die hard.[44]

Neoconservative aspersions of this "appeasement," however, missed an important historical point about the United States' long-term infatuation with communism and its relationship with war. By concentrating so much on the Soviet threat, few policymakers could contemplate either the Cold War's end or the irrelevancy of long-held deterrence theories. "It jarred people," George Shultz recalled, "to think about no nuclear weapons." Fear had inhibited creative thinking about how the Cold War might conclude. One member of the conservative group Accuracy in Media illustratively called upon the president to understand that Gorbachev "is a communist and that he intends to carry out the goal of world domination by communism." The rote repetition of such outmoded clichés evoked nearly a half century's worth of willfully self-imposed fears and anxieties.[45]

A deeper fear, however, pervaded these national security debates as Reagan's time in the White House came to a close. If the "Gipper" had restored the nation's honor through massive spending to prepare for war, what would happen if the Soviet Union no longer posed an existential threat? By defining US prestige and credibility in martial terms, Reagan had set the nation up for future disappointment, if not despair. He had made war central to American identity. Yet the decades-long conflict for which Americans believed they had sacrificed so much soon would be over. Could the nation sustain its reputation, its honor, if war no longer was central to its integrity? In many ways, Reagan's faith in war was about to inspire new questions—and new fears—about war with the Soviet Union's collapse. Perhaps most fundamentally, what was war's purpose once the Cold War came to a close?

PART VI

War to Create Order

CHAPTER 20

Desperately Seeking Stability

A news reporter stands amid olive-drab army tents, razor-edged concertina wire, and sand-colored Humvees. Music blares in the background as the camera pans across a desert landscape before settling on a frustrated journalist, unhappy with her first take. She composes herself and then, as if ready to ask a question, states: "They say you exorcised the ghost of Vietnam with a clear moral imperative." The camera cuts quickly to three soldiers garbed in the iconic "chocolate-chip" fatigues that US personnel wore during Operation Desert Storm. "We liberated Kuwait," one declares emphatically, before he and his buddies whoop and holler in glee. A squad of soldiers descends upon the camera crew, singing Lee Greenwood's "Proud to Be an American."

Once more the camera cuts, this time to a helicopter pilot crooning off key as he flies above. Then again to another soldier, arms raised and wearing a makeshift turban scarf, singing as well. As the shot pans out to a group of drinking and roaring servicemen, Greenwood's soppy patriotic refrain is overtaken by a uniformed disc jockey spinning Public Enemy's "Can't Do Nuttin' for Ya, Man!" The soldiers, now with a full head of steam, circle into a martial thrash pit, violently dancing as the shouting hits fever pitch. Then in unison, they bellow "Trained warrior! Trained warrior!"[1]

This opening scene from David Russell's film *Three Kings* well captured the euphoria of the American armed forces' 1991 victory in Iraq. With the Cold War's end, the triumph appeared to vindicate Reagan's massive defense expenditures of the 1980s, the cherry on top of a decades-long conflict successfully prevailed. Across the nation, policymakers and citizens alike exulted in their military achievement. President George H. W. Bush gushed over America's "magnificent fighting forces" and hailed their victory as one "for all mankind." Journalist Rick Atkinson called the "relentlessly successful military campaign" a "42-day juggernaut," while one senior British officer pronounced Desert Storm "one of the greatest victories that we've ever experienced, certainly in our lives and possibly in history."[2]

The fictional *Three Kings* journalist, however, intimated something amiss in this moment of martial jubilation. Why were people asking about Vietnam while celebrating such a decisive military victory in Iraq? Perhaps because the president himself had brought it up. With the dust still settling as Desert Storm came to its rapid conclusion, Bush declared, "By God, we've kicked the Vietnam syndrome once and for all." The president was referring to a phenomenon by which the lost war had created an "isolationist current" within the US foreign-policy establishment. Writing in the aftermath of Saigon's fall, neoconservative critic Norman Podhoretz lamented the "slow erosion of our own sense of political value in response to the Communist challenge." To Podhoretz, the US defeat in Vietnam didn't mean intervention had been a mistake. Rather, the nation had to renew its commitment—and its responsibility—to protect the world from "the most determined and ferocious and barbarous enemies of liberty."[3]

While Bush congratulated himself for vaporizing Vietnam's ghosts, others worried that Desert Storm might create its own "Iraq Syndrome" by lowering the threshold for going to war. Congressman David R. Obey (D-WI) warned that the conflict should not "make the world safe for ill-advised wars." Fellow Representative John Lewis (D-GA) added, "I hope we don't get used to war being so easy. War is not a cure-all." Such cautionary talk, though, gained little purchase in the heady days when yellow ribbons and American flags were dotting the nation's landscape.[4]

The linkages between Vietnam and Iraq offered yet another view into the fraught relationship between faith in war and fear of war. Desert Storm suggested the merits of putting faith in Cold War military solutions for a new post–Cold War era. Reinvigorated and building on its success in Iraq, the nation and its armed forces could "end violence and impose order." And yet unshakable fears persisted. The Soviet empire may have collapsed, but the world, Americans were told, was still a dangerous place stubbornly resistant to US influence. What if Desert Storm was a one-off, an unrepeatable triumph? What if the Vietnam quagmire represented the true character of war, a future where internecine conflicts sapped American strength while exposing weaknesses within the world's sole remaining superpower? In this light, Iraq forewarned as much as it validated.[5]

Even before the Gulf War ended, political commentator Thomas L. Friedman was calling for a "new, stable balance of power in the gulf." As the journalist supposed, such a balance would emanate from "Washington's political influence in the region," which after America's imminent victory would be "greater than any other time in the postwar era." Friedman acknowledged the undertaking's likely costs. Some "outside power," he proposed, "is going to have to sit indefinitely on the horizon to make sure that Iran does not take advantage of the power vacuum in Iraq to reassert dominance." No doubt who that outside power should be.[6]

Friedman's call for stability, enticingly simple if Iraqis ousted Saddam Hussein, concealed deeper fears back home. Across Washington, policy elite worried that the post–Cold War era might be resistant to a stable, US-led world order. With Saddam remaining in power after Desert Storm, military victory seemed somehow incomplete. Thus the calls for a persisting US presence in the Middle East. Bush himself worried of "potential instability" across the globe that merited renewed fealty to the military-industrial complex. A new liberal world did not guarantee peace. In fact, the world appeared as dangerous as ever.[7]

Thus, despite the Cold War's end, US policymakers sensed an uncertain future. Their vision of a peaceful international system led by an unrivaled United States looked curiously vulnerable. Regional enemies imperiled American dominance, even without support from erstwhile Soviet benefactors. New requirements for maintaining global stability threatened to erase any economic peace dividends. Proposed defense reductions drew sharp criticism. Fearful observers worried that Pentagon budget and manpower cuts might weaken the nation's ability to undertake "more demanding missions" necessitated by regional threats. As one analysis cautioned, "formidable" opponents like Iraq not only would become more powerful in the future but might attack on shorter notice than any imagined Soviet invasion in the Cold War era.[8]

If military victories like Desert Storm weren't as definitive as first assumed, perhaps new threats could be diminished through building global economic ties. With the United States leading, agrarian societies, once susceptible to communist influence, could be shepherded into the modern, techno-industrial world. Perhaps, more than a few social scientists mused, earlier modernization theorists had met their time, when societies around the globe would follow in the footsteps of the Cold War's victor. Since the former Soviet Union had become a "minefield of nationalist grievances and aspirations," then a rational, modernizing approach to US foreign policy might promise the stability for which Washington policymakers yearned.[9]

Certainly, an economic component subsidized this faith in America's example. A cornerstone of Clinton-era policies assumed that global communism's death knell would reopen markets formerly off limits behind the Iron Curtain. Taking its cue from liberal international-relations theories, Clinton's administration extolled a faith that economic interdependence among democratic nations was the best way to avoid war. Indeed, some editorialists in the 1990s argued that the Cold War's real story was not the triumph over communism but the "triumph of an ambitious American economic vision," one rooted in the foundations of US history. To more than a few political forecasters, global security actually meant American economic security.[10]

But this faith in the United States' ability to serve as an example for those emerging from the yoke of Soviet oppression misrepresented a key aspect of recent history. The American-led Cold War order had relied on coercive means. The US government had supported regime-changing coups, leveled Asian lands through carpet-bombing, and imposed economic sanctions with little regard for humanitarian consequences. The liberal order had a decidedly "illiberal" feel to it. Moreover, prioritizing American economic interests over global liberal ideals hardly inspired those less fortunate. The nation might applaud a new Pax Americana rising in the Cold War's aftermath, but activists from Latin America to the Middle East soon would condemn the brutal nature of the United States' neo-imperial projects.[11]

If critics knocked US foreign policy from abroad, so too did they at home. Aggrieved ultra-conservatives believed Washington policymakers weren't doing nearly enough to "guarantee 'peace and security' for future generations." The global "anticommunist revolution," they argued, should be extended beyond the Cold War contest. In their view, the Vietnam syndrome hadn't been kicked at all. To some marginalized, increasingly bitter veterans, a feckless government and unpatriotic antiwar movement had betrayed them, the failures in Vietnam highlighting inherent weaknesses of a multiracial American society. Fearing their own loss of privilege, veterans with ties to the white power movement placed their own warped faith in militia activities targeting the US government. Such dangerous fantasies ultimately would lead to acts of domestic terrorism, further expanding the notion of national security "threats" in the Cold War's wake.[12]

These threats, both foreign and domestic, suggested that any reluctance to engage militarily overseas might lead to perilous vulnerabilities. Optimists held to their faith that the Cold War's end would produce a "peace dividend," that revenues formerly spent on war could be redirected to "roads, clean air, education, housing and foreign economic aid." Yet old fears endured. On the eve of Desert Storm, Defense Secretary Dick Cheney warned that redeeming any peace dividend would result in an outbreak of war in the Middle East. At least in the short term, Cheney argued, preparation for war must take precedence over defense budget reductions. No wonder some political scientists maintained that the so-called Vietnam Syndrome—American's aversion, in the years after the Vietnam War, to defense commitments overseas—had been a "myth" all along. If policymakers could broadcast threats in compelling fashion, Americans likely would support almost any use of military power abroad.[13]

Not surprisingly, debates over military interventionism and the United States' global obligations became political fodder. Columnist George Will blasted liberals for their false claims of "the reflexive militarism of the right." Rather, Will contended, conservative realists understood that military power had three functions—"deterrence and coercion and reassurance." Will believed the final function, reassurance, offered a sense of security needed in uncertain times. Moreover, the journalist felt that historians reflected his thinking in condemning liberal antiwar romantics. Writing in 1995, Yale classics historian Donald Kagan confidently maintained that "the only thing more common than predictions about the end of war has been war itself." To hard-power advocates like Will, a secure world order guaranteed by Pax Americana would cost far less than "the ubiquity of war."[14]

Both the Bush and Clinton administrations apparently found merit in Will's argument. As they struggled to define an overarching grand strategy to replace George Kennan's guiding light of containment, the US armed forces spread across the globe. American military interventions spiked in the post–Cold War era. But for what overarching purpose? What global response was needed when the "Evil Empire" had been defeated? In a 1990 news conference with West German Chancellor Helmut Kohl, Bush warned that, with the Soviet Union in its death throes, "The enemy is unpredictability. The enemy is instability." Improved global stability, he believed, required increased US military activity.[15]

A key problem here was one of language. What followed containment? The White House wasn't sure. Bush's secretary of state, James Baker, proposed an American-centric answer. "Beyond containment lies democracy," Baker claimed. "The time of sweeping away the old dictators is passing fast; the time of building up the new democracies has arrived." The Clinton team spoke similarly, expressing faith that trade liberalization, backed by political warfare against "countries of concern," would offer coherence to US foreign relations in the 1990s. Yet, as one scholar has argued, these efforts lacked a "grand metanarrative to justify or explain the projection of power." In the end, Washington couldn't articulate a Kennanesque vision for military interventionism in the post–Cold War era. The best wary policymakers could offer was "stability."[16]

From a narrow Western perspective, the Cold War *had* provided stability. Nuclear war had been averted. Communism had been contained. America had retained its superpower status. And yet peace still seemed elusive. Already new dangers were emerging from the shadows, ones in which states themselves no longer were the central drivers of violence. Indeed, the concept of "failing states" introduced the prospect of an unstable world, in which violence was unrestrained by Cold War superpowers. Perhaps earlier policymakers who feared the nonalignment movement had been right all along. In due course, old fears took on new forms. Chairman of the Joint Chiefs John M. Shalikashvili, speaking during Clinton's second term, captured these apparent dangers. As the Cold War ended and the world found itself "unshackled from the fear of global war," the general shared, "we also found ourselves with failing states, humanitarian tragedies, ethnic conflicts and regional bullies, all capable of damaging our interests if left to their own devices."[17]

Within this chaotic international environment, persistent nuclear threats added fuel to already burning fear-based fires. The possibility of nuclear war seemed heightened by irrational "rogue" actors obtaining weapons from the former Soviet empire. Senior officials claimed the United States confronted "a bigger proliferation danger than we've ever faced before." Critics thus rebuked the Clinton administration for not limiting the sale of sensitive technologies to potential adversaries. (Defense industrialists, worried about profit losses in a post–Cold War era, proved far less circumspect.) One Clinton detractor scolded the White House for allowing China to ship advanced weaponry to Pakistan and Iran and for turning a blind eye to Beijing's "proliferation practices." Could it be the world was safer when mutually assured destruction theories prevailed? Given neither Bush nor Clinton could "tame" these "rogue states and nuclear outlaws," it certainly appeared that way.[18]

The struggle to find a strategic heir to containment proved not just a policy problem but a cultural one as well. A generational faith in war and anticommunism had left Americans uncertain of the future, since they no longer had an identifiable enemy with which to contrast themselves. A senior advisor to Mikhail Gorbachev surely had it right when alleging the Cold War's end would be a "terrible thing" for the United States because it would "deprive" the nation of an enemy. In fact, Americans had spent most of the era defining their identity in comparative terms. "Good" Americans were fervent anticommunists. What would the nation now stand for if it had nothing to stand against?[19]

Thus, as Americans entered the twentieth century's final decade, they strained to reconceptualize their relationship with war. Global transformations were pushing them into new foreign-policy territory where ideology seemed less important—perhaps even irrelevant—to local actors freed from the Cold War superpower competition. This fear of the strategic unknown may help explain the amplified talk of liberal values and humanitarian concerns driving US policy in the 1990s. Spreading democracy after the Soviet Union's collapse, analysts mused, could create an ever-enlarging "zone of peace." Faith in liberal idealism appeared justified, the theory went, because democracies rarely fought each other. The "phenomenon of growing interdependence" supposedly decreased "the appeal of war." The coming decade, however, would put into question the merits of such optimism.[20]

These divisions between foreign-policy idealists and realists would become increasingly visible as the grand strategic arc of containment reached its endpoint. Throughout the 1990s, Americans continued to debate war's utility, if not its relevancy. Yet war lurked in the background, promising service on behalf of the state. Policy elite thus retained their faith in force, believing it vital for establishing order and maintaining stability given what the Cold War competition had wrought. War, though, remained a fickle servant. As US policymakers would be reminded again and again in the coming decade, military interventionism was an ineffective tool for generating global stability.

CHAPTER 21

War in an Era of Triumphant Liberalism

In a region many Americans still believed to be the locus point of Cold War threats, nationalist sentiments bubbling from within Eastern Europe during the late 1980s appeared to be driving events as much as Gorbachev's domestic policies. Certainly, the Bush administration felt that way. Having won the 1988 election, Reagan's vice president came to power just as Gorbachev was losing his grip on his. Liberalization in Soviet satellite states began outpacing the Kremlin's ability to manage transformational change. Worse, the general secretary's aims of reforming the Soviet economic and political systems, dubbed *perestroika*, appeared powerless at stemming the rising turmoil. The Baltic states' calls for independence, Bush recalled, "posed what the Soviets saw as a mortal threat to the integrity of the Union itself."[1]

Meanwhile, Polish nationalism, inspired by the 1980 Solidarity movement, found a voice not just in Europe but around the globe. Clamoring for lower food prices and relief from crippling debt, disaffected Poles mounted an ideological offensive that cast doubt on socialism itself. Like earlier Moscow leaders who worried about the spreading "contagion" of Solidarity, Gorbachev feared that rising nationalist sentiments in Poland would spread throughout the republics before economic reforms took hold. While promising a "profound transformation of the Soviet federation," the general secretary warned of "the enormous danger" posed by "manifestations of nationalism" that could lead to ethnic conflict and threaten the Russian state's very integrity. Sovietologists wondered aloud if Gorbachev could "guide the passions he's aroused."[2]

Thus, at the very moment when Cold War victory appeared within reach, Washington elite were caught by the moment's irony. An enduring faith in their cause had led them to the precipice of a fragmented, unstable new world order, one potentially more dangerous than the last. They long had championed nationalism as a bulwark against communism. Now, the "ideals of western democracy—tolerance, civility, freedom, opportunity"—seemed unable to contain nationalism's worst excesses. Nor did the transition to a global market economy inspire optimism, rather concerns of economic frustrations leading to increased political instability. In a sign of changing times, US policymakers agreed with the St. Petersburg mayor who feared that "disenchantment and dissatisfaction with democracy" would set in if local authorities and new state leaders failed to stop inflation and falling living standards.[3]

The president shared these concerns. Despite signs of the Cold War coming to a peaceful end, Bush remained cautious—"prudent," he called it. While critics disparaged him as "timid," Bush tried to navigate a middle course, worried Gorbachev and his reformers had unleashed something they no longer could control. Flak came from both sides. Some detractors faulted Bush for being too eager to use military force for imposing "an excessively ambitious, American-centered 'new world order.'" Others condemned him for being too slow to act, for engaging in "calculated neglect of democracy and human rights" as ethnic conflicts emerged in the early 1990s. All the while, the president feared long-standing global relationships might descend into chaos and violence, weakening American influence and power in the process.[4]

A collapsing Soviet Union thus offered few pretexts for triumphant self-congratulation. Old fears resided in Cold Warriors like National Security Advisor Brent Scowcroft, who argued in early 1989 that the "Cold War is not over" and cast doubt on Gorbachev's "peace offensive." The retired air force general denounced Kremlin plans to—as he saw it— "unmake NATO" through a false campaign of disarmament, leaving the western alliance facing a "more serious threat than ever before." As a distrustful Scowcroft recalled, despite Gorbachev's attempts to "kill us with kindness," the general secretary "remained a communist," committed to the Soviet Union's "socialist future."[5]

Public pressures encouraged the president to share Scowcroft's wariness. To many Americans, Bush seemed to lack his predecessor's swagger, his willingness to stand up to threats, regardless of their potency. Back in 1987, *Newsweek* had run a cover story, "Fighting the Wimp Factor," arguing that Bush suffered "from a potentially crippling handicap—a perception that he isn't strong enough or tough enough for the challenges of the Oval Office. That he is, in a single mean word, a wimp." Fears of looking weak reinforced those of Gorbachev pulling the wool over Americans' eyes. Of course, fear of being branded a "wimp" led politicians like Bush and Governor Michael Dukakis to publicly demonstrate their machismo. "Who can spend the most for weapon systems," one political analyst noted, "and who will respond most swiftly to any aggression anywhere on earth?"[6]

As Bush took heat for not acting more forcefully, his administration strived to end the Cold War peacefully. Fears of what would replace the collapsing international system vied with faith that the United States might now be able to reshape the globe as the world's sole remaining superpower. Obviously, the White House exercised only so much influence. Bush's team might have plans to build a "new world order," but only leaders inside the disintegrating Soviet Union could ensure a peaceful transition to a new post–Cold War era.[7]

Americans were not alone in eyeing the future warily. West Germans worried not only about constructing a new post–Cold War national identity, but also keeping their economy from crumbling as former East Germans streamed westward in late 1989. The dramatic dismantling of the Berlin Wall that November seemed a fitting coda to a global contest that had once been localized on German soil. But in Bonn and Washington alike, policymakers braced for surging violence as the East German state gave way. Would revolutionaries protesting Erich Honecker's Socialist Unity Party of Germany remain peaceful after its collapse?

More broadly, what would a reintegrated Germany look like after being divided for so long? From Jerusalem to Moscow, long-suppressed fears of Germany's Nazi past resurfaced as reunification plans took shape.[8]

Similar fears in Washington led Bush to commit himself to a non-negotiable stance: a reunified Germany must be tied to the West and, ultimately, included in the NATO alliance. The president realized the "strategic ramifications of German reunification were understandable causes for Soviet trepidation"—they were—but saw an alliance with Germany as crucial to preserving US influence on the continent. If Bush "hoped to encourage stability in Eastern Europe as it changed," then he needed a strong regional partner with which to ally. Reflecting old fears, Prime Minister Margaret Thatcher bluntly spoke of restraining the "German juggernaut," but Bush would not be denied. American interests took precedence over British uncertainties.[9]

"The Iron Lady" might be forgiven for her anxieties. They had prevailed across the Cold War years. Decades earlier, Nikita Khrushchev had dryly noted, "We have a saying here: 'Give a German a gun; sooner or later he will point it at Russians.'" Back home, singer-satirist Tom Lehrer hummed "MLF Lullaby," a critique of US plans to include Germany in a nuclear-armed Multilateral Force. As Lehrer had sung in 1965, "Once all the Germans were warlike and mean / But that couldn't happen again / We taught them a lesson in 1918 / And they've hardly bothered us since then." Weapons manufacturers proved far less circumspect, perceiving a coming windfall by selling arms to an expanded NATO. As one observer put it, companies like Lockheed Martin had "an emotional commitment to NATO expansion."[10]

As pundits debated NATO's purpose after the Warsaw Pact collapse, the Soviet Union's imminent downfall offered a rare opportunity for solidifying US influence around the world, especially for those espousing a faith in American power abroad. As Scowcroft recalled, "Suddenly, everything was open to reconsideration." Yet new challenges quickly emerged. NATO enlargement might incentivize domestic reforms within former Soviet states, but it also risked reviving Russian fears of encirclement. As the US ambassador to the United Nations,

Madeleine Albright, warned, the administration and its allies had to harmonize "three seemingly competing objectives: to revitalize NATO, to avoid antagonizing Russia by feeding nationalist tendencies, and to calm growing fears in Central and Eastern Europe."[11]

Albright's counsel suggested how the reconstruction of post–Cold War Europe might be seen as an unwelcome sequel to the peace settlements following World War II, when the collapse of an older order spurred the pursuit of a stable replacement. But as in 1945, competing visions of the future collided. Just as Gorbachev hoped to stabilize his country and then return it to a position of strength, Helmut Kohl, chancellor of the newly unified Germany, similarly pursued policies to rebuild his state's political and economic power. All the while, Bush strived for order to maintain US influence in a rapidly changing Europe. Behind all of this, fears persisted that, if NATO did not maintain a strong military presence, Russian armed forces might return to Eastern Europe.[12]

If the White House retained its faith to manage these competing priorities, Bush and his team remained reticent in declaring the Cold War won. Despite prevailing evidence of the USSR's impending collapse, the administration demurred, old fears clinging to the US national security establishment like barnacles to a rusted warship. What if the Soviet Union's breakup led to "catastrophe"? What if the republics devolved into anarchy and pulled the United States into another European war? What if Russia, excluded from European integration, responded militarily? As fears mounted, George Kennan surmised difficulties in accepting the Cold War's peaceful ending. As the father of containment offered, members of the Bush administration could neither ignore the past nor "allow themselves to be the captives of all its emotional traumas."[13]

If US policymakers weren't traumatized by the past, they certainly were drawing lessons from it. To them, NATO had provided security during the Cold War and must continue to do so in the future. Thus, twice during the 1990s the United States would lead efforts to enlarge NATO. Multilateral defense arrangements still made sense in the post–Cold War world, especially if they facilitated US hegemony in Europe. At the time, however, enlargement advocates spoke less of protecting

American continental interests and more of spreading democratic, liberal values in former Soviet client states. This even as military officers in Germany were "trying to define new missions now that the old threat is gone." As one noted, "The soldiers don't know what their duty is any more." American GIs would share these doubts throughout the 1990s.[14]

Brent Scowcroft felt more certain, declaring the Cold War would be over "when the Soviets accepted a united Germany in NATO." But wars never conclude so neatly. Despite favoring enlargement of NATO, at least some American analysts worried that its expansion in Eastern Europe might goad Russia into more aggressive action and aggravate the transition to a new era. They were right to be concerned. Many Russians—among them a young KGB officer, Vladimir Putin—saw the Berlin Wall's collapse as a humiliating defeat. Putin recalled that the Cold War's end and a united Germany's rise illuminated how the Soviet Union had suffered a "terminal disease without a cure, namely paralysis. Paralysis of power." To like-minded Russians, Gorbachev and his successor, Boris Yeltsin, had abandoned the Soviet cause, allowing the United States to fill a vacuum created by the USSR's collapse.[15]

Still, both Bush and Clinton spoke often of "enlargement" and "engagement," intimating an activism to post–Cold War grand strategy. Of course, Americans long had seen NATO as an extension of the US defense establishment. The Soviet Union's demise, though, threatened to eliminate the rationale for engagement. If the communist peril had faded, then why the need to employ American armed forces across the globe? To Clinton, a forward-leaning foreign policy could combine ideals as well as interests. Despite "no looming threat on the horizon," the United States and its allies could provide global leadership by extending "the reach of security and prosperity to the new democracies in Europe that once were on the other side of the cold war." Security analysts fretted about the 1990s becoming a period of "strategic pause," but neither Bush nor Clinton was ready to relinquish the nation's authority over the international system, regardless of what that system looked like.[16]

This focus on an enlarged, retooled NATO underlined continuing tensions between faith and fear. Washington elite retained their faith in expanding democracy globally, yet fears of a still dangerous world cultivated a demand for alliances and "collective engagement." While critics wondered why military alliances were necessary given so few adversaries, Bush warned NATO must not "disperse out of euphoria." Clinton equally worried a "gray zone of insecurity" might reemerge in Europe without a strong alliance. A new American grand strategy would replace deterrence of current threats with prevention of future ones. In this calculus, the threat of would-be aggressors required collective security and military readiness that only alliances like NATO could offer.[17]

After a failed coup attempt against Gorbachev in August 1991, the deck seemed stacked against the long-term viability of the Soviet state, further stimulating debates over European security and NATO's future. Gorbachev argued that the plotters "wanted to strike a blow at the vanguard of democracy," seeking to upend "the democratic transformation of the country." Yet when Yeltsin assumed leadership of the new Russian Republic in December, the Soviet empire's demise felt somehow unsatisfying. Perhaps fears of what came next precluded a celebratory mood. Perhaps the transition lacked a defining moment like the symbolic tearing down of the Berlin Wall two years earlier. Or perhaps suspicions got the best of Americans who worried Yeltsin might not differ from his hardline communist predecessors who ran the Soviet military machine.[18]

Despite persistent fears of what lay ahead, Bush's national security team couldn't help but be relieved by the largely peaceful ending of the Cold War or swayed by a prevailing sense of "triumphant liberalism." Writing in early 1990, historian John Lewis Gaddis noted that the "abrupt erosion of superpower authority" in Europe had "created unexpected opportunities for geopolitical 'grand designers.'" The moment called for bold ideas. Thus, while cautious advisors like James Baker worried about the unpredictability of newly independent republics, more audacious Americans claimed the time had come to create a truly "liberal international order."[19]

With the receding Soviet threat, however, new and lesser enemies would have to suffice in justifying America's continuing relationship with war. Bush already had set the claim by authorizing an invasion of Panama back in 1989. Denouncing General Manuel Noriega's corrupt dictatorship, the president offered a host of reasons for sanctioning the largest military operation since Vietnam: facilitating democracy and human rights, protecting Panamanian and American civilians, and disrupting international drug trafficking. That Noriega seemed to be "thumbing his nose" at the US presence in Latin America only further incentivized Bush to war. As Joint Chiefs Chairman Colin Powell alleged, American credibility once more was on the line. To ignore the challenge from a "third-rate dictator" would be "intolerable," an "affront to the country." Old assumptions retained their relevance in the new world order.[20]

In late December, Bush launched Operation Just Cause. More than 25,000 US armed forces descended upon the small isthmus country. Within hours, the Panama Defense Forces had yielded, though it would take nearly two more weeks to capture Noriega himself. Senior military officers, with bitter Vietnam memories still fresh in their minds, extolled the superior power they had brought to bear. With fewer than thirty US casualties, defense officials savored the victory. Yet inside the Pentagon, underwhelmed critics dubbed the invasion "Operation Just Because," while those outside DC labeled Bush a belligerent "gringo meddler." Perhaps smaller wars in places like Grenada and Panama were not as homeopathic as White House officials hoped them to be.[21]

Looking back, Pentagon leaders might have been more circumspect over their Just Cause victory. While they took satisfaction that the operation "represented a bold new era in American military force projection," they passed over the looting and rioting following the US invasion. Nor did they consider whether the Noriega threat had demanded such a massive display of military force. (Of course, such adventures fit within a long imperial history, with the US military invading Panama twenty-four times between 1856 and 1989.) And while policymakers believed winning the "war on drugs" was vital to the nation's health, they equivocated on whether Panama's new civilian government materially advanced such an ambitious goal. It wouldn't be the last time Washington elite focused on applying military force while failing to plan for what would come afterward.[22]

While Noriega played his role as a small-time film-noir gangster, Saddam Hussein emerged from central casting as the villainous lead. The brutal dictator looked the modern-day stand-in for Hitler or Stalin. (Didn't he too have a mustache?) Naturally, such analogies could justify, even mandate, military action for fear of being labeled an appeaser. One contemporary critic equated words like "Hitler" and "madman" to "warspeak." Saddam, though, had helped trigger such language through his own aggressive action. In the aftermath of the Iran-Iraq War, he took a belligerent stance toward Israel and the United States, all while tightening his reign at home to limit anti-regime dissent. He also looked south, to oil-rich Kuwait, whose petroleum could help rebuild his military arsenal and bolster his teetering economy. In early August 1990, Iraqi forces leaped across their southern border and occupied Kuwait.[23]

The invasion sparked a new round of fears in Washington. The White House worried that Saddam might attack Saudi Arabia, engulfing the entire region in war. CIA director William Webster expressed concern over the Iraqi dictator now controlling some "twenty percent of the world's oil reserves," with another twenty percent only "a few miles away." More broadly, Saddam's bold move into Kuwait—what Bush deemed "naked aggression"—suggested that local actors, finally decoupled from the Cold War competition, might feel emboldened to use war for their own purposes, unconstrained by superpower benefactors. As in Panama, US credibility once again seemed endangered. Bush commenced upon building an international coalition while compelling the UN Security Council to demand Iraq "immediately and unconditionally" withdraw its forces from Kuwait.[24]

As the United States prepared, almost inevitably, for war, a renewed faith in airpower arose from the Vietnam ashes. Given technological advances in global positioning systems, advocates spoke in tantalizing terms about "precision" bombing. Newspapers shared alluring diagrams of America's "air armada" alongside armament checklists, ostensibly so that readers could keep score at home. How could Iraq withstand an aerial assault, air acolytes posited, when fighter jets—with names like "Thunderbolt," "Fighting Falcon," and "Wild Weasel"—were fitted with high-speed cannons, gravity bombs, and laser- and TV-guided missiles? Here was a new form of war porn for American viewers raised on Rambo and Braddock.[25]

Airpower advocates deemed their operational theories capable of harnessing these awesome technologies. Air Force strategists like John Boyd and John Warden resurrected long-held dreams of avoiding messy ground warfare by means of airpower properly applied. Boyd spoke of greater speed in decision-making processes to paralyze an adversary. Meanwhile, Warden laid out a model of concentric rings—"subsystems," he called them—to target an enemy's military forces, its population and "organic essentials," and its leadership. These theorists deemed air forces uniquely suited to attacking an adversary physically and psychologically, even morally, all with greater efficiency than ground troops. As Desert Storm launched, Boyd and Warden apparently had met their moment. Winged warriors would deliver victory quickly and emphatically.[26]

In Iraq's deserts, for a brief moment in early 1991, war seemed useful again. Hawks declared that military force, not economic sanctions, had forced Saddam's hand. Fears of a "major influx of casualties" overloading military hospitals went unrealized in a 100-hour ground campaign that rivaled any Hollywood action movie. Senior air force officers like General Buster Glosson crowed that "we had revolutionized the way war would be fought in the future." Back home, journalists promoted equally triumphant narratives. One foreign correspondent thought Desert Storm had established "with clarity the strength and scope of American muscle in the post–Cold War era." Once more, war became meaningful, invigorating, virtuous. The patriotism inspired by war, quite simply, felt good.[27]

Yet fears of Iraq turning into another Vietnam quagmire demanded Bush preserve limited political goals while the Pentagon planned its exit strategy. The White House wanted clear messaging: the forces liberating Kuwait would "do their job quickly, massively and decisively. And when their mission is completed, they will go home." US troops overstaying their Middle East welcome, the president worried, might feed into Saddam's intention to "fan Arab-Israeli tensions." Americans were not there to engage in a decades-long nation-building project. Neoconservative critics not surprisingly lambasted Bush for yielding to the "power of fear and defeatism." Now wasn't the time, they claimed, for "postwar timidity and restraint."[28]

While numerous politicos supported the liberation of Iraq after that of Kuwait, Saddam remaining in power hinted that airpower advocates hadn't quite delivered on their grandiose promises. If John Warden had guaranteed "strategic paralysis" of the enemy, why were Iraqi Republican Guard units continuing to resist even after absorbing punishing blows from the air? Why did it take a ground invasion to compel the regime's withdrawal from Kuwait? Airpower acolytes had pledged they could force an end to hostilities by targeting an enemy's willpower, but their accomplishments in Iraq seemed incomplete at best. Warden's wingmen had disrupted Saddam's military forces for sure, but they hardly had "decapitated" the regime's political leadership.[29]

Most contemporary Americans took scant notice of airpower's limitations. They were too busy being entertained. With a twenty-four-hour news cycle, war became perpetual theater, one critic calling Desert Storm a "Pentagon trade show with live ammunition." Viewers were consuming war as part of their daily lives, commercials and all. Yet in seeking a wide audience, networks like CNN blurred the lines between informative news, governmental propaganda, and martial entertainment. Pentagon spokesmen proved willing participants, the Gulf War a golden media event for communicating military relevance in the post–Cold War era. As one observer wryly noted, uniformed staff officers knew how to "stage fireworks displays" over places like Baghdad.[30]

While the Iraq war entertained, it also helped launch a faith-based "revolution in military affairs" that captivated national security analysts throughout the 1990s. The "defense transformation" movement allured with promises of recasting wars and the military organizations that fought them. Advocates spoke of skirmishes within the "microelectronics domain," of technological innovations multiplying warfighting capabilities, and of overwhelming military power enabled by "precision warfare." Army leaders pledged to field a "digitized" division by decade's end, one "more deployable and more strategically agile." Still others imagined achieving "full-spectrum dominance" across all military realms. It was all so appealing, all so addictive.[31]

The allure of futuristic conceptions like "network centric warfare" shrouded an unrealistic faith within military communities. Converts envisioned future wars with few American casualties and little collateral damage. Taking Boyd's theories to the extreme, they spoke of achieving "rapid dominance" thanks to unprecedented command of battlefield information. Military leaders would control warfighting armed with "total knowledge." And, predating Secretary of Defense Donald Rumsfeld's bold claims about the 2003 Iraq invasion, US armed forces would channel modern technology to defeat their adversaries through "shock and awe." Perhaps the Napoleonic-era theorist Carl von Clausewitz had become an anachronism. Harnessing new tech would prevail over the fog and friction of war.[32]

Saddam's political survival after Desert Storm, however, challenged this techno-faith in war's potential. Bush wanted to use force in limited, constrained ways. Marching on Baghdad and occupying Iraq, he recalled, "would instantly shatter our coalition, turning the whole Arab world against us, and make a broken tyrant into a latter-day Arab hero." Yet when Saddam brutally suppressed Kurdish and Shi'a rebellions as American troops departed, Bush committed to humanitarian and policing missions that portended uncomfortable conversations about the use of military power in the 1990s. How long, worried Pentagon officials asked, would US forces remain to contest future Iraqi aggression? At the time, no one could be certain. In hindsight, both Saddam and Bush were creating conditions for an open-ended American military commitment in the Middle East with far greater, long-term political impact than either ever intended.[33]

Moreover, for all the talk about kicking the Vietnam syndrome, why was Saddam still in power? Emotional Vietnam vets expressed gratitude for a "rapid end to the hostilities," one feeling "vindicated with our nation and our military." Yet a sense of dissatisfaction pervaded postwar discourse. Why couldn't the United States, in this unipolar moment, demand an unconditional surrender of its enemy? Might it be because the Bush administration was too "passive" in its approach to the brutal Iraqi dictator? If so, then what was the point of going to war? As one observer noted, with Saddam defying the United States and the UN, the president faced "the question of what the Gulf War accomplished, and even what it was all about in the first place." Vietnam veterans might thank Bush for allowing the military "to do what it was trained to do," but many Americans felt the president had achieved an "incomplete success."[34]

Of course, Desert Storm's termination only highlighted the numerous challenges facing Bush's team. Wars have a nasty habit of not ending when their architects expect. Desert Storm was no different. The implications of leaving US troops in Iraq and undertaking a "peacemaking" role for which they were unprepared sounded unappealing. Middle East experts at State and on the National Security Council feared a weakened Iraq might crumble in the war's aftermath, left powerless to check Iranian expansionism in the region. Meanwhile, Saudi militants like Osama bin Laden saw the deployment of so many American "infidels" to holy lands as an affront to Islamic tenets. Maybe a Middle Eastern quagmire had not been avoided after all.[35]

And what did this desert episode suggest for neoconservatives who would later affirm the benefits of "regime change" wars? For them, the Iraq war's partial victory supported their fear-based claims that global crisis had become a "permanent condition." In their view, both Bush and Clinton misjudged in believing that "containing" Saddam would keep Americans safe. The dictator's insufferable defiance not only threatened unfettered access to Middle East oil, but jeopardized the United States' geopolitical standing by exhausting the nation's prestige and credibility. Saddam's insolence reinforced long-standing neoconservative predilections and revitalized faith in their core ideals and principles. Only by bringing democracy to the Middle East, even at the point of a gun, would the Iraq impasse be broken and the region's problems solved.[36]

Desert Storm's uncertain end thus obscured already convoluted discussions over America's larger relationship with war. In the post–Cold

War era, US policymakers cast about for a new "strategic paradigm" with little resolution. The Gulf War hardly had served as a beacon. Nor did it conform neatly to the Cold War's European ending. If the main communist threat had dissipated because of fundamental flaws within the Soviet system, rather than from Reagan's massive military buildup, wasn't Americans' faith in war misplaced? Policy hawks didn't think so. Writing in 1995, historian Richard Pipes noted that "hard-liners" believed all along that they "had it right." But had they? Had they not, in fact, overstated fears, deriding any skepticism over going to war as unpatriotic? Surely, the Hitler of Baghdad remaining in power, they grumbled, justified renewed commitments to projecting military power abroad.[37]

In an era of triumphant liberalism, then, war once more offered hope of providing purpose to policy. As during the Cold War, Washington hawks held faith in military power—properly applied—deterring, even preventing, future threats, this time against rogue states, brutal dictators, or fanatical terrorists. In fact, the Bush team spent its remaining time in office seeking "a model for the use of force," a strategic vision that might be "applied universally to other crises." Iraq, however, disappointed as a template for future interventions. If wars didn't end as intended, neither did they conform to theoretical archetypes.[38]

Bush's search for practical models assumed a sense of urgency as defense analysts and political scientists deduced that mankind had reached the "end of history" with the Cold War's end. That phrase, coined by State Department official Francis Fukuyama in 1989, implied the world was entering a new epoch. Democratic capitalism had triumphed over authoritarian communism, leaving, in Fukuyama's words, no "viable systematic alternatives to Western liberalism." Such thinking might have been celebratory, but it also inferred a great deal of anxiety about what came next. For Bush and his immediate successor, an "end of history" also posed difficult questions about America's relationship with war. If liberalism had triumphed, then what need for war?[39]

Military predominance advocates avoided these uncomfortable hypotheses by arguing instead that preserving and enforcing the new liberal world order required a "continuation of US armed supremacy." To them, Desert Storm had proved the need for an enduring regional presence, perhaps beyond Iraq's borders. Despite the Gulf War victory, economist Leonard Silk maintained in early 1991, America faced "threats of civil wars and regional wars" from the Middle East to Eastern Europe, all while contending with "economic, financial and social problems" at home. As Silk argued, Americans were coming to realize that "this is not the same world an all-powerful United States faced half a century ago after the defeat of Germany and Japan." If Silk was right, then war remained as relevant as ever.[40]

CHAPTER 22

War in a Globalized World

As a one-term president, George H. W. Bush didn't profit from the televised Gulf War saga that only momentarily animated his "soaring popularity" and left liberals "in mourning." Perhaps this was because the 1991 war looked to some "like a tactical triumph but a strategic draw at best." Bush was out of power, but Saddam still in. Regional stability had been secured, but the Iraqi leader obstructed weapons inspectors, elevating fears that his bacteriological and chemical weapons programs were proceeding, hidden from sight. Desert Storm's follow-up, Operation Provide Comfort, required international troops and thousands of tons of humanitarian relief supplies to protect the Iraqi Kurdish population from Saddam's wrath. American pilots patrolled "no-fly zones," providing additional security. Despite the Gulf victory, Bill Clinton would be bequeathed, if not a war, then a stubborn political-military headache.[1]

Clinton's vision of national security, perhaps like Jimmy Carter's, challenged, if ever so briefly, Americans' faith in war. Critics doubted the new president was up to his task. The first president since World War II with no personal military experience, and one who had actively opposed the war in Vietnam, Clinton inspired vitriol among the uniformed ranks and within veterans' organizations, some of whom felt the president had an "anti-military bias." On the campaign trail in 1992, the Arkansas governor repeatedly defended his draft record, promising to "be a good president for America's veterans." A year into the White House, Clinton remained on the defensive against those who felt that "he, his wife and other closer advisors still loathe the military." One vet even claimed the new president actively engaged in "discrimination against veterans," an unenviable perception for any commander-in-chief.[2]

Clinton's support for homosexual men and women openly serving in uniform didn't help matters. Vocal detractors spit disgust over the armed forces being used as a laboratory for social equality programs that would undermine readiness and "good order and discipline." The Joint Chiefs publicly fought Clinton, with the Chief of Naval Operations arguing that gays were "fine" as long as they stayed closeted. As the admiral claimed, if homosexual service members came out and got "proactive, it'll be really nasty." The service chiefs feared the spread of AIDS and the mass resignation of religious recruits, and the enlisted ranks feeling "uncomfortable sharing group showers" or being on "a dance floor at a military social club next to a homosexual couple." As the decade wore on, policy analysts worried that commanders were engaging in "witch hunts" and, under Clinton, that work and living conditions within the military ranks had deteriorated due to the "don't ask, don't tell" policy.[3]

This lack of faith in Clinton as commander-in-chief surely preoccupied the president as he began crafting an overarching foreign policy for the 1990s. At its core, that policy focused on creating a globally interconnected liberal-capitalist order, yet one undeniably dominated by the United States. If Francis Fukuyama had correctly depicted liberalism's triumph, then backing a worldwide transformation to democratic governance seemed the logical next step. Democracy promotion, economic growth, and national security conjoined once more at the global level. And because of post–Cold War developments, whereby threats could emerge from Eastern Europe to the Middle East, "the security perimeter of the United States could not be geographically bounded."[4]

Clinton's team accordingly embraced a globalist approach. National Security Advisor Anthony Lake believed that expanding global free markets not only would inspire democratic growth abroad but would replace containment as an organizing principle of US grand strategy. So finding a new strategic framework mattered. In Lake's estimation, Cold War divisions had "given way to a confusing tangle of problems that prevent us from setting clearly defined goals for our foreign policy." The demise of the global communist threat, however, did not relieve the United States of its international responsibilities. As Lake argued, "our interests and ideals compel us not only to be engaged, but to lead." Thus, containment's doctrinal successor "must be a strategy of enlargement—enlargement of the world's free community of market democracies." A faith in the universality of American-style institutions underwrote this new strategic framing.[5]

So too the projection of military power. Lake realized that transnational problems—refugees, terrorism, weapons of mass destruction, and rogue states—threatened a stable global economy. The administration therefore would "maintain and modernize the finest military in the world so that we can deter aggression—and counter it when the need arises." Expanding democracy's reach while containing regional threats like Iran and Iraq required a continually sharpened sword. Clinton might hope to temper America's faith in war by concentrating more on economic than military might, but he could not escape the promises of war's utility.[6]

Still, the prominence of economics in presidential remarks suggested that war might prove less important to Clinton's vision of global security than that of his immediate predecessors. As just one example, his support of the North American Free Trade Agreement (NAFTA) with Canada and Mexico rested upon conviction that a new economic order offered an "opportunity to remake the world." Prosperity and democracy, Clinton argued, went hand-in-hand. Not surprisingly, talk of a "Western Hemisphere–wide free trade system" elicited fearmongering from the usual suspects. Conservative Patrick Buchanan, for instance, blasted the president for undermining the "nation's economic health, its geopolitical reach, even its moral character." As the headline for one Buchanan editorial ran, "America First, NAFTA Never." Globalism clearly had its limits.[7]

Yet while Buchanan charged Clinton with endangering the American dream, it is worth asking if the new administration truly was "contemptuous" of national independence and the security upon which it rested. It's unlikely. Rather, Clinton and Lake viewed US economic competition and enlargement through a global lens. They spoke often of building "successful market economies" that would promote democracy abroad while strengthening the economy at home. Critics may have used "globalization" as a cudgel with which to beat the president, but the term hardly equated to abrogating America's role as *the* international economic powerhouse.[8]

Military activists expressed their discomfort with Clinton's shift in priorities. They railed against policies in which economic matters overshadowed martial ones for sustaining America's global leadership in the post–Cold War era. As historian Douglas Brinkley, by no means a militarist, noted during Clinton's second term, the president appeared "more interested in helping Toys 'R' Us and Nike to flourish in Central Europe and Asia than in dispatching Marines to quell unrest in economically inconsequential nations." The activists shouldn't have fretted. Economic interdependence, in fact, had not lessened Washington's faith in the utility of war. Rather, the administration relied upon military means to secure that interdependence. Managing economic globalization while engaging in "preventive diplomacy" required access abroad to defuse potential crises. And only military power guaranteed access to foreign lands.[9]

Clinton had not long to wait for international crises to find him. Leaning into his economic predilections, he worked with the International Monetary Fund (IMF) to provide billion dollars' worth of credit to the Yeltsin government, fears of a collapsing Russian economy overtaking those of the once-dreaded Soviet military machine. But if Washington elite too often misplaced their faith in military might, so too did Clinton overestimate his faith in the power of democratic capitalism to inspire economic reform overseas. In Russia, Yeltsin struggled mightily to privatize state-owned assets. Corruption flourished. Russia's central bank became mired in a scandal over misused IMF funding. According to one account, inflation was running at 2,500 percent by the end of 1992. No wonder Clinton worried that a collapsing Russian economy might destabilize all of Eastern Europe.[10]

Clinton's fears morphed easily into an expanded, global concept of "national security." Defense became assertive, with the nation's military forces underwriting free-flowing trade across the planet. What's more, despite liberalism's Cold War triumph, policy analysts stressed about a coming economic catastrophe. Under headlines like "Is Capitalism Doomed?" they worried about America's economic strength eroding in the Cold War's wake. As one Rand forecaster shuddered, "a global economy bites the hegemon that feeds it, destroying the hegemon's relative dominance and shattering the very foundation upon which interdependence rests." Such a dangerous world plainly needed "America's security leadership."[11]

The White House and the Pentagon certainly thought so. Because the world was "no longer a simple place with clear choices," Clinton argued, American forces had to operate continuously around the globe to ensure the nation's "extended security." In the process, "forward" became one of the administration's favorite adjectives when discussing military affairs. The US armed forces, employing a "forward strategy," would support a posture of "forward engagement" that required troops to be "forward deployed." Arguments for such a global reach, however, failed to answer a fundamental question. Beyond vague warnings about rogue states and regional instabilities, what kind of threat—and from where—did the United States really face?[12]

Enlargement, of course, presumed expansion, and when a force expands it often meets resistance. Thus, while Clinton's national security strategy proposed being "actively engaged in global affairs," not all global actors welcomed that engagement. American troops soon found out the hard way on the Horn of Africa. Clinton had inherited from Bush a humanitarian aid mission in Somalia, code-named Operation Restore Hope, that was directed at alleviating mass starvation caused by years of bloody civil war. The task seemed well aligned with the new administration's priorities, especially since protecting oil tankers off the Somali coast was of economic significance to American companies. With UN involvement, Restore Hope seemed to represent a perfect opportunity to further global peacekeeping, demonstrate American benevolence overseas, and showcase Clinton's commitment to international leadership. These lofty intentions disintegrated in the streets of Mogadishu.[13]

By the summer of 1993, Somalia had become a pit of vipers. Warlords and their troops roamed the capital. Humanitarian assistance ground to a halt. When Clinton authorized US Army ranger and special forces units to capture militia leader Mohamed Farrah Aidid, "enlargement" suddenly assumed new meaning. Then, in October, a raid against Aidid and his "thugs" went awry. Militiamen shot down three Blackhawk helicopters. AK-47 fire ripped across cramped and narrow city streets. Casualties mounted as surrounded Americans fought off waves of militia attacks. A raid intended to last only an hour resulted in eighteen American deaths and seventy-three wounded. Journalists once more heard echoes of Vietnam. Within weeks, US commanders were declaring they had "backed down from offensive operations." Within months, Secretary of Defense Les Aspin had resigned. Enlargement had come at a high, high cost in the violent streets of Mogadishu.[14]

With polling mixed over whether the administration should retain a presence in eastern Africa, veteran diplomat Richard Holbrooke warned against becoming bogged down in "Vietmalia." Such doubts help explain Clinton's reluctance to intervene and stop a massive "killing spree" in Rwanda the following year. The internecine violence in which Hutu militias slaughtered some 800,000 ethnic Tutsis devastated the Central African country, with one observer justifiably describing the massacre as "low-tech genocide." The UN Secretary General, Boutros Boutros-Ghali, condemned the international community's inaction as "a scandal." Yet Clinton held back, doing nothing to curb the slaughter. While the president would later regret his failure to act, he took little political heat at the time for sidestepping another African tragedy. Americans' faith in war, it seemed, had its limits. So too did those forward-deployed soldiers who, in fact, could not "promote an international security environment of trust, cooperation, peace and stability" as Clinton's national security strategy had promised.[15]

Looking back, the disconnect between strategic rhetoric and reality is palpable. Enlargement and extended security depended on projecting American military power abroad, on preparedness for war deterring future threats. Yet the global landscape stubbornly resisted US influence taking root. Saddam's Iraq defied containment efforts. Russian political and economic woes imperiled European stability. Decades of "poor economic performance" left Africa an "unstable environment." Nuclear proliferation among weak states—or, worse, non-state actors—loomed dangerously in the background. All the while, critics feared a "rash of global deployments" taking a heavy toll on US troops and equipment, the spate of peacekeeping operations blunting preparations for "real" combat. What good was war if it bequeathed only more war?[16]

Clinton appeared to be asking just that question. In the aftermath of the Somalia experience, he hoped to narrow the armed forces' "peacekeeping" role over fears that post-conflict stabilization and humanitarian missions were degrading military effectiveness. He was not alone. Critics denounced a "foreign policy as social work" approach. Others asked how genocide in Central Africa, horrible for sure, had anything to do with US national security. As one political scientist noted, "philanthropy" was not grand strategy. Nor was the exercise of military power resolving political problems that gave rise to humanitarian tragedies in the first place. In a frequent refrain among senior military officers, General Wesley K. Clark, looking back upon the Somalia debacle, declared emphatically that Americans "should never look to our military to do police work."[17]

Yet involvement in Haiti's civil war suggested an enduring compulsion to engage militarily, at least in the Western Hemisphere. In September 1994, US forces invaded the small Caribbean island, a "model failed state" in one estimation. The plan aimed to restore democratically elected Jean-Bertrand Aristide to office, the victim of a military coup back in late 1991. In the intervening years, Haiti had devolved into a humanitarian nightmare, owing in no small part to UN sanctions targeting the military regime. Hoping to avoid a full-scale intervention, Clinton dispatched former President Carter to Port-au-Prince for last-minute negotiations as US troops prepared to deploy. The threat of invasion worked. The junta backed down, Aristide resumed the presidency, and American soldiers and marines arrived in Haiti not as invaders but as peacekeepers overseeing the transition of power.[18]

The accomplishments of Operation Uphold Democracy raised familiar concerns about the merits of interventionism. Even before Clinton made his decision to cancel the invasion plans, Senator John Glenn (D-OH) had worried about an exit strategy. "We could prevail militarily, but then what do you do? How do you establish order? . . . And how do you get out?" Even the operational code name implied questions about the military's post–Cold War mission. Was democracy promotion the new raison d'être of the American armed forces? Jeane Kirkpatrick had her doubts. The former UN ambassador thought invading and occupying countries like Haiti—all in the name of "restoring democracy"—"deadly serious and deeply disturbing in both theory and practice." To her, Haiti posed "no threat to international peace and security or to vital US interests." Relying on "international altruism" to justify military action against lesser-developed countries rested on bad theory and worse policy.[19]

The turmoil in Haiti—and Kirkpatrick's denunciations—hinted at problems within the new world order. In short, the new international system appeared as fragile as, and even more so than, the Cold War era. Preparation for war thus seemed essential for maintaining order. We might argue then that Washington elite in the 1990s feared instability more than anything else. An unstable global order could undermine a hierarchical system in which the United States ranked first. Failed and failing nation-states could disrupt the globalized economy. Protracted occupations could overburden the armed forces. Anarchic civil societies could become breeding grounds for future terrorists. Given such bleak possibilities, war now looked like a last-ditch safeguard against potential nightmare scenarios resulting from the collapse of the Cold War system.

Not surprisingly, war also remained linked to notions of national credibility and prestige. Bush, for instance, had painted the Iraqi invasion of Kuwait as "the first assault on the new world that we seek," a test for "America and the world" to "stand up to aggression." While alarming, the crisis offered, in the president's words, "a rare opportunity to move toward an historic period of cooperation." Some analysts, though, worried future conflicts might be far messier than Desert Storm. Writing in its aftermath, two British military historians cautioned that the "West may not find many conflicts with principles so clear-cut" or "enemies so ready to take on Western military power on its own terms."[20]

The muddled strategic environment of the mid-1990s seemed to bear out such concerns. James Woolsey, head of the CIA under Clinton, testified in 1993 that the Cold War's end had not, in fact, left behind a safer world. "We have slain a large dragon, but we live now in a jungle filled with a bewildering variety of poisonous snakes." Those serpents were roaming freely in "failed states," where violence and anarchy threatened not only their own citizens but regional stability as well. In Afghanistan, for instance, a whole generation had grown up knowing nothing but war thanks to the Soviet invasion and the civil conflict that followed. The potential for disorder rose precipitously. Contemporary analysts viewed war's consequences in stark terms, from refugee flows to human-rights abuses, from collapsing economies to increased ethnic strife. The stability of Cold War Europe appeared comparatively blissful in hindsight.[21]

Yet nothing was new here. Beyond Europe, the Cold War always had been more violent than most Americans grasped. Now, as in past decades, policy elite retained their faith in military force guaranteeing the world remained "open" to the United States politically and, just as importantly, economically. As such, the US armed forces still could help build "long-term" commitments to partner states or, put another way, engage in generational neo-imperialism. While arguably resting on a broad faith in American authority overseas, such prescriptions also drew upon fears that local ills, exacerbated by state weaknesses, would disproportionately injure regional and international politics.[22]

Still, faith in American power remained difficult to challenge, especially when so many believed the United States had singlehandedly "won" the Cold War. Should not the nation take advantage of this "unipolar moment" for fear it might be fleeting? Charles Krauthammer thought so. When the political pundit judged America the "center of world power" and the "unchallenged superpower," fellow neoconservatives hailed the new epoch as a rare opportunity to remake the world in their image. With Soviet communism's demise, few opponents seemed capable of contesting an American-led global restructuring. The US armed forces finally had the freedom to span the globe with few consequences. It was a heady moment. As Krauthammer boasted, there was "no prospect in the immediate future of any power to rival the United States."[23]

No wonder Republicans laid into the president for his talk of multilateralism. While Clinton spoke of building international networks and of working through organizations like the UN, his political opponents were aghast that he had "squandered American credibility and undermined our preeminence around." Chair of the Republican National Committee Haley Barbour argued that the administration had "no foreign policy at all." Future Vice President Dick Cheney called Clinton's team "one of the least competent of the 20th century," while Jeane Kirkpatrick assailed the administration for depending too much on multilateralism. "We can only do good in the world, if we have the power to do good," she argued. "But that power is being neglected and dissipated." Apparently, working alongside allies on common ground reeked of weakness.[24]

Lest we think that Republicans alone disapproved of Clinton's restraint, many Democrats equally chafed at its self-imposed limits. Now was the moment, some argued, for using military force to reshape the world. As just one example, Madeleine Albright, secretary of state during Clinton's second term, seconded Henry Kissinger, who believed that "America's preponderant position rendered it the indispensable component of international stability." In many ways, Albright and Kissinger were following Cold War blueprints, seeing international problems in military shades. Diplomacy worked only if reinforced by the threat of war. Albright acknowledged that America's "well-being depended on being integrated internationally." An activist global role, though, depended upon a willingness to apply military force when needed.[25]

Albright's Czechoslovakian background no doubt colored her view of the United States playing a global role lest chaos reign. As she argued, the Cold War's end may have "thawed the ground," but that meant "all the worms were crawling out" now that ethnic conflicts had been unfrozen.

In this view, the US-Soviet competition had kept the forces of disorder at bay. Now, in this unipolar moment, only the United States could act decisively to thwart new, destabilizing threats. Not all policy analysts were so sanguine about America flexing its military muscles to fill the void left by the Soviet collapse. Political commentator Fareed Zakaria, for instance, worried that "bluster about American hegemony" could become "self-defeating." In Zakaria's view, gloating over US dominance only invited challenges to such global leadership.[26]

Conservatives like William Kristol and Robert Kagan, however, tended to agree with Albright, arguing that American foreign policy should aspire to "benevolent global hegemony." To Kristol and Kagan, this hegemony, far from "hubristic or morally suspect," could serve as a "guide to action." Never mind that President William McKinley had spoken in similar imperial terms as the twentieth century opened, declaring US policy toward the Philippines one of "benevolent assimilation." Kristol and Kagan believed that most world powers welcomed America's "global involvement" and preferred its authority to any undemocratic alternatives. Perhaps unsurprisingly, then, they called for additional defense spending—$60–$80 billion each year—to preserve the nation's role as "global hegemon." Given this defense budget "crisis," talk of Cold War peace dividends seemed naive at best, dangerous at worst.[27]

Of course, not all Democrats followed Albright's lead and readily disputed Kristol and Kagan's interventionistic hyper-nationalism. Reacting to language of the United States being an "indispensable nation," Senator John Kerry (D-MA) asked aloud, "Why are we adopting such an arrogant, obnoxious tone?" Across the political aisle, libertarian Llewellyn Rockwell, Jr. claimed that such phrases made America look like a "swaggering B-movie villain." As Rockwell argued, if Americans were indispensable, then everyone else was "dispensable, meaning expendable." Even allies criticized the Clinton administration for mistaking "global leadership" with simple "bullying." Perhaps others around the globe weren't so welcoming of American hegemony as Kristol and Kagan surmised.[28]

These policy debates held consequences for military leaders still seeking a strategic lodestar to guide them through the post–Cold War era. The doctrine of "full-spectrum dominance," asserting that the armed forces could prepare for larger wars while still engaging in peacekeeping operations, promised to facilitate the nation's grand strategic aims. Yet the expansion of noncombat missions left many uniformed leaders questioning what all this meant for America's relationship with war. Deploying military assistance to locales devastated by natural disasters made for good press, but some commanders worried this "mission creep" undermined their readiness for war.[29]

And what to make of claims that the United States, in its unipolar moment, had a "responsibility to protect" victims of state persecution? The theory, abbreviated to "R2P," presupposed the virtue of interventionism. Critics, though, questioned Uncle Ben Parker's notion that with great power comes great responsibility. Not only did R2P threaten to turn the US military into a global police force, but the concept raised larger questions about state sovereignty and humanitarian-based protections. What, for instance, was the trigger for activating R2P? Was the responsibility legal or moral? And, given how the United States projected power, did R2P reinforce existing notions that only military instruments could resolve international political problems? The theory of R2P would gain fuller prominence in the early 2000s, when it would end up faltering in practice during the frustratingly inconclusive wars in Afghanistan and Iraq.[30]

Despite his lack of foreign-policy experience, Clinton appreciated the domestic drivers behind these new post–Cold War debates. Most notably, he had to contend with the unremitting criticism of neoconservatives clamoring for a bolder foreign policy agenda. Only international dominance, in their view, assured true national security. They had set the argument back in 1992. During Bush's final year in office, the "Defense Planning Guidance" embraced a simple principle: "no peer rival." Written under the auspices of Paul Wolfowitz, future architect of the 2003 Iraq invasion, the internal policy memorandum argued that the nation's first priority was deterring "potential competitors from even aspiring to a larger regional or global role." Of course, only the Pentagon, in Wolfowitz's view, could provide such assurances.[31]

Leaked to the *New York Times*, the document generated fierce pushback. Journalist Patrick Tyler surmised that with its focus on "benevolent domination by one power," the White House had articulated "the clearest rejection to date of collective internationalism." As Tyler rightly noted, the leaked draft conspicuously avoided mention of the United Nations. Democrats condemned the guidance as an excuse for ever larger defense budgets. Meanwhile, Republican Pat Buchanan thought the document little more than a "formula for endless American intervention in quarrels and war when no vital interest of the United States is remotely engaged." For a fleeting moment, the nation's faith in war became contested space.[32]

But how radical was the Defense Planning Guidance? Not as much as critics claimed. Ever since 1945, Americans had assumed a forceful posture in foreign policy, seeing forward engagement as essential to national security. Policymakers would work with foreign allies when convenient, but they hardly were shy about acting alone when they thought it necessary. "American primacy" had driven every administration, even before Truman had articulated his doctrine setting the Cold War's ideological groundwork. White House occupants like Clinton might occasionally argue for greater restraint, but they hardly disavowed their faith in war as an insurance policy to global primacy. Arguably, the Defense Planning Guidance raised ire only because the Bush team was saying the quiet part out loud.[33]

Five years later, conservatives no longer hesitated in vocalizing their appetite for a more aggressive foreign policy. The Project for a New American Century, founded in 1997, boasted a veritable who's-who list of policymakers and intellectuals intent on tying military strength to "moral clarity." Among its founders, the DC think tank included Dick Cheney, Norman Podhoretz, Donald Rumsfeld, and Paul Wolfowitz. Depicting Clinton's foreign policy as "adrift," the project's statement of principles called for increasing defense spending, promoting "the cause of political and economic freedom abroad," and challenging "regimes hostile to our interests and values." Later analysts would contend, with merit, that George W. Bush's policy of preemptive regime change traced its lineage back to the Project for a New American Century.[34]

Below the surface, long-standing fears were driving these neoconservative critiques. The Defense Planning Guidance, for example, registered the failure of democracy in Russia, the rising threat from China, and the nuclear arms race between India and Pakistan as frightening developments. An added fear hit home in April 1995. When a car bomb struck the Alfred P. Murrah Federal Building in Oklahoma City, killing 168 and wounding another 680, fears of domestic terrorism ran rampant. Might the nation be reliving the 1983 film *The Day After*, now in a different guise, in which a mortal threat stabbed "directly at America's heretofore invulnerable and innocent heartland"? Not surprisingly, both policymakers and media outlets immediately looked abroad, assuming the perpetrators were disciples of "Mideast terrorism." To their shock, and likely dismay, the criminals turned out to be Americans, products of the anarchist militia movement in Michigan.[35]

The Oklahoma City attack inspired a new wave of fear, complicating definitions of "war" and, with them, conceptions of American unity and inner strength. A "home-grown extremist group" spread panic among foreign-policy analysts who worried that Americans would have to learn "to face terrorism from anyone, anywhere." They spoke in direful terms. "The threat the United States now faces," one contended, "is far more complex and fragmented than anything we have contended with before." Others expressed concern over the "threat within," a clear allusion to anxieties that had fueled the McCarthy-era Red Scare. This domestic menace, with seemingly few connections to US foreign policy, further obscured Clinton administration attempts to even define the word "terrorism" and the threat it posed.[36]

Terrorism historically had relied on a fear of weak actors unleashing disproportionate damage on their intended targets. But what did the Oklahoma City bombing actually represent? Was terrorism an individual criminal undertaking, an act of war, or a political statement by a non-state actor? Regardless, Clinton elevated combating terrorism as a "top national security objective." He appeared to have little choice. Two years after the attack, the *Los Angeles Times* reported that "many Americans still fear terrorist attacks by paramilitary groups." Such anxieties made sense given that analysts were warning of domestic terrorists gaining weapons "as sophisticated as a third-world country"—or, worse, were actually experimenting with weapons of mass destruction.[37]

These fears of domestic and international terrorists getting hold of nuclear weapons reached back to the Bush administration, which, following in Reagan's footsteps, had sought cuts in the number of available nuclear devices and delivery systems. Bush had signed two Strategic Arms Reduction Treaties with Russia, hoping to "tame the nuclear beast." Mostly aimed at reducing stockpiles and lessening the chances of accidental war, the treaties took on new significance as analysts increasingly worried about nuclear proliferation in the wake of the Soviet Union's collapse. Once more, the DC elite spoke of attaining "stability" and of the threat that criminal dissemination posed to the international order. As Clinton himself warned, the danger to American security had increased thanks to forces "operating both beyond and within our own borders."[38]

Fears of an international landscape littered with Cold War nuclear detritus extended to Asia as well, where one of communism's last refuges was eagerly developing its own atomic arsenal. By 1993, it became clear Pyongyang was producing plutonium for a nuclear-weapons program. Clinton considered military action, but with Seoul inside the firing range of thousands of North Korean artillery tubes, war plainly was too risky. Diplomacy would have to suffice. The following year, the US-North Korea Agreed Framework stipulated the exchange of food and energy aid from the United States for North Korea's compliance with the Non-Proliferation Treaty. In its wake, with Pyongyang's nuclear program temporarily frozen, fears should have subsided. Yet in late 1999 Republican politicians like Senator Mitch McConnell (R-KY) began fundraising off the Korean nuclear threat, asking supporters for a "generous emergency gift of $25 or more . . . to protect our country from a potentially devastating nuclear attack." Allegedly, Republicans were doing what Clinton would not: taking action to "preserve, protect and defend the United States of America."[39]

McConnell's political opportunism actually reflected contemporary fears of nuclear war. Back in 1991, Tom Clancy's novel *The Sum of All Fears* showcased the dangers of nuclear proliferation when Palestinian terrorists recover a lost Israeli warhead and plan to detonate it at the Super Bowl. Only through last-minute efforts by CIA deputy director Jack Ryan is nuclear war averted. Four years later, Tony Scott's film *Crimson Tide* pitted the executive officer of a US nuclear submarine against his hawkish commander, intent on carrying out an erroneous missile launch order. In one tense scene at the captain's mess, as officers discuss the military theories of Carl von Clausewitz, Denzel Washington's character reflects that "the true nature of war is to serve itself." His captain is amused but clearly unconvinced, and the crew ultimately mutinies to abort the missile launch.[40]

If Denzel was correct in arguing that "in the nuclear world, the true enemy is war itself," then might nuclear weapons not be the stabilizing force policymakers long supposed them to be? Both Bush and Clinton worried over Ukraine's nuclear weapons falling into the wrong hands as Russia's political future seemed precarious in the 1990s. Deterring states from nuclear war was one thing. Deterring non-state actors and terrorist organizations was something quite different. As the decade unfolded, nuclear proliferation and international instability would increasingly appear to be two related and immensely dangerous phenomena.[41]

Thus, despite the supposed triumph of liberalism, there was little dismantling of the US military machine in the Cold War's aftermath. Policymakers saw no choice but to retain their faith in war. Globalization apparently necessitated a global American presence, justifying an explosion of military interventions abroad. Instability festered in nearly all regions of the world, demanding an expansion of "forward-operating" bases. The "enlargement" of free-market economies required a global flow of goods, guaranteed only by the show or threat of force.[42]

The larger story of the 1990s thus became inscribed by an unremitting faith in war, one reinforcing perennial debates about where and under what conditions to carry out that faith mission. Yes, Clinton oversaw a cursory effort to scale back the US military, but the larger philosophical context of the decade was a question of how—not whether—the United States should conduct itself militarily within its unipolar moment. Consequently, in an era of liberal globalization, national security became an international undertaking.

CHAPTER 23

War on the Cheap?

While most Americans in the 1990s centered their attention on globalization's economic aspects—a "worldwide convergence of supply and demand," as one analyst put it—the nation's faith in war hummed perceptibly in the background. After the fiasco in Somalia, President Clinton surely remained reluctant to send large numbers of US troops into combat. But Americans' apprehensions about a dangerous world were countered by faith in their own unrivaled military power. The challenge, then, was facing these dangers while preserving the nation's competitive advantages within an increasingly integrated global economy. As one study has argued, Clinton wanted "liberal hegemony on the cheap."[1]

Political pressures, along with military-industrial complex influences, weakened Clinton's position. Former director of the National Security Agency William E. Odom, for instance, called for "more military muscle, not less" in the mid-1990s. For the retired army general, "America could not solve its problems at home unless it [met] challenges abroad." Guns were merely "an overhead cost."[2]

What followed the Soviet Union's collapse seemed to reaffirm arguments for added American muscle. As ethnic violence swelled in a splintering Yugoslavia—a process begun by the 1974 constitution's decentralization of power and Tito's death in 1980—the Clinton team found it increasingly difficult to turn away from the Balkans bloodshed. Nationalist fervor replaced communist rule, motivating Slovenia and Croatia to declare their independence in 1991. The secessions inspired waves of violence that even accomplished military historians found difficult to track. Yugoslavia's federal army briefly attacked Slovenia. An internecine, four-year war followed between Croatia and its rebellious Serb minority. Evidence of ethnic cleansing seeped into the American press. Worse was yet to come.³

As for Bosnia-Herzegovina, the ethnically mixed country immediately devolved into vicious civil war following its secession in 1992. Bosnian Serbs, declaring their own independence for fear of domination by Bosnia's Muslim majority, waged war on Bosnian Croats and Muslim Slavs. Once more, the Yugoslav army entered the fray and, along with Serbian troops, laid siege to the capital city of Sarajevo. In early 1993, yet another civil war broke out, this one between Bosnia's Croatian and Muslim populations. Two years later, Bosnian Serb forces killed over 8,000 Muslims at the town of Srebrenica in eastern Bosnia, one of the worst mass civilian killings since the Holocaust. The conflicts were as dizzying as they were destructive.⁴

The intense violence generated by these long-suppressed ethnic rivalries threatened to destabilize not just the Balkans but all of Eastern Europe. Eerie specters of the continent's descent into World War I hovered above Washington policy debates. Moreover, the deteriorating situation raised questions about theories that democracy would lead to peace. Instead, the process of democratization within the ethnically plural republics of former Yugoslavia appeared to be provoking war rather than promoting peace. As the response from the UN and United States evolved from humanitarian relief missions, to the establishment of no-fly zones, to, ultimately, a NATO air campaign, fear and faith again contended for ascendancy among the foreign-policy establishment in Washington, DC. If the Balkans were potentially disintegrating into ethnic and nationalistic chaos, then only war, it seemed, could prevent its spread.⁵

Clinton, however, hesitated jumping into this ethnic cauldron. Perhaps Bush's secretary of state, James Baker, had it right: the United States owned "no dog in this fight." Other Republicans weren't so sure. Senator Richard Lugar (R-IN) berated the president for abandoning

"American leadership and decisiveness in favor of 'multilateralism' and the desire to pursue consensus." To Lugar, allowing aggressors to "defy the international community with impunity" exposed the West as "all bark and no bite." Yet such political bellicosity failed to answer a fundamental question. Was violence in the Balkans truly relevant to US national security?[6]

As reports of ethnic cleansing came into sharper view, humanitarian concerns seemed to render that question increasingly moot. For many Americans, the United States could not stand idly by while another European genocide unraveled in front of their eyes. (Few were willing to discuss their tolerance of similar crimes against humanity in Rwanda.) Still, senior officials demurred. Chairman of the Joint Chiefs Colin Powell resisted pressures to intervene militarily, telling a National Security Council staffer, "I'm doing everything I can to keep the United States out of getting involved in the Balkans." The ghosts of Vietnam, Beirut, and Somalia still roamed the Pentagon halls.[7]

But as the language from media outlets evolved from "civil war" to "ethnic cleansing" to "genocide," it became increasingly untenable for Clinton's White House to remain aloof. Tales of sexual brutality and targeted killings joined the stories of indiscriminate violence. Though still shaken by the fiasco in Mogadishu, the president asked to review military options. And, among the cacophony, some observers spied a chance to craft a grand strategy for the new millennium. Perhaps defeating local aggression and preventing genocidal policies could be, even with Russia's help, a new form of containment. As in the past, however, interventionists focused far more on the symptoms of war than on its causes. Meanwhile, Clinton was finding out that not all internal conflicts had military solutions.[8]

The president also faced a domestic challenge: convincing skeptical Americans that a military commitment was required despite the Cold War's end. Were Yugoslav problems, critics asked, really American ones? Should the United States act as a "global constabulary"? Pulled in two directions, Clinton chose what was—at least politically—the safest middle ground, calling for NATO air strikes against Serbian forces while avoiding any military options entailing the deployment of American ground forces. We might call the approach "discount enlargement." The president spoke publicly of a "moral imperative" to act and how preventing a wider war in Europe was "important to America's national interest." Yet he also declared his intentions not "to put our troops in Kosovo to fight a war." Bombing campaigns apparently did not qualify as war.[9]

The NATO airstrikes, however, did accomplish two aims. For Clinton, they demonstrated the continuing viability of the European alliance. NATO still had purpose in the post–Cold War era, perhaps even an expanded one. They also led, however fitfully, to the 1995 Dayton Accords. While the ceasefire terms ended hostilities—and provided for a NATO peacekeeping force, further cementing the alliance's new security role—they were far less successful in establishing a sense of unity among the multiethnic Balkan states. Not surprisingly, faith-based interventionists claimed victory. Thanks to America's "active involvement," one Eastern European specialist gushed, the "fatigued parties" now could see "the wisdom of not resuming full-scale wars." Here was a *mission civilisatrice* for the new century.[10]

Despite the self-congratulatory praise Dayton inspired, the 1990s, in many ways, became an era of strategic drift. Senior military leaders questioned their cosmic purpose with the defeat of their decades-long enemy. Batman had lost his Joker, it seemed. What came next? Did the future lie in technology and network-centric warfare or in peacekeeping operations in the Middle East or Eastern Europe? To what threat should the armed forces adapt with their chief competitor now bested? In short, what strategic concept would replace containment? Even the commander-in-chief quipped that he needed to find the right "bumper sticker" for this new era.[11]

The Balkans, however, weren't quite done with the Clinton administration. Though some 6,000 American soldiers remained in Bosnia after Dayton, Serbian President Slobodan Milošević soon resumed his cleansing campaign against ethnic Albanians in Kosovo. Once more, mass killings and deportations engulfed the region. Once more, Clinton turned to airpower in hopes of limiting the costs of war. In March 1999, US and NATO aircraft launched Operation Allied Force, a seventy-eight-day air campaign that included more than 10,000 strike sorties. By June, Yugoslav and Serb forces agreed to cease hostilities and withdraw from Kosovo, while NATO established yet another regional peacekeeping force. Upon its completion, Secretary of Defense William Cohen judged Allied Force "the most precise application of airpower in history." Coercive military power, it seemed, once again had imposed order where none had existed.[12]

Cohen's immodest assessment resurrected the age-old faith of airpower winning wars on the cheap. The Supreme Allied Commander of NATO, General Wesley K. Clark, noted how even in the modern era, ground combat "retained the possibility of turning nasty and unpredictable at close quarters." But like its counterparts in Vietnam, Operation Allied Force conveyed a mixed message. The military operation needed no ground component, yet air force officers' frustrations spilled into the press. Air leaders complained of political micromanagement—a popular Vietnam-era refrain—and of operating without a clear military strategy. Clark himself shared "that we could not guarantee any specific level of damage from the air, much less predict it." Meanwhile, air analysts wondered if and how their target selections had materially halted the ethnic cleansing.[13]

More importantly, critics doubted airpower's role in forcing Milošević to concede. General Clark may have argued that the Serbian leader only respected "the threat of military force," or columnists, like William Safire, that military ultimatums could "create new diplomatic facts." But others were far less sanguine. Former National Security Advisor Zbigniew Brzezinski, for example, thought Milošević's capitulation resulted more from Russian diplomatic pressure than from American military might. Perhaps it was not the NATO alliance that had brought down the "Butcher of the Balkans" after all.[14]

Clinton's economical way of war in the Balkans raised one final question. Did America's involvement amount to coercion or to actual war? In the post–Cold War decade, neither policymakers nor senior military leaders were quite certain. The distinction mattered, ostensibly, given that Congress should have been involved in any decision taking the nation to war. Wesley Clark parsed the differences by judging Allied Force an example of "modern war—limited, carefully constrained in geography, scope, weapons, and effects. Every measure of escalation was excruciatingly weighed. . . . And 'victory' was carefully defined." The NATO commander might have added an important impulse of "modern" war. Any leader who threatened war purportedly risked humiliation by not following through if those threats were ignored. Credibility remained as relevant as ever.[15]

Framing also mattered. Clark argued that, to "maintain momentum" in modern war, military leaders required "favorable images on TV." But something deeper played in as well. The American public long had conceived of war as a crusade of good versus evil. During the Cold War, that construct had garnered public support by envisioning its adversary as malevolent communist hordes intent on global domination. But it was far more difficult for the public to see how the Balkan wars served US geopolitical interests. Did supporting human rights by itself truly meet the threshold for military interventionism? Throughout much of the 1990s, Americans simply didn't know.[16]

Thus, when Clinton authorized the firing of cruise missiles against Sudan and Afghanistan in 1998, retaliatory strikes against al-Qaeda forces which had attacked US embassies in Kenya and Tanzania, many citizens struggled to connect the dots. The president declared Americans were the "targets of terrorism," largely because of their "unique leadership responsibilities in the world." Yet such language failed to clarify. Why were US missiles being launched into Afghanistan against a Saudi exile for an attack in East Africa? As further questions arose over possibly faulty intelligence and suppression of dissent within the administration—not all were convinced that Sudan was an appropriate target—critics wondered what "reliable information" had led the United States to launch its weapons of war.[17]

Clinton also took heat from those seeing his reliance on cruise missiles as weakness, as a risk-averse, ineffective approach to war that realized few lasting gains. Detractors knocked the president (and the armed forces) for concentrating too much on "force protection" and not enough on mission accomplishment. If senior leaders were unwilling to suffer casualties in war, then did the rationale for going to war hold up? General Clark, not missing an opportunity to speak out, faulted "the political climate in Washington, where it was feared that casualties might discredit [any military] campaign." Avoiding bloodshed in war might be admirable, but also illusory.[18]

Others expressed worries that if war no longer could be separated from populations, its utility might now be circumscribed. One senior British officer envisioned a new era of conflict, "war amongst the people," in which civilians became "targets, objectives to be won, as much as an opposing force." Like-minded officers feared that increasing urbanization around the globe would make it more difficult for commanders to conduct military operations without causing horrific levels of civilian collateral damage. Within a Balkans context, Clark even suggested "there was no military answer to the problem of urban warfare in Belgrade."[19]

Indeed, to purchase an end to fighting in the Balkan nations, the Dayton Accords "locked in ethnic divisions and partitions." The agreement also required some 60,000 NATO-led troops to enforce it, suggesting that wars might not truly end when outright hostilities did. Similar partitioning along ethnic lines would resurface in Iraq in the new millennium, as occupying Americans forcibly segregated Iraqi communities as a way to decrease sectarian violence. As one Iraqi scholar has argued, such "divide-and-rule policies" only "generated sectarian categories by which to implement new forms of rule" and open "new vacuums of power."[20]

These experiences suggest that Clinton's faith in war on the cheap had been misplaced all along. Political opponents predictably condemned his emphasis on "cruise missile hegemony." They lambasted his policy of containing Iraq militarily and economically. And they mocked as "pinpricks" his aerial bombing of the country in 1996, and again in 1998, after Saddam quashed internal revolts. Yet those same critics remained reluctant to send large contingents of US ground combat troops back into Iraq, even after Saddam rebuffed UN weapons inspectors at decade's end. Former Under Secretary of Defense Paul Wolfowitz might argue that "containment did nothing for the Iraqi people," but the suffering of Middle Easterners so far from home wasn't enough to inspire Americans to support another invasion. The best Clinton could muster was a four-day bombing campaign in 1998, Operation Desert Fox, which hardly broke the "cheat and retreat" cycle into which both Washington and Baghdad had fallen.[21]

Conservatives no doubt agreed that Saddam was an "outlaw in his own neighborhood," as Defense Secretary William Cohen labeled him, but they were willing to take the extra steps to ensure his demise. As William Kristol and Robert Kagan put it simply in early 1998, "Saddam Hussein must go." Others, taking a swing at the acolytes of airpower, doubted the "value of bombing to coerce Iraq" or "reform Iraq's ways." More had to be done. The threat, they alleged, justified preemptive war. Such martial talk, soon to gain traction after 9/11, presaged the Bush administration's support for "regime change" wars, leading to one of the nation's worst foreign-policy decisions.[22]

In the end, the dangers facing post–Cold War America appeared as perilous as ever. War on the cheap would not suffice. Clinton remained wary of becoming embroiled in local conflicts, but inescapably they kept pulling him in. Perhaps the United States had not kicked its "Vietnam Syndrome" after all. Indeed, critics lambasted Clinton for his "shameful" decision to lift the US trade embargo against Vietnam more than twenty years after the last American troops had departed. For apprehensive policy elite, the relatively weak enemies of the 1990s posed just as much danger as the strong ones of the Cold War era. Enlargement decidedly had not been a "cheap" strategic alternative to the containment of communism.[23]

Nor did America's global dominance guarantee order in the new world. Take for instance the continuing Israeli-Palestinian conflict which festered well outside the limits of US power and influence. A September 1993 declaration for Palestinian self-rule in the Gaza Strip, the Oslo Accords, offered hope of peace finally coming to the Middle East. Yet the assassination of Israeli Prime Minister Yitzhak Rabin two years later by an Israeli extremist who opposed the accords derailed the process. So too did continuing violence in the West Bank and the rise of hard-right conservatives like Benjamin Netanyahu. Fearful Americans worried that the Middle East's "mix of religion and violence" might spread into the United States. The Israeli consul general in New York even suggested that donations to Israeli settlements could end up in the hands of terrorists and finance evil militants tearing the region apart.[24]

The Palestinian "problem" reinforced predictions about the decline of nation-state wars that abounded at the close of the century, suggesting that new forms of war would be just as chaotic as any conventional conflict. There was no shortage of pundits willing to weigh in. Writing in 1991, Israeli military historian Martin van Creveld predicted that the world was "entering an era, not of peaceful economic competition between trading blocks, but of warfare between ethnic and religious groups." American Samuel Huntington agreed, foreseeing a "clash of civilizations" coming to "dominate world politics." As the political scientist put it, the "central axis of world politics" was likely to be "conflict between the 'West and the rest.'" Outside academia, commentators like Robert Kaplan predicted a "coming anarchy" in which "worldwide, demographic, environmental, and societal stress" became the "real 'strategic' danger."[25]

These gloomy analyses, so authoritatively presented, left Americans with an unpleasant conclusion. Although the United States now called itself the world's sole remaining superpower, order had not been achieved at the Cold War's close. Worse, America's traditional relationship with war might be coming to an end. (Alas, it wasn't.) As van Creveld shared, military power of the present was "simply irrelevant as an instrument for extending or defending political interests" in the future. With a global clash of civilizations on the horizon, such proclamations epitomized fears that war and its consequences had inspired since the very first days of the Cold War era.[26]

In such a chaotic environment, it made sense that Clinton would joke, "Gosh, I miss the Cold War." Of course, that bygone era hadn't been nearly as serene as imagined by nostalgic politicians. The bipolar competition between the United States and the Soviet Union may have offered a sense of stability, but from a global perspective, the Cold War had always been an immensely violent era. Still, wistful observers feared the coming age of "untamed anarchy" and the consequent loss of international order. Despite "winning" the Cold War, Americans were still afraid of "flying blind" in such a "dangerous world."[27]

What did this mean for how Americans thought about their faith in war and the overall utility of force? The incoming Bush administration certainly believed preparation for war vital to survival in the new millennium. As National Security Advisor Condoleezza Rice argued, the best way to "renew America's leadership in the world" was by "boosting military readiness and morale." New reasons for existential fears, however, lurked just around the corner. The Cold War may be over. But Americans' faith in and fear of war were about to be put into overdrive.[28]

Conclusion
War for War's Sake

Let us return, one final time, to Douglas MacArthur. It's 1951, and it has been six months since President Truman relieved him of command in Korea. Ever eying the Washington political scene, the retired general has agreed to speak at the American Legion's national convention in Miami. He could not have asked for a friendlier venue. He tells his welcoming veteran audience how they inspire him because they advocate "no partisan cause." And then, without pause, the general launches into a full-throated attack on civilian policymakers and their mishandling of US military policy. The speech is pure MacArthur. Soaring rhetoric matched by biting criticism, delivered with supreme confidence in his own carefully crafted persona. He shares his faith in American principles and values and warns that the nation must regain that faith so it can "reassert itself to guide the world toward reason and right."

Yet MacArthur speaks also of fear. He castigates "our leaders" for reducing the nation's military strength after World War II and then reversing the process "to rearm with no less precipitate haste under the pressure of an artificially aroused fear psychosis throughout the land." And while he wants to "avoid being drawn into unreasonable and unnecessary expenditures for armament," he also hopes to "regain military faith in ourselves and the policies upon which our victories in the past have always rested." The general's concluding remarks are clear.

The United States must rebuild its military power to reclaim the faith of its citizens and of peoples around the world.[1]

While addressing the role of power, MacArthur no doubt viewed the unfolding Cold War drama as an ideological struggle pitting democratic values against communist treachery. He was not alone. The DC elite he so easily disparaged likewise based their policy views and strategic assumptions upon ideological convictions. But ideology explains only so much. From a more instinctual, even emotional level, persistent tensions between faith in and fear of war and its consequences played a significant role in Cold War decision-making. Those tensions shaped how policymakers and regular Americans alike conceived of the ideological battle of good versus evil.[2]

The dualisms between faith and fear matter because they endure. For better or worse, the Cold War paradigm has cast a long shadow over US foreign policymaking. In this sense, the historian John Lewis Gaddis now seems to have been premature in judging, back in 2005, that the Cold War was "a necessary contest that settled fundamental issues once and for all." The Soviet-American ideological contest may have been settled, but China soon would become a convenient stand-in as the prevailing communist bogeyman. When added to the threats from terrorism, a resurgent Russia, and an unrelenting Israeli-Palestinian conflict, it is no wonder that faith and fear have remained a constant in Americans' approach to foreign policy and grand strategy in the twenty-first century.[3]

Nor did the Cold War's end prove that war itself had become an "anachronism," in Gaddis's words. Despite its victory, the United States barely had the chance to reap any "peace dividends." Looking back, one wonders if there was any genuine effort to procure such rewards. Not long after the 1991 Gulf War, the *New York Times* posited that America's "go-it-alone" attitude was a "consequence of straining to justify extravagant military spending." The newspaper took Pentagon planners to task for conjuring threats in order to preserve the military-industrial complex. Little since has changed. With minor editing, MacArthur's American Legion speech from 1951 could be used today by any aspiring politicians seeking to burnish their national security credentials.[4]

War remains with us because we have inherited Cold War tendencies toward viewing the world in black-and-white terms, where every threat seems existential to the global American project. Despite their checkered history with what war delivered them, Americans' faith never truly wavered, even after the debacle in Vietnam. Calls for military crusades against evil still resonate. Hence the parallels between George W. Bush's Global War on Terror and the Truman Doctrine, the latter warning that if Americans faltered in their leadership, they might "endanger the peace of the world." A faith in democracy promotion underwritten by military might. A fear of consequences if the global crusade failed. So little had changed during the intervening decades.[5]

Arguably, the failure of war to produce global stability, that long-coveted Cold War policy aim, only exacerbated Americans' fears. In truth, their faith in war had been misplaced all along. Deploying military force overseas rarely resulted in enhanced control, prestige, or status. Battlefield exploits seldom translated into lasting political gain. War, as a foreign-policy tool, continued to defy direction. Thus, when faith in war faltered, fear of war's consequences elevated.[6]

To see how old tensions between faith and fear rippled into the twenty-first century, we need look no further than the September 11 attacks on US soil and the subsequent "war on terror." Though Americans' initial reactions to 9/11 were undergirded by a desire for revenge, just as their reactions to Pearl Harbor had been, the faith-and-fear dichotomy persisted as trumpeters along the Potomac summoned the nation to war. Fear of America under attack merged effortlessly with faith that military power could extinguish terror across the globe, all while, in some eyes, helping reconstruct anarchic regions like the Middle East. The terrorist attacks, while traumatic, seemingly had granted the United States a moral authority not seen since World War II.[7]

If Reagan had defeated one "evil empire" at Cold War's end, perhaps George W. Bush could do the same in a dangerous new world order bequeathed to him by his elders. Moral crusaders, however, tend toward militancy, and Bush proved no different. His fear of another terrorist attack, of global disorder challenging American hegemony, only intensified a personal religious faith justifying his call to arms. Yet imposing order—or at least Bush's attempts to do so—exacted a heavy price. The president's global war consumed the national security state, rapidly dissolving any moral authority imparted by the 9/11 attacks. Fear of disorder led to the practice of "coerced consent," leaving little room for opposition, either domestically or abroad. In fearful Americans' eyes, the world had slipped back into a familiar black-and-white, us-versus-them Cold War paradigm.[8]

The attacks also revived long-simmering, stereotypical fears that Muslim Arabs, in literary critic Edward Said's words, might "take over the world." Middle East scholars advising the Bush administration spoke of Islam's "rejection of modernity" and of Islamic extremists' "preemptive fundamentalism." The clash of civilizations that Samuel Huntington predicted in the early 1990s appeared eerily to have materialized. Others rationalized that Islamist terrorism, while making headlines, was a "persistent problem, but one involving small numbers of fanatics." Such analyses, however, hardly comforted the White House as it contemplated potential scenarios of these "fanatics" armed with weapons of mass destruction.[9]

In many ways, 9/11 punctured Americans' sense of what war meant, while reinforcing long-held notions of defending against the savage "other." While some conjectured that terrorism was best understood as a criminal act rather than one of war, the president adopted bellicose language, calling al-Qaeda and its ilk "heirs of all the murderous ideologies of the 20th century." Here were new barbarians at the gates, radicals who couldn't be accommodated, who offered "nothing more than bleakness, paranoia, and a volatile avidity for violence." Not surprisingly, senior American diplomats in the late 1940s, fearing Soviet control of the European continent in the wake of World War II, had spoken analogously of a "barbarian invasion of Europe."[10]

The emergence of these post-9/11 threats seemed to transcend the Cold War while paralleling its long experience. Vice President Dick Cheney may have identified a "fundamental shift" to a new era after September 11th, but old verities remained. As in the Cold War, Americans again were reminded that power did not ensure security.

"Terrorism" replaced "communism" as the synonym for evil, despite Secretary of State Colin Powell's pleas to avoid such facile comparisons. Policy elite feared that all terrorist networks somehow were connected, just as their predecessors had believed Moscow controlled all communist movements during the Cold War. Meanwhile, business leaders advocated for a "Marshall-like plan for those moderate regimes in the Muslim world willing to commit to the war against fanaticism."[11]

While a Marshall Plan for the new millennium sounded appealing, the gross intelligence failure associated with 9/11 made the attacks all the more frightening. Some argued that fear and "hysteria spread to and infected parts of the national security establishment." Others felt that "turning commercial airlines into guided missiles" challenged basic definitions of the term "security risk." As US troops descended into Afghanistan and Iraq, still others wondered how young GIs could draw the lines between al-Qaeda terrorists and local organizations like the Afghan Taliban or the Iraqi Ba'ath Party. And, in all this, what did it even mean that the United States' enemy was "terrorism"? Some weren't sure. "Declaring war on 'terror,'" one military strategist quipped, was "like declaring war on air power."[12]

The debate over terminology mattered little to Americans who saw themselves as victims in the immediate aftermath of 9/11. This victimization, though, not only justified an aggressively violent self-defense. It also inhibited Americans from asking if the incessant projection of US military power was containing enemies or provoking them. Nor does it seem that Bush's team thought all that deeply about potential long-term consequences of a militarized foreign policy that focused more on reciprocating violence than restraining it. In senior officials' minds, Americans were the victims, pure and simple. And to those like Defense Secretary Donald Rumsfeld, victimhood, like appeasement, only invited more attacks.[13]

The administration's call for vengeance no doubt expressed the blood-lust of many Americans as they scoured the wreckages in New York, Pennsylvania, and Washington, DC. Below the surface, though, deep fears persisted. The 2001 Authorization of Military Force that Bush secured from Congress would frame the US reply to terrorism as "war," suggesting that law enforcement or counterterror responses would be insufficient for meeting the new global threat. Yet old questions resurfaced about Americans' relationship with war. What would be the purpose of a global war on terror? To exact retribution? To prevent further attack? To promote democracy abroad? And might not a strategy based on overreaction and fear aggravate the terror problem instead of redressing its underlying causes?[14]

Ultimately, the Bush administration would go further than simply exacting vengeance, arguing, implicitly if not outright, that it could repair "failed states" and return order to the international system. Moreover, this imposed stability, so the White House claimed, would come with the added benefits of preventing rogue actors from acquiring and potentially using weapons of mass destruction. As a consequence, faith and fear merged to build a fragile consensus on America's relationship with war in the new century. After the strategic drift of the 1990s, war against terror could provide a grand strategic framework to finally replace the ideology of Cold War containment.[15]

Countless faith-based assumptions undergirded the American enterprises in Afghanistan and Iraq supporting Bush's terror paradigm. Most of these assumptions, like those that had buttressed America's Cold War policies, were founded on a misreading of history, a view of the past that dismissed earlier failures in grand strategy and foreign policy. Critics might resurrect the ghosts of Vietnam as both wars went sour, but White House officials only doubled down in their faith that war would see them through.[16]

Perhaps the greatest assumption was the belief in Bush's team that there were few, if any, limits to American military power. Regime change in Iraq was one thing; the president himself saw "the liberation of Iraq [as] a crucial advance in the campaign against terror." Yet he went further, advancing the notion that Saddam's fall would spark democratic reform across the entire Middle East. And as the mission in Afghanistan evolved from countering terrorism to building a new nation, the administration kept doggedly to its faith that, while undermining the Taliban through aid and reconstruction efforts, America would also be combating terrorism across the globe. In the aftermath of 9/11, anything seemed possible to those still viewing the United States as a unipolar power... even "geopolitical dominance."[17]

In both wars, senior policymakers also shared a faith that American power would inspire local populations to reject malicious leaders. Their conviction that US military power could transform "traditional" societies harkened back to the Cold War faith in modernization theory. Under enlightened American supervision, the thinking went, Afghanistan and Iraq would commit to economic growth and social progress, leading to regional stability. Soon, however, reality stepped in. In Afghanistan, combat veteran Bing West denounced the American military being turned into a "gigantic Peace Corps," avoiding risk and handing out "billions of dollars in projects." In Iraq, journalist Dexter Filkins recalled after Saddam's fall that Iraq hadn't become a springboard for democracy but rather a "theater of revenge, each murder inspiring another and then another."[18]

As failures mounted, faith endured. For Bush, democracy and capitalism were universal, even inevitable, traits desired by all. The president nurtured this devotion, born of personal prayer and broader lessons gleaned from America's Cold War "victory." And his faith made sense to the nation he led. As historian Odd Arne Westad has argued, "most Americans still believed that they could only be safe if the world looked more like their own country and if the world's governments abided by the will of the United States." Presumptions and convictions became reinforcing. Americans didn't occupy. They liberated. When Americans went to war, they left liberal democracies behind, not broken societies. At home, war inspired unity and patriotism, not division and a veteran community questioning the worth of their sacrifices.[19]

The experience of these wars told a far different story. Bush's "with us or against us" challenge had an imperial tone to it, dismissing local dynamics that made such choices far trickier than the president imagined. In both Afghanistan and Iraq, US troops entered into a "moral morass," just as they had during earlier conflicts. To civilians on the ground caught in the whirlwind of bloody fighting, liberation looked more like "democratization by force." As death tolls mounted and social fabrics frayed, local political order remained elusive. One journalist covering the Afghanistan war saw little more than "broken alliances . . . faltering hopes . . . [and] the rude exposure of foreign agendas." As Iraq collapsed into a state of outright civil war, it was evident that American military power had hardly brought about a brighter tomorrow.[20]

While policymakers proselytized their faith in American power, interventionists in the White House made public their fears that the United States would not be safe until it had planted democratic seeds around the globe, especially the Middle East. Economist Paul Krugman suggested that politicians were "hoping for fear" and exploiting terrorism for their own political agendas. The president certainly leaned into the rhetoric. Wasn't the world, according to Bush, facing an "axis of evil"? Perhaps because of these fears, others preached Americans to renew their "fighting faith" in liberalism since the war on terrorism was just as important as the battle against communism. Cynics must have wondered if Afghanistan and Iraq were being made safe for *American* democracy and little more.[21]

Contemporary fears loomed so large that Bush even argued that the United States had to go to war to *prevent* war, ostensibly judging diplomacy, coercive or otherwise, as insufficient for ridding the world of evil. The resultant Bush Doctrine elevated regime change as a primary tool in the nation's foreign-policy kitbag. Neoconservatives like Paul Wolfowitz long had advocated such aggressive thinking and ultimately won Bush over as the administration put Iraq in its crosshairs. Unencumbered by qualms about unilateralism, the United States would act unilaterally and preemptively, all in the name of "democracy promotion." As the president warned, "If we wait for threats to fully materialize, we will have waited too long." Fear rarely entails patience.[22]

Critics did emerge, hinting at limits to the faith-fear relationship. Paul Krugman skewered the Bush Doctrine for being "based on delusions of grandeur about America's ability to dominate the world through force."

Other critics pointed to Israel, as Ariel Sharon's government appeared to be using Bush's playbook for justifying its own "anti-terrorist offensive" against Palestinians in the West Bank. Still others questioned a doctrine that, by 2004, already had failed its first test in Iraq. Yet even as public denunciations grew louder, far too few citizens at home asked if the terrorist threat had been overrated. In short, Americans had believed the hype.[23]

So too had the US armed forces, albeit in a different way. Military officers, in the Pentagon and overseas, espoused their faith in counterinsurgency tactics compensating for any muddled strategy put forth by civilian policymakers, a sort of shortcut to broader political objectives. Yet as one US Army publication correctly noted, "a simple aggregation of tactical actions does not in itself constitute a strategy." In both the Middle East and Central Asia, the disconnects between Bush's grand ideas and military strategy widened. Looking back, it's hard to give senior officers a passing grade for matching military might to political purpose. The lack of strategic coherence is unmistakable. Of course, these officers weren't solely to blame since White House officials, as they had done in Vietnam, were asking their war managers to accomplish far more than they ever could.[24]

That didn't stop combat commanders, at least early on, from trying to compensate for the bad strategy handed down to them. Hoping to gain a sense of security in two war-torn countries, they sent out waves of "presence patrols." They engaged in counterterrorism missions, humanitarian support projects, and traditional combat operations. The pace was frenetic. Yet few of these soldiers or marines had much training—let alone predisposition—for the "non-kinetic," civic-minded missions they were being asked to perform. Most felt vulnerable among the populations they ostensibly were there to protect. Frustrations mounted. As one veteran recalled, he and his peers became increasingly "embittered that their efforts to build schools and support orphans did not somehow settle long-standing religious and ethnic hatreds and local blood feuds." The fact that these same GIs had only a "superficial understanding of local politics" didn't help matters.[25]

The mounting failures, increasingly obvious to the American public, did not deter the clerics of counterinsurgency theory from promising salvation. Foremost among them, General David Petraeus and his acolytes undertook a massive salesmanship campaign to rescue America's wars from the jaws of defeat. Few epitomized this faith in counterinsurgency more than John Nagl, a mid-career army officer whom fawning journalists compared to Lawrence of Arabia. Nagl had been among the authors of a new doctrine aimed at countering overseas insurgencies. But he had embraced a mission far beyond Iraq or Afghanistan. In 2008, Nagl would argue that "winning the Global War on Terror [would] require an ability not just to dominate land operations, but to change entire societies." Petraeus's biographer followed suit, citing the general's challenge to a young American officer to help "change the culture of the Afghan military." Faith had become hubris.[26]

Unfortunately, American vanity could not fill the yawning gaps between theory and practice. The US troop presence generated its own violence and civilian displacement. Intelligence on the enemy remained unclear. In many places, Americans couldn't even agree on whom they were fighting, despite lofty conceptual claims that "human terrain" was the "decisive terrain." Few metrics of progress held up under scrutiny, with one of Petraeus's own senior advisors conceding that she wasn't even sure there was an "over-arching strategy" to which their efforts contributed. Worse, far worse, the longer Americans remained, the more some began to view civilians around them as less than human. One veteran recalled being unimpressed after seeing photos of US soldiers violating Iraqi prisoners at the Abu Ghraib prison complex. Since "most of us hated the Iraqis so much," he shared, "we didn't really care.... They were the enemy, all of them, the whole fucking country, maybe even the kids."[27]

Such attitudes, reminiscent of the American experience in Vietnam, surely perpetuated local insurgencies rather than countering them. Senior officers, though, counseled patience. While they admitted that their wars were lasting longer than anticipated, perhaps even becoming "generational," their faith in final victory endured, even in the face of countervailing evidence. In truth, the longer Americans stayed—and the more mistakes they made—the more the locals' awe of US power eroded. The White House chimed in, claiming that the "only thing to fear was a failure of will." Yet young soldiers and marines serving overseas, increasingly victims of deadly ambushes and IED attacks, likely feared more than well-worn political catchphrases.[28]

But Bush had identified a key "lesson" from Vietnam: only a unified nation at home could sustain a long war abroad. Thus, the administration linked patriotism to support for its wars. In the aftermath of 9/11, it wasn't hard to argue that the United States was acting as a global force for good. As the wars in Afghanistan and Iraq ground on, though, "war-based patriotism" took on a cruel, jingoistic vibe. Self-righteous patriots labeled dissent "immoral" and opponents to the war on terror "soft." Dissenters pushed back against this "mandatory faux patriotism" sustaining war with a mixture of "apathy and anemic soldier adulation." Veterans themselves denigrated the "lobotomized patriotism" that led to many leaving the service in disgust. Bush's wars had not been nearly as redemptive as the president had hoped.[29]

They were, though, less destabilizing at home than in the regions to which US forces deployed. Afghan and Iraqi civilians, many of them victims of the war's violence, did not see Americans as liberators but rather mostly as occupiers. Critics asked how the nation should "square the tales of American cruelty with the promise of democracy" that US troops supposedly were bringing with them. When General Stanley McChrystal pledged a "government in a box" to Afghans living under American protection, the Cold War faith in martial modernizing efforts resurrected itself with little irony and less historical understanding of the limits to American power overseas.[30]

Deep fears sustained this mislaid faith. It was nearly impossible to shake persistent fears that terrorists once again would attack the American homeland if only given the chance. Five years after 9/11, fears of "Islamic terrorism," according to some journalists, had been "woven into the fabric" of American life. Franklin Graham, son of the famed Cold War evangelist, maligned Islam as a "very evil and wicked religion."

Scholars wrote of dispersed yet globally integrated terrorist networks "capable of disintegrating and reconvening in different forms when challenged." Following the White House's lead, many Americans mimicked the president in asserting "they hate us for what we are." Critics may have rolled their eyes at this "dangerous claptrap" sustaining Bush's invasive wars of choice, but the anxieties felt real nonetheless.[31]

These metastasized fears bled into policy debates. Some suggested that Cold War deterrence theories could be resurrected for the latest global war, even though it was "harder to deter terrorists than it was to deter a Soviet attack." In the aftermath of 9/11, few policymakers were willing to diminish any terrorist network's ability to project power or to question intelligence assets overstating the danger of "substate" threats. It was far easier (and more popular) to speak in apocalyptic terms. Thus, neoconservative chickenhawk Frederick Kagan could argue in 2007 that "victory" in Iraq was "vital to America's security. Defeat will likely lead to regional conflict, humanitarian catastrophe, and increased global terrorism." Taking a cue from Cold War polemics, it was better to fight terrorism—like communism—abroad than at home.[32]

Of course, such framing presumed an unquenchable hunger to slay monsters abroad. With little comprehension—and much indifference—from the American public, the United States began waging war for war's sake. Here was a rejuvenated post–Cold War paradox. As Americans increasingly became "at peace with being at war," they worried little about the long-term costs and consequences of what Bush's policies had wrought. Journalist Anand Gopal, covering the long war in Afghanistan, had it right: "The war on terror had become an end in itself, the ultimate self-fulfilling prophecy."[33]

And if military leaders had difficulty defining "war" in this new age, the public mostly was content to remain aloof from such thorny conversations and simply accede to government wishes. They, along with their representatives, willingly circumscribed their own civil liberties with the 2001 USA Patriot Act. Cold War fears of malicious fifth-columnists seeking to destroy America from within were resurrected by those preaching security through limiting individual freedoms. One of the few dissenters,

Senator Russ Feingold (D-WI), recoiled at the irony of a war against terror being used to justify antidemocratic behavior at home. Feingold defended his vote against the Patriot Act by pointing to the massive expansion of government authority having little to do with national security. As the senator noted, the whole tenor of the legislation was "Let's grab as much as we can given the fear of terrorism."[34]

With neither their faith in war realized nor their fears of war dampened, Americans since 9/11 have failed to reconsider their largely dysfunctional relationship with war. Even when recent history suggests that their faith in war is misplaced, fear keeps them from too critically reexamining why that might be the case. Few Americans today, for instance, view the 2003 invasion of Iraq as a good idea that made them any safer. Yet despite the failures that followed, both there and in Afghanistan, many policymakers and senior military leaders still imagine US troops as agents of sweeping societal transformation overseas. Dissenting views survive only along the political margins. In short, there is "inertia" in how we think about our relationship with war.[35]

Of course, policy skeptics have raised their voices, as they did in the Cold War, asking why a nation so willing to apply its military power doesn't exert greater influence abroad. Others have criticized how the United States tends to overreact to "marginally relevant" security threats that, viewed holistically, amount to a kind of "foreign policy hypochondria." In spite of these judgments, there has been little desire or incentive for opposing defense budget increases that, in truth, have no real grand strategy to justify them. Even as the nation outspends its rivals on "defense" by considerable margins, there are strategic analysts such as Eliot A. Cohen who claim that these outlays are hardly enough because of "underlying weaknesses in the American position." How increased budget outlays might make us feel any safer, we are never told.[36]

Upon taking office, Barack Obama sought to recalibrate US grand strategy and foreign policy. Yet war continued unabated, now with armed drones and special-forces teams as the new administration's weapons of choice. No doubt Obama hoped to avoid the political costs of large US troop deployments or the revulsion to episodes like Abu

Ghraib that Bush had endured. But such tactics came with high costs. Military options seemed more attractive. Legislative and judicial oversight languished. Targeted killings pushed the boundaries of ethical wartime behavior. In the process, war became more "invisible," more expansive, more persistent.[37]

As Obama strove to get America's enduring conflicts off the front pages, the language and tactics of war may have changed, but not Washington's faith in war. In Afghanistan, the White House recommitted its efforts for fear the state would collapse if US troops withdrew. Under pressure from both Pentagon officials and congressional hawks, Obama even authorized a "surge" in hopes of stabilizing an uncertain political situation. Meanwhile, despite a controversial departure from Iraq, Obama quickly ordered US troops to return to the Middle East. A Syrian civil war and threats posed by the Islamic State had pulled the United States back in. Nevertheless, critics were quick to blame Obama for a decline in American credibility, further incentivizing aggressive policies for shoring up the administration's political right flank.[38]

At the same time, as if continued fighting in Afghanistan and Syria wasn't enough, the White House championed a strategic "pivot" to Asia, suggesting the need for a new post–Cold War "peer competitor" to justify the nation's obsession with war. While senior US senators howled that the threat from the Islamic State could not be overstated, academics surmised that China soon would be attempting to "dominate Asia," thus requiring an American response. A new Red Scare spread across media outlets, a dismay that hardly has diminished since the Obama presidency. Lest readers miss the point, editorialists argued in plain language that Cold War "nostalgia" was fueling this "dangerous anti-China consensus." Others spoke of "failed deterrence" and of how China soon would "rule the seven seas and five oceans." The response seemed inescapable. Spend more on defense to protect the United States from yet another national security bogeyman.[39]

How can all this be sustainable? The costs of war accrue year after year—and not just at home—forcing Americans to spend billions of tax dollars on defense mechanisms that don't alleviate any of their insecurities. An ever-expanding defense budget drives deficit spending, while many of war's costs remain hidden as they fund private military contractors who aren't easily tracked through traditional accounting methods. As in the Cold War, fear has remained lucrative for the military-industrial complex and for politicians whose constituencies depend on defense-related jobs. All the while, enough strategy "experts" calling for a "substantially larger military" provide a veneer of respectability for those hawking peace through unrestrained strength.[40]

Such calls, however, often dismiss the fact that US defense expenditures alone constituted nearly forty percent of total military spending worldwide in 2022. Surely this faith in disproportionate budget outlays producing security attests to the exaggerated fears underlying American foreign policy. Behind these notions wasn't just a "forever war" mentality, but an "everywhere war" one as well. Such a reckless faith in war fails to account for the costs or the potential harm it imposes on others. Returning to the architect of containment, George Kennan submitted during the mid-1980s that the United States would "continue to harm our own interests as much as we benefit them if we continue to employ the instruments of coercion in the international field without a better understanding of their significance and possibilities." Four decades later, Kennan's warning has stood the test of time.[41]

Still, fiscal arguments take us only so far. We need to realize that despite war's brutality, it remains an attractive human behavior. Donald Trump's first presidency showcased for Americans how the masculine appeal of war endures. Trump embraced the illusion of tough leaders who wielded big sticks and protected the nation by cowing its enemies into submission. Even as he railed against his predecessors for wasting time and resources on failed wars, the president crafted a façade of "militarized masculinity" and "male nationalism" that enlivened his base of supporters. In the process, Trump, as had his forerunners, inverted the old Clausewitzean dictum by making politics a continuation of war rather than the opposite.[42]

And under Trump, fascination with war, like everything else, could transform into entertainment for popular consumption. Trump surrounded himself with retired generals, forever "fascinated with raw military might." He exulted in the power that the US armed forces extended to the commander-in-chief. He called for extravagant military parades that critics reviled as "popular in tin-pot dictatorships." Yet for all his bluster, Trump's adulation of military power seemed linked inherently to fears of a dangerous world. The president repeatedly invoked the threats posed by terrorism and immigration, one feeding off the other. No doubt he also saw political benefits in stigmatizing Muslims, telling one CNN host that "I think Islam hates us." Trump might scorn endless wars, but he has clearly found them useful.[43]

Moreover, Trump's national security advisor, General H. R. McMaster—supposedly one of the "adults" in the chaotic White House—followed his boss's militaristic lead. After his brief stint with the administration, McMaster penned a policy-prescriptive book arguing that Americans, far too focused on "victimhood," "forgot *that they had to compete* to keep their freedom, security, and prosperity." Neoconservative scholar Robert Kagan agreed, noting how "low-cost military involvements," unfairly equated with "forever wars," actually were preserving a "general peace." In such a dystopian worldview, where anyone anywhere might be a potential threat, were there any other options besides a permanent global US military presence?[44]

Besides demonstrating little imagination to alternatives beyond endless wars, McMaster and Kagan's views suggest something fundamental about how Americans see the world. In short, we are deeply afraid of instability. In succumbing to these fears, as military historian Lawrence Freedman tells us, we miss war's fundamental character, that "any exercise of power is inherently unstable." Arguably, long-term consequences accumulate apace to our fears. At the risk of being paralyzed by uncertainty, we tend to rely almost exclusively on our faith in military force to provide some sense of surety in a dangerous world.[45]

Breaking this cycle will be a difficult task. Fear is not necessarily a "spontaneous emotion." It often requires cultivation. But fear need not define us or our foreign policy. Yes, we need to protect the state in an uncertain world. Given a bloody war in Ukraine, Iran's nuclear ambitions, and the relentless Israeli-Palestinian conflict, it is unlikely that international power politics will end any time soon. But we need more balanced, more honest discussions on the tensions between the "promise and peril" of war. We need to be more reflective about war's consequences, not simply to render our unconscious consent for the militarization of American foreign policy. We need to reevaluate our "hyperactive foreign policy," which, in large part, can be seen as a destructive legacy of both 9/11 and the Cold War that preceded it. Most of all, we need a more pragmatic approach to our relationship with war.[46]

Exaggerated hopes and fears lead to paranoia in the guise of realism. In the process, Americans institutionalize permanent war and seek military solutions for nearly all political problems. There isn't much incentive to think otherwise. Frankly, it is risky for any politician to honestly evaluate what our armed forces actually can accomplish and chance the sin of not supporting them. Far easier is it to participate in the enamored infatuation of the troops encouraged by "savior generals" like Petraeus and McMaster. But when these "secular saints" pen puff pieces on "America's awesome military" and how our security can be assured only through increased defense appropriations, such sentiments carry important implications. A more candid review of the past demonstrates that our faith in war extinguishing all threats has been misplaced for a long, long time.[47]

These embedded expectations of what war can provide have led to a central paradox: we need war to conquer our fears, but fear obliges us to excessively prepare for war. Perhaps this is the greatest legacy of the long Cold War. Military might may have reinforced Americans' notions of exceptionality, but that martial power only rarely translated into true security, either at home or abroad. The recent COVID-19 global pandemic suggests that our faith in military dominance may not, in fact, be well suited for future threats, not all of which will emanate from state or non-state actors. Will increased defense budgets or additional aircraft carriers, for instance, safeguard us from the ravages of climate change? Perhaps our faith in war is why so many commentators fell so easily into comparing fighting a pandemic with wartime mobilization.[48]

Ultimately, we need to embrace a more clear-headed worldview, to judge potential adversaries based on their true strengths and weaknesses, not on our own faith and fears. The world will always be a dangerous place. And war, most likely, will remain an inherent part of the state. It's how we react to dangers, real and perceived, that matters. As one critic rightly put it, "anarchy is what states make of it," at least for "great" powers like the United States. Panic and despair need not drive US foreign policy. And continually asking for "more and better military power" will only reinforce a never-ending cycle of global violence perpetuated by the world's largest military machine.[49]

In the end, if we believe arguments that the Cold War never ended, then these tensions between faith and fear have the potential to lead into a never-ending spiral, falsely validating and then perpetuating an irreversible militarization of American foreign policy. Faith in war and raw military power need not govern our foreign policy. Fear of war need not consign us to a future of existential insecurities. Such a twisted relationship with faith and fear, if left unbroken, can only preordain the nation to a militarized way of life bounded by the grimness of war.[50]

Notes

INTRODUCTION

1. For an operational review of MacArthur in the Southwest Pacific, see Williamson Murray and Allan R. Millet, *A War to Be Won: Fighting the Second World War* (Cambridge, MA: Belknap Press, 2000), 204–9. Operation Cartwheel in Ronald H. Spector, *Eagle against the Sun: The American War with Japan* (New York: Free Press, 1985), 226. Douglas MacArthur, *Reminiscences* (New York: McGraw-Hill, 1964), 193. Of the memoir, reviewer William Styron remarked that it may have been "the only autobiography by a great man which is almost totally free of self-doubt." *New York Review of Books*, 8 October 1964. RGD, passim.
2. "Text of Statement by MacArthur: Model Conquering Army Basic Cause of Surrender," *New York Times*, 16 October 1945. Occupation mission in Sayuri Guthrie-Shimizu, "Japan, the United States, and the Cold War, 1945–1960," in *The Cambridge History of the Cold War*, Vol. I, *Origins*, ed. Melvyn P. Leffler and Odd Arne Westad (New York: Cambridge University Press, 2010), 247.
3. "Democracy Is Seen as Gaining," *New York Times*, 27 June 1947. Changing patterns in Jennifer M. Miller, "Narrating Democracy: Historical Narratives, the Potsdam Declaration, and Japanese Rearmament, 1945–50," in *The Power of the Past: History and Statecraft*, ed. Hal Brands and Jeremi Suri (Washington, DC: Brookings Institution Press, 2016), 104.
4. Governor Homer Adkins quoted in Stephanie Hinnershitz, *Japanese American Incarceration: The Camps and Coerced Labor During World War II* (Philadelphia: University of Pennsylvania Press, 2021), 39. Attorney General U. S. Webb quoted in Jay Feldman, *Manufacturing Hysteria: A History of Scapegoating, Surveillance, and Secrecy in Modern America* (New York: Pantheon, 2011), 166. Order 9066 on p. 178.
5. Murrow quoted in Lisa M. Mundey, *American Militarism and Anti-Militarism in Popular Media, 1945–1970* (Jefferson, NC: McFarland, 2012), 37. MacArthur in William Appleman Williams, *The Tragedy of American Diplomacy* (New York: Norton, 1959), 273. Hostile power in John W. Spanier, *The Truman-MacArthur Controversy and the Korean War* (Cambridge, MA: Harvard University Press, 1959), 76.
6. For an intellectual diplomatic history that does consider the role of war and its relationship to foreign policy, see David Milne, *Worldmaking: The*

Art and Science of Diplomacy (New York: Farrar, Straus & Giroux, 2015). On Cold War as a substitute for war, see Robert L. Scott, "Cold War and Rhetoric: Conceptually and Critically," in *Cold War Rhetoric: Strategy, Metaphor, and Ideology*, ed. Martin J. Medhurst, Robert L. Ivie, et al. (New York: Greenwood, 1990), 11. Exceptionalism in Arnold A. Offner, "Liberation or Dominance? The Ideology of U.S. National Security Policy," in *The Long War: A New History of U.S. National Security Policy since World War II*, ed. Andrew J. Bacevich (New York: Columbia University Press, 2007), 40.

7. Tensions in Odd Arne Westad, *The Global Cold War* (New York: Cambridge University Press, 2007), 9, 27–28. Werner Levi, "Ideology, Interests, and Foreign Policy," *International Studies Quarterly* Vol. 14, No. 1 (March 1970): 7, 13.

8. Chosen nation in Andrew Preston, *American Foreign Relations: A Very Short Introduction* (New York: Oxford University Press, 2019), 24. Robert Kagan speaks of a "universalistic nationalism" in *Dangerous Nation* (New York: Knopf, 2006), 42. Exceptionalism in Mark Philip Bradley and Mary L. Dudziak, "Introduction," in *Making the Forever War: Marilyn B. Young on the Culture and Politics of American Militarism*, ed. Mark Philip Bradley and Mary L. Dudziak (Amherst: University of Massachusetts Press, 2021), 7. Intolerant in Christopher Layne, *The Peace of Illusions: American Grand Strategy from 1940 to the Present* (Ithaca, NY: Cornell University Press, 2006), 120. Ideology surviving in Ralph B. Levering, *The Cold War: A Post-Cold War History*, 3rd ed. (Malden, MA: Wiley Blackwell, 2016), xv. Threat of force in Patrick Porter, *The False Promise of Liberal Order: Nostalgia, Delusion and the Rise of Trump* (Medford, MA: Polity, 2020), 2.

9. Wilsonian deals in Amos Perlmutter, *Making the World Safe for Democracy: A Century of Wilsonianism and Its Totalitarian Challengers* (Chapel Hill: University of North Carolina Press, 1997), 5, 30. Internationalism in Christopher McKnight Nichols, "Woodrow Wilson, W.E.B. DuBois, and Beyond: American Internationalists and the Crucible of World War I," in *Rethinking American Grand Strategy*, ed. Elizabeth Borgwardt, Christopher McKnight Nichols, and Andrew Preston (New York: Oxford University Press, 2021), 179; and Kenneth N. Waltz, *Man, the State, and War: A Theoretical Analysis* (New York: Columbia University Press, 1954, 2001), 117. Christopher Hemmer argues that "Wilson rejected any simple dichotomy between realism and idealism." *American Pendulum: Recurring Debates in U.S. Grand Strategy* (Ithaca, NY: Cornell University Press, 2015), 23. "Forum Discusses Wilsonian Theme," *New York Times*, 9 January 1956.

10. On relative definitions of "national security," see Barry Buzan, *People, States, and Fear: The National Security Problem in International*

Relations (Brighton: Wheatsheaf, 1983), 18; and Barry R. Posen, *Restraint: A New Foundation for U.S. Grand Strategy* (Ithaca, NY: Cornell University Press, 2014), 3. Ideology and geopolitics in Colin S. Gray, *War, Peace and International Relations*, 2nd ed. (London: Routledge, 2007), 218. On realism see Layne, *The Peace of Illusions*, 15–17. On Wilsonianism, see p. 118. American expansion in Williams, *The Tragedy of American Diplomacy*, 94. (Of course the means to achieve that expansion was military.) Dangerous place in John J. Mearsheimer, *The Tragedy of Great Power Politics* (New York: Norton, 2001, 2014), xi.

11. Benjamin Miller and Ziv Rubinovitz argue that the international system served as "the selector of competing ideas on national security." This system, in turn, "determined US grand strategy." *Grand Strategy from Truman to Trump* (Chicago: University of Chicago Press, 2020), 4, 51–52. Historian Melvyn P. Leffler, while acknowledging the crucial roles of memory and agency, maintains that the Cold War came about because of "conditions in the international system." *For the Soul of Mankind: The United States, the Soviet Union, and the Cold War* (New York: Hill & Wang, 2007), 8, 57–58, 70, 79. Taking one step further, Mearsheimer even argues that the "main causes of war are located in the architecture of the international system." *The Tragedy of Great Power Politics*, 337. See also Heonik Kwon, *The Other Cold War* (New York: Columbia University Press, 2010), 24.

12. Williams, *The Tragedy of American Diplomacy*, 57. Hans J. Morgenthau, *Politics among Nations: The Struggle for Power and Peace* (New York: Knopf, 1948, 1961), 27. On the pursuit of power, see Posen, *Restraint*, 21. Raw and extraregional in Layne, *The Peace of Illusions*, 3, 4. See also, pp. 7–9, 32–33, 36. On "dominant power" see Mearsheimer, xv.

13. On the role of ideology, see John Lamberton Harper, *The Cold War* (New York: Oxford University Press, 2011), 244; and Naoko Shibusawa, "Ideology, Culture, and the Cold War," in *The Oxford Handbook of the Cold War*, ed. Richard H. Immerman and Petra Goedde (New York: Oxford University Press, 2013), 32–49.

14. On human motives, see Azar Gat, *The Causes of War and the Spread of Peace: But Will War Rebound?* (New York: Oxford University Press, 2017), 51, 68; and Margaret MacMillan, *War: How Conflict Shaped Us* (New York: Random House, 2020), xii. In a sense, I am following Waltz's lead of tying systems to "man" and "human motivations." *Man, the State, and War*, 12, 14. For a similar line of argument, see Robert Dallek, "National Mood and American Foreign Policy: A Suggestive Essay," *American Quarterly*, Vol. 34, No. 4 (Autumn, 1982): 339–61.

15. On "desires" see Campbell Craig and Fredrik Logevall, *America's Cold War: The Politics of Insecurity* (Cambridge, MA: Belknap, 2009), 58. Fears in Paul Boyer, *By the Bomb's Early Light: American Thought and Culture*

at the Dawn of the Atomic Age (New York: Pantheon, 1985), 66. Journalist Norman Cousins wrote in 1945 that the atomic era "brought less hope than fear. It is a primitive fear, the fear of the unknown—the fear of forces man can neither channel nor comprehend." Quoted in Robert A. Jacobs, *The Dragon's Tail: Americans Face the Atomic Age* (Amherst: University of Massachusetts Press, 2010), 8.

16. Rational means in Gat, v. We might ask, however, how "rational" military means truly are when used to achieve whatever interests a nation's leaders define. "Excerpts from Testimony by Generals Bradley and Vandenberg," *New York Times*, 20 October 1949.

17. Chaos and influence in Tom Engelhardt, *A Nation Unmade by War* (Chicago: Haymarket, 2018), 22.

18. On cognitive perspectives in foreign policy, see Nikolas Gvosdev, Jessica D. Blankshain, and David A. Cooper, *Decision-Making in American Foreign Policy: Translating Theory into Practice* (New York: Cambridge University Press, 2019), 91, 94.

19. On religion, see William Inboden, *Religion and American Foreign Policy, 1945–1960: The Soul of Containment* (New York: Cambridge University Press, 2008); and Andrew Preston, *Sword of the Spirit, Shield of Faith: Religion in American War and Diplomacy* (New York: Knopf, 2012). On the global challenges of religious and ethnic nationalism in the Cold War see Carole K. Fink, *Cold War: An International History* (Boulder, CO: Westview, 2014), 2.

20. Harold Lasswell, *Essays on the Garrison State* (New Brunswick, NJ: Transaction, 1997), 20. On strategy, see Antulio J. Echevarria II, *Military Strategy: A Very Short Introduction* (New York: Oxford University Press, 2017), 2. Colin S. Gray defines strategy as the "bridge" between policy and armed combat. "Why Strategy Is Difficult" in *Strategic Studies: A Reader*, ed. Thomas G. Mahnken and Joseph A. Maiolo (New York: Routledge, 2014), 43. War as usable in Hew Strachan, *The Direction of War: Contemporary Strategy in Historical Perspective* (New York: Cambridge University Press, 2013), 43.

21. Defense and security in David Vine, *The United States of War: A Global History of America's Endless Conflicts, from Columbus to the Islamic State* (Oakland: University of California Press, 2020), xxiv. Cultural meaning in Roy Scranton, "What Good Is Dissent?" in *Paths of Dissent: Soldiers Speak Out against America's Misguided Wars*, ed. Andrew Bacevich and Daniel A. Sjursen (New York: Metropolitan, 2022), 97–98. On "strategic culture," see Christopher McKnight Nichols and Andrew Preston, "Introduction," in *Rethinking American Grand Strategy*, 11–12; and Adrian R. Lewis, *The American Culture of War: The History of U.S. Military Force from World War II to Operation Iraqi Freedom* (New York: Routledge, 2007), 5. Meaning-making in Melani McAlister, *Epic Encounters: Culture,*

Media, and U.S Interests in the Middle East since 1945, rev. ed. (Berkeley: University of California Press, 2001, 2005), 5.
22. James H. Lebovic, *The Limits of U.S. Military Capability: Lessons from Vietnam and Iraq* (Baltimore: Johns Hopkins University Press, 2010), 2. Christopher Preble, *The Power Problem: How American Military Dominance Makes Us Less Safe, Less Prosperous and Less Free* (Ithaca, NY: Cornell University Press, 2009), 5.
23. "Jackson Charges Nixon Disparages Kennedy Loyalty," *New York Times*, 4 October 1960. Periphery in Engelhardt, *A Nation Unmade by War*, 29. Xenophobia in Preble, 10. Promises of war in MacMillan, *War*, 46.
24. On the fear of "what's beyond" see John Lewis Gaddis, *On Grand Strategy* (New York: Penguin, 2018), 94. Hobbes in Azar Gat, *War in Human Civilization* (New York: Oxford University Press, 2006), 5, 13. See also Jan H. Blits, "Hobbesian Fear," *Political Theory*, Vol. 17, No. 3 (August 1989): 417–31.
25. Mearsheimer, 2, 32, 42. Ideology in Walter LaFeber, *America, Russia, and the Cold War, 1945–1990*, 6th ed. (New York: McGraw-Hill, 1991), 22. On China, see Chen Jian, *Mao's China and the Cold War* (Chapel Hill: University of North Carolina Press, 2001), 7–9; and Jeremy Friedman, *Shadow Cold War: The Sino-Soviet Competition for the Third World* (Chapel Hill: University of North Carolina Press, 2015), 19–20.
26. On defining fear, see Ralph K. White, *Fearful Warriors: A Psychological Profile of U.S.-Soviet Relations* (New York: Free Press, 1984), 88–90, 98–99. On realistic versus neurotic fears, see pp. 112–13, 116–17, 136. See also Elaine Tyler May, *Fortress America: How We Embraced Fear and Abandoned Democracy* (New York: Basic, 2017), 2, 5. Paranoia in Kwon, *The Other Cold War*, 139. On grand strategy, see McKnight Nichols and Preston, "Introduction," 1, 6–7.
27. Fear of surprise attacks and aggression in Leffler, *For the Soul of Mankind*, 48. "Pearl Harbor Day Marked in Hawaii," *New York Times*, 8 December 1951.
28. Absolute security in Layne, *The Peace of Illusions*, 119. Charles Edel, "Extending the Sphere: A Federalist Grand Strategy," in *Rethinking American Grand Strategy*, 83. Americans long have wrestled with this "security dilemma." As their enemies opposed US military-laced expansionism, Americans intensified their faith in war and, at the same time, their fears of war's expansion. Thus, the safer they tried to make themselves, the less safe they actually felt.
29. Total defense and continuous security in Michael S. Sherry, *In the Shadow of War: The United States since the 1930s* (New Haven, CT: Yale University Press, 1995), 4–6, 32–33. Ingo Trauschweizer, *Maxwell Taylor's Cold War: From Berlin to Vietnam* (Lexington: University Press of Kentucky, 2019), 30. Insecurity in Layne, 10, 19. Threats in Perlmutter, *Making*

the World Safe for Democracy, 2–3. War as "ever present" in Bradley and Dudziak, *Making the Forever War*, 6.

30. Propaganda in Susan A. Brewer, *Why America Fights: Patriotism and War Propaganda from the Philippines to Iraq* (New York: Oxford University Press, 2009), 7. Information policy officer quoted in Nicholas J. Cull, *The Cold War and the United States Information Agency: American Propaganda and Public Diplomacy, 1945–1989* (New York: Cambridge University Press, 2008), 34–35. Breeding obedience in William H. McNeill, *The Pursuits of Power: Technology, Armed Force, and Society since 1000* (Chicago: University of Chicago Press, 1982), 380. Barry Goldwater, *Conscience of a Conservative* (Shepherdsville, KY: Victor, 1960), 88.

31. Exploiting in May, *Fortress America*, 71. Fifth columnists in Feldman, *Manufacturing Hysteria*, 199. Solidarity in H. W. Brands, *The Devil We Knew: Americans and the Cold War* (New York: Oxford University Press, 1993), v. "McCarthy Asserts Budenz Named Red in Acheson Office," *New York Times*, 26 April 1950. "Partisan Fires Fanned by 'Communist' Charges," *New York Times*, 30 April 1950. "Anti-Red Board Begins Its Duties," *New York Times*, 2 November 1950.

32. "Designs Offered on Bomb Havens," *New York Times*, 18 September 1955. Jack Raymond, "The 'Military-Industrial Complex': An Analysis," *New York Times*, 22 January 1961.

33. John Lewis Gaddis, *The Cold War: A New History* (New York: Penguin, 2005), 3, 98, 102. In many ways, both the United States and Soviet Union relied on multiple, cogenerating fears: of internal and external enemies, of their own leaders not taking existential threats seriously, and of their safety being undermined and their nation destroyed. For an alternate take to Gaddis, see Frank Costigliola, *Roosevelt's Lost Alliances: How Personal Politics Helped Start the Cold War* (Princeton, NJ: Princeton University Press, 2012), 4.

34. On Clausewitz, see Strachan, *The Direction of War*, 46, 54. Interaction in Miguel Centeno and Elaine Enriquez, *War & Society* (Malden, MA: Polity, 2016), 4, 173. John Keegan, *The History of Warfare* (New York: Knopf, 1993), 3, 11–12. I tend to agree with Colin Gray's definition of war as "organized violence *threatened* [my emphasis] or waged for political purpose." It allows us to think about faith and fear more comprehensively, about how "war" became more all-encompassing in the post-1945 era. For Gray's definition, and several competing ones, see Ian Speller, "Introduction to the Second Edition," in David Jordan, James D. Kiras, et al., *Understanding Modern Warfare*, 2nd ed. (New York: Cambridge University Press, 2016), 2–3.

35. Stephen Wertheim, *Tomorrow, the World: The Birth of U.S. Global Supremacy* (Cambridge, MA: Belknap Press, 2020), 80, 82. Justin Hart,

Empire of Ideas: The Origins of Public Diplomacy and the Transformation of U.S. Foreign Policy (New York: Oxford University Press, 2013), 9.

36. Social cohesion in Centeno and Enriquez, 17. Systemic in Fink, *Cold War*, 55.
37. George F. Kennan, "'Let Peace Not Die of Neglect,'" *New York Times*, 25 February 1951. George F. Kennan, *American Diplomacy* (Chicago: University of Chicago Press, 1984), xi. It is notable that Kennan's views of foreign policy—and, more importantly, his "fears"—changed considerably from 1946 to 1947, when he articulated the original formulation of containment, and 1950 to 1951, when he became one of the nation's chief critics of how those ideas of containment were interpreted, applied, and militarized.
38. On Americans' sense of destiny, see Odd Arne Westad, *The Cold War: A World History* (New York: Basic, 2017), 15–16. Innocence in Richard W. van Alstyne, *The Rising American Empire* (Chicago: Quadrangle, 1960), 205. "Empire in Denial" in Vine, *The United States of War*, 9. See also Prasenjit Duara, "The Cold War and the Imperialism of Nation-States," in Immerman and Goedde, 90. On animus against the United States, see Reinhold Niebuhr, "Why They Dislike America," *New Leader*, 12 April 1954, 3–5.
39. Hal Brands, *What Good Is Grand Strategy? Power and Purpose in American Statecraft from Harry S. Truman to George W. Bush* (Ithaca, NY: Cornell University Press, 2104), 3. Aspirations and capabilities in Gaddis, *On Grand Strategy*, 21. See also Nathan K. Finney and Francis J. H. Park, "A Brief Introduction to Strategy," in *On Strategy: A Primer*, ed. Nathan K. Finney (Fort Leavenworth, KS: Combat Studies Institute Press, 2020), 4, 8. On interests versus threats, see Hemmer, *American Pendulum*, 3, 10, 14.
40. "Power" defined in military terms in Mearsheimer, *The Tragedy of Great Power Politics*, 56. Grand strategy as producing security in Posen, *Restraint*, 1. For a rejoinder, see Kevin Narizny, *The Political Economy of Grand Strategy* (Ithaca, NY: Cornell University Press, 2007), 9. On grand strategy as a "creature of modern warfare," see McKnight Nichols and Preston, "Introduction," 8.
41. Arthur Bryant, "Co-existence—But Not Surrender," *New York Times*, 6 February 1955. On militarization as a process by which a "society organizes itself for the production of violence," see Catherine Lutz, citing Michael Geyer, "Militarization," in *A Companion to the Anthropology of Politics*, ed. David Nugent and Joan Vincent (Malden, MA: Blackwell, 2007), 320.
42. For a focus on these regional actors, and the interconnections of these areas, see as two examples Lorenz Lüthi, *Cold Wars: Asia, The Middle East, Europe* (New York: Cambridge University Press, 2020); and

Ang Cheng Guan, *Southeast Asia's Cold War: An Interpretive History* (Honolulu: University of Hawaii Press, 2018).

43. Gray areas in Robert Strausz-Hupé, William R. Kintner, et al., *Protracted Conflict: A Challenging Study of Communist Strategy* (New York: Harper & Row, 1959), 53. Peripheral in Michael E. Latham, *The Right Kind of Revolution: Modernization, Development, and U.S. Foreign Policy from the Cold War to the Present* (Ithaca, NY: Cornell University Press, 2011), 29.

44. James Reston, "Eisenhower Would Aid Allies, Defend West, Prevent Wars," *New York Times*, 28 December 1950. For a similar argument, see James Reston, "Now U.S. Must Anticipate Many 'Little Wars,'" *New York Times*, 23 July 1950. Violence in Paul Thomas Chamberlin, *The Cold War's Killing Fields: Rethinking the Long Peace* (New York: Harper-Collins, 2018), 3, 6–7. Anxieties in Marilyn B. Young, "The Age of Global Power," in Bradley and Dudziak, *Making the Forever War*, 22. Influence in Douglas J. Macdonald, *Adventures in Chaos: American Intervention in the Third World* (Cambridge, MA: Harvard University Press, 1992), 44.

45. Direction of history in Robert J. McMahon, "Introduction," in *The Cold War in the Third World*, ed. Robert J. McMahon (New York: Oxford University Press, 2013), 2. "Civilizing mission" in Sara Lorenzini, *Global Development: A Cold War History* (Princeton, NJ: Princeton University Press, 2019), 10. Self-determination in Shibusawa, "Ideology, Culture, and the Cold War," 38. Priya Chacko argues that the Cold War conflict was one to prove the "universal applicability" of competing ideologies throughout the Third World. "Indira Gandhi, the 'Long 1970s,' and the Cold War," in *India and the Cold War*, ed. Manu Bhagavan (Chapel Hill: University of North Carolina Press, 2019), 178.

46. Experiment in Stephen Kotkin, *Armageddon Averted: The Soviet Collapse, 1970–2000* (New York: Oxford University Press, 2008), 6. Yet this competition also was linked to access of markets and materials. Robert J. McMahon, "Introduction: The Challenge of the Third World," in *Empire and Revolution: The United States and the Third World since 1945*, ed. Peter L. Hahn and Marry Ann Heiss (Columbus: Ohio State University Press, 2001), 3, 7. Liberal ideas and capitalist institutions in Norman A. Graebner, Richard Dean Burns, and Joseph A. Siracusa, *America and the Cold War, 1941–1991: A Realist Interpretation*, Vol. 1 (Santa Barbara, CA: Praeger, 2010), 3; and Michael Howard, *The Invention of Peace: Reflections on War and International Order* (New Haven, CT: Yale University Press, 2000), 86. "Long peace," citing John Lewis Gaddis, in Kwon, *The Other Cold War*, 17.

47. For an argument on balancing a globalized approach with a US perspective, see Daniel Bessner and Fredrik Logevall, "Recentering the United States in the Historiography of American Foreign Relations," *Texas National Security Review*, Vol. 3, No. 2 (Spring 2020): 38–55.

48. William O. Douglas, "The Black Silence of Fear," *New York Times*, 13 January 1952. "An Appeal for Calm," in *America in the World: A History in Documents from the War with Spain to the War on Terror*, ed. Jeffrey A. Engel, Mark Atwood Lawrence, and Andrew Preston (Princeton, NJ: Princeton University Press, 2014), 178–79.
49. "Excerpts from Fulbright Talk on Cold War Effect," *New York Times*, 6 April 1964. "Faulkner's Fears," in Engel, Lawrence, and Preston, 192. Economic concerns in Lloyd Gardner, *Spheres of Influence: The Great Powers Partition Europe, from Munich to Yalta* (Chicago: Ivan R. Dee, 1993), 63.
50. We might argue that Americans' fears have led to the pursuit of solutions through the only thing they truly believed in: stockpiling the military technology and hardware to inflict violence. Indeed, Chris Hedges maintains that fear has stopped Americans "from objecting to government spending on a bloated military. Fear means we will not ask unpleasant questions of those in power." *The Greatest Evil Is War* (New York: Seven Stories, 2022), 167.
51. "In Search of Security," *New York Times*, 19 March 1950.
52. Reinhold Niebuhr, *The Irony of American History* (Chicago: University of Chicago Press, 1952, 2008), 109, 113, 130. See also LaFeber, *America, Russia, and the Cold War*, 46–47. We should note, however, that in the 1930s and early 1940s Niebuhr was a rather passionate interventionist, and even in the early Cold War era was supportive of broader containment policies.
53. Of course, we might argue that at least some Americans came to love war in the 1940s. War had been good to them, at least compared to those Europeans and Asians who suffered mightily during the global conflict. In many ways, World War II gave the world to the United States and, thus, the faith necessary to rule it.

CHAPTER 1

1. Theodore H. White, *In Search of History: A Personal Adventure* (New York: Warner, 1978), 228–29.
2. "The Texts of the Official Statements and Orders Issued about the Surrender of Japan," *New York Times*, 2 September 1945.
3. White, *In Search of History*, 230.
4. Absolute condition and increased obligation in William C. Martel, *Victory in War: Foundations of Modern Strategy*, rev. ed. (New York: Cambridge University Press, 2011), 176, 184. On victory and power, see Keith Lowe, *Savage Continent: Europe in the Aftermath of World War II* (New York: St. Martin's, 2012), 179.
5. Tom Engelhardt, *The End of Victory Culture: Cold War America and the Disillusioning of a Generation*, rev. ed. (Amherst: University of

Massachusetts Press, 2007), 10. Status in Tony Judt, *Postwar: A History of Europe since 1945* (New York: Penguin, 2005), 7.

6. Daniel Sargent, "Oasis in the Desert? America's Human Rights Rediscovery" in *The Breakthrough: Human Rights in the 1970s*, ed. Jan Eckel and Samuel Moyn (Philadelphia: University of Pennsylvania Press, 2014), 128. Liberal ideas in Levering, *The Cold War*, 11; and David B. Woolner, *The Last 100 Days: FDR at War and at Peace* (New York: Basic, 2017), 74, 119. On fears among FDR's advisors, see John Lewis Gaddis, *The United States and the Origins of the Cold War, 1941–1947* (New York: Columbia University Press, 1972, 2000), 199. On problems of translating victory to the international system, see Martel, *Victory in War*, 25, 33, 39.

7. Costigliola, *Roosevelt's Lost Alliances*, 2–3. Gardner, *Spheres of Influence*, 237. Stalin quoted in Benn Steil, *The Marshall Plan: Dawn of the Cold War* (New York: Simon & Schuster, 2018), 10.

8. "Text of President's Message on the State of the Union and Transmitting the Budget," *New York Times*, 22 January 1946. Markets in Brands, *The Devil We Knew*, 10–11. Fears of depression in Gaddis, *The United States and the Origins of the Cold War*, 189. Job losses in Michael Brenes, *For Might and Right: Cold War Defense Spending and the Remaking of American Democracy* (Amherst: University of Massachusetts Press, 2020), 6. US economy in Derek Leebaert, *Grand Improvisation: America Confronts the British Superpower, 1945–1957* (New York: Farrar, Straus & Giroux, 2018), 33. British debt in Steil, *The Marshall Plan*, 21.

9. Churchill quoted in Steil, 15. On Europe, see May Elise Sarotte, *The Collapse: The Accidental Opening of the Berlin Wall* (New York: Basic, 2014), 4; and Lowe, *Savage Continent*, 10, 27. Political stability and social reform in Judt, *Postwar*, 82–83. On Chinese civil war, see Jian, *Mao's China and the Cold War*, 20–22.

10. Truman quoted in David Ekbladh, *The Great American Mission: Modernization and the Constructions of an American World Order* (Princeton, NJ: Princeton University Press, 2010), 77–79. Javitz on p. 109. See also Jason C. Parker, *Hearts, Minds, Voices: US Cold War Public Diplomacy and the Formation of the Third World* (New York: Oxford University Press, 2016), 29–30. Global economy in Derek S. Reveron, Nikolas K. Gvosdev, and Mackubin Thomas Owens, *US Foreign Policy and Defense Strategy: The Evolution of an Incidental Superpower* (Washington, DC: Georgetown University Press, 2015), 16.

11. On New Deal, see Williams, *The Tragedy of American Diplomacy*, 173, 190, 194–95, 267. Participatory democracy in Lorenzini, *Global Development*, 23. On links to security, see Elizabeth Borgwardt, "Franklin Roosevelt, the New Deal, and Grand Strategy: Constructing the Postwar Order," in Borgwardt, McKnight Nichols, and Preston, *Rethinking American Grand Strategy*, 201, 208. For a specific example with the TVA,

see Ekbladh, *The Great American Mission*, 8, 41. On a "New Deal synthesis," see Michael J. Hogan, *The Marshall Plan: America, Britain, and the Reconstruction of Western Europe, 1947–1952* (New York: Cambridge University Press, 1987), 22.

12. FDR views in Hemmer, *American Pendulum*, 34–35. FDR's faith in Levering, *The Cold War*, 12–13. Hope of cooperation in Steil, *The Marshall Plan*, 4–5. Machinery in David Ryan and David Fitzgerald, "Introduction," in *Not Even Past: How the United States Ends Wars*, ed. David Fitzgerald, David Ryan, and John M. Thompson (New York: Berghahn, 2020), 1. Collective security in Miller, *Grand Strategy from Truman to Trump*, 61. Vladislav M. Zubok, *A Failed Empire: The Soviet Union in the Cold War from Stalin to Gorbachev* (Chapel Hill: University of North Carolina Press, 2007), 14–15. Leahy and Vandenberg quoted in Norman A. Graebner, Richard Dean Burns, and Joseph M. Siracusa, *America and the Cold War, 1941–1991: A Realist Interpretation*, Vol. 1 (Santa Barbara, CA: Praeger, 2010), 73.

13. Pearl Harbor in Preston, *American Foreign Relations*, 71; and Douglas T. Stuart, *Creating the National Security State: A History of the Law That Transformed America* (Princeton, NJ: Princeton University Press, 2008), 2, 7–8, 40–41. Bases in Layne, *The Peace of Illusions*, 45. "Free security" in Craig and Logevall, *America's Cold War*, 13, 20. Relative concept in Buzan, *Peoples, States, and Fear*, 18. On how this led to a "bunker mentality," see May, *Fortress America*, 1, 14.

14. Holland M. Smith in "Scores Demobilization," *New York Times*, 6 October 1946. See also Sidney Shalett, "Army Seeks a Way out of Its Morale Crisis," *New York Times*, 13 January 1946. Lemay in Trevor Albertson, *Winning Armageddon: Curtis LeMay and Strategic Air Command, 1948–1957* (Annapolis, MD: Naval Institute Press, 2019), 44.

15. Andrew J. Bacevich, *The New American Militarism: How Americans Are Seduced by War* (New York: Oxford University Press, 2013), 15. On choices for internationalism, see Wertheim, *Tomorrow, the World*, 3–5. Imposing democracy in Stephen D. Krasner, *How to Make Love to a Despot: An Alternative Foreign Policy for the Twenty-First Century* (New York: Liveright, 2020), 186.

16. Bernard Brodie, *War and Politics* (New York: Macmillan, 1973), 345. See also Preston, *American Foreign Relations*, 72–73. Bases in Vine, *The United States of War*, 141, 156, 161, 169.

17. Harold Callender, "Why a Free Europe Is Vital to Us," *New York Times*, 7 January 1951. For a classic essay on this theme, see Geir Lundestad, "Empire by Invitation? The United States and Western Europe, 1945–1952," *Journal of Peace Research*, Vol. 23, No. 3 (September 1986): 263–77. Unparalleled opportunity in Layne, *The Peace of Illusions*, 39. Power vacuum in Henry Kissinger, *Diplomacy* (New York: Simon &

Schuster, 1995), 424. Economic interests in Vine, 165. John Mueller argues that few defense analysts took time to question whether conquest was in Russia's best interests. *The Stupidity of War: American Foreign Policy and the Case for Complacency* (New York: Cambridge University Press, 2021), 34.

18. Hans Morgenthau, "What the Big Two Can, and Can't, Negotiate," *New York Times*, 20 September 1959. On this relation to political power, see Morgenthau, *Politics among Nations*, 11, 27–28.

19. Incompatible aspirations in Gaddis, *The Cold War: A New History*, 6, 7. On links to World War II, see Perlmutter, *Making the World Safe for Democracy*, xi. Lorenz Lüthi argues that there was a three-way ideological conflict between imperialism, communism, and liberal democracy/capitalism. *Cold Wars*, 3, 4. Fear in Graebner, Burns, and Siracusa, *America and the Cold War*, Vol. 1, 3–4. Christine Hong argues that US militarism was framed as "a means to a future." *A Violent Peace: Race, U.S. Militarism, and Cultures of Democratization in Cold War Asia and the Pacific* (Stanford, CA: Stanford University Press, 2020), 18.

20. John G. Norris, "Economic Phases of Cold War a Factor in Military Program," *Washington Post*, 3 January 1949. See also Quincy Home, "More of the Good Things of Life for More and More People," *New York Times*, 21 June 1959. On wartime production, see *Maury Klein Call to Arms: Mobilizing America for World War II* (New York: Bloomsbury, 2013). Stephen E. Ambrose, *Band of Brothers: E Company, 506th Regiment, 101st Airborne from Normandy to Hitler's Eagle's Nest* (New York: Simon & Schuster, 1992), 224.

21. Seeking evil enemies in Brands, *The Devil We Knew*, vi. National security in Stuart, *Creating the National Security State*, 27. Civil religion in Raymond Haberski, Jr., *God and War: American Civil Religion since 1945* (New Brunswick, NJ: Rutgers University Press, 2012), 4–5; and Haberski, "Just War as Ideology: A Militant Ecumenism of Catholics and Evangelicals," in *Ideology in U.S. Foreign Relations: New Histories*, ed. Christopher McKnight Nichols and David Milne (New York: Columbia University Press, 2022), 263. On the greatest generation, see Elizabeth D. Samet, *Looking for the Good War: American Amnesia and the Violent Pursuit of Happiness* (New York: Farrar, Straus & Giroux, 2021).

22. On development as competing forms of intervention, see Bradley R. Simpson, *Economists with Guns: Authoritarian Development and U.S.-Indonesian Relations, 1960–1968* (Stanford, CA: Stanford University Press, 2008), 6. President John F. Kennedy's national security advisor Walt Rostow would assert that the United States had a "special responsibility of leadership" in assisting those "hard-pressed states on the periphery of the Communist bloc." "The Challenge of Modernization," in Engel, Lawrence, and Preston, *America in the World*, 219. See also Michael E.

Latham, *Modernization as Ideology: American Social Science and "Nation Building" in the Kennedy Era* (Chapel Hill: University of North Carolina Press, 2000), 2, 56–57; and Ekbladh, *The Great American Mission*, 40.
23. Power politics in Nicholas John Spykman, *America's Strategy in World Politics: The United States and the Balance of Power* (New York: Harcourt, Brace, 1942), 26. Prevailing narrative in Costigliola, *Roosevelt's Lost Alliances*, 8. Future national security advisor Walt Rostow believed the United States had a "special responsibility" to protect the free world. In Mark A. Haefele, "Walt Rostow's Stages of Economic Growth: Ideas and Actions," in *Staging Growth: Modernization, Development, and the Global Cold War*, ed. David C. Engerman, Nils Gilman, et al. (Amherst: University of Massachusetts Press, 2003), 90. But historian Barbara W. Tuchman warned, at the height of the Reagan presidency, that "the responsibility of power often fades as its exercise augments." *The March of Folly: From Troy to Vietnam* (New York: Knopf, 1984), 32.

CHAPTER 2

1. Gaddis, *The United States and the Origins of the Cold War*, 32, 42, 45. New world system in Odd Arne Westad, "The Cold War and the International History of the Twentieth Century," in Leffler and Westad, *The Cambridge History of the Cold War*, Vol. I, 3. On Orwell, see Lawrence Freedman, *Strategy: A History* (New York: Oxford University Press, 2013), 145–46.
2. Wilson regarded the Russian undertaking as a "competing form of internationalism." In Westad, *The Cold War*, 29. Competing ideologies in Gaddis, ibid., 47, 49. Mistake in David C. Engerman, "Ideology and the origins of the Cold War, 1917–1962," *The Cambridge History of the Cold War*, Vol. I, 23, 27. Symbolic basis for conflict in John Lewis Gaddis, *We Now Know: Rethinking Cold War History* (New York: Oxford University Press, 1998), 6. Universalistic notions in Kagan, *Dangerous Nation*, 42.
3. Lenin quoted in Westad, *The Global Cold War*, 50–51. Comintern in Guan, *Southeast Asia's Cold War*, 14–16. Lorenz M. Lüthi, *The Sino-Soviet Split: Cold War in the Communist World* (Princeton, NJ: Princeton University Press, 2008), 19. Vijay Prashad, *Red Star over the Third World* (London: Pluto, 2017), 77, 127.
4. Lenin to American Workers, 22 August 1918, and A. Mitchell Palmer on eradicating Bolshevism, April 2020, in *The Cold War: A History in Documents and Eyewitness Accounts*, ed. Jussi Hanhimäki and Odd Arne Westad (New York: Oxford University Press, 2004), 3–4, 6. Permanent revolution in Harry and Bonaro Overstreet, *What We Must Know about Communism* (New York: Norton, 1958), 93, 95. Class-conscious in Prashad, 37. Vanguard in Fink, *Cold War*, 11. Intelligence in Feldman, *Manufacturing Hysteria*, 68. Imperialism in Kenneth N. Waltz, *Theory of International*

Politics (Reading, MA: Addison-Wesley, 1979), 27. On Bolsheviks, see Orlando Figes, *Revolutionary Russia, 1891–1991: A History* (New York: Metropolitan, 2014), 66, 78–124. Lamberton Harper, *The Cold War*, 31. Stalin seemingly would inherit this revolutionary paradigm. Zubok, *A Failed Empire*, xxiv, 51.

5. Twisted brains in "The Communist Threat," *Washington Post*, 13 May 1922. Critics in Eric F. Goldman, "The Second Outburst," *New York Times*, 18 September 1955; and "Nation Is Depicted in 'Chronic Crisis,'" *New York Times*, 3 April 1954. Disease in Thomas A. Bailey, *America Faces Russia: Russian-American Relations from Early Times to Our Day* (Gloucester, MA: Peter Smith, 1964), 248. On party's limited impact and appeal, see Ellen Schrecker, *Many Are the Crimes: McCarthyism in America* (New York: Little, Brown, 1998), 12, 56; and Richard M. Fried, *Nightmare in Red: The McCarthy Era in Perspective* (New York: Oxford University Press, 1990), 12. Domestic reactions in Feldman, *Manufacturing Hysteria*, 75, 77, 91, 100.

6. Feldman, 90, 127. Hoover quoted on p. 188. Weak in Bailey, 267. Barry M. Goldwater, *Why Not Victory? A Fresh Look at American Foreign Policy* (New York: McGraw-Hill, 1962), 24–25. On policymakers speaking about defending civilization, rather than promoting it, see Benjamin A. Coates, "American Presidents and the Ideology of Civilization," in Nichols and Milne, *Ideology in U.S. Foreign Relations*, 60.

7. Edward Crankshaw, "Is the Man in the Kremlin Another Hitler?" *New York Times*, 4 July 1948. See also "Hitler Was Just an Amateur," *Los Angeles Times*, 11 December 1949. Nazism in Preston, *American Foreign Relations*, 8. Kennan, *American Diplomacy*, 171. See also John Mueller, *Overblown: How Politicians and the Terrorism Industry Inflate National Security Threats, and Why We Believe Them* (New York: Free Press, 2006), 74. Of note, these fears also were coupled with a faith that America alone could provide leadership in a volatile postwar world. Fink, *Cold War*, 30, 39.

8. Henry Steele Commager, "An Inquiry Into 'Appeasement,'" *New York Times*, 11 February 1951. On Munich, see Yuen Foong Khong, *Analogies at War: Korea, Munich, Dien Bien Phu, and the Vietnam Decisions of 1965* (Princeton, NJ: Princeton University Press, 1992), 11. On appeasement, see Mearsheimer, *The Tragedy of Great Power Politics*, 163–64. World domination in Levering, *The Cold War*, 29. Complacency in Mueller, *The Stupidity of War*, 18. In short, Americans gained faith in war from World War II while losing faith in diplomacy from Munich.

9. LeMay in Albertson, *Winning Armageddon*, xvii, 134, 143. See also Melvin G. Deaile, *Always at War: Organizational Culture in Strategic Air Command, 1946–62* (Annapolis, MD: Naval Institute Press, 2018), 102. Ike quoted in Engel, Lawrence, and Preston, *America in the World*, 195.

See also Martin J. Sherwin, *Gambling with Armageddon: Nuclear Roulette from Hiroshima to the Cuban Missile Crisis, 1945–1962* (New York: Vintage, 2020), 76; and Petra Goedde, *The Politics of Peace: A Global Cold War History* (New York: Oxford University Press, 2019), 26.

10. Warren Weaver, Jr., "Hanley Denounces U.S. 'Appeasement,'" *New York Times*, 6 October 1950. See also W. H. Lawrence, "Stevenson Report Hit by Ferguson," *New York Times*, 18 September 1953. Threatening in Bradley and Dudziak, *Making the Forever War*, 29. Innocence in van Alstyne, *The Rising American Empire*, 205. See also Joseba Zulaika, *Terrorism: The Self-Fulfilling Prophecy* (Chicago: University of Chicago Press, 2009), 9.

11. Quasi allies and disquieting conclusions in Bailey, *America Faces Russia*, 308, 320. On Potsdam, see Fredrik Logevall, "American Grand Strategy: How Grand Has It Been? How Much Does It Matter?" in Borgwardt, McKnight Nichols, and Preston, *Rethinking American Grand Strategy*, 449; Zubok, *A Failed Empire*, 29; David M. Edelstein, *Over the Horizon: Time, Uncertainty, and the Rise of Great Powers* (Ithaca, NY: Cornell University Press, 2017), 134; and Aleksandr Fursenko and Timothy Naftali, *Khrushchev's Cold War: The Inside Story of an American Adversary* (New York: Norton, 2006), 21–22.

12. Arthur M. Schlesinger, Jr., *The Vital Center: The Politics of Freedom* (New York: Houghton Mifflin, 1949), 9. K. A. Cuordileone, *Manhood and American Political Culture in the Cold War* (London: Routledge, 2012), 2, 6, 7–8. Arthur M. Schlesinger, Jr., "The Vital Center: 50 Years Later," *Society*, Vol. 35, No. 4 (1998): 53. Spykman spoke of "total war" being "permanent war." *America's Strategy in World Politics*, 40.

13. FDR in Robert J. O'Neill, "Alliances and International Order," in *The Limitations of Power: Essays Presented to Professor Norman Gibbs on His Eightieth Birthday*, ed. John H. Hattendorf and Malcolm H. Murfett (New York: St. Martin's, 1990), 73; and Woolner, *The Last 100 Days*, 14, 31. On the UN, see Goedde, *The Politics of Peace*, 6–7; and Wertheim, *Tomorrow, the World*, 100, 118–19, 138, 140–41. On the UN's precursor, see Susan Pedersen, *The Guardians: The League of Nations and the Crisis of Empire* (New York: Oxford University Press, 2015).

14. Impacts of World War II and cautious expansionist in Mearsheimer, *The Tragedy of Great Power Politics*, 198–99. Zubok, *A Failed Empire*, 2, 5. Stalin's agenda in Vladimir O. Pechatnov, "The Soviet Union and the World, 1944–1953," in Leffler and Westad, *The Cambridge History of the Cold War*, Vol. I, 98. Soviet exasperation in Levering, *The Cold War*, 4–5. World War III in Judt, *Postwar*, 120–21.

15. On Marxist thought, see Waltz, *Man, the State, and War*, 126, 128; and Peter Singer, *Marx: A Very Short Introduction* (New York: Oxford University Press, 2018), 64, 77. Suspicion in Gaddis, *We Now Know*, 25, 29.

On paradox of Stalinist thought, see Curt Cardwell, "The Cold War," in *America in the World: The Historiography of American Foreign Relations since 1941*, 2nd ed., ed. Frank Costigliola and Michael J. Hogan (New York: Cambridge University Press, 2014), 107; and Lüthi, *Cold Wars*, 18, 24. Radicalized visions in Figes, *Revolutionary Russia*, 147.

16. Fears of German aggression in Figes, 192, 210; Christian F. Ostermann, *Between Containment and Rollback: The United States and the Cold War in Germany* (Stanford, CA: Stanford University Press, 2021), 8–9; and Donald A. Carter, *Forging the Shield: The U.S. Army in Europe, 1951–1962* (Washington, DC: Center of Military History, 2015), 35. Stalin quoted in Jonathan Haslam, *Russia's Cold War: From the October Revolution to the Fall of the Wall* (New Haven, CT: Yale University Press, 2011), 17. War trophy in Laszlo Borhi, "The Soviet Union, the United States and Eastern Europe: 1941–1953," in *The Routledge Handbook of American Military and Diplomatic History: 1865 to the Present*, ed. Antonio S. Thompson and Christos G. Frentzos (New York: Routledge, 2013), 177. Social system in Gardner, *Spheres of Influence*, x. Fears in Anne Applebaum, *Iron Curtain: The Crushing of Eastern Europe, 1944–1956* (New York: Doubleday, 2012), 250; and Leffler, *For the Soul of Mankind*, 26–27, 30, 52, 55. On Germany, see Judt, *Postwar*, 145; and Zubok, *A Failed Empire*, 8–9.

17. On the socialist camp, see Lüthi, *Cold Wars*, 69, 71, 72, 89. Red Army in Applebaum, *Iron Curtain*, xxviii, xxix, 51; and Figes, *Revolutionary Russia*, 230. Puppets in Overstreet, *What We Must Know about Communism*, 263. Integration in Craig and Logevall, *America's Cold War*, 37–39, 60; and Applebaum, *Iron Curtain*, xxv. Repression in Krasner, *How to Make Love to a Despot*, 171. On US misestimations, see Williams, *The Tragedy of American Diplomacy*, 227, 228.

18. Edward Crankshaw, "The Question: 'Does Stalin Want War?'" *New York Times*, 31 August 1952. Drew Middleton, "Do the Men in the Kremlin Want War?" *New York Times*, 28 March 1948. Churchill's Iron Curtain Speech, March 1946, in *The Cold War: A Global History with Documents*, 2nd ed., ed. Edward H. Judge and John W. Langdon (Boston: Prentice Hall, 2010), 286. On contemporary views, see R. J. Reinhart, "Americans' Views as the Iron Curtain Descended," *Gallup Vault*, 2 March 2021. Of note, Stalin himself said in March 1945 that the Soviet Union needed "an ideology of preparedness not only for defense but also for attack." In Haslam, *Russia's Cold War*, 30. Norman M. Naimark argues that Stalin had no immediate postwar plans other than security. *Stalin and the Fate of Europe: The Postwar Struggle for Sovereignty* (Cambridge, MA: Belknap, 2019), 6, 11, 13. See also Miller, *Grand Strategy from Truman to Trump*, 89; and Zubok, 18–19, 21.

19. Helms and CIA report in Tim Weiner, *Legacy of Ashes: The History of the CIA* (New York: Doubleday, 2007), 9, 41. Assessing the Red Army

in Hemmer, *American Pendulum*, 43; and Carter, *Forging the Shield*, 40–41, 49.
20. Naimark, 9. Pitiful in Williams, 230. Russian concerns in Kotkin, *Armageddon Averted*, 43–44, 46.
21. For biographies of Kennan, see John Lewis Gaddis, *Kennan: An American Life* (New York: Penguin, 2011), and Frank Costigliola, *Kennan: A Life between Worlds* (Princeton, NJ: Princeton University Press, 2023). Snapshot in Steil, *The Marshall Plan*, 28–29. Piecemeal in David Milne, "Grand Strategies (or Ascendant Ideas) since 1919," in Borgwardt, McKnight Nichols, and Preston, *Rethinking American Grand Strategy*, 150. Reliance on military in Miller, 66–68.
22. Telegram in Hanhimäki and Westad, *The Cold War*, 108–11. For analysis, see Costigliola, *Roosevelt's Lost Alliances*, 410–17; and Lüthi, *Cold Wars*, 25, 68.
23. X-Article, 1947, in Judge and Langdon, *The Cold War*, 294–302.
24. Insecurity in Hemmer, *American Pendulum*, 45, 46; and LaFeber, *America, Russia, and the Cold War*, 63. Costigliola speaks of a "Russian status anxiety" in *Roosevelt's Lost Alliances*, 17. Steady pressure in John Lewis Gaddis, *Strategies of Containment: A Critical Appraisal of American National Security Policy during the Cold War*, rev. ed. (New York: Oxford University Press, 1982, 2005), 48. Security and domination in George F. Kennan, *The Kennan Diaries*, ed. Frank Costigliola (New York: Norton, 2014), 204. Encirclement in White, *Fearful Warriors*, 12. On states' quest for power and dominance, see Morgenthau, *Politics Among Nations*, 5, 9.
25. Bohlen quoted in John L. Harper, "Friends, Not Allies: George F. Kennan and Charles E. Bohlen," *World Policy Journal*, Vol. 12, No. 2 (Summer, 1995): 83. On Bohlen at State, see Robert R. Bowie and Richard H. Immerman, *Waging Peace: How Eisenhower Shaped an Enduring Cold War Strategy* (New York: Oxford University Press, 1998), 46; and Costigliola, *Roosevelt's Lost Alliances*, 6, 358. On analyzing Soviet intentions, see Edelstein, *Over the Horizon*, 136; and Steil, *The Marshall Plan*, 48.
26. Walter H. Waggoner, "Acheson Tells Bitter Marine to Have Faith in U.S. Ideals," *New York Times*, 4 March 1951. William S. White, "Acheson Says West Won Unity to Face Menace of Soviet," *New York Times*, 1 June 1950. Milton Bracker, "Acheson Exhorts Americas to Meet Soviet Peril 'Now,'" *New York Times*, 28 March 1951. See also Gardner, *Spheres of Influence*, 264. Notably, Acheson also realized that exaggerating threats could be useful as a "bludgeon" to force top officials into making decisions and then carrying them out. In Graebner, Burns, and Siracusa, *America and the Cold War*, Vol. 1, 185. On containment, see Alexander L. George and Richard Smoke, *Deterrence in American Foreign Policy: Theory and Practice* (New York: Columbia University Press, 1974), 22–23. Pattern in Narizny, *The Political Economy of Grand Strategy*, 10.

27. Expectations of war in Melvyn P. Leffler, "The Emergence of an American Grand Strategy, 1945–1952," in Leffler and Westad, *The Cambridge History of the Cold War*, Vol. I, 73; and Layne, *The Peace of Illusions*, 56–57. On US strategy at this time, see Russell F. Weigley, *The American Way of War: A History of United States Military Policy and Strategy* (New York: Macmillan, 1973), 365, 367–68; and Hal Brands, *The Twilight Struggle: What the Cold War Teaches Us about Great-Power Rivalry Today* (New Haven, CT: Yale University Press, 2022), 18. Geography in Colin S. Gray, "Geography and Grand Strategy," in Hattendorf and Murfett, *The Limitations of Power*, 125–27. Middle ground in Brands, *What Good Is Grand Strategy?* 17.
28. Novikov, 27 September 1946, in Hanhimäki and Westad, *The Cold War*, 111–14. He also argued that the US armed forces had been placed in service of "ruling circles" bent on supporting "reactionary forces" abroad. On Novikov, see also Levering, *The Cold War*, 31–32; and Martin Sixsmith, *The War of Nerves: Inside the Cold War Mind* (New York: Pegasus, 2022), 72–75. Strangulation in Hemmer, *American Pendulum*, 47. On US bases, see David Vine, *Base Nation: How U.S. Military Bases Abroad Harm America and the World* (New York: Metropolitan, 2015), 3, 10–11.
29. Clifford/Elsey Report in Edelstein, *Over the Horizon*, 145–47; Graebner, Burns, and Siracusa, *America and the Cold War*, Vol. 1, 113–14; and Layne, *The Peace of Illusions*, 54. Us versus them in Masuda Hajimu, *Cold War Crucible: The Korean Conflict and the Postwar World* (Cambridge, MA: Harvard University Press, 2015), 7. Language of force in Levering, *The Cold War*, 39.
30. "Roots of the Truman Doctrine," *Washington Post*, 16 March 1947. Doctrine in Lamberton Harper, *The Cold War*, 64; and Graebner, Burns, and Siracusa, 118–20. Language in Arnold A. Offner, "Liberation or Dominance? The Ideology of U.S. National Security Policy," in Bacevich, *The Long War*, 8. Dennis Merrill argues that although "it reflected America's faith in progress, Truman's doctrine also betrayed an existential fear of modernity." "The Truman Doctrine: Containing Communism and Modernity," *Presidential Studies Quarterly*, Vol. 36, No. 1 (March 2006): 28.
31. Frederick L. Schuman, "The Truman Doctrine," *New York Times*, 8 May 1947. Wallace and Taft quoted in LaFeber, *America, Russia, and the Cold War*, 55. Marshall in Brewer, *Why America Fights*, 146–47. Open-ended in Gaddis, *Strategies of Containment*, 23. Multiple audiences in Macdonald, *Adventures in Chaos*, 68–70, 73, 259.
32. Judge and Langdon, *The Cold War*, 292.
33. German recovery in Hogan, *The Marshall Plan*, 2, 18, 26. Dislocation from William L. Clayton in Steil, *The Marshall Plan*, 112. Deteriorating, integration, and Stalin in Leffler, *For the Soul of Mankind*, 62–65,

75. Industrial areas in Brands, *What Good Is Grand Strategy?* 27. Revival in Carolyn Woods Eisenberg, *Drawing the Line: The American Decision to Divide Germany, 1944–1949* (New York: Cambridge University Press, 1996), 313. See also William I. Hitchcock, "The Marshall Plan and the Creation of the West," in Leffler and Westad, *The Cambridge History of the Cold War*, Vol. I, 154–74. Military-centric in Miller, *Grand Strategy from Truman to Trump*, 77. Development in Ethan B. Kapstein, *Seeds of Stability: Land Reform and US Foreign Policy* (New York: Cambridge University Press, 2017), 45, 133.

34. Marshall quoted in Judge and Langdon, *The Cold War*, 294. Costs in Lorenzini, *Global Development*, 24. Global aspects in Robert J. McMahon, *Colonialism and the Cold War: The United States and the Struggle for Indonesian Independence, 1945–49* (Ithaca, NY: Cornell University Press, 1981), 227. Douglas Little, *American Orientalism: The United States and the Middle East since 1945*, 3rd ed. (Chapel Hill: University of North Carolina Press, 2008), 53. On the role of Western Europe, see Hogan, *The Marshall Plan*, 179, 192.

35. William M. Blair, "Taft Doubts Value of Marshall Plan," *New York Times*, 31 December 1947. Military footing and Taft in Brenes, *For Might and Right*, 38–39. See also Stephen Kinzer, *The Brothers: John Foster Dulles, Allen Dulles, and Their Secret World War* (New York: Times Books, 2013), 91. Harold Callender Paris, "We Expect Too Much from the Marshall Plan," *New York Times*, 23 January 1949. For a larger assessment of the plan, see Steil, *The Marshall Plan*, 342, 369. Contrary to Taft's objections, both the Truman Doctrine and the Marshall Plan were explicitly couched as antidotes to militarism.

36. David Chidester, *Authentic Fakes: Religion and American Popular Culture* (Berkeley: University of California Press, 2005), 222. Kagan, *Dangerous Nation*, 130–31. On similar McKinley-era expansion, see Brewer, *Why America Fights*, 15.

37. "Exiles Will Pierce the Iron Curtain in New Radio Broadcast Tomorrow," *New York Times*, 3 July 1950. See also Applebaum, *Iron Curtain*, 459–60. Psychological warfare in Edward L. Bernays, "Saving the Voice of America," *Washington Post*, 2 May 1953. Laura A. Belmonte, *Selling the American Way: U.S. Propaganda and the Cold War* (Philadelphia: University of Pennsylvania Press, 2010), 49, 71, 82, 179. VOA in Dina Fainberg, *Cold War Correspondents: Soviet and American Reporters on the Ideological Frontlines* (Baltimore: Johns Hopkins University Press, 2020), 22.

38. Hogan, *The Marshall Plan*, 337, 380, 382, 393, 419. Steil, *The Marshall Plan*, 90–92, 207.

39. CIA in Richard H. Immerman, *The Hidden Hand: A Brief History of the CIA* (Malden, MA: Wiley Blackwell, 2014), 23. In a "manifesto of peace"

signed by two past secretaries of state, a former Supreme Court justice, and even First Lady Eleanor Roosevelt, the Washington elite pledged their support in the Italians' "struggle to maintain their freedom and their dignity in a world that is again darkened with the threat of oppression and slavery." In "Pleas to Italy Ask Vote against Reds," *New York Times*, 8 April 1948. On elections, see Judt, *Postwar*, 88; Lowe, *Savage Continent*, 276, 278, 291–92; and Naimark, *Stalin and the Fate of Europe*, 122–23, 136–39, 146–49. Arnaldo Cortesis, "Danger of Communism Still Grave in Italy," *New York Times*, 25 April 1948.

40. Pincher in Steven L. Rearden, *Council of War: A History of the Joint Chiefs of Staff, 1942–1991* (Washington, DC: Joint History Office, 2012), 71. Clay in Sixsmith, *The War of Nerves*, 106–7.

41. "U.S. 'Imperialism' Scored in Moscow," *New York Times*, 22 January 1949. "Red China Assails U.S. 'Aggression,'" *New York Times*, 30 June 1950. See also Lorenzini, *Global Development*, 28. "Soviet Hits at U.S. on Troops in Egypt," *New York Times*, 14 March 1946. See also Rashid Khalidi, *Sowing Crisis: The Cold War and American Dominance in the Middle East* (Boston: Beacon, 2010), 35. Lüthi, *Cold Wars*, 387. Molotov quoted in Steil, *The Marshall Plan*, 132.

42. Cominform in Judge and Langdon, *The Cold War*, 303. Bases in Hanhimäki and Westad, *The Cold War*, 51. See also Guan, *Southeast Asia's Cold War*, 37.

43. Little choice in Burton Hersh, *The Old Boys: The American Elite and the Origins of the CIA* (New York: Scribner's, 1992), 221–22. Moral obligations in Michael B. Oren, *Power, Faith, and Fantasy: America in the Middle East, 1776 to the Present* (New York: Norton, 2007), 482; and Craig and Logevall, *America's Cold War*, 78–79. Victims in Zubok, *A Failed Empire*, 46. Oil and trade in Levering, *The Cold War*, 22–23. On Britain and France, see Gaddis, *Now We Know*, 164.

44. Acheson quoted in Little, *American Orientalism*, 123, 127. On the Greek Civil War, see Jaqueline L. Hazelton, *Bullets Not Ballots: Success in Counterinsurgency Warfare* (Ithaca, NY: Cornell University Press, 2021), 48–57; Jonathan M. House, *A Military History of the Cold War, 1944–1962* (Norman: University of Oklahoma Press, 2012), 53–60, 75; and Svetozar Rajak, "The Cold War in the Balkans, 1945–1956," in Leffler and Westad, *The Cambridge History of the Cold War*, Vol. I, 203–8. As would become a common refrain, US advisors' advice and support barely altered the government's repressive policies. On Britain's withdrawal, see Miller, *Grand Strategy from Truman to Trump*, 55, 88. Derek Leebaert, *The World after the War: America Confronts the British Superpower, 1945–1957* (London: Oneworld, 2018), 34, 84, 372. Misestimating the threat in Brands, *The Devil We Knew*, 18–21; Mara E. Karlin, *Building Militaries*

in Fragile States: Challenges for the United States (Philadelphia: University of Pennsylvania Press, 2018), 21, 23–24; and Judt, *Postwar*, 127. Leebaert argues that the US aid and military presence proved effective. *Grand Improvisation*, 91–92.

45. Shoring up in Bailey, *America Faces Russia*, 336. On Turkey, see Edelstein, *Over the Horizon*, 141–44. Soviet actions in Zubok, *A Failed Empire*, 36–40. Mastery in Graebner, Burns, and Siracusa, *America and the Cold War*, Vol. 1, 2.

46. Barnet Nover, "The Real Test: Moscow's Unfinished Task," *Washington Post*, 1 January 1946. On Iran, see Khalidi, *Sowing Crisis*, 50–51, 53; James A. Bill, *The Eagle and the Lion: The Tragedy of American-Iranian Relations* (New Haven, CT: Yale University Press, 1988), 32, 33, 50–52; and Edelstein, *Over the Horizon*, 138–41. Global interests in William L. Cleveland and Martin Bunton, *A History of the Modern Middle East*, 6th ed. (Boulder, CO: Westview, 2016), 262. Soviet objectives and Tudeh party in Zubok, *A Failed Empire*, 40–45. Mark J. Gasiorowski, "Why Did Mosaddeq Fail?" in *Mohammed Mosaddeq and the 1953 Coup in Iran*, ed. Mark J. Gasiorowski and Malcolm Byrne (Syracuse, NY: Syracuse University Press), 208–9, 220. Oil interests in John Foran, "Discursive Subversions: *Time* Magazine, the CIA Overthrow of Musaddiq and the Installation of the Shah," in *Cold War Constructions: The Political Culture of United States Imperialism, 1945–1966*, ed. Christian G. Appy (Amherst: University of Massachusetts Press, 2000), 158–59.

47. On creation of Israel, see Lüthi, *Cold Wars*, 60, 188, 190; Rashid Khalidi, *The Hundred Years' War on Palestine: A History of Settler Colonialism and Resistance, 1917–2017* (New York: Metropolitan Books, 2021), 9, 24, 32, 34; Little, *American Orientalism*, 21, 25, 26; and Cleveland and Bunton, 255. US recognition in Peter L. Hahn, *Caught in the Middle East: U.S Policy toward the Arab-Israeli Conflict, 1945–1961* (Chapel Hill: University of North Carolina Press, 2004), 50, 62–63; and Little, 82, 84, 87. Arab-Israeli relations in Oren, *Power, Faith, and Fantasy*, 496–97. Encroachment in Salim Yaqub, *Containing Arab Nationalism: The Eisenhower Doctrine and the Middle East* (Chapel Hill: University of North Carolina Press, 2004), 23; and Hahn, 2–3, 18, 44.

48. US policy elite in "Aid for Israel Is Asked," *New York Times*, 29 October 1948. Hard core in "Morgenthau See Israel Soviet Foe," *New York Times*, 2 November 1948. Exaggerated fears in Gaddis, *Now We Know*, 167. US interests in Hahn, *Caught in the Middle East*, 20–23, 68–69, 76. Of note, Morgenthau's view was in the minority and contested by a rare show of State-Defense agreement that supporting Israel would be detrimental to US interests. Truman made his decision to support the new state against the overwhelming anti-Israel consensus within his administration.

For more, see John B. Judis, *Genesis: Truman, American Jews, and the Origins of the Arab/Israeli Conflict* (New York: Farrar, Straus & Giroux, 2015).

49. Militarization in Lüthi, *Cold Wars*, 209; and Little, *American Orientalism*, 125. Liability in John J. Mearsheimer and Stephen M. Walt, *The Israel Lobby and U.S. Foreign Policy* (New York: Farrar, Straus & Giroux, 2007), 49–55, 95–96. Hahn, 99, 110. Yaqub, *Containing Arab Nationalism*, 25. Asset in Khalidi, *The Hundred Years' War on Palestine*, 80. Exacerbating in Khalidi, *Sowing Crisis*, 1.

CHAPTER 3

1. Goldwater also called it a "war of a more deadly nature than any we have fought before." *Why Not Victory?* 23, 173. Resolve in Richard Ned Lebow and Janice Gross Stein, *We All Lost the Cold War* (Princeton, NJ: Princeton University Press, 1994), 300, 355.
2. William O. Douglas, "The Black Silence of Fear," *New York Times*, 13 January 1952. Security threats in Mueller, *The Stupidity of War*, 23. Politics of militarization in David Fitzgerald, *Militarization and the American Century: War, the United States and the World since 1941* (London: Bloomsbury Academic, 2022), 4. For a contemporary view, see Alfred Vagts, *A History of Militarism* (New York: Meridian, 1959).
3. Walter Lippmann, "The Cold War: A Study of U.S. Foreign Policy," *Los Angeles Times*, 7 September 1947. Walter Lippmann, "The Cold War: A Study of U.S. Foreign Policy—III," *Los Angeles Times*, 9 September 1947. Monstrosity and exhaustion in Milne and Logevall in Borgwardt, McKnight Nichols, and Preston, *Rethinking American Grand Strategy*, 151, 450. On Lippmann, see Chamberlin, *The Cold War's Killing Fields*, 43; Craig and Logevall, *America's Cold War*, 83–85; and Graebner, Burns, and Siracusa, *America and the Cold War*, Vol. 1, 112, 129.
4. JCS in Bowie and Immerman, *Waging Peace*, 99. Limited resources in Jonathan M. House, *A Military History of the Cold War, 1962–1991* (Norman: University of Oklahoma Press, 2020), 16.
5. Dulles in Kinzer, *The Brothers*, 168. Henry in "World Seen Split by Two Ideologies," *New York Times*, 18 July 1949. Graham quoted in Kristin Kobes Du Mez, *Jesus and John Wayne: How White Evangelicals Corrupted a Faith and Fractured a Nation* (New York: Liveright, 2020), 26. On Graham, see Inboden, *Religion and American Foreign Policy*, 277; Preston, *Sword of the Spirit, Shield of Faith*, 421, 469; and Haberski, *God and War*, 106. Evil in Jolyon Mitchell and Joshua Rey, *War and Religion: A Very Short Introduction* (New York: Oxford University Press, 2021), 101. We might also note, however, that until the 1960s, religion was a main source of pacifism and peace movements and thus a main source of internationalism.

6. Sherry, *In the Shadow of War*, 161. "'Cold War' Termed a Spiritual Clash," *New York Times*, 16 June 1952. On Vatican and pacifism, see Goedde, *The Politics of Peace*, 97, 99, 102, 112–13. Armageddon and Graham, Spellman in Stephen J. Whitfield, *The Culture of the Cold War*, 2nd ed. (Baltimore: Johns Hopkins University Press, 1996), 78, 81, 94. Militarized Christianity in Mundey, *American Militarism and Anti-Militarism in Popular Media*, 52; and Preston, *Sword of the Spirit, Shield of Faith*, 371–72. On religion in the US military, see James Gilbert, *Redeeming Culture: American Religion in an Age of Science* (Chicago: University of Chicago Press, 1997), 121–46.
7. Sacred focus in Chidester, *Authentic Fakes*, 49. Kennan in Porter, *The False Promise of Liberal Order*, 49. See also Preston, 424–25. Muscular in Kobes Du Mez, *Jesus and John Wayne*, 11. Hoover quoted in Kwon, *The Other Cold War*, 71. Spiritual mobilization in Preston, 382. Military and economic alone might in Inboden, 155. On similar arguments during the Reagan administration, see Greg Grandin, *Empire's Workshop: Latin America, the United States, and the Rise of the New Imperialism* (New York: Metropolitan, 2006), 231.
8. On the 1947 act, see LaFeber, *America, Russia, and the Cold War*, 68; House, *A Military History of the Cold War, 1944–62*, 86–87; and Reveron, Gvosdev, and Owens, *US Foreign Policy and Defense Strategy*, 55–59. Not everyone was pleased with unifying the nation's security system. Senior naval officers worried about diminished influence in an overcentralized command structure, while George C. Marshall feared the NSC would undermine traditional State Department prerogatives. See Stuart, *Creating the National Security State*, 129–30. CIA in Immerman, *The Hidden Hand*, 19–21; Stuart, 141, 268, 270; and Weiner, *Legacy of Ashes*, 54, 63. Mansfield in Brandon Wolfe-Hunnicutt, *The Paranoid Style in American Diplomacy: Oil and Arab Nationalism in Iraq* (Stanford, CA: Stanford University Press, 2021), 39. Rational in Amy B. Zegart, *Flawed by Design: The Evolution of the CIA, JCS, and NSC* (Stanford, CA: Stanford University Press, 1999), 8.
9. "Governor Blasts at Godless States," *Los Angeles Times*, 2 May 1949. NSC-68 quoted in Ernest R. May, ed., *American Cold War Strategy: Interpreting NSC 68* (Boston: Bedford, 1993), 25, 26, 33–34, 51, 80–81. On NSC-68, see Hemmer, *American Pendulum*, 54–55; Bowie and Immerman, *Waging Peace*, 18–19; McAlister, *Epic Encounters*, 51–52; and Jerry W. Sanders, *Peddlers of Crisis: The Committee on the Present Danger and the Politics of Containment* (Boston: South End Press, 1983), 27–31, 42–43, 86–89.
10. Exaggeration in Lüthi, *Cold Wars*, 27, 29. "No people in history," NSC-68 claimed, "have preserved their freedom who thought that by not being strong enough to protect themselves they might prove inoffensive to their enemies." May, 41, 54. Kennan in Edelstein, *Over the Horizon*,

149–50. Power in Aaron L. Friedberg, *In the Shadow of the Garrison State: America's Anti-Statism and Its Cold War Grand Strategy* (Princeton, NJ: Princeton University Press, 2000), 11; Bruce Kuklick, *Blind Oracles: Intellectuals and War from Kennan to Kissinger* (Princeton, NJ: Princeton University Press, 2006), 47–48; Gaddis, *Strategies of Containment*, 81.

11. Paranoia in Westad, *The Cold War*, 69. NSC 20/4 in Bowie and Immerman, *Waging Peace*, 12–13; Graebner, Burns, and Siracusa, *America and the Cold War*, Vol. 1, 148–49; and Layne, *The Peace of Illusions*, 62–63. Alarmist militarism in Craig and Logevall, *America's Cold War*, 4. See also Kennan, *The Kennan Diaries*, xxix, 217; and Hemmer, *American Pendulum*, 48–49. Faith in expanding interests and Kennan's critique in Gaddis, *Strategies of Containment*, 31, 96. Anti-militarism in Mundey, *American Militarism and Anti-Militarism in Popular Media*, 13.

12. Offensive in Miller, *Grand Strategy from Truman to Trump*, 79–80; Bowie and Immerman, *Waging Peace*, 21. Link to Korean War in Hajimu, *Cold War Crucible*, 112. Panic in Andrew J. Bacevich, *The Limits of Power: The End of American Exceptionalism* (New York: Metropolitan, 2008), 113. Defense budget in Craig and Logevall, 134; and Rebecca Lissner, *Wars of Revelation: The Transformative Effects of Military Intervention on Grand Strategy* (New York: Oxford University Press, 2021), 34. Strategic defense in Lewis, *The American Culture of War*, 114, 137; and Goldwater, *Conscience of a Conservative*, 104. Security versus defense and power projection in Andrew J. Bacevich, "Changing the Subject: How the United States Responds to Strategic Failure," in Fitzgerald, Ryan, and Thompson, *Not Even Past*, 200. Liberation in Milne in Borgwardt, McKnight Nichols, and Preston, *Rethinking American Grand Strategy*, 152–53. Levering, *The Cold War*, 44.

13. Defining interests in Hemmer, *American Pendulum*, 57. In George Marshall's words, the United States must "keep itself militarily strong and use this strength to promote world order." In Frank A. Settle, Jr., "To Harness Atomic Power: Marshall and Nuclear Weapons," in *George C. Marshall and the Early Cold War: Policy, Politics, and Security*, ed. William A. Taylor (Norman: University of Oklahoma Press, 2020), 108. Niebuhr in Gat, *The Causes of War and the Spread of Peace*, 111; and Niebuhr, *The Irony of American History*, 131–32. See also Inboden, *Religion and American Foreign Policy*, 93; and Kinzer, *The Brothers*, 85. Security dilemma in Waltz, *Theory of International Politics*, 186; and Gat, 114, 116–18. Breeding war in Gat, *War in Human Civilization*, 97, 99.

14. On Germany, see Eisenberg, *Drawing the Line*, 9–11, 14, 47, 79, 120, 166, 200–201, 237, 316; Layne, *The Peace of Illusions*, 68–69; Zubok, *A Failed Empire*, 62; Williams, *The Tragedy of American Diplomacy*, 143; and Kennan, *The Kennan Diaries*, 233.

15. Blockade in House, *A Military History of the Cold War, 1944-62*, 118-19; and Pechatnov in Leffler and Westad, *The Cambridge History of the Cold War*, Vol. I, 106-7. On Soviet views, see Applebaum, *Iron Curtain*, 253; and Zubok, *A Failed Empire*, 76. Truman quoted in Eisenberg, *Drawing the Line*, 440. Brandt in Hanhimäki and Westad, *The Cold War*, 99. Naimark, *Stalin and the Fate of Europe*, 157, 190. Clay in Naimark, 165; and LaFeber, *America, Russia, and the Cold War*, 77.

16. Monopoly in Guy Oakes, *The Imaginary War: Civil Defense and American Cold War Culture* (New York: Oxford University Press, 1994), 13; and Eisenberg, *Drawing the Line*, 441-42. Status quo in George and Smoke, *Deterrence in American Foreign Policy*, 109. Short-term expedient in Steil, *The Marshall Plan*, 277. Hanson W. Baldwin, "Airlift as a Weapon," *New York Times*, 19 December 1948. A decade later, after yet another crisis in Berlin, where the Soviets constructed a wall dividing the city, John F. Kennedy would sigh that it was "a hell of a lot better than a war." In W. R. Smyser, *Kennedy and the Berlin Wall* (Lanham, MD: Rowman & Littlefield, 2009), 106.

17. Outcomes of Berlin in Judt, *Postwar*, 147, 149; and Fink, *Cold War*, 72. As British Foreign Secretary Ernest Bevin persuasively argued in Berlin's aftermath, if Washington offered "concrete evidence of American determination to resist further Communist encroachment," Europeans could avoid future provocations. In Timothy Andrews Sayle, *Enduring Alliance: A History of NATO and the Postwar Global Order* (Ithaca, NY: Cornell University Press, 2019), 13. On the Atlantic Charter, see Wertheim, *Tomorrow, the World*, 112-14; and Jeremi Suri, "Freedom as Ideology," in Nichols and Milne, *Ideology in U.S. Foreign Relations*, 292.

18. Article 5 in House, *A Military History of the Cold War, 1944-62*, 131. C. L. Sulzberger, "Foreign Affairs: The Cold War Role of a Rearmed Germany," *New York Times*, 10 November 1954. See also Carter, *Forging the Shield*, 171-72; and Zubok, *A Failed Empire*, 77. Forward defense in Mira Rapp-Hooper, *Shields of the Republic: The Triumph and Peril of America's Alliances* (Cambridge, MA: Harvard University Press, 2020), 49-50, 53. Fear of Soviets in Sayle, *Enduring Alliance*, 2-3, 11; and Gardner, *Spheres of Influence*, 262-63. Collective security in Layne, *The Peace of Illusions*, 99, 105. On doubts over collective security, see Sayle, 17. On simplifications of "isolationism," see Hemmer, *American Pendulum*, 28-29; and Wertheim, *Tomorrow, the World*, 9, 34, 44, 49. Kennan quoted in Hanhimäki and Westad, *The Cold War*, 129.

19. Zhukov quoted in Hanhimäki and Westad, 86-87. Paniushkin in ibid., 135; and Engel, Lawrence, and Preston, *America in the World*, 177-78. *Pravda* in Fursenko and Naftali, *Khrushchev's Cold War*, 34. See also Wilfried Loth, *Overcoming the Cold War: A History of Détente, 1950-1991*,

trans. Robert F. Hogg (New York: Palgrave, 2002), 30, 32. On the economic component in these debates, see Judt, *Postwar*, 354–55. Grand Alliance in Fink, *Cold War*, 73.

20. Stimulating confrontation in Eisenberg, *Drawing the Line*, 460. NATO plans in Francis J. Gavin, *Nuclear Weapons and American Grand Strategy* (Washington, DC: Brookings Institution Press, 2020), 112–16. General Wesley K. Clark later would bemoan how such a "defensive" organization like NATO had elevated "conflict termination" over "victory." The truth, clearly, was more complicated. *Waging Modern War: Bosnia, Kosovo, and the Future of Combat* (New York: Public Affairs, 2001), 4.

21. "Chennault Sees War in Loss of China," *Washington Post*, 26 June 1949. See also Graebner, Burns, and Siracusa, *America and the Cold War*, Vol. 1, 10. On Chinese civil war, see Guan, *Southeast Asia's Cold War*, 52–54. "Lean in" in Jian, *Mao's China and the Cold War*, 44, 48, 50.

22. Acheson quoted in Mearsheimer, *The Tragedy of Great Power Politics*, 326. On limits of US power, see Macdonald, *Adventures in Chaos*, 77, 109. Accusations in Engelhardt, *The End of Victory Culture*, 61. Nightmare in Thomas K. Robb and David James Gill, *Divided Allies: Strategic Cooperation against the Communist Threat in the Asia-Pacific during the Early Cold War* (Ithaca, NY: Cornell University Press, 2019), 47. "Red Threat to India Seen," *New York Times*, 14 December 1949. If the national security state was formalized in 1947, then the events of 1949 arguably validated Americans' faith in that state by offering proof of the global threat. The great evils in China and Russia had emerged, many believed, and Satan had shown himself.

23. On India, see David C. Engerman, *The Price of Aid: The Economic Cold War in India* (Cambridge, MA: Harvard University Press, 2018), 6, 40. Erez Manela, *The Wilsonian Moment: Self-Determination and the International Origins of Anticolonial Nationalism* (New York: Oxford University Press, 2007), 217. Robert J. McMahon, *The Cold War on the Periphery: The United States, India, and Pakistan* (New York: Columbia University Press, 1994), 6, 13–14, 32–33. Nehru quoted on p. 37.

24. A. M. Rosenthal, "Reds in China Held Peril to Neighbors," *New York Times*, 2 October 1949. See also Simpson, *Economists with Guns*, 23–24, 31; and McMahon, *Colonialism and the Cold War*, 74, 137–39, 315–16. Revolutionary in Jian, *Mao's China and the Cold War*, 4. Kennan in Robb and Gill, *Divided Allies*, 52. On early domino theories, see Fredrik Logevall, *Embers of War: The Fall of an Empire and the Making of America's Vietnam* (New York: Random House, 2012), 222–23. John Mackinlay, *The Insurgent Archipelago: From Mao to bin Laden* (New York: Columbia University Press, 2010, 49). For the Soviet view, see Fursenko and Naftali, *Khrushchev's Cold War*, 82.

25. Domination in Chamberlin, *The Cold War's Killing Fields*, 99. Analysts in Craig and Logevall, *America's Cold War*, 105. See also Hajimu, *Cold War Crucible*, 162. Revolution in Chen Jian, "China, the Third World, and the Cold War," in McMahon, *The Cold War in the Third World*, 86. On early Sino-American relations, see Lüthi, *Cold Wars*, 117, 121, 122; Gordon H. Chang, *Friends and Enemies: The United States, China, and the Soviet Union, 1948–1972* (Stanford, CA: Stanford University Press, 1991), 16, 21; and Lüthi, *The Sino-Soviet Split*, 33, 39.
26. Role of peasants in Kapstein, *Seeds of Stability*, 93–94. General Albert Wedemeyer quoted in Andrew J. Birtle, *U.S. Army Counterinsurgency and Contingency Operations Doctrine, 1942–1976* (Washington, DC: Center of Military History, 2006), 38. MRS staff member Ken Twitchell in Inboden, *Religion and American Foreign Policy*, 202. On 30 January 1949, Representative Kennedy gave a speech arguing that "the vital interest of the United States in the independent integrity of China" was being "sacrificed." Philip J. Durkin Testimonial Dinner, Online Archives, JFK Speeches, John F. Kennedy Presidential Library and Museum.
27. On Chinese, see Chang, *Friends and Enemies*, 173. Japanese in Engelhardt, *The End of Victory Culture*, 49. Racism in Patrick Porter, *Military Orientalism: Eastern War through Western Eyes* (New York: Oxford University Press, 2013), 2–3, 31, 37, 40. Yellow Peril in Wen-Qing Ngoei, *Arc of Containment: Britain, the United States, and Anticommunism in Southeast Asia* (Ithaca, NY: Cornell University Press, 2019), 36. General Adna Chaffee quoted in Samuel Moyn, *Humane: How the United States Abandoned Peace and Reinvented War* (New York: Farrar, Straus & Giroux, 2022), 111. See also White, *In Search of History*, 214.
28. On Guomindang policies, see Lüthi, *Cold Wars*, 120; and Hajimu, *Cold War Crucible*, 48–53. Americans tended to excuse or overlook oppressive, even reckless, GMD policies in China. General Wedemeyer quoted in Graebner, Burns, and Siracusa, *America and the Cold War*, Vol. 1, 163. Bomb in Hemmer, *American Pendulum*, 52–53.
29. Maoist revolutionary warfare in William C. Martel, *Grand Strategy in Theory and Practice: The Need for an Effective American Foreign Policy* (New York: Cambridge University Press, 2015), 134–37. Eqbal Ahmad, "Revolutionary Warfare and Counterinsurgency," in *Guerrilla Strategies: An Historical Anthology from the Long March to Afghanistan*, ed. Gérard Chaliand (Berkeley: University of California Press, 1982), 233, 236. NSC report in Graebner, Burns, and Siracusa, 164.
30. On Japan, see Hajimu, *Cold War Crucible*, 40–41. For an excellent overview, see Jennifer M. Miller, *Cold War Democracy: The United States and Japan* (Cambridge, MA: Harvard University Press, 2019). Rivalry and control in Brenda Gayle Plummer, *In Search of Power: African Americans*

in the Era of Decolonization, 1956–1974 (New York: Cambridge University Press, 2012), 87. Decolonization in Kwon, *The Other Cold War*, 24, 26. Confrontational in Stephen G. Rabe, "Cold War Presidents: Dwight D. Eisenhower, John F. Kennedy, Lyndon Baines Johnson, and Richard M. Nixon," in Costigliola and Hogan, *America in the World*, 157.

31. Europeans in Cary Fraser, "Decolonization and the Cold War," in Immerman and Goedde, *The Oxford Handbook of the Cold War*, 475; and Paul Kennedy, *The Rise and Fall of the Great Powers: Economic Change and Military Conflict from 1500 to 2000* (New York: Random House, 1987), 392. Fanon in Hanhimäki and Westad, *The Cold War*, 368; and Westad, *The Global Cold War*, 85. On use of violence, see Goedde, *The Politics of Peace*, 8, 162–64.

32. Williams, *The Tragedy of American Diplomacy*, 161. On economic aspects, see also Wertheim, *Tomorrow, the World*, 64–65, 71, 77; and Sumner H. Slighter, "We Can Win the Economic 'Cold War', Too," *New York Times*, 13 August 1950. Fears in Edelstein, *Over the Horizon*, 122.

CHAPTER 4

1. Fetish in Whitfield, *The Culture of the Cold War*, vii. Social warfare in Hajimu, *Cold War Crucible*, 202. Cabell Phillips, "Broader Loyalty Tests Proposed for U.S. Jobs," *New York Times*, 19 February 1950. Fear in Schrecker, *Many Are the Crimes*, 99. Blacklists in Thomas Doherty, *Cold War, Cool Medium: Television, McCarthyism, and American Culture* (New York: Columbia University Press, 2003), 33.

2. "'Deceit' Laid to Truman by McCarthy," *Washington Post*, 7 May 1950. Murrey Marder, "Senator Charges President with 'Shrinking Show of Weakness,'" *Washington Post*, 8 December 1954. Stuffed shirt in George Gallup, "Tactics of McCarthy Provoke Sharp Reactions among Voters," *Washington Post*, 17 August 1951. Loss of China in LaFeber, *America, Russia, and the Cold War*, 87. Egg-sucking in John Tirman, *The Deaths of Others: The Fate of Civilians in America's Wars* (New York: Oxford University Press, 2011), 72. Godless in Preston, *Sword of the Spirit, Shield of Faith*, 413.

3. Colleen M. O'Connor, "'Pink Right Down to Her Underwear,'" *Los Angeles Times*, 9 April 1990. On political climate, see Schrecker, xii. White, *In Search of History*, 394. One year after Ike's inauguration, Nixon declared that "if it were not for the Communist threat, the free world could live in peace." "Japan's Disarming Wrong, Nixon Says," *New York Times*, 19 November 1953.

4. Vandenberg in Feldman, *Manufacturing Hysteria*, 198. Supporting war in Goedde, *The Politics of Peace*, 157. Lasswell, *Essays on the Garrison State*, 69. War criminals and Ike in May, *Fortress America*, 21–22. Friedberg

argues that "domestic constraints" actually prevented the worst excess of McCarthyism. *In the Shadow of the Garrison State*, 4.

5. Neurosis in Whitfield, *The Culture of the Cold War*, 38. Office of Armed Forces Information and Education, "*Know Your Communist Enemy*," (Washington, DC: US Government Printing Office, 1954), 1–15, 2–8, 2–20, 6–15.

6. Surveillance in Andrea Friedman, *Citizenship in Cold War America: The National Security State and the Possibilities of Dissent* (Amherst: University of Massachusetts Press, 2014), 81. Charles Grutzner, "Harriman Predicts Attack by G.O.P. as 'Soft' on Reds," *New York Times*, 26 October 1954. Moral flabbiness in "Rivals To Soft, Hanley Declares," *New York Times*, 22 October 1950. On softness, see Craig and Logevall, *America's Cold War*, 8–9, 64, 66; and Schrecker, *Many Are the Crimes*, 131, 220. Kennan in Sixsmith, *The War of Nerves*, 133.

7. McCarthy in Judge and Langdon, *The Cold War*, 319. John D. Connaughton, "Mr. McCarthy Commended: Believed to Possess Moral Force in Attacking Communism," *New York Times*, 12 March 1954. Truman in Doherty, *Cold War, Cool Medium*, 14. Soft in Cuordileone, *Manhood and American Political Culture in the Cold War*, vii–viii. Conformity in Fried, *Nightmare in Red*, 29. Robert A. Heinlein, *Starship Troopers* (New York: Four Square, 1959, 1961), 27.

8. Transgressions and maladjustment in Cuordileone, 29, 74, 76; and Sixsmith, *The War of Nerves*, 210–11. Report in Friedman, *Citizenship in Cold War America*, 33–34. "Senators Ask Full-Scale Probe On '3750' Perverts in Agencies," *Washington Post*, 20 May 1950. During testimony, the head of the Washington, DC, vice squad estimated there were some "5000 homosexuals in the district" and that 75 percent of them were employed by the government. Of note, another Metropolitan Police officer presented evidence of a purported communist plan "to sabotage and damage the Capital of the United States in the event of war with Russia."

9. Charles Mohr, "Goldwater Gibes at Faint-Hearted," *New York Times*, 6 March 1964. Superiority in Jeremi Suri, *Power and Protest: Global Revolution and the Rise of Détente* (Cambridge, MA: Harvard University Press, 2005), 101. Cuordileone, 19, 24, 49. Passivity in Thomas Waldman, *Vicarious Warfare: American Strategy and the Illusion of War on the Cheap* (Bristol, UK: Bristol University Press, 2021), 120.

10. Timmerman in "Dixie Governors Defy Rights Law," *Chicago Defender*, 7 September 1957. Black violence in May, *Fortress America*, 75. On Ike's relationship with the civil-rights movement, see William I. Hitchcock, *The Age of Eisenhower: America and the World in the 1950s* (New York: Simon & Schuster, 2018), 242–43, 370–71. Ellison in Hong, *A Violent Peace*, 49.

11. "NAACP Pledges Crackdown on Communism at Confab," *The Chicago Defender*, 1 July 1950. "Plan to Combat NAACP Urged," *Washington*

Post, 3 October 1958. Of note, while the decree may not have made much headway with segregationists, it did lead to the NAACP ruthlessly purging itself of CPUSA members. On race, see Hajimu, *Cold War Crucible*, 22, 204–5, 216; Friedman, *Citizenship in Cold War America*, 5; and Whitfield, *The Culture of the Cold War*, 22.

12. 1952 act in Elizabeth R. Escobedo, *From Coveralls to Zoot Suits: The Lives of Mexican American Women on the World War II Home Front* (Chapel Hill: University of North Carolina Press, 2013), 137. 1950 act in Feldman, *Manufacturing Hysteria*, 223–24; and Hitchcock, *The Age of Eisenhower*, 121. Churches in Murrey Marder, "McCarran-Walter Act Called 'Affront' to U.S. Conscience," *Washington Post*, 29 October 1952. McCarran Act in "Alien Bill Veto Is Overridden by House," *Washington Post*, 27 June 1952.

13. HUAC and instrument in Goedde, *The Politics of Peace*, 1–2, 55. The WSP formed in 1961. Neutrality in Whitfield, 10. FBI in Feldman, *Manufacturing Hysteria*, 191. Masters in Engelhardt, *The End of Victory Culture*, 99.

14. Haynes Johnson and Harry Katz, *Herblock: The Life and Work of the Great Political Cartoonist* (New York: Norton, 2009), 115. Scandrett in Feldman, *Manufacturing Hysteria*, 202. Hofstadter in Hemmer, *American Pendulum*, 144. See also Kinzer, *The Brothers*, 105. Subversive Activities Control Board in Jay Walz, "Board Overrules Reds' Challenge," *New York Times*, 24 April 1951.

15. Susan H. Swetnam, "Look Wider Still: The Subversive Nature of Girl Scouting in the 1950s," *Frontiers: A Journal of Women Studies*, Vol. 37, No. 1 (2016): 90–114. Menken in Christopher A. Preble, *Peace, War, and Liberty: Understanding U.S. Foreign Policy* (Washington, DC: Cato Institute, 2019), 113.

16. Whitfield, *The Culture of the Cold War*, 45, 49, 56.

17. Lasswell, *Essays on the Garrison State*, 32, 34, 53, 56. Of note, at the time he wrote this essay, Laswell was a World War II interventionist, arguing that if the nation didn't intervene to stop Hitler, Germany would become so powerful as to force the United States into becoming a "garrison state," thus harming American freedom at home because of the need to hunker down and empower the presidency. He coined the term in "Sino-Japanese Crisis: The Garrison State versus the Civilian State," *China Quarterly* Vol. XI, No. 2 (Fall 1937): 643–49. See also Alex Roland, "The Military-Industrial Complex: Lobby and Trope," in Bacevich, *The Long War*, 339–40; Ekbladh, *The Great American Mission*, 64; and Friedberg, *In the Shadow of the Garrison State*, 54.

18. "Hoffman Reports Gain in 'Cold War,'" *New York Times*, 8 December 1949. Putman in "U.S. Seen Becoming a 'Garrison State,'" *New York Times*, 12 October 1950. Hal Brands argues, unpersuasively if not

incredulously, that this "vigilance" actually strengthened American society rather than corrupting it. *The Twilight Struggle*, 194.
19. Amy J. Rutenberg, *Rough Draft: Cold War Military Manpower Policy and the Origins of Vietnam-Era Draft Resistance* (Ithaca, NY: Cornell University Press, 2019), 3, 41, 69. On UMT, see James Burk, "The Changing Moral Contract for Military Service," in Bacevich, *The Long War*, 421–22; William A. Taylor, *Military Service and American Democracy: From World War II to the Iraq and Afghanistan Wars* (Lawrence: University Press of Kansas, 2016), 35, 37, 42; Friedberg, 152–61; and William A. Taylor, "The Obligation to Serve: Marshall and Universal Military Training," in Taylor, *George C. Marshall and the Early Cold War*, 25–31.
20. Instrument in Emile Simpson, *War from the Ground Up: Twenty-First-Century Combat as Politics* (New York: Oxford University Press, 2013), 10.
21. Control in Preston, *American Foreign Relations*, 84. Risk and uncertainty in Edelstein, *Over the Horizon*, 20. Intangible in Fursenko and Naftali, *Khrushchev's Cold War*, 540. Defining security in Buzan, *Peoples, States, and Fear*, 74, 88–89. Family in Elaine Tyler May, *Homeward Bound: American Families in the Cold War Era*, rev. ed. (New York: Basic, 1988, 2008), 85. On knowledge related to how Americans saw themselves, see Fainberg, *Cold War Correspondents*, 3.
22. On containment's success, see Craig and Logevall, *America's Cold War*, 3, 101; and Graebner, Burns, and Siracusa, *America and the Cold War*, Vol. 1, 150–51.

CHAPTER 5

1. Jack Randolph, "Source of Aggression," *Washington Post*, 20 July 1950.
2. Message in Clay Blair, *The Forgotten War: America in Korea, 1950–1953* (New York: Times Books, 1987), 395. "Text of Replies by MacArthur," *New York Times*, 3 December 1950. See also Steven Casey, *Selling the Korean War: Propaganda, Politics, and Public Opinion, 1950–1953* (New York: Oxford University Press, 2008), 207–8. MacArthur also noted that the Chinese intervention was "one of the most offensive acts of international lawlessness of historical record." In Max Hastings, *The Korean War* (New York: Simon & Schuster, 1987), 132. Hanson Baldwin, "Whole Asian Struggle Enters a New Phase," *New York Times*, 3 December 1950. Inevitable in Wada Haruki, trans. Frank Baldwin, *The Korean War: An International History* (Lanham, MD: Rowman & Littlefield, 2014), 170.
3. MacArthur quoted in Casey, *Selling the Korean War*, 53. McCarthy in Masuda Hajimu, *Cold War Crucible: The Korean Conflict and the Postwar World* (Cambridge, MA: Harvard University Press, 2015), 88;

and Stanley Sandler, *The Korean War: No Victors, No Vanquished* (Lexington: University Press of Kentucky, 1999), 9. Prearranged plan in Hastings, *The Korean War*, 131. Turning point in Ellen Schrecker, *Many Are the Crimes: McCarthyism in America* (New York: Little, Brown, 1998), 286. Truman quoted in William Stueck, *The Korean War: An International History* (Princeton, NJ: Princeton University Press, 1995), 43.

4. Roy K. Flint, "Task Force Smith and the 24th Division: Delay and Withdrawal, 5–19 July 1950," in *America's First Battles, 1776–1965*, ed. Charles E. Heller and William A. Stofft (Lawrence: University Press of Kansas, 1986), 266. See also Hastings, *The Korean War*, 19. Hajimu, 1–2, 8. On the intermingling of local, regional, and international dynamics of this war, see Elspeth O'Riordan, *Understanding the Cold War: History, Approaches and Debates* (Cham, Switzerland: Palgrave Macmillan, 2022), 110.

5. On Stalin and the Korean War, see Jonathan Haslam, *Russia's Cold War: From the October Revolution to the Fall of the Wall* (New Haven, CT: Yale University Press, 2011), 120; Zubok, *A Failed Empire*, 80; Hajimu, *Cold War Crucible*, 137–38, 148; and O'Riordan, *Understanding the Cold War*, 113–14. Global conspiracy in Sandler, *The Korean War*, 52.

6. "Eisenhower Backs Invasion if Needed," *New York Times*, 21 July 1950. Fears of a ruse in Albertson, *Winning Armageddon*, 35; and Deaile, *Always at War*, 125.

7. Truman to Acheson, 7 December 1956, in *Affection and Trust: The Personal Correspondence of Harry S. Truman and Dean Acheson, 1953–1971* (New York: Knopf, 2010), 157. Legitimacy and orchestrated offensive in Hastings, *The Korean War*, 57, 59. Handbook in Brewer, *Why America Fights*, 142.

8. On vital interests, see Gaddis, *Now We Know*, 82. See also William Manchester, *American Caesar: Douglas MacArthur, 1880–1964* (New York: Little, Brown, 1978), 547, 550; and Bryan R. Gibby, *Korean Showdown: National Policy and Military Strategy in a Limited War, 1951–1952* (Tuscaloosa: University of Alabama Press, 2021), 2. Acheson speech in Judge and Langdon, *The Cold War*, 321; Hajimu, *Cold War Crucible*, 91; and Stueck, *The Korean War*, 30. Bruce Cumings argues that Acheson was "seeking ambiguity" and trying to keep communists and allies alike "guessing about what the United States would do if South Korea or Taiwan were attacked." *The Korean War: A History* (New York: Modern Library, 2011), 72.

9. Bradley quoted in Blair, *The Forgotten War*, 84. Westad calls Korea an "entirely avoidable war" yet clearly one that militarized the larger Cold War. *The Cold War*, 159. World War III and Gallup polling in Hajimu, *Cold War Crucible*, 3, 61, 69. Rationality in Gaddis, *On Grand Strategy*, 54–55; and Gvosdev, Blankshain, and Cooper, *Decision-Making in American Foreign Policy*, 30, 32.

10. B. H. Liddell Hart, *Defence of the West* (Greenwood, CT: Greenwood, 1950), 76.
11. On Mao's aims, see Jian, *Mao's China and the Cold War*, 54; and Gregg A. Brazinsky, *Winning the Third World: Sino-American Rivalry during the Cold War* (Chapel Hill: University of North Carolina Press, 2017), 47–49. Truman quoted in Haruki, *The Korean War*, 150. On strategic debates over Korea, see Lissner, *Wars of Revelation*, 22–23, 39. Racial issues in Tirman, *The Deaths of Others*, 86–87; and Thomas Borstelmann, *The Cold War and the Color Line: American Race Relations in the Global Arena* (Cambridge, MA: Harvard University Press, 2001), 105. Kennan, *American Diplomacy*, 169. Rollback in Bowie and Immerman, *Waging Peace*, 31. Changes in containment policies in Hal Brands, "Getting Grand Strategy Right: Clearing Away Common Fallacies in the Grand Strategy Debate," in Borgwardt, McKnight Nichols, and Preston, *Rethinking American Grand Strategy*, 30, 33.
12. On Mao, see Jian, *Mao's China and the Cold War*, 87, 90, 95, 116; and Hajimu, *Cold War Crucible*, 108, 123–25, 139, 141–43, 175. Hardliners and debate in Hajimu, 93–96, 98. Truman quoted in Stueck, *The Korean War*, 183.
13. JCS in Blair, *The Forgotten War*, 785–86. MacArthur quoted in Jared Dockery, "Return to the Pentagon: Marshall and the Korean War," in Taylor, *George C. Marshall and the Early Cold War*, 205. On his public statements, see Sandler, *The Korean War*, 137–38; Casey, *Selling the Korean War*, 230–31; and Haruki, 124–27, 169.
14. Truman quoted in Hajimu, 63. Imposing will in Hastings, *The Korean War*, 198–99. On issues with the concept of "total victory," see Kennan, *American Diplomacy*, 102; and Martel, *Victory in War*, 131. Civil-military relations in House, *A Military History of the Cold War, 1944–1962*, 444.
15. "World War III? Mao Challenges U.N.," *New York Times*, 3 December 1950. Atomic weapons in Lawrence Freedman and Jeffrey Michaels, *The Evolution of Nuclear Strategy*, 4th ed. (London: Palgrave Macmillan, 2019), 97. Truman limiting the war in Casey, *Selling the Korean War*, 234. Rand analyst Paul Kecskemeti, *Strategic Surrender: The Politics of Victory and Defeat* (Stanford, CA: Stanford University Press, 1958), 26. Exaggerating in Brewer, *Why America Fights*, 145.
16. On the term "limited war," see Beatrice Heuser, *War: A Genealogy of Western Ideas and Practices* (New York: Oxford University Press, 2022), 55. Brodie quoted in Barry H. Steiner, *Bernard Brodie and the Foundations of American Nuclear Strategy* (Lawrence: University Press of Kansas, 1991), 154. Later historians tended to agree with Brodie. One argued that the Korean War led to "a departure from historic habits" seeking outright annihilation of the enemy, while another claimed that, culturally, "Americans could not adjust to limited, defensive wars of attrition." Departure in Weigley, *The American Way of War*, xi. Attrition in Lewis, *The American*

Culture of War, 210. Yalu in Sandler, *The Korean War*, 183. Beech quoted in Casey, *Selling the Korean War*, 63. Police action on p. 97.

17. Revolutionary movement, citing Robert Taylor, in Guan, *Southeast Asia's Cold War*, 51. Why Korea? in Hajimu, *Cold War Crucible*, 152. On limited war, see Centeno and Enriquez, *War & Society*, 90; and Hastings, *The Korean War*, 64. Notions of success in Khong, *Analogies at War*, 101–2.

18. James Reston, "Now U.S. Must Anticipate Many 'Little Wars,'" *New York Times*, 23 July 1950. Robert E. Osgood, *Limited War: The Challenge to American Security* (Chicago: University of Chicago Press, 1957), 1–2. See also Antulio J. Echevarria II, *War's Logic: Strategic Thought and the American Way of War* (New York: Cambridge University Press, 2021), 71, 74. Initiative in Freedman and Michaels, *The Evolution of Nuclear Strategy*, 103.

19. Modifying behavior in Echevarria, *Military Strategy*, 57. China in Gaddis, *Now We Know*, 107–8.

20. Instruments in Robert L. O'Connell, *Of Arms and Men: A History of War, Weapons, and Aggression* (New York: Oxford University Press, 1989), 305. On Osgood, see Echevarria, ibid.

21. Tie in Steven Casey, *When Soldiers Fall: How Americans Have Confronted Combat Losses from World War I to Afghanistan* (New York: Oxford University Press, 2014), 104, 124. Bernard Brodie, *Strategy in the Missile Age* (Princeton, NJ: Princeton University Press, 1959), 311. Artificial in Kecskemeti, *Strategic Surrender*, 250. Not valuing victory and MacArthur in Donald Stoker, *Why America Loses Wars: Limited War and US Strategy from the Korean War to the Present* (New York: Cambridge University Press, 2019), 8, 11.

22. Clark quoted in Gibby, *Korean Showdown*, 274. On issues with stalemates, see Haruki, *The Korean War*, 213. Its relationship to negotiations, Stueck, *The Korean War*, 342; and Gibby, 338.

23. Liddell Hart, *Defence of the West*, 320–21. Concessions, citing General Matthew Ridgway, in Gibby, *Korean Showdown*, 52. Stoker seemingly agrees with Ridgway. See *Why America Loses Wars*, 106–7. Ike quoted in Freedman and Michaels, 144. On North Korea's destruction, see Benjamin R. Young, *Guns, Guerrillas, and the Great Leader: North Korea and the Third World* (Stanford, CA: Stanford University Press, 2021), 15; and Haruki, 293.

24. On translating power into influence, and Truman's difficulty in explaining this to the American public, see Hastings, *The Korean War*, 206. Not surprisingly, the Soviets were asking similar questions. O'Riordan, *Understanding the Cold War*, 31–32.

25. Hanson Baldwin, "War or Peace: Some Basic Issues," *New York Times*, 18 April 1954. On Baldwin, see also Friedberg, *In the Shadow of the Garrison State*, 62.

26. Trauschweizer, *Maxwell Taylor's Cold War*, 3. Osgood, *Limited War*, 5, 8. For an alternate view that placed less faith in the theory of limited war, see Thomas C. Schelling, *The Strategy of Conflict* (Cambridge, MA: Harvard University Press, 1963), 190–93.
27. Rehearsal in Hastings, *The Korean War*, 10. Budget and reforms in Lüthi, *Cold Wars*, 98. Modernization in Ekbladh, *The Great American Mission*, 9; and Gregg Andrew Brazinsky, "Koreanizing Modernization: Modernization Theory and South Korean Intellectuals," in Engerman, Gilman, et al., *Staging Growth*, 252–55. Rhee in Hajimu, *Cold War Crucible*, 76–77, 79. On difficulties leveraging local allies, see Lebovic, *The Limits of U.S. Military Capability*, 208.
28. Cement in Sayle, *Enduring Alliance*, 31. See also Stueck, *The Korean War*, 25. NATO in O'Riordan, *Understanding the Cold War*, 88, 91. Why Korea? in Bradley and Dudziak, *Making the Forever War*, 42, 45–46. Tydings quoted in Hajimu, 149.
29. Ike and Dulles in Hitchcock, *The Age of Eisenhower*, 96. Fursenko and Naftali, *Khrushchev's Cold War*, 17–20, 22–23, 241. Tobias Rupprecht, *Soviet Internationalism after Stalin: Interaction and Exchange between the USSR and Latin America during the Cold War* (New York: Cambridge University Press, 2015), 1–5.
30. "New Soviet Regime Held Up as Threat," *New York Times*, 14 March 1953. "Adenauer Advises West Not to Relax," *New York Times*, 7 March 1953. "Eden Urges West Not to Shift Policy over Stalin Death," *New York Times*, 13 March 1953. "Text of Anthony Eden's Address before the Foreign Policy Association," ibid.
31. On debates over how to deal with the Soviet transition to power, see Bowie and Immerman, *Waging Peace*, 109, 117. Peace initiative Zubok, *A Failed Empire*, 86, 91, 94. Bury you in Fursenko and Naftali, 232. Faith in the communist system in O'Riordan, *Understanding the Cold War*, 130. Conspiracy in Overstreet, *What We Must Know about Communism*, 58–59.
32. Acheson quoted in Bradley and Dudziak, *Making the Forever War*, 19. Zero-sum in Gaddis, *Strategies of Containment*, 210; and Costigliola, *Roosevelt's Lost Alliances*, 4; Lost victory in Sandler, *The Korean War*, 14. Balance of terror in Kwon, *The Other Cold War*, 19.
33. Globalizing local conflicts in Lüthi, *Cold Wars*, 14, 27. Power differentials in Mario Del Pero, "Incompatible Universalisms: The United States, the Soviet Union, and the Beginning of the Cold War," in *The Routledge Handbook of the Cold War*, ed. Artemy M. Kalinovsky and Craig Daigle (New York: Routledge, 2014), 3. On paradoxes, see Bradley and Dudziak, 85.
34. Blair, *The Forgotten War*, 78.
35. John Foster Dulles, "A Policy of Boldness," *Life*, 19 May 1952, 146, 148, 151. John Foster Dulles, "Policy for Security and Peace," *Foreign Affairs*,

Vol. 32, No. 3 (April 1954): 355, 58. See also Craig and Logevall, *America's Cold War*, 145–46; Leffler, *For the Soul of Mankind*, 111; and Graebner, Burns, and Siracusa, *America and the Cold War*, Vol. 1, 212–14. On Dulles's earlier views, see Bowie and Immerman, 61; Preston, *Sword of the Spirit, Shield of Faith*, 455; and Kinzer, *The Brothers*, 80–82.

36. Rollback in Blair, *The Forgotten War*, 327. Moral superiority in Ostermann, *Between Containment and Rollback*, xi–xii. Dulles quoted in Kinzer, 106. We might note here how Dulles was pushing back against a strong public desire for retrenchment and demobilization in 1945–1946 and in the early Cold War years.
37. Poll in Gibby, *Korean Showdown*, 135. Ridgway in Stueck, *The Korean War*, 211.
38. Tensions in Hanson W. Baldwin, "The MacArthur Ouster," *New York Times*, 12 April 1951. Acheson in Chamberlin, *The Cold War's Killing Fields*, 149. MacArthur in Hemmer, *American Pendulum*, 58. See also House, *A Military History of the Cold War, 1944–1962*, 200. Stoker is far more sympathetic to the general. See *Why America Loses Wars*, 48, 51, 60–61. Kennan, however, was far more worried by the implications of those supporting MacArthur after he was relieved of command. See Kennan, *The Kennan Diaries*, 283–84.
39. Economic closure and ideology in Layne, *The Peace of Illusions*, 79. Consensus in Lissner, *Wars of Revelation*, 24–26. Bohlen quoted in Leebaert, *Grand Improvisation*, 256. For an example of the Korean War transforming US policies along more interventionist lines, see McMahon, *The Cold War on the Periphery*, 123–25.

CHAPTER 6

1. Reinhold Niebuhr, *The World Crisis and American Responsibility: Nine Essays* (New York: Association Press, 958), 116–17. This was Niebuhr's "tragedy"—that to do good, we sometimes need to do evil—and he talked about it from the 1930s on.
2. "Will It Be Welfare or Weapons?" *Los Angeles Times*, 14 December 1950. See also Christopher A. Preble, *John F. Kennedy and the Missile Gap* (Dekalb: Northern Illinois University Press, 2004), 28. Airpower in Sandler, *The Korean War*, 8–9; and Gibby, *Korean Showdown*, 77–78. Defraying human costs in Lewis, *The American Culture of War*, 32, 69.
3. James M. Gavin, *War and Peace in the Space Age* (London: Hutchinson, 1959), 124. Strategic targets in Edward Kaplan, *To Kill Nations: American Strategy in the Air-Atomic Age and the Rise of Mutually Assured Destruction* (Ithaca, NY: Cornell University Press, 2015), 69. Technology in Lewis, 38.

4. Obsolescence in Alex Roland, *Delta of Power: The Military-Industrial Complex* (Baltimore: Johns Hopkins University Press, 2021), 32.
5. Truman quoted in Fred Kaplan, *The Bomb: Presidents, Generals, and the Secret History of Nuclear War* (New York: Simon & Schuster, 2020), 6. Vandenberg in David Alan Rosenberg, "The Origins of Overkill: Nuclear Weapons and American Strategy, 1945–1960," in *Strategy and Nuclear Deterrence*, ed. Steven E. Miller (Princeton, NJ: Princeton University Press, 1984), 123. Incorporating in Freedman and Michaels, *The Evolution of Nuclear Strategy*, x. On relation to NATO, see Sayle, *Enduring Alliance*, 24.
6. William S. White, "Defense of Europe Is Clearly Mapped, Bradley Discloses," *New York Times*, 30 July 1949. On the atomic battlefield and the pentomic idea, see Trauschweizer, *Maxwell Taylor's Cold War*, 66, 71, 82; Ingo Trauschweizer, *The Cold War U.S. Army: Building Deterrence for Limited War* (Lawrence: University Press of Kansas, 2008), chapter 3; and Jonathan M. House, *Combined Arms Warfare in the Twentieth Century* (Lawrence: University Press of Kansas, 2001), 207–10. Seventh Army in Carter, *Forging the Shield*, 101–2, 212.
7. NSC-30 in *Foreign Relations of the United States, 1948, The United Nations*, Vol. I, Part 2 (Washington, DC: US Government Printing Office, 1976), 626. See also Craig and Logevall, *America's Cold War*, 97. Strauss quoted in James H. Lebovic, *Flawed Logics: Strategic Nuclear Arms Control from Truman to Obama* (Baltimore: Johns Hopkins University Press, 2103), 23. On earlier AEC debates, see Eric Schlosser, *Command and Control: Nuclear Weapons, the Damascus Incident and the Illusion of Safety* (New York: Penguin, 2013), 78–79, 81.
8. Harry Schwartz, "Soviet Exploits Its New 'Sputnik Diplomacy,'" *New York Times*, 20 October 1957. Vulnerable in Freedman and Michaels, 172–73. Teller quoted in Fred Kaplan, *The Wizards of Armageddon* (New York: Simon & Schuster, 1983), 135. LBJ in Fursenko and Naftali, *Khrushchev's Cold War*, 151. *Life* in Hitchcock, *The Age of Eisenhower*, 377.
9. Panic and little threat in LaFeber, *America, Russia, and the Cold War*, 197. Missiles in Lüthi, *Cold Wars*, 342. Test ban in Benjamin P. Greene, *Eisenhower, Science Advice, and the Nuclear Test-Ban Debate, 1945–1963* (Stanford, CA: Stanford University Press, 2007), 131–33. Arms race in Freedman and Michaels, 195.
10. Inaugural remarks in Lamberton Harper, *The Cold War*, 110. Ike's priorities in Robert J. McMahon, "US National Security Policy from Eisenhower to Kennedy," in Leffler and Westad, *The Cambridge History of the Cold War*, Vol. I, 289–91. On McCarthyism, see Hitchcock, 119–20, 128, 144–45.

11. Hanson W. Baldwin, "Are We Safe from Our Own Atomic Bombs?" *New York Times*, 16 March 1958. Incident in Schlosser, *Command and Control*, 122, 186–87. Accidental escalation in Todd A. Sechser and Matthew Fuhrmann, *Nuclear Weapons and Coercive Diplomacy* (New York: Cambridge University Press, 2017), 10; and Freedman and Michaels, 60.
12. On New Look, see Brands, *The Devil We Knew*, 46–47; and McMahon, "US National Security Policy from Eisenhower to Kennedy," 293–96. Striking power on p. 293. Political condition and qualitative aspects in Jeffrey Lewis and Ankit Panda, "How Much Is Enough? Revisiting Nuclear Reliability, Deterrence, and Preventive War," in *The Fragile Balance of Terror: Deterrence in the New Nuclear Age*, ed. Vipin Narang and Scott D. Sagan (Ithaca, NY: Cornell University Press, 2022), 124. Dulles argued that "passions" could not always be "suppressed by foreign guns." In Gaddis, *Strategies of Containment*, 131. Soviet 1953 test in Weiner, *Legacy of Ashes*, 75. On what was required to deter, see Freedman and Michaels, 417.
13. Elie Abel, "Ridgway Cool to 'New Look' and Doctrine of Retaliation," *New York Times*, 16 April 1954. William S. White, "Democrats Brand New Look Defense Unsafe for Nation," *New York Times*, 31 March 1954. Solvency in Leffler, *For the Soul of Mankind*, 100, 113. See also Hitchcock, 97–98, 101. Massive retaliation in Gaddis, *Strategies of Containment*, 145.
14. National security questions in Bowie and Immerman, *Waging Peace*, 96–97. On relation to New Look, see O'Riordan, *Understanding the Cold War*, 138, 139–141. Deterring in Bernard Brodie, "The Development of Nuclear Strategy" in Miller, *Strategy and Nuclear Deterrence*, 13.
15. Hanson W. Baldwin, "Much More Than the H-Bomb Is Needed," *New York Times*, 18 August 1957. Elie Abel, "Dulles Redefines War Risk Policy for Saving Peace," *New York Times*, 18 January 1956. Schelling, *The Strategy of Conflict*, 9. Unthinkable in Sherwin, *Gambling with Armageddon*, 89. On persuasion and threats, see Kaplan, *The Bomb*, 82; and George and Smoke, *Deterrence in American Foreign Policy*, 78. On deterrence, see Freedman, *Strategy*, 159; and David J. Lonsdale, "Strategy," in David Jordan, James D. Kiras, et al., *Understanding Modern Warfare* (New York: Cambridge University Press, 2008), 51. Gavin, *Nuclear Weapons and American Grand Strategy*, 10.
16. Weigley, *The American Way of War*, 398. Political ends in Jenna E. Higgins, "Deterrence and Strategy," in Finney, *On Strategy*, 182. Preemptive action in Echevarria, *Military Strategy*, 47, 48.
17. Henry A. Kissinger, *Nuclear Weapons and Foreign Policy* (New York: Harper, 1957), 31, 139, 141, 145, 147.
18. James Gavin, "War and Peace: Limited Strife Idea Held Folly," *Los Angeles Times*, 20 October 1958. See also Gavin, *War and Peace in the Space Age*, 24. Bernard Brodie, "Implications for Military Policy," in *The Absolute Weapon: Atomic Power and World Order*, ed. Bernard Brodie (New

York: Harcourt, Brace, 1946), 74. On defeat and victory, see Howard, *The Invention Peace*, 88; and Brands, *The Twilight Struggle*, 18. Zubok argues that Soviet leaders were wrestling with similar issues. *A Failed Empire*, 153.
19. Brodie, *Strategy in the Missile Age*, 309. Quoted in Steiner, *Bernard Brodie and the Foundations of American Nuclear Strategy*, 15. On credibility and perception, see Higgins, 181; Lewis and Panda, "How Much Is Enough?" 127; and Miller, *Grand Strategy from Truman to Trump*, 40. Expected punishment in Robert Jervis, "Deterrence and Perception," in Miller, *Strategy and Nuclear Deterrence*, 58.
20. Brodie in Freedman and Michaels, *The Evolution of Nuclear Strategy*, 62; and Steiner, 12. Gat has argued that "conflict is about deterrence no less than it is about actual fighting." *The Causes of War and the Spread of Peace*, 43. Rigidified in George and Smoke, 7. Schelling, *The Strategy of Conflict*, 200. On brinkmanship, see White, *Fearful Warriors*, 73; and Sechser and Fuhrmann, *Nuclear Weapons and Coercive Diplomacy*, 38, 95.
21. Rusk quoted in O'Riordan, *Understanding the Cold War*, 274. John W. Dower, *The Violent American Century: War and Terror since World War II* (Chicago: Haymarket, 2017), 9. Deterrence failing in Freedman and Michaels, 672. Stephen W. Walt, "America Has an Unhealthy Obsession with Credibility," *Foreign Policy*, 29 January 2022. John Lewis Gaddis has described credibility as "a state of mind, not an objective, independently measured reality." Gaddis, *Now We Know*, 151. On this, see also McMahon, "Introduction: The Challenge of the Third World," in Hahn and Heiss, *Empire and Revolution*, 5; and Layne, *The Peace of Illusions*, 166.
22. William S. White, "Threat to Security in Defense Inquiry Feared by Johnson," *New York Times*, 11 October 1949. William S. White, "Strategic Bombing Is Ruthless, Futile, Admiral Declares," *New York Times*, 12 October 1949. On interservice rivalries, see House, *A Military History of the Cold War, 1944–1962*, 95; and Schlosser, *Command and Control*, 84–87. Navy revolt in Kaplan, *The Bomb*, 6–7, 16–18. On defense budget, see Lissner, *Wars of Revelation*, 42. World War II bombing in Moyn, *Humane*, 122–23, 125, 132.
23. Robert Alden, "Korea Shows Limits of Air Power; Enemy Keeps on Despite Bombings," *New York Times*, 27 December 1952. Early airpower theory in David J. Lyle, "Strategy in the Air," in Finney, *On Strategy*, 51, 53, 55–56. On a "misguided faith" in airpower, see Vine, *The United States of War*, 191. World War II consensus in Centeno and Enriquez, *War & Society*, 111. MacArthur quoted in Lissner, 47. On limits of airpower in Korea, see Gibby, *Korean Showdown*, 93; and Hastings, *The Korean War*, 255–56, 258. Air Staff report in Deaile, *Always at War*, 73.
24. "Strategic Air Command Confident," *Los Angeles Times*, 27 November 1958. On coercion, see Freedman and Michaels, 234; Sechser and Fuhrmann, 5; and Mearsheimer, *The Tragedy of Great Power Politics*,

106, 108. Centers and obsolete in Echevarria, *War's Logic*, 32, 48. See also Kaplan, *To Kill Nations*, 24, 29, 83–84. Shortening wars in Echevarria, *Military Strategy*, 67, 71. Shortcut and expectations in Tami Davis Biddle, *Rhetoric and Reality in Air Warfare: The Evolution of British and American Ideas about Strategic Bombing, 1914–1945* (Princeton, NJ: Princeton University Press, 2002), 139, 289. On problems of airpower influencing political will, see Lewis, *The American Culture of War*, 55.

25. Harold B. Hinton, "LeMay Opposes Cut in Global Bombers as Too Great a Risk," *New York Times*, 6 June 1953. On SAC mission, see Rosenberg, "The Origins of Overkill," 128–31; and Albertson, *Winning Armageddon*, 76, 131–32. Cult in Kaplan, *The Bomb*, 14. SAC officer in Deaile, *Always at War*, 181. Bases in Allan R. Millet, Peter Maslowski, and William B. Feis, *For the Common Defense: A Military History of the United States from 1607 to 2012*, rev. ed. (New York: Free Press, 2012), 446. Twenty-four hours a day in Deaile, 106.

26. Primary deterrent in "LeMay Says War Peril Is Rising," *New York Times*, 25 April 1958. LeMay quoted in Kenneth D. Rose, *One Nation Underground: The Fallout Shelter in American Culture* (New York: New York University Press, 2001), 20. Legitimate targets in Daniel Ellsberg, *The Doomsday Machine: Confessions of a Nuclear War Planner* (New York: Bloomsbury, 2017), 274. See also Albertson, *Winning Armageddon*, xv; Howard, *The Invention of Peace*, 76; and Allan M. Winkler, *Life under a Cloud: American Anxiety about the Atom* (New York: Oxford University Press, 1993), 60. On strategic plan, SIOP-62, see Kaplan, *The Bomb*, 27–28. On Japan, see Moyn, *Humane*, 135.

27. Counterforce in Kaplan, *The Bomb*, 19–20, 81. Ellsberg on p. 37. See also Freedman, *Strategy*, 163–64, 167. Coercion in Echevarria, *War's Logic*, 82, 86–87. Thomas Schelling advocated the "exploitation of force potential force" as part of US strategy. *The Strategy of Conflict*, 5. McNamara and no cities in Kuklick, *Blind Oracles*, 107–9; and Kaplan, *To Kill Nations*, 34, 177–78. Absorbing first blows in Albertson, 19.

28. Hanson W. Baldwin, "The Effects of Russia's Bomb on Our Military Strategy," *New York Times*, 25 September 1949. On Dulles's "massive retaliation" speech, see Judge and Langdon, *The Cold War*, 328–29; and Kaplan, *The Wizards of Armageddon*, chap. 11. Monopoly in Kecskemeti, *Strategic Surrender*, 123. Orgy on p. 253. Bolt in Lebovic, *Flawed Logics*, 67. Damage limitation in Freedman and Michaels, *The Evolution of Nuclear Strategy*, 319. On MAD, see Campbell Craig, "The Nuclear Revolution: A Product of the Cold War, or Something More?" in Immerman and Goedde, *The Oxford Handbook of the Cold War*, 366–67, 369. Brendan Rittenhouse Green argues that MAD did not necessarily constrain the superpowers. See *The Revolution That Failed: Nuclear Competition, Arms Control, and the Cold War* (New York: Cambridge University Press,

2020), 2–7. Of note, Khrushchev held similar doubts about nuclear war's utility, even as nuclear weapons promised the Soviet Union strategic parity with the United States. See Fursenko and Naftali, *Khrushchev's Cold War*, 39; and Zubok, *A Failed Empire*, 126–29.

29. Boyer, *By the Bomb's Early Light*, 14. Brodie in Kaplan, *The Wizards of Armageddon*, 26; and Steiner, *Bernard Brodie and the Foundations of American Nuclear Strategy*, 28, 46. Victims in Sarah E. Robey, *Atomic Americans: Citizens in a Nuclear State* (Ithaca, NY: Cornell University Press, 2022), 12. Spies on pp. 92–94. See also Paul Rubinson, *Redefining Science: Scientists, the National Security State, and Nuclear Weapons in Cold War America* (Amherst: University of Massachusetts Press, 2016), 5, 65. John D. Morris, "House Body to Sift Spying for Russia by Atomic Scientists," *New York Times*, 2 September 1948. "Atomic Spy Report Will Shock Public, Official Declares," *New York Times*, 26 September 1948. Misguided in C. P. Trussell, "House Body Plans to Expose Details of Atomic Spying," *New York Times*, 18 September 1948.

30. Strategy intellectuals in Echevarria, *War's Logic*, 57. On Rand, see Freedman, *Strategy*, 146–48; and Kuklick, 33, 34. Senior officers quoted in Sharon Ghamari-Tabrizi, *The Worlds of Herman Kahn: The Intuitive Science of Thermonuclear War* (Cambridge, MA: Harvard University Press, 2005), 48. On technology and civil-military relations, see Samuel P. Huntington, *The Soldier and the State: The Theory and Politics of Civil-Military Relations* (Cambridge, MA: Belknap Press, 1957), 2–3, 7–9. Morris Janowitz, *The Professional Soldier: A Social and Political Portrait* (New York: Free Press, 1960), 135, 217, 258.

31. Brodie, *Strategy in the Missile Age*, 7, 9. See also Echevarria, *War's Logic*, 66–69, 75; and Steiner, 130. Kissinger, *Nuclear Weapons and Foreign Policy*, 16. See also Kuklick, 190–92. Edward Teller, "A New Look at War-Making," *New York Times*, 7 July 1957. See also Rubinson, 76–92. Political payoffs in Kecskemeti, *Strategic Surrender*, 257.

32. Guilty in Ghamari-Tabrizi, *The Worlds of Herman Kahn*, 83. Charts in Kaplan, *The Wizards of Armageddon*, 226. On Kahn and his theories, see Echevarria, *War's Logic*, 95, 99–102, 104–5; and Freedman and Michaels, *The Evolution of Nuclear Strategy*, 165–66, 316–17. Unthinkable in Eliot Fremont-Smith, "What If the Balance of Terror Goes Out of Balance?" *New York Times*, 9 June 1965.

33. Limited nuclear war in Stoker, *Why America Loses Wars*, 32. Stabilizing force in Ryan W. Kort, "Contemporary Strategic Theories and Their Influence on Doctrine," in Finney, *On Strategy*, 77. Retaliation in Kaplan, *The Wizards of Armageddon*, 31, 81, 85.

34. On World War II, see Craig and Logevall, *America's Cold War*, 51–55. See also Williams, *The Tragedy of American Diplomacy*, 229. Signaling in Echevarria, *War's Logic*, 79. How much in Lebow and Gross Stein, *We*

All Lost the Cold War, 357; and Brodie, "The Development of Nuclear Strategy," 9.

35. On H-bomb, see Lüthi, *Cold Wars*, 337. Links to containment in Leffler, *For the Soul of Mankind*, 139, 142. Triad in House, *A Military History of the Cold War, 1944–1962*, 383; and Millet, Maslowski, and Feis, *For the Common Defense*, 476. Genocide in Freedman and Michaels, 88. Walter H. Waggoner, "Connally Favors Hydrogen Bombs to Protect Peace," *New York Times*, 29 January 1950.

36. Russell Baker, "U.S. Reconsidering 'Small-War' Theory," *New York Times*, 11 August 1957. See also Rosenberg, "The Origins of Overkill," 141. On Korea, see Greene, *Eisenhower, Science Advice, and the Nuclear Test-Ban Debate*, 42. Indochina in Logevall, *Embers of War*, 499–500; and George and Smoke, *Deterrence in American Foreign Policy*, 259–60. Osgood, *Limited War*, 257.

37. Broken-back warfare in Waldo Drake, "Red Berlin Threat May Revise U.S. Military Policy," *Los Angeles Times*, 13 January 1959; and Stoker, 153. Jeff Schogol, "The Story of the 'Davy Crockett,'" *Task & Purpose*, 19 September 2022. See also Millet, Maslowski, and Feis, *For the Common Defense*, 484; and Schlosser, *Command and Control*, 265.

38. Stalin and unusable in Gaddis, *The Cold War: A New History*, 57. Mao in Lüthi, *The Sino-Soviet Split*, 137; and Freedman and Michaels, 389–91, 397. Symbolic power in Lüthi, *Cold Wars*, 167; and Tami Davis Biddle, "Shield and Sword: U.S. Strategic Forces and Doctrine Since 1945," in Bacevich, *The Long War*, 140. Sechser and Fuhrmann question the "coercive utility of nuclear weapons" in *Nuclear Weapons and Coercive Diplomacy*, 8, 12–13.

39. Bullet in Greene, 44. On the crisis, see Hitchcock, *The Age of Eisenhower*, 205–9; Chang, *Friends and Enemies*, 116–42; and Sechser and Fuhrmann, 188–94. Ike's views in Craig and Logevall, 151–52. On tactical nuclear weapons' relationship to credibility, see Hemmer, *American Pendulum*, 68.

40. Hanson W. Baldwin, "U.S. Joint Chiefs Split on A-Bomb," *New York Times*, 21 April 1955. The Chief of Naval Operations leaked that the JCS favored an all-out attack on China. See George and Smoke, *Deterrence in American Foreign Policy*, 291–92. Retaliation in Freedman and Michaels, 58. For an overview of Sino-American relations after the Korean War, see Tao Wang, *Isolating the Enemy: Diplomatic Strategy in China and the United States, 1953–1956* (New York: Columbia University Press, 2021).

41. Staten Island in George and Smoke, 267. General Lawrence Kuter quoted in Kaplan, *To Kill Nations*, 130. On the crisis, see Jian, *Mao's China and the Cold War*, 163–204; and M. H. Halperin, *The 1958 Taiwan Straits Crisis: A Documented History* (Santa Monica, CA: Rand Corporation, 1966). De-escalation in Sechser and Fuhrmann, 197–200. Lessons in

Laurence S. Kuter, "The Meaning of the Taiwan Strait Crisis," *Air Force*, Vol. 42, No. 4 (March 1959). Firepower in John G. Norris, "Starfighters on Formosa," *Air Force*, Vol. 42, No. 1 (January 1959).

42. Imagining in Robey, *Atomic Americans*, 2, 15. Policy implications in Sherwin, *Gambling with Armageddon*, 49, 67. Lippmann quoted in Gretchen Heefner, *The Missile Next Door: The Minuteman in the American Heartland* (Cambridge, MA: Harvard University Press, 2012), 38.

43. Truman quoted in Gaddis, *The Cold War*, 53. Inflating numbers in Casey, *When Soldiers Fall*, 101. Visions of collective death in Eva Horn, "The Apocalyptic Fiction: Shaping the Future in the Cold War," *Understanding the Imaginary War: Conflict, Thought, and Nuclear Conflict, 1945–90*, ed. Matthew Grant and Benjamin Ziemann (Manchester, UK: Manchester University Press, 2016), 47. On contemporary complaints about moralism in policy decision-making, see Joseph S. Nye, Jr., *Do Morals Matter? Presidents and Foreign Policy from FDR to Trump* (New York: Oxford University Press, 2020), 2. Saving Americans in Winkler, *Life under a Cloud*, 27. Red or dead in Freedman and Michaels, 122.

44. "The Unwanted War," *Collier's*, 27 October 1951, 17. Of note, the issue included articles as if they were written as of 1960 and showed how "war would be fought and won." Appeal in Goedde, *The Politics of Peace*, 48. Ike in Lebovic, *Flawed Logics*, 26.

45. Walter Lippmann, "The Big Bombs," *Washington Post*, 6 April 1954. On Bravo test and *Lucky Dragon* incident, see Gaddis, *Now We Know*, 226–27; Greene, *Eisenhower, Science Advice, and the Nuclear Test-Ban Debate*, 52–55, 66–69; and Winkler, 94.

46. Terror weapons Gaddis, *Now We Know*, 103. Psychological in Freedman and Michaels, 25, 200. On ecological aspects of testing, see Sarah Alisabeth Fox, *Downwind: A People's History of the Nuclear West* (Lincoln: University of Nebraska Press, 2014). Hong called the Marshall Islands a "sacrificial... proving ground" for the bomb. *A Violent Peace*, 123.

47. Albert Wohlstetter, "The Delicate Balance of Terror" in Mahnken and Maiolo, *Strategic Studies*, 230. See also Rittenhouse Green, *The Revolution That Failed*, 28–31. C. Wright Mills, *The Causes of World War Three* (New York: Simon & Schuster, 1958), 4. Ellsberg, *The Doomsday Machine*, 51, 63, 73, 136–37. Ellsberg additionally would report that fallout estimates were "a fantastic underestimate." p. 140.

48. John Hersey, *Hiroshima* (New York: Knopf, 1946, 1965), 40. Einstein-Russell Manifesto in Hanhimäki and Westad, *The Cold War*, 281–82. "The 36-Hour War," *Life*, 19 November 1945. Bulletin in Boyer, *By the Bomb's Early Light*, 64; and Winkler, *Life under a Cloud*, 40–41.

49. Bosley Crowther, "Monsters Again," *New York Times*, 6 May 1956. Films in Whitfield, *The Culture of the Cold War*, 224; Doherty, *Cold War, Cool Medium*, 151–52; and Robert A. Jacobs, *The Dragon's Tail: Americans*

Face the Atomic Age (Amherst: University of Massachusetts Press, 2010), 12–14, 34–36.
50. Federal Civil Defense Administration, *Bert the Turtle Says Duck and Cover* (Washington, DC: US Government Printing Office, 1951). See also Edward M. Geist, *Armageddon Insurance: Civil Defense in the United States and Soviet Union* (Chapel Hill: University of North Carolina Press, 2019), 75; and Heefner, *The Missile Next Door*, 44–45. *Atomic War!* No. 1, November 1952. Radiation and superheroes in Matthew J. Costello, *Secret Identity Crisis: Comic Books and the Unmasking of Cold War America* (New York: Continuum, 2009), 1.
51. "Bomb Shelters Urged," *New York Times*, 13 January 1959. De facto targets in Rose, *One Nation Underground*, 8. Geist, 244–45. US Department of Defense, *Fallout Protection: What to Know and Do about Nuclear Attack* (Washington, DC: US Government Printing Office, 1961), 42. See also Kaplan, *The Wizards of Armageddon*, 310–11. Bigelow quoted in Robey, *Atomic Americans*, 117. Minutemen in Heefner, *The Missile Next Door*, 2.
52. Kahn in Ghamari-Tabrizi, *The Worlds of Herman Kahn*, 35. Balancing and mass panic in Oakes, *The Imaginary War*, 8, 41–42. Panic prone in Robey, *Atomic Americans*, 44. *Twilight Zone* in Jacobs, *The Dragon's Tail*. See also Freedman and Michaels, 325.
53. Maryland Civil Defense Agency, "The H-Bomb and You," 1954. On contemporary administration officials calling "every home a fortress," see May, *Fortress America*, 37–41.

CHAPTER 7

1. Ultra-modern in Jacobs, 33. On Ike's "integrated grand strategy," see Bowie and Immerman, *Waging Peace*, 4–5; and Trauschweizer, *Maxwell Taylor's Cold War*, 76. Procommunists and leftists in Piero Gleijeses, *Shattered Hope: The Guatemalan Revolution and the United States, 1944–1954* (Princeton, NJ: Princeton University Press, 1991), 101. Questionable value of covert operations in John Prados, "Cold War Intelligence History," in Immerman and Goedde, *The Oxford Handbook of the Cold War*, 419; and Immerman, *The Hidden Hand*, 50–51. Intimidation in Michael Grow, *U.S. Presidents and Latin American Interventions: Pursuing Regime Change in the Cold War* (Lawrence: University Press of Kansas, 2008), 1.
2. Vine, *The United States of War*, 201. Bullet in Waldman, *Vicarious Warfare*, 87. W. H. Lawrence, "Kennedy Says U.S. Must Regain Lead in 'Fight for Peace,'" *New York Times*, 8 September 1960. See also Fursenko and Naftali, *Khrushchev's Cold War*, 338. Kennedy on defense in Graebner, Burns, and Siracusa, *America and the Cold War*, Vol. 1, 254. For

an overview on covert actions, see Lindsey A. O'Rourke, *Covert Regime Change: America's Secret Cold War* (Ithaca, NY: Cornell University Press, 2018).

3. A full copy of the Doolittle Report can be found at https://www.cia.gov/readingroom/. See also Feldman, *Manufacturing Hysteria*, 253; and Brands, *The Devil We Knew*, 61. On precedent for the future, see Stephen G. Rabe, *The Killing Zone: The United States Wages War in Latin America*, 2nd ed. (New York: Oxford University Press, 2016), 52; and John Prados, "The Central Intelligence Agency and the Face of Decolonization under the Eisenhower Administration," in *The Eisenhower Administration, the Third World, and the Globalization of the Cold War*, ed. Kathryn C. Statler and Andrew L. Johns (Lanham, MD: Rowman & Littlefield, 2006), 34–35.

4. Patrick Porter argues that the United States "outcompeted the Soviet Union with coups, election meddling, alliances with authoritarians." *The False Promise of Liberal Order*, 73. Operations in Vine, 202. Business interests and capitalist development in Grandin, *Empire's Workshop*, 25–27. Vine argues there was a "frequent conflation of the economic interests of U.S. businesses and elites with U.S. 'national security.'" *The United States of War*, 73. Nourishing revolutionary violence in Lorenzini, *Global Development*, 52, 172.

5. Free world in Hitchcock, *The Age of Eisenhower*, 153. Worldwide in scope on p. 152. Pax Americana in David Talbot, *The Devil's Chessboard: Allen Dulles, the CIA, and the Rise of America's Secret Government* (New York: Harper, 2015), 241. Regime change in Vincent Bevins, *The Jakarta Method: Washington's Anticommunist Crusade & the Mass Murder Program that Shaped Our World* (New York: PublicAffairs, 2020), 45. Projecting in Gaddis, *On Grand Strategy*, 56. France in Lüthi, *Cold Wars*, 103; and Judt, *Postwar*, 88, 153.

6. Reforms in Hal Brands, *Latin America's Cold War* (Cambridge, MA: Harvard University Press, 2010), 16; and Grandin, *Empire's Workshop*, 42–44. On United Fruit, see Rabe, *The Killing Zone*, 38; Gleijeses, *Shattered Hope*, 86, 92, 93; and Grow, *U.S. Presidents and Latin American Interventions*, 11–12. On links to communism, see Sarah Foss, "Community Development in Cold War Guatemala: Not a Revolution but an Evolution," in *Latin America in the Global Cold War*, ed. Thomas C. Field, Jr., Stella Krepp, and Vanni Pettinà (Chapel Hill: University of North Carolina Press, 2020), 127. Outpost in Stephen Schlesinger and Stephen Kinzer, *Bitter Fruit: The Story of the American Coup in Guatemala*, rev. ed. (Cambridge, MA: Harvard University Press, 1982, 2005), 11. Beachhead in "Wiley Scores Guatemala," *New York Times*, 17 October 1953. State Department in Grow, 17. Early apprehensions and CIA assessments in Nick Cullather, *Secret History: The CIA's Classified*

Account of Its Operation in Guatemala, 1952–1954, 2nd ed. (Stanford, CA: Stanford University Press, 2006), 14–17, 22–25, 35.

7. Credibility in Grow, 18. Arms shipment in Fursenko and Naftali, 61–62. Christian G. Appy, "Eisenhower's Guatemalan Doodle, or: How to Draw, Deny, and Take Credit for a Third World Coup," in Appy, *Cold War Constructions*, 194. Atom bomb in Gleijeses, *Shattered Hope*, 299.

8. "Guatemalan Coup Hailed by Dulles," *Los Angeles Times*, 1 July 1954. On CIA planning, see Cullather, *Secret History*, 7–8, 40–45, 152–55. On consequences, see Rabe, *The Killing Zone*, 50–56. Hubris in Gleijeses, *Shattered Hope*, 361.

9. On Mosaddegh as an anti-interventionist, see Bill, *The Eagle and the Lion*, 56. On US actions being more than just part of an anticommunist crusade, see Maziar Behrooz, "The 1953 Coup in Iran and the Legacy of the Tudeh," and William. Roger Louis, "Britain and the Overthrow of the Mosaddeq Government" in Gasiorowski and Byrne, *Mohammed Mosaddeq and the 1953 Coup in Iran*, 125, 128. Nationalization in Ervand Abrahamian, *The Coup: 1953, the CIA, and the Roots of Modern U.S.-Iranian Relations* (New York: New Press, 2013), 31, 81; and John Foran, "Discursive Subversions: *Time* Magazine, the CIA Overthrow of Musaddiq, and the Installation of the Shah," in Appy, *Cold War Constructions*, 181–82. AIOC in Giuliano Garavini, *The Rise and Fall of OPEC in the Twentieth Century* (New York: Oxford University Press, 2019), 82. British in Ali Rahnema, *Behind the 1953 Coup in Iran: Thugs, Turncoats, Soldiers, and Spooks* (New York: Cambridge University Press, 2015), 20; and Louis, 135–36, 137.

10. Dulles quoted in Little, *American Orientalism*, 216. Oil concerns in Garavini, 84–85. Conflation in Abrahamian, 4. Power vacuum in Cleveland and Bunton, *A History of the Modern Middle East*, 277. Hanson W. Baldwin, "Military Void in Mid-East," *New York Times*, 3 March 1953. Lev Vasiliev, "Soviet Plot to Steal Iran," *Los Angeles Times*, 19 April 1953.

11. Persistent US fears in Louis and Mark J. Gasiorowski, "The 1953 Coup d'État against Mosaddeq," in Gasiorowski and Byrne, 151, 231. CIA assessments in Abrahamian, *The Coup*, 174, 175–76. CIA operations in Rahnema, 86. Mosaddegh assessments in Mary Ann Heiss, "Real Men Don't Wear Pajamas: Anglo-American Cultural Perceptions of Mohammed Mosaddeq and the Iranian Oil Nationalization Dispute," in Hahn and Heiss, *Empire and Revolution*, 181–85; and Foran, 164, 172. On the Shah's return, see Weiner, *Legacy of Ashes*, 92. On the coup's success, see Rahnema, 249–53, 274–76. Coverage in Abrahamian, 199–200. Implications in Latham, *The Right Kind of Revolution*, 143–46, 148.

12. C. P. Trussell, "Soviet on War Basis, Gen. Ridgway Warns," *New York Times*, 26 April 1955. Obliging a presence in Kissinger, *Diplomacy*, 551. The fact that Americans were so unfamiliar with many of these areas

did not help matters. See Leebaert, *Grand Improvisation*, 57. Warsaw Pact in Zubok, *A Failed Empire*, 102. Finally, we might see Americans' faith in covert action as similar to their faith in "war," since covert action often deployed elements of warfare even as it was a means of securing US objectives while hopefully avoiding full-scale war.

13. Walter Lippmann, "Hungary and the Middle East," *Washington Post*, 6 November 1956. Use of violence in Applebaum, *Iron Curtain*, 88. Uprising in Csaba Békés, *Hungary's Cold War: International Relations from the End of World War II to the Fall of the Soviet Union* (Chapel Hill: University of North Carolina Press, 2022), 107, 116, 125. Costs in Fink, *Cold War*, 98–99. Swapna Kona Nayunu, "The Soviet Peace Offensive and Nehru's India, 1953–1956," in Bhagavan, *India and the Cold War*, 37, 44. Khrushchev in O'Riordan, *Understanding the Cold War*, 133. See also Zubok, *A Failed Empire*, 117.

14. Murrey Marder, "Ike Deplores Soviet Force in Hungary," *Washington Post*, 26 October 1956. Liberation in Carroll Kilpatrick, "Peace Gaining under Ike, Foreign Policy Plank Says," *Washington Post*, 20 August 1956. RFE in Dezso Saly, "Broadcasting to Hungary," *New York Times*, 17 December 1956. On RFE, see Belmonte, *Selling the American Way*, 74. Avoiding risk in Békés, 150–152. Domination in Sixsmith, *The War of Nerves*, 180–82. Diabolical, citing a British diplomat, in Judt, *Postwar*, 322–23. Czechoslovakia in House, *A Military History of the Cold War, 1944–1962*, 235–36.

15. On crisis, see Hahn, *Caught in the Middle East*, 194–209. Arms deal in Cleveland and Bunton, 294–96. Dulles quoted in James L. Gelvin, *The Israel-Palestine Conflict: A History*, 4th ed. (New York: Cambridge University Press, 2021), 182–83. Diverting attention from Hungary in Yaqub, *Containing Arab Nationalism*, 51; and Leebaert, *Grand Improvisation*, 473. On the dam project, see Hitchcock, *The Age of Eisenhower*, 306–9. On the military operation, see House, ibid., 350–52.

16. Oil reserves in Salim Yaqub, "The Cold War and the Middle East," in McMahon, *The Cold War in the Third World*, 11. Anderson quoted in Little, *American Orientalism*, 61. Oil and nationalism on p. 172. On oil as a strategic asset since World War I, see Garavini, 14–15. British interests in McMahon, "US National Security Policy from Eisenhower to Kennedy," 306–9. French interests in Guy Laron, *Origins of the Suez Crisis: Postwar Development Diplomacy and the Struggle over Third World Industrialization, 1945–1956* (Baltimore: Johns Hopkins University Press, 2013), 154–55, 172. Losing Cairo in Lüthi, *Cold Wars*, 35. On US objectives after the Suez crisis, see Malik Mufti, "The United States and Nasserist Pan-Arabism," in *The Middle East and the United States: History, Politics, and Ideologies*, 6th ed., ed. David W. Lesch and Mark L. Haas (New York: Routledge, 2018), 93–94.

17. John D. Morris, "President Signs Mideast Doctrine," *New York Times*, 10 March 1957. Doctrine in Judge and Langdon, *The Cold War*, 347. See also Hahn, *Caught in the Middle East*, 156, 224–27. Radicalism in Little, *American Orientalism*, 78. On benevolence, see McAlister, *Epic Encounters*, 81–82.
18. Ideology in O'Riordan, *Understanding the Cold War*, 243. Resistance in Lüthi, *Cold Wars*, 43. Political allegiance in Yaqub, *Containing Arab Nationalism*, 2, 5, 58–59. On fears of Soviet inroads, see Little, *American Orientalism*, 132–33; and Hitchcock, 338. Moderating behavior in Jason Brownlee, *Democracy Prevention: The Politics of the U.S.-Egyptian Alliance* (New York: Cambridge University Press, 2012), 17.
19. Crisis in Paul Thomas Chamberlin, "The Cold War in the Middle East," in Kalinovsky and Daigle, *The Routledge Handbook of the Cold War*, 168. Ike quoted in Douglas Little, "His Finest Hour? Eisenhower, Lebanon, and the 1958 Middle East Crisis," in Hahn and Heiss, *Empire and Revolution*, 29. Radical in Little, *American Orientalism*, 93. Stability in Howard, *The Invention of Peace*, 52. Dulles quoted in Mufti, 106. One USIA report agreed, stating that "supercharged nationalism has become a dangerous threat to orderly progress." In Parker, *Hearts, Minds, Voices*, 102.
20. Ike quoted in Little, *American Orientalism*, 27. See also Yaqub, *Containing Arab Nationalism*, 13. Kennan, *The Kennan Diaries*, 307. On Arab views, see Bill, *The Eagle and the Lion*, 128, 129.
21. Ike quoted in Little, *American Orientalism*, 218. Support for authoritarians in Yaqub, *Containing Arab Nationalism*, 116. Reinforcement and aid in Bill, 113, 114; and Rahnema, *Behind the 1953 Coup in Iran*, 3. Latin America in Garavini, *The Rise and Fall of OPEC in the Twentieth Century*, 53, 60. "Mideast Plan Scored," *New York Times*, 14 January 1957.
22. Ceylon and Lodge in Mary L. Dudziak, *Cold War Civil Rights: Race and the Image of American Democracy* (Princeton, NJ: Princeton University Press, 2000), 31, 131. Propaganda in Brazinsky, *Winning the Third World*, 150; and Belmonte, *Selling the American Way*, 160. Clout and appeal in McMahon, "Introduction: The Challenge of the Third World," in Hahn and Heiss, *Empire and Revolution*, 6–7.
23. Allen Drury, "Fulbright Lashes at Foreign Policy," *New York Times*, 7 August 1958. "Excerpts from Address by Fulbright," ibid. See also Williams, *The Tragedy of American Diplomacy*, 12. On militarization, see Fitzgerald, *Militarization and the American Century*, 3. For a chart on defense expenditures, see Paul M. Kennedy, *The Rise and Fall of the Great Powers: Economic Change and Military Conflict from 1500 to 2000* (New York: Random House, 1987), 384.
24. Violence on periphery in Hong, *A Violent Peace*, 225. Geneva in Hitchcock, *The Age of Eisenhower*, 268–69. Ike quoted in Levering, *The Cold War*, 76. Open Skies in Greene, *Eisenhower, Science Advice, and the Nuclear Test-Ban Debate*, 83–86. Inspecting bases in Howard

Handleman, "No Real Hope of Cold War's End Held on Eve of Geneva Talks," *Washington Post*, 23 October 1955.

25. Struggle in Rupprecht, *Soviet Internationalism after Stalin*, 23. "Khrushchev Stresses Peaceful Coexistence," *New York Times*, 22 February 1958. See also Zubok, *A Failed Empire*, 95, 104–5. On China's reaction, see Lüthi, *The Sino-Soviet Split*, 47, 76. Relation to India in Nayudu, "The Soviet Peace Offensive and Nehru's India, 1953–1956," 43. The managing editor of *Foreign Affairs* saw things differently, regarding the Cold War's new phase as one of "competitive coexistence." In Johanna Rainio-Niemi, "Neutrality as an Instrument for a Small State Manouevring and the Globalisation of Neutrality in the Cold War," in *Margins for Manoeuvre in Cold War Europe: The Influence of Smaller Powers*, ed. Laurien Crump and Susanna Erlandsson (London: Routledge, 2020), 175.

26. Great Leap in Lüthi, *Cold Wars*, 80; Jeremy Friedman, *Shadow Cold War: The Sino-Soviet Competition for the Third World* (Chapel Hill: University of North Carolina Press, 2015), 2, 7, 49; and Lorenz Lüthi, "The Sino-Soviet Split and Its Consequences," in Kalinovsky and Daigle, *The Routledge Handbook of the Cold War*, 75–78. On links to militarization, see Covell F. Meyskens, *Mao's Third Front: The Militarization of the Cold War* (New York: Cambridge University Press, 2020), 20–22; and Brazinsky, *Winning the Third World*, 166–67. Frederick Kempe argues that "Mao had shocked Khrushchev with his readiness for war with the U.S., irrespective of the devastation it might bring." *Berlin 1961: Kennedy, Khrushchev, and the Most Dangerous Place on Earth* (New York: Putnam, 2011), 42. American fears in Brazinsky, 185. Rapprochement Lüthi, *The Sino-Soviet Split*, 10.

27. Encirclement in Lüthi, *Cold Wars*, 124. Nehru quoted on p. 168. Sihanouk in Kinzer, *The Brothers*, 198. Dulles in Guan, *Southeast Asia's Cold War*, 74. See also Graebner, Burns, and Siracusa, *America and the Cold War*, Vol. 2, 316. On SEATO membership see Khong, *Analogies at War*, 80.

28. Polyzoides, "Nehru Lets Anger Override Reason," *Los Angeles Times*, 23 April 1955. Molotov in Brazinsky, *Winning the Third World*, 83. Sukarno in Kinzer, 218. Goldwater, *Conscience of a Conservative*, 96–97. On alliance networks, see Rapp-Hooper, *Shields of the Republic*, 5, 47–48.

29. On independence and anticolonialism, see Guan, 6–7, 14. Westad, *The Global Cold War*, 397–98. War creating new political orders in Howard, *The Invention of Peace*, 10. Frantz Fanon, trans. Richard Philcox, *The Wretched of the Earth* (New York: Grove, 1961, 2004), 46, 51. See also Lowe, *Savage Continent*, 368. Atlantic Charter in Thomas J. Hamilton, "Anti-Colonialism Now a Vital World Force," *New York Times*, 9 August 1956. See also Costigliola, *Roosevelt's Lost Alliances*, 134–35, 159.

30. On preference for conservative leaders and misunderstanding the differences between nationalism and communism, see Bevins, *The Jakarta Method*, 49, 80, 122, 157, 181–82; and Rabe, *The Killing Zone*, 119.
31. Opportunity in W. Averell Harriman, "What the Africans Expect of Us," *New York Times*, 9 October 1960. George Padmore, *Pan-Africanism or Communism? The Coming Struggle for Africa* (New York: Roy, 1956, 1971), 15. As Penny M. Von Eschen argues, US policymakers feared "that resentment of American racism might cause Asian and African peoples to seek closer relations with the Soviet Union." In "Who's the Real Ambassador? Exploding Cold War Racial Ideology," in Appy, *Cold War Constructions*, 113. See also Plummer, *In Search of Power*, 100. On Congo, see Lise Namikas, *Battleground Africa: Cold War in the Congo, 1960–1965* (Stanford, CA: Stanford University Press, 2013); and Jessica M. Chapman, *Remaking the World: Decolonization and the Cold War* (Lexington: University Press of Kentucky, 2023), 108–43.
32. Preservation in Craig and Logevall, *America's Cold War*, 8. Existential enemies in Dower, *The Violent American Century*, 25. May lead to war in "Sargeant Asks Aid to Undo Fear of US," *New York Times*, 30 January 1952.
33. "Text of Eisenhower's Farewell Address," *New York Times*, 18 January 1961. On congress, see Roland, *Delta of Power*, 18. Brenes argues that a "new political economy" would come into being during the 1950s, one centered around the military-industrial complex. *For Might and Right*, 4–5, 110.
34. "Text of General Eisenhower's Address to the American Legion Convention," *New York Times*, 26 August 1952. See also Bowie and Immerman, *Waging Peace*, 49.

CHAPTER 8

1. Intellectuals in Rupprecht, *Soviet Internationalism after Stalin*, 136–37, 171, 186.
2. Castro's rise in Westad, *The Global Cold War*, 170–74. Revolution and reforms in Thomas C. Wright, *Latin America in the Era of the Cuban Revolution and Beyond*, 3rd ed. (Santa Barbara, CA: Praeger, 2018), xvi, 16, 21. Rival model to a US system in Bevins, *The Jakarta Method*, 230. On Cuba and Guatemala, see Grandin, *Empire's Workshop*, 45.
3. Model in Ryan Irwin, "Through the Looking Glass: African National Congress and the Tricontinental Revolution, 1960–1975," in *The Tricontinental Revolution: Third World Radicalism and the Cold War*, ed. R. Joseph Parrott and Mark Atwood Lawrence (New York: Cambridge University Press, 2022), 153. US fears in Grow, *U.S. Presidents and Latin American Interventions*, 41–42. Economic aspects in Rabe, *The Killing*

Zone, 62–64. Castro's anti-Americanism in Jones, *The Bay of Pigs* (New York: Oxford University Press, 2008), 11, 12. Chapman argues that the revolutionary example showed one way to contest the "heavily militarized American project of neoimperialism." *Remaking the World*, 5.

4. Castro quoted in Tad Szulc, "Red Influence Growing in Cuba behind Facade of the Revolution," *New York Times*, 2 August 1960. Worried observers in Robert S. Allen and Paul Scott, "Latin Storm Stirring in Cold War," *Los Angeles Times*, 28 December 1961. Embassy in Grow, 51. Fortress and cancer in Lebow and Stein, *We All Lost the Cold War*, 21.

5. Fulbright in Jones, 65, 67. Moscow not wanting war in Fursenko and Naftali, *Khrushchev's Cold War*, 306. Third camp in Wright, 34. Journalist Herbert Matthews on p. 41. Eric Gettig, "Cuba, the United States, and the Uses of the Third World Project, 1959–1967," in Field, Krepp, and Pettinà, *Latin America in the Global Cold War*, 241, 262.

6. Alexander Hamilton, James Madison, and John Jay, *The Federalist Papers* (New York: New American Library, 1961), 87. See also Edel, "Extending the Sphere," in Borgwardt, McKnight Nichols, and Preston, *Rethinking American Grand Strategy*, 84. Monroe Doctrine in Alan McPherson, *A Short History of U.S. Interventions in Latin America and the Caribbean* (Malden, MA: Wiley Blackwell, 2016), 17. Roosevelt and Platt in Rabe, *The Killing Zone*, 1, 5–8, 12. Wood quoted on p. 5.

7. Good Neighbor in Rabe, *The Killing Zone*, 16–19. Missiles in Teishan A. Latner, *Cuban Revolution in America: Havana and the Making of a United States Left, 1968–1992* (Chapel Hill: University of North Carolina Press, 2018), 75. Goldwater, *Why Not Victory?* 92–93. On building US supremacy in Latin America, see also Kagan, *Dangerous Nation*, 302–3.

8. On "Latin America's revolutionary twentieth century," see Greg Grandin, "What Was Containment? Short and Long Answers from the Americas," in McMahon, *The Cold War in the Third World*, 27–28. Negligible on p. 31. See also Rabe, *The Killing Zone*, xxxvi—xxxvii. Training in O'Riordan, *Understanding the Cold War*, 220. Rusk in Sherwin, *Gambling with Armageddon*, 161–62.

9. On leadup, see Jones, *The Bay of Pigs*, 3, 14–15, 21–22. Drew Pearson, "Makeshift Armada Invaded Cuba," *Washington Post*, 6 May 1961. Drew Pearson, "How CIA Staged Cuban Fiasco," *Washington Post*, 5 May 1961. Operation in David Patrick Houghton, *The Decision Point: Six Cases in U.S. Foreign Policy Decision Making* (New York: Oxford University Press, 2013), 88–93. No part worked on p. 90.

10. Ike distancing in Sherwin, 126–27. Immediate aftermath in Jones, 126–31.

11. Jones, 98, 122, 124. On Guatemala, see Hitchcock, *The Age of Eisenhower*, 167.

12. On Mongoose, see Rabe, *The Killing Zone*, 74. Vendetta in Jones, *The Bay of Pigs*, 132. Revolt and coup, citing Ted Shackley, on pp. 156–57. Missiles on p. 160. For a Soviet view of the planning, see Fursenko and Naftali, 426.
13. Nick B. Williams, "Cuba: We Must Do It Ourselves," *Los Angeles Times*, 13 August 1961. Convinced of US invasion in Lebow and Stein, *We All Lost the Cold War*, 30–31. On post-9/11 preemptive war, see Martel, *Grand Strategy in Theory and Practice*, 319.
14. Weak in Preston, *American Foreign Relations*, 96–97. Joseph A. Loftus, "Report Is Somber," *New York Times*, 7 June 1961. Kempe, *Berlin 1961*, 175–76, 211, 224–59. Immature on p. 235. Beat the hell on p. 258. Fursenko and Naftali, 349, 367.
15. Vulnerabilities in Waldman, *Vicarious Warfare*, 41.
16. Tad Szulc, "Eisenhower Backs Hemispheric Drive for Development," *New York Times*, 24 February 1960. On some issues with these assumptions, see Joe Renouard, *Human Rights in American Foreign Policy: From the 1960s to the Soviet Collapse* (Philadelphia: University of Pennsylvania Press, 2016), 18.
17. Mike Mansfield, "The Basic Problem of Latin America," *New York Times*, 4 December 1960. Economic and military power in Mark Atwood Lawrence, "Explaining the Rise to Global Power: U.S. Policy toward Asia and Africa since 1941," in Costigliola and Hogan, *America in the World*, 245; and Rebecca Lissner and Mira Rapp-Hooper, *An Open World: How American Can Win the Contest for the Twenty-First-Century Order* (New Haven, CT: Yale University Press, 2020), 46.
18. Chester Bowles, *Promises to Keep: My Years in Public Life, 1941–1969* (New York: Harper & Row, 1971), 253, 343, 344.
19. Goldwater, *Why Not Victory?* 69, 85. Conflation in Grandin, "What Was Containment?" 33–36. JCS in Brands, *Latin America's Cold War*, 33. Contemporary historian Williams, *The Tragedy of American Diplomacy*, 5.
20. Ernesto Che Guevara, "Reminiscences of the Cuban Revolutionary War," in Chaliand, *Guerrilla Strategies*, 172. See also Michelle D. Paranzino, "'Two, Three, Many Vietnams': Che Guevara's Tricontinental Revolutionary Vision" in Parrott and Lawrence, 282–93; and Wright, *Latin America in the Era of the Cuban Revolution and Beyond*, 82. On armed struggle, see Tanya Harmer, "The Cold War in Latin America," in Kalinovsky and Daigle, *The Routledge Handbook of the Cold War*, 140. On Cuba in the American imagination, see Latner, *Cuban Revolution in America*, 7–8, 13, 17.
21. Goldwater, *Conscience of a Conservative*, 95. See also Goldwater, *Why Not Victory?* 91. Collective security and Lemnitzer in Felix Belair, Jr., "Defense Leaders Demand Arms Aid," *New York Times*, 9 June 1961. Links between economic and military aid in Simpson, *Economists with Guns*, 63, 67–68, 70.

22. Grandin, *Empire's Workshop*, 43. Imperial violence on p. 4. On action-reaction, see Brands, 3–4, 7, 9; Rabe, *The Killing Zone*, xxxix; and Wright, 187–88. On strengthening the radicals, see Williams, 4.
23. New Frontier in "Text of Address by Kennedy Accepting Party Nomination," *Washington Post*, 16 July 1960.

CHAPTER 9

1. "Text of Eisenhower's Farewell Address," *New York Times*, 18 January 1961. See also Hemmer, *American Pendulum*, 64.
2. Flexible response in Robert J. McMahon, "US National Security Policy from Eisenhower to Kennedy," in Leffler and Westad, *The Cambridge History of the Cold War*, Vol. I, 303–5; and Trauschweizer, *The Cold War U.S. Army*, 121. On Kennedy's campaigning, supported by Generals Ridgway and Taylor, see Preble, *John F. Kennedy and the Missile Gap*, 76, 147, 161. Calibration in Brands, *The Twilight Struggle*, 59.
3. "Kennedy Hopeful on Russian Amity," *New York Times*, 4 November 1960. Bowles, *Promises to Keep*, 346.
4. "Text of Kennedy's Inaugural Outlining Policies on World Peace and Freedom," *New York Times*, 21 January 1961. Romanticist view in Arthur M. Schlesinger, Jr., *Robert Kennedy and His Times* (Boston: Houghton Mifflin, 1978), 417–18.
5. Symington in Fursenko and Naftali, *Khrushchev's Cold War*, 250. For similar fear-mongering, see p. 254. America's favor in Kaplan, *The Bomb*, 44. Intelligence sources in Craig and Logevall, *America's Cold War*, 175. On gap, see Stephen F. Knott, *Coming to Terms with John F. Kennedy* (Lawrence: University Press of Kansas, 2022), 93–97; and Preble, 8–10, 54–57. Jack Raymond, "Kennedy Defense Study Finds No Evidence of a 'Missile Gap,'" *New York Times*, 7 February 1961. Don Shannon, "Missiles Gap Exists between Russia, U.S.," *Los Angeles Times*, 8 February 1961.
6. Deterrence in Trauschweizer, *Maxwell Taylor's Cold War*, 105. On the political vulnerabilities coming from the Bay of Pigs and their relation to the missile crisis, see Graham T. Allison, *Essence of Decision: Explaining the Cuban Missile Crisis* (Boston: Little, Brown, 1971), 187–88.
7. Rabe argues that both Khrushchev and Castro believed the United States intended to invade Cuba. *The Killing Zone*, 76. On multiple reasons for deploying missiles, see Don Munton and David A. Welch, *The Cuban Missile Crisis: A Concise History*, 2nd ed. (New York: Oxford University Press, 2012), 22–24, 26, 34; and Allison, 40, 41. Khrushchev quoted in Zubok, *A Failed Empire*, 146. On Castro probing limits of risk, see Fursenko and Naftali, 428.
8. Roscoe Drummond, "Red Brinksmanship," *Washington Post*, 17 September 1962. Fursenko and Naftali, 434–64. On Khrushchev wanting to "equalize the strategic balance of power" see Lebow and Stein, *We All Lost*

the Cold War, 39. The earlier 1960 U-2 incident suggested that reputation also was part of the faith-and-fear paradigm. Fursenko and Naftali, 290.

9. On McNamara's support of a "no cities" doctrine, see Gaddis, *The Cold War: A New History*, 79; and Freedman and Michaels, *The Evolution of Nuclear Strategy*, 305–6. Type of threat in Munton and Welch, 53. "Surgical" strikes in Allison, *Essence of Decision*, 124–26. British papers cited in Sherwin, *Gambling with Armageddon*, 346.

10. Air strikes and LeMay in Kaplan, *The Bomb*, 67, 68–69. Turkey exchange on pp. 73–74; and Allison, 43. Failure in Sherwin, 276. JFK's skepticism of the chiefs in Schlesinger, *Robert Kennedy and His Times*, 449–50; and Munton and Welch, *The Cuban Missile Crisis*, 98. Of note, "quarantine" was the administration's euphemism for a blockade, which is what it actually imposed. Yet a blockade was legally an act of war, and by that point the administration wanted to keep the crisis in hand.

11. Miscalculation in Knott, 99. Political consequences in Lebow and Stein, 98; and Sherwin, 272. McNamara quoted in Allison, *Essence*, 131. Taylor in Kaplan, *The Bomb*, 67. Credibility in Layne, *The Peace of Illusions*, 127. Humiliation in Fredrik Logevall, *Choosing War: The Lost Chance for Peace and the Escalation of War in Vietnam* (Berkeley: University of California Press, 1999), 244.

12. Hanson W. Baldwin, "Will There Be War?" *New York Times*, 28 October 1962.

13. "A Time for Diplomacy," *New York Times*, 28 October 1962. McNamara quoted in Stoker, *Why America Loses Wars*, 121. Control in Sherwin, 39. Beijing in Lüthi, *The Sino-Soviet Split*, 227. Diplomacy in Morgenthau, *Politics among Nations*, 539–40.

14. "An Appeal for Détente," in Engel, Lawrence, and Preston, *America in the World*, 253–54. Leffler, *For the Soul of Mankind*, 182.

15. LTBT in Goedde, *The Politics of Peace*, 88–93; and Loth, *Overcoming the Cold War*, 77–78. Goldwater, *Conscience of a Conservative*, 113. Baiting in Goldwater, *Why Not Victory?* 162. On critics, see Lebovic, *Flawed Logics*, 44–46; and Rubinson, *Redefining Science*, 93–119. Of note, China also criticized limitations. See Lüthi, *The Sino-Soviet Split*, 254. Dirksen quoted in Knott, *Coming to Terms with John F. Kennedy*, 118. "Chiefs Say Soviet Will Test in Air," *New York Times*, 4 September 1963.

16. Superiority in Gavin, *Nuclear Weapons and American Grand Strategy*, 59. Political calculations in Miller, *Grand Strategy from Truman to Trump*, 115. NPT on p. 132. Eve Edstrom, "LBJ Urges Ratification Of A-Treaty," *Washington Post*, 10 July 1968. Kahn in Freedman and Michaels, 333. Rohan Mukherjee, "Nuclear Ambiguity and International Status: India in the Eighteen-Nation Committee on Disarmament, 1962–1969," in Bhagavan, *India and the Cold War*, 127, 130–31, 145.

17. Sabotage in Rabe, *The Killing Zone*, 77, 79. Soviet weapons procurement in Haslam, *Russia's Cold War*, 210. Kennan, meanwhile, worried that "if

we acted as though war were inevitable, we would help to make it that." Kennan, *The Kennan Diaries*, 402.
18. Economic reform in Edwin L. Dale, Jr., "The Cold War That Is Only Beginning," *New York Times*, 22 May 1960. Reformist intervention in Macdonald, *Adventures in Chaos*, 44. Modernization and civilizing mission in Michael E. Latham, "Modernization, International History and the Cold War World," and Michael Adas, "Modernization Theory and the American Revival of the Scientific and Technological Standards of Social Achievement and Human Worth," in Engerman, Gilman, et al., *Staging Growth*, 6, 35.
19. JFK and promoting reform in Kapstein, *Seeds of Stability*, 48, 50, 192. Alliance for Progress in Rabe, 86–88. Values and paternalism in Lorenzini, *Global Development*, 64, 66. Radicalism in Latham, *The Right Kind of Revolution*, 126. Awaken in Grandin, *Empire's Workshop*, 49.
20. On the Peace Corps, see Elizabeth Cobbs Hoffman, "Decolonization, the Cold War, and the Foreign Policy of the Peace Corps," in Hahn and Heiss, *Empire and Revolution*, 123–48. Faith in the state in Lorenzini, 6. Community development in Latham, *Modernization as Ideology*, 112. Military autocracies in David Johnson Lee, *The Ends of Modernization: Nicaragua and the United States in the Cold War Era* (Ithaca, NY: Cornell University Press, 2021), 6, 32. Paternalism and racism in Latham, 127, 128. US official on p. 105. Ryan M. Irwin, "Decolonization and the Cold War," in Kalinovsky and Daigle, *The Routledge Handbook of the Cold War*, 91. Universalistic in Brands, *Latin America's Cold War*, 22.
21. On markets, see McMahon, *Colonialism and the Cold War*, 143; and Leebaert, *Grand Improvisation*, 189. Roscoe Drummond, "Alliance for Progress Provides Plan but No Working Machinery," *Los Angeles Times*, 16 August 1962. Security in Latham, *The Right Kind of Revolution*, 131. CIA's Douglas Blaufarb quoted in Kapstein, *Seeds of Stability*, 165.
22. On modernization, see Latham, *Modernization as Ideology*, 4–5, 6; and Nils Gilman, "Modernization Theory, the Highest Stage of American Intellectual History," in Engerman, Gilman, et al., *Staging Growth*, 61–62. Competing models in Lorenzini, 68. Enlightened in Rabe, *The Killing Zone*, 91. Backyard and blow up on p. 90. See also Chapman, *Remaking the World*, 30. Economic gap in Mark H. Haefele, "Walt Rostow's Stages of Economic Growth: Ideas and Action," in Engerman, Gilman, et al., 91.
23. Rostow quoted in Little, *American Orientalism*, 195; and Hanhimäki and Westad, *The Cold War*, 352. Would not survive in James Bassett, "Cold War Victory, Vital, Tower Says," *Los Angeles Times*, 1 December 1961.
24. Land reform in Kapstein, *Seeds of Stability*, 171, 175. Threat in Schlesinger and Kinzer, *Bitter Fruit*, 77, 88. Latham, *The Right Kind of Revolution*, 167.

25. Militarization in Herbert L. Matthews, "When Generals Take Over in Latin America," *New York Times*, 9 September 1962. See also Grandin, 48, 102. Brian D'Haeseleer, *The Salvadoran Crucible: The Failure of US Counterinsurgency in El Salvador, 1979–1992* (Lawrence: University Press of Kansas, 2017), 47–48. Decade in Chapman, *Remaking the World*, 30. Laboratory in Sarah Ross, "Community Development in Cold War Guatemala," in Field, Krepp, and Pettinà, *Latin America in the Global Cold War*, 124. Terrorism in Wright, *Latin America in the Era of the Cuban Revolution and Beyond*, 189.

26. Political tools in Lorenzini, *Global Development*, 13, 15. Control in Latham, *The Right Kind of Revolution*, 6; and Rabe, *The Killing Zone*, 92–93, 95. On limits of the Alliance, see Parker, *Hearts, Minds, Voices*, 168. Franklin A. Lindsay, "Unconventional Warfare," *Foreign Affairs*, Vol. 40, No. 2 (January 1962), 266, 268.

27. Will Kern, "Reservists Toughened for New, Deadly Role," *Los Angeles Times*, 9 September 1962. See also Engelhardt, *The End of Victory Culture*, 165. Alasdair Spark, "The Soldier at the Heart of the War: The Myth of the Green Beret in the Popular Culture of the Vietnam Era," *Journal of American Studies*, Vol. 18, No. 1 (April 1984): 29–48. The idea of armed social workers persisted. See Julian D. Alford, "Operational Design for ISAF in Afghanistan: A Primer," *Joint Forces Quarterly* (Second Quarter, 2009): 92–98.

28. Nucleus in House, *A Military History of the Cold War, 1962–1991*, 35. On *foco*, see Michelle Getchell, "Cuba, the USSR, and the Non-Aligned Movement," in Field, Krepp, and Pettinà, *Latin America in the Global Cold War*, 160; Paranzino, "'Two, Three, Many Vietnams,'" 299–300; and Wright, 83, 94. Che's demise in Rabe, 82–83.

29. On 1958 crisis, see Rapp-Hooper, *Shields of the Republic*, 68–69. Ulbricht and refugee crisis in Kempe, *Berlin 1961*, xxi, 4, 47, 117, 140. Uncontrolled border, citing Ambassador Mikhail Pervukhin, in Gaddis, *Now We Know*, 143. Manpower drain in Goedde, *The Politics of Peace*, 119. East German survival in Fursenko and Naftali, *Khrushchev's Cold War*, 217. Crisis and checkpoint confrontation in Carter, *Forging the Shield*, 406–27.

30. White House advisors, Adenauer, and Khrushchev in Fursenko and Naftali, 384–85. Vienna on p. 365.

31. Acheson quoted in Gaddis, *Now We Know*, 146. See also Kempe, *Berlin 1961*, 140–45, 275. Kissinger, *Diplomacy*, 593; and quoted in Kempe, 303.

32. Overreact in Kempe, 312. JFK quoted in Loth, *Overcoming the Cold War*, 63. "Text of Kennedy Speech on Berlin," *Los Angeles Times*, 26 July 1961. Limited-strike planning in "Thinking the Unthinkable," in Engel, Lawrence, and Preston, *America in the World*, 242–44; and Kaplan, *The Bomb*, 50–53.

33. Brandt in Goedde, 193. Atomic Death in Benjamin Ziemann, "German angst? Debating Cold War anxieties in West Germany, 1945–90," in Grant and Ziemann, *Understanding the Imaginary War*, 123–24. On NATO, see Carter, *Forging the Shield*, 240–41; Gavin, *Nuclear Weapons and American Grand Strategy*, 119–20; and Biddle, "Shield and Sword," in Bacevich, *The Long War*, 168. Instability in Sayle, *Enduring Alliance*, 118. Murrey Marder, "U.S. Hopes for NATO Bolstering," *Washington Post*, 23 July 1961.
34. Testing ground in William J. Jorden, "Kennedy Pledges Support to Laos," *New York Times*, 16 March 1961. W. H. Lawrence, "Kennedy Alerts Nation on Laos," *New York Times*, 24 March 1961. Bowles, *Promises to Keep*, 335. On Laos's relation to Berlin, see Lebow and Stein, *We All Lost the Cold War*, 22–23. Moscow's stance toward Laos in Fursenko and Naftali, 323–29. For a fuller treatment, see Seth Jacobs, *The Universe Unraveling: American Foreign Policy in Cold War Laos* (Ithaca, NY: Cornell University Press, 2012).
35. Hitchcock, *The Age of Eisenhower*, 196–97. Kissinger quoted in David J. Rothkopf, *National Insecurity: American Leadership in an Age of Fear* (New York: PublicAffairs, 2014), 184. Enslaved in Jack Raymond, "Pledge to SEATO Restated by U.S.," *New York Times*, 26 May 1960.
36. Paul Grimes, "Nehru Denounces Neutrality Foes," *New York Times*, 16 January 1960. See also Andrew J. Rotter, "Feeding Beggars: Class, Caste, and Status in Indo-U.S. Relations, 1947–1964," in Appy, *Cold War Constructions*, 70. To UN in McMahon, *The Cold War on the Periphery*, 173. Cold War fears on p. 152. Nonalignment in Engerman, *The Price of Aid*, 49; and Chapman, *Remaking the World*, 44–45, 50. Fears of Soviet Influence in Pallavi Raghavan, "Journeys of Discovery: The State Visits of Jawaharlal Nehru and Liaquat Al Khan to the United States," in Bhagavan, *India and the Cold War*, 19–20, 28. SEATO in Lüthi, *Cold Wars*, 30. On local issues, see Andrew J. Rotter, "South Asia," in Immerman and Goedde, *The Oxford Handbook of the Cold War*, 212, 215–19.
37. On Washington's stance toward India, see McMahon, 38, 40, 49–50. Chinese aggression in Raymond, "Pledge to SEATO Restated by U.S." Flirtation with China in Robert Trumbull, "New Blow for SEATO," *New York Times*, 27 November 1962.
38. Reshaping institutions in Shawn F. McHale, *The First Vietnam War: Violence, Sovereignty, and the Fracture of the South 1945–1956* (New York: Cambridge University Press, 2021), 2, 14–15.

CHAPTER 10

1. Groping in Marshall D. Shulman, "A Continuing Challenge," *New York Times*, 5 April 1964. On modernization assumptions, see Latham, *The*

Right Kind of Revolution, 47–49, 53, 61. Stabilizers in Kapstein, *Seeds of Stability*, vii–viii.

2. Security in Latham, 22. Unchallenged in Lorenzini, *Global Development*, 7. Williams, *The Tragedy of American Diplomacy*, 14, 15, 66.

3. Competing visions of development in Simpson, *Economists with Guns*, 4. Direct competition in Peggy and Pierre Street, "Battle in the 'Peaceful' Cold War," *New York Times*, 23 October 1960. Mao in Brazinsky, *Winning the Third World*, 306–7. On the Cambodian genocide, see Alexander Laban Hinton, *Why Did They Kill? Cambodia in the Shadow of Genocide* (Berkeley: University of California Press, 2004). Development as a weapon in David C. Engerman, "West Meets East: The Center for International Studies and Indian Economic Development," in Engerman, Gilman, et al., *Staging Growth*, 200, 202.

4. Alternative in Guan, *Southeast Asia's Cold War*, 62–63. Courting aid in Chapman, *Remaking the World*, 43. As Latham notes, locals' "diverse visions of development did not fit easily into the more rigid U.S. conceptions of modernization." *The Right Kind of Revolution*, 67.

5. Conference in Lüthi, *Cold Wars*, 278–85; and Bevins, *The Jakarta Method*, 53–59. On control, see Bradley R. Simpson, "Southeast Asia in the Cold War," in McMahon, *The Cold War in the Third World*, 48. Common strategies in Guan, 78–79. "Excerpts from the Opening Speeches at the Asian-African Conference in Bandung," *New York Times*, 20 April 1955. China's goals at Bandung in Brazinsky, *Winning the Third World*, 76, 100.

6. Issues in Jason C. Parker, "Small Victory, Missed Chance: The Eisenhower Administration, the Bandung Conference, and the Turning of the Cold War," in Statler and Johns, *The Eisenhower Administration, the Third World, and the Globalization of the Cold War*, 156. Wright in Duncan White, *Cold Warriors: Writers Who Waged the Literary Cold War* (New York: Custom House, 2019), 417. Links to Taiwan in Parker, *Hearts, Minds, Voices*, 80. Eisenhower administration in Borstelman, *The Cold War and the Color Line*, 96; and Westad, *The Global Cold War*, 103. Disarmament in Yaqub, "The Cold War and the Middle East," in McMahon, 14. Indifference in "Powell, Dulles Differ on Bandung Versions," *Washington Post*, 6 May 1955. Collapse of spirit in Lüthi, *Cold Wars*, 281.

7. Bowles, *Promises to Keep*, 247. Sufficient in Bevins, 41. Inspiration in Anton Harder, "Promoting Development without Struggle: Sino-Indian Relations in the 1950s," in Bhagavan, *India and the Cold War*, 166, 167. On Nehru and nonalignment, see Lüthi, *Cold Wars*, 288–89. Nicholas J. Cull and B. Theo Mazumdar argue that the Soviets "actively sought to manipulate" Third World nonalignment, but the same could be said of the Americans. "Propaganda in the Cold War," in Kalinovsky and Daigle,

The Routledge Handbook of the Cold War, 331. For instance, see Guan, *Southeast Asia's Cold War*, 85.
8. Nehru and model in Engerman, "West Meets East," 204–5. Tito in Applebaum, *Iron Curtain*, 254, 392, 412; and Sixsmith, *The War of Nerves*, 123–24. Cominform in Noel Malcolm, *Bosnia: A Short History* (London: Papermac, 1996), 194. A. H. Raskin, "Meany Says Nehru and Tito Aid Reds," *New York Times*, 14 December 1955. Truman quoted in Mark Atwood Lawrence, "The Rise and Fall of Nonalignment," in McMahon, *The Cold War in the Third World*, 139. On Bush, see Stephen Tankel, *With Us and against Us: How America's Partners Help and Hinder the War on Terror* (New York: Columbia University Press, 2018), 3, 19.
9. State Department in Raghavan, "Journeys of Discovery," 21. NSC in Lissner, *Wars of Revelation*, 53. On Brazil, see Stella Krepp, "Brazil and Non-Alignment," in Field, Krepp, and Pettinà, *Latin America in the Global Cold War*, 103; and Thomas E. Skidmore, *The Politics of Military Rule in Brazil, 1964–1985* (New York: Oxford University Press, 1988).
10. A. M. Rosenthal, "India's Economy Now at a Critical Stage," *New York Times*, 29 September 1957. Radicalism in Latham, *The Right Kind of Revolution*, 70. Economic failure in Priya Chacko, "Indira Ghandi, the 'Long 1970s,' and the Cold War," in Bhagavan, *India and the Cold War*, 182. Poverty in Nick Cullather, *The Hungry World: America's Cold War Battle against Poverty in Asia* (Cambridge, MA: Harvard University Press, 2010), 134, 135, 139. Economic offensive in Engerman, *The Price of Aid*, 126.
11. Irwin Suall, "Alternative to Communism," *New York Times*, 16 August 1961. Evil in Williams, *The Tragedy of American Diplomacy*, 129. Defensive expansion in Lamberton Harper, *The Cold War*, 23. Little choice in Parker, *Hearts, Minds, Voices*, 84, 87.
12. On disarmament and development, see Krepp, 104; and Waheguru Pal Singh Sidhu, "The Accidental Global Peacekeeper," in Bhagavan, *India and the Cold War*, 93. Drew Pearson, "Is Nasser Acting Hitlerish with Diplomats?" *Washington Merry-Go-Round*, 19 September 1956. Nasser in Chapman, *Remaking the World*, 82; and Yaqub, *Containing Arab Nationalism*, 32. Engulfment in Guan, *Southeast Asia's Cold War*, 80. Repressive in Latham, 90.
13. On partition, see Lüthi, *Cold Wars*, 164, 165. Internal issues in Sugata Bose and Ayesha Jalal, *Modern South Asia: History, Culture, Political Economy*, 2nd ed. (New York: Routledge, 1997), 158, 202. American responses to India in McMahon, *The Cold War on the Periphery*, 343–44.
14. Instability in McMahon, 9, 19–20. A. M. Rosenthal, "Communism's No. 1 Target in Asia," *New York Times*, 20 November 1955. Warmongering in

A. M. Rosenthal, "India: A Case History in the 'Cold War,'" *New York Times*, 5 February 1956.

15. On the lead-up to the 1962 war, see Srinath Raghavan, "A Missed Opportunity? The Nehru-Zhou Enlai Summit of 1960," in Bhagavan, 100–125. Arrogance and JFK in Chapman, *Remaking the World*, 58–60. Strengthening ties in Engerman, *The Price of Aid*, 207–9. China in Brazinsky, *Winning the Third World*, 186–91. Advisor Robert Komer quoted in McMahon, *The Cold War on the Periphery*, 287.

16. Khrushchev in Hanhimäki and Westad, *The Cold War*, 358–60. Overextension in Vladislav Zubok, "Cold War Strategies/Power and Culture—East: Sources of Soviet Conduct Reconsidered," in Immerman and Goedde, *The Oxford Handbook of the Cold War*, 311–12. White House anxieties in Latham, *The Right Kind of Revolution*, 41, 42; and McMahon, 219–20. NSAM 124 in Heuser, *War*, 31. Anticolonial nationalism in Raghavan, "Journeys of Discovery," 2. On Wilson, see David Steigerwald, "The Reclamation of Woodrow Wilson?" in *Paths to Power: The Historiography of American Foreign Relations to 1941*, ed. Michael J. Hogan (New York: Cambridge University Press, 2000), 174; and Manela, *The Wilsonian Moment*, 5, 10.

17. British report in Hajimu, *Cold War Crucible*, 74. Khrushchev in Judge and Langdon, *The Cold War*, 360. Goldwater, *Why Not Victory?* 83.

18. "Moscow's 'New' Line," *New York Times*, 27 July 1953. On Soviet development, see Lorenzini, *Global Development*, 42–43, 48.

19. Peace-building in Mitchell and Rey, *War and Religion*, 85. Castroite in Grow, *U.S. Presidents and Latin American Interventions*, 80. Background in Rabe, *The Killing Zone*, 13, 97–104. Another Cuba in Grow, 80.

20. Exaggerated in Grow, 81. Political situation in Kyle Longley, "U.S. Troops as an Instrument in Foreign Policy: The Dominican Republic in 1965 and Grenada in 1983," in Thompson and Frentzos, *The Routledge Handbook of American Military and Diplomatic History*, 297–300. Military operation in House, *A Military History of the Cold War, 1962–1991*, 60–66. 1990s on p. 67.

21. Frank Church, "How Many Dominican Republics and Vietnams Can We Take On?" *New York Times*, 28 November 1965. Of note, Nixon argued that "a democratic government was probably not the best kind for Indonesia" because the communists were so well organized. See Bevins, *The Jakarta Method*, 64–65.

22. "Johnson Proffers Vast Dominican Aid Program," *Los Angeles Times*, 16 May 1965. Far East Command in Birtle, *U.S. Army Counterinsurgency and Contingency Operations Doctrine*, 129. On "good governance," see Hazelton, *Bullets Not Ballots*, 8. Thanks to Professor Pablo Ben, San Diego State University, for sharing his ideas on the United States as an armed branch of capitalism.

23. Breeding ground in Kapstein, *Seeds of Stability*, 40. On reformist interventionism, see pp. 52, 72. Goldwater, *Why Not Victory?* 171. On Goldwater, no being alone in his critique, see Kapstein, 73.
24. Kennan and Acheson in Rabe, 24, 28. On Kennan, see also Brenda Gayle Plummer, "Race and the Cold War," in Immerman and Goedde, *The Oxford Handbook of the Cold War*, 503.
25. Jerry A. Rose, "The Peasant Is the Key to Vietnam," *New York Times*, 8 April 1962. Edward M. Kennedy, "Hungry Peasants Hold Latin America's Fate," *Los Angeles Times*, 26 September 1961.Victims or revolutionaries in Johnson Lee, *The Ends of Modernization*, 69, 78. Villages in Cullather, *The Hungry World*, 74, 78. See also Nick Cullather, "The War on the Peasant: The United States and the Third World," in McMahon, *The Cold War in the Third World*, 192–207; and Westad, *The Global Cold War*, 400.
26. Land reform as a "weapon" in Kapstein, *Seeds of Stability*, 106, 95. Schlesinger, *Robert Kennedy and His Times*, 463, 466. Rostow in Gaddis, *Strategies of Containment*, 222. See also Schlesinger, 460. On security emphasis, see Richard A. Hunt, *Pacification: The American Struggle for Vietnam's Hearts and Minds* (Boulder, CO: Westview, 1995), 15.
27. On paradoxes, see Del Pero, "Incompatible Universalisms," in Kalinovsky and Daigle, *The Routledge Handbook of the Cold War*, 6; Cullather, *The Hungry World*, 8, 79; and Rabe, *The Killing Zone*, 111. Violent anticommunism in Bevins, 5–6. McCarthyism in White, *In Search of History*, 396.
28. Problems with development in Lorenzini, *Global Development*, 87. Imperialism in O'Riordan, *Understanding the Cold War*, 206–7; and Chapman, *Remaking the World*, 123. On counterinsurgency, see Simpson, "Southeast Asia in the Cold War," 59; and Hazelton, *Bullets Not Ballots*, 2, 5. For a comparison to similar problems in America's more recent wars, see Buddhika Jayamaha, "When Grunts Complain," Bacevich and Sjursen, *Paths of Dissent*, 123.

CHAPTER 11

1. McNamara, *In Retrospect*, 30.
2. Fears in Hemmer, *American Pendulum*, 74. Nolting quoted in Brazinsky, *Winning the Third World*, 243. McNamara in Houghton, *The Decision Point*, 152.
3. Conquer in Harry G. Summers, Jr., *On Strategy: A Critical Analysis of the Vietnam War* (Novato, CA: Presidio, 1982), 87. See also Lüthi, *Cold Wars*, 160. Ho in Chapman, *Remaking the World*, 146. Nationalists in Lowe, *Savage Continent*, 268. Fear of China in Brazinsky, *Winning the Third World*, 3.

4. On LBJ, see Gaddis, *Strategies of Containment*, 210. Barry Goldwater, "If Communism Triumphs It Will Be Because We Chose Surrender," *Los Angeles Times*, 23 April 1961. On image, see David W. P. Elliott, "Wag the Dog: Vietnam and the Cold War," in *The Cold War—Reassessments*, ed. Arthur L. Rosenbaum and Chae-Jin Lee (Claremont, CA: Keck Center for International and Strategic Studies, 2000), 66.
5. Regroupments and control in Karl Hack, *The Malayan Emergency* (New York: Cambridge University Press, 2022), 5. Theater-wide in Leebaert, *Grand Improvisation*, 128. On the British campaign, see House, *A Military History of the Cold War, 1944–1962*, 304–16.
6. Local conditions in Craig and Logevall, *America's Cold War*, 277. China in "Malaya Says Reds Halt War, Try Subversion," *Washington Post*, 28 March 1959. MCP and Chin Peng in Guan, *Southeast Asia's Cold War*, 19, 41. Ethnic aspects in Donald Mackay, *The Malayan Emergency, 1948–60: The Domino That Stood* (London: Brassey's, 1997), 21, 42. On the emergency receiving a "sympathetic" reading among Americans, see D'Haeseleer, *The Salvadoran Crucible*, 24–26.
7. JFK from 1954 in Knott, *Coming to Terms with John F. Kennedy*, 127. Kennedy in "What Next? 'Falling Dominoes,'" *New York Times*, 25 August 1963. On expansion see Schlesinger, *Robert Kennedy and His Times*, 725; and Chapman, *Remaking the World*, 165.
8. Marc J. Selverstone, *The Kennedy Withdrawal: Camelot and the American Commitment to Vietnam* (Cambridge, MA: Harvard University Press, 2022), 46, 136. On Malaya, see Ngoei, *Arc of Containment*, 9, 67, 82.
9. Walter Lippmann, "The 'Domino Theory' Seems to Be Working in Asia—but in Reverse," *Los Angeles Times*, 25 April 1965. De Gaulle in Logevall, *Choosing War*, 176. John Foster Dulles on despotism in Hanhimäki and Westad, *The Cold War*, 213. Asian dominoes in Hitchcock, *The Age of Eisenhower*, 177. On JCS views at this time, see Brazinsky, *Winning the Third World*, 58. Hypnosis in Tuchman, *The March of Folly*, 251.
10. Chain reaction from Dulles in Fredrik Logevall, "The Indochina Wars and the Cold War, 1945–1975," in Leffler and Westad, *The Cambridge History of the Cold War*, Vol. II, 288. On sovereignty, see Larry Berman, "From Intervention to Disengagement: The United States in Vietnam," in *Foreign Military Intervention: The Dynamics of Protracted Conflict*, ed. Ariel E. Levite, Bruce W. Jentleson, and Larry Berman (New York: Columbia University Press, 1992), 26. Civil war in Carolyn Woods Eisenberg, *Fire and Rain: Nixon, Kissinger, and the Wars in Southeast Asia* (New York: Oxford University Press, 2023), 18.
11. Martin Evans, *Algeria: France's Undeclared War* (New York: Oxford University Press, 2012), xii, xvi, 183, 335, 337, 349. House, *A Military History of the Cold War, 1944–1962*, 296–97.

12. Dirty and reduced in Andrew Pham, *The Eaves of Heaven: A Life in Three Wars* (New York: Three Rivers, 2008), 55–57. James Walker Trullinger, Jr., *Village at War: An Account of Revolution in Vietnam* (New York: Longman, 1980), 61, 98. On Greene, see White, *Cold Warriors*, 368.
13. On US relationship with France, see Pierre Asselin, "Fueling the World Revolution: Vietnamese Communist Internationalism, 1954–1975," in Parrott and Lawrence, *The Tricontinental Revolution*, 117. Instability in Stoker, *Why America Loses Wars*, 160; and Bradley and Dudziak, *Making the Forever War*, 87. On Americans assuming a fundamental weakness in Vietnamese societies, see Mark Bradley, "Slouching toward Bethlehem: Culture, Diplomacy, and the Origins of the Cold War in Vietnam," in Appy, *Cold War Constructions*, 27. Principles in David Galula, *Pacification in Algeria* (Santa Monica, CA: Rand Corporation, 1963, 2006), 246–47. On issues with Galula's writings, see Grégor Mathias, *Galula in Algeria: Counterinsurgency Practice versus Theory* (Santa Barbara, CA: Praeger, 2011).
14. Laboratory in Trauschweizer, *Maxwell Taylor's Cold War*, 110. Fishel in James M. Carter, "'Shaky as All Hell': The U.S. and Nation Building in South Vietnam," in Thompson and Frentzos, *The Routledge Handbook of American Military and Diplomatic History*, 254. Pentagon in Khong, *Analogies at War*, 94. On Diem, see Chapman, *Remaking the World*, 156–58.
15. On issues with French civilizing mission, see Michael G. Vann and Liz Clarke, *The Great Hanoi Rat Hunt: Empire, Disease, and Modernity in French Colonial Vietnam* (New York: Oxford University Press, 2019), 8, 15, 16, 56. Nationalism in McHale, *The First Vietnam War*, 3–5. Manipulation in Kathryn C. Statler, "Building a Colony: South Vietnam and the Eisenhower Administration, 1953–1961," in Statler and Johns, *The Eisenhower Administration, the Third World, and the Globalization of the Cold War*, 102. Development in Ekbladh, *The Great American Mission*, 10. Test case in Mueller, *The Stupidity of War*, 47.
16. Internationalism in Asselin, "Fueling the World Revolution," 115, 122, 136. Client state in Statler, "Building a Colony," 101, 110; and Jessica M. Chapman, "Vietnam and the Global Cold War," in Kalinovsky and Daigle, *The Routledge Handbook of the Cold War*, 109, 110. On "contested nationalism" and Saigon authoritarianism, see Heather Marie Stur, *Saigon at War: South Vietnam and the Global Sixties* (New York: Cambridge University Press, 2020), 13, 17, 27, 31. Corruption and land reform in Pham, *The Eaves of Heaven*, 65, 69.
17. Foreign assistance in Kapstein, *Seeds of Stability*, 136. On Huk support, see Hajimu, *Cold War Crucible*, 272–73. On the Huk rebellion, see Collen Woods, *Freedom Incorporated: Anticommunism and Philippine Independence in the Age of Decolonization* (Ithaca, NY: Cornell University Press,

2020); Lessons from Americans in Macdonald, *Adventures in Chaos*, 181–84.

18. Stimulate in Mark Moyar, *A Question of Command: Counterinsurgency from the Civil War to Iraq* (New Haven, CT: Yale University Press, 2009), 107. Margins in Kapstein, 155. Contradictions in Guan, *Southeast Asia's Cold War*, 65. Magsaysay in House, *A Military History of the Cold War, 1944–1962*, 249–55. Civic action and security in Christopher Capozzola, *Bound by War: How the United States and the Philippines Built America's First Pacific Century* (New York: Basic, 2020), 248–49.

19. Ed Meagher, "U.S. General in Viet-Nam Optimistic," *Washington Post*, 6 March 1963. Strategic hamlets in Peter Arnett, "Viet-Nam Defenses Imperiled," *Washington Post*, 30 March 1963. Warren Unna, "Peasant Is Uncertain Element of Viet-Nam," *Washington Post*, 19 May 1963. McNamara in Ekbladh, *The Great American Mission*, 201. On strategic hamlets, see House, *A Military History of the Cold War, 1962–1991*, 112–13; Latham, *The Right Kind of Revolution*, 140–41; and Latham, *Modernization as Ideology*, 152, 154.

20. Vulnerable and underdevelopment in Richard N. Goodwin, *Triumph or Tragedy: Reflections on Vietnam* (New York: Random House, 1966), 14. External aggression in Khong, *Analogies at War*, 233–34. Control in J. C. Wylie, *Military Strategy: A General Theory of Power Control* (Annapolis, MD: Naval Institute Press, 1967, 1989), 41, 66, 89. See also Echevarria, *War's Logic*, 136–37. On control and power, see Waltz, *Theory of International Politics*, 189, 191.

21. Advisors in House, *A Military History of the Cold War, 1962–1991*, 118. Unknowable in Goodwin, *Triumph or Tragedy*, 12. On cultural terrain, see Christian Tripodi, *The Unknown Enemy: Counterinsurgency and the Illusion of Control* (New York: Cambridge University Press, 2021), 2, 19, 135. Thomas Powers, "Ten Thousand Mile Mistake," *London Review of Books*, 18 February 2021.

22. Bowles, *Promises to Keep*, 404, 417. Values in Belmonte, *Selling the American Way*, 2. See also Nathan J. Citino, "Modernization and Development," in Kalinovsky and Daigle, *The Routledge Handbook of the Cold War*, 123–24. On LBJ, see Bevins, *The Jakarta Method*, 106; and Borstelman, *The Cold War and the Color Line*, 173.

23. American boys in Chapman, *Remaking the World*, 170. Jim VandeHei, "Bush Calls Democracy Terror's Antidote," *Washington Post*, 9 March 2005. See also Little, *American Orientalism*, 8. Contest over values in Brands, *The Twilight Struggle*, 25; and Andrew J. Bacevich, *The Age of Illusions: How America Squandered Its Cold War Victory* (New York: Metropolitan, 2020), 112.

24. Robert B. Semple, Jr., "Dr. King Scores Poverty Budget," *New York Times*, 16 December 1966. Summers, *On Strategy*, 171.

25. LBJ in Frank Costigliola, "US Foreign Policy from Kennedy to Johnson," in Leffler and Westad, *The Cambridge History of the Cold War*, Vol. II, 126; and Khong, *Analogies at War*, 49. Credibility on p. 57. See also Stoker, *Why America Loses Wars*, 220; Fredrik Logevall, *The Origins of the Vietnam War* (Harlow: Pearson Education, 2001), 45–46; and Levering, *The Cold War*, 125. Pressing on in Logevall, *Embers of War*, 710. Rusk in Berman, "From Intervention to Disengagement," 40. Soldiers dying in Brands, *The Devil We Knew*, 28.
26. McNamara, *In Retrospect*, 107. Signaling in Lebovic, *The Limits of U.S. Military Capability*, 129. Humphrey and credibility in Craig and Logevall, *America's Cold War*, 234, 275–76. Humphrey actually believed the administration could cut losses in 1965, the "year of minimum political risk." Local leaders in Gaddis, *The Cold War: A New History*, 129–38.
27. James R. McDonough, *Platoon Leader* (Novato, CA: Presidio, 1985), 92. Marine Samuel. B. Griffith quoted in Hong, *A Violent Peace*, 139. Civilian noncombatants in Tirman, *The Deaths of Others*, 123, 128. Spirit in Stur, *Saigon at War*, 75.
28. "Excerpts from Senate Exchange on Vietnam War," *New York Times*, 26 April 1967. On concerns about Vietnam damaging US standing abroad, see Engelhardt, *The End of Victory Culture*, 196.
29. On US military strategy, see Gregory A. Daddis, *Westmoreland's War: Reassessing American Strategy in Vietnam* (New York: Oxford University Press, 2014). Inability to build capable local army forces Pham, *The Eaves of Heaven*, 85, 108, 116. Will in Goodwin, *Triumph or Tragedy*, 53.
30. Lee Lescaze, "U.S. and Vietnam: Test in Battle, Tension at the Top," *Washington Post*, 11 February 1968. LBJ in James H. Lebovic, *Planning to Fail: The US Wars in Vietnam, Iraq, and Afghanistan* (New York: Oxford University Press, 2019), 62. On the Tet offensive, see William Thomas Allison, *The Tet Offensive: A Brief History with Documents* (New York: Routledge, 2008). For an overview of the antiwar movement, see Penny Lewis, *Hardhats, Hippies, and Hawks: The Vietnam Antiwar Movement as Myth and Memory* (Ithaca, NY: Cornell University Press, 2013).
31. John Wayne, "His Hat Is Off to 'Green Berets,'" *Los Angeles Times*, 28 January 1968. Renata Adler, "'Green Berets' as Viewed by John Wayne," *New York Times*, 20 June 1968. Kevin Thomas, John Wayne, "'Green Berets' in Multiples," *Los Angeles Times*, 3 July 1968. On the film and reactions to it, see Kobes Du Mez, *Jesus and John Wayne*, 54–59.
32. Peter Manseau, "Fifty Years Ago, a Rag-Tag Group of Acid-Dropping Activists Tried to 'Levitate' the Pentagon," *Smithsonian Magazine*, 20 October 2017. Cost tolerance in Lissner, *Wars of Revelation*, 13. "Hoover Says Reds Use Black Power," *New York Times*, 6 January 1968. See also Feldman, *Manufacturing Hysteria*, 284; and Whitfield, *The Culture of the*

Cold War, 65. LBJ in Bradley and Dudziak, *Making the Forever War*, 71. Consensus in Craig and Logevall, 242.

33. Mortal danger in Craig and Logevall, 242. Clifford quoted in Leslie H. Gelb with Richard K. Betts, *The Irony of Vietnam: The System Worked* (Washington, DC: Brookings Institution, 1979), 176. See also Lissner, *Wars of Revelation*, 91. Soviets in Westad, *The Cold War*, 336.
34. Ties in Ngoei, *Arc of Containment*, 10. Purges and perpetrators in Geoffrey B. Robinson, *The Killing Season: A History of the Indonesian Massacres, 1965–66* (Princeton, NJ: Princeton University Press, 2018), 4–7. Death estimates on pp. 120–21.
35. McNamara in Bevins, 160. Kill lists on p. 156. On US attitudes, see Simpson, *Economists with Guns*, 172–74, 189–90. See also Guan, *Southeast Asia's Cold War*, 120–24; and Chamberlin, *The Cold War's Killing Fields*, chapter 8.
36. Self-determination in Daniel H. Weiss, *In That Time: Michael O'Donnell and the Tragic Era of Vietnam* (New York: PublicAffairs, 2019), 120, 161. Deaths in Eisenberg, *Fire and Rain*, 41.

CHAPTER 12

1. Sharp quoted in Michael E. Weaver, *The Air War in Vietnam* (Lubbock: Texas Tech University Press, 2022), 274. On target selections, see Brian D. Laslie, *Air Power's Lost Crusade: The American Air Wars of Vietnam* (Lanham, MD: Rowman & Littlefield, 2021), 67–71.
2. Objectives in Mark Clodfelter, *The Limits of Airpower: The American Bombing of North Vietnam* (New York: Free Press, 1989), 75, 108, 113. Lack of consensus on p. 101. See also Trauschweizer, *Maxwell Taylor's Cold War*, 156.
3. Strategic bombing in Deaile, *Always at War*, 66. Giulio Douhet, trans. Dino Ferrari, *The Command of the Air* (Washington, DC: Office of Air Force History, 1921, 1983), 9, 15. On coercive airpower, see David Jordan, "Air and Space Power," in David Jordan, Kiras, et al., *Understanding Modern Warfare*, 198.
4. Advisors and CIA in Kaplan, *The Wizards of Armageddon*, 335. Sharp in Weaver, 289. Kenneth H. Williams, ed., *LeMay on Vietnam* (Washington, DC: Air Force History and Museums Program, 2017), 14, 23. Bomb tonnage in Jacob Van Staaveren, "The Air War against North Vietnam," in *The United States Air Force in Southeast Asia, 1961–1973* (Washington, DC: Office of Air Force History, 1977), 89; and Millet, Maslowski, and Feis, *For the Common Defense*, 521–22.
5. LBJ quoted in George C. Herring, *LBJ and Vietnam: A Different Kind of War* (Austin: University of Texas Press, 1994), 31. Ground troops in Lissner, *Wars of Revelation*, 84. IDA and not working in Laslie, 93.

6. Fierce independence in Harrison E. Salisbury, "North Vietnam Spirit Found High," *New York Times*, 15 January 1967. Long odds in Harrison E. Salisbury, "Hanoi Propaganda Stresses Tradition," *New York Times*, 30 December 1966. Waitress in Harrison E. Salisbury, "Hanoi during an Air Alert," *New York Times*, 28 December 1966. Furious in "Hanoi Dispatches to Times Criticized," *New York Times*, 1 January 1967. See also Tirman, *The Deaths of Others*, 162–65. On Salisbury being used by Hanoi to support its "diplomatic struggle," see Pierre Asselin, "National Liberation by Other Means: US Visitor Diplomacy in the Vietnam War," *Past & Present* (August 2024).
7. Psychological in Millet, Maslowski, and Feis, 530. Equating in Harrison E. Salisbury, "Asians Call Raids Damaging to U.S.," *New York Times*, 3 July 1966. General Edward Lansdale quoted in Clodfelter, 138. Halt in Wayne Thompson, *To Hanoi and Back: The United States Air Force and North Vietnam, 1966–1973* (Washington, DC: Air Force History and Museums Program, 2000), 151–52.
8. Sharing publicly in Robert J. Donovan, "Nixon on Vietnam: Dewey or Eisenhower Tactics?" *Los Angeles Times*, 7 July 1968. McNamara in Goodwin, *Triumph or Tragedy*, 27. Disorder in Jeffrey Kimball, *Nixon's Vietnam War* (Lawrence: University Press of Kansas, 1998), 51. Coercing on p. 62.
9. Hard liner and advisability in James Reston, "Mr. Nixon Looks beyond the Election Campaign," *New York Times*, 25 September 1968. Richard M. Nixon, "Asia after Viet Nam," *Foreign Affairs*, Vol. 46, No. 1 (October 1967): 114, 123.
10. Resolved in Gaddis, *Strategies of Containment*, 264–65. Crucé in Heuser, *War*, 214.
11. Madman in William Burr and Jeffrey P. Kimball, *Nixon's Nuclear Specter: The Secret Alert of 1969, Madman Diplomacy, and the Vietnam War* (Lawrence: University Press of Kansas, 2015), 53; and Jeffrey Kimball, *The Vietnam War Files: Uncovering the Secret History of Nixon-Era Strategy* (Lawrence: University Press of Kansas, 2004), 14–18. On Ike, see Freedman and Michaels, *The Evolution of Nuclear Strategy*, 112–13. Dramatic in Thomas A. Schwartz, *Henry Kissinger and American Power: A Political Biography* (New York: Hill & Wang, 2020), 84.
12. Bombing assumptions in Eisenberg, *Fire and Rain*, 147, 149. Kissinger in Kaplan, *The Bomb*, 104. Coercive escalation in Lebovic, *Planning to Fail*, 52. Quickly in Burr and Kimble, 244. Alert on pp. 110–14. Haldeman on p. 115.
13. Nixon quoted in Eisenberg, 404. Linebacker in House, *A Military History of the Cold War, 1962–1991*, 164–65. On proportionality, see Gaddis, *On Grand Strategy*, 105. "Urge End to War: U.S. Clerics Decry the Bombing and Urge End to Vietnam War," *New York Times*, 23 December 1972.

James Reston, "Power without Pity," *New York Times*, 27 December 1972.

14. Southern politics in Stur, *Saigon at War*, 3, 7, 183. Reunification bid on p. 24. Advisor George Ball quoted in Berman, "From Intervention to Disengagement," in Levite, Jentleson, and Berman, *Foreign Military Intervention*, 35. Popular support in Lebovic, *The Limits of U.S. Military Capability*, 37. Robert S. Elegant, "South Vietnamese Forces Still Inadequate to Defend Nation," *Los Angeles Times*, 23 June 1968.

15. Juan de Onis, "Nixon Puts 'Bums' Label on Some College Radicals," *New York Times*, 2 May 1970. Kissinger in Daniel L. Sargent, *A Superpower Transformed: The Remaking of American Foreign Relations in the 1970s* (New York: Oxford University Press, 2015), 48–49. Nixon in Eisenberg, *Fire and Rain*, 169.

16. Fundamentalist in Anthony Lewis, "The Kissinger Mystery," *New York Times*, 10 May 1971. Disastrous in "What Should We Do Now?" *Look*, 9 August 1966, 26. Weary in Robert B. Semple, Jr., "Nixon and Vietnam: He Tries, amidst Conflicting Pressures, to End an Ugly War," *New York Times*, 14 September 1969. Kissinger quoted in Eisenberg, *Fire and Rain*, 119. On prestige, see pp. 335–36; and Robert K. Brigham, "After the Fall of Saigon: Strategic Implications of America's Involvement in Vietnam," in Ryan and Fitzgerald, *Not Even Past*, 89. Unclear victory in Goodwin, *Triumph or Tragedy*, 51.

17. On diplomatic compromises and consent, see Suri, *Power and Protest*, 2, 43, 129–30, 166. Moral authority in Stur, *Saigon at War*, 8, 113. Stabilizing in Jussi M. Hanhimäki, *The Rise and Fall of Deétente: American Foreign Policy and the Transformation of the Cold War* (Washington, DC: Potomac, 2013), xv. Changing paradigm in Sargent, *A Superpower Transformed*, 9.

18. On threat to stability, see Svetlana Savranskaya and William Taubman, "Soviet Foreign Policy, 1962–1975," in Leffler and Westad, *The Cambridge History of the Cold War*, Vol. II, 144–45. Leadup in Loth, *Overcoming the Cold War*, 95–101. Counterrevolution on p. 96. Brezhnev quoted in Hanhimäki and Westad, *The Cold War*, 259. Dubček in Fink, *Cold War*, 139–40.

19. Reluctance in Zubok, *A Failed Empire*, 207–8. China's reaction in Lüthi, *Cold Wars*, 131; and Sergey Radchenko, "Untrusting and Untrusted: Mao's China at a Crossroads, 1969," in *Trust, but Verify: The Politics of Uncertainty and the Transformation of the Cold War Order, 1969–1991*, ed. Martin Klimke, Reinhild Kreis, and Christian F. Ostermann (Stanford, CA: Stanford University Press, 2016), 20. NATO in House, *A Military History of the Cold War, 1962–1991*, 245. Clyde H. Farnsworth, "People of Prague Scream Defiance at the Tanks," *New York Times*, 22 August 1968. Aftermath in Suri, *Power & Protest*, 202–4.

20. Sovereignty in Lüthi, *Cold Wars*, 86. Doctrine in Savranskaya and Taubman, 145–46. Dominoes in Zubok, *A Failed Empire*, 207. David Binder, "The 'Brezhnev Doctrine' Sows Fears about Where Moscow Will Hit Next," *New York Times*, 20 April 1969. Threat of force in "The Brezhnev Doctrine," *New York Times*, 28 September 1968.
21. On reducing burdens and tensions, see Michael Cotey Morgan, *The Final Act: The Helsinki Accords and the Transformation of the Cold War* (Princeton, NJ: Princeton University Press, 2018), 51–52, 55.
22. B. H. Liddell Hart, *Strategy*, 2nd ed. (New York: Praeger, 1954, 1967), 351, 366. Kennan, *American Diplomacy*, 144. Kennan conceded that "military victory" made "possible but by no means assures" any positive achievement from war.
23. Brands, *The Twilight Struggle*, 144–45. Appeasement in Zubok, *A Failed Empire*, 192.

CHAPTER 13

1. Shell and exploiting in Henry Raymont, "Nixon Aide Affirms U.S. Will Press for China Ties," *New York Times*, 6 September 1969. Community in Brazinsky, *Winning the Third World*, 310. Taiwan on p. 315.
2. Harry Schwartz, "Sino-Soviet Relationships Still an Enigma," *New York Times*, 6 September 1959. China criticisms in Fursenko and Naftali, *Khrushchev's Cold War*, 495–96. On split, see Lüthi, *The Sino-Soviet Split*, 6; and Friedman, *Shadow Cold War*, 180, 183.
3. Chauvinism in Meyskens, *Mao's Third Front*, 43. Monolithic in O'Riordan, *Understanding the Cold War*, 119.
4. Split in Tibor Szamuely, "U.S.-China Alliance: It Could Preserve Peace," *Los Angeles Times*, 23 March 1969. Fracturing in Lissner, *Wars of Revelation*, 69.
5. Preventive in "Sino-Soviet Tensions," *New York Times*, 1 September 1969. On China and Vietnam, see Meyskens, 63–64. Nixon, quoted by Kissinger to Zhou Enlai, in Chris Tudda, *A Cold War Turning Point: Nixon and China, 1969–1972* (Baton Rouge: Louisiana State University Press, 2012), 91.
6. Tom Braden, "High-Priced Détente," *Washington Post*, 12 December 1971. Realism versus anticommunism in Preston, *Sword of the Spirit, Shield of Faith*, 423. Artificial and zero-sum in Milne, "Grand Strategies (or Ascendant Ideas) since 1919," in Borgwardt, McKnight Nichols, and Preston, *Rethinking American Grand Strategy*, 156.
7. Objectives in Julian E. Zelizer, "Détente and Domestic Politics," *Diplomatic History*, Vol. 33, No. 4 (September 2009): 653–57; O'Riordan, *Understanding the Cold War*, 310; and Lebow and Gross Stein, *We All Lost the Cold War*, 173. Era in Craig Daigle, "The Era of Détente," in

Kalinovsky and Daigle, *The Routledge Handbook of the Cold War*, 197. On Vietnam, see Eisenberg, *Fire and Rain*, 66.

8. Second-rate and decline in Sargent, *A Superpower Transformed*, 43, 48.

9. Dusko Doder, "Jackson Attacks Soviet Detente in Scathing Speech," *Washington Post*, 5 June 1973. See also Zelizer, 657–58. William F. Buckley, Jr., "Say It Isn't So, Mr. President," *New York Times*, 1 August 1971. On eroding consensus for détente, see O'Riordan, *Understanding the Cold War*, 329.

10. Barry Goldwater, "The Imminence of World War III," *Los Angeles Times*, 13 July 1969. See also Goldwater, *Why Not Victory*, 22. Godless in Preston, *Sword of the Spirit, Shield of Faith*, 413.

11. Kissinger in Brands, *The Twilight Struggle*, 142–43. Confrontation in Jian, "China, The Third World, and the Cold War," in McMahon, *The Cold War in the Third World*, 94. On détente, see Craig and Logevall, *America's Cold War*, 261–63. Relation to Vietnam in Eisenberg, *Fire and Rain*, 314, 468.

12. Departure in Goedde, *The Politics of Peace*, 210. On relaxing tensions, see Preston, *American Foreign Relations*, 98; and Leffler, *For the Soul of Mankind*, 191. Meaning of security in Morgan, *The Final Act*, 108–10. Limits in Schwartz, *Henry Kissinger and American Power*, 299. On cooperation and competition, see O'Riordan, *Understanding the Cold War*, 319, 326. Of note, the American ambassador in Belgium wondered if NATO required a new "political reason," if not identity, to survive détente. Sayle, *Enduring Alliance*, 153.

13. Victory in Richard M. Nixon, *No More Vietnams* (New York: Arbor House, 1985), 102. Nixon quoted in Engel, Lawrence, and Preston, *America in the World*, 279. On violence in Cambodia and Laos, see Eisenberg, *Fire and Rain*, 192, 205.

14. Diplomatic isolation in Chapman, *Remaking the World*, 178. On paradox of US bombing, see Eisenberg, 425. U. S. Grant Sharp, *Strategy for Defeat: Vietnam in Retrospect* (San Rafael, CA: Presidio, 1978), 268.

15. Nixon quoted in Engel, Lawrence, and Preston, 286. Differences in Sargent, "Oasis in the Desert?" in Eckel and Moyn, *The Breakthrough*, 134. On need for cooperation, see Schwartz, 67–69. Border conflict in Jian, *Mao's China and the Cold War*, 239–42. Chalmers M. Roberts, "Sino-Soviet Border Clash: Kremlin Might Let Its Military Try to Teach China a Lesson," *Washington Post*, 17 August 1969.

16. Encirclement in Lüthi, *Cold Wars*, 529. See also Craig Daigle, *The Limits of Détente: The United States, the Soviet Union, and the Arab-Israeli Conflict, 1969-1973* (New Haven, CT: Yale University Press, 2012), 26. Blade in Tudda, *A Cold War Turning Point*, 20. Status quo in Figes, *Revolutionary Russia*, 261. Brezhnev in O'Riordan, *Understanding the Cold War*, 305.

17. Stanley Karnow, "U.S. Insists It Yielded Nothing to China," *Washington Post*, 2 March 1972. Summit in Daigle, *The Limits of Détente*, 220–22, 264–65. Radical turn in Carroll Kilpatrick, "Nixon Sees Brezhnev in Kremlin," *Washington Post*, 23 May 1972. Murrey Marder, "Summit: New Patterns," *Washington Post*, 23 May 1972. Walter Laqueur, "A Meeting in Moscow," *Washington Post*, 21 May 1972.
18. SALT I components in Davis Biddle, "Shield and Sword," in Bacevich, *The Long War*, 167; Graebner, Burns, and Siracusa, *America and the Cold War*, Vol. 2, 350–53; and Lebovic, *Flawed Logics*, 64–67, 74–89. On negotiations, see Loth, *Overcoming the Cold War*, 110–15.
19. Sufficiency, centerpiece and doubts in Freedman and Michaels, *The Evolution of Nuclear Strategy*, 431, 436, 438. Parity in Chalmers M. Roberts, "SALT Talks Reopen Today in Less Optimistic Mood," *Washington Post*, 15 March 1971. Stability in Rittenhouse Green, *The Revolution That Failed*, 89–91. Doubts in Arvid Schors, "Trust and Mistrust and the American Struggle for Verification of the Strategic Arms Limitation Talks, 1969–1979," in Klimke, Kreis, and Ostermann, *Trust, but Verify*, 85–92.
20. William F. Buckley, Jr., "Nixon's Soft Line on Arms," *Los Angeles Times*, 30 May 1971. Capitulation in Bacevich, *The Age of Illusions*, 36. "Where We Stand on SALT," in *Alerting America: The Papers of the Committee on the Present Danger*, ed. Charles Tyroler II (Washington, DC: Pergamon-Brassey's, 1984), 16–17. For view of the "hawks," see Levering, *The Cold War*, 144.
21. Differing interpretations in Hemmer, *American Pendulum*, 85. Containment and control, citing Gaddis, in Michael Kofman, "Continuity and Change in Russian Grand Strategy," in *Before and After the Fall: World Politics and the End of the Cold War*, ed. Nuno P. Monteiro and Fritz Bartel (New York: Cambridge University Press, 2021), 174–75.
22. Immoral and inhumane in Tom Wicker, "A Needed Debate," *New York Times*, 9 July 1974. Links to Watergate in Hanhimäki, *The Rise and Fall of Détente*, 77. Kissinger in Schwartz, *Henry Kissinger and American Power*, 219. On domestic critics, see Hemmer, 86. It is worth mentioning that the origins of the scandal were rooted in the war, specifically the "leaking" of the Pentagon Papers.
23. Sydney H. Schanberg, "Kennedy, in India, Terms Pakistani Drive Genocide," *New York Times*, 17 August 1971. On genocide and reactions, see Sargent, *A Superpower Transformed*, 82–91. For an excellent overview, see Gary J. Bass, *The Blood Telegram: Nixon, Kissinger and a Forgotten Genocide* (New York: Vintage, 2013).
24. Encirclement and treaty in Lüthi, *Cold Wars*, 179. China in Schwartz, 150. Psychological on p. 153. Geopolitical interests in Sargent, 83. Power play on p. 88.

25. Cambodia in Sarah B. Snyder, "Human Rights and the Cold War," in Kalinovsky and Daigle, *The Routledge Handbook of the Cold War*, 242–43.
26. C. L Sulzberger, "Can the U.N. Make Nations Behave?" *New York Times*, 25 October 1972. Fears and civil wars in Brigham, "After the Fall of Saigon," 92–94. On atrocities and US priorities, see Chamberlin, *The Cold War's Killing Fields*, 343. Cambodia and Laos in Guan, *Southeast Asia's Cold War*, 160.
27. On détente not extending to Latin America, see Tanya Harmer, *Allende's Chile and the Inter-American Cold War* (Chapel Hill: University of North Carolina Press, 2011), 150. Election and outcome on pp. 2, 4, 50–51, 63. Mortal on p. 35. Nixon on p. 60. Allende actually hoped for "cooperative relations" with the United States. See Grow, *U.S. Presidents and Latin American Interventions*, 96.
28. CIA and credit blockade in Lubna Z. Qureshi, "U.S. Clandestine Operations in Chile, 1970–1973," in Thompson and Frentzos, *The Routledge Handbook of American Military and Diplomatic History*, 288–94. See also Weiner, *Legacy of Ashes*, 308–17. Infection in LaFeber, *America, Russia, and the Cold War* 273. Disinformation in Bevins, *The Jakarta Method*, 171. Nixon quoted in Wright, *Latin America in the Era of the Cuban Revolution and Beyond*, 149.
29. Contempt in Rabe, *The Killing Zone*, 123. Scream on p. 133. See also Laurence Stern, "CIA's 'Massive' Chile Role Told," *Los Angeles Times*, 5 December 1975. Kissinger quoted in Immerman, *The Hidden Hand*, 90. On Pinochet, see Rabe, 142–44; and Kyle Burke, *Revolutionaries for the Right: Anticommunist Internationalism and Paramilitary Warfare in the Cold War* (Chapel Hill: University of North Carolina Press, 2018), 67.
30. Chile and détente in Grandin, *Empire's Workshop*, 59. Kissinger quoted in Harmer, 69, 251. Richard Reston, "Colby Denies Any Direct CIA Role in Overthrow of Allende," *Los Angeles Times*, 14 September 1974.
31. Nixon in Harmer, 170. Georgie Anne Geyer, "The Breakaway to the South—U.S. Losing Latin America," *Los Angeles Times*, 18 February 1973. Power in Grow, 104. On Pinochet, see Renouard, *Human Rights in American Foreign Policy*, 90.
32. Economy in Westad, *The Cold War*, 396. De-ideologize in Brands, *The Devil We Knew*, 123. Raw power in Lamberton Harper, *The Cold War*, 167. On doctrine, see Lissner, *Wars of Revelation*, 100–101; and Michael Mandelbaum, *The Four Ages of American Foreign Policy: Weak Power, Great Power, Superpower, Hyperpower* (New York: Oxford University Press, 2022), 314–15. Self-reliance in Don Oberdorfer, "U.S. Bars New Asia War Role," *Washington Post*, 26 July 1969. Burden sharing and avoiding Vietnams in Murrey Marder, "Hill Leaders Hail New Asian Policy," *Washington Post*, 27 July 1969.

33. Weapons sales in House, *A Military History of the Cold War, 1962–1991*, 255; Bill, *The Eagle and the Lion*, 209; and Little, *American Orientalism*, 144. Shah lobbying in Chapman, *Remaking the World*, 229. Stability in Brands, *What Good Is Grand Strategy?* 82. Drew Middleton, "U.S. Global Military Role: Are Forces Big Enough?" *New York Times*, 17 March 1974.
34. On Angola, see Westad, *The Global Cold War*, 228–40; Piero Gleijeses, "Cuba and the Cold War, 1959–1980," in Leffler and Westad, *The Cambridge History of the Cold War*, Vol. II, 335–40; and Chapman, *Remaking the World*, 183–210. William Safire, "Cold War II," *New York Times*, 29 December 1975.
35. "The Inaugural Address," *New York Times*, 21 January 1969.

CHAPTER 14

1. Richard D. Lyons, "Nixon Says Paris Accord Can Bring Lasting Peace," *New York Times*, 21 February 1973. "Excerpts from President Nixon's Address to the Legislature of South Carolina," *New York Times*, 21 February 1973. Carolyn Eisenberg argues the "Paris Peace Agreement was never about 'peace.'" *Fire and Rain*, 498.
2. Military-industrial in Brenes, *For Might and Right*, 124. Recruiting in Matthew S. Muehlbauer and David J. Ulbrich, *Ways of War: American Military History from the Colonial Era to the Twenty-First Century* (New York: Routledge, 2014), 485. On critics of the AVF, see Taylor, *Military Service and American Democracy*, 141. The best overview on the AVF is THE Beth Bailey, *America's Army: Making the All-Volunteer Force* (Cambridge, MA: Belknap, 2009).
3. Scapegoating in Yến Lê Espiritu, *Body Counts: The Vietnam War and Militarized Refuge(es)* (Berkeley: University of California Press, 2014), 109. On blame, see Gregory A. Daddis, "Mired in a Quagmire: Popular Interpretations of the Vietnam War," *Orbis*, Vol. 57, No. 4 (Autumn 2013): 532–48.
4. Pham, *The Eaves of Heaven*, 226. Appeals in Sarah Thelen, "The Importance of Being Popular: Richard Nixon, Henry Kissinger, and Domestic Support for the Vietnam War," in Fitzgerald, Ryan, and Thompson, *Not Even Past*, 39.
5. Liquidation and borders in Lüthi, *Cold Wars*, 213, 217. Rostow in Little, *American Orientalism*, 187. Land over peace on p. 268. Blockade in Cleveland and Bunton, *A History of the Modern Middle East*, 321.
6. Fighting and LBJ in Oren, *Power, Faith, and Fantasy*, 524–27. Pan-Arabism in Immerman and Goedde, *Oxford Handbook of the Cold War*, 253. Ceasefire in Lüthi, *Cold Wars*, 222. Beijing in Friedman, *Shadow Cold War*, 159.

7. Eshkol in Michael B. Oren, *Six Days of War: June 1967 and the Making of the Modern Middle East* (New York: Oxford University Press, 2002), 169. Infiltrators on p. 306. Nasser on p. 319. Soviet aid in Khalidi, *Sowing Crisis*, 120–21. On Palestinians, see Cleveland and Bunton, 328–29, 341–42; Khalidi, *The Hundred Years' War on Palestine*, 96–98, 122–23; and Little, 280–81. Soviet support in House, *A Military History of the Cold War, 1962–1991*, 183–84.
8. Consciousness in Khalidi, *The Hundred Years' War on Palestine*, 109. Settler-colonial on p. 106. On Arab nationalism, see Hahn, *Caught in the Middle East*, 4. Roots in Lebow and Gross Stein, *We All Lost the Cold War*, 173. Era in Craig Daigle, "The Era of Détente," in Kalinovsky and Daigle, *The Routledge Handbook of the Cold War*, 150–52. Liability in Little, *American Orientalism*, 103; and Oren, *Power, Faith, and Fantasy*, 502. Geostrategic in William B. Quandt, "How American Middle East Policy Is Made," in Lesch and Haas, *The Middle East and the United States*, 8.
9. Détente in Lebow and Gross Stein, 221. Nasser in Chapman, *Remaking the World*, 99; and Brownlee, *Democracy Prevention*, 21.
10. Sadat's plans in Daigle, *The Limits of Détente*, 284–87, 294–97. Forest and bloody in Charles Mohr, "Suez Strategy: An Israeli View of Egyptian Mistakes," *New York Times*, 28 October 1973. Heavy toll in John W. Finney, "U.S. Aides See Eventual Israeli Victory," *New York Times*, 10 October 1973. On US Army reforms, see House, 192, 195; Thomas E. Ricks, *The Generals: American Military Command from World War II to Today* (New York: Penguin, 2012), 337–38; and Trauschweizer, *The Cold War U.S. Army*, 202.
11. Out of hand in Bernard Gwertzman, "Kissinger Says U.S. and Soviet Have Acted to Keep War Restricted to Mideast," *New York Times*, 3 October 1973. On Kissinger's aims, see Oren, *Power, Faith, and Fantasy*, 533–35. Nuclear escalation in Little, *American Orientalism*, 107. Restraint in Khalidi, *Sowing Crisis*, 127. Palestinians on p. 133. See also Hanhimäki, *The Rise and Fall of Détente*, 86–87. Extend in Daigle, *The Limits of Détente*, 5.
12. On détente, see Daigle, 329–31. Oil as a weapon in Leonard Silk, "Political Aspects of World Oil Crisis," *New York Times*, 14 November 1973. On OPEC, see Lorenzini, *Global Development*, 120; and Craig and Logevall, *America's Cold War*, 280. Prices in Jeremy Black, *War since 1945* (London: Reaktion, 2004), 100. Increased US presence in Andrew J. Bacevich, *America's War for the Greater Middle East: A Military History* (New York: Random House, 2016), 5. Public opinion in Victor McFarland, *Oil Powers: A History of the U.S.-Saudi Alliance* (New York: Columbia University Press, 2020), 126–32.
13. Siberia in Kotkin, *Armageddon Averted*, 15–16. Oil crisis in Little, *American Orientalism*, 65, 68–70; and Cleveland and Bunton, 408. On

American reactions, see Garavini, *The Rise and Fall of OPEC in the Twentieth Century*, 217–21, 233. Garavini calls this episode an "oil revolution," not a "shock." See p. 361.

14. House, *A Military History of the Cold War, 1962–1991*, 196. Occupation in Chapman, *Remaking the World*, 101. Arms race in Daigle, *The Limits of Détente*, 89.
15. Schlesinger quoted in Drew Middleton, "U.S. Reviewing Its World Military Posture after Saigon's Fall," *New York Times*, 5 May 1975. Tragedy in Espiritu, *Body Counts*, 18. Habit in Keegan, *The History of Warfare*, 385.
16. Damage in William J. Duiker, "Military Power and Revolutionary War in Vietnam," in Hattendorf and Murfett, *The Limitations of Power*, 227. Officer critiques in Echevarria, *War's Logic*, 143. On conceptions of veterans' homecomings, see John A. Wood, *Veteran Narratives and the Collective Memory of the Vietnam War* (Athens, OH: Ohio University Press, 2016), 74–94. Of note, Americans didn't really grapple with the actual implications of the question "Was the war in Vietnam necessary?" Instead, the focus ultimately rested on curing the supposed "Vietnam Syndrome."
17. Rod MacLeish, "The Mayaguez Ordeal," *Washington Post*, 20 May 1975. Power and will in Tom Wicker, "Raising Some Mayaguez Questions," *New York Times*, 16 May 1975. On the rescue mission, see William P. Head, "Mayaguez: The Final Tragedy of the U.S. Involvement in the Vietnam War," *Journal of Third World Studies*, Vol. 29, No. 1 (Spring 2012): 57–80. *Time* on p. 71. See also Daniel P. Bolger, *Americans at War: 1975–1986, An Era of Violent Peace* (Novato, CA: Presidio, 1988), 19–94; and Houghton, *The Decision Point*, 62–68.
18. Ford quoted in Nye, *Do Morals Matter?* 101. Obligation in Amanda C. Demmer, *After Saigon's Fall: Refugees and US-Vietnamese Relations, 1975–2000* (New York: Cambridge University Press, 2021), 48. On narratives, see Espiritu, *Body Counts*, 2, 7, 46, 81.
19. Richard Bergholz, "Ford Assails War Powers Act of 1974," *Los Angeles Times*, 3 December 1977. Act in Grandin, *Empire's Workshop*, 62. Antimilitarism in Brenes, *For Might and Right*, 15, 64. On the CIA's "Team B" pushing back against this antimilitarism, see Greg Grandin, *Kissinger's Shadow: The Long Reach of America's Most Controversial Statesman* (New York: Metropolitan, 2015): 165–69.
20. On human rights' links to US policy, see Renouard, *Human Rights in American Foreign Policy*, 14, 16. High point in Sarah B. Snyder, *Human Rights Activism and the End of the Cold War: A Transnational History of the Helsinki Network* (New York: Cambridge University Press, 2011), 30. Act in O'Riordan, *Understanding the Cold War*, 306–7; and Morgan, *The Final Act*, 6, 11–12. On Soviet views, see Zubok, *A Failed Empire*, 237–38. On critics, see Daigle, "The Era of Détente," 203.

21. Ersatz in Flora Lewis, "Not a Treaty, but a Declaration of Intentions in Europe," *New York Times*, 27 July 1975. Buildup in Drew Middleton, "As U.S. Arms Outlays Slow, Soviet Intentions Are a Big Question," *New York Times*, 19 March 1974. See also Aaron Donaghy, *The Second Cold War: Carter, Reagan and the Politics of Foreign Policy* (New York: Cambridge University Press, 2021), 29. Critics in Renouard, 99. George W. Ball, "Capitulation at Helsinki," *Atlantic Community Quarterly*, Vol. 13, No. 3 (Fall 1975): 286. On Soviet fears, see Loth, *Overcoming the Cold War*, 8. Andrew Preston argues that Helsinki marked détente's decline. *American Foreign Relations*, 109.

22. On the Jackson-Vanik bill, see Barbara J. Keys, *Reclaiming American Virtue: The Human Rights Revolution of the 1970s* (Cambridge, MA: Harvard University Press, 2014), 104, 106; and Snyder, 39. Soviet response in Morgan, *The Final Act*, 170–71; and Donaghy, 23, 32, 35. Breakdown in Murrey Marder, "Hill Blamed for Setback," *Washington Post*, 17 February 1975.

23. Ford in Leffler, *For the Soul of Mankind*, 253. John W. Finney, "Ford-Reagan Race Focusing on Arms Issue," *New York Times*, 11 May 1976. Coalition in Donaghy, 23; Lamberton Harper, *The Cold War*, 184, 187; and Preston, *Sword of the Spirit, Shield of Faith*, 563. Kissinger in Rabe, *The Killing Zone*, 145, 154; Snyder, 28, 35; and Sargent, "Oasis in the Desert?" 138. Precise balance in Kissinger, *Diplomacy*, 812.

24. On Ostpolitik, see Goedde, *The Politics of Peace*, 197–98, 216; Graebner, Burns, and Siracusa, *America and the Cold War*, Vol. 2, 348; and Judt, *Postwar*, 498–99. Treaties in Lüthi, *Cold Wars*, 430–31. Kissinger to Nixon, February 1970, in Hanhimäki and Westad, *The Cold War*, 338. On Kissinger's fears, see Hanhimäki, *The Rise and Fall of Détente*, 65; and Hope M. Harrison, "Berlin and the Cold War Struggle over Germany," in Kalinovsky and Daigle, *The Routledge Handbook of the Cold War*, 67.

25. Inordinate in Donaghy, *The Second Cold War*, 1. Emulation and foundation in Hemmer, *American Pendulum*, 89, 90. On Carter's policy outlook, see Sargent, *A Superpower Transformed*, 11; and Donaghy, 2, 19, 34. "Transcript of Foreign Affairs Debate between Ford and Carter," *New York Times*, 7 October 1976.

26. Criticism in Craig and Logevall, *America's Cold War*, 291. Militarization in Sherry, *In the Shadow of War*, 341. Humanitarian purpose in Derek Chollet and James Goldgeier, *America between the Wars, from 11/9 to 9/11: The Misunderstood Years between the Fall of the Berlin Wall and the Start of the War on Terror* (New York: PublicAffairs, 2008), 224. Soft power in Nancy Mitchell, "The Cold War and Jimmy Carter," in Leffler and Westad, *The Cambridge History of the Cold War*, Vol. III, 73. Arms control in Snyder, *Human Rights Activism and the End of the Cold War*, 85. Brezhnev on p. 90. Tony Judt lays out the Soviet human-rights context in *Postwar*, 559–61.

27. "Text of President's Commencement Address at Notre Dame on Foreign Policy," *New York Times*, 23 May 1977.
28. On speech, see Donaghy, *The Second Cold War*, 46. Brzezinski in Graebner, Burns, and Siracusa, Vol. 2, 402. Moral issues in Keys, *Reclaiming American Virtue*, 3–4, 240. Abusive regimes in Lorenzini, *Global Development*, 158. Links in Sargent, "Oasis in the Desert?" 133. We might also note that many Americans also worried that any de-militarization efforts would have harmed the already struggling economy during the 1970s.
29. The Committee of Santa Fe, *A New Inter-American Policy for the Eighties* (Washington, DC: Council for Inter-American Security, 1980), iii, 1, 2. Jeane Kirkpatrick, "Dictatorships and Double Standards," *Commentary*, Vol. 68, No. 5 (1 November 1979): 45. She also howled that Carter's administration seemed "willing to negotiate anything with anyone anywhere." See also Grandin, *Empire's Workshop*, 66; Latham, *The Right Kind of Revolution*, 181; and O'Riordan, *Understanding the Cold War*, 365.
30. On dissidents, see Sanders, *Peddlers of Crisis*, 3. Brzezinski in Leffler, *For the Soul of Mankind*, 284, 323. Power in Lloyd C. Gardner, *The Long Road to Baghdad: A History of U.S. Foreign Policy from the 1970s to the Present* (New York: New Press, 2008), 36. Vance in Miller, *Grand Strategy from Truman to Trump*, 135, 145. On the debate between power and diplomacy, see Donaghy, 25.
31. Martin Tolchin, "Carter Warns Soviet Its Military Policies Imperil Cooperation," *New York Times*, 18 March 1978. On opposing advisor viewpoints, see Mitchell, 69.
32. Laurence Stern, "Vance and Brzezinski Defend Administration's Foreign Policy Record," *Washington Post*, 2 May 1979. On arc, see Little, *American Orientalism*, 151; and Gardner, *The Long Road to Baghdad*, 37, 53.
33. Jonathan Kandell, "Antinuclear Movement Growing in West Europe," *New York Times*, 2 August 1977. Of note, Alvin M. Weinberg argued "nuclear people" had made a "Faustian bargain with society" that pitted "atomic peace" against the possession of massive nuclear arsenals. "Social Institutions and Nuclear Energy," *Science*, Vol. 177, No. 4043 (7 July 1972): 33–34.

CHAPTER 15

1. CIA, naval officers, and Buckley in Schors, "Trust and Mistrust and the American Struggle for Verification of the Strategic Arms Limitation Talks," 93–94. On SALT II negotiations, see William Burr and David Alan Rosenberg, "Nuclear Competition in an Era of Stalemate, 1963–1975," in Leffler and Westad, *The Cambridge History of the Cold War*, Vol. II, 106–8; and Loth, *Overcoming the Cold War*, 150–55. Charles Mohr,

"Joint Chiefs Support Arms Treaty but Urge Higher Nuclear Spending," *New York Times*, 12 July 1979.
2. Exchange and SALT II in Kaplan, *The Bomb*, 132–35, 138. Concerns over SALT II in Davis Biddle, "Shield and Sword," 170–71. Jackson in Donaghy, *The Second Cold War*, 67, 69. Nitze in "Is SALT II a Fair Deal for the United States?" in Tyroler, *Alerting America*, 162, 163.
3. Reagan in Miller, *Grand Strategy from Truman to Trump*, 143. Stability in Lebovic, *Flawed Logics*, 92–93. Parity in Miller, *Strategy and Nuclear Deterrence*, 209. On MAD, see Rittenhouse Green, *The Revolution That Failed*, 122–23. Abiding and unilateral, citing Senator Steve Symms (R-ID), in Donaghy, 66, 263–64.
4. Hatch in Donaghy, 55. John M. Goshko, "Reagan Aids GOP against Panama Canal Treaties," *Washington Post*, 30 October 1977.
5. Goldwater in David S. Broder and Bill Peterson, "Credibility of U.S. Hurt, Critics Say," *Washington Post*, 16 December 1978. George F. Will, "Crawling Away from Taiwan," *Washington Post*, 4 September 1977. On diplomatic relations with China, see Donaghy, 49–50; Guan, *Southeast Asia's Cold War*, 167; and Chen Jian, "China and the Cold War after Mao," in Leffler and Westad, *The Cambridge History of the Cold War*, Vol. III, 189–90. Deng in Brazinsky, *Winning the Third World*, 335. Clinton and appeasement in Chollet and Goldgeier, *America between the Wars*, 259.
6. Principal threat in "Common Sense and the Common Danger" in Tyroler, *Alerting America*, 3. Rostow in Sanders, *Peddlers of Crisis*, 10.
7. Well-being in Tyroler, *Alerting America*, 5. Accommodation on p. 89. Decisive steps on p. 91. Doomsday in Donaghy, *The Second Cold War*, 38. On CPD influence within the Reagan administration, see Graebner, Burns, and Siracusa, *America and the Cold War*, Vol. 2, 443–44; and Grandin, *Empire's Workshop*, 141.
8. Expansion, citing Rostow, and drive, in Sanders, 254–55. Report in Tyroler, *Alerting America*, 39–93. James Reston, "'The Present Danger,'" *New York Times*, 17 November 1978.
9. Middle East order in Andrew Bowen, "The Golan Negotiations: US-Syrian Relations and the Failure to Achieve a Comprehensive Peace," in Lesch and Haas, *The Middle East and the United States*, 159. Crisis of capitalism in Lorenzini, *Global Development*, 143. For a superb overview, see Elisabeth Leake, *Afghan Crucible: The Soviet Invasion and the Making of Modern Afghanistan* (New York: Oxford University Press, 2022).
10. Aaron David Miller, "The Long Dance: Searching for Arab-Israeli Peace," *Wilson Quarterly* (Spring 2008): 39. On the larger meaning of the two countries' relationship, see Shaul Mitelpunkt, *Israel in the American Mind: The Cultural Politics of US-Israeli Relations, 1958–1988* (New York: Cambridge University Press, 2018).

11. Murrey Marder, "Carter Embraces Sadat Visit," *Washington Post*, 17 November 1977. On lead-up to Camp David, see Douglas Little, "The Cold War in the Middle East: Suez Crisis to Camp David Accords," in Leffler and Westad, *The Cambridge History of the Cold War*, Vol. II, 322–24.
12. "Text of Camp David 'Framework' Accord," *New York Times*, 27 March 1979. See also Cleveland and Bunton, *A History of the Modern Middle East*, 384; and Brownlee, *Democracy Prevention*, 31–37. Arab reactions in Lüthi, *Cold Wars*, 240, 501. Carter worries in Little, *American Orientalism*, 110. Begin on p. 289.
13. West Bank in Little, 289–91. Brilliance in Hedrick Smith, "After Camp David Summit, a Valley of Hard Bargaining," *New York Times*, 6 November 1978. Charter in Gelvin, *The Israel-Palestine Conflict*, 214. PLO vow in Don A. Schanche, "Arab Reaction Mixed—from Joy to Rage," *Los Angeles Times*, 19 September 1978. On limits of accords, see Graebner, Burns, and Siracusa, Vol. 2, 411–12.
14. Warsaw Pact in Levering, *The Cold War*, 186. On the coup and invasion, see Larry P. Goodson, *Afghanistan's Endless Wars: State Failure, Regional Politics, and the Rise of the Taliban* (Seattle: University of Washington Press, 2001), 55–58; and Thomas Barfield, *Afghanistan: A Cultural and Political History* (Princeton, NJ: Princeton University Press, 2010), 225–33.
15. "Transcript of President's Speech on Soviet Military Intervention in Afghanistan," *New York Times*, 5 January 1980.
16. "Soviet Invasion of Afghanistan Derails Détente," *New York Times*, 6 January 1980. Carter's actions in Donaghy, 77–78; and Kaplan, *The Bomb*, 140–41. Malcolm W. Browne, "As Detente Falters, U.S. Military Looks to Chemical War Capability," *New York Times*, 24 February 1980. CPD in Sanders, *Peddlers of Crisis*, 278. Of note, the reinstatement of Selective Service registration in 1980 also was part of Carter's responses to the Soviet invasion of Afghanistan.
17. PD-59 in Donaghy, 105–7. Thinkable and slaughter in Dan A. Ebener, "Directives 58 and 59 Are War Strategies," *New York Times*, 17 August 1980. *Pravda* in Anthony Austin, "Soviet Calls the U.S. Strategy Shift on Nuclear War an 'Ominous' Sign," *New York Times*, 8 August 1980. Defense analysts in "A Debate: Are U.S. Defenses Ready, Rusty or Adequate?" *New York Times*, 12 October 1980.
18. Regional crisis in Chamberlin, *The Cold War's Killing Fields*, 435, 438. Don Oberdorfer, "Brzezinski Urges Allies to Respond," *Los Angeles Times*, 13 March 1980. See also Donaghy, 14. On Moscow's fears, see Lüthi, *Cold Wars*, 510; Rodric Braithwaite, *Afghansty: The Russians in Afghanistan 1979–89* (New York: Oxford University Press, 2011), 37–38, 47; and Zubok, *A Failed Empire*, 260, 262. Islamic threat in Gregory

Feifer, *The Great Gamble: The Soviet War in Afghanistan* (New York: HarperCollins, 2009), 3. Gromyko in O'Riordan, *Understanding the Cold War*, 339.

19. On defensive nature, see Geoffrey Warner, "Geopolitics and the Cold War," in Immerman and Goedde, *The Oxford Handbook of the Cold War*, 78; and Leffler, *For the Soul of Mankind*, 336. Soviet fears in Feifer, 50; and Lüthi, *Cold Wars*, 511. Brzezinski quoted in Donaghy, *The Second Cold War*, 94. Terence Smith, "Carter Tells Soviet to Pull Its Troops Out of Afghanistan," *New York Times*, 30 December 1979. William Safire, "The Second Cold War," *New York Times*, 10 January 1980.

20. Islam as a weapon, citing Richard Dekmegian, in Fatema Mernissi, "Palace Fundamentalism and Liberal Democracy: Oil, Arms and Irrationality," *Development and Change*, Vol. 27, No. 2 (April 1996): 260. See also Belmonte, *Selling the American Way*, 106; and Kwon, *The Other Cold War*, 68.

21. Carter in Donaghy, 2. On 1979, see Hemmer, *American Pendulum*, 94–95; House, *A Military History of the Cold War, 1962–1991*, 72; Grandin, *Empire's Workshop*, 66; and Wright, *Latin America in the Era of the Cuban Revolution and Beyond*, 163. Wilfried Loth argues that through a "combination of sanctions and containment gestures, Carter practically ended American détente policy." *Overcoming the Cold War*, 162.

22. "Transcript of President's State of the Union Address to Joint Session of Congress," *New York Times*, 24 January 1980. See also Gary Sick, "The United States in the Persian Gulf: From Twin Pillars to Dual Containment," in Lesch and Haas, *The Middle East and the United States*, 240. On deterrence, see Echevarria, *Military Strategy*, 53.

23. Leslie H. Gelb, "Beyond the Carter Doctrine," *New York Times*, 10 February 1980. See also McFarland, *Oil Powers*, 227–31. Congress unlikely in Brigham, "After the Fall of Saigon," in Ryan and Fitzgerald, *Not Even Past*, 92. On doctrine, see Bacevich, *America's War for the Greater Middle East*, 29; and Vine, *The United States of War*, 246–47.

24. Don Oberdorfer, "Crises Lead Carter to Shift toward Reactive Foreign Policy," *Washington Post*, 28 January 1980. Peace's sake in Oren, *Power, Faith, and Fantasy*, 540.

CHAPTER 16

1. Satan in William Borders, "Hostage Issue Is Troubling Few in Iran," *New York Times*, 21 April 1980. Turbans in John Kifner, "Impasse over the Hostages," *New York Times*, 10 December 1979. Coverage in Narges Bajoghli, "American Media on Iran: Hostage to a Worldview," *Anthropology*, Vol. 11, No. 3 (2019): 31–32. On ABC, see also James G. Blight, Janet M. Lang, et al., *Becoming Enemies: U.S.-Iran Relations and the Iran-Iraq War, 1979–1988* (London: Rowman & Littlefield, 2012), 38.

2. Journalist Robert Dyk quoted in Bajoghli, 32. Political Islam and loss of ally in Malcolm Byrne, *Iran-Contra: Reagan's Scandal and the Unchecked Abuse of Presidential Power* (Lawrence: University Press of Kansas, 2014), xix, xx, xxi, 28. Friction in Bill, *The Eagle and the Lion*, 170.
3. Militant republic and arsenal in Cleveland and Bunton, *A History of the Modern Middle East*, 355. "Transcript of the President's News Conference on Crisis over Hostages in Iran," *New York Times*, 29 November 1979.
4. Guardian in William Borders, "Handling of Hostage Issue Alters U.S. Image Abroad," *New York Times*, 5 November 1980. On the coup, see Cleveland and Bunton, 278. Communism in Khalidi, *Sowing Crisis*, 170–73; and Chapman, *Remaking the World*, 219. Carter quoted in Hanhimäki, *The Rise and Fall of Détente*, 130.
5. Brzezinski quoted in O'Riordan, *Understanding the Cold War*, 335. Carter in Donaghy, *The Second Cold War*, 83. On internal aspects of the revolution, see Bill, 234–35, 297.
6. Khomeini philosophy in Chapman, *Remaking the World*, 236. Relation to communism on p. 212. Drifting in Daniel Pipes, "Khomeini, The Soviet and U.S.," *New York Times*, 27 May 1980. Emile A. Nakleh, "'Islamic Revolution': Dangerous Export," *Washington Post*, 22 October 1979. On Khomeini's political priorities, see Blight et al., *Becoming Enemies*, 36; Lüthi, *Cold Wars*, 327, 503–4. Anti-Sovietism on p. 505. See also Westad, *The Global Cold War*, 291, 299. Student on p. 295.
7. Islamization in Cleveland and Bunton, 367–68. Loss in Bill, *The Eagle and the Lion*, 257. Reversing revolution on p. 303. Steven R. Weisman, "'Fanatics' in Regime in Teheran Blamed by Carter for Crisis," *New York Times*, 5 July 1980. Specialist in Norman Kempster, "Carter Caught between 2 Forces on Iran Response," *Los Angeles Times*, 2 December 1979.
8. "A Tale of Carter and the 'Killer Rabbit,'" *New York Times*, 30 August 1979. Criticisms in Donaghy, 67, 91, 109. Carter as hostage in O'Riordan, 337.
9. Carter in "This Rescue Attempt 'Became a Necessity and a Duty,'" *Washington Post*, 26 April 1980. Humanitarian mission Betty Glad, *An Outsider in the White House: Jimmy Carter, His Advisors, and the Making of American Foreign Policy* (Ithaca, NY: Cornell University Press, 2009), 267. On Eagle Claw, see Houghton, *The Decision Point*, 172–74.
10. Readiness in George C. Wilson and Michael Getler, "Anatomy of a Failed Mission," *Washington Post*, 27 April 1980. Sad symbols in Richard Harwood, "Series of Mishaps Defeated Rescue in Iran," *Washington Post*, 26 April 1980. Haynes Johnson, "America the Gulliver Mired in Impotence Again," *Washington Post*, 26 April 1980. Richard Halloran, "Army Rates Six of 10 Divisions Unready to Fight," *New York Times*, 9 September 1980. George F. Will, "'Do Not Scoff at U.S. Power'—Why Not?" *Los Angeles Times*, 1 May 1980.

11. Richard Burt, "Report Charges 'Major' Mistakes On Iran Mission," *New York Times*, 6 June 1980. On military reforms, see Charles G. Cogan, "Desert One and Its Disorders," *Journal of Military History*, Vol. 67, No. 1 (January 2003): 201–16. Vance in Glad, 264. Aide Rick Hernandez quoted in Elaine Kamarck, "The Iranian Hostage Crisis and Its Effect on American Politics," *Brookings*, 4 November 2019.
12. Douglas E. Kneeland, "Reagan Says Carter Acted Too Late with Iran Mission," *New York Times*, 1 May 1980. Fearful and shambles in Donaghy, *The Second Cold War*, 92, 95. See also Hanhimäki, *The Rise and Fall of Détente*, 139–40.
13. Lou Cannon, "Reagan Hits President on Soviet Policy," *Washington Post*, 1 April 1976. See also Hanhimäki, 198–201; and Brenes, *For Might and Right*, 191. Anticommunism in James Mann, *The Rebellion of Ronald Reagan: A History of the End of the Cold War* (New York: Penguin, 2009), 17–19. On defense spending and military superiority, see William Inboden, *The Peacemaker: Ronald Reagan, the Cold War, and the World on the Brink* (New York: Dutton, 2022), 39.
14. Supremacy in Robert D. Schulzinger, "Détente in the Nixon-Ford years, 1969–1976," in Leffler and Westad, *The Cambridge History of the Cold War*, Vol. II, 391. On battle over détente, see Mann, 23. World revolution in Donaghy, 125. Howell Raines, "Reagan Calls Arms Race Essential to Avoid a 'Surrender' or 'Defeat,'" *New York Times*, 19 August 1980.
15. Instability in Artemy M. Kalinovsky, "The Cold War in South and Central Asia," in Kalinovsky and Daigle, *The Routledge Handbook of the Cold War*, 185. On détente as a system, see Gaddis, *The Cold War: A New History*, 189, 198–200. Illusion and principles in Steven V. Roberts, "Reagan, in Chicago Speech, Urges Big Increases in Military Spending," *New York Times*, 18 March 1980. For a critique of "soft power," see Eliot A. Cohen, *The Big Stick: The Limits of Soft Power & the Necessity of Military Force* (New York: Basic, 2016), 15, 19.
16. "Carter Warns of 'Crisis of Confidence,'" *Los Angeles Times*, 16 July 1979. See also Haberski, *God and War*, 114–15. Critics in Joshua Muravchik, "The Think Tank of the Left," *New York Times*, 26 April 1981.
17. On the role of popular culture, see Susan Jeffords, *The Remasculinization of America: Gender and the Vietnam War* (Bloomington: Indiana University Press, 1989), 116–143. "Transcript of the Presidential Debate between Carter and Reagan in Cleveland," *New York Times*, 29 October 1980. "'Let Us Begin an Era of National Renewal,'" *New York Times*, 21 January 1981.
18. Warmonger in Brenes, 185. Bumbling and fears in E. J. Dionne, Jr., "Fear of War or Weakness Resonating in Campaign," *New York Times*, 24 October 1980.

CHAPTER 17

1. On Carter's weakness, see Graebner, Burns, and Siracusa, *America and the Cold War*, Vol. 2, 432. Spending in Kaplan, *The Bomb*, 147. Identifiable in Sarah B. Snyder, "Compartmentalizing US Foreign Policy: Human Rights in the Reagan Years," in *The Reagan Moment: America and the World in the 1980s*, ed. Jonathan R. Hunt and Simon Milesand Simon Miles (Ithaca, NY: Cornell University Press, 2021), 195. On human rights, see Keys, *Reclaiming American Virtue*, 273–74.
2. Buildup in Beth A. Fischer, "US Foreign Policy under Reagan and Bush," in Leffler and Westad, *The Cambridge History of the Cold War*, Vol. III, 270. See also Christopher J. Fuller, "Reagan and the Evolution of US Counterterrorism," in Hunt and Miles, 69. On defense spending, see Graebner, Burns, and Siracusa, 441. "Reagan Calls Vietnam War a 'Noble Cause,'" *Los Angeles Times*, 18 August 1980.
3. Guidance in Hemmer, *American Pendulum*, 98. Anticommunism in Inboden, *The Peacemaker*, 4. Hedrick Smith, "Reagan, What Kind of World Leader," *New York Times*, 16 November 1980.
4. Warmonger in Smith, "Weinberger Said to Offer Reagan Plan to Regain Atomic Superiority," *New York Times*, 14 August 1981. "Reagan Remark Stirs European Furor," *Washington Post*, 21 October 1981.
5. Buildup in Michael De Groot, "Global Reaganomics: Budget Deficits, Capital Flows, and the International Economy," in Hunt and Miles, 88. Moratorium in James Graham Wilson, *The Triumph of Improvisation: Gorbachev's Adaptability, Reagan's Engagement, and the End of the Cold War* (Ithaca, NY: Cornell University Press, 2014), 20. Brezhnev on p. 44. Vessey in Simon Miles, *Engaging the Evil Empire: Washington, Moscow, and the Beginning of the End of the Cold War* (Ithaca, NY: Cornell University Press, 2020), 35–36.
6. On Mahan, see Echevarria, *War's Logic*, 13–14; Bacevich, *The Age of Illusions*, 38–39; and Kennan, *American Diplomacy*, 6. Morgenthau, *Politics among Nations*, 73, 77.
7. Albert Wohlstetter, "His Defense Spending Will Help Redress a Perilous Imbalance," *Los Angeles Times*, 22 March 1981. Horrendous in Owen Ullmann, "Weidenbaum Decries Growth of Spending for Defense," *Los Angeles Times*, 27 August 1982. See also Levering, *The Cold War*, 192.
8. "C.I.A. Sees Stagnation in Soviet," *New York Times*, 31 May 1983. "C.I.A. Analysts Now Said to Find U.S. Overstated Soviet Arms Rise," *New York Times*, 3 March 1983. See also Immerman, *The Hidden Hand*, 142–44. On Haig, see Craig and Logevall, *America's Cold War*, 311. Weinberger in Wilson, *The Triumph of Improvisation*, 95. On Soviet economy, see Kotkin, *Armageddon Averted*, 124; Mearsheimer, *The Tragedy of Great Power Politics*, 149; and Haslam, *Russia's Cold War*, 328–29.

9. David Gold and Robert De Grasse, Jr., "Economic Recovery vs. Defense Spending," *New York Times*, 20 February 1981. Wallets in Leslie H. Gelb, "Conflict in Reagan's Favorite Goals," *New York Times*, 23 August 1981. On debt, see Brands, *What Good Is Grand Strategy?* 105. Social programs in De Groot 87; and Brenes, *For Might and Right*, 25, 233. Kirkland in Donaghy, 136.
10. Imperialists in Nate Jones, ed., *Able Archer 83: The Secret History of the NATO Exercise That Almost Triggered Nuclear War* (New York: New Press, 2016), 16. Hedrick Smith, "Brezhnev Rebuts Reagan View of U.S.-Soviet Rivalry," *New York Times*, 21 November 1981.
11. Strength in Leffler, *For the Soul of Mankind*, 346. The Committee of Santa Fe, *A New Inter-American Policy for the Eighties*, 1–3, 17, 52. See also Grandin, *Empire's Workshop*, 70.
12. Proof in Wertheim, *Tomorrow, the World*, 162. On exceptionalism, see Nye, *Do Morals Matter?* 55. Young in Bradley and Dudziak, *Making the Forever War*, 34.
13. Vincent Canby, "'Rambo' Delivers a Revenge Fantasy," *New York Times*, 26 May 1985. Complex in Fuller, "Reagan and the Evolution of US Counterterrorism," 69. GI Joe and *Top Gun* in Benjamin Griffin, *Reagan's War Stories: A Cold War Presidency* (Annapolis, MD: Naval Institute Press, 2022), 8, 106. Brute force in Lawrence Christon, "Imperiled Masculinity and Screen Warriors," *Los Angeles Times*, 22 June 1986.
14. Principle in Christon. Tests in Robert D. Dean, *Imperial Brotherhood: Gender and the Making of Cold War Foreign Policy* (Amherst: University of Massachusetts Press, 2001), 3. Alsop in Hitchcock, *The Age of Eisenhower*, 399.
15. Gaddis, *The Cold War: A New History*, 217. Peace through strength in Donaghy, 118. Follow-through in Leslie H. Gelb, "Reagan, Power and the World," *New York Times*, 13 November 1983. On links between Reagan and Roosevelt, see Robert G. Kaiser, "Why Can't the Democrats Get at Reagan?" *Washington Post*, 13 November 1983; and David A. Smith, *Cowboy Presidents: The Frontier Myth and U.S. Politics since 1900* (Norman: University of Oklahoma Press, 2021).
16. Hussein in Cleveland and Bunton, *A History of the Modern Middle East*, 443. Iran-Iraq war in Peter L. Hahn, *Mission Accomplished? The United States and Iraq since World War I* (New York: Oxford University Press, 2012), 70–71. Zealots and crimping in Robert C. Toth, "Analysts Fear Impact of Iran-Iraq War Will Spread," *Los Angeles Times*, 22 July 1981. Soviet aid in Robert K. Brigham, ed., *The United States and Iraq since 1990: A Brief History with Documents* (West Sussex, UK: Wiley-Blackwell, 2014), 5–6. On access to oil, see Monica Duffy Toft and Sidita Kushi, *Dying by the Sword: The Militarization of US Foreign Policy* (New York: Oxford University Press, 2023), 98.

17. On the aging politburo, see Kotkin, *Armageddon Averted*, 50–51, 53; and Jones, *Able Archer 83*, 18. Harrison E. Salisbury, "The Russia Reagan Faces," *New York Times*, 1 February 1981.
18. Toft and Kushi argue that in the post-Reagan years, "the United States grew to prefer the direct use of force over threats or displays of force." *Dying by the Sword*, 19.

CHAPTER 18

1. Low-intensity conflict in David Fitzgerald, *Learning to Forget: US Army Counterinsurgency Doctrine and Practice from Vietnam to Iraq* (Stanford, CA: Stanford Security Studies, 2013), 60. Memo in Mark Atwood Lawrence, "Rhetoric and Restraint: Ronald Reagan and the Vietnam Syndrome," in Hunt and Miles, *The Reagan Moment*, 178. Of course, the defense buildup also focused on enhancing US nuclear forces. See Miles, *Engaging the Evil Empire*, 37.
2. Focus and weapons systems in Frederick W. Kagan, *Finding the Target: The Transformation of American Military Policy* (New York: Encounter, 2006), 61. Deep battle in Christopher Tuck, "Land warfare," in Jordan, James D. Kiras, et al., *Understanding Modern Warfare*, 98. Muehlbauer and Ulbrich, *Ways of War*, 487. Rapid and violent in Trauschweizer, *The Cold War U.S. Army*, 226.
3. NSDD-32 in "Doctrine," *New York Times*, 15 January 1984. On the directive, Donaghy, *The Second Cold War*, 129, 150–51; Wilson, *The Triumph of Improvisation*, 31–32; and William Inboden, "Grand Strategy and Petty Squabbles: The Paradox and Lessons of the Reagan NSC," in Brands and Suri, *The Power of the Past*, 163–64.
4. Carterism in Norman Podhoretz, "The Neo-Conservative Anguish over Reagan's Foreign Policy," *New York Times*, 2 May 1982. On Reagan's portrayal of Carter, see William Michael Schmidli, "Reframing Human Rights: Reagan's 'Project Democracy' and the US Intervention in Nicaragua," in Hunt and Miles, *The Reagan Moment*, 239. Expansionism in Inboden, *The Peacemaker*, 138.
5. Haig in Snyder, *Human Rights Activism and the End of the Cold War*, 139; and Weiner, *Legacy of Ashes*, 388. Support base on p. 389. Center in Immerman, *The Hidden Hand*, 160. On fear and terrorism, see Echevarria, *Military Strategy*, 76.
6. Commandos in official trailer, *The Delta Force*, dir. Menahem Golan (Cannon Group, 1986). Fiction in Vincent Canby, "Screen: 'Delta Force,'" *New York Times*, 14 February 1986. For an excellent movie analysis, see McAlister, *Epic Encounters*, 225–29.
7. On low-intensity conflict and direct versus indirect, see Fitzgerald, *Learning to Forget*, 68–74. Teen-age patriots Vincent Canby, "Cockeyed at 'Red

Dawn,'" *New York Times*, 16 September 1984. Clancy in Bacevich, *The New American Militarism*, 117. War college in Griffin, *Reagan's War Stories*, 140.

8. Israeli actions in Chamberlin, "The Cold War in the Middle East," in Kalinovsky and Daigle, *The Routledge Handbook of the Cold War*, 174; and Shai Feldman, "Israel's Involvement in Lebanon: 1975–1985," in Levite, Jentleson, and Berman, *Foreign Military Intervention*, 132–35. On US intervention, see Little, *American Orientalism*, 246. Missions in Bolger, *Americans at War*, 208. Rocket fire on p. 244.

9. Death tolls in Lüthi, *Cold Wars*, 518. Demonstrating strength in Brownlee, *Democracy Prevention*, 47. On projecting power, see Bacevich, *America's War for the Greater Middle East*, 68, 76.

10. Pressures in Little, *American Orientalism*, 247, 248. White House debate in Inboden, *The Peacemaker*, 239–42; and John Gans, *White House Warriors: How the National Security Council Transformed the American Way of War* (New York: Liveright, 2019), 82. "Transcript of President Reagan's News Conference on the Attack in Beirut," *New York Times*, 25 October 1983. Cut and run in Lüthi, 518. Convincing in Jack Nelson, "The Beirut Bombings," *Los Angeles Times*, 25 October 1983. Sara Fritz and Karen Tumulty, "Troops 'Like Cheese in Trap,' a Father Says," *Los Angeles Times*, 30 December 1983.

11. Elimination in Gelvin, *The Israel-Palestine Conflict*, 220. On the PLO, see Khalidi, *The Hundred Years' War on Palestine*, 142, 150. Intifada in Cleveland and Bunton, 452–53. Leverage in Fitzgerald, *Learning to Forget*, 67. On Soviet issues in the region, see Oren, *Six Days of War*, 43; and Mandelbaum, *The Four Ages of American Foreign Policy*, 350.

12. Symbolic and resolve in Grow, *U.S. Presidents and Latin American Interventions*, 154. Power and morale on p. 155. On linkages between Lebanon and Grenada, see Inboden, *The Peacemaker*, 243; Weiner, *Legacy of Ashes*, 391–93; and Lawrence, "Rhetoric and Restraint," 179. For an overview, see Longley, "U.S. Troops as an Instrument in Foreign Policy," in Thompson and Frentzos, *The Routledge Handbook of American Military and Diplomatic History*, 301–2.

13. William Pfaff, "Grenada: The Question Is Really Colonialism," *Los Angeles Times*, 13 November 1983. Soviet leaders in Zubok, *A Failed Empire*, 275. Clear-cut in Bolger, *Americans at War*, 351.

14. On Reagan savoring the Grenada victory, see Donaghy, 199. Industrial warfare and peace operations in Mackinlay, *The Insurgent Archipelago*, 66. Young in Bradley and Dudziak, *Making the Forever War*, 167.

15. Reagan in Hedrick Smith, "Men at War: From Beirut to Grenada, The Price of Power Rises," *New York Times*, 30 October 1983. Peacekeeping in Steven Metz, *Iraq & the Evolution of American Strategy* (Washington, DC:

Potomac, 2008), 63, 65. On increasing commitments linked to avoiding global reverses, see Brands, *The Twilight Struggle*, 87.
16. Sara Fritz, "'New Vietnam' Fears Fading in Congress," *Los Angeles Times*, 14 July 1985. See also Braithwaite, *Afghansty*, 331–32. Inflicting pain in Feifer, *The Great Gamble*, 131. Bleeders in Victor Sebestyen, *Revolution 1989: The Fall of the Soviet Empire* (New York: Pantheon, 2009), 199–200.
17. Goading in "Discretion in Aid to Afghans," *Los Angeles Times*, 16 May 1985. Reprisals in Hassan Kakar, *Afghanistan: The Soviet Invasion and the Afghan Response, 1979–1982* (Berkeley: University of California Press, 1995), 257. Soviet faith in force in Barfield, *Afghanistan*, 237–38. CIA in Weiner, *Legacy of Ashes*, 420; and Robert Rakove, "The Central Front of Reagan's Cold War: The United States and Afghanistan," in Hunt and Miles, *The Reagan Moment*, 325.
18. Fears in Barfield, 233–35. Impotent in Artyom Borovik, *The Hidden War: A Russian Journalist's Account of the Soviet War in Afghanistan* (New York: Grove, 1990), 13. On military operations, see the Russian General Staff, *the Soviet-Afghan War: How a Superpower Fought and Lost*, ed. and trans. Lester W. Grau and Michael A. Gress (Lawrence: University Press of Kansas, 2002).
19. For a short overview, see Bill, *The Eagle and the Lion*, 304–6. Saddam's aims in Lüthi, *Cold Wars*, 506–7. US support to Iraq in Little, *American Orientalism*, 249. De-designated in Bacevich, *America's War for the Greater Middle East*, 90. Iran support on p. 94.
20. CIA analyst Bruce Riedel quoted in Blight et al., *Becoming Enemies*, 104. US strategic aims on p. 309. See also Byrne, *Iran-Contra*, 30–31. War's consequences in Hahn, *Mission Accomplished?* 73–75.
21. David Lamb, "Governments Facing Challenges: Islamic Fundamentalism a Growing Force in Mideast," *Los Angeles Times*, 10 January 1983. See also Chamberlin, *The Cold War's Killing Fields*, 529, 530. On holy wars, see Mitchell and Rey, *War and Religion*, 35. Commitment in Judith Miller, "Moslem World Is Unsettled by Surge in Fundamentalism," *New York Times*, 18 December 1983. Palestinian nationalism in Salim Yaqub, "The Cold War and the Middle East," in McMahon, *The Cold War in the Third World*, 17–18.
22. Faith in Chamberlin, 557. Weapons sales in Josh Pollack, "Saudi Arabia and the United States, 1931–2002," *Middle East Review of International Affairs*, Vol. 6, No. 3 (September 2002): 83. For a broader overview of the relationship, see McFarland, *Oil Powers*, 7, 9, 43–107. Bernard Gwertzman, "U.S. Plans to Sell Advanced Missiles to Saudi Arabia," *New York Times*, 11 March 1986.
23. Tool in Khalidi, *Sowing Crisis*, 19–20, 22. See also Rashid Khalidi, "The Superpowers and the Cold War in the Middle East," in Lesch and Haas,

The Middle East and the United States, 124–26. On violence toward Muslims, see John Bodnar, *Divided by Terror: American Patriotism after 9/11* (Chapel Hill: University of North Carolina Press, 2021), 215–44. On the subject of using religion as an ideological tool during the early Cold War era, we might suggest that an ill-informed faith in war combined with an overwhelming fear of communism that blinded Americans to the potential future pitfalls of such policies.

24. Religious faith in Griffin, *Reagan's War Stories*, 49. On NSDD-75, see Wilson, *The Triumph of Improvisation*, 66–71; Inboden, "Grand Strategy and Petty Squabbles," 165–66; and Mann, *The Rebellion of Ronald Reagan*, 30. Internal administration debates in Donaghy, 168–70. Internal affairs in Robert C. Toth, "Economic Squeeze of Soviets Ordered," *Los Angeles Times*, 16 March 1983.

25. "Transcript of President's State of Union Address to Congress," *New York Times*, 7 February 1985. Cost-effective in Gregory A. Fossedal, "What Does the Reagan Doctrine Really Mean?" *New York Times*, 18 June 1988. See also Hemmer, *Pendulum*, 100. Transcend in O'Riordan, *Understanding the Cold War*, 391. Hunt and Miles, *The Reagan Moment*, 29. Soviet leaders in Donaghy, 171; and Sebestyen, *Revolution 1989*, 82.

26. Communist threat in Byrne, *Iran-Contra*, 8–11, 21–22. On counterinsurgency, see D'Haeseleer, *The Salvadoran Crucible*, 4–10. Counterrevolutionaries in Grow, *U.S. Presidents and Latin American Interventions*, 114. Shultz in Gil Troy, *Morning in America: How Reagan Invented the 1980s* (Princeton, NJ: Princeton University Press, 2005), 243. For a superb overview, see Mateo Jarquín, *The Sandinista Revolution: A Global Latin American History* (Chapel Hill: University of North Carolina Press, 2024).

27. Kirkpatrick in Shirley Christian, "Nicaragua Week in the Capital," *New York Times*, 18 April 1985. See also Grandin, *Empire's Workshop*, 72–73. On Munich, see Lebovic, *The Limits of U.S. Military Capability*, 8.

28. Doctrine in Brigham, "After the Fall of Saigon," in Ryan and Fitzgerald, *Not Even Past*, 95. On the modified doctrine that followed, see Walter LaFeber, "The Rise and Fall of Colin Powell and the Powell Doctrine," *Political Science Quarterly*, Vol. 124, No. 1 (Spring 2009): 71–93.

29. Bob Woodward, *The Commanders* (New York: Simon & Schuster, 1991), 117. Support in Christopher Layne, "The Weinberger Doctrine," *Los Angeles Times*, 6 December 1984. Vietnam's relevance in Lebovic, 2. Summers in Echevarria, *War's Logic*, 148.

30. Moral struggle in Grandin, *Empire's Workshop*, 81. Dominoes and land reform in Rabe, *The Killing Zone*, 173. George Skelton, "Reagan Sees Hemispheric Threat in Salvador Conflict," *Los Angeles Times*, 5 March 1983. Enemy hands in D'Haeseleer, 65–67.

31. USS *Honduras* in Vine, *Base Nation*, 101–2; and Byrne, *Iran-Contra*, 23. Kissinger Commission report in Grow, 187.

32. On support to Contras, see Jack Devine and Amanda Mattingly, "The Iran-Contra Affair and the Afghan Task Force: Lessons in Covert Action," in *Routledge Handbook of US Counterterrorism and Irregular Warfare*, ed. Michael A. Sheehan, Erich Marquardt, and Liam Collins (London: Routledge, 2022), 213–14. Slaughter in Bevins, *The Jakarta Method*, 219. Mercenaries in House, *A Military History of the Cold War, 1962–1991*, 73. Dictatorship in Grandin, 71. Opposition and human rights in Schmidli, "Reframing Human Rights," 241–42; and John H. Coatsworth, "The Cold War in Central America, 1975–1991," in Leffler and Westad, *The Cambridge History of the Cold War*, Vol. III, 212–14. Church in Graebner, Burns, and Siracusa, *America and the Cold War*, Vol. 2, 472.
33. Jim Mann, "Communism Spread by Force, President Charges," *Los Angeles Times*, 15 April 1984. Pledge in Simon Miles, "Peace through Strength and Quiet Diplomacy: Grand Strategy Lessons from the Reagan Administration," in Monteiro and Bartel, *Before and After the Fall*, 68. Contradictions in Brands, *Latin America's Cold War*, 185, 190, 192. Local consequences in Rabe, 170. Credibility in Grow, *U.S. Presidents and Latin American Interventions*, 127. D'Haeseleer claims the "US experience in El Salvador confirms that outside intervention in civil wars exacerbates an already volatile situation and extends the bloodshed." *The Salvadoran Crucible*, 164.
34. For a contemporary overview of Iran-Contra, see "Key Sections of Document: The Making of a Political Crisis," *New York Times*, 19 November 1987. Boland in Rabe, *The Killing Zone*, 169. On scheme, see Byrne, *Iran-Contra*, 3, 162–63, 186. Ignorance in Immerman, *The Hidden Hand*, 130.
35. Paramilitary and harnessing in Burke, *Revolutionaries for the Right*, 153, 196. Reagan quoted on p. 138. Freedom fighters in Sara Fritz, "Reagan Doctrine Seen as a Policy Watershed," *Los Angeles Times*, 31 August 1986. On the CIA, see Vine, *The United States of War*, 250; and Byrne, 56, 57, 59.
36. Exaggeration in Mueller, *Overblown*, 67. Enemy of humanity in, oddly enough, Christopher Dickey, "U.S.-Nicaraguan Relations Show Signs of Improvement," *Washington Post*, 12 June 1980. Bloc in Brands, 157.
37. Amnesia, citing North, in Byrne, *Iran-Contra*, 253. Henry Steele Commager, "Real Threat to U.S. Stems from Historical Ignorance," *Los Angeles Times*, 27 May 1984.

CHAPTER 19

1. Faith in Haslam, *Russia's Cold War*, 330. Salesman in David Hoffman, "Public Skeptical of Contra Aid, Spending Increase for Pentagon," *Washington Post*, 16 March 1986. On support, see Tom Shales, "Reagan,

Looking Good," *Washington Post*, 25 April 1985. For an example of Reagan's "standard" speeches, see Graebner, Burns, and Siracusa, *America and the Cold War*, Vol. 2, 442.

2. Empire speech in Donaghy, *The Second Cold War*, 171. Salvation in Inboden, *The Peacemaker*, 200. Evangelicals in Griffin, *Reagan's War Stories*, 55. On the Cold War as a contest between religious faiths, see Chidester, *Authentic Fakes*, 107.

3. Evil in the world in Donaghy, 171. George Skelton, "Reagan Visits DMZ, Lauds GI Defenders," *Los Angeles Times*, 13 November 1983. Gromyko quoted in Zubok, *A Failed Empire*, 276.

4. Reluctance in Inboden, *The Peacemaker*, 9. Reagan in "Evil Empire . . . Come In, Evil Empire," *New York Times*, 17 January 1984.

5. Confrontational in Hemmer, *American Pendulum*, 101. Peace through strength in Wilson, *The Triumph of Improvisation*, 15. On arms control, see Miles, *Engaging the Evil Empire*, 51. Diplomacy in Donaghy, 15. Shultz in Miles, "Peace through Strength and Quiet Diplomacy," 67.

6. Freedoms and ideas in Inboden, 10–11. On Reagan being more sympathetic to the Soviets, see Haslam, *Russia's Cold War*, 332.

7. Deterrence in Posen, *Restraint*, 75. Reagan quoted in Fischer, "US Foreign Policy under Reagan and Bush," 277.

8. On START, see Graebner, Burns, and Siracusa, Vol. 2, 468–69. Soviet economic problems in Donaghy, 132–33.

9. Shield in Hanhimäki and Westad, *The Cold War*, 308. Star Wars in Graebner, Burns, and Siracusa, Vol. 2, 470. Avenge and transcend in Freedman and Michaels, *The Evolution of Nuclear Strategy*, 518–20. Faith in technology in Griffin, *Reagan's War Stories*, 145. MAD in Fink, *Cold War*, 209. Uncertainties in Bacevich, *The Limits of Power*, 41.

10. Awesome and ABM Treaty in Donaghy, 173–74. Abolition in Bernard Weinraub, "Reagan Foresees an End to A-Arms," *New York Times*, 5 November 1985.

11. Caspar W. Weinberger, "Strategic Defense Initiative," *Los Angeles Times*, 9 July 1985. Cartoonist in ibid. On ABM Treaty, see Mandelbaum, *The Four Ages of American Foreign Policy*, 348. Asimov in Griffin, *Reagan's War Stories*, 151.

12. Pentagon support in Kaplan, *The Bomb*, 155. Cowboy in Inboden, *The Peacemaker*, 151. Soviet reactions in Zubok, 273; and Donaghy, 181–83, 192. Gromyko on p. 251. See also Charles Mohr, "'Star Wars' Dispute," *New York Times*, 17 October 1985. Arms race in Lamberton Harper, *The Cold War*, 213. Jonathan Fuerbringer, "U.S. Deficit in 1985 to be $180 Billion, Reagan Aide Says," *New York Times*, 24 January 1984.

13. On Able Archer, see Miles, *Engaging the Evil Empire*, 80–83. Soviet leadership in Jones, *Able Archer 83*, 26. Cover in Kaplan, *The Bomb*, 161.

14. Debates in Jones, 34–35. Scary in Sam Roberts, "NATO Exercise Unwittingly Put Soviets on 'Hair Trigger' in '83, Analysis Suggests," *New York Times*, 10 November 2015. Reagan quoted in Donaghy, *The Second Cold War*, 215.
15. Weinberger in Edward Tabor Linenthal, *Symbolic Defense: The Cultural Significance of the Strategic Defense Initiative* (Urbana: University of Illinois Press, 1989), 67. Robert Shogan, "Nuclear Freeze Movement Emerges as Political Test," *Los Angeles Times*, 17 April 1982. Time and polling in J. Michael Hogan and Ted J. Smith III, "Polling on the Issues: Public Opinion and the Nuclear Freeze," *Public Opinion Quarterly*, Vol. 55, No. 4 (Winter 1991): 535, 538. On the freeze campaign, see Charles Chatfield, "American Insecurity: Dissent from the 'Long War,'" in Bacevich, *The Long War*, 486–88.
16. Fallout and syndromes in Hugh Middleton, "Epidemiology: The Future Is Sickness and Death," and J. E. Coggle and Patricia J. Lindop, "Medical Consequences of Radiation Following a Global Nuclear War," in *The Aftermath: The Human and Ecological Consequences of Nuclear War*, ed. Jeannie Peterson (New York: Pantheon, 1983), 54–55, 60. Sagan in Rubinson, *Redefining Science*, 175–81. Jonathan Schell, *The Fate of the Earth* (New York: Knopf, 1982), 50, 65.
17. On movie, see Heefner, *The Missile Next Door*, 149–50; and Andrew Hunt, *We Begin Bombing in Five Minutes: Late Cold War Culture in the Age of Reagan* (Amherst: University of Massachusetts Press, 2021), 112–20. Viewership in Kaplan, *The Bomb*, 159. Glenn Collins, "Students Voice Fear and Hopelessness in Talks the Day after 'The Day After,'" *New York Times*, 22 November 1983. Diary in Griffin, *Reagan's War Stories*, 111. Poll in Lamberton Harper, *The Cold War*, 215.
18. Roundtable in Dan Sullivan, "After the Shock of 'The Day After,'" *Los Angeles Times*, 22 November 1983. A version of the conversation can be found on YouTube under "'The Day After' Nuclear War/Deterrence Discussion Panel—ABC News 'Viewpoint' (November 20 1983)."
19. Sun Ra Arkestra, "Nuclear War," *Nuclear War*, Atavistic Records, 1982. Call-and-response in Paul Youngquist, *A Pure Solar World: Sun Ra and the Birth of Afrofuturism* (Austin: University of Texas Press, 2106), 238. Songs in Cull and Mazumdar, "Propaganda in the Cold War," in Kalinovsky and Daigle, *The Routledge Handbook of the Cold War*, 334. See also *WarGames*, dir. John Badham (Metro-Goldwyn-Mayer, 1983), in which a military computer accidentally believes a game simulation is the start of World War III.
20. Lack of meetings in Donaghy, 212. Arthur Macy Cox, *Russian Roulette: The Superpower Game* (New York: Times Books, 1982), 5. Robert Jervis, "War and Misperception," *The Journal of Interdisciplinary History*, Vol. 18, No. 4 (Spring 1988): 675. W. Averell Harriman, "If the Reagan

Pattern Continues, America May Face Nuclear War," *New York Times*, 1 January 1984.

21. Ruling circles, citing Chernenko, in Wilson, *The Triumph of Improvisation*, 73. Fears of SDI in Inboden, *The Peacemaker*, 364. Harvey Miles, "Religious Authorities Ask Reagan, Mondale to Repudiate 'Armageddon Ideology' on Nuclear War," *Los Angeles Times*, 24 October 1984.

22. Reagan in "'That Neither Likes the Other's System Is No Reason Not to Talk,'" *Washington Post*, 17 January 1984. On improvisation and peace, see Wilson, 6, 13.

23. Sufficiency in Wilson, 4. See also Friedberg, *In the Shadow of the Garrison State*, 346. On Gorbachev, see Zubok, *A Failed Empire*, 282; and O'Riordan, *Understanding the Cold War*, 394–95.

24. Framework in Wilson, 75. Dialogue in Donaghy, *The Second Cold War*, 155. On Shultz, see Mann, *The Rebellion of Ronald Reagan*, 242–51.

25. On multiple issues, see Cardwell, "The Cold War," in Costigliola and Hogan, *America in the World*, 112.

26. Fear in Leffler, *For the Soul of Mankind*, 358. Hardliners in Wilson, 5. Socialism in Kotkin, *Armageddon Averted*, 56–57. Doubts in Kaplan, *The Bomb*, 165. Quayle in Mann, 263. CIA specialist, Robert M. Gates, on p. 38.

27. Molly Moore, "Perle Berates U.S. Allies in NATO as 'Mealy-Mouthed,'" *Washington Post*, 2 February 1987. "The Light and Darkness of Richard Perle," *New York Times*, 16 March 1987. Richard N. Perle, "Like Putting the K.G.B. into the Pentagon," *New York Times*, 30 June 1987. Shred and naive in Sidney Blumenthal, "Perle and the Diminished Dream: The Long, Frustrating Crusade for SDI," *Washington Post*, 25 November 1987. Prince in Jim Hoagland, "Old Foes, New Friends," *Washington Post*, 2 April 1992. On Perle, see Alan Weisman, *Prince of Darkness Richard Perle: The Kingdom, the Power and the End of Empire in America* (New York: Union Square, 2007).

28. On the KAL 007 disaster, see Miles, *Engaging the Evil Empire*, 57–58; and Sebestyen, *Revolution 1989*, 84–85. Barbarism in "Transcript of President Reagan's Address on Downing of Korean Airliner," *New York Times*, 6 September 1983. Anthony Lewis, "Why Reagan Blinked," *New York Times*, 2 October 1986.

29. Soviet resistance to reforms in Kotkin, 65–66, 74, 82. For a critical view of Gorbachev, see Gaddis, *The Cold War: A New History*, 230–33. Leffler, *For the Soul of Mankind*, 461.

30. Burden in Bill Keller, "Civil War Goes On," *New York Times*, 16 February 1989. Aide in Sebestyen, 152. Loss of faith in Braithwaite, *Afghantsy*, 274, 278. Extracting in Feifer, *The Great Gamble*, 238.

31. Proxies in House, *A Military History of the Cold War, 1962–1991*, 362. Balance in Carter Malkasian, *The American War in Afghanistan: A*

History (New York: Oxford University Press, 2021), 32. Civil War on p. 36. Wounds in Leffler, 403.
32. Consequences in Leffler, 411; and Rakove, "The Central Front of Reagan's Cold War," in Hunt and Miles, *The Reagan Moment*, 339. On effects of support to mujahedeen, see Anand Gopal, *No Good Men among the Living: America, the Taliban, and the War through Afghan Eyes* (New York: Picador, 2014), 56–57, 60. Scorched earth and younger generation in Kakar, *Afghanistan*, 225, 295.
33. On the Taliban's rise and oil fields, see Ahmed Rashid, *Taliban: Militant Islam, Oil and Fundamentalism in Central Asia*, 2nd ed. (New Haven, CT: Yale University Press, 2010), 13, 25, 35, 163; and Goodson, *Afghanistan's Endless Wars*, 77–81, 92. Students and jihad in Stephen Tanner, *Afghanistan: A Military History from Alexander the Great to the War against the Taliban* (Philadelphia: Da Capo, 2009), 279.
34. "'Mr. Gorbachev, Open This Gate, Tear Down This Wall,'" *Los Angeles Times*, 12 June 1987. For an analysis, see Mann, *The Rebellion of Ronald Reagan*, 117–21, 212–13.
35. On Soviet thinking, see Hemmer, *American Pendulum*, 104–5. Deficit spending in Bacevich, *The Limits of Power*, 39–40. Reagan once noted that "defense is not a budget item." In Artemy M. Kalinovsky and Craig Daigle, "Explanations for the End of the Cold War," in Kalinovsky and Daigle, *The Routledge Handbook of the Cold War*, 376.
36. Isolation in Westad, *The Cold War*, 528. Economic issues in Zubok, *A Failed Empire*, 268. Destroy in Sebestyen, *Revolution 1989*, 230. Liabilities in Lüthi, *Cold Wars*, 572. Reagan in Donaghy, 270.
37. Peace dividend in Zubok, *A Failed Empire*, 332. Economic challenges on pp. 313, 327. Economic crisis and socialist democracy in Vladislav M. Zubok, *Collapse: The Fall of the Soviet Union* (New Haven, CT: Yale University Press, 2021), 4, 42. On security through cooperation, see O'Riordan, *Understanding the Cold War*, 398.
38. Polish Crisis in Lüthi, *Cold Wars*, 544–50. Warsaw Pact in Mann, 173–75; and Fritz Bartel, "Overcoming Stagnation: Global Finance and the Search for 'New Thinking' on the End of the Cold War," in Monteiro and Bartel, *Before and After the Fall*, 39.
39. Trust in Leffler, 448. Soviet elites and promises in Kotkin, *Armageddon Averted*, 27, 29–30. On relation to Soviet economic woes, see Zubok, *Collapse*, 62. William Safire, "'The Risks of Distrust,'" *New York Times*, 9 December 1987.
40. Strategic-arms experts in Brent Scowcroft, John Deutch, and R. James Woolsey, "A Way out of Reykjavik," *New York Times*, 25 January 1987. On summit meetings, see Kaplan, *The Bomb*, 171, 172; Sarah B. Snyder, "'No Crowing': Reagan, Trust, and Human Rights," in Klimke, Kreis, and Ostermann, *Trust, but Verify*, 48–54; Loth, *Overcoming the Cold War*,

191–93; and Inboden, *The Peacemaker*, 410–17. Nixon, Kissinger, and Scowcroft in Griffin, *Reagan's War Stories*, 116–17.

41. Appeasement in Philip M. Kaiser, "Reagan Is No Chamberlain," *New York Times*, 5 February 1988. Will and Krauthammer in Dinesh D'Souza, "Reagan's Misguided Heirs Forget What He Stood For," *Washington Post*, 23 November 1997. Phillips in "U.S. Conservatives Assail Reagan Over Arms Treaty," *Los Angeles Times*, 6 December 1987. On overlooking something "fundamental about Gorbachev," see Donaghy, 255. Peace offensive in Sergey Radchenko, "Mikhail Gorbachev: The Anatomy of New Thinking," in Monteiro and Bartel, *Before and After the Fall*, 53.

42. On abolition, see Wilson, *The Triumph of Improvisation*, 101–2. On Chernobyl, see ibid., 105–6; Lüthi, *Cold Wars*, 566; and Sebestyen, *Revolution 1989*, 180–82. Breath in Radchenko, "Mikhail Gorbachev," 50. Velikhov in Robert Scheer, "A Legacy of Ruin: Inside Chernobyl," *Los Angeles Times*, 9 April 1987. On victory, see Zubok, *A Failed Empire*, 288.

43. Summit, in Donaghy, *The Second Cold War*, 286; Wilson, 135–38; and Hemmer, *American Pendulum*, 102. On SDI, see Fink, *Cold War*, 234. "'A Decision Which Offers a New Hope for Our Children,'" *Washington Post*, 24 March 1983. Though Reagan spoke these words during his first term, he appears to have genuinely embraced them by his second. Gaddis, *The Cold War: A New History*, 226.

44. Maureen Dowd, "Washington Summit Song Is Off Key for Weinberger," *New York Times*, 12 December 1987. George. F. Will, "Drunk on Détente," *Washington Post*, 13 December 1987. Jan Kalicki, "A Re-Nuclearization of Europe?" *Los Angeles Times*, 16 February 1988. Helen Dewar, "Kissinger Backs Pact, with Misgivings," *Washington Post*, 24 February 1988. See also Mann, *The Rebellion of Ronald Reagan*, 286–87.

45. Concentrating on communists in Williams, *The Tragedy of American Diplomacy*, 289. On appeasement, see Khong, *Analogies at War*, 175, 189. Shultz in Donaghy, 285. Accuracy in Media in James Gerstenzang, "Conservatives Hit Reagan on Treaty," *Los Angeles Times*, 5 December 1987.

CHAPTER 20

1. *Three Kings*, dir. David O. Russell (Warner Bros., 1999).
2. "Bush Text: 'Victory for All Mankind,'" *Los Angeles Times*, 28 February 1991. Rick Atkinson, "U.S. Victory Is Absolute," *Washington Post*, 1 March 1991. British officer in ibid.
3. "Kicking the 'Vietnam Syndrome,'" *Washington Post*, 4 March 1991. Norman Podhoretz, "Making the World Safe for Communism," *Commentary*, April 1976. On the syndrome, see George C. Herring, "The Vietnam

Syndrome," in *The Columbia History of the Vietnam War*, ed. David L. Anderson (New York: Columbia University Press, 2011), 409–30.
4. Obey and Lewis in "Kicking the 'Vietnam Syndrome.'"
5. Violence and order in Bacevich, *America's War for the Greater Middle East*, 131. Linkages in Gardner, *The Long Road to Baghdad*, 2, 92–94.
6. Thomas L. Friedman, "What the United States Has Taken On in the Gulf, Besides a War," *New York Times*, 20 January 1991.
7. Bush quoted in Jeffrey A. Engel, "George H. W. Bush: Strategy and the Stream of History," in Borgwardt, McKnight Nichols, and Preston, *Rethinking American Grand Strategy*, 303. On military enforcement and the liberal order, see Toft and Kushi, *Dying by the Sword*, 191. We might also ask if a successful grand strategy equals "peace," "stability," or, depending on the definitions of these key terms, something else.
8. Analysis in Michael R. Gordon, "Pentagon Drafts Strategy for Post–Cold War World," *New York Times*, 2 August 1990. Demanding missions in James Flanigan, "A New Military for the Post–Cold War Era," *Los Angeles Times*, 16 September 1990. On threats, see Lissner, *Wars of Revelation*, 110–11. New requirements in Bacevich, *The Age of Illusions*, 66. On deepening unease this caused, see Chollet and Goldgeier, *America between the Wars, from 11/9 to 9/11*, xiii.
9. On military decisions not being final, see Kennan, *American Diplomacy*, 129. Minefield in Zubok, *Collapse*, 51. On the 1990s "renaissance of modernization theory," see Robert M. Marsh, "Modernization Theory, Then and Now," *Comparative Sociology*, Vol. 14 (2014): 261–83.
10. On liberal theories, see Miller, *Grand Strategy from Truman to Trump*, 19, 23, 169–70. Mearsheimer, *The Tragedy of Great Power Politics*, 9. See also Anna Geis, Lothar Brock, and Harald Müller, "From Democratic Peace to Democratic War?" *Peace Review*, Vol. 19, No. 2 (June 2007): 157–63. Foundations in Kagan, *Dangerous Nation*, 39. Triumph in Benjamin Schwarz, "Why We're Stuck with Being No. 1," *Los Angeles Times*, 9 June 1997. See also Benjamin Schwarz, "Capitalism Is the Cold War Winner," *Los Angeles Times*, 6 February 1995.
11. Coercion, "illiberal," and *Pax Americana* in Porter, *The False Promise of Liberal Order*, 6, 7, 21. On illiberal sentiments being linked to "war-based patriotism," see Bodnar, *Divided by Terror*, 11. Criticisms came from Europe as well, with French Foreign Minister Hubert Vedrine defining the United States as a "hyperpower." "To Paris, U.S. Looks Like a 'Hyperpower,'" *New York Times*, 5 February 1999.
12. Guarantee and revolution in Burke, *Revolutionaries for the Right*, 7, 9. See also Fitzgerald, *Militarization and the American Century*, 143. The best treatment on this topic is Kathleen Belew, *Bring the War Home: The White Power Movement and Paramilitary America* (Cambridge, MA: Harvard University Press, 2018).

13. Peace dividend in Seymour Melman, "What to Do with the Cold War Money," *New York Times*, 17 December 1989. Melissa Healy, "Cold War's 'Peace Dividend' Is in Jeopardy, Cheney Warns," *New York Times*, 5 December 1990. Richard A. Brody and Richard Morin, "From Vietnam to Iraq: The Great American Syndrome Myth," *Washington Post*, 31 March 1991. On contemporary arguments that America pulling back would lead to increased regional conflicts, see Layne, *The Peace of Illusions*, 27.
14. George Will, "Always a War," *Washington Post*, 16 July 1995. Will was citing historian Sir Michael Howard regarding war's three functions. Donald Kagan, *On the Origins of War and the Preservation of Peace* (New York: Doubleday, 1995), 1.
15. Interventions in Lissner, *Wars of Revelation*, 151. Military activity in Porter, 104. "Excerpts from the News Conference Held by Bush and Kohl," *New York Times*, 26 February 1990. See also Lissner, 116. For a superb overview of the US military in this era, see David Fitzgerald, *Uncertain Warriors: The United States Army between the Cold War and the War on Terror* (New York: Cambridge University Press, 2024).
16. Baker quoted in Samuel P. Huntington, *The Third Wave: Democratization in the Late Twentieth Century* (Norman: University of Oklahoma Press, 1991), 284. Liberalization in "Superpowerdom: Is It the Mantle America Needs to Wear?" *Los Angeles Times*, 27 November 1994. Metanarrative and countries of concern in Liam Kennedy, *Afterimages: Photography and U.S. Foreign Policy* (Chicago: University of Chicago Press, 2016), 93.
17. Shalikashvili in "'Success Can Breed Forgetfulness,'" *Washington Post*, 28 September 1997.
18. Rogue states in Mueller, *Overblown*, 122. Jim Mann, "New U.S. Nuclear Policy to Focus on 'Rogue' Regimes," *Los Angeles Times*, 10 May 1994. Technologies in Lally Weymouth, "Good News for Rogue States," *Washington Post*, 4 February 1994. Lally Weymouth, "Chinese Take-Out," *Washington Post*, 12 August 1993. Taming outlaws in Stephen Rosenfeld, "The Menace of Rogue States," *Washington Post*, 7 June 1996. MAD in Brands, *The Twilight Struggle*, 61.
19. Georgi Arbatov quoted in John Dumbrell, *Clinton's Foreign Policy: Between the Bushes, 1992–2000* (London: Routledge, 2009), 22. See also Bacevich, *The Age of Illusions*, 2. Seeking to replace containment in Toft and Kushi, *Dying by the Sword*, 178.
20. On a "nonideological age," see Metz, *Iraq & the Evolution of American Strategy*, 54. Humanitarian in Kennedy, *Afterimages*, 94. Zone and interdependence in David Callahan, *Between Two Worlds: Realism, Idealism, and American Foreign Policy after the Cold War* (New York: HarperCollins, 1994), 5, 6.

CHAPTER 21

1. Nationalism in Kotkin, *Armageddon Averted*, 107. See also John-Thor Dahlburg, "Nationalism Stirs Turmoil in a Collapsing Soviet Union," *Los Angeles Times*, 7 October 1991. On liberalization, see Snyder, *Human Rights Activism and the End of the Cold War*, 7, 37, 53. Economy in Zubok, *Collapse*, 125. George Bush and Brent Scowcroft, *A World Transformed* (New York: Knopf, 1998), 140.
2. On Poland, see Sebestyen, *Revolution 1989*, 21, 40–41. Solidarity in Zubok, *A Failed Empire*, 265–66. Contagion on p. 41. See also Judt, *Postwar*, 627–28. Of note, Polish anti-communists of the 1980s were not simply right-wing populists of their day, nor were they forerunners to authoritarian leaders like Hungarian Prime Minister Viktor Orban. Critiques of socialism in Zubok, *Collapse*, 15; and Kotkin, 19. Bill Keller, "Gorbachev Warns on Ethnic Unrest," *New York Times*, 2 July 1989. Sovietologists Colette Schulman and Marshall D. Schulman, "Gorbachev's Latest Gamble," *New York Times*, 30 July 1989.
3. Economic frustrations in Roger Cohenpirna, "An Empty Feeling Is Infecting Eastern Europe," *New York Times*, 21 March 1993. St. Petersburg mayor Anatoly A. Sobchak in Dahlburg.
4. R. W. Apple, Jr., "Prudent Meets Timid," *New York Times*, 15 October 1989. Critics in Stephen S. Rosenfeld, "World Cops and Ethnic Violence," *Washington Post*, 12 April 1991. Middle road in Dumbrell, *Clinton's Foreign Policy*, 23. Chaos and power in Engel, "George H. W. Bush," 295; and Wilson, *The Triumph of Improvisation*, 148.
5. John M. Broder, "'Cold War Is Not Over,' Bush Advisor Cautions," *Los Angeles Times*, 23 January 1989. Bush and Scowcroft, *A World Transformed*, 13–14. See also Sarotte, *The Collapse*, 121; and Sebestyen, *Revolution 1989*, 265.
6. Margaret Garrard Warner, "George Bush: Fighting the 'Wimp Factor,'" *Newsweek*, 19 October 1987. "George Bush's Wimp Label a Misnomer," *Los Angeles Times*, 23 October 1987.
7. On peaceful transition, see Wilson, 157.
8. Sarotte, *The Collapse*, 179–80. Jackson Diehl, "Prospect of Reunified Germany Raises Concern in Israel," *Washington Post*, 2 February 1990. David Remnick, "Soviets Are Haunted by Fear of Powerful Unified Germany," *Washington Post*, 12 February 1990.
9. Bush and Scowcroft, *A World Transformed*, 44, 186. Influence in Ostermann, *Between Containment and Rollback*, x. On NATO, see Wilson, 174, 184. Insistence on ties to Germany in Graebner, Burns, and Siracusa, *America and the Cold War*, Vol. 2, 497. Thatcher in Helga Hafterdorn, "The Unification of Germany, 1985–1991," Leffler and Westad, *The Cambridge History of the Cold War*, Vol. III, 343.

10. Khrushchev in Leffler, *For the Soul of Mankind*, 163. Tom Lehrer, "MLF Lullaby," *That Was the Year That Was*, Reprise Records, 1965. Jeff Gerth and Tim Weiner, "Arms Makers See Bonanza in Selling NATO Expansion," *New York Times*, 29 June 1997. See also Renouard, *Human Rights in American Foreign Policy*, 74.
11. Thomas L. Friedman, "NATO's Difficult Career Change," *New York Times*, 9 June 1991. Bush and Scowcroft, 230. Albright in Mary Elise Sarotte, "The Historical Legacy of 1989: The Arc to Another Cold War?" in Monteiro and Bartel, *Before and after the Fall*, 296. NATO in James Goldgeier and Joshua Shifrinson, "The United States and NATO after the End of the Cold War: Explaining and Evaluating Enlargement and Its Alternatives," ibid., 274–75.
12. On competing models for the future, see Mary Elise Sarotte, *1989: The Struggle to Create Post–Cold War Europe* (Princeton, NJ: Princeton University Press, 2009), 5–9. Persistent fears in Thomas L. Friedman, "NATO Tries to Ease Security Concerns in Eastern Europe," *New York Times*, 7 June 1991.
13. Fears in Kotkin, *Armageddon Averted*, 170, 181. Reticence in Engel, "George H. W. Bush," 298, 300. Douglas Jehl and John M. Broder, "Soviet Collapse Likely, Bush's Aides Conclude," *Los Angeles Times*, 28 August 1991. George F. Kennan, "After the Cold War," *New York Times*, 5 February 1989.
14. Hegemony in Layne, *The Peace of Illusions*, 111, 113. Client states in Joshua R. Shifrinson, "NATO Enlargement and US Foreign Policy: The Origins, Durability, and Impact of an Idea," *International Politics*, Vol. 57, No. 3 (June 2020): 345. Soldiers quoted in Craig R. Whitney, "Cold War Past, Germans Ask Why Army Is Still Necessary," *New York Times*, 23 June 1992.
15. Bush and Scowcroft, *A World Transformed*, 299. On Putin, see Miles, *Engaging the Evil Empire*, 136–39.
16. Enlargement in Christopher Layne and Benjamin C. Schwarz, "The Perils of Stability," *New York Times*, 3 October 1993. Lack of threat in Metz, *Iraq & the Evolution of American Strategy*, 53. Alison Mitchell, "Clinton Girding For Stiff Debate On NATO Issue," *New York Times*, 27 May 1997. Pause in Kagan, *Finding the Target*, 176. On enlargement and engagement, see Dumbrell, *Clinton's Foreign Policy*, 42–43; Martel, *Grand Strategy in Theory and Practice*, 312–14; and James Mark, Bogdan C. Iacob, Tobias Rupprecht, and Ljubica Spaskovska, *1989: A Global History of Eastern Europe* (New York: Cambridge University Press, 2019), 152.
17. Collective engagement in Hemmer, *American Pendulum*, 113. Bush quoted in Sayle, *Enduring Alliance*, 223. Alison Mitchell, "Clinton Urges

NATO Expansion in 1999," *New York Times*, 23 October 1996. Aggressors in Robert W. Tucker and David C. Hendrickson, *The Imperial Temptation: The New World Order and America's Purpose* (New York: Council on Foreign Relations Press, 1992), 49. Deterrence versus prevention in Rapp-Hooper, *Shields of the Republic*, 102–4. On a retooled NATO, see Chollet and Goldgeier, *America between the Wars*, 124–25.

18. Long-term viability in Michael Scammell, "Will the Coup Kill Communism?" *New York Times*, 21 August 1991. "Gorbachev's Speech to Russians," *New York Times*, 24 August 1991. Fears of hardliners and a return to authoritarianism in Zubok, *Collapse*, 215; and Mark, Iacob, Rupprecht, and Spaskovska, *1989*, 119.

19. Triumphant in Kwon, *The Other Cold War*, 5. John Lewis Gaddis, "One Germany—in Both Alliances," *New York Times*, 21 March 1990. Baker in Zubok, *Collapse*, 342. Liberal order in Lissner and Rapp-Hooper, *An Open World*, 11. See also Lüthi, *Cold Wars*, 596.

20. On Panama, see Barry Mowell, "Operation Just Cause: The U.S. Invasion of Panama," in Thompson and Frentzos, *The Routledge Handbook of American Military and Diplomatic History*, 315–22. Powell in Grow, *U.S. Presidents and Latin American Interventions*, 180.

21. On Just Cause, see Martel, *Victory in War*, 215–30. Relation to Vietnam in Woodward, *The Commanders*, 163. Operation Just Because in Andrew Cockburn, "Because We Could," *The Nation*, 8 November 2004. R. W. Apple, Jr., "Bush's Trap on Panama: Can He Avoid Label of a Gringo Meddler?" *New York Times*, 11 May 1989. Homeopathic in Bradley and Dudziak, *Making the Forever War*, 59.

22. Bold era and looting in Brian McAllister Linn, *The Echo of Battle: The Army's Way of War* (Cambridge, MA: Harvard University Press, 2007), 220. Twenty-four invasions in Vine, *The United States of War*, 129. David E. Pitt, "Panama to Assist the U.S. on Drug War," *New York Times*, 11 January 1990. Democratic nation building in Grandin, *Empire's Workshop*, 191–92.

23. Hitler analogies in H. W. Brands, "Neither Munich nor Vietnam: The Gulf War of 1991," in Brands and Suri, *The Power of the Past*, 79–82; and Raymond Cohen, "Crush Iraqi War Power or No Deal," *Los Angeles Times*, 3 October 1990. Warspeak in Howard Rosenberg, "The Pen as Sword in Gulf . . . Situation," *Los Angeles Times*, 28 September 1990. Saddam's actions in Hahn, *Mission Accomplished?* 89–91.

24. Webster in Little, *American Orientalism*, 255. R. W. Apple, Jr., "Naked Aggression: Bush Suggests Action by U.N.," *New York Times*, 3 August 1990. No constraints in Engel, "George H. W. Bush," 305. Coalition and UN in Joseph Stieb, *The Regime Change Consensus: Iraq in American Politics, 1990–2003* (New York: Cambridge University Press, 2021), 21. On

the Cold War still informing Saddam's decision-making, see Daniel Chardell, "The Origins of the Iraqi Invasion of Kuwait Reconsidered," *Texas National Security Review*, Vol. 6, No. 3 (Summer 2023): 51–78.

25. Precision in Lewis, *The American Culture of War*, 341. Technology in Stephen Biddle, *Military Power: Explaining Victory and Defeat in Modern Battle* (Princeton, NJ: Princeton University Press, 2004), 132. Diagram in John M. Broder, "U.S. Air Power Has Formidable Options in Gulf," *Los Angeles Times*, 24 August 1990.

26. On Boyd and Warden, see Kort, "Contemporary Strategic Theories and Their Influence on Doctrine," in Finney, *On Strategy*, 71, 78; Echevarria, *War's Logic*, 177, 185–87, 197–98, 205; Echevarria, *Military Strategy*, 23, 90–91; and Freedman, *Strategy*, 196–98.

27. On economic sanctions, see Bush and Scowcroft, *A World Transformed*, 404, 439. On Bush's decision to go to war, see H. W. Brands, "George Bush and the Gulf War of 1991," *Presidential Studies Quarterly*, Vol. 34, No. 1 (March 2004): 113–31. Influx in Sandra Friedland, "State Readies Plan to Treat Casualties Of Gulf War," *New York Times*, 3 February 1991. Glosson in Lewis, *The American Culture of War*, 347. Muscle in Jim Hoagland, "Bush's America: Welcome to the Post-Gulf World," *Washington Post*, 3 March 1991.

28. Vietnam links in Brigham, "After the Fall of Saigon," in Ryan and Fitzgerald, *Not Even Past*, 98–99. Go home in David Ryan, "The Ironies of Overwhelming 'Victory': Exits and the Dislocation of the Gulf War," in Ryan and Fitzgerald, 116. Fanning tensions in Bush and Scowcroft, 346. Charles Krauthammer, "Good Morning, Vietnam," *Washington Post*, 19 April 1991.

29. On limits to airpower, see Kagan, *Finding the Target*, 111, 113, 138–39; and Echevarria, *Military Strategy*, 90–91.

30. News cycle in Thomas B. Rosenstiel, "CNN: The Channel to the World," *Los Angeles Times*, 23 January 1991. Trade show and fireworks in Lewis Lapham, *Theater of War: In Which the Republic Becomes an Empire* (New York: New Press, 2002), 132. News and propaganda in Brewer, *Why America Fights*, 234. Media event in McAlister, *Epic Encounters*, 239. Consuming war in Fitzgerald, *Militarization and the American Century*, 181. Most Americans watching Desert Storm unfold on television focused more on military operations (the force) than on the overriding purpose of the mission (the goal).

31. RMA in Art Pine, "Military Nears Revolution in Weapons, War Strategy," *Los Angeles Times*, 19 March 1996. See also Bacevich, *The Age of Illusions*, 74; and Freedman, *Strategy*, 216–18. Recasting in Williamson Murray and MacGregor Knox, "Thinking about Revolutions in Warfare," in *The Dynamics of Military Revolution, 1300–1500*, ed. MacGregor Knox and Williamson Murray (New York: Cambridge University Press,

2001), 7. Innovations in Lissner, *Wars of Revelation*, 15. Microelectronics in Roland, *Delta of Power*, 106. Precision warfare in Dower, *The Violent American Century*, 73. Digitized in Kagan, 203, 239. Dominance in Tuck, "Land Warfare," in Jordan, James D. Kiras, et al., *Understanding Modern Warfare*, 110.

32. Network centric in Kagan, *Finding the Target*, 255–60. Richard K. Ullman and James P. Wade, Jr., *Rapid Dominance: A Force For All Seasons* (London: Royal United Services Institute for Defence Studies, 1998), 1–3, 12–19. See also Fitzgerald, *Learning to Forget*, 111–12. Harnessing in Bradley Graham, "Battle Plans for a New Century," *Washington Post*, 21 February 1995.

33. Limited and constrained in Metz, *Iraq & the Evolution of American Strategy*, 29. Bush and Scowcroft, *A World Transformed*, 464. See also Gardner, *The Long Road to Baghdad*, 89. Rebellions in Stieb, *The Regime Change Consensus*, 65–70; and Bacevich, *America's War for the Greater Middle East*, 138. Open-ended in Lissner, 140.

34. First place in William Pfaff, "Bombs Will Never Hurt Him," *Los Angeles Times*, 26 July 1992. Vets in "Overcoming the Vietnam Syndrome," *Los Angeles Times*, 11 March 1991. Passive in Robin Wright, "Drift Seen in U.S. Policy toward Iraq," *Los Angeles Times*, 18 January 1992. On requirements after Desert Storm, see Hahn, *Mission Accomplished?* 117. Incomplete in Gans, *White House Warriors*, 112.

35. Peacemaking in Bush and Scowcroft, 488. Challenges facing Bush in Stieb, 40–42. On bin Laden, see Little, *American Orientalism*, 311.

36. Neoconservatives and permanent in Bacevich, *The New American Militarism*, 71, 75, 77. Oil and geopolitics in Douglas J. Little, "Impatient Crusaders: The Making of America's Informal Empire in the Middle East," in Costigliola and Hogan, *America in the World*, 226. Regime change and democracy in Stieb, 51.

37. Paradigm in Metz, 29. Questions over the Soviet collapse in Craig and Logevall, *America's Cold War*, 353, 355; Kotkin, *Armageddon Averted*, 2, 168; and Loth, *Overcoming the Cold War*, 218–21. On the Cold War's ending having little meaning in Asia or the Middle East, see Lüthi, *Cold Wars*, 563. Richard Pipes, "Misinterpreting the Cold War: The Hard-Liners Had It Right," *Foreign Affairs*, Vol. 74, No. 1 (January–February 1995): 154–60.

38. Purpose in Toft and Kushi, *Dying by the Sword*, 176. Bush and Scowcroft, 491.

39. Francis Fukuyama, "The End of History?" *The National Interest*, No. 16 (Summer 1989): 3–18. See also Daniel Bessner, "A Bad Breakup: The Discontents of Francis Fukuyama, *The Nation*, 1/8 May 2023; and Latham, *The Right Kind of Revolution*, 188–89. For a contemporary view on the political aspects of fear, see Judith N. Shklar, "The Liberalism of Fear,"

in *Liberalism and the Moral Life*, ed. Nancy L. Rosenblum (Cambridge, MA: Harvard University Press, 1989).

40. Supremacy in Porter, *The False Promise of Liberal Order*, 38. On the supposed need for a presence in the Middle East, see Hahn, *Mission Accomplished?* 113–14. Leonard Silk, "The 'New Order' Is a Tall Order for the U.S.," *New York Times*, 17 March 1991.

CHAPTER 22

1. Soaring popularity in Dov S. Zaheim, "Is the Vietnam Syndrome Dead?" *New York Times*, 4 March 1991. Tactical triumph in Ricks, *The Generals*, 384. Bush out of power, see p. 386; and Melvyn P. Leffler, *Confronting Saddam Hussein: George W. Bush and the Invasion of Iraq* (New York: Oxford University Press, 2023), 15–16. Post Desert Storm in Hahn, 108–9, 114–16.
2. Dan Balz, "Clinton Faces Draft Issue," *Washington Post*, 26 August 1992. John Wheeler, "Clinton Has to Shed His Anti-Military Bias," *Los Angeles Times*, 5 January 1994.
3. Order and discipline in John H. Cushman, "Top Military Officers Object to Lifting Homosexual Ban," *New York Times*, 14 November 1992. Eric Schmitt, "Joint Chiefs Fighting Clinton Plan to Allow Homosexuals in Military," *New York Times*, 23 January 1993. Andrew Sullivan, "Undone by 'Don't Ask, Don't Tell,'" *New York Times*, 9 April 1998. On laboratory, see Jacqueline E. Whitt and Elizabeth A. Perazzo, "The Military as a Social Experiment: Challenging a Trope," *Parameters*, Vol. 48, No. 2 (Summer 2018): 5–12. See also Taylor, *Military Service and American Democracy*, 159–62; and Beth Bailey, "The Politics of Dancing: 'Don't Ask, Don't Tell,' and the Role of Moral Claims," *Journal of Policy History*, Vol. 25, No. 1 (2013): 89–113.
4. Transformation in Chollet and Goldgeier, *America between the Wars*, 37. Perimeter in Hemmer, *American Pendulum*, 117.
5. Organizing principle in Toft and Kushi, *Dying by the Sword*, 142. Anthony Lake, "The Reach of Democracy," *New York Times*, 23 September 1994. "Excerpts from the Remarks of Anthony Lake," in Brigham, *The United States and Iraq since 1990*, 75. American-style in Jeremi Suri, *Liberty's Surest Guardian: Rebuilding Nations after War from the Founders to Obama* (New York: Free Press, 2011), 6.
6. Transnational problems in Lake, "The Reach of Democracy."
7. Remake in Bacevich, *The Age of Illusions*, 95. On NAFTA, see Dumbrell, *Clinton's Foreign Policy*, 37, 50–53; and Mandelbaum, *The Four Ages of American Foreign Policy*, 392–94. Hemisphere trade system in "NAFTA: Clinton's Defining Task," *Washington Post*, 20 July 1993. Patrick Buchanan, "America First, NAFTA Never," *Washington Post*, 7 November 1993.

8. Clinton in Douglas Brinkley, "Democratic Enlargement: The Clinton Doctrine," *Foreign Policy*, No. 106 (Spring 1997): 125.
9. Brinkley, 125. David E. Sanger, "Clinton to Rekindle Old Debate on Trade Interdependence," *New York Times*, 9 September 1997. Military commitments in Layne and Schwarz, "The Perils of Stability." Preventive and access in Dumbrell, 41.
10. On IMF, see Nye, *Do Morals Matter?* 138. On Yeltsin transition and inflation, see Padma Desai, "Russian Retrospectives on Reforms from Yeltsin to Putin," *Journal of Economic Perspectives*, Vol. 19, No. 1 (Winter 2005): 96–98. David E. Sanger, "Clinton Endorses I.M.F. Plan to Help Russia Pay Debts," *New York Times*, 1 June 1998.
11. Expanding national security in Andrew J. Bacevich, *American Empire: The Realities and Consequences of U.S. Diplomacy* (Cambridge, MA: Harvard University Press, 2002), 121; and Grandin, *Empire's Workshop*, 194. Benjamin C. Schwarz, "Is Capitalism Doomed?" *New York Times*, 23 May 1994. We might note that the global remit of national security wasn't Clinton's doing—it had been there since FDR and Truman.
12. Simple place in James D. Boys, *Clinton's War on Terror: Redefining US Security Strategy, 1993–2001* (Boulder, CO: Lynne Rienner, 2018), 79. Extended security in Andrew Preston, "National Security as Grand Strategy: Edward Mead Earle and the Burdens of World Power," in Borgwardt, McKnight Nichols, and Preston, *Rethinking American Grand Strategy*, 247. Strategy in Vine, *Base Nation*, 5. Engagement in Reveron, Gvosdev, and Owens, *US Foreign Policy and Defense Strategy*, 114. Deployed in Vine, *The United States of War*, 259. On fundamental questions, see Hemmer, *American Pendulum*, 114.
13. The White House, *A National Security Strategy of Engagement and Enlargement* (Washington, DC: US Government Printing Office, 1994), ii. Restore Hope in Muehlbauer and Ulbrich, *Ways of War*, 499.
14. On Aidid, see Chollet and Goldgeier, *America between the Wars*, 72–75. Echoes in Keith Richburg, "Interventions in Somalia," *Washington Post*, 6 October 1993. Offensive operations in Keith Richburg, "U.S. Halts Somalia Drive," *Washington Post*, 14 October 1993. For a contemporary report, see Rick Atkinson, "Deliverance from Warlord's Fury," *Washington Post*, 7 October 1993. The best overall history remains Mark Bowden, *Black Hawk Down: A Story of Modern War* (New York: Atlantic Monthly Press, 1999).
15. Polling and Holbrooke in Haberski, *God and War*, 184. Killing spree, citing Samantha Powers, in Chollet and Goldgeier, 91. Administration reaction on pp. 92–93; and in David L. Phillips, *Liberating Kosovo: Coercive Diplomacy and U.S. Intervention* (Cambridge, MA: MIT Press, 2012), 187–90. Keith Richburg, "The World Ignored Genocide, Tutsis Say," *Washington Post*, 8 August 1994. Low-tech and scandal in Roger Winter, "Journey into Genocide: A Rwanda Diary," *Washington Post*, 5 June

1994. The White House, *A National Security Strategy of Engagement and Enlargement*, 8.

16. Benjamin F. Bobo, "A Research Agenda for the NEPAD Initiative: A Note," *Journal of Third World Studies*, Vol. 23, No. 1 (Spring 2006): 81. Rash and spate in Art Pine, "Global Tasks Take Toll on U.S. Military," *Los Angeles Times*, 19 March 1995.

17. Eric Schmitt, "U.S. Set to Limit Role of Military in Peacekeeping," *New York Times*, 29 January 1994. Stabilization and humanitarian missions in Gray, *War, Peace and International Relations*, 252. Social work in Chollet and Goldgeier, 113. Philanthropy and application in Posen, *Restraint*, 56–57. Clark, *Waging Modern War*, 55.

18. Failed state in Millet, Maslowski, and Feis, *For the Common Defense*, 616. On Haiti background, see Chollet and Goldgeier, 95–99; and Mandelbaum, *The Four Ages of American Foreign Policy*, 403–4.

19. Glenn quoted in Dumbrell, *Clinton's Foreign Policy*, 73. Promotion on p. 76. On codename, see Art Pine, "Pentagon May Be Losing Operation Code Name Battle," *Los Angeles Times*, 12 November 1994. Jeane Kirkpatrick, "Why It's Smart to Bet on a Haiti Invasion," *Los Angeles Times*, 21 August 1994.

20. Bush in Engel, Lawrence, and Preston, *America in the World*, 333. Lawrence Freedman and Efraim Karsh, *The Gulf Conflict, 1990–1991: Diplomacy and War in the New World Order* (Princeton, NJ: Princeton University Press, 1993), 442. They also noted how future circumstances might not be so favorable to Western military application.

21. Woolsey in Mueller, *Overblown*, 118. Violence and anarchy and its consequences in Gerald B. Helman and Steven R. Ratner, "Saving Failed States," *Foreign Policy*, No. 89 (Winter, 1992–1993): 3–5. Generation in Goodson, *Afghanistan's Endless Wars*, ix.

22. Openness in Bacevich, *American Empire*, 3–4. Armed forces making commitments in Karlin, *Building Militaries in Fragile States*, 4, 8, 108. State weakness in Goodson, xiii.

23. Freedom of action in Lissner, *Wars of Revelation*, 123. Charles Krauthammer, "The Unipolar Moment," *Foreign Affairs*, Vol. 70, No. 1 (1990/1991): 23–33. See also Miller, *Grand Strategy from Truman to Trump*, 178. No prospect in Chollet and Goldgeier, *America between the Wars*, 25. On unilateralism as an ideology, see Christopher McKnight Nichols, "Unilateralism as Ideology," in Nichols and Milne, *Ideology in U.S. Foreign Relations*, 190–91. Fleeting in Toft and Kushi, *Dying by the Sword*, 189.

24. Robert Shogan, "GOP's Big Guns Rake Clinton on Foreign Policy," *Los Angeles Times*, 28 July 1994.

25. Henry Kissinger, *Does America Need a Foreign Policy? Toward a Diplomacy for the 21st Century* (New York: Simon & Schuster, 2001), 17. See

also Hemmer, *American Pendulum*, 120. Reshaping diplomacy and force in Tim Judah, *Kosovo: War and Revenge* (New Haven, CT: Yale University Press, 2000), 228; and Bacevich, *The New American Militarism*, 2. Well-being and activist role in Chollet and Goldgeier, 149. Application of force in Bacevich, *American Empire*, 48–49.

26. Albright in Chollet and Goldgeier, 56. Fareed Zakaria, "The Vision Thing," *New York Times*, 21 August 1996.
27. William Kristol and Robert Kagan, "Toward a Neo-Reaganite Foreign Policy," *Foreign Affairs*, 1996, Vol. 75, No. 4 (July-August, 1996): 20–21, 23. On McKinley, see Stuart Creighton Miller, *"Benevolent Assimilation": The American Conquest of the Philippines, 1899–1903* (New Haven, CT: Yale University Press, 1982).
28. Kerry in Preble, *The Power Problem*, 32. Llewellyn H. Rockwell, Jr., "U.S. Deludes Itself as Being Indispensable," *Los Angeles Times*, 15 April 1997. Bullying from Lloyd Axworthy, Canadian Foreign Minister, in "White House Defining Vital U.S. Interests," *New York Times*, 29 July 1996.
29. Full-spectrum dominance in Paul Richter, "Pentagon Plans Bigger Noncombat Role," *Los Angeles Times*, 3 April 1997. See also Preston, *American Foreign Relations*, 114. On uncertain strategic aims, see Rupert Smith, *The Utility of Force: The Art of War in the Modern World* (New York: Knopf, 2007), 15. Natural disasters in Gordon Adams and Shoon Murray, "An Introduction to Mission Creep," in *Mission Creep: The Militarization of US Foreign Policy?* ed. Gordon Adams and Shoon Murray (Washington, DC: Georgetown University Press, 2014), 9.
30. Trigger and ambiguities of R2P in Jennifer Welsh, "The Responsibility to Protect: Dilemmas of a New Norm," *Current History*, Vol. 111, No. 748 (November 2012): 294. See also Warren Hoge, "Intervention, Hailed as a Concept, Is Shunned in Practice," *New York Times*, 20 January 2008; and Heuser, *War*, 163. The theory originated from criticisms of a global failure to intervene and halt the genocides in Rwanda (1994) and Srebrenica (1995) and then coalesced with the 2001 report by the International Commission on Intervention and State Sovereignty. In the 1990s, debates among academics, policymakers, and practitioners used terms like "humanitarian intervention" and the "right to intervene," while the term "R2P" gained prominence later. Ironically, this happened only as the wars in Afghanistan and then Iraq were seemingly making R2P irrelevant. Mary Elizabeth Walters, correspondence with author, 2 July 2024. On a "capability gap" in performing R2P, see Gordon Adams, "The Institutional Imbalance of American Statecraft," in Adams and Murray, *Mission Creep*, 24.
31. Guidance in Roland, *Delta of Power*, 97–98. See also Chollet and Goldgeier, *America between the Wars*, 44–47.

32. Patrick E. Tyler, "U.S. Strategy Plan Calls for Insuring No Rivals Develop," *New York Times*, 8 March 1992. Democrats and Buchanan in Chollet and Goldgeier, 45.
33. On DPG continuities and American primacy, see Hal Brands, "Choosing Primacy: U.S. Strategy and Global Order at the Dawn of the Post–Cold War Era," *Texas National Security Review*, Vol. 1, No. 2 (March 2018): 9–33.
34. PNAC in Brigham, *The United States and Iraq Since 1990*, 90–92. Steven R. Weisman, "Pre-emption: Idea with a Lineage Whose Time Has Come," *New York Times*, 23 March 2003.
35. DPG fears in Chollet and Goldgeier, 45. Serge Schmemann, "New Images of Terror: Extremists in Heartland," *New York Times*, 24 April 1995. On the bombing, see Feldman, *Manufacturing Hysteria*, 301; and Boys, *Clinton's War on Terror*, 89–91, 103.
36. Anyone, anywhere in Mark D. W. Edington, "Now for the New Threat," *New York Times*, 22 April 1995. "The Threat within Takes Center Stage," *Los Angeles Times*, 24 April 1995. Definitions in Boys, 6, 10.
37. Challenges of defining terrorism in Bruce Hoffman, *Inside Terrorism* (New York: Columbia University Press, 1998), 27–29. See also Krasner, *How to Make Love to a Despot*, 33, 39. Combating terrorism in Toft and Kushi, 200. Sophisticated in Heather Knight, "Domestic Terrorism Seen as Becoming More Violent," *Los Angeles Times*, 19 April 1997. Jessica Stern, "Terrorism Multiplied," *Washington Post*, 17 July 1996.
38. Tame in Serge Schmemann, "It Would Reduce Atom Arsenals about 75%," *New York Times*, 4 January 1993. Stability in Bush and Scowcroft, *A World Transformed*, 45. On START, see Lebovic, *Flawed Logics*, 190–96. Proliferation on p. 197. John F. Harris, "Clinton Criticizes Congress for Delay on Post-Bombing Anti-Terrorism Bill," *Washington Post*, 1 June 1995.
39. On North Korea, see Kaplan, *The Bomb*, 200, 216–19, 221; Dumbrell, *Clinton's Foreign Policy*, 117–22; and Rapp-Hooper, *Shields of the Republic*, 114–15. Don Van Natta, Jr., "G.O.P. Letter Plays On Nuclear Threat," *New York Times*, 4 September 1999.
40. Tom Clancy, *The Sum of All Fears* (Thorndike, ME: Thorndike Press, 1991). *Crimson Tide*, dir. Tony Scott (Hollywood Pictures, 1995). On war serving only itself, see also Keegan, *A History of Warfare*, 21.
41. Ukraine in Zubok, *Collapse*, 392. Proliferation fears in Freedman and Michaels, *The Evolution of Nuclear Strategy*, 547, 587; and Gavin, *Nuclear Weapons and American Grand Strategy*, 83–84.
42. Interventions in Moyn, *Humane*, 226; and Toft and Kushi, *Dying by the Sword*, 192–94. Bases in Vine, *Base Nation*, 52–54. On globalization, see Bacevich, *The Age of Illusions*, 4–5; and Mandelbaum, *The Four Ages of American Foreign Policy*, 390–91. Requiring a global US presence in

Pamela Harriman, "With World Power Comes Global Responsibility," *Los Angeles Times*, 8 March 1996. On connections between globalization and humanitarianism, see Sargent, "Oasis in the Desert?" in Eckel and Moyn, *The Breakthrough*, 130.

CHAPTER 23

1. Convergence in Robert J. Samuelson, "'Globalization' on the March," *Washington Post*, 15 October 1997. Globalization and integration in Chollet and Goldgeier, *America between the Wars*, 42, 148. Cheap in Toft and Kushi, 194.
2. Pressures in Preble, *The Power Problem*, 23. William E. Odom, "More Military Muscle, Not Less," *New York Times*, 17 February 1993.
3. Communism's collapse in Sabrina P. Ramet, *Thinking about Yugoslavia: Scholarly Debates about the Yugoslav Breakup and the Wars in Bosnia and Kosovo* (New York: Cambridge University Press, 2005), 35, 55–59; and Paul Hockenos, *Homeland Calling: Exile Patriotism & the Balkan Wars* (Ithaca, NY: Cornell University Press, 2003), 4. For an overview of the violence in Eastern Europe, see Mandelbaum, 404–9; Black, *War Since 1945*, 155–57; and Judah, *Kosovo*, 34–38. Ethnic cleansing in Judt, *Postwar*, 674–76. On the 1970s and early 1980s, see Tone Bringa, "The Peaceful Death of Tito and the Violent End of Yugoslavia," in *Death of the Father: An Anthropology of the End in Political Authority*, ed. John Borneman (New York: Berghahn, 2004), 148–93.
4. Violence in Bosnia-Herzegovina in Fink, *Cold War*, 274–76. Srebrenica in Elizabeth Pond, *Endgame in the Balkans: Regime Change, European Style* (Washington, DC: Brookings Institution Press, 2006), 5. Of note, the International Criminal Tribunal for the former Yugoslavia ruled the massacre to be a genocide.
5. Plural states in Marie-Janine Calic, *The Great Cauldron: A History of Southeastern Europe*, trans. Elizabeth Janik (Cambridge, MA: Harvard University Press, 2019), 528. Sebastian Rosato, "The Flawed Logic of Democratic Peace Theory," *American Political Science Review*, Vol. 97, No. 4 (November 2003): 585–602. Evolution and disintegration in Martel, *Victory in War*, 252–53.
6. Baker in Pond, 30. Norman Kempster, "Lugar Blasts Clinton on Global Leadership," *Los Angeles Times*, 25 June 1993. On the ethnic violence as it related to self-determination, see Mark, Iacob, Rupprecht, and Spaskovska, *1989*, 198–209.
7. "In The Shadow of the Holocaust," *Washington Post*, 25 September 1994. Powell in Gans, *White House Warriors*, 124–25.
8. Indiscriminate in Hockenos, *Homeland Calling*, 113. Media in Noel Malcolm, *Bosnia: A Short History* (London: Papermac, 1996), 244–45.

Symptoms and causes on p. 242. Language evolution and sexual violence in Dubravka Žarkov, *The Body of War: Media, Ethnicity, and Gender in the Break-up of Yugoslavia* (Durham, NC: Duke University Press, 2007), 5–6, 116. Internal conflicts in Andrew J. Bacevich and Eliot A. Cohen, "Introduction," in *War over Kosovo: Politics and Grand Strategy in a Global Age*, ed. Andrew J. Bacevich and Eliot A. Cohen (New York: Columbia University Press, 2001), xi. "Recruiting Russia for the New Containment," *Los Angeles Times*, 1 February 1993.

9. R. W. Apple, Jr., "Preaching to Skeptics," *New York Times*, 16 September 1994. Benjamin Schwarz, "Leave the Little Wars Alone," *Los Angeles Times*, 8 June 1992. Constabulary in Bacevich, *American Empire*, 74. On Clinton's strategy "requiring minimal blood and only modest treasure," see Andrew J. Bacevich, "Neglected Trinity: Kosovo and the Crisis in U.S. Civil-Military Relations," in Bacevich and Cohen, 172. Clinton quoted in Dumbrell, *Clinton's Foreign Policy*, 94. Bombing campaign in Ivo H. Daalder and Michael E. O'Hanlon, *Winning Ugly: NATO's War to Save Kosovo* (Washington, DC: Brookings Institution Press, 2000), 2.

10. On NATO, see James Kurth, "First War of the Global Era: Kosovo and U.S. Grand Strategy," in Bacevich and Cohen, *War over Kosovo*, 74–83; and Bacevich, *America's War for the Greater Middle East*, 169. On debates over Dayton's accomplishments, see Steven E. Meyer, "The Dayton Accords: Anchor to the Past or Bridge to the Future? "*Politeia*, Vol. 2, No. 4 (2012): 51–66. Ivo John Lederer, "Bosnia: Precedents of Peace," *Washington Post*, 17 December 1995. We might note that the US commitment to Vietnam, if not modernization theory more broadly, was heir to the French mandate of *mission civilisatrice*.

11. On drift and labels, see Dumbrell, 41–42, 62. Search for a new strategy in Haberski, *God and War*, 181, 182–83.

12. Imposing order in Layne, *The Peace of Illusions*, 130. On coercive airpower, see Daniel L. Byman and Matthew C. Waxman, "Kosovo and the Great Air Power Debate," in Mahnken and Maiolo, *Strategic Studies*, 147, 151. On diplomatic efforts before the air campaign, see Phillips, *Liberating Kosovo*, 89–108; and Chollet and Goldgeier, *America between the Wars*, 211–19. On Allied Force, see William M. Arkin, "Operation Allied Force: 'The Most Precise Application of Air Power in History," in Bacevich and Cohen, 1–37; and Daalder and O'Hanlon, *Winning Ugly*, 101–3. Cohen in Mary Elizabeth Waters, "A Tantalizing Success: The 1999 Kosovo War," *The Strategy Bridge*, 9 July 2021.

13. Faith in airpower in Michael Dugan, "Airpower Can Succeed without Deciding," *Los Angeles Times*, 28 April 1993. Clark, *Waging Modern War*, 10, 299. Frustrations in William M. Arkin, "Objective: Kosovo," *Washington Post*, 25 April 1999. Cleansing in Arkin, "Operation Allied Force," 9. See also Craig R. Whitney, "NATO Chief Admits Bombs Fail to Stem Serb Operations," *New York Times*, 28 April 1999.

14. Clark, *Waging Modern War*, 108, 153. William Safire, "Lessons of Bosnia," *New York Times*, 21 February 1994. Brzezinski in Echevarria, *Military Strategy*, 60. Limits of airpower in Daalder and O'Hanlon, 211–12. For a less optimistic account of Allied Force, see Iain King and Whit Mason, *Peace at Any Price: How the World Failed Kosovo* (Ithaca, NY: Cornell University Press, 2006). On Milošević backing down, see Judah, *Kosovo*, 279–80. "Stop the Butcher of the Balkans," *New York Times*, 15 April 1992.
15. Coercion in Bacevich, "Neglected Trinity," 183. Clark, *Waging Modern War*, xxiv, 7. Humiliation in Judah, *Kosovo*, 311.
16. Clark, 87. Framing in Kennedy, *Afterimages*, 113. On human rights, see Brigham, "After the Fall of Saigon," in Ryan and Fitzgerald, *Not Even Past*, 100.
17. Strikes in Malkasian, *The American War in Afghanistan*, 48. Clinton in Bacevich, *America's War for the Greater Middle East*, 205. Reliable information in James Risen, "To Bomb Sudan Plant, or Not," *New York Times*, 27 October 1999.
18. Force protection in Serge Schmemann, "Not Taking Losses Is One Thing. Winning Is Another," *New York Times*, 3 January 1999. Clark, *Waging Modern War*, 303. On avoiding bloodshed, see Howard, *The Invention of Peace*, 102; and Waldman, *Vicarious Warfare*, 10.
19. Smith, *The Utility of Force*, xiii, 6, 7. Clark, 318.
20. Locked in in Porter, *The False Promise of Liberal Order*, 87. On Dayton, see Judah, *Kosovo*, 120–23; and Pond, *Endgame in the Balkans*, 140–43. Kali J. Rubaii, "Tripartheid: How Sectarianism Became Internal to Being in Anbar, Iraq," *Political and Legal Anthropology Review*, Vol. 42, No. 1 (2019): 127. To date, Kosovo Force (KFOR) is NATO's longest running deployment except for the Cold War–era deployment in Western Germany.
21. Cruise missile in Hemmer, *American Pendulum*, 39. Pinprick in Milne, "Grand Strategies (or Ascendant Ideas) since 1919," in Borgwardt, McKnight Nichols, and Preston, *Rethinking American Grand Strategy*, 163. On containment of Iraq, see Hahn, *Mission Accomplished?* 120–23. Wolfowitz in Thomas E. Ricks, *Fiasco: The American Military Adventure in Iraq* (New York: Penguin, 2006), 18. Desert Fox implications in Stieb, *The Regime Change Consensus*, 179–83. Cheat and retreat Brigham, *The United States and Iraq since 1990*, 50.
22. Cohen in Brownlee, *Democracy Prevention*, 65. William Kristol and Robert Kagan, "Bombing Iraq Isn't Enough," *New York Times*, 30 January 1998. Eric Schmitt, "U.S. Weighs the Value of Bombing to Coerce Iraq," *New York Times*, 16 November 1997. On the lead-up to the 2003 Iraq invasion, see Hahn, 138–45. Preemptive war in Moyn, *Humane*, 229.
23. Dangers and weakness in Freedman and Michaels, *The Evolution of Nuclear Strategy*, 554–57. Susan Carpenter McMillan, "Wrong Time, Wrong Man to Lift Embargo," *Los Angeles Times*, 8 February 1994.

24. On Oslo, see Oren, *Power, Faith, and Fantasy*, 575–77. Gaza violence in Clyde Haberman, "Israel Sees New Delays to Palestinian Self-Rule," *New York Times*, 14 December 1993. Fears of violence and donations in Joe Sexton, "Assassination of Rabin Raises Alarm over Role of Kahane's Violent Followers in U.S.," *New York Times*, 13 November 1995.
25. Martin van Creveld, *The Transformation of War* (New York: Free Press, 1991), ix. Samuel P. Huntington, "The Coming Clash of Civilizations or, the West against the Rest," *New York Times*, 6 June 1993. See also Samuel P. Huntington, "The Clash of Civilizations?" *Foreign Affairs*, Vol. 72, No. 3 (Summer, 1993): 22–49; and Oren, 572–73. Robert D. Kaplan, "The Coming Anarchy," *Atlantic*, February 1994, 46.
26. Van Creveld, 27. On the need to mobilize for the future threat, see Preston, *American Foreign Relations*, 120–21; and Latham, *The Right Kind of Revolution*, 192.
27. Joke in Ann Devroy and R. Jeffrey Smith, "Clinton Reexamines Foreign Policy under Siege," *Washington Post*, 17 October 1993. On anarchy and loss of order, see John J. Mearsheimer, "Why We Will Soon Miss the Cold War," *Atlantic*, Vol. 266, No. 2 (August 1990): 35–36. On fears of an "unbalanced" multipolar system, see Mearsheimer, *The Tragedy of Great Power Politics*, 335, 338; and Waltz, *Theory of International Politics*, 104–5, 126. Judith Miller, "Flying Blind in a Dangerous World," *New York Times*, 6 February 2000.
28. Rice quoted in Leffler, *Confronting Saddam Hussein*, 34.

CONCLUSION

1. "Text of MacArthur's Legion Address Criticizing Defense Policies," *New York Times*, 18 October 1951.
2. Melvyn Leffler argues that leaders in Washington and Moscow "viewed developments through ideological prisms." *For the Soul of Mankind*, 233. Convictions and assumptions in Christopher McKnight Nichols and David Milne, "Introduction," in McKnight Nichols and Milne, *Ideology in U.S. Foreign Relations*, 2–3. Fear and ideology in Andrew Preston, "The Fearful Giant: National Insecurity and U.S. Foreign Policy," in ibid., 172–74.
3. Dualisms in Sherry, *In the Shadow of War*, 57. Gaddis, *The Cold War: A New History*, ix. On fearmongering over China, see Cohen, *The Big Stick*, 99, 107. In 2014, Admiral Samuel Locklear warned Americans of "talking ourselves into conflict with China." Quoted on p. 103.
4. Gaddis, 262. "America Only," *New York Times*, 10 March 1992.
5. On the Cold War not, in fact, ending, see Khalidi, *Sowing Crisis*, xv, 218, 219. On war's promises being different than what delivered, see Lawrence LeShan, *The Psychology of War: Comprehending Its Mystique and Its*

Madness (Chicago: Noble Press, 1992), 29. Truman Doctrine in Judge and Langdon, *The Cold War*, 292. Jackson Lears, "How a War Became a Crusade," *New York Times*, 11 March 2003. See also Little, *American Orientalism*, 318. On democracy promotion, see Gary J. Bass, "Despot Watch," *New York Times*, 12 October 2008; and Hemmer, *American Pendulum*, 27.

6. On control, see Chamberlin, *The Cold War's Killing Fields*, 17; and Krasner, *How to Make Love to a Despot*, 175. Status in Brazinsky, *Winning the Third World*, 8. War as a "reasonable and manageable tool" in MacMillan, *War*, 82. On a generally flawed approach after World War II, see Jeremi Suri, "What American Century?" *Foreign Policy*, 17 July 2020.

7. Pearl Harbor in Gardner, *The Long Road to Baghdad*, 7; and Mueller, *Overblown*, 59. Trauma in Bodnar, *Divided by Terror*, 17. Moral authority in Bradley and Dudziak, *Making the Forever War*, 171. Andrew Bacevich argues that fighting a "global war" helped "to remove limits on the exercise of American power." *America's War for the Greater Middle East*, 221. On Bush focusing globally, see Leffler, *Confronting Saddam Hussein*, 57. Calls for war in Lapham, *Theater of War*, 137.

8. On Bush engaging in a "militant, moral crusade," see Latham, *The Right Kind of Revolution*, 201; and Metz, *Iraq & the Evolution of American Strategy*, 81. Coerced consent in Porter, *The False Promise of Liberal Order*, 101. Attempts at ordering on pp. 60, 113.

9. Said in Little, *American Orientalism*, 35. Bernard Lewis, *The Crisis of Islam: Holy War and Unholy Terror* (New York: Modern Library 2003), 120, 138. See also Little, 36. Fanatics in Fareed Zakaria, "Economics Trumps Politics," in *Conflict after the Cold War: Arguments on Causes of War and Peace*, 5th ed., ed. Richard K. Betts (New York: Routledge, 2017), 52–53. Fear of WMD in Miller, *Grand Strategy from Truman to Trump*, 199.

10. On rhetoric of terrorism, see John A. Lynn, *Battle: A History of Combat and Culture* (Boulder, CO: Westview, 2003), 318–19. Bush quoted in Alex Lubin, *Never-Ending War on Terror* (Oakland: University of California Press, 2021), 26. Accommodation and bleakness in Cohen, *The Big Stick*, 134, 137. Conceptualization of barbarians in Wayne E. Lee, *Barbarians and Brothers: Anglo-American Warfare, 1500–1865* (New York: Oxford University Press, 2011), 3. Senior diplomat W. Averell Harriman quoted in Gardner, *Spheres of Influence*, 255.

11. Power and security in Brands, *What Good Is Grand Strategy?* 152. Cheney in Hemmer, *American Pendulum*, 132. Terrorism replacing communism in Dower, *The Violent American Century*, 101. Powell in Little, *American Orientalism*, 320. Marshall Plan in Hanhimäki and Westad, *The Cold War*, 659. Of note, Bush too called for a "Marshall Plan" for Afghanistan. See Malkasian, *The American War in Afghanistan*, 83. Stephen Tankel

argues that 9/11 "provided a new organizing principle for US foreign policy; winning the War on Terror." *With Us and against Us*, 57.

12. Hysteria in Thomas E. Ricks, "Fear Factor," *New York Times*, 7 October 2012. Missiles and risks in Freedman and Michaels, *The Evolution of Nuclear Strategy*, 606–7. Blurred lines in Craig Whitlock, *The Afghanistan Papers: A Secret History of the War* (New York: Simon & Schuster, 2021), 19, 23; and Malkasian, 54. Strategist in Mark Danner, "Taking Stock of the Forever War," *New York Times*, 11 September 2005.

13. Defensive rhetoric in Toft and Kushi, *Dying by the Sword*, 254; and Zulaika, *Terrorism*, 7–8. Containing or provoking in Sherry, *In the Shadow of War*, 498; and Lebow and Gross Stein, *We All Lost the Cold War*, 4. On reciprocating threats, see May, *Fortress America*, 58. Weakness inviting attack in Leffler, *Confronting Saddam Hussein*, 62, 89.

14. Vengeance in Malkasian, *The American War in Afghanistan*, 59. AUMF in Stoker, *Why America Loses Wars*, 2. Competing purposes in Jeffrey H. Michaels, *The Discourse Trap and the US Military: From the War on Terror to the Surge* (New York: Palgrave Macmillan, 2013), 19, 37. See also Krasner, *How to Make Love to a Despot*, 94. Overreaction in Mueller, *Overblown*, 7.

15. Failed states in Latham, *The Right Kind of Revolution*, 1. WMDs in Metz, 106. Fragile consensus in Lebovic, *Planning to Fail*, 72. Krasner maintains that the Bush administration assumed that "consolidated democracy was possible in all countries," p. 217.

16. While faith was at play, Adam Wunische argues that "fear induced by 9/11 was detrimental to the objective analysis of the international events that followed." *Unwinnable Wars: Afghanistan and the Future of American Armed Statebuilding* (Cambridge, UK: Polity, 2024), ix.

17. No limits in Andrew Bacevich, "Introduction: Reflections on Military Dissent," in Bacevich and Sjursen, *Paths of Dissent*, 1, 5. On those very limits, see Lebovic, *The Limits of U.S. Military Capability*, 17, 20. Bush quoted in Little, *American Orientalism*, 308. On regime change sparking broader reform, see Stieb, *The Regime Change Consensus*, 210–11. Afghanistan nation building in Whitlock, *The Afghanistan Papers*, 14, 30; and Malkasian, 8, 249. Defeating terrorism in Leffler, *Confronting Saddam Hussein*, 58. Dominance in Layne, *The Peace of Illusions*, 2.

18. Modernization in Latham, 2–3. Bing West, *The Wrong War: Grit, Strategy, and the Way out of Afghanistan* (New York: Random House, 2011), xiii. Dexter Filkins, *The Forever War* (New York: Knopf, 2009), 77.

19. Odd Arne Westad, "The Cold War and America's Delusion of Victory," *New York Times*, 28 August 2017. On occupation, see Gardner, *The Long Road to Baghdad*, 205. Leaving behind in Lebovic, *Planning to Fail*, 82.

20. Morass in Gopal, *No Good Men among the Living*, 133. Alliances and agendas on p. 147. Bush quoted in Gardner, 264. Democratization in

Miller, *Grand Strategy from Truman to Trump*, 189. On debate over the term "civil war" in Iraq, see Michaels, *The Discourse Trap and the US Military*, 135–37.
21. Paul Krugman, "Hoping for Fear," *New York Times*, 14 August 2006. Axis of evil in Engel, Lawrence, and Preston, *America in the World*, 361–62. Andrew Bacevich argues that one axis, Iran, actually gained influence and stature during Bush's war against terror. *The Limits of Power*, 159. Peter Beinart, "A Fighting Faith," *New Republic*, 12 December 2004.
22. Prevent in Steven R. Weisman, "Pre-emption: Idea with a Lineage Whose Time Has Come," *New York Times*, 23 March 2003. Ridding evil in Bodnar, *Divided by Terror*, 33. Bush Doctrine in Martel, *Grand Strategy in Theory and Practice*, 321; and Grandin, *Empire's Workshop*, 160, 194. On long tail of regime change, see Stieb, 9. Wolfowitz in Milne, "Grand Strategies (or Ascendant Ideas) since 1919," in Borgwardt, McKnight Nichols, and Preston, *Rethinking American Grand Strategy*, 164–65. Materialize in Bacevich, *America's War for the Greater Middle East*, 244.
23. Paul Krugman, "A Deliberate Debacle," *New York Times*, 12 December 2003. Thomas Henriksen, "The Bush Doctrine: The Line Begins to Look Less Solid," *Newsday*, 21 April 2002. Ronald Brownstein, "Count Bush's Doctrine of Preemption as a Casualty of the Iraq War," *Los Angeles Times*, 17 May 2004. Overrated in Gat, *The Causes of War and the Spread of Peace*, 235. Hype in Robert Malley and Jon Finer, "The Long Shadow of 9/11: How Counterterrorism Warps U.S. Foreign Policy," *Foreign Affairs*, Vol. 97, No. 4 (July-August 2018): 60–62.
24. Aggregation in Finney and Park, "A Brief Introduction to Strategy," in Finney, *On Strategy*, 3. Political purpose in Andrew J. Bacevich, "Changing the Subject: How the United States Responds to Strategic Failure," in Fitzgerald, Ryan, and Thompson, *Not Even Past*, 207. On lack of a coherent strategy, see Whitlock, 100, 105; and West, *The Wrong War*, xx. On Vietnam, see Gregory A. Daddis, "Out of Balance: Evaluating American Strategy in Vietnam, 1968–72," *War & Society*, Vol. 32, No. 3 (October 2013): 252–70.
25. Presence patrols in Daniel A. Sjursen, *Patriotic Dissent: America in the Age of Endless War* (Berkeley, CA: Heyday, 2020), vii. See also West, 8, 58. Lack of training in Lebovic, *Planning to Fail*, 117. On numerous missions, see Malkasian, *The American War in Afghanistan*, 109–112, 175, 196. Veteran Jason Dempsey, "The Accountability-Avoidance Two-Step," in Bacevich and Sjursen, *Paths of Dissent*, 139. See also Christopher D. Kolenda, *Zero-Sum Victory: What We're Getting Wrong about War* (Lexington: University Press of Kentucky, 2021), 223–24.
26. "Professor Nagl's War," *New York Times*, 11 January 2004. See also Fred Kaplan, *The Insurgents: David Petraeus and the Plot to Change the American Way of War* (New York: Simon & Schuster, 2013), 79–80, 141–52.

Nagl quoted in Gian Gentile, "What I Learned in Baghdad," in Bacevich and Sjursen, *Paths of Dissent*, 242. On the drafting of new doctrine, see Conrad C. Crane, *Cassandra in Oz: Counterinsurgency and Future War* (Annapolis, MD: Naval Institute Press, 2016). Paula Broadwell and Vernon Loeb, *All In: The Education of General David Petraeus* (New York: Penguin, 2012), 195.

27. On treatment of civilians, see Metz, *Iraq & the Evolution of American Strategy*, 156. Violence and displacement in Lebovic, *The Limits of U.S. Military Capability*, 65, 70. Lack of intelligence in C. J. Chivers, *The Fighters: Americans in Combat in Afghanistan and Iraq* (New York: Simon & Schuster, 2018), 131; and Peter Mansoor, *Baghdad at Sunrise: A Brigade Commander's War in Iraq* (New Haven, CT: Yale University Press, 2008), 164. Advisor Emma Sky, *The Unraveling: High Hopes and Missed Opportunities in Iraq* (London: Atlantic Books, 2015), 256. Problems measuring progress in West, *The Wrong War*, 178; and Gopal, *No Good Men among the Living*, 273. Terrain in Rothkopf, *National Insecurity*, 78. Of course, "human terrain" really was only seen from a military perspective, not a cultural-anthropological one. Veteran Roy Scranton, *We're Doomed. Now What? Essays on War and Climate Change* (New York: Soho, 2018), 118.

28. Perpetuate in Ahmed S. Hashim, *Insurgency and Counter-Insurgency in Iraq* (Ithaca, NY: Cornell University Press, 2006), 272. Awe erosion in Leffler, *Confronting Saddam Hussein*, 234. On patience and generational wars, see Kolenda, 2; Layne, *The Peace of Illusions*, 122; and Stieb, 213. White House paraphrased in Gardner, *The Long Road to Baghdad*, 30. Ambushes in Chivers, 215.

29. On "redemption through violence," see Kennedy, *Afterimages*, 168. On global force, see Lubin, *Never-Ending War on Terror*, 8–9. Immoral, citing Peter Beinart, in Lapham, *Theater of War*, 161. Soft in Metz, 124. War-based patriotism in Bodnar, *Divided by Terror*, 4. Faux patriotism in Sjursen, *Patriotic Dissent*, 75. Lobotomized in Erik Edstrom, "As American as It Gets," in Bacevich and Sjursen, 41.

30. Edward Wong, "Battle for Falluja Rouses the Anger of Iraqis Weary of the U.S. Occupation," *New York Times*, 22 April 2004. See also McAlister, *Epic Encounters*, 299–300. Civilian casualties in Bodnar, *Divided by Terror*, 104. American cruelty in Frank Rich, "It Was the Porn That Made Them Do It," *New York Times*, 30 May 2004. McChrystal in Chivers, 251. On the limits of democratic institutions producing democracy, see Howard, *The Invention of Peace*, 86.

31. Fabric in Alessandra Stanley, "All Terrorism All the Time," *New York Times*, 12 August 2006. Graham in Kobes Du Mez, *Jesus and John Wayne*, 219. Networks in Mackinlay, *The Insurgent Archipelago*, 102, 141. Hate us and claptrap in Mueller, *The Stupidity of War*, 92. Tom Engelhardt argues

that this hate rhetoric endures because "in our world, there is only one type of barbarism: theirs." *A Nation Unmade by War*, 37. Wars of choice in Vine, *The United States of War*, xiv.

32. Deterrence in Eric Schmitt and Thom Shanker, "U.S. Adapts Cold-War Idea to Fight Terrorists," *New York Times*, 18 March 2008. Paul R. Pillar, "The American Perception of Substate Threats," *Cato Institute*, 13 May 2020. Kagan in Brigham, *The United States and Iraq since 1990*, 217.

33. Indifference in Bacevich, "Introduction," in Bacevich and Sjursen, *Paths of Dissent*, 15. At peace with war in David Carr, "The Wars We Choose to Ignore," *New York Times*, 26 May 2008. On John Quincy Adams warning against going "abroad in search of monsters to destroy," see Vine, 74. On dismissing the damages and costs of war, see Bodnar, *Divided by Terror*, 6; and Mueller, *Overblown*, 29–30. Gopal, *No Good Men among the Living*, 133.

34. Defining "war" in Brian McCallister Linn, *The Echo of Battle*, 3. On the Patriot Act, see Lubin, *Never-Ending War on Terror*, 55–56. Antidemocratic behavior in Bodnar, *Divided by Terror*, 15. Robert E. Pierre, "Wisconsin Senator Emerges as a Maverick," *Washington Post*, 27 October 2001.

35. Polling in Dave Lawler, "20 years on, most Americans say Iraq invasion was the wrong decision," *Axios*, 18 March 2023. Inertia in Preble, *Peace, War, and Liberty*, 99. On military leaders' "unwarranted and baseless" optimism, see Whitlock, *The Afghanistan Papers*, 94; and, in Iraq, Ricks, *Fiasco*, 110.

36. Influence in Rothkopf, *National Insecurity*, 239. See also Engelhardt, *A Nation Unmade by War*, 5, 10, 21; and Kolenda, *Zero-Sum Victory*, 4, 9. Hypochondria in Ted Galen Carpenter, *Smart Power: Toward a Prudent Foreign Policy* (Washington, DC: Cato Institute, 2008), 6. Cohen, *The Big Stick*, 64–65.

37. Recalibration in David Fitzgerald and David Ryan, "Failing to End: Obama and Iraq," in Fitzgerald, Ryan, and Thompson, *Not Even Past*, 142. Unabated in Peter Baker, "Obama's War on Terror," *New York Times*, 17 January 2010. Peter W. Singer, "Do Drones Undermine Democracy?" *New York Times*, 22 January 2012. On special forces, see Jennifer D. Kibbe, "The Military, the CIA, and America's Shadow Wars," in Adams and Murray, *Mission Creep*, 212–17. Oversight in Toft and Kushi, *Dying by the Sword*, 225. Morality in Echevarria, *Military Strategy*, 83, 86; and Lubin, 95. Revulsion and invisible in Dexter Filkins, "Did Making the Rules of War Better Make the World Worse?" *New Yorker*, 6 September 2021. Attractive in Heefner, *The Missile Next Door*, 9. Persistent and expansive war in Moyn, *Humane*, 4, 8, 280.

38. Front pages in Moyn, 284. Language in Hemmer, *American Pendulum*, 154. Fear of collapse and hawks in Whitlock, 201, 228. Surge in Malkasian,

The American War in Afghanistan, 233–36. Syria in Toft and Kushi, 238–39. Criticism in Cohen, *The Big Stick*, 167, 168, 171, 178.

39. Douglas T. Stuart, *The Pivot to Asia: Can It Serve as the Foundation for American Grand Strategy in the 21st Century?* (Carlisle Barracks, PA: US Army War College Press, 2016). On Chinese domination, see Mearsheimer, *The Tragedy of Great Power Politics*, 360–61, 401. Senators in Mueller, *The Stupidity of War*, 130–31. Ana Swanson, "Red Scare Grows in Washington, Now With China as Boogeyman," *New York Times*, 21 July 2019. Jeet Heer, "Cold War Nostalgia Fuels a Dangerous New Anti-China Consensus," *The Nation*, 15 March 2021. Seven seas in Gordon G. Chang, "Preparing for War with China, U.S. Shrinks Its Navy," *Newsweek*, 4 April 2023. Gordon G. Chang, "America's Failed Deterrence of China Has Left Us with Only Bad Options," *Newsweek*, 30 October 2023.

40. Costs in Vine, *The United States of War*, 281; and Bacevich, *The Limits of Power*, 147, 156. Deficit spending in Porter, *The False Promise of Liberal Order*, 164, 169. Lucrative in Dower, *The Violent American Century*, 95. Substantial in Cohen, *The Big Stick*, 195.

41. Einar H. Dyvik, "Countries with the Highest Military Spending 2022," *Statista*, 29 August 2023. See also Gat, *The Causes of War and the Spread of Peace*, 213; and Craig and Logevall, *America's Cold War*, 361–63. Everywhere war in Waldman, *Vicarious Warfare*, 110. Exaggerated fears in May, *Fortress America*, 7, 9–11. Michiko Kakutani, "Human Costs of the Forever Wars, Enough to Fill a Bookshelf," *New York Times*, 26 December 2014. Kennan, *American Diplomacy*, 89.

42. Masculinity in Kobes Du Mez, *Jesus and John Wayne*, 3. Male nationalism in Moyn, *Humane*, 66. On Trump and his relationship with war, see Whitlock, *The Afghanistan Papers*, 245. Clausewitz in Keegan, *The History of Warfare*, 32.

43. Entertainment in Engelhardt, *A Nation Unmade by War*, 50. See also Lubin, *Never-Ending War on Terror*, 6. Retired generals in Gordon Adams, "Donald Trump's Military Government," *New York Times*, 10 December 2016. Max Fisher, "Trump's View of Military," *New York Times*, 4 March 2017. On Trump's "cultish attachment to hard power," see Porter, 138. Tin-pot in Jason Berger, "Trump's Military Parade Would Turn U.S. Troops into Toy Soldiers," *Washington Post*, 16 February 2018. Terrorism and immigration in Miller, *Grand Strategy from Truman to Trump*, 239. Maggie Haberman, "Trump Rekindles Campaign Threat of Islamic Peril," *New York Times*, 16 April 2019. "I Think Islam Hates Us," *New York Times*, 26 January 2017. On Trump and endless wars, see William M. Arkin with E. D. Cauchi, *The Generals Have No Clothes: The Untold Story of Our Endless Wars* (New York: Simon & Schuster, 2021), 5.

44. William D. Hartung, "The Generals In Trump's Cabinet Aren't 'Adults in the Room,'" *In These Times*, 7 March 2017. H. R. McMaster,

Battlegrounds: The Fight to Defend the Free World (New York: Harper, 2020), 4, 443. Italics in original. Robert Kagan, "A Superpower, Like It or Not: Why Americans Must Accept Their Global Role," *Foreign Affairs*, Vol. 100, No. 2 (March-April 2021): 28–38. Anyone anywhere in Rothkopf, *National Insecurity*, 307–8.

45. Imagination in David Ryan and David Fitzgerald, "Introduction," in Ryan and Fitzgerald, *Not Even Past*, 8. Fareed Zakaria, "U.S. Foreign Policy Needs to Get over Its Fear of Instability," *Washington Post*, 8 July 2021. Lawrence Freedman, "Strategic Studies and the Problem of Power," in Mahnken and Maiolo, *Strategic Studies*, 19. Paralyzed in Gaddis, *On Grand Strategy*, 13. Of note, Melvyn Leffler argues that "Fear, power, and hubris led to war" in Iraq. *Confronting Saddam Hussein*, 146.

46. Spontaneous in Sanders, *Peddlers of Crisis*, 2. Promise and peril in Sherry, *In the Shadow of War*, 108. On power politics, see Scott T. Davis, "A Brief History of Strategy," in Finney, *On Strategy*, 19. Hyperactive in Preble, *The Power Problem*, 169. See also Vine, 16. Stephen Wertheim, "The Legacy of 9/11," *Prospect*, 14 July 2021.

47. Exaggerated hopes and fears in Leffler, *For the Soul of Mankind*, 456, 458. Institutionalized in Porter, 116. Extinguishing on p. 160. Military solutions in Trauschweizer, *Maxwell Taylor's Cold War*, 207; and Vine, 308. Realism in Dower, 11. Paranoia in Kotkin, *Armageddon Averted*, 192. Savior generals in Kelley Beaucar Vlahos, "Lessons from the Anti-Petraeus," *American Conservative*, 22 August 2013. Secular saints in Susan Bryant, Brett Swaney, and Heidi Urben, "From Citizen Soldier to Secular Saint: The Societal Implications of Military Exceptionalism," *Texas National Security Review*, Vol. 4, No. 2 (Spring 2021): 12. David Petraeus and Michael E. O'Hanlon, "America's Awesome Military," *Brookings*, 30 September 2016. For an alternate view, see Jeremi Suri, "History Is Clear: America's Military Is Way Too Big," *New York Times*, 30 August 2021.

48. On strength not being a function of military power, see Preble, *The Power Problem*, 3. See also Posen, *Restraint*, xii, 24, 33. Lawrence Freedman, "Coronavirus and the Language of War," *New Statesman*, 11 April 2020.

49. Inherent in Michael Howard, *The Causes of War*, 2nd ed. (Cambridge, MA: Harvard University Press, 1983), 25. Anarchy, citing Alexander Wendt, Gat, *The Causes of War and the Spread of Peace*, 123. More and better in Cohen, *The Big Stick*, xii. On panic and fear not needing to drive policy, see Gregory W. Meeks, "Anti-China Rhetoric Distracts Washington—and Boosts Beijing," *Foreign Policy*, 26 June 2023; and Michael Brenes, "American Hegemony Is Morally Bankrupt. We Need a Just Alternative," *Jacobin*, 20 December 2022.

50. Stephen Kotkin, "The Cold War Never Ended: Ukraine, the China Challenge, and the Revival of the West," *Foreign Affairs*, 6 April 2022. On "perpetuating politics of insecurity," see Craig and Logevall, *America's Cold War*, 11; and Edstrom, "As American as It Gets," 35.

Index

For the benefit of digital users, indexed terms that span two pages (e.g., 52–53) may, on occasion, appear on only one of those pages.

ABC News, 225, 261–262
Able Archer 83 exercise, 259–260
ABM treaty. *See* Anti-Ballistic Missile Treaty
absolute security, 10
Abu Ghraib prison complex, 336, 339–340
Acheson, Dean, 39–40, 46, 57, 86, 143, 155
    Korean War and, 75–76, 84
ACLU. *See* American Civil Liberties Union
Adenauer, Konrad, 83, 142
Afghanistan, 148, 308
    Carter and, 218–220
    CIA and, 246
    civil war in, 267
    cruise missile strikes on, 322
    Reagan and, 246, 249–250
    Taliban and, 267–268, 331
    US invasion of, 332–334, 337, 339
    USSR and, 216–220, 246–247, 266–267
Afred P. Murrah Federal Building, 313
Africa, 118
Aidid, Mohamed Farrah, 305
AirLand Battle, 240–241, 245
airpower, 55–56, 295
    in Balkans, 319–321
    deterrence and, 95–96
    faith in, 95–96, 176–177, 293–295
    fear of, 95–96, 176–177
    Korean War and, 87–88
    Operation Desert Storm and, 184
    Vietnam War and, 175–177, 180
    in World War II, 176
Albania, 182–183
Albright, Madeline, 4, 12, 288–289, 309–310

Algeria, 162
    France and, 163
Ali, Mohammed, 148
Alien (film), 237
Allende, Salvador, 195–196
Alliance for Progress, 138–141
Alsop, Joseph, 237
Ambrose, Stephen, 28
American Civil Liberties Union (ACLU), 2
American exceptionalism, 85, 103–104, 236
American Legion, 67–68
American Legion Convention of 1952, 119
Anderson, Robert, 112–113
Andropov, Yuri, 238
Anglo-Persian Oil Company, 110
Angola, 197–198
anti-Americanism, 225–226
Anti-Ballistic Missile Treaty (ABM treaty), 258–259
anticolonialism, 77, 118, 148–149
anticolonial nationalism, 152
anticommunism, 63, 90, 108, 128–129, 139–140, 281
    civil rights movement and, 66
    dictators and, 153
    neoconservative movement and, 253
    Reagan and, 229–230
    religion and, 50–51
    segregationism and, 66
    support for anticommunist governments, 45–46
    violent, 156
    white supremacists using, 65–66
anti-imperialism, 129, 152–153
anti-Sovietism, 227
antiwar movement, 170–171, 181
Arab nationalism, 112–114

Arbenz, Jacobo, 109–110, 126–127, 140
Aristide, Jean-Bertrand, 306
Asimov, Isaac, 258–259
Aspin, Les, 305
Aswan High Dam, 112
Atkinson, Rick, 277–278
Atlantic Charter, 55, 117–118
Atomic Energy Commission, 89
Atomic War! (comic), 105
atomic weapons, 10, 21–23, 80, 88–89
   Air Force and, 95
   Carter and, 218–219
   decision making over, 98
   fear and, 90–91
   Israel and, 202–203
   limited war and, 79, 92–93
   moral ambiguities over, 102
   Osgood on, 79–80
   Reagan and, 233
   tactical, 100
   terrorism and, 314
   testing of, 137
   USSR and, 59
Authorization of Military Force (2001), 331–332
Azerbaijan, 47

Ba'ath Party, 331
Bacevich, Andrew, 26
Baker, James, 282–283, 318–319
balance of power, 84
balance of terror, 84, 102–104
Baldwin, Hanson W., 55, 73–74, 81–82, 90–91, 110, 136
   on deterrence, 92
Baldwin, Roger N., 2
Balkans, 322
   Clinton and, 318–321
   ethnic cleansing in, 319
   ethnic violence in, 318
   nationalism in, 317–318
   NATO airstrikes in, 319–321
Ball, George, 206
Bandung Conference, 148–149
Bangladesh, 211
Barbour, Haley, 309
Barkley, Alben W., 9–10
Batista, Fulgencio, 123
Bay of Pigs, 126–127, 134, 135

Beech, Keyes, 79
Begin, Menachem, 216–217
Beirut truck bombings, 242–243, 250
Berlin Airlift, 54–55
Berlin Wall
   crisis and construction of, 142–143, 185–186
   dismantling of, 287–288, 290, 291
Bigelow, Albert, 105
Block, Herbert, 67
Blood, Archer, 193
Bohlen, Charles, "Chip," 39, 86, 87
Bolivia, 141–142
Bolshevik Revolution, 30–31
Bosch, Juan, 153–154
Bosnia-Herzegovina, 318, 320–321
Boutros-Ghali, Boutros, 305
Bowles, Chester, 129, 133, 144, 149, 166–167
Boyd, John, 294, 296
Boyer, Paul, 97
Bradley, Omar N., 6, 76
   atomic weapons and, 88–89
Brands, Hal, 13–14
Brandt, Willy, 54, 143–144, 207–208, 268
Brazil, 149–150
Brezhnev, Leonid, 182–183, 190–191, 235
   death of, 238
   SALT II and, 213
Brinkley, Douglas, 303
brinksmanship, 94, 135
Brodie, Bernard, 26–27, 79, 80, 93–94, 97–98
Brown v. Board of Education, 115
Bryant, Arthur, 14
Brzezinski, Zbigniew, 209–211, 214
   on Afghanistan, 219
   on Iran, 226–227
   on Milošević, 321
Buchanan, Patrick, 302, 312
Buckley, William F., 192, 212–213, 261–262
Bulletin of the Atomic Scientists (magazine), 104
Bush, George H. W., 277–278, 285, 286–287, 289–291, 300
   Defense Planning Guidance and, 311–312

Bush, George H. W. (*Continued*)
   Iraq and, 293–297, 307–308
   Panama and, 291–292
   START and, 314
   use of force models and, 298
Bush, George W., 149, 167, 312–313, 329–332
   "axis of evil" and, 334
   Global War on Terror and, 329
   patriotism used by, 337
Bush Doctrine, 334–335

Cambodia, 117, 148, 204–205
   bombing of, 180
   genocide in, 194
   incursion into, 189
   Vietnam invasion of, 216
Camp David Accords, 216–217
Canada, 302
"Can't Do Nuttin' for Ya, Man!" (song), 277
capitalism, 139
Carter, Jimmy, 194, 208, 212, 230–231
   Afghanistan and, 218–220
   Camp David Accords and, 216–217
   China and, 214
   containment and, 208, 220
   defense budgets and, 213–215, 218, 232
   Haiti and, 306
   human rights and, 210
   Iran and, 216, 221, 225–228
   Israel and, 216
   militarization and, 208–209
   military readiness and, 228
   Notre Dame speech, 209–211
   nuclear weapons and, 218–219
   Panama Canal and, 213–214
   Reagan debate with, 231
   as reluctant belligerent, 220–221
   SALT II and, 212–213, 218
   Wake Forest speech, 210–211
Carter Doctrine, 220–221, 241
Castle Bravo atomic test, 103
Castro, Fidel, 118, 123, 124–128, 185–186
   CIA and, 126, 137–138
The Causes of World War Three (Mills), 103–104
Center for Strategic and International Studies, 191

Central Intelligence Agency (CIA), 44, 51
   Afghanistan and, 246, 267
   "Bleeders" group in, 246
   Castro and, 126–127, 137–138
   Chile and, 195–196
   Contras and, 251
   Counterterrorism Center, 241–242
   covert actions by, 107–108
   Cuba and, 126–127, 137–138
   Dominican Republic and, 153–154
   Iran and, 110–111
   Iran-Contra affair and, 252–253
   paramilitary actions and, 108–109
   on USSR economy, 234–235
   on Vietnam air strikes, 176
Chamberlain, Neville, 32–33
Chamoun, Camille, 113–114
Cheney, Dick, 281, 309, 312–313, 330–331
Chennault, Claire L., 56–57
Chernenko, Konstantin, 238
Chernobyl nuclear accident, 271
Chiang Kai-shek, 101
Chile, 195–196
China, 2–3, 21, 23–24
   Carter and, 214
   civil war in, 56–59
   communism and, 56–59
   Cultural Revolution in, 148
   encirclement fears in, 117
   Great Leap Forward in, 116, 148
   India and, 145, 151–152
   Korean War and, 73–77, 87
   Nixon and, 185–186, 190–191
   Pakistan and, 145
   as peer competitor, 340
   proliferation and, 283
   Taiwan and, 101
   USSR and, 56–57
Chinese Communist Party, 30–31
Chin Peng, 160
Church, Frank, 154, 251–252
Churchill, Winston, 23–24
   "Iron Curtain" speech, 36–37
CIA. *See* Central Intelligence Agency
civil defense, 105–106
civil liberties, 338–339
civil-military tensions, 77–78
civil rights movement, 65–66

Clancy, Tom, 242, 315
Clark, Mark, 81
Clark, Wesley K., 306, 321–323
clash of civilizations, 325, 330
von Clausewitz, Carl, 296, 315
Clay, Lucius, 44–45, 54
Clifford, Clark, 40–41, 171
Clinton, Bill, 208–209, 282, 283, 290–291, 300, 317
   Balkans and, 318–321
   cruise missile hegemony and, 323–324
   foreign policy of, 301–303, 312–313
   Haiti and, 306–307
   homosexual service members and, 301
   Iraq and, 297, 323–324
   military reductions and, 316
   multilateralism and, 309
   national security vision of, 300–301, 304, 305
   peacekeeping and, 306
   al-Qaeda strikes under, 322
   Russia and, 303
   Somalia and, 304–305
   terrorism and, 313–314
coercive escalation, 180
Cohen, Eliot A., 339
Cohen, William, 320–321, 324
Colby, William W., 196
Cold War, 3–8, 11, 13, 328
   changing security structures in early, 25
   containment strategy in, 38–40
   end of, 289–290, 308
   as existential conflict of systems, 28
   Germany division and, 54–55
   Global South and, 14–15
   as ideological competition, 27–28
   Kennan impact on strategies in, 37–38
   militarization of policy in, 33
   Morgenthau, Hans, on, 27
   opening markets after, 280
   stability in, 283
   start of, 30
   as zero-sum game, 84
collective alliances, 117
collective security, 130
Collier's (magazine), 102–103
colonialism, 57–58, 162–163
   Africa and, 118

Comintern. *See* Third Communist International
Commager, Henry Steele, 254
Committee of Santa Fe, 210, 236
Committee on the Present Danger, 192, 214–215
communism, 28–29
   anti-imperialism confused with, 129
   Asia and, 57–58
   China and, 56–59
   development and, 148
   fears of, 11, 31–32
   homosexuality and, 65
   India and, 151
   Kennan on, 38
   Korean War and, 76–78
   Latin America and, 125, 128–129
   nationalist social reforms conflated with, 129
   permanent revolution of, 31
   the Philippines and, 164–165
   red scare and, 31
   revolutionary thinking of, 35
   Rostow on, 140
   sexual equality and, 65
Communist Control Act (1954), 68
communist imperialism, 63–64
Communist Information Bureau (Cominform), 45, 149
Communist Party
   Chinese, 30–31
   Indonesian, 171–172
   Malayan, 159–160
   Texas outlawing membership in, 68
Congo, 118
conscription, 69
containment, 13, 38–40
   Carter and, 208, 220
   covert operations for, 108
   Eisenhower and, 90
   Global South and, 108
   Korean War and, 76–77
   militarizing, 52–53
   origins of strategy, 38
   Osgood on, 79
   spiritual mobilization and, 51
Contras, 249–253
counterinsurgency doctrine, 130–131, 335
   cultural landscapes and, 165–166

counterinsurgency doctrine (*Continued*)
  the Philippines and, 164–165
counterterrorism missions, 335
covert operations, 107–108
Covid-19 pandemic, 343
Cox, Arthur Macy, 262
van Creveld, Martin, 325
Crimson Tide (film), 315
Croatia, 317–318
cruise missile hegemony, 323–324
Crusade in Europe (Eisenhower), 128
Cuba, 123–125, 127
  CIA and, 126–127, 137–138
  Congo and, 118
  missile deployment in, 134–135
Cuban Missile Crisis, 126, 134–136
cultural meaning, war and, 7–8
Cultural Revolution, 148
Czechoslovakia, 112
  Prague Spring, 182–183
  USSR invasion of, 182–183

Daoud, Mohammed, 217–218
Davy Crocket weapon, 100–101
The Day After (film), 261–262, 313
Dayton Accords, 320–321, 323
decolonization, 14, 117–118, 138, 144, 152, 153
Defense Planning Guidance, 311–313
defense transformation movement, 295–296
defensive expansion, 150
de Gaulle, Charles, 161
delayed fallout, 260–261
The Delta Force (film), 242
demobilization, 26, 28
democracy, 2–4
  markets and, 139
  war to promote, 334
democratic capitalism, 139, 141, 144
denaturalization, 66
Deng Xiaoping, 214
Department of Defense, "Know Your Enemy" series, 63–64
de-Stalinization, 116
détente, 187–198, 216
  Afghanistan war and, 218
  expansionist, 202
  Helsinki Act and, 206–207

deterrence, 92, 119, 180, 233
  airpower and, 95–96
  faith in, 97, 99
  limited war and, 93
  Reagan and, 257
  US Air Force and, 95–96
development, 14–15, 28–29
  communism and, 148
  security and, 147
"Dictatorship and Double Standards" (Kirkpatrick), 210
Diem, Ngo Dinh, 163–165
Dien Bien Phu, 100, 160
Dirksen, Everett, 137
dissent, 8
Dominican Republic, 153–154
domino theory, 158–162
Doolittle, James H., 108
The Doomsday Machine (Ellsberg), 103–104
Douglas, Helen Gahagan, 63
Douglas, William O., 16, 49
Douhet, Giulio, 176
Dower, John, 94
Doyle, Clyde, 66–67
Dr. Strangelove (film), 104
Duan, Le, 189–190
Dubcek, Alexander, 182
Duck and Cover (film), 105
Dukakis, Michael, 287
Dulles, Allen, 110, 112
Dulles, John Foster, 50, 53, 83, 99, 109–110, 117
  on Arab nationalism, 113–114
  on deterrence, 92
  on massive retaliation, 91
  militancy of, 85
Durbrow, Elbridge, 39

East Germany, 112, 207–208
  Berlin Wall crisis and, 142
  collapse of, 287–288
East Pakistan, 193
economic aid programs
  modernization and, 130
  nation building and, 129
economic globalization, 303
economic instability, 23–24, 42–43
Egypt, 112

Israel attacking, 201
Israel blockade by, 200–201
Israel meeting with, 216
Einstein, Albert, 104
Eisenhower, Dwight D., 14–15, 33, 93, 115–116, 128
  Africa and, 118
  CIA and, 107
  containment and, 90
  covert operations under, 108
  Cuba and, 126
  Egypt and, 112
  farewell address, 119, 132
  Hungary and, 112
  India and, 149–150
  interventionism and, 114
  Iran and, 110
  Khrushchev and, 83
  Korean War and, 75–76
  Latin America and, 109
  long-range missiles and, 90
  McCarthy and, 62–63
  Middle East and, 112–113
  missile gap claims and, 133–134
  New Look policy, 91, 110–111
  nuclear weapons and, 79–80, 99–100, 102–103
  regime reinforcement policy, 114
  Taiwan and, 101
Eisenhower Doctrine, 113
Ellison, Ralph, 65–66
Ellsberg, Daniel, 96–97, 103–104
El Salvador, 140–141, 251, 254
Elsey, George, 40–41
embassy bombings of 1998, 322
end of history, 298
Eshkol, Levi, 201
essential security, 26–27
ethnic cleansing, 319
European Recovery Program. *See* Marshall Plan
everywhere war, 341
exceptionalism, 85, 103–104
ExComm, 134–136
Executive Order 9066, 2
expansionist détente, 202

failed states, 283, 332
Fail-Safe (film), 104

faith, 5–6, 8
  in airpower, 95–96, 176–177, 293–295
  in American innocence, 13
  in American power, 13, 308–309
  defining, 7
  in deterrence, 97, 99
  Hollywood and, 237
  militarization and, 234–235
  in military power, 26
  national security and, 7–8
  revolution in military affairs and, 295–296
Fanon, Frantz, 60, 117–118
The Fate of the Earth (Schell), 260–261
Faulkner, William, 16
FBI. *See* Federal Bureau of Investigation
fear, 5–8
  in airpower, 95–96, 176–177
  atomic weapons and, 90–91
  business uses of, 11
  of communism, 11, 31–32
  cultivation of, 342–343
  foreign policy shaped by, 9
  of instability, 307
  international system and, 9
  neoconservative uses of, 236
  patriotism and, 67–68
  political uses of, 10–11
  US Global South policy and, 144
Federal Bureau of Investigation (FBI), 66–67
Feingold, Russ, 338–339
Ferguson, Homer, 33–34
Filkins, Dexter, 333
Fishel, Wesley, 163
flexible response, 82
foco theory, 141–142
Ford, Gerald R., 204–208, 229–230
Foreign Affairs (magazine), 38, 85, 141
  Nixon and, 178–179
foreign aid, 148
foreign policy
  Clinton and, 301–303, 312–313
  fear shaping, 9
  militarization of, 14, 49, 52–53, 141, 229
  neoconservative agendas for, 311–312
  realism and, 187
  segregationism and, 115

forever war, 341–342
Formosa, 57, 86. *See also* Taiwan
forward defense, 55–56
forward strategy, 304
France
  Algeria and, 162–163
  Indochina and, 100, 162, 163
  Vietnam and, 161–164
free-market capitalism, 28
free trade, 43
Friedman, Milton, 235
Friedman, Thomas L., 279
Front de libération nationale, 162
Fukuyama, Francis, 298, 301
Fulbright, J. William, 16, 115, 124
full-spectrum dominance, 311

Gaddis, John Lewis, 11–12, 237–238, 291, 328
Gates, Thomas S., Jr., 145
Gavin, James, 87–88, 93
Gaza Strip, 201, 217, 244, 324–325
Gelb, Leslie, 221
Geneva Accords on Indochina (1954), 117, 144
Geneva summit, 270
genocide, 306
  in Cambodia, 194
  in former Yugoslavia, 318–319
  in Rwanda, 305
Germany
  Berlin Wall crisis in, 142
  Cold War and, 54
  division of, 54–56
  reunification of, 287–289
Gibson, Mel, 237
G.I. Joe, 237
Girl Scouts, 67–68
Glenn, John, 307
global involvement, 310
globalism, 302
globalization, 22–23, 302–303, 315–316
  liberal, 316
global market economy, 286
global periphery, 115–116
Global South, 116
  Cold War and, 14–15
  containment policies and, 108
  development programs and, 14–15

fear in US policy in, 144
Global War on Terror, 329, 336
Glosson, Buster, 294
Godzilla (film), 104
Golan Heights, 202
Goldwater, Barry, 10–11, 31–32, 49, 65, 130, 152–153, 159
  on China, 214
  on collective alliances, 117
  on détente, 188–189
  on Latin America and communism, 125, 129
  nuclear limits opposed by, 137
  on sources of communism, 155
  Vietnam and, 159
Good Neighbor Policy, 125
Gopal, Anand, 338
Gorbachev, Mikhail, 268, 283–284, 289, 290
  Afghanistan and, 264, 266–267
  coup attempt against, 291
  defense spending and, 264
  economic collapse fears of, 268–269
  liberalization and, 285
  peace offensive, 286
  Poland and, 285–286
  Reagan meeting with, 270–272
  reforms by, 264–266, 269
  rise to power, 263–264
Graham, Billy, 50–51
Graham, Franklin, 337–338
Grandin, Greg, 130–131
gray areas, 14–15
Great Depression, 23
Great Leap Forward, 116, 148
Great Society, 166–167
Great War. *See* World War I
Greece, 41, 45–46
The Green Berets (film), 170
Greene, Graham, 162–163
Greenwood, Lee, 277
Grenada, 244–245
Gromyko, Andrei, 219, 255–256, 259
Guatemala, 109–110, 123, 139–141
Guevara, Ernesto, "Che," 60, 129–130, 141–142
Gulf War. *See* Operation Desert Storm
Guomindang, 58

INDEX

Haig, Alexander, 232, 234–235, 238, 241–242
Haiti, 306–307
Hajima, Masuda, 74
Haldeman, H. R., 180
Hamilton, Alexander, 125
Harkins, Paul D., 165
Harriman, W. Averell, 262
Hartford Courant (newspaper), 16
Hatch, Orrin, 213–214
Heinlein, Robert A., 64–65
Helms, Richard, 37
Helsinki Consultations, 206
Helsinki Final Act, 206–207
Henry, Leland, 50
Hersey, John, 104
Hiroshima (Hersey), 104
Hitler, Adolf, 32–33
Ho Chi Minh, 159
Ho Chi Minh Trail, 175–176
Hoffmann, Paul G., 68–69
Hofstadter, Richard, 67
Holbrooke, Richard, 305
Hollywood, war and, 237
homosexuality, 65
homosexual service members, 301
Honduras, 251
Honecker, Erich, 287–288
Hoover, J. Edgar, 31–32, 51, 170–171
House, Jonathan, 203–204
House Un-American Activities Committee (HUAC), 66–67, 97
Hudson Institute, 98–99
Hukbalahap rebellion, 164–165
humanitarian support projects, 335
human rights, 206
   Reagan and, 251–252
human terrain, 166
Humphrey, Hubert, 168
Hungary, 34
   Soviet crackdown in, 111–112
Huntington, Samuel, 325, 330
Hussein, Saddam, 238, 247, 279, 293, 294–296, 300, 305–306, 324, 333
Hutus, 305
hydrogen bombs, 99–100, 106

ideology, 5
   Cold War as competition of, 27–28

IMF. *See* International Monetary Fund
Immigration and Nationality Act (1952), 66
imperialism, 31, 57–58, 60, 125, 129–130
   puppet-government, 36
India, 111–112, 145, 211
   China and, 145, 151–152
   communism and, 151
   economy of, 150
   independence of, 57
   neutrality and, 149–150
   Non-Alignment Movement and, 149
   partition of, 151
   SEAO and, 117
   USSR and, 193–194
Indochina
   France and, 100, 162, 163
   Geneva Accords on, 117, 144
Indonesia, 148, 152–153, 171–172
Indonesian Communist Party (PKI), 171–172
INF treaty. *See* Intermediate-Range Nuclear Forces Treaty
instability
   economic, 23–24, 42–43
   fear of, 307
   internal, 130–131
   in USSR, 268
Institute of Defense Analysis, 177
Intermediate-Range Nuclear Forces Treaty (INF treaty), 271
internal instability, 130–131
Internal Security Act (1950), 66
internationalism, 4
International Monetary Fund (IMF), 303
international system
   fear and, 9
   Wilson vision of, 30
interventionism, 14–15, 108, 114, 125, 282–283
   human rights and, 206
   internal instability as pretext for, 130–131
   in Latin America, 196
   reformist, 138, 155
   South Asia and, 145
interventionistic hypernationalism, 310
intifada, 244

Iran, 45–47, 110, 197, 211, 216, 219, 220–221, 225–226, 238, 297, 342–343
  Brzezinski on, 226–227
  hostage rescue attempt in, 228
  USSR and, 227
Iran-Contra affair, 252–254
Iranian Revolution, 221, 225
Iran-Iraq War, 247–248, 252–253, 293
Iraq, 238, 247, 278–279, 293–297, 305–308, 323–324, 331
  US invasion of, 332–334, 336, 337, 339
Iraq Syndrome, 278
"Is America Becoming Number Two?" (Committee on the Present Danger), 215
Islam, 248, 337–338
Islamic fundamentalism, 247–248
Islamic State, 340
Israel, 200–201, 324–325, 342–343
  atomic weapons and, 202–203
  creation of, 47–48
  Egypt meeting with, 216
  Gaza and, 217, 244
  Lebanon and, 242–244
  Palestinians and, 201–202
  Six-Day War and, 201
  West Bank and, 217, 244, 334–335
Italy, 23–24
  elections of 1948, 44–45
  US missiles in, 90

Jackson, Henry M., "Scoop," 188, 207, 213
Japan
  rearmament calls for, 60
  surrender of, 21
  after World War II, 1–2
Japanese Americans, internment of, 2–3
Javits, Jacob, 24
Jefferson, Thomas, 3
Jervis, Robert, 262
Jim Crow policies, 65–66
Johnson, Louis, 94–95
Johnson, Lyndon, 4, 89–90
  Dominican Republic and, 153–154
  Great Society agenda, 166–167
  Nuclear Non-Proliferation Treaty and, 137
  Six-Day War and, 201
  Vietnam and, 159, 166–170, 177–178
Joint Chiefs of Staff, 51, 69, 77–78, 129, 130
  Taiwan and, 101
Jordan, 201

Kagan, Donald, 282, 324, 342
Kagan, Frederick, 338
Kagan, Robert, 310
Kahn, Herman, 97–99, 102, 105–106, 259–260
Kaplan, Robert, 325
Keegan, John, 12
Kennan, George, 4, 13, 32, 37–40, 42, 44, 49–53, 57–58, 64, 184, 282, 289, 341
  Korean War and, 76–77
  on Latin America, 155
  on Middle East, 114
  on militarization, 52–53
Kennedy, Edward M., "Ted," 155–156, 193
Kennedy, John F., 8, 107, 131, 133
  American University address, 136–137
  Bay of Pigs and, 126
  Berlin Wall crisis and, 142–143
  Cuba and, 127, 137–138
  Cuban Missile Crisis and, 134–137
  deterrence and, 134
  India and, 149–150
  Khrushchev and, 127–128
  Laos and, 144
  Latin America and, 138
  Limited Test Ban Treaty and, 137
  missile gap claims by, 133–134
  modernization programs and, 139–140
  presidential campaign, 131–132
  Vietnam and, 160–161, 163
Kennedy, Robert, 156
Kenya, US embassy bombing in, 322
Kerry, John, 310
Khan, Yahya, 193–194
Khmer Rouge, 194, 204–205
Khomeini, Ruhollah, (Ayatollah), 225–227, 238, 247
Khrushchev, Nikita, 83–84, 93, 112, 135–136, 185–186, 288
  Berlin and, 142

INDEX 471

Cuba and, 124, 127
East Germany and, 142–143
Hungary and, 111–112
Kennedy, J. F., and, 127–128
missiles deployed to Cuba by, 134–135
national-liberation movement and, 152–153
peaceful coexistence call by, 115–116
Kim Il Sung, 74–75, 77
King, Martin Luther, Jr., 167
Kirkland, Lane, 235
Kirkpatrick, Jeane, 210, 250–251, 307, 309
Kissinger, Henry, 4, 97–98, 144, 188–190, 193–194, 309
   Berlin Wall Crisis and, 143
   China and, 185–186
   on *The Day After*, 261–262
   deterrence and, 179–180
   German relations normalization and, 207–208
   on human rights advocates, 207
   on limited war, 92–93
   realism and, 187
   Vietnam War and, 181–182
   on Watergate, 193
   Yom Kippur War and, 202–203
"Know Your Enemy" series (Department of Defense), 63–64
Kohl, Helmut, 282, 289
Korean War, 2–3, 38, 44
   Acheson and, 75–76, 84
   China and, 73–77, 87
   communism and, 76–78
   containment and, 76–77
   defense budgets and, 53
   Eisenhower and, 75–76
   globalizing, 84
   limited war and, 79–80
   MacArthur and, 73–74, 77–78, 80
   Mao and, 76–77
   start of, 73–74, 77
   Truman and, 75–78
   United States becoming world power and, 86
Kosovo, 319–321
Krauthammer, Charles, 270–271, 308–309
Kristol, William, 310, 324
Krugman, Paul, 334–335

Kurds, 296
Kuter, Laurence S., 101–102
Kuwait, 277, 293, 295, 307–308

Lake, Anthony, 301–303
land reform, 164
Lansdale, Edward, 164–165
Laos, 149–150, 189
   coup in, 144
Laqueur, Walter, 191
Lasswell, Harold, 7, 63, 68–69
Latham, Michael E., 140
Latin America
   communism and, 125, 128–129
   Eisenhower and, 109
   foco in, 141–142
   interventionism in, 196
   Kennedy, J., and, 138
   militarization in, 140–141
   modernization in, 140–141
   regime reinforcement policies and, 114
Leahy, William D., 23, 25
Lebanon, 113–114, 245
   Israel and, 242–244
   US marines in, 242–243
Leffler, Melvyn, 266
Lehrer, Tom, 288
LeMay, Curtis, 26, 33, 95–97, 135
Lemnitzer, Lyman L., 130
Lenin, Vladimir, 30–31
Lescaze, Lee, 169–170
Lewis, Anthony, 265–266
Lewis, John, 278
liberal globalization, 316
liberalism, 3–6, 24, 298
liberty, 3
Liddell Hart, Basil, 76, 81, 184, 201
Life (magazine), 85, 89–90, 104
Limited Test Ban Treaty, 137
limited war, 78–81, 85–86
   atomic weapons and, 79, 92–93
   deterrence and, 93
   stalemates in, 93
Lippmann, Walter, 49–50, 102, 103, 161
localized wars, 81
Lockheed Martin, 288
Lodge, Henry Cabot, 115
Long, Russell, 169
long-range missiles, 90

"Long Telegram" (Kennan), 38–39
Los Angeles Times (newspaper), 110, 127
low-intensity conflict, 240, 242, 246, 248–249, 253–254
Luce, Henry, 12
Lucky Dragon (fishing trawler), 103
Lugar, Richard, 318–319

MacArthur, Douglas, 1–3, 86
  on air power, 95
  American Legion convention speech, 327–328
  end of World War II and, 21–23, 26–27
  firing of, 77–78
  Korean War and, 73–74, 77–78, 80
MacLeish, Rod, 204–205
MAD. *See* mutually assured destruction
madman theory, 179–180
Magsaysay, Ramon, 165
Mahan, Alfred Thayer, 234
Malaya, 160
Malayan Communist Party, 159–160
Malenkov, Georgy, 83–84
Manchuria, 86
Mansfield, Mike, 51, 128–129
Mao Zedong, 9, 56–60, 100–102, 185–186
  Cultural Revolution and, 148
  Great Leap Forward and, 116, 148
  Korean War and, 76–77
  SEATO and, 117
Marder, Murrey, 191
Marshall, George C., 41–43, 68–69
Marshall Plan, 24, 41, 42, 44
Marxism, 35
massive retaliation, 80, 91, 93
Mayaguez (ship), 204–205
McCarran, Patrick, 66, 74
McCarthy, Joseph R., 11, 62–65, 156, 214–215
McCarthyism, 62–65, 67, 90, 115
McChrystal, Stanley, 337
McConnell, Mitch, 314–315
McDonough, James R., 168–169
McFarlane, Bud, 243
McGovern, George, 169
McKinley, William, 310
McMaster, H. R., 342–343
McNamara, Robert, 96–97, 130, 135–136, 158, 165, 168, 171–172

Mearsheimer, John, 9
Mencken, H. L., 67–68
Mexico, 302
Meyer, Edward C., 228
Meyer, Nicholas, 261
Meyner, Robert B., 4
Middle East, 47, 114
  National Security Council and, 247
  regime reinforcement policies and, 114
  terrorism in, 241–242
  US presence in, 112–113
  USSR and, 201
militarization, 33, 130
  Carter and, 208–209
  of containment, 52–53
  faith and, 234–235
  of foreign policy, 14, 49, 52–53, 141, 229
  in Latin America, 140–141
  spiritual, 51
militarized masculinity, 237, 341
militarized modernization, 155–156
militarized nation-building, 57–58
military activism, 27
military-industrial complex, 119, 240–241
military interventionism, 14–15, 282–283
military readiness, 228
Mills, C. Wright, 103–104
Milošević, Slobodan, 320–321
Minuteman missiles, 105
missile defense, 257–258
missile gap, 133–134
missile silos, 105
"MLF Lullaby" (song), 288
modernity, Third World and, 148
modernization, 14–15, 28–29, 118–119, 139–141, 147, 150–151, 333
  as civilizing mission, 138
  economic aid programs and, 130
  in Latin America, 140–141
  militarized, 155–156
  social reforms and, 140
  Vietnam and, 163
  violence in, 156
Mogadishu, Somalia, 305
Molotov, Vyacheslav, 45, 117
Mondale, Walter, 256
Monroe Doctrine, 125
moral crusaders, 329–330

Moral Re-Armament, 58–59
Morgenthau, Hans J., 5, 27, 234
Morgenthau, Henry, Jr., 47–48
Mosaddegh, Mohammad, 110–111, 226
Moscow Summit, 191
multilateralism, 309
 global security and, 208
Murrow, Edward R., 2–3
mutually assured destruction (MAD), 97

NAACP. *See* National Association for the Advancement of Colored People
NAFTA. *See* North American Free Trade Agreement
Nagl, John, 336
Nagy, Imre, 111–112
Nasser, Gamal Abdel, 112, 114, 150–151, 202
 Israel blockade by, 200–201
 Six-Day War and, 201
Nasserism, 113
National Association for the Advancement of Colored People (NAACP), 66
National Association of Evangelicals, 255
National Association of Manufacturers, 68–69
National Committee for a Sane Nuclear Policy (SANE), 260
National Council of Churches of Christ, 66
nationalism, 14, 150–151
 anticolonial, 152
 Arab, 112–114
 in Balkans, 317–318
 Bandung Conference and, 148–149
 communism conflated with, 129
 interventionistic, 310
 Palestinian, 244
 Third World, 117–118
 Vietnam and, 163–164
national liberationism, 60
national liberation movements, 117–118, 152–153
national security, 4–5, 7–8, 53
 Clinton vision of, 300–301, 304, 305
 as national interest, 28
National Security Act (1947), 51
National Security Council, 51–53, 59–60
 atomic weapons and, 89

 on India, 149–150
 Iran-Contra affair and, 252–253
 Middle East and, 247
 New Look and, 91–92
National Security Strategy Directives, 241
nation-building, militarized, 57–58
NATO. *See* North Atlantic Treaty Organization
Naval War College, 242
Nehru, Jawaharlal, 57, 117, 145, 149, 150–151
Nena (band), 262
neoconservative movement, 210, 213, 214–215, 230, 235–236, 265, 272
 anticommunism and, 253
 Bush Doctrine and, 334
 foreign policy agenda of, 311–312
 national security strategies and, 241
 unipolar moment and, 308–309
Netanyahu, Benjamin, 324–325
network centric warfare, 296
neutralism, 148–149
New Deal, 24
New Guinea, 1
"A New Inter-American Policy for the Eighties" (Committee of Santa Fe), 236
New Look policy, 91–92, 94–95, 110–111, 132
New York Times (newspaper), 17, 27, 44
 on Afghanistan, 148
 Defense Planning Guidance document and, 312
 on India, 151
 on national-liberation rhetoric, 153
 on nuclear war, 136
 on Pele, 265
 on Reagan national security strategy, 241
 on Vietnam, 177
Nicaragua, 220, 249–254
Niebuhr, Reinhold, 17, 53–54, 87
9/11. *See* September 11, 2001, terrorist attacks
99 Luftballons (song), 262
Nitze, Paul, 52–53, 213, 215
Nixon, Richard, 8, 11, 178–179, 183, 205–206
 anticommunism and, 63

Nixon, Richard (*Continued*)
  Buckley and, 192
  Cambodia and, 180, 189
  Chile and, 195
  China and, 185–186, 190–191
  coercive escalation and, 180
  détente and, 187–189, 192–193
  excessive force and, 179–180
  faith in military power, 179–181
  missile gap claims and, 133–134
  realism and, 187
  resignation of, 204
  US Air Force and, 180
  Vietnam and, 178–181, 199
  Watergate and, 193
Nixon Doctrine, 197, 246
no-fly zones, 300, 318
Nolting, Frederick, 158
Non-Aligned Movement, 149–151, 153
Noriega, Manuel, 291–293
Norris, Chuck, 237, 242, 256
North, Oliver, 252–253
North Africa, 162
North American Free Trade Agreement (NAFTA), 302
North Atlantic Treaty Organization (NATO), 117, 143–144
  Able Archer 83 exercise, 259–260
  Balkans airstrikes by, 319–321
  after Cold War, 288–290
  creation of, 55–56
  Dayton Accord enforcement and, 323
  enlargement of, 288–291
  German reunification and, 288, 290
  Lehrer on, 288
  Soviet reactions to, 56
North Korea, 73–74, 81
  nuclear weapons program, 314–315
North Vietnam, 159
  bombing of, 168, 175–177, 180, 189–190
Novikov, Nikolai, 40–41
NSC 20/4, 52–53
NSC-68, 52–54, 213
NSDD-32, 241
NSDD-75, 248–249
nuclear disarmament movement, 260–261
nuclear freeze movement, 260–261
Nuclear Non-Proliferation Treaty, 137
nuclear proliferation, 283, 314
nuclear war, 96, 104, 136, 260–261
"Nuclear War" (song), 262
nuclear weapons. *See* atomic weapons
Nuclear Weapons Freeze Campaign, 260

Obama, Barack, 339–340
  pivot to Asia and, 340
Obey, David R., 278
October War. *See* Yom Kippur War
Odom, William E., 317
oil embargo, 203
Oklahoma City bombing, 313–314
On the Beach (film), 104
On Thermonuclear War (Kahn), 98–99
OPEC. *See* Organization of Petroleum Exporting Countries
Open Skies proposal, 115–116
Operation Allied Force, 320–321
Operation Cartwheel, 1
Operation Desert Fox, 323–324
Operation Desert Storm, 277–281, 294–297, 307–308
Operation Eagle Claw, 228–229, 234, 242
Operation Just Cause, 292
Operation Provide Comfort, 300
Operation Restore Hope, 304–305
Operation Rolling Thunder, 168, 175–176
Operations Linebacker I and II, 180
Operation Uphold Democracy, 307
Operation Urgent Fury, 244–245
Organization of Petroleum Exporting Countries (OPEC), 203
Orwell, George, 30
Osgood, Robert, 79–80, 82, 100
Oslo Accords, 324–325
Ostpolitik, 207–208

Pahlavi, Mohammad Reza (Shah), 197, 216
Pakistan, 117, 145, 148, 151, 193–194, 211, 246
Palestine Liberation Organization (PLO), 217, 244
Palestinian nationalism, 244
Palestinians, 201–204, 324–325, 334–335, 342–343
Palmer, A. Mitchell, 31

Pan-Africanism, 118
Panama, invasion of, 291–292
Panama Canal, 213–214
pan-Arabism, 162, 201
Paniushkin, Alexander, 56
paramilitary actions, 108–109
paranoia, 343
Paris Peace Accords, 189–190, 199, 200–201
Patriot Act (2001), 338–339
patriotism, 8
   Bush, G. W., use of, 337
   fear and, 67–68
   performative, 68
Pax Americana, 280–282
PBSuccess, 109–110
peace activism, 66–67
   nuclear freeze advocacy by, 260
Peace Corps, 138–139, 141
peace dividend, 269, 281, 328
peacekeeping, 305–306
peacemaking, 297
Pearl Harbor, 9–10
   US security fears after, 25
Pearson, Drew, 150–151
perestroika, 285
performative patriotism, 68
periphery, 14–15, 115–118
Perle, Richard N., 265
Petraeus, David, 336, 343
the Philippines, 310
   communism and, 164–165
   Huk rebellion in, 164–165
Phillips, Howard, 270–271
Phillipsburg Youth Forum, 4
Pincher, 44–45
Pinochet, Augusto, 195–196
Pipes, Richard, 297–298
PKI. *See* Indonesian Communist Party
Platt Amendment (1901), 125
PLO. *See* Palestine Liberation Organization
Podhoretz, Norman, 278, 312–313
Poland, 285–286
"A Policy of Boldness" (Dulles, J. F.), 85
political mobilization, 59–60
Potsdam Conference, 34
poverty
   radicalism and, 150
   war and, 155

Powell, Colin, 291–292, 319, 330–331
power politics, 29
Powers, Thomas, 166
Prague Spring (1968), 182–183
Pravda (newspaper), 45, 56, 218–219
preemption, 33
presence patrols, 335
Presidential Directive 59, "Nuclear Weapons Employment Policy," 218–219
Project for a New American Century, 312–313
proletarian internationalism, 58–59
"Proud to Be an American" (song), 277
psychological warfare, 10–11, 43–44
Public Enemy, 277
puppet-government imperialism, 36
Putin, Vladimir, 290
Putman, Claude, 68–69

al-Qaeda, 322, 330, 331
Quayle, Dan, 264–265
The Quiet American (Greene), 162–163

R2P. *See* responsibility to protect
Ra, Sun, 262
Rabin, Yitzhak, 324–325
racial violence, 65–66
radicalism, poverty and, 150
Radio Free Europe, 43–44, 112
Rand Corporation, 97–98, 103–104
rational means, 6
Reagan, Ronald, 210, 229–231, 271
   Afghanistan and, 246, 249–250
   American exceptionalism and, 236
   Carter debate with, 231
   Central America policies, 252–253
   on *The Day After*, 261
   defense budgets and, 213–214, 264
   deterrence and, 257
   economic policies, 235
   El Salvador and, 251
   "evil empire" speech, 255
   foreign policy and, 232
   "freedom fighters" supported by, 249–250
   Gorbachev and, 263–264, 270, 271–272
   Grenada and, 245
   human rights and, 251–252

Iran-Contra affair and, 252–254
Iraq and, 247
Lebanon and, 243
low-intensity warfare and, 242, 246, 248–249
military buildup and, 233–234
moderating of, 263
national security strategies, 241
Nicaragua and, 249–253
nuclear arsenal and, 233–234
peacekeeping and, 245
reelection campaign, 254
remilitarization program, 237–238
SALT II and, 213
SDI and, 257–258
START and, 257
State of the Union Address of 1985, 249
strategic guidance, 233
on Vietnam War, 232–233
in West Berlin, 268
Reagan Doctrine, 249
realism
foreign policy and, 187
paranoia as, 343
"Red Menace" fears, 65–66
Red Scare, 31, 62, 67, 90, 115, 340
Red Storm Rising (Clancy), 242
reformist intervention, 138, 155
regime change wars, 297
regime reinforcement policy, 114
responsibility to protect (R2P), 311
Reston, James, 79–80, 178–180, 215
revolutionary nationalism, 77
revolution in military affairs, 295–296
Reykjavik summit, 270
Rhee, Syngman, 82
Rice, Condoleezza, 326
Ridgway, Matthew, 85–86, 91, 111
Rockwell, Llewellyn, Jr., 310
Roosevelt, Franklin D., 2, 10, 22–23, 25, 34–35
Good Neighbor Policy, 125
Roosevelt, Theodore, 125, 237–238
Rostow, Eugene V., 214–215
Rostow, Walt, 140, 156, 200–201
Rumsfeld, Donald, 296, 312–313, 331
Rusk, Dean, 94, 125–126, 167–168
Russell, Bertrand, 104
Russell, David, 277–278

Russia
financial rescue of, 303
after USSR collapse, 291
Rutenberg, Amy, 69
Rwanda, 305

SAC. *See* Strategic Air Command
Sadat, Anwar, 202, 216–217
Safire, William, 197–198, 219–220, 269–270
Sagan, Carl, 260–262
Said, Edward, 330
Salisbury, Harrison, 177, 238
SALT. *See* Strategic Arms Limitation Talks
SALT II treaty, 212–213
Sandinista National Liberation Front, 249–250, 252–253
SANE. *See* National Committee for a Sane Nuclear Policy
Sarajevo, Bosnia, 318
Sargent, Daniel, 22–23
satellites, 89–90
Saudi Arabia, 197, 248, 293
Scandrett, Richard, 67
Schell, Jonathan, 260–261
Schelling, Thomas
on brinksmanship, 94
on deterrence, 92
Schlesinger, Arthur M., Jr., 34
Schlesinger, James R., 204
Schwarzenegger, Arnold, 237
Scott, Tony, 315
Scowcroft, Brent, 286–287, 290
SDI. *See* Strategic Defense Initiative
SEATO. *See* South East Asia Treaty Organization
Second Taiwan Crisis, 101–102
Segal, Steven, 237
segregationism
anticommunism and, 66
foreign policy and, 115
self-determination, 4, 152
Senate Foreign Relations Committee, 83, 115
September 11, 2001, terrorist attacks, 329–331, 337
Serbia, 318, 320–321
Shalikashvili, John M., 283
Sharon, Ariel, 334–335

INDEX

Sharp, U. S. Grant, 175–176, 189–190
"The Shelter" (television episode), 105–106
Sherry, Michael, 50–51
"Shrimp" device, 103
Shultz, George P., 248–250, 256, 257, 261–264, 272
Sihanouk (Prince), 117
Silk, Leonard, 298–299
Sinai Peninsula, 201–202
Sino-Soviet alliance, fears of, 57–58
Sino-Soviet split, 185–187
Sino-Vietnamese war (1979), 216
Six-Day War, 201
Slovenia, 317–318
Smith, Holland M., 26
social reforms
    communism conflated with, 129
    modernization and, 140
Solidarity movement, 285–286
Solomon Islands, 1
Somalia, 304–306
"The Sources of Soviet Conduct" ("X Article") (Kennan), 38–40, 49–50
South East Asia Treaty Organization (SEATO), 117, 145, 193–194
South Korea
    politics of, 82
    United Nations defense of, 73–74
South Vietnam, 159, 163, 165–169, 200
    collapse of, 204
Soviet Union. *See* Union of Soviet Socialist Republics
Spanish-American War, 125
Special Forces, 141, 170, 242
Spellman, Francis Cardinal, 50–51
Spider-Man, 105
spiritual militarization, 51
Sputnik (satellite), 89–90, 158, 237
Srebenica, Bosnia, 318
The Stages of Economic Growth (Rostow), 140
Stalin, Joseph, 9, 23, 25, 32, 34–35
    Azerbaijan and, 47
    as cautious expansionist, 35
    death of, 83
    insecurities of, 36
    Korean War and, 75
    Marshall Plan and, 42

"The Sources of Soviet Conduct" and, 40
    views of, 37
    Yugoslavia and, 149
Stallone, Sylvester, 237
Starship Troopers (Heinlein), 64–65
START. *See* Strategic Arms Reduction Talks
state sovereignty, 206
Stevenson, Adlai E., 33–34
Stockholm Appeal, 102–103
Straits of Tiran, 200–201
Strategic Air Command (SAC), 95–96
Strategic Arms Limitation Talks (SALT), 191, 212–213, 215, 218
Strategic Arms Reduction Talks (START), 257, 314
strategic coercion, 96–97
strategic defense, 258–259
Strategic Defense Initiative (SDI), 257–259, 262–263, 265
strategic nuclear deterrent forces, 233
strategic sufficiency, 263–264
strategy, 13–14
Strauss, Lewis, 89
Subversive Activities Control Board, 11, 67
Sudan, 322
Suez Canal, 112, 202
Suez Crisis, 112–113
Suharto, 171–172
Sukarno, 117, 150–151, 171
Summers, Harry S., Jr., 167, 250–251
The Sum of All Fears (Clancy), 315
sunk-cost fallacies, 167–168
supply-side economics, 235
Symington, Stuart, 133–134
Syria, 201–202
    civil war in, 340

tactical atomic weapons, 100
Taft, Robert, 41–43
Taiwan, 101–102, 185, 214
Taliban, 267–268, 331
Tanzania, US embassy bombing in, 322
Task Force Smith, 74
tax cuts, 235
Taylor, Maxwell, 82, 135–136
technology, war and, 87–88

Teller, Edward, 89–90, 98
terrorism, 241–242, 313–314, 328, 329, 337–338
　Iraq and, 247
Tet offensive, 169–170, 181–182
Thatcher, Margaret, 257, 288
thermonuclear weapons, 103
Thieu, Nguyen Van, 180–181
Third Communist International (Comintern), 30–31
Third World, modernity and, 148
Third World nationalism, 117–118
Thomas, Kevin, 170
Three Kings (film), 277–278
Thunder Out of China (White), 21
Tibet, 151–152
Time (magazine), 21
Timmerman, George Bell, Jr., 65–66
Tito (Josip Broz), 149–151, 317–318
Top Gun (film), 237
total defense, 10
total war, 81–82, 103–104
Tower, John G., 140
trade, global security and, 208
trade liberalization, 282–283
Truman, Harry S., 23–25, 34, 39–42, 46, 52, 86
　atomic weapons and, 88–89, 98
　China and, 57
　Israel and, 47
　Korean War and, 74–78
　McCarthy and, 62–65
Truman Doctrine, 41–43, 45–46, 329
Trump, Donald, 341–342
Tudeh party, 110–111
Turkey, 41, 45–47
　missiles in, 90, 135
Tutsis, 305
The Twilight Zone (television series), 105–106
Tydings, Millard, 82–83
Tyler, Patrick, 312

Ukraine, 342–343
　nuclear weapons and, 315
Ulbricht, Walter, 142
uncommitted nations, 150
Union of Soviet Socialist Republics (USSR), 9, 30
　Able Archer and, 259–260
　Afghanistan and, 216–220, 246–247, 266–267
　aging and deaths of leaders of, 238
　Arabs and, 47–48
　atomic bomb tests, 59
　Azerbaijan and, 47
　China and, 56–57
　collapse of, 284, 286–289
　coup attempt in, 291
　Cuba and, 124, 135
　Czechoslovakia and, 182–183
　decentralization efforts in, 266, 269
　defense budgets, 264
　domestic politics in, 268–269
　Eastern Europe ambitions of, 23
　economy of, 234–235, 269
　expansionist détente policy, 202
　expansion of western borders by, 35
　fear of encirclement in, 35–36
　Germany and, 54–55
　Hungary and, 111–112
　India and, 193–194
　instability in, 268
　Kennan on, 38
　Korean airliner shot down by, 265–266
　Korean War and, 75
　Marshall Plan and, 42–43
　Middle East and, 201
　NATO reactions in, 56
　nuclear weapons buildup, 187–188
　oil supplies, 203
　postwar relations with, 25
　psychological warfare and, 10–11
　remains of, 280
　revolutionary thinking and, 35
　satellite states of, 36
　Shultz on economy of, 264
　unipolar moment, 296–297, 308–311, 316
United Fruit Company, 109, 140
United Nations
　creation of, 34–35
　Korean War and, 73–74, 81
　Rwanda and, 305
　Somalia and, 304–305
United States
　Afghanistan invaded by, 332–334, 337, 339
　becoming world power, 86

INDEX

defense institution reorganization, 51
defensive expansion policies, 150
global base network of, 26–27
as global hegemon, 310
Grenada and, 244–245
interpretations of Marxism in, 35
Iraq invaded by, 332–334, 336, 337, 339
Middle East presence of, 112–113
nuclear strategy of, 218–219
Panama and, 213–214, 291–292
al-Qaeda bombing embassies of, 322
R2P and, 311
regime reinforcement policies, 114
security fears after Pearl Harbor, 25
withdrawal from Vietnam, 200
universal military training, 69
US Air Force
    deterrence and, 95–96
    Iraq and, 294
    Nixon and, 180
    strategy theorists in, 294
USA Patriot Act (2001), 338–339
US-North Korea Agreed Framework, 314–315
"US Relations with the USSR" (national-security directive), 248–249
USS Missouri (ship), 21–23, 26–27, 46–47
USSR. *See* Union of Soviet Socialist Republics

Vance, Cyrus, 210, 229
Vandenberg, Arthur H., 25, 63
Vandenberg, Hoyt, 88
Vanik, Charles A., 207
Venezuela, 114
Vessey, John, 233–234
victimhood, 331, 342
Vienna Summit (1961), 127–128, 142
Vietnam, 3, 100, 158, 160–161, 204, 208
    Cambodia invaded by, 216
    France and, 161–164
    modernization and, 163
    nationalism and, 163–164
    population resettlement in, 165
    refugees from, 205
Vietnam syndrome, 278, 281, 296–297, 324
Vietnam War
    airpower and, 175–177, 180
    Cambodia and, 189
    Clinton and, 300–301
    end of, 199–200
    Johnson, L., and, 159, 166–170, 177–178
    movement against, 170–171, 181
    Nixon and, 178–181, 199
    Operation Desert Storm and, 278, 281
    political impacts of, 169
    Reagan on, 232–233
    Sino-Soviet split and, 186–187
    start of, 159
    Tet offensive, 169–170, 181–182
    US ground troops deployed in, 168, 177
    veterans of, 204
violent anticommunism, 156
The Vital Center (Schlesinger, A. M., Jr.), 34
Voice of America, 43–44
Voorhis, Horace, "Jerry," 63
voting rights, 65–66

Wallace, Henry, 41–42
war, 5–8
    cultural meaning and, 7–8
    defining, 12
    democracy promotion and, 334
    everywhere, 341
    failure to produce stability of, 329
    forever, 341–342
    Hollywood and, 237
    limited, 78–81, 85–86, 92–93
    localized, 81
    low-intensity, 240, 242, 246, 248–249, 253–254
    national credibility and, 307–308
    nuclear, 96, 104, 136, 260–261
    poverty and, 155
    regime change, 297
    technology and, 87–88
    on terror, 329, 338
    total, 81–82, 103–104
    utility of, 92
Warden, John, 294–295
War Powers Act (1973), 205–206
War Relocation Authority, 2
Warsaw Pact, 111–112, 182–183, 217–218, 245
    collapse of, 288–289

Warsaw Pact (*Continued*)
    costs of sustaining, 264
    tensions in, 269
Warsaw Treaty Organization, 111
Washington, Denzel, 315
Washington Post (newspaper), 28, 41, 47, 67, 143–144, 169–170, 191
    on Bay of Pigs, 126
    on Cuba missile deployment, 134
Washington summit, 271
Watergate, 193, 204, 205–206
Wayne, John, 169–170
Weaver, Sigourney, 237
Webster, William, 293
Weigley, Russel F., 92
Weinberger, Caspar W., 232–235, 238, 250–251, 260, 272
    on strategic defense, 258–259
Weinberger Doctrine, 250
West, Bing, 333
Westad, Odd Arne, 333
West Bank, 201, 217, 244, 324–325, 334–335
West Berlin, 142–144, 268
West Germany, 83, 143–144, 207–208, 287–288
White, Theodore H., 21–22
white supremacists, anticommunism used by, 65–66
Why Korea? (film), 79, 82–83
Wiesel, Elie, 261–262
Wiley, Alexander, 83
Will, George, 214, 228, 270–272, 282
Williams, Nick B., 127
Williams, William Appleman, 5, 60–61, 147

"Will There Be War?" (Baldwin, H.), 136
Wilson, Woodrow, 30
Wohlstetter, Albert, 103–104, 234
Wolfowitz, Paul, 311–313, 323–324, 334
Women Strike for Peace, 66–67
Wood, Leonard, 125
Woodward, Bob, 250–251
Woolsey, James, 308
World Bank, 112
World Peace Council, 102–103
World War I, 30–31
World War II, 3–4, 9–10
    airpower in, 176
    demobilization after, 26
    economic precarity after, 23–24
    end of, 1, 21
    Soviet influence during, 34
    world order after, 22–23
The Wretched of the Earth (Fanon), 117–118
Wright, Richard, 148–149

X Article. *See* "The Sources of Soviet Conduct"

Yalta Conference, 23
Yalu River, 79
"Yellow Peril" fears, 59, 65–66
Yeltsin, Boris, 290–291, 303
Yom Kippur War, 202–203
Young, Marilyn, 236, 245
Yugoslavia
    neutrality and, 149
    splintering of, 317–318

Zakaria, Fareed, 309–310
Zhukov, Georgy, 56